Front Cover: Hong Kong Scouts on their way to the first post-war St. George's Day parade in the Botanical Garden in Hong Kong, 1946 (right), Hong Kong Scouts in the Tiananmen Square in Beijing, 2010 (left),

Scouting in Hong Kong

1910-2010

Citizenship training in colonial and Chinese contexts

Scouting in Hong Kong, 1910-2010:

Citizenship training in colonial and Chinese contexts

© 2024 Paul Kua

Email: p.kua@oxon.org

First edition (hardcover): July 2011
(Hong Kong: Scout Association of Hong Kong)

Email: info@scout.org.hk

Second edition (paperback, ebook): May 2024
(London: Propius Press)

Email: propiuspress@pm.me

ISBN 978-962-7835-69-1 (hardcover)

ISBN 978-1-7384360-3-3 (paperback)
ISBN 978-1-7384360-4-0 (ebook)

Scouting in Hong Kong
1910-2010

Citizenship training in colonial and Chinese contexts

Paul Kua

Second Edition

London: Propius Press
2024

Contents

Forward

First edition of this book, *Scouting in Hong Kong, 1910-2010*, relying heavily on a doctoral dissertation, was published in 2011 by Scout Association of Hong Kong, when the Hong Kong youth movement celebrated its centenary.[1]

Despite a reasonably large print run, copies of this hardcover edition are largely sold out, though they are still available in most public and academic libraries in Hong Kong and some leading ones around the world.[2]

This second edition, retitled *Scouting in Hong Kong, 1910-2010: Citizenship training in colonial and Chinese contexts*, is issued in 2024 in paperback and ebook formats. The paperback edition, being a full-color publication with numerous illustrations, is somewhat costly. Readers are encouraged to opt for the environmentally-responsible ebook edition, which is more economical and full-text searchable, and has navigation aids.

The second edition contains corrections, revisions, new writeups, and extra illustrations and footnotes, drawing from additional sources and more recent studies, including two subsequent books in Chinese on the same topic by this author.[3] The same chapter structure of the first edition and, to the extent possible, similar pagination are kept. The Appendices now include information up to 2023 and the bibliography and index have been updated and cleaned up. However, *no* attempt has been made in Chapter 6 to extend coverage of history of Hong Kong Scouting beyond the cut-off year of the first edition, i. e., 2010.

Both the first and the second editions are available for free partial preview on Google Books.

Paul Kua
London, UK
May 2024

---

[1] Paul Kua, *Scouting in Hong Kong, 1910-2010* (Hong Kong: Scout Association of Hong Kong, 2011).

[2] For a *partial* listing of availability in university and public libraries in Asia, Europe and America see the World Catalogue (https://search.worldcat.org/title/986217641).

[3] Paul Kua 柯保羅, *A Century of Hong Kong Scouting, an Illustrated History* 香港童軍百年圖史 (Hong Kong: Scout Association of Hong Kong, 2012); Paul Kua 柯保羅, *Hong Kong Scout Stories* 香港童軍故事 (Hong Kong: Joint Publishing, 2019).

Acknowledgement

This book was completed with the kind support and generous help of many people, inside and outside Scouting.

Appreciation is due to Pau Shiu-hung and Anthony Chan, two successive Chief Commissioners of Scout Association of Hong Kong, who had offered their full support in the research phase, enabling me to set up Hong Kong Scout Archives, and allowing unrivaled access to association documents. Later Chief Commissioners, when approached, had also been consistently helpful. Staff members, esp. Evita Lee, Kathy Wong, Florine Fung, Cara Mok, Summy Fung, Dick Tuen, Van So, Kenny Ho, Mendy Chiu, Anita Fok and Shing Chi-hung, cheerfully gave their time in many supportive tasks.

I want to thank many who had offered useful sources, photographs and memorabilia and/or sat through interviews conducted in Hong Kong, Canada and Britain: Robin Bolton, Dr. Stuart Braga, James Chan, Chan Pak-lam, Thomas Chan, Dr. Chau Cham-son, Nelson Cheng, Cheung Kam-chuen, Francis Chin, Stephen Ching, Sammy Chiu, Robert Chow, Fung Yuen, Dr. Hari Harilela, William Ho Chung-keung, Nancy Ho, Kenneth Ho Wing Yee, Jenny Hounsell, John Hui, Anthony Hung, Ku Ka-chit, Kwan Kee, William Kwan, Andrew Lai Gar-yan, Lai Yuk-shu, Herbert Lau, Garson Lee, Dr. Solomon Lee Kui-nang, Lee Wah-sun, Leung Sze-on, Oswald Lim, Gregory Loh, Francis Loo, Loo Sai Kung, Dr. Mak Wai-ming, Philip Mo, Jason Ng, Ng Siu-hong, Anne Ozorio, Sheila Potter, Stephen Quah, Joseph Shek, Yoken Sin, Jan van der Steen, Louis Tam, Thomas Tam, Tang Nim-chi, Patrick Tse, Tse Ping-fui, Tsin Chi-ming, Alexander Wong, Ambrose Wong, Wong Chun, Philip Wong, Wong Shiu-kwong, Yau Yu-kai, Yeung Chun-man, Yip Kam-fat, Patrick Yip, and Roger Yu. In different ways, they have all contributed to my research and understanding of Hong Kong Scouting.

The staff of Gilwell Archives (later Scout Association Heritage Service), National Archives, British Library and SOAS Archive in London; Public Records Office, Hong Kong University Library, Chinese University Library, Central Library, and St. Andrew's Church in Hong Kong; and Beijing National Library, Shanghai Library, and Central Library in Taipei, etc., have been helpful. In particular, I would like to thank Paul Moynihan and Patricia Styles of Gilwell Archives and Peter Ford of the Heritage Service, Bernard Hui at Public Records Office and Rev. Kenchington of St. Andrew's Church.

Most Scout-related illustrations came from Hong Kong Scout Archives and Scout Association of Hong Kong. Gilwell Archives was a key source for early photographs. Public Records Office supplied some images of leaders and events in Hong Kong. Information Services Department granted permission to use a photograph from the 1971 *Hong Kong Annual Report*. St. Andrew's Church provided photographs of B-P's only visit to Hong Kong. The photograph of Boy Scouts on their way to their first post-war parade in 1946 was taken by the U. S. Navy. The author's collection of Scout badges, medals, photographs, postcards, memorabilia and cigarette cards and those of other collectors already mentioned here proved useful as illustrative materials. Gratitude is due to all for enriching this book with so many instructive and interesting illustrations.[4]

I would like to express my deep gratitude to Prof. David Pomfret, primary supervisor of my doctoral study at the University of Hong Kong, for his critical guidance during the successive drafts of the dissertation entitled "Scouting in Hong Kong: Citizenship Training in a Chinese Context, 1910-2007," on which this book was largely based. Special thanks are due to Dr. Peter Cunich, my other supervisor, who has patiently read through all chapters multiple times and offered many helpful comments. I have learned a lot from both and sincerely hope that some of the learning is reflected in this work. I thank Prof. Clyde Binfield for letting me present a paper on this subject at a conference in Birmingham in 2006. I am indebted to Prof. Allen Warren, Prof. John Carroll, Dr. Xu Guo-qi and Dr. Bert Becker for their thorough examiners' reports, insightful questions, and helpful suggestions on how to improve the dissertation and turn it into a book.

Last but not least, I would like to thank all my loved ones and friends for bearing with me in good humor throughout my years of research and writing. In more occasions than I care to recall, I have imposed upon them discussions on my study or disappeared during trips or gatherings with them for side visits to archives and libraries or writing duties. In particular, I would like to acknowledge my debt to my wife Jolia and my daughter Valerie. Jolia lived through this project on a daily basis. The book could not have been completed without her love, patience, advice and support.

---

4   Copyright holders are acknowledged at the bottom of the captions when known, except for the cigarette cards, postcards, and more common badges and medals.

Tables and graphs

Tables

Graphs

Abbreviations

APR	*The Advance Party Report* (of the British Boy Scouts Association)
ARP	Air Raid Precaution (as in the ARP Despatch Corps)
BAAG	The British Army Aid Group
B-P	Robert S. S. Baden-Powell
BSA	Boy Scouts of America
CM	*The China Mail*
CSO	Community Service Organisation (a unit of the Scout Association)
FOS	Friends of Scouting (a subsidiary of the Scout Association)
HKDP	*Hong Kong Daily Press*
HKSH	*The Hong Kong Sunday Herald*
HKT	*The Hongkong Telegraph*
IDU	Island Development Unit (an experimental mixed Venture Troop)
KMT	*Kuomintang* (the Chinese Nationalist Party) (國民黨)
KSYP	*Kung Sheung Yat Po* (工商日報)
MTB	Motor Torpedo Boat
NSO	National Scout Organization
PLA	People's Liberation Army
POR	The *Policies, Organisation, and Rules* (a Scout publication)
PRC	People's Republic of China
ROC	Republic of China
RTHK	Radio Television Hong Kong
SAR	The Special Administrative Region (of Hong Kong)
SCAA	South China Athletic Association
SCMP	*South China Morning Post*
SMA	*Scouts musulmans algériens* (Muslim Scouts in Algeria)
SSU	Service Scout Unit (s)
VDC	The Volunteer Defence Corps
WAGGGS	World Association of Girl Guides and Girl Scouts
WKYP	*Wah Kiu Yat Po* (華僑日報)
WOSM	World Organization of the Scout Movement
YMCA	Young Men's Christian Association
YWCA	Young Women's Christian Association

Romanization

Romanization of names or phrases in Chinese is often included in this book. Romanization of Chinese texts in Mandarin, or *Putonghua*, the national dialect, is problematic given the existence of multiple Romanization methods. The difficulty is complicated in this study by the fact that some terms used are customarily Romanized based on other Chinese dialects (e.g., Hokkien/Minnan, Shanghainese, and esp. Cantonese, native dialect for most Chinese in Hong Kong) which also have multiple Romanization schemes. The pinyin system, increasingly accepted, is generally used. However, in many cases the terms are Romanized using other methods such as the Wade-Giles system for Mandarin and the Yale or the Hong Kong Government systems for Cantonese. This is often done when the terms in question are better known in their original forms, when they appeared in these forms in the source documents, when they should appear in such forms given their contexts, or when the Chinese characters are not known and transliteration into pinyin could not be reliably performed.

Hence, Chiang Kai-shek (蔣介石, Wade-Giles Romanization) will not become Jiang Jie Shi, Quah Cheow-cheong (柯昭章, Romanized based on Hokkien) will not be renamed Ke Zhao Zhang, and Chau Cham-son (周湛燊, Romanized based on Cantonese) will not be called Zhou Zhan Shen. Similarly, place names such as Wongneichong (黃泥涌) will not be labeled Huang Ni Yong and Guangdong (廣東) could be Kwangtung, Guangdong or even, loosely, Canton; and the newspaper *Kung Sheung Yat Po* (工商日報) will not be referred to as *Gong Shang Ri Bao*. Even with one system, a Romanized form could represent a multitude of Chinese characters. With multiple systems for several dialects, this problem is worse. Hence, Chinese characters, where known, are often provided in parenthesis next to the term, the first or most appropriate occasion it occurs.

Scouting in Hong Kong
1910-2010

Citizenship training in colonial and Chinese contexts

Introduction

Robert S. S. Baden-Powell.

To most Scouts around the world, Scouting's origins could be summed up as "one man," "one book" and "one island," facts repeated in numerous official histories published by Scout associations in many countries over the years: Scouting was founded by Robert S.S. Baden-Powell (B-P), the hero of the Siege of Mafeking in 1899-1900, and started with an experimental camp for boys organized by him at the Brownsea Island in Dorset in Southwest England in 1907, followed by the publication in serial form of his *Scouting for Boys* in 1908. But the movement's origins went beyond these superficial facts, and were rooted in a complex combination of ideas, personalities and organizations, including Baden-Powell and his scouting experience in the military, Ernest Thompson Seton and his naturalism and American Indian symbolism in *The Birch-bark Roll of the Woodcraft Indians* issued in 1907, militarism, social control, imperialism, social Darwinism, the Edwardian cult of national efficiency, the National Service League, and the Boys' Brigade Movement.[1]

Scouting promised to be a panacea for many social ills and political concerns of the time, including the perceived physical degeneration of urbanized youth, the malaise of young people incarcerated in schools, spiritual ambiguity in an increasingly secular society, the military unpreparedness of Britain, and even the decline of the British Empire. Though it owed much of its initial success to these contemporary concerns and pre-existing efforts to address them, such as the work done by the Boys' Brigade and the Young Men's Christian Association (YMCA), Scouting's proposed training in citizenship, character and patriotism appealed to a broad spectrum of people in many countries. Within years of its founding, this youth movement grew like wildfire, first in England, then around the world. The first UK Scout census reported 108,000 members in 1910; the world census claimed 1,019,000 members in 1922, and 10,462,000 members in 1966. Today, the World Organization of the Scout Movement (WOSM), the official world body for Scouting, boasts of having 28 million members. Scouting can legitimately claim to be a global (or at least a truly transnational) movement—there are only six

---

1   See Paul Kua 柯保羅, *Hong Kong Scout Stories* 香港童軍故事, 15-28. .

countries in the world in which it is not available.

This book deals with the development of the Hong Kong Scout Movement from 1910 to 2010, primarily as a subject of enquiry in itself, and secondarily as an analytical tool which may shed light upon the broader history of Hong Kong society, whose development and that of the movement were closely intertwined. By reconstructing the evolution of Scouting from a niche movement for a handful of British boys in the expatriate community before the First World War to a fully indigenized and co-educational mass movement in the post-colonial Hong Kong society, it fills a gap in the historical studies of Scouting around the world. By analyzing how the youth movement and the (re)construction of its particular brand of citizenship training largely reflected the development of the community, it adds to our understanding of the political, cultural and social history of Hong Kong, often influenced by that of China. By demonstrating the uniqueness of the movement's evolution in its colonial context, as opposed to, say, in other former French or British colonies, it provides useful comparative insights into the history of imperialism and colonial youth movements. By exploring the options available to and choices made by local Scouting since Hong Kong's retrocession of sovereignty to China, it compliments other studies on decolonization and post-colonial citizenship. The book relied heavily on a recent dissertation,[1] but the two have significant differences in both structure and content. While the dissertation has five substantive chapters, the book has six, with the last three covering somewhat different time periods. Some analyses in the original academic study have been abbreviated or taken out in the book; while new narratives of general interest, updated information, new appendices, an index, and numerous illustrations have been added.

Scouting for Boys by B-P, 1908.

Existing literature on the history of Scouting

The history of the Scout Movement has attracted many academic investigations and general studies, as interest in cultural, social, youth and colonial history has burgeoned in recent decades. Many of these

The Birch-bark Roll by Seton, 1907.

---

1   Paul Kua, "Scouting in Hong Kong: Citizenship Training in a Chinese Context, 1910-2007," Ph. D. thesis, the Univ. of Hong Kong, 2010.

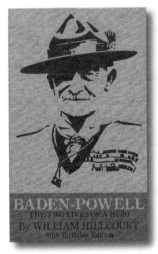

Hillcourt's *Two Lives of a Hero.*

have dealt with Scouting in larger, mostly western, contexts such as the United States, Britain, Canada, France and Germany, shedding lights on the movement where it originated or grew strongly. Some have studied smaller or non-western environments, especially those which were part of the colonial empires of some western countries, supplying refreshing comparative insights. A few have attempted to cover Scouting in China. However, while many aspects of the political, cultural and social history of Hong Kong have been studied throughout the years, the history of Hong Kong Scouting has to date not attracted any academic attention.

Studies on the two closely-related topics of British Scouting and Baden-Powell have so far attracted the most research interest. These can, in turn, be subdivided into what will be termed "sympathetic narratives," "revisionist critiques," and "balanced analyses." Many works could be classified as sympathetic narratives. Aitken, Neilly, and Begbie issued popular publications soon after Mafeking idolizing Baden-Powell.[1] Later books by Aitken, Wade, Kiernan, Reynolds, Everett, Collis, Hillcourt, and Freedman, often officially-sanctioned, also tend to glorify the movement and perpetuate the legends surrounding the Chief Scout.[2] These studies were typically published before or in the 1960s and mostly narratives as opposed to critical analyses. The most comprehensive book is William Hillcourt's *Two Lives.* This is a definitive biography of Baden-Powell, and has benefited from unrivaled access to primary materials, including more than two thousand letters which Baden-Powell wrote to his mother, and Lady Baden-Powell's own diaries and collection of her husband's papers. However, perhaps due to the co-authorship of Lady Baden-Powell, this book shied away from anything that might be considered unfavorable. The basis of Baden-Powell's initial world-wide

1   W. Francis Aitken, *Baden-Powell: The Hero of Mafeking* (London: Partridge, 1900); J. Emerson Neilly, *Besieged with B-P: Siege of Mafeking* (London: Pearson's, 1900); and Harold Begbie, *The Story of Baden-Powell: The Wolf That Never Sleeps* (London: Richards, 1900).

2   Francis Aitken, *The Chief Scout: Sir Robert Baden-Powell*(London: S.W. Partridge, 1912); Eileen K. Wade, *Twenty-One Years of Scouting: The Official History of the Boy Scout Movement From its Inception* (London: C. Arthur Pearson, 1929); R. H. Kiernan, *Baden-Powell* (Philadelphia: David McKay, 1938); E. E. Reynolds, *Baden-Powell: A Biography of Lord Baden-Powell of Gilwell* (London: Oxford Univ. Press, 1943); and *The Scout Movement* (London: Oxford Univ. Press, 1950); Percy Everett, *The First Ten Years* (Ipswich, The East Anglian Daily Times, 1948); Henry Collis, et. al.'s *B-P's Scouts: an Official History of the Boy Scouts Association* (London, Collins, 1961); Hillcourt, *Baden-Powell: The Two Lives of a Hero* (Boy Scouts of America, 1964); and Russell Freedman, *Scouting with Baden Powell* (New York: Holiday House, 1967).

fame was his performance at the siege of Mafeking. *Two Lives* focused on tales that portrayed Baden-Powell in a heroic light, without alluding to the doubtful military value of the siege or his possible mistreatment of the natives. Hillcourt also did not mention Vane, the first commissioner for London who had started a parallel movement claimed to be less militaristic, though, to be fair, he did point to the fact that "some of the pacifists set up a splinter group."[1]

A postcard depicting B-P the Defender of Mafeking.

Revisionist critiques include early works by Hamilton, Vane, the pseudonymous author "Captain Noemo," and more recent studies by Gardner, Hynes, Pakenham, Brendon, Rosenthal, Nasson and Searle.[2] The earlier works were issued by contemporary critics who spoke up against overwhelmingly popular views. More recent books reflect revisionist views of earlier history, part of a broader trend of debunking myths related to Edwardian heroes and imperialists, based on re-interpretation of primary sources. A representative work is Michael Rosenthal's *The Character Factory*, a part-biography of Baden-Powell and part-history of the movement. The author adopted Pakenham's claim that Baden-Powell had caused the death of many indigenous people during

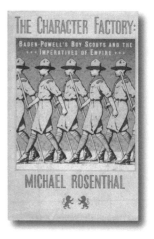

Rosenthal's *The Character Factory.*

---

1   Hillcourt, *Two Lives of a Hero*, 296. Besides Mafeking and Vane's pacifist movement, another issue which might be interesting to compare is Baden-Powell's sexuality/sexual orientation, which again is treated very differently by the sympathetic, revisionist and balanced studies. But this issue has less relevance in the context of Hong Kong Scouting.

2   Angus Hamilton, *The Siege of Mafeking* (London: Methuen, 1900); Captain Noemo, *The Boy Scout Bubble: A Review of a Great Futility* (London, 1912); Sir Francis Vane, *The Boy Knight: Essays and Addresses on the Evolution of the Boy Scout Movement* (The Council of National Peace Scouts, 1910); Brian Gardner, *Mafeking: A Victorian Legend* (New York: Harcourt, Brace & World, 1967); Samuel Hynes, *The Edwardian Turn of Mind* (Princeton: The Princeton Univ. Press, 1968); Thomas Pakenham, *The Boer War* (London: Weidenfeld, 1979); Piers Brendon, *Eminent Edwardians* (New York: Houghton Mifflin, 1979); Michael Rosenthal, *The Character Factory: Baden-Powell and the Origins of the Boy Scout Movement* (New York: Pantheon Books, 1986); Bill Nasson, *The South African War* (London: Arnold, 1999); G.R. Searle, *A New England: Peace and War, 1886-1918* (Oxford: Clarendon, 2003).

Jeal's *Baden-Powell*.

the siege by imposing a ruthless leave-here-or-starve-here food policy on the local Baralongs and other African refugees. The indirect killing of natives was, of course, a serious charge against the future Chief Scout of a worldwide youth movement with members from all races. Rosenthal also devoted a chapter to militarism in Scouting, and quoted Vane's accusation that "the [Scout] Council…was almost entirely recruited from ex-generals or colonels," resulting in "a military cabal controlling a great educational movement."[1] Elsewhere, he portrayed Baden-Powell as a shrewd opportunist who took advantage of the war spirit. To Rosenthal, the charge of militarism was substantiated by the participation of many Boy Scouts in the First World War.

Reacting to the sympathetic narratives and sometimes also to the later revisionist assessments, some researchers published more balanced analytical accounts. Key books include those by Springhall, Gillis, MacDonald and Jeal.[2] There are also scholarly articles by Wilkinson, Warren, Springhall, Summers, MacKenzie, Pryke, and Dedman, typically more focused on specific issues such as militarism, nationalism, and masculinity.[3] An important study is Tim Jeal's *Baden-Powell*, by far the most thorough treatment of early British Scouting and its founder, written with works by Reynolds, Hillcourt, and especially Rosenthal in

---

1   Rosenthal, *The Character Factory*, 206.

2   John Springhall, *Youth, Empire, and Society: British Youth Movements, 1883-1940* (London: Croom Helm, 1977); John R. Gillis, *Youth and History: Tradition and Change in European Age Relations, 1760-the Present* (New York: Academic Press, 1974); Robert H. MacDonald, *Sons of the Empire: The Frontier and the Boy Scout Movement, 1890-1918* (Toronto: Univ. of Toronto, 1993); Tim Jeal, *Baden-Powell* (London: Hutchinson, 1989).

3   Paul Wilkinson, "English Youth Movements, 1908-1930," *Journal of Contemporary History*, 4, Apr. 1969; Allen Warren, "Sir Robert Baden-Powell, the Scout Movement and Citizen Training in Great Britain, 1900-1920," *The English Historical Review*, Apr. 1986, 376-398; "Baden-Powell: A Final Comment," *The English Historical Review*, Apr. 1986, 948-950; John Springhall, "The Boy Scout, Class, and Militarism in Relation to British Youth Movements, 1908-1930," *International Review of Social History*, 1971, 125-58; "Baden-Powell and the Scout Movement before 1920: Citizen Training or Soldiers of the Future," *The English Historical Review*, 1987; and "Building Character in the British Boy: The Attempt to Extend Christian Manliness to Working-class Adolescents, 1880-1914," in J. A. Mangan and James Walvin (eds.), *Manliness and Morality* (Manchester: Manchester Univ., 1987); Anne Summers, "Scouts, Guides and VADs: A Note in Reply to Allen Warren," *The English Historical Review*, Oct. 1987, 943-947; John M. MacKenzie, "The Imperial Pioneer and the British Masculine Stereotype in Late Victorian and Edwardian Times," in J. A. Mangan and James Walvin (eds.), *Manliness and Morality*; Sam Pryke, "The Popularity of Nationalism in the Early British Boy Scout Movement," *Social History*, Oct. 1998, 309-324; Martin Dedman, "Baden-Powell, Militarism, and the 'Invisible Contributors' to the Boy Scout Scheme, 1904-1920," *Twentieth Century British History*, 1993, 201-233; and "the Boy Scouts and the 'Girl' Question," *Sexualities*, 2001, 191-210.

mind. Jeal carefully re-examined evidence on Mafeking and concluded that Baden-Powell was a resourceful military leader who made the best of a difficult situation and dealt with the needs of many as judiciously as possible, given his predicaments and prevailing racist values. He argued that accusations of starvation and genocide were not substantiated. Jeal also dealt with Vane extensively, detailing his personal styles and prejudices, his difficult working relationship with Chief Commissioner Sir Edmond Elles and J. A. Kyle, vacillation and indecision of Baden-Powell in the matter, and reasons behind the early demise of Vane and subsequent decline of the pacifist British Boy Scouts organization. Unlike the sympathetic accounts, which simply omitted any mention of Vane, or the revisionist treatments, which only quoted Vane in support of their criticisms, *Baden-Powell* made good efforts to deal with this difficult episode both thoroughly and in a balanced manner.

As Scouting gained popularity beyond the British Isles, a large quantity of literature of varying quality documented these experiences. Many studies dealt with western nations, including those by Macleod, Nicholson, Mechling, Peterson, Townley, Murray, Wagner, Sterne, and Dean on America; Radey, Bragg, Thériault and Bernier on Canada; Laneyrie, Baubérot, Bouchet, and Guérin on France; Biagioli on Italy; Seidelmann on Germany, and van der Steen on Netherlands.[1] Murray's

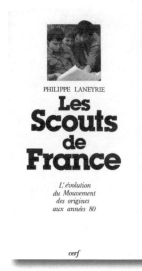

PHILIPPE LANEYRIE

Les Scouts de France

L'évolution du Mouvement des origines aux années 80

cerf

Laneyrie's *Les Scouts de France*.

---

1   David Macleod, *Building Character in the American Boy: the Boy Scouts, YMCA, and their Forerunners, 1870-1920* (Wisconsin: Univ. of Wisconsin, 2004); Edwin Nicholson, *Education and the Boy Scout Movement in America* (NY: Columbia Univ., 1941); Jay Mechling, *On My Honor: Boy Scouts and the making of American youth* (Chicago: Univ. of Chicago, 2001); Robert W. Peterson, *The Boy Scouts: An American Adventure* (Forbes, 1985); Alvin Townley, *Legacy of Honor: The Values and Influence of America's Eagle Scouts* (NY: Thomas Dunne, 2007); William D. Murray, *The History of the Boy Scouts of America* (NY: Boy Scouts of America, 1937); Carolyn Ditte Wagner, "The Boy Scouts of America: A Model and a Mirror of American Society," Ph. D. thesis, Johns Hopkins Univ., 1978; Wendy C. Sterne, "The Formation of the Scouting Movement and the Gendering of Citizenship," Ph. D. thesis, Univ. of Wisconsin, 1993; John Dean, "Scouting in America, 1910-1990," D. Ed. thesis, Univ. of S. Carolina, 1992; Kerry-Anne Radey, "Young Knights of the Empire: Scouting Ideals of Nation and Empire in Interwar Canada," MA thesis, Laurentian Univ., 2003; Ross Andres Bragg, "The Boy Scout Movement in Canada: Defining Constructs of Masculinity for the Twentieth Century," MA thesis, Dalhousie Univ., 1995; Raphaël Thériault, "Former des homes, des Chrétiens, des Citoyens: Le Project d'Éducation des Scouts du Petit Séminaire de Québec, 1933-1970," M.A. thesis, Univ. of Laval, 2000; Claire Bernier, *Histoire du scoutisme et guidisme francophones en Alberta de 1931 à 1988* (Edmonton: Les Éditions Duval, 1995); Philippe Laneyrie, *Les Scouts de France: L'évolution du Mouvement des origins aux années 80* (Paris: Cerf, 1985); Arnaud Baubérot, *L'invention du Scoutisme Chrétien: Les Eclaireurs Unionistes De 1911 à 1921* (Les Bergers et Les Mages, 1997); H. Bouchet, *Le Scoutisme et L'individualité* (Librairie Felix Alcan, 1933); Christian Guérin, *L'utopie Scouts de France, 1920-1995: histoire d'une identité collec-*

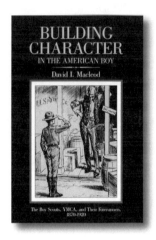

Macleod's *Building Character in the American Boy.*

book is an earlier attempt at a narrative history of Scouting in America. Sterne analyzes the gendered nature of U. S. Scouting, supplying hints for understanding of Scouting and Guiding in Hong Kong. Radey discusses nationalism and imperialism in Canadian Scouting, illustrating the tensions of a movement professed to be both national and imperial, and offering lessons for understanding Scouting for Chinese boys in British Hong Kong. Laneyrie examines French Scouting, providing insights on the significance of Catholic Scouting in Hong Kong. Biagioli reviews the growth of Scouting in Umbria in central Itlay before 1928, when Fascist *Balilla* largely replaced it. Seidelmann's study of German Scouting covers its early development, demise due to Nazism, and re-emergence postwar. The Italian and the German experiences shed lights on the development of politicized Scouting in Nationalist China.

David Macleod's *Building Character* is representative of a balanced analytical history of youth movements in a developed western country. According to Macleod, middle-class male in America promoted character-building organizations such as Scouting and YMCA's boys' work as institutions of social control in the hope of countering the perceived harmful impacts of city living on middle-class boys. He analyzes how the Boy Scouts of America (BSA) gained institutional supports, volunteer leaders and youngsters over the years, and offers insights on internal dissensions and organizational politics of the BSA, including the struggle between voluntarism and professionalization. Many of these issues, as it turned out, have applications for Hong Kong Scouting, albeit in somewhat different contexts, and often different time periods.

Some recent works have focused on Scouting in non-western and colonial contexts, where indigenous religions or lack of religiousness prevailed over Christianity and indigenous people(s) greatly outnumbered the ruling Europeans. These include works on Scouting in Africa, Indochina, India, Singapore and Japan by Parsons, Bancel, Derouiche, Raffin, Tan and Wan, Watt, Rau, and Proctor.[1] The books on

tive catholique et sociale (Fayard, 1997); Enrico Biagioli, *Origini e nascita dello Scautismo in Umbria (1910-1928)* (Selvazzano: T. Zaramella, 2010); Karl Seidelmann, *Die Pfadfinder in der deutschen Jugendgeschichte* (Hannover: Schroedel Verlag, 1977); Jan van der Steen, *Padvinders:100 Jaar Scouting in Netherland* (Zutphen: Walburg, 2010).
1   Timothy H. Parsons, *Race, Resistance, and the Boy Scout Movement in British Colonial Africa* (Athens: Ohio Univ., 2004); Nicolas Bancel, Daniel Denis, Youssef Fates, *De l'Indochine à l'Algérie: la Jeunesse en mouvements des deux côtés du mirroir colonial, 1940-1962* (Paris: Éditions La Découverte, 2003); Mohamed Derouiche, *Scou-*

§ Introduction | 22

Scouting in Japan and Singapore both provide useful comparative information for the analyses in the current book. Rau's and Watt's studies analyze the struggle with admission of native boys into early Indian Scouting, supplying good parallels for the Hong Kong colonial context. Works by Derouiche, Bancel and Raffin discuss Scouting for native boys and nationalism versus imperialism in the former French colonies of Algeria and Indochina, issues which are quite instructive for this study.

Timothy Parsons' book examines, among other things, how the Fourth Scout Law on international brotherhood was applied in British Africa. The central theme is race, but religion, gender, colonial education, role of youth movements in politics, nationalism and decolonization are also touched on. It documents the reluctance of colonial and Scout authorities to admit African boys, the development of parallel movements for native youngsters, the eventual merger of the two types, and some post-colonial challenges. This study's treatments of how the ideals of the transnational youth movement were adapted to fit local contexts and how an institution of social control fared amidst the emerging nationalism of the colonies provide valuable insights for reading Scouting in Hong Kong and analyzing its evolving membership policies over time.

Scouting in Singapore by Tan and Wan.

A few studies deal with Scouting in China, which heavily influenced Scouting in Hong Kong in the interwar and the early postwar years. Fan provides an early narrative account of Chinese Scouting. Qin emphasizes political control of Scouting by the Nationalist Party. Rong studies Chinese Scouting in Guangdong from 1915 to 1938, highlighting the growing influence of the Nationalists. Hwang's article reviews the state's control over the individual body through youth organizations such as the Nationalist Boy Scouts and the Communist Young Pioneers in

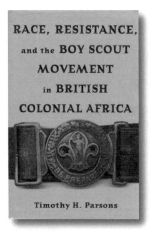

tisme école du patriotisme (Alger: Enterprise Nationale du Livre, 1985); Anne Raffin, *Youth Mobilization in Vichy Indochina and its Legacies, 1940-1970* (Lanham: Lexington Books, 2005); Timothy H. Parsons, "The Consequences of Uniformity: The Struggle for the Boy Scout Uniform in Colonial Kenya," *Journal of Social History*, Winter 2006, 361-383; "No More English than the Postal System: the Kenya Boy Scout Movement and the Transfer of Power," *Africa Today*, 61-80; Carey A. Watt, "The Promise of 'Character' and the Spectre of Sedition: The Boy Scout Movement and Colonial Consternation in India, 1908-1921," *South Asia*, 1999, 37-62; C. Subba Rau, *Scouting in India: What It Is and What It Might Be* (Tumkur: Tumkur District Scout Council, 1933); Tammy M. Proctor, "A Separate Path: Scouting and Guiding in Interwar South Africa," *Comparative Studies in Society and History*, July 2000, 605-631; Kevin Y. L. Tan & Wan Meng-Hao, *Scouting in Singapore, 1910-2000* (Singapore: Singapore Scout Association, 2002); Scout Association of Japan, *History of Scout Movement in Japan* 日本ボーイスカウト 運動史 (Tokyo: ボーイスカウト日本連盟, 2005).

Parson's Race, Resistance and the Boy Scout Movement.

*75 Years of Hong Kong
Scouting* by Leung,
Leung and Wu.

China, in the context of similar phenomena in Nazi Germany, Fascist Italy and Communist Soviet Union. Choi's thesis studies how the Nationalists established effective control over Scouting and tried to politicize and militarize it, while expanding it through incorporating its program into the school curriculum.[1] These works provide useful insights into the development of politicized Scouting in China, which for a period of time had spilled over into the Hong Kong movement.

There is currently no scholarly study on the history of Hong Kong Scouting. Up to now, the most substantive effort was *75 Years of Hong Kong Scouting* (香港童軍七十五) by Leung, Leung and Wu.[2] This brief work contains many photos, a chronology, short write-ups, a bibliography with thirty-four sources, and no footnotes. It is an uncritical institutional narrative history rather than a primary source-based analytical history (though, to be fair to these authors, the former rather than the latter had been their intention from the start). Nevertheless, it provides some useful background information and a starting point for further research in the initial stages of this study.

Given this lack of secondary sources dealing directly with the history of Hong Kong Scouting, this book relied heavily on a large number and variety of primary sources. The Hong Kong Scout Archives in Hong Kong has a large quantity of administrative documents, photographs, magazines and other publications, mostly postwar and of uneven usefulness. The British Scout Archives at Gilwell in London has a much more selective collection of documents and photographs which are often quite valuable and mostly from the pre-war years. An excellent source for public records on Scouting and the history of Hong Kong in general is the National Archives at Kew Garden in London, while the Public

1   Fan Xiao-liu 范曉六 (ed.), *Zhong Guo Tong Zi Jun Shi* 中國童子軍史 (History of Scouting in China) (Shanghai: 225 Tong Zi Jun Shu Bao Shi, 1935); Rong Zi-han 榮子菡, "Guang Dong Tong Zi Jun Yan Jiu 廣東童子軍研究: 1915-1938 (A Study on the Boy Scouts of Guangdong)," M. Phil. thesis, Jinan Univ., 2002; Qin Sui-ling 秦穗齡, "Tong Zi Jun Yu Xian Dai Zhong Guo De Qing Shao Nian Xun Lian 童子軍與現代中國的青少年訓練 (1911-1949) (Scouting and Youth Training in Modern China, 1911-1949)," M. Phil. thesis, National Taiwan Normal Univ., 2004; Hwang Jinlin, "Authority over the Body and the Modern Formation of the Body," in Peter Zarrow (ed.), *Creating Chinese Modernity: Knowledge and Everyday Life, 1900-1940* (New York: Peter Lang, 2006), 183-212; Choi Sze Hang, "The Scouts Movement and the Construction of New Citizenship in Republican China (1912-1937)," M. Phil. thesis, Lingnan Univ., 2008.
2   Leung Siu-kei 梁肇祺, Leung Wai-fan 梁惠芬, Wu Po-sau 胡寶秀 (eds.), *75 Years of Hong Kong Scouting, 1911-1986* 香港童軍七十五 (Hong Kong: the Scout Association of Hong Kong, 1987).

Records Office in Hong Kong also has many relevant government documents, mostly postwar. The Hong Kong collections of the libraries of the University of Hong Kong, the Chinese University of Hong Kong and other Hong Kong academic and public libraries have good supplies of contemporary newspaper reports on Scouting and publications of schools, churches, and other organizations which have Scout Groups. Literally thousands of newspaper articles in English and Chinese from the 1910s through to the postwar decades were consulted. These were particularly helpful for the earlier chapters, since administrative documents covering this period tended to be scarce. Verbal histories collected from old Hong Kong Scouts during interviews conducted in Hong Kong, Canada, and Britain have also proved useful, especially for the later chapters. Other archives and libraries in Hong Kong, Britain, North America, Singapore, Shanghai, Beijing, Taipei, and Mumbai have also yielded some useful primary sources on Scouting in Hong Kong, China, and other colonial and non-colonial contexts.

Theme, motives and identities

In this book, the author has tried to combine the professed aim of Scouting (citizenship), the key motives for supporting the movement (religious conversion, secular education, governance and war) and the most relevant differentiating identities (race, class, gender and age) to analyze the experience of young people involved in Hong Kong Scouting throughout the years. In a sense, citizenship has been considered by some to be a form of social-political identity similar to race, class, and so on. But for our purpose here, it functioned largely as a recurring theme of the Scout Movement, while the motives as driving forces which underpinned its development, and the identities as analytical categories which informed and impacted upon it over time.

Of course, citizenship has different meanings in different contexts. Manfred Liebel notes that "it is a product of the emergence of predominantly urban societies and the demands of the residents to no longer leave public affairs to a high-handed ruling class, but to take them into their own hands."[1] Traditionally, most people would associate it

---

1   Manfred Liebel, "Citizenship from Below: Children's Rights and Social

with political and civil rights and duties, democracy and participation. T. H. Marshall broadened the definition of modern citizenship to include civil rights (e.g., personal freedom), political rights (e.g., right to vote), and also social rights (e.g., economic welfare), which had developed historically in that order.[1] While in some states, the concept of citizenship is closely related to that of nationalism, in many states or empires with a multitude of nationalities, a distinction between the two must be made. Furthermore, with increasing globalization and transnationalism, the concepts of global, dual and post-national citizenship, as opposed to citizenship of a single state, have also been gaining acceptance.[2]

The meanings of citizenship are further complicated in Hong Kong. As a British colony with a predominantly Chinese population, does citizenship apply to the tiny minority of European British, the small group of mostly Chinese British nationals, or the large number of non-British Chinese? As Hong Kong was often largely dependent on China, Chinese nationalism has consistently been a relevant issue in Hong Kong. Benedict Anderson has argued that nationality, nation-ness and nationalism are but "cultural artefacts of a particular kind" which came "into historical being" and "their meanings have changed over time," even though they often command "profound emotional legitimacy" at a particular point in time.[3] How could or should Chinese nationalism be accommodated? Could Chinese nationalism's meanings change or be modified to suit Hong Kong's needs? More specifically, in a city-state associated strongly with the pursuit of material wealth, have economic rights historically been more relevant than civil and political ones? As a society of immigrants, should some deviation from the idealized concept of citizenship and a transient sense of belonging be expected? After the reunification of a capitalist Hong Kong with a Communist China, what sort of post-colonial citizenship could emerge and how should it be nurtured? Are Agnes S. Ku and Ngai Pun correct in suggesting that

Movements," in Antonella Invernizzi and Jane Williams (eds.), *Children and Citizenship* (London: Sage Publications, 2008), 32.

1   T. H. Marshall, "Citizenship and Social Class," in Bryan S. Turner and Peter Hamilton (eds.), *Citizenship: Critical Concepts* (New York: Routledge, 1994), Vol. II, 5-43.

2   Thomas Faist, "The Fixed and Porous Boundaries of Dual Citizenship," in Thomas Faist and Peter Kivisot (eds.), *Dual Citizenship in Global Perspective: From Unitary to Multiple Citizenship* (New York: Palgrave, 2007), 1-44.

3   Benedict Anderson, *Imagined Communities* (New York: Verso, 1991), 4.

"the formation and reformation of citizenship in Hong Kong...show a *sui generis* path that is perhaps rather distinct from Western and other models and experiences"?[1]

The colonial authorities tended to take a pragmatic view of the matter. Bryan Turner concludes that "citizenship in Hong Kong was never intended to be a nation-building exercise."[2] The evolving formulation of citizenship throughout the years was nothing more than "conditional or provisional citizenship."[3] Frequently, the Chinese were considered denizens rather than citizens. The people in Hong Kong often refer to themselves as *shimin* (市民 people of the city) instead of *gongmin* (公民 citizen), reflecting their perception of their limited civic roles.[4] More recently, young "Hongkongers" would be "aligned more toward world market conditions than toward the moral meaning of citizenship in a particular nation."[5] This substitution of a discourse of the state by a discourse of the market was encouraged by the colonial government, but also justified to some extent by rapidly rising per capita income levels from the 1970s onward.[6] The post-colonial government of Hong Kong also appears to subscribe to views which would emphasize economic rights ahead of political or civil ones, again suggesting the perceived validity of a narrowly-defined concept of citizenship.[7]

From day one, Scouting was positioned by its promoters as a new and better scheme for citizenship training. Baden-Powell's first edition of *Scouting for Boys* issued in 1908 has the subtitle "*A Handbook for Instruction in Good Citizenship*." Even before that, in a small booklet issued in 1907, he clearly stated that the object of the Boy Scouts Scheme was "to help in making the rising generation, of whatever class or creed, into good citizens at home or for the colonies."[8] Sam Pryke

In this section:

A selection of cigarette cards depicting Scout proficiency badges for some "citizenship" skills.

"Ambulance"

1   Agnes S. Ku and Ngai Pun, "Remaking citizenship in Hong Kong," in Agnes S. Ku, et. al. (eds.), *Remaking Citizenship in Hong Kong: Community, Nation and the Global City* (London: RoutledgeCurzon, 2004), 2.
2   Bryan S. Turner, "Making and Unmaking Citizenship in Neo-liberal Times," in Ku et al. (eds.,) *Remaking Citizenship in Hong Kong*, xix.
3   Ibid.
4   Leung Hon-chu, "Politics of Incorporation and Exclusion: Immigration and Citizenship Issues," in Ku et al. (eds.), *Remaking Citizenship in Hong Kong*, 100.
5   Aihwa Ong, *Flexible Citizenship: the Cultural Logics of Transnationality* (Durham: Duke Univ. Press, 1999), 119.
6   Gordon Mathews, Eric Kit-wai Ma, and Tai-lok Lui, *Hong Kong, China: Learning to Belong to a Nation* (London: Routledge, 2008), 17.
7   "Popularity of Tsang drops after June 4 comments," *SCMP*, May 27, 2009.
8   Baden-Powell, R. S. S., *Boy Scouts: A Suggestion* (London, 1907).

"Boatman"

argues that "the nationalism of the Scouts" was not academic, but "central to the organization and informed virtually every aspect of its ethos and practice."[1] Regardless of how one views the success of Scouting as a scheme for citizenship training, one must accept that it is nevertheless the most important recurring theme of the movement. In fact, its leaders had created early on many proficiency badges to recognize boys for achieving certain standards in a variety of skills considered useful for good citiznes. These presumably prepared Boy Scouts to live up to what was expected of them, and serve the nation or people in need in both military and civilian situations. Many of these badges were depicted in cigarette cards issued in the early part of the 20th century, when such cards were popular promotional tools for tobacco companies. A few of these cards are illustrated on the pages in this section.

What is being claimed versus what is being practiced is, of course, subject to interpretation. Some historians have asked questions about the fundamental nature of Scouting in practice, debating, for example, whether militarism was the key driver in the early years. Allen Warren suggests a broader view, arguing that "by 1910 and 1911...the three strands of citizen training—the militaristic, the educational and the Christian—had been brought together in the official thinking behind the Boy Scout Movement, each coexisting more or less easily with another and in a variety of permutations at local level."[2] According to him, Baden-Powell, as the popular soldier-hero, was sought by many with different views as model of their ideals:

> *To those concerned with "militaristic" citizenship training he brought a support for corporate and organic notions of society, an emphasis on duty, honour and self-sacrifice as against the allegedly selfish and disrupting effects of socialist teaching. To those concerned with the religious training of the young, his outdoor training methods, tapping as they did profound feelings of disillusion and alienation within the urban world, brought new opportunities of reviving the flagging energies of church or inter-denominational work amongst the young, once anxieties about the spiritual objectives of the movement had been allayed. Finally, for*

1   Pryke, "The Popularity of Nationalism...," 310.
2   Warren, "Sir Robert Baden-Powell...," 390.

those concerned with training for democratic citizenship, Baden-Powell's scouting method with its emphasis on play, individual character development, and child-centered education through the medium of the troop or patrol offered an alternative to patterns of education which seemed to concentrate exclusively on rote learning imposed by the teachers and which appeared to have failed demonstrably in their aims of equipping children to face the adult world.[1]

Therefore, Scouting's success was to some extent depended on its ability to hold these different elements in a sort of "constructive tension," and to become "the most comprehensively acceptable voluntary attempt" at "a national training for the young in citizenship."[2]

This concept of the all-encompassing nature of the movement seems to explain well why Scouting had broad appeals in Hong Kong. Arthur Waley, besides bringing Chinese poetry to the English-speaking world, has made some insightful comments on Chinese-British interactions. Writing in 1942, he noted a turning-point in Sino-British relationship in the early twentieth century, when some British intellectuals went to China "not to convert, trade, rule or fight, but simply to make friends and learn."[3] As it turns out, a modified version of Warren's and Waley's lists of motives, namely "to convert, educate, rule or fight," describes aptly the main reasons why many supported Hong Kong Scouting, all in the name of citizenship training. In the colonial setting in which the ruled Chinese far outnumbered the ruling Europeans, it is necessary to add a motivation related to governance to Warren's emphasis upon military, religious, and educational factors.

"To convert" youngsters in a religious sense was an important motive for churches who viewed citizenship in God's kingdom essential. But, to most others, citizenship of a more secular nature was desired: "To educate" students more holistically was why schools, educationalists, teachers, and parents supported Scouting. "To rule," or the perceived benefits of boys trained in Scouting for effective governance, ensured that the ruling elite, members of the ruling race, and Chinese who shared

"Rescuer"

---

1 Ibid., 397.

2 Ibid., 398.

3 Arthur Waley, "A Debt to China," reprinted in Hsiao Ch'ien (ed.,) *A Harp with a Thousand Strings: A Chinese Anthology in Six Parts* (London, 1944), 342.

the benefits of a politically stable colony, were all supportive. "To fight," or the perceived effectiveness of Scout training in preparing boys for military-related tasks, was important among the authorities, the military, and the community, especially when war threats were imminent. Politics, patriotism and nationalism, British and Chinese, tended to enter into play for the last two motives. As will be shown, different motives were relevant at different phases of the development of local Scouting, though "to rule" tended to be the most important one much of the time.

Pryke rightly observes that "the reasons why boys liked the Scouts is rather obvious...they were attracted by the games, the camping, the uniform and the camaraderie."[1] For them, "to play" in the game of Scouting was the main reason why they joined. Citizenship training was little more than a convenient excuse by which the approvals for participation might be won from parents and other adults. This has not been added as a fifth motive since the focus of the study is on analyzing what prompted adults to support Scouting. The aim is to try to understand how Scouting as a scheme for the socialization of youth provided the space for adult anxieties and their desires to influence the next generation to play out. Furthermore, the fact that "to play" has been the invariable reason for youngsters throughout all periods also makes an analytical review of their motivation somewhat redundant and uninteresting.

However, as David M. Pomfret points out, youngsters in Scouting did not simply accept idealized constructs handed down by the adults in a passive manner, as the latter attempted "to colonise urban pre-adulthood" and to influence the former.[2] They tended to negotiate their own responses and create their individualized experiences according to what they view as relevant. In turn, the adults would adjust their approaches in order to remain effective in their intercessions.[3] This dynamic was notable throughout the history of Scouting, in Hong Kong or elsewhere: young people continued "to play," while the adults continued to attempt "to convert, educate, rule or fight" through Scouting.

Citizenship training in local Scouting in colonial and post-colonial times as a component of the overall educational process must be

"Marksman"

---

1   Pryke, "The Popularity of Nationalism...," 310.

2   David M. Pomfret, *Young People and the European City: Age Relations in Nottingham and Saint-Etienne, 1890-1940* (Aldershot: Ashgate, 2004), 292.

3   Ibid., 292-293.

viewed in the context of China. The importance of Chinese politics and the evolving relationship between Britain, Hong Kong and China cannot be over emphasized. In the late interwar years, for instance, Chinese nationalism was accepted if not openly encouraged in Hong Kong, when a common enemy and a rising nationalism among local Chinese made this policy expedient. After Second World War, caught between the struggles of the Chinese Nationalists and Communists, education and Scouting focused on "detaching students from their indigenous nationality and local politics and molding them into residents or subjects rather than citizens."[1] Cultural rather than political identification with China was encouraged. Denationalized Scouting was not a "reactionary" program invented by the Scout organization, but supplemented civics education in the schools, both aimed at producing what Thomas Tse calls a "deformed citizenry."[2] Just before and after decolonization, citizenship training in the schools and in Scouting was transformed again, as renationalization occurred, if only hesitantly and in an *ad hoc* manner. Hong Kong youth was again taught to identify with China as a modern political reality and the motherland, not just an ancient cultural construct.

"Coast Watchman"

The term "youth" refers to young people collectively, a period of development for a person, the process of "growing up," or a life stage between childhood and adulthood. Youth implies semi-dependence, or a transition between dependence and independence. However, a more precise definition is evasive, and often changes based on time, location and circumstance. A young person could be defined differently using physical, religious, cultural, social, or legal milestones that were in vogue. "Growing up" could reflect a complex interplay of biological, social, cultural, economical, and psychological forces. Youth as a life stage could depend on the prevailing views of childhood and adulthood as life stages. Sometimes, the two pre-adult stages could be merged. Others have suggested that the pre-adult stages did not always exist in history.[3]

A wealth of literature has emerged around the argument that age groups have histories, and that, at any point in time, different groupings

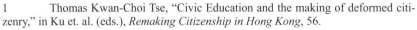

1   Thomas Kwan-Choi Tse, "Civic Education and the making of deformed citizenry," in Ku et. al. (eds.), *Remaking Citizenship in Hong Kong*, 56.
2   Ibid., 54.
3   Philippe Ariès claimed that childhood as a life stage was not "discovered" in Europe until the thirteenth century. See Philippe Ariès, *Centuries of Childhood*, trans. Robert Baldick (Middlesex: Penguin Books, 1962), 30.

"Pilot"

of youth or, over time, same groupings, could have different experiences. Works by Ariès, Demos, and Gillis in the 1960s and 1970s are considered pioneering efforts. Recently, Ariès' sources, methodologies, and theses have been criticized by some, but as Hiner points out, "no one has successfully challenged his essential point that childhood is not an immutable stage of life…that childhood as an experience and a social category is part of the historical process and subject to change over time."[1] Given the impressive amount of scholarly works on youth history in recent decades, it would appear that many historians agree that youth as a life stage is likewise not immutable, but a dynamic social construction with different meanings for different societies at a given time and evolving meanings over time.

Driving youth's different and evolving meanings are inequalities experienced by subsets of youth, within a country, across nations, or over time. These inequalities are, in turn, due to identities such as race, ethnicity, class, religion, gender, sexual orientation, age, and nationality. Boris and Janssens label these as "complicating categories," or "systems of domination or…inequality."[2] Religion, for example, has played a pivotal role in history and is arguably the most significant category in terms of impacts on historical developments. Identities provide a useful framework for understanding the experience of youth and their inequalities in history. Such inequalities could come as inclusion versus exclusion, unequal treatments, and differentiated perceptions. For instance, a young person may be excluded from education based on gender or age, treated unequally in the job market based on race or class, or perceived differently in marriage or life in general based on gender or race.

To the extent that the history of Scouting is concerned with the experience of young people in Scouting, it is a specialized field in youth history. The differentiated experience of young people in Hong Kong Scouting was often driven by four identities, namely race, class, gender and age. Other identities are important elsewhere. Religion and sexual orientation, for example, feature prominently in American Scouting. The BSA has a policy of not admitting atheists, as highlighted in a

1   N. Ray Hiner and Joseph M. Hawes (eds.), *Growing Up in America: Children in Historical Perspective* (Urbana: Univ. of Illinois, 1985), xvi-xvii.
2   Eileen Boris and Angélique Janssens (ed.), *Complicating Categories: Gender, Class, Race and Ethnicity* (Cambridge: Univ. of Cambridge, 1999), International Review of Social History, Supplement 7, 6.

recent case involving expulsion of an Eagle Scout because of his avowed atheism.[1] There is also a policy of excluding gay people, which has been challenged several times, culminating in a decision by the Supreme Court in *Boy Scouts of America vs. Dale* in 2000, confirming that the BSA as a private association has "First Amendment right of expressive association," and could decide to exclude gay people if it chose to do so.[2]

Class is often a relevant identity in history. Arthur Marwick defines a "class" as a socio-economic aggregate distinguishable by its wealth, social standing, power, or opportunities.[3] The relationship between the many and the few, the have-nots and the haves, the proletariat and the bourgeoisie, the underprivileged and the privileged provides a useful framework for the study of past societies. Marx went further, and claimed that class was the predominant category and supplied most explanations to historical developments. Class matters in the context of youth. Young people from different social classes could have very different "growing-up" experiences. In the last few centuries, while upper-class youngsters in many countries have enjoyed years of leisure and education, lower-class youth often experienced an abbreviated schooling and years of servitude under the apprenticeship system.

Similarly, class matters in Scouting. The movement was founded on the ideal that boys of all classes could be trained to be better citizens, though in practice it often only reached boys from mostly middle-class backgrounds, in Britain, America and elsewhere. Likewise, class played an important role as an entry barrier to Hong Kong Scouting until the last years of the interwar period and the postwar decades.

Race could function similarly to class as an identity in a multi-racial environment, such as between the European and the colonial races in a colony, or between the black and the white people in America. One could enjoy access to wealth, social standing, power, and opportunities by simply belonging to the "right" racial aggregate. The interaction between the slaves and the masters, the "inferior" race and the "superior"

"Missioner"

1   Darrell Lambert, "How I Got Booted out of the BSA," *The Humanist*, Jan.-Feb, 2003, 7-9.
2   John C. O'Quinn, "How Solemn is the Duty of the Mighty Chief: Mediating the Conflict of Rights in Boy Scouts of America v. Dale," *Harvard Journal of Law and Public Policy*, Fall 2000, 323.
3   Arthur Marwick, *The New Nature of History: Knowledge, Evidence, and Language* (Hampshire: Palgrave, 2001), 219.

one, the colonized and the colonizing supplies insights for better under-standing of a society. Inequalities among youth based on race are common. In many societies, youth unemployment among minorities would typically be more severe. Chief Justice Warren, in the Supreme Court case of *Brown vs. Board of Education*, declared that segregated schools were illegal as "to separate [African-Americans] from others...solely because of their race generates a feeling of inferiority."[1] Yet, many states actively or passively supported segregated schools for black and white children, years after *Brown*.

In the history of Scouting, race often counted, in colonial and non-colonial settings. Black American Boy Scouts suffered discrimination just as their non-Scout brethren did in the community. Natives in many colonies, including Vietnamese, Indians, Black Africans and Hong Kong Chinese, were effectively prohibited from joining Scouting in the earlier years. Some, when allowed to participate, were given differentiated, "second-class," status.

Gender has emerged as a key identity in historical scholarship in the last few decades. Joan Scott defines gender as a "constitutive element of social relationship based on perceived differences between the sexes" and as "a primary way of signifying relationships of power."[2] Perceived differences between the sexes, often culturally or socially constructed rather than biologically determined, drove social organizations which, in turn, legitimized power of one over the other and unequal treatments. Much like class or race, one's gender could affect one's access to wealth, social standing, power and opportunities. The gender perspective has provided a rich source for historical analysis. Inequalities among youth based on gender have been widespread. Though schools in the seventeenth century were not monopolized by one class, they were monopolized by a single sex. Even girls from families where boys went to college would be given no education. Fénelon complained that while boys were educated for years, girls were left "willy-nilly to the guidance of ignorant or indiscreet mothers," not even taught to read or write.[3]

"Camper"

---

1   Michael J. Friedman, "The Brown vs. Board of Education Decision," http://usinfo.state.gov/usa/civilrights/brown/overview.htm (accessed Oct. 18, 2004)..
2   Joan Scott, "Gender: a useful category of historical analysis," *Gender and the Politics of History* (New York: Columbia Univ. Press, 1988), 42.
3   Ariès, *Centuries of Childhood*, 319.

Scouting was gendered from day one as it started as a movement for boys only. Efforts to associate girls soon followed, in response to British girls' demands, but only in segregated Guides organizations. Up until the late 1970s, the Hong Kong Scout and Guide Movements offered differentiated training within the two segregated schemes, though eventually this gender barrier was crossed, when girls were integrated into the boys' movement. Because the inclusion or exclusion of girls in the movement has been an issue from day one, this study will from time to time refer to the history of local Guiding, even though its main focus remains the history of Scouting. It should be noted that in some countries, such as Indonesia, America and China, the term Scouting has always applied to both boys and girls. Hong Kong followed Britain and conventionally refers to Scouting for boys and Guiding for girls, until the former became coeducational. In our analyses, the term Scouting is sometimes also used liberally to cover both Scouting and Guiding.

"Wirelessman"

Age has often been an important identity in the context of "vulnerable" younger or older people. Widespread discriminatory employment practices based on age eventually led to anti-age-discrimination laws in many countries. These often protect older workers from being treated unequally based on age, but sometimes also apply to younger people. Among young people, age-based policies for youth often have in mind their protection from adult exploitation. The most common of these are the child-labor laws. Amidst concerns with child prostitution, evangelists and moralists obtained legal reforms in Britain in the late nineteenth century to successively increase girls' "age of consent" from ten to twelve, to thirteen, and then to sixteen.[1]

In Scouting, age played a role in inclusion and treatment. Younger boys were barred in the early days. Wolf Cubs, when eventually introduced for younger boys, were given a differentiated training program. The older Senior and Rover Scouts, when added, were also given different objectives. In the 1980s, age played a role again, when a pre-Cub section was introduced, targeting even younger children.

The four main identities outlined, besides functioning separately, could also work jointly. For example, age and race (and, in a sense,

---

1   Roger Cox, *Shaping Childhood: Themes of Uncertainty in the History of Adult-Child Relationships* (London: Routledge, 1996), 149-150.

"Signaller"

class) came into play in local Scouting, when, in the interwar years, Chinese boys were admitted as Boy Scouts but not as Wolf Cubs, a section initially dominated by British and Eurasian boys, who were typically from wealthier families. Similarly, race and gender both mattered, when Chinese girls were initially excluded from Hong Kong Guiding and were then required to wear a Chinese-style uniform, while Chinese boys joined local Scouting years earlier, and were allowed to wear the same, westernized, uniform as their European counterparts.

How these identities work to drive differentiated experience of youth depends on mutually-influencing interactions between the "serving" and the "served" parties. In early 1900s, Baden-Powell had only intended to include boys in Scouting. Gender would have acted as an identity for exclusion. However, Guiding came into existence because girls in Britain demanded admission, and took it on themselves to attend for the first time a Boy Scout rally at the Crystal Palace.[1] Similarly, many years later, girls were admitted to the all-boys Scout Movement both in Britain and in Hong Kong largely because there were demands from the youthful participants for mixed training as opposed to the single-sex programs offered by the separate Scout and Guide organizations.

A narrative and analytical history

This work is, at the same time, a narrative and analytical history of Hong Kong Scouting. In this regard, it is different from many institutional histories produced by Scout Associations around the world. For our purpose, a narrative account could range in meaning from a mere chronicle of events to a historical study which is more focused on the "what," "when" and "how"; while an analytical account would pay more attention to the "so what" and "why" and/or analyze structures and consequently be more explanatory or even predictive. The difference between the two is often one of degree, not kind. Mark Philips suggests that "the varieties of narrative and non-narrative modes…exist…along a continuum."[2] W. H. Dray points out that "narrative histories need not be, and never are in fact for long, mere chronicles," as "they character-

---

1   Hillcourt, *Two Lives of a Hero*, 294-295.
2   Mark Phillips, "On Historiography and Narrative," *Univ. of Toronto Quarterly*, 53, 1983-84, 157.

istically offer what might be called 'running explanations' of events they narrate."[1] On the other hand, as J. P. Kenyon puts it, one could hardly expect to find in analytical studies just the explanations, as it would be necessary to establish first "what actually happened."[2]

Historians who chose to revisit topics already well-researched are often faced with the necessity of adopting a selective, thematic and analytical approach. With the narrative history of British Scouting well established by the likes of Reynolds and Hillcourt, Rosenthal and Mac-Donald could be quite selective in their choice of topic and more-or-less analytical in their approach. This is, unfortunately, more difficult in cases such as Hong Kong where good narrative histories of Scouting are lacking. While it is not the intention of this study to provide a comprehensive chronicle of the history of Scouting in Hong Kong (such a task would be too tedious, uninteresting and, at any rate, impossible, in view of the fact that a large quantity of administrative documents are missing), it is necessary, so to speak, first to ascertain "what actually happened." As there has been no extensive, primary source-based, treatment of Hong Kong Scouting to date, a key task of this study is to establish a well-substantiated narrative history by asking the "who, what, how and when" questions. In other words, work similar to though perhaps more limited in scale than that done by Reynolds, Hillcourt and Murray on the history of British and American Scouting, however mundane, needs to be attempted in the context of the history of Hong Kong Scouting.

Some challenge the rationales behind an analytical approach to history. A. J. P. Taylor notes that while "it is the fashion nowadays to seek profound causes for great events," this may not be possible: "perhaps the war which broke out in 1914 had no profound causes...In July 1914 things went wrong. The only safe explanation is that things happened because they happened."[3] If this is possible with such a momentous occurrence as the Great War, it is certainly also possible with relatively trivial developments in a youth movement in the colonial outpost of Hong Kong. In the history of Scouting, some things could have hap-

---

1   W. H. Dray, "Narrative versus analysis in history," in Robert M. Burns (ed.), *Historiography: Critical Concepts in Historical Studies* (Taylor & Francis, 2005), 344.
2   Quoted in Dray, "Narrative versus analysis in history," 344
3   As quoted in L. J. Butler and Anthony Gorst (eds.), *Modern British History: A Guide to Study and Research* (London: L. B. Tauris, 1997), 7.

pened randomly, with no profound driving forces behind them. Still, it is desirable to at least try to produce a suitable analytical history of Hong Kong Scouting by addressing the "why and so what" questions, where possible. Work similar in nature to that of Jeal, MacDonald, Macleod, Parsons and Rosenthal on Scouting in Britain and elsewhere needs to be attempted in the context of the Scout Movement in Hong Kong.

In trying to analyze past events, one must, of course, be aware of the possible limitations imposed by what some historians called "presentism," through which present-day values and perspectives are applied in interpreting the past. But, as Hélène Bowen Raddeker argues, "the past doing the determining is already the product of our interpretation… in history it is inevitable that the present will teleologically determine (our representations of) the past."[1] All one can do is to make an honest effort to see past events using (one's interpretation) of past values and perspectives. Attempts have been made in this direction, for example, in trying to understand issues related to racism, militarism, class-based prejudices and sexual discrimination throughout the history of Scouting in the colonial context of British Hong Kong.

In this study there is a need to balance the dual requirements of a more-or-less holistic (though by no means comprehensive) narrative history of Hong Kong Scouting and an analytical account of that history. Considerable effort is devoted to establishing the relevant "who, what, how, and when" of the movement and its general historical contexts, although much attention is also paid to exploring the possible "why and so what" of this history, bearing in mind, of course, that not all events were necessarily driven by "profound causes." To avoid being too selective with facts and consequently unduly biasing subsequent analyses, an inclusive attitude is generally adopted when establishing the narrative history, which does occupy a substantial portion of this study.

Periodization

Not everyone is a fan of periodization. Some have argued that periodization *per se* is an anachronism in the postmodern age. After all, "nowa-

---

1   Hélène Bowen Raddeker, *Sceptical History: Feminist and Postmodern Approaches in Practice* (London: Routledge, 2007), 53.

days we seem to inhibit a kind of global space which has denied succession in favor of simultaneity and it should be obvious that there is no periodization without succession."[1] But there are periodization schemes of a less-ambitious sort. Ludwig von Mises points out that "the ages of history as distinguished by historians" are rather different from "the stage schemes of the philosophy of history" in that the former aims only at "classifying historical phenomena," while the latter often have predictive claims. The periodization scheme employed in this study is clearly the former, an attempt at "classifying historical phenomena" in Scouting "into artificial sub-divisions," and does not have any pretense to predicting the next stage or anything at all about the future.[2]

Any periodization scheme has to start and end somewhere. In the case of this study, choosing a start date was relatively easy. Informal Scouting began in Hong Kong in 1910, and formal Scouting in 1913. While one could conceivably call for some background analysis before the 1910s, most would agree that it is reasonable to start the account in 1910. The choice of 2010 as the end date requires a bit more elaboration. After all, ending it in, say, 1977, when local Scouting became independent of the British movement, might enable more objective assessments of the people and the events. Furthermore, most public documents from before this date would be available, as access to British and Hong Kong public records are both generally based on the "thirty-year" rule.[3] On the other hand, as far as this author is concerned, most administrative documents up till the 2000s are readily accessible from the Hong Kong Scout Archives. The year 2010 was also the centenary of Hong Kong Scouting, as marked by the issuance of a centenary medallion,[4] making it a convenient cutting off point. Perhaps more importantly, stretching the period under review to the 2000s enables this study to analyze several key developments, namely the admission of girls, the creation of a new section for younger (pre-Cub) children, and the development of Scouting

Hong Kong Scout Centenary Medallion, 2010-11.

H. K. Scout Archives.

---

1   Vladimir Biti, "Periodization as a Technique of Cultural Identification," in John Neubauer (ed.), *Cultural History After Foucault* (New York: Aldine de Gruyter, 1999), 177.
2   Ludwig von Mises, *Theory and History: An Interpretation of Social and Economic Evolution* (Auburn: Ludwig von Mises Institute, 2007), 170.
3   Special access was kindly granted on several recent record series dated from 1978 to 1991 by the Hong Kong Public Records Office at the last stage of this study.
4   This medallion was awarded to members who had served in a series of official centenary events between December 2010 and December 2011.

since the retrocession of sovereignty in 1997. The benefits of being able to address questions related to gender, age and nationalism in Scouting in the most recent decades far outweighed the handicaps imposed by a lack of some public records from this period.

Breaking the history of a continuous movement into discreet periods is by definition an arbitrary if necessary task. Historical events are not always easily grouped into clear-cut "eras." Cutoffs in this study took into account tenures of key leaders (Chief Scouts and commissioners), important external events (such as the two world wars), pivotal internal ones (such as the demise and re-launch of the movement and the independence of Hong Kong Scouting from the British movement) and the four motives and four identities, already noted. Based on these periodization criteria, six phases in the history of Hong Kong Scouting over the last century were identified. This periodization scheme becomes the chapter structure for Chapters 1 to 6.

First joint Scout parade in Hong Kong at St. Joseph's College, March 1915.

H. K. Scout Archives.

Chapter 1 deals with the first decade of the movement, when informal Scouting was started in an Anglican church, and formal Scouting was launched in a Catholic school. Sir Francis May, governor at the time, became the first Chief Scout for a short while. Citizenship training meant preparing a small number of British boys for God and the empire. Militarism, religion, sectarianism, and Chinese nationalism all mattered. Racial exclusion through British nationality requirements and cadet enrollment rules, age-based inclusion through Wolf Cubs, and gendered treatment through later and segregated training for girls in Guiding created differentiated experiences for youth in Scouting, defined broadly to include Guiding. In particular, though no formal color bar existed, race, assuming the veil of the nationality restriction, acted as a discriminating identity to effectively exclude most Chinese and a majority of Portuguese boys from the movement. "To fight" was for a brief period of time a key motivation for supporting Scouting, when war broke out in Europe. Photographic evidence will be included throughout this book. In this section, one photograph from each of the periods (the one featured on the spread before each chapter) is included here as illustrations.

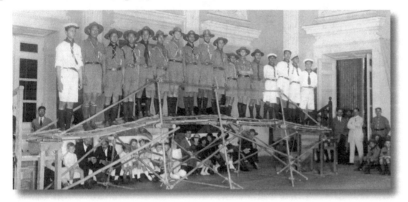

First Scout Jamboree/exhibition at the City Hall, April 1923.

H. K. Scout Archives.

The first interwar decade, when Scouting was re-launched, limited racial inclusion occurred, and the movement grew modestly in some schools, churches, and other organizations, is covered in Chapter 2. Governors Stubbs and Clementi were Chief Scouts, and citizenship training was redefined to include non-British Chinese elites as partners for effective colonial governance, especially after the strikes in the 1920s, first through removal of the British nationality restriction and then by way of an adapted Scout Promise in Chinese which accommodated Chinese nationalistic sentiments. "To rule" became the dominant motivation for the authorities' support. Though race *per se* became less of an issue, class and age were still important *de facto* discriminating categories for Chinese boys, and gender played a role in Guiding's programming and also its later availability to Chinese girls.

Chapter 3 reviews the later interwar years and the period of Japanese occupation, when Scouting grew strongly and became indigenized just before the war, and then disappeared as it was prohibited under the Japanese. Governors Peel, Caldecott, Northcote and, very briefly, Young were Chief Scouts. The movement featured inclusive though largely segregated training, promoted as a realization of the ideal of the worldwide Scout brotherhood. Chinese nationalism mattered greatly, first to be avoided as "politics" and then, as Japan became common enemy of Britain and China, to be embraced as "patriotism" and appropriate dual loyalty. Scouting's citizenship training increasingly meant preparing middle-class native Chinese boys "to fight."

Boy Scouts greeted Duke of Gloucester at Government House, April 1929.

H. K. Scout Archives.

Chapter 4 studies the first two postwar decades, when Scouting was re-started, systematically "denationalized," extended to underprivileged Chinese boys, and eventually became a localized mass movement. Governors Young, Grantham, and Black were Chief Scouts. Chinese nationalism was again important, and was tolerated in the immediate postwar years, and then methodically removed from 1949, after the Communists gained control of China. The Scout Promise called for increasingly detached allegiance to China, requiring only doing one's duty to "the territory in which [one was] living." Class as a discriminating identity was gradually resolved, as the poor, the orphaned and those judged to be "juvenile delinquents" were welcomed into the movement. In the interest of colonial governance, citizenship training took on a denationalized form, even as local Scouting continued to expand and became a mass youth movement.

Scouts on the way to the Botanical Garden for the first post-war parade, April 1946.

Official photograph, U. S. Navy.

Chapter 5 examines the developments from 1964 to 1977, when Scouting rose up to internal and external challenges, grew through various reforms, and obtained early independence from British Scouting. Under Governors Trench and MacLehose and new Chinese Commissioners, Scouting adopted locally-devised planned growth and British-centric reforms. In response to perceived needs of the community subsequent to the disturbances of the 1960s, the local movement also expanded its scope to cover young people who were not Scouts. The members were required to commit to do their duty to "the native territory," giving expressions to a growing sense of Hong Kong identity. Finally, with encouragement from Britain and blessing of the colonial authority, the Hong Kong branch broke away from British Scouting and became an independent member of WOSM, two decades before Hong Kong was handed over to China.

MacLehose met the Scouts, incl. female Venture Scouts, in Kowloon, April 1979.

H. K. Scout Archives.

Chapter 6 covers trends in the post-independence years, when Scouting wrestled with coeducation, infantilization, relevance and tentative renationalization in the postcolonial era. British-appointed governors Youde, Wilson and Patten and Chinese-sanctioned Chief Executives Tung and Tsang were Chief Scouts, though the latter tended to be less involved than their British predecessors. Gender barriers were crossed as girls were integrated into Scouting. Age as a differentiating category was also challenged, as Scouting reached out to younger, pre-Cub-age children. Citizenship training à la Scouting assumed the character of educating young people, including girls and children, for the less sexist and more precocious modern community. Local Scouting continued to expand healthily, despite declines in the movement elsewhere. After decolonization, Hong Kong Scouts were required to commit to do their duty to "the country," finally aligning their promise with that of most countries. New meanings for citizenship training were slowly reconstructed and negotiated, as China replaced Britain as the sovereign country, though a considerable amount of self-government was allowed under the so-called "one country, two systems (一國兩制)" principle.

Hong Kong Scouts, incl. Cub Scouts, visited Tiananmen Sqaure in Beijing, China, July 2010.

H. K. Scout Archives.

This proposed periodization scheme appears reasonable. The First World War conveniently broke up periods one and two. Succession of Clementi by Peel in 1930 is a good divide between periods two and three. The Japanese occupation neatly broke up periods three and four. Trench as the Chief Scout and Lo the new Commissioner in early 1960s, when important challenges had to be met, marked the beginning of period five. The independence of the Hong Kong Scout Movement in 1977 heralded in period six, the last period being reviewed. Just as importantly, these time periods also make sense in terms of the relevance of the analytic categories of race, class, gender, and age and the motives of "to convert, educate, rule or fight." For example, race as a discriminating identity was largely removed in the interwar years covered by periods two and three, class in the first postwar decades or period four, and gender from the 1970s through to the post-colonial decade or period six. Similarly, "to fight" was the most relevant motive in the pre-war periods one and three. "To rule" was the key driver in the postwar periods two and four. And "to educate" became the most important consideration in the most recent phases, or periods five and six.

The book by necessity chose to include certain events (in certain ways) and exclude others. Positivists like Leopold von Ranke wanted history to be written "*wie es eigentlich gewesen ist* (like it actually has been)," or objectively with facts only.[1] E. H. Carr argues that Ranke's requirement is often inadequate, as accuracy is a necessary but not a sufficient condition of good history; and even impossible, as historians must select the facts to include and interpret them based on some conceptual frameworks.[2] Peter Burke points out that "historical narrators…are not omniscient or impartial and…other interpretations besides theirs are possible."[3] There is no such thing as *the* history of Hong Kong Scouting. Indeed, it could be argued that each Scout unit (a group, a district, a region, the training team, etc.) and even each Scout in Hong Kong has its/his/her own history. Some of these histories have in fact been compiled into substantial volumes.   This work is only *a* history of Scouting in Hong Kong written from a particular perspective.

While first published by the Scout Association, it is not meant to be an institutional hagiography or official history. It is rather a narrative and analytical history aimed at both general readers and readers with specific interests in the history of Scouting and the history of Hong Kong. The narratives and analyses developed here attempt to cover the "what, how, when and who" as well as the "why and so what" of the Hong Kong Scout Movement using a large volume of primary sources. It tried to sort out and interpret many facts related to the development of Scouting in Hong Kong from 1910 to 2010 based on the theme of citizenship training for youth and its defining categories, especially that of race, class, gender, and age, in a Chinese context, both colonial and post-colonial. By doing so, it hopes to enrich our understanding of the histories of Scouting, youth, citizenship education, the colonies, the British Empire, decolonization, China and Hong Kong.

---

1   As quoted in Murray Rae, *History and Hermeneutics* (New York: T & T Clark, 2005), 85

2   E. H. Carr, *What is History?* (Hampshire: Palgrave, 1961), 4-6.

3   Peter Burke, "History of Events and the Revival of Narrative," in Peter Burke (ed.), *New Perspectives on Historical Writing* (Cambridge: Polity Press, 1991), 239.

BOY SCOUTS PARADE
MARCH 20, 1915

Chapter 1

Hesitant Start and Early Demise

1910-1919

Chapter 1
Hesitant Start and Early Demise
1910-1919

European Boy Scouts in Tsingtao, 1908.

Gilwell Archives.

Previous Page:

Anstruther and Lady May inspected the Boy Scouts and Wolf Cubs in Hong Kong's first joint parade at St. Joseph's College, March 20, 1915.

H. K. Scout Archives.

Scouting came to the British colony of Hong Kong just a few years after it started in Britain. Informal Scout training was introduced in 1910. The first formal Boy Scout Troop was started in late 1913, and it was registered with the British headquarters in 1914. This was a few years later than elsewhere in the British Empire and in British communities in China. Boy Scouts had appeared in Canada, Australia, New Zealand and South Africa in 1908, and in India and Singapore in 1909. There were European Boy Scouts in Tsingtao in 1908, Tientsin had a local Scout association affiliated with the British association in 1909, and Wei Hai Wei and Shanghai had set up similar organizations by 1911.

In these early years, Scouting prepared a few British boys in the colonial outpost of Hong Kong for citizenship in God's kingdom and the British Empire. Sir Frederick Lugard, a military man whose "stay in Hong Kong was but a brief interlude in a brilliant African career," was the governor from 1907 to March 1912.[1] Sir Francis Henry May succeeded him in July 1912 and stayed till September 1918. They both played a relatively minor role in local Scouting, and the latter was the first Chief Scout of Hong Kong for a brief period of time. Scouting prides itself as an international brotherhood. Yet, except for a short time, due to the exclusion of many youngsters based on rules imposed by the colonial authority along both racial and nationality lines, the movement served only a small minority of British Portuguese and Chinese youth. Scouting teaches duty to God. Yet Christian sectarian prejudices had retarded the start and hastened the end of local Scouting. The movement has been praised by its enthusiasts (and accused by its detractors) as militaristic. Yet, as shall be shown, war waged by the empire provided an

---

1   G. B. Endacott, *A History of Hong Kong* (Hong Kong: Oxford Univ. Press, 1973), 269.

excuse first for excluding non-British Chinese and Portuguese and even older British European (and non-Portuguese) boys and later for abandoning Scouting entirely. In short, a particular vision of nationality, religion and empire informed a rather exclusionary approach to enrollment in and the eventual demise of the movement in this early period.

First Boy Scouts in Hong Kong

In 1910, some within the expatriate community in Hong Kong called for Boy Scout Troops in the colony, similar to those established in significant numbers in Britain and other parts of the empire. In response, two expatriate Protestant churches proposed to each set up a unit for their boys. Informal Scouting began in May 1910 when one of these started "something better"—a Christian Boys' Brigade Corps for British boys which adopted Scout training methods.[1]

Though Hong Kong was a few years late in taking up Scouting, its popularity in Britain had generated some local interests. By 1909, British Scouting activities were regularly reported by the local English papers. A few illustrative examples would suffice. In May 1909, the *South China Morning Post* (*SCMP*) noted that five thousand Boy Scouts were to march through streets of Glasgow on Empire Day. In September, the *China Mail* (*CM*) reported on the thirty thousand Scouts at the Crystal Palace parade, labeled the "King's Hope." In the same month, a piece entitled "Making Manly Men: Quarter of a Million Boy Scouts Enrolled," appeared in the *Hong Kong Telegraph* (*HKT*). In January 1910, the *Hong Kong Daily Press* (*HKDP*) noted Baden-Powell's retirement to devote himself full-time to the burgeoning Boy Scout Movement.[2]

The earliest reference to the need to establish Scouting *in Hong Kong* appeared in the *SCMP* on March 9, 1910, in an article entitled "Boy

OGDEN'S CIGARETTES.

THE KING'S BADGE.

A card depicting The King's Scout Badge, approved by Edward VII.

---

1   Much of this section is based on Paul Kua, "Boys' Brigade, YMCA, and early Scouting in Hong Kong and Singapore, 1909-1918: Christian Boy's Work in two Non-Christian British Colonies," a paper presented at the conference "*Christian Youth Movements: Their History and Significance*," sponsored by the Royal Historical Society and the YMCA of England, held at the Univ. of Birmingham, on February 17-19, 2006.
2   The *South China Morning Post (SCMP)*, May 26, 1909; the *China Mail (CM)*, September 7, 1909; the *Hong Kong Telegraph (HKT)*, September 8, 1909; *Hong Kong Daily Press (HKDP)*, January 25, 1910.

Scouts: Corps Wanted in Hong Kong," which pointed out that "Baden-Powell's scoutey [*sic*] boys are all the 'go' with the younger generation at home," and asked: "Could not some enthusiast take up the matter here?...The idea should include every eligible boy in the colony, and the Government might induce the schools to take up the scheme."[1] It should be noted that this call was for Scouting (not another youth movement), was expansive in nature (for "every eligible boy"), and was aimed at the schools (not, say, the churches). Interestingly, what eventually materialized was different on all three counts. Later that month, another editorial lamented that "no response has yet been made to the idea mooted in the 'South China Morning Post' of starting a corps of Boys Scouts in Hongkong," and reported Baden-Powell's claim that well-trained Boy Scouts would potentially make good colonists.[2]

BOY SCOUTS.

Corps Wanted in Hongkong.

While the volunteer movement is so much on the ebb in this colony, writes a correspondent, it may not be inopportune to suggest the establishment of a corps of boy scouts. Baden Powell's scoutey boys are all the

First public appeal for Boy Scouts in Hong Kong. *SCMP, March 9, 1910.*

The appeals from the *SCMP* for Scouting eventually elicited a response, though not exactly in the form that it was expecting. Rev. H. O. Spink, a recent arrival from England and chaplain of St. Andrew's Church, the Anglican Church for Europeans in Kowloon, wrote in late March that he could do "better" by establishing "a really efficient company of the Boys' Brigade," as it would include "in its programme all that is attempted by the boy scouts," but would also offer extra training "calculated to help the moral and spiritual life of a boy."[3] At that time, most British boys lived on Hong Kong Island, though some (including a

1   *SCMP*, March 9, 1910.
2   *SCMP*, March 21, 1910.
3   *SCMP*, March 24, 1910.

number from military families in the Whitfield Barracks across the street from the church) were in Kowloon. Spink thought that there were not enough boys nearby for a satisfactory company, but still hoped that one could be started by autumn. Spink's preference for the Boys' Brigade instead of Boy Scouts perhaps echoed that of more religious-minded contemporaries in England.[1] While his claim that the brigade was "better" was possibly partly motivated by his church affiliation, it was not totally unfounded. The Boys' Brigade was older, had at the time a more substantial presence in the empire, and did have "more" to offer, at least in terms of spiritual training.

St. Andrew's Church, with the Whitfield Barracks in the background.

The Boys' Brigade had inspired and facilitated early Scouting. The brigade, founded by Sir William Smith in 1884, had become international by 1900. Baden-Powell spoke with Smith at length in 1903 on "the B[oys'] B[rigade], the Boy, the Boy-messengers of Mafeking and much else," and was made an honorary vice-president of the brigade.[2] In 1904, when Smith noted proudly that there were 54,000 brigade boys, Baden-Powell observed that "if the work really appealed to the boys they should have ten times that number," and suggested "scouting" as the solution.[3] In 1906, the *Boys Brigade Gazette* published Baden-Powell's Scout scheme.[4] Even the famous Brownsea Island camp in 1907 owed

---

1   One of whom had complained that there were "no prayers in many scout camps" and declared that "the objective of Sir William Smith" was much sounder. See *The Times*, September 8, 1909.

2   Jeal, *Baden-Powell*, 360.

3   Rosenthal, *The Character Factory,* 52-53.

4   Wilkinson, "English Youth Movements," 12.

BB's Founder's Badge, featuring a portrait of Sir William Smith.

Robin Bolton.

a few debts to Smith: ten out of twenty-one participants were brigade boys; and two brigade captains secured the equipment needed.[1] It might be said that Scouting started as a training program for the brigade.

However, though Baden-Powell might have originally intended that Scouting should be implemented by youth organizations such as the Boys' Brigade and the YMCA, many boys decided that they wanted only to be Boy Scouts, and nothing else. By 1908, independent Baden-Powell Scout Troops had mushroomed throughout Britain. B-P had to introduce a measure of order by setting up local committees to register troops, appoint leaders, conduct tests, and award badges. Willingly or otherwise, the boys' own initiatives had forced B-P to adjust his strategy, a fact illustrative of the negotiated nature of the relationship between the "serving" adults and the "served" youth. A year later, Baden-Powell approached Smith about a merger, predicting that they could achieve "nothing more than very partial results...working as separate organizations."[2] However, Smith refused to join due to the secular nature of Scouting, though he admitted that it was "an excellent thing...within the Boys' Brigade..., *as an interesting and helpful adjunct to its regular work.*"[3] From this point on, Scouting and Boys' Brigade went their separate paths, the latter adopting the former as a training method, and the former growing rapidly as an independent movement.

The interest of the local expatriate community in Scouting appears to have arisen primarily from beliefs in its military value. In 1910, the *SCMP* argued that Scouting would prepare youngsters to become volunteer soldiers, by producing "successive 'year-waves' of young British humanity...all fit citizens, and imbued with the worthy ideals such training will ensure."[4] The *HKT* chimed in with a piece entitled "Boy Scouts for Hongkong: A Feeder for the Volunteers," which lamented the lack of local interest in the Volunteers, and concluded that Scout training would be "a valuable assistance to our Volunteers."[5] To its supporters, then, Scouting would ideally function almost as a cadet program for the Volunteers. This attitude no doubt owed much to the fact that, in those

1   Hillcourt, *Two Lives of a Hero*, 266-267.
2   J. Springhall, B. Fraser, and M Hoare, *Sure and Stedfast. A history of the Boys Brigade, 1883 to 1983* (London: Collins, 1983), 102.
3   Ibid., 103, italics added.
4   *SCMP,* April 11, 1910.
5   *HKT*, May 3, 1910.

days, many British in the colony were military personnel or their family members. However, support for a Volunteers Corps fed by Boy Scouts was also driven by the on-going debates over colonial contributions to the cost of the British military presence. In 1908, the *Hongkong Weekly Press* called for a reduction of the military contribution.[1] In 1911, unofficial Legislative Councilors jointly objected to what they viewed as an excessive share of the colonial military expenses.[2] The Volunteer Corps, made up of part-time soldiers who held down day jobs, represented a much more cost-effective alternative to a large professional army.

BOYS' BRIGADE AND SCOUTS.

To-day's Opening Ceremony.

The first company of the Boys' Brigade and Scouts, in connection with St Andrew's Church, Kow-

Inauguration of the "Boys' Brigade and Scouts."
SCMP, May 11, 1910.

The earliest evidence of local Scouting activities came in April 1910, when Spink advocated a Boys' Brigade Corps with Scout training in Kowloon, and Rev. Hickling of the Union Church suggested a Boy Scout Troop on Hong Kong Island. Early press reports often failed to make well-informed distinctions between the two troops, and tended to label them interchangeably or to treat them as one and the same. The *SCMP* noted that "this movement" (labeled as the "Boys' Brigade and Scouts,") was "decidedly catching on in the Colony."[3] The *CM* declared that "two of the most promising movements in England...are the Boys' Brigade and the Baden-Powell Scouts," and expressed vague hopes of "great things for the two Companies...to be formed."[4] On May 11, 1910, the "first company of the Boys' Brigade and Scouts" was inaugurated at St. Andrew's Church, as twenty-eight boys were inspected by Sir Henry

1 The *Hongkong Weekly Press and China Overland Trade Report*, September 28, 1908.
2 *Hong Kong Hansard*, February 23, 1911.
3 *SCMP*, April 28, 1910.
4 *CM*, April 30, 1910.

May, the acting governor.[1] The Star Ferry Company granted free passes to boys living on the Hong Kong Island on Wednesday afternoons, so that they could attend the weekly meetings, suggesting community support of Scout training. The *SCMP* praised Rev. Spink for having "taken up the cause of the Baden-Powell Boy Scout Movement."[2] That same evening, Hickling met with a dozen boys to discuss the formation of a second Boy Scout company at the Union Church, a non-denominational Protestant church for Europeans on the Hong Kong Island.[3] These Hong Kong Boy Scouts and their Kowloon counterparts were to have similar uniforms, and would engage in "healthy rivalry," "friendly emulation and…occasionally… combined operations."[4]

The Union Church (front right), viewed from the Peak on Hong Kong, with Victoria Harbor in the background.

The English press was enthusiastic about local Scouting, despite some criticism of its racial and religious exclusivity. The *SCMP* declared that "the Boy Scout Movement" had solved what it labeled as "the boy problem," as children could be kept off the street and taught healthy exercise and clean living.[5] It went on to note that though there were twenty-eight boys at St. Andrew's and twelve at the Union Church, parents should encourage more boys to enroll as "there should be more than forty boy scouts available in this Colony."[6] The table on the next page provides some insights on how many boys were potentially avail-

1	*SCMP*, May 11, 1910.
2	*SCMP*, May 12, 1910.
3	*HKT*, May 12, 1910.
4	*SCMP*, May 12, 1910; *CM.* May 12, 1910.
5	*SCMP*, May 13, 1910.
6	Ibid.

able at the time. Out of 450,000 people in the colony, less than 1% were British. While there were close to 34,700 Chinese boys, there were less than 240 British boys, 60% of whom were living on the Hong Kong Island.[1] Therefore, forty boys interested in Scouting actually constituted a very high percentage of eligible British boys. Contrary to the press' conjecture, there could not be many more Boy Scouts, unless the net was cast wider, beyond the British boys.

	Male		Male &
	All	*Boys 5-15*	Female
Chinese	283,276	34,687	438,873
Europeans/Americans	4,111	647	7,743
British	2,157	239	3,761
Other Non-Chinese	2,365	170	3,482
Total	289,752	35,504	450,098

Hong Kong Population by Race, Gender, and Age, 1911

Sources: Tables 2-4, 20-21, the *Hong Kong: Report on the Census of the Colony for 1911* (Hong Kong: Census Office, 1911).

BOY SCOUT MOVEMENT.
The formation of a Boy Scouts Brigade in Hongkong is a sign of the times. Why not form a Chinese section and thus give an opportunity to native lads of acquiring that strength of body and character, which is synonymous with a rigid military training. Chinese lads can appreciate discipline as well as European children

CASUAL CRITIC.

An appeal for Scouting for the Chinese boys.

HKT, April 30, 1910.

The large number of Chinese boys clearly offered the greatest opportunity for growth. A "casual critic" in the *HKT*, while praising the founding of "a Boy Scouts Brigade," asked in April 1910 for "a Chinese section," arguing that "Chinese lads can appreciate discipline as well as European children."[2] But, as it turned out, a Chinese troop was not to appear until years later. It seems that, for the time being, a Chinese section

---

1   *Hong Kong: Report on the Census of the Colony for 1911*, Tables 37, 38.
2   *HKT*, April 30, 1 910.

was far from the minds of these first promoters, and not in tune with the *Zeitgeist* of the colonial community.

Weeks later, the same newspaper lamented that the first initiatives were associated with churches, as Boy Scouts should be "wholly unsectarian, unconnected…with any religious body."[1] This preference for separation of church and Scouting was again ahead of its time. The Christian influence in local Scouting would remain strong for decades. Given that only European boys, predominantly Christian, were served in this period, this complaint may seem puzzling. It might have been motivated by the newspaper's genuine concern for the religious neutrality of Scouting as a matter of principle, but it was also likely driven by worries about Protestant (Anglican) connections, since the *HKT* tended to have a notable Catholic bias, and was to become a staunch supporter of Catholic Scouting later, notwithstanding its religious nature.

The St. Andrew's boys in Brigade Scout uniforms in front of the matshed church hall, c. 1912.

Boys' Brigade Gazette.

At any rate, Spink's brigade met both his personal needs and the perceived needs of the British community. Early appeals were clearly for a Boy Scout Troop—there was no popular demand for the Boys' Brigade. Though the unit set up at St. Andrew's was registered in Britain as the 1st Hong Kong Boys' Brigade Company, it was known to most local people as the Hong Kong Boy Scouts.[2] The *HKT*, covering its inauguration, elaborated on "this 'Scout' system of training invented…

---

1   *HKT*, May 12, 1910.
2   The *Boys' Brigade Gazette,* June 1, 1912, 145.

by…Baden-Powell."[1] When King George became president of the Boy Scouts, the *SCMP* noted that "the Hong Kong corps" was also flourishing.[2] To the community, Scouting was introduced. Spink, having founded a religiously-oriented brigade company with Scout training, had satisfied the community's call for a secular Scout Troop. A group photograph taken around this time of the St. Andrew's boys in their brigade Scout uniforms shows that there were twenty-seven boys, some of whom apparently quite young and perhaps not yet of "Scout" age.

But religion, or rather sectarian conflicts arising from it, soon led to difficulties encountered by the proposed troop on the Hong Kong Island. A second meeting at the Union Church had to be cancelled, as only two boys showed up—a curious development, given that a dozen boys had expressed interest earlier, and there was a lot of publicity in all the English newspapers at the time.[3] After the unsuccessful meeting, Hickling wrote to the *CM,* indicating that he had decided not to pursue the idea further, and recommended that interested boys on the Island should join the Kowloon brigade. He noted that though a Hong Kong company had originally been proposed based on the geographical divide of the Victoria Harbor, some had perceived this plan to be driven by interdenominational rivalry. He pointed out that "some of this bitterness has already appeared, making for sectarian jealousy rather than Colonial union and cooperation," which he had no intention of replicating.[4] Hickling's thinly veiled accusation implicated the Anglican community of

Victoria Harbor, viewed from Hong Kong Island, with the less urbanized Kowloon Peninsula across the harbor.

1   *HKT,* May 12, 1910.
2   *SCMP*, June 21, 1910.
3   *SCMP*, May 19, 1910.
4   *CM,* May 18, 1910.

A Brigade Scout Badge, 1st Class.

Robin Bolton.

the colony. Between the first meeting and the second, it would appear that most interested boys had withdrawn. Though the British population was small, sectarian rivalry between Anglicans and non-conformists was strong enough to jettison this project before it was launched. Ironically, then, religious and sectarian considerations not only delayed the formation of the first Boy Scout Troop by substituting it with a Boys' Brigade Company, it would also appear to have prevented the establishment of a proposed second boys corps (and the first Boy Scout Troop).

The St. Andrew's Boys' Brigade stayed active in the next two years, but contemporary reports focused on typical Scout activities and never mentioned brigade-style spiritual training. The brigade in Britain had adopted its own Scout uniform to be used in Scout activities and a Scout badge to be awarded based on passing a test. Photographic and documentary evidences indicate that St. Andrew's boys often wore the brigade Scout uniforms, and some were called "Scouts," presumably because they had passed the requisite test. In May 1910, at the first parade, Spink, assisted by his lieutenants R. J. Brown, P. Wilkie, Witchell and Wilks, put thirty-two boys through many gymnastic exercises. In October, they held their annual camp at "Seaton," owned by Tse Tsan Tai (謝纘泰), a republican revolutionary and the founder of the *SCMP*, who could be viewed as the first Chinese supporter of local Scouting. In December, Spink took the boys on an outing to the New Territories. In March 1911, another gymnastic display was held, confirming again the impression that Spink was "a firm believer in muscular Christianity." In October, the corps had its second annual camp at Taipo, and the boys assisted in a church bazaar. In March 1912, another inspection occurred,

Lugard met the St. Andrew's boys, March 1912.

St. Andrew's Church.

when Lugard presented a gymnastic medal to "Scout" Johnston, days before the governor's departure for Africa.[1] All these would have been considered normal activities of a secular Boy Scout Troop. There was little evidence that the corps had a large amount of spiritual training and was, therefore, "better than Scouting."

Tse Tsan Tai.

Baden-Powell's first and only visit

Baden-Powell visited Hong Kong in April 1912 and, after a few days of indecision, finally met with the brigade boys of St. Andrew's. A year later, however, the Brigade Corps was replaced by a Cadet Corps attached to the Volunteers, then considered by many in the empire as a more effective junior military scheme for boys, despite Baden-Powell's arguments otherwise.

In April 1912, Baden-Powell's whirlwind tour of inspection of Boy Scouts around the world took him to Hong Kong, where his visit was enthusiastically anticipated by the local Boy Scouts, though such feeling was apparently not reciprocated. In early April, the *SCMP* noted Baden-Powell's imminent visit and claimed that "everything points to a warm welcome being extended by the local corps of Boy Scouts attached to St. Andrew's Church."[2] According to Crowther Smith, a local solicitor involved with the brigade, extensive preparations had been made by the Boy Scouts. An initial plan to camp out at their headquarters the night before so they could greet the founder on his arrival in the morning of April 16 was canceled at the last minute, when a telegram indicated that the general's visit was unofficial, and he would rather not be met at the pier. Instead, he was received by the *aide-de-camp* of Claud Severn, the officer administering the government.[3] On his first day, Baden-Powell toured the principal streets and went to "tiffin" with Severn. At night, he took a river steamer and left for Canton, just when news of the tragic sinking of the *Titanic* was rapidly being circulated around the world, and reported in great details by all Hong Kong English newspapers.

Claud Severn.

PRO 7-2-41

1   *SCMP*, May 19, October 28, October 29, December 21, and December 28, 1910; March 8, October 9, and October 19, 1911; March 12, 1912.
2   *SCMP*, April 10, 1912.
3   *CM*, November 25, 1911.

The Hong Kong-Canton river steamer, 1910s.

Baden-Powell was clearly not in a hurry to see the Boy Scouts in Hong Kong, though he was often eager to meet them in other places. When he landed in New York, he was met "on the wharf…[by] a smart little troop of Boy Scouts."[1] When his ship entered the harbor of Yokohama, a steamer crowded with Boy Scouts came out to see him. In Shanghai, Baden-Powell inspected Scout Troops at the British Consulate, gave a long speech, dined with the Scout Council members, and also watched a camp display.[2] He went to Australia in May, after his visit to Hong Kong, and upon landing in Brisbane, "he proceeded immediately by motor-car" to inspect several hundred Boy Scouts.[3]

Even after his arrival, uncertainties surrounded his itinerary as far as meeting the Boy Scouts was concerned. The *CM* enquired at Government House as to whether "any demonstration is to be given by the Boys' Scouts in honour of the visit," and was told that "up to that time nothing had been definitely arranged, but on a decision being come to the Press would be informed."[4] Later, a reporter was told by Crowther Smith that an official inspection of the Boy Scouts would not be held by the general. One may imagine the disappointment of Smith and the St. Andrew's Boy Scouts. Some of them might and probably did interpret this as an intentional slight on the part of Baden-Powell.

On April 19, after his return from Canton, Baden-Powell, accompanied by Severn, finally met with the Boy Scouts. Around thirty

1   Robert Baden-Powell, *Boy Scouts beyond the Seas: My World Tour* (London: C Arthur Pearson Ltd., 1913), Chapter 2.
2   *CM*, April 16, 1912.
3   The *West Australian*, May 13, 1912.
4   *CM*, April 16, 1912.

boys in smart Boys' Brigade Scout uniforms marched from the ferry wharf on Hong Kong Island to Government House, where "they went through various movements and gymnastic exercises," directed by Spink and Smith.[1] Then the Chief Scout addressed them briefly. Photographs of this historic event were taken by Miss Kate Spink, Rev. Spink's sister, who came to Hong Kong with her brother to help take care of the vicarage.[2] As Baden-Powell never returned to Hong Kong in his lifetime, these photographs of the 1912 parade and inspection at Government House were the only photographic evidence of the founder with his Boy Scouts in Hong Kong.

B-P addressed (above) and inspected (left) the "Boys Brigade and Scouts" at Government House, April 19, 1912.

St. Andrew's Church.

Though Scouting had in some sense begun in Hong Kong, it did not receive the unreserved endorsement of the leader of the movement. How can this curious turn of events be explained, and what does it reveal about the nature of the Scout movement in this outpost of empire? It is unlikely that the fact that this visit was "unofficial" would discourage Baden-Powell from receiving the boys as soon as he arrived. After all, his visit to Shanghai was also unofficial. From the initial response given by the government spokesman, it seemed that B-P was in two minds as to whether to inspect the brigade boys, and had taken some time to consider the matter. Comments made later by Baden-Powell about his encounter with the Hong Kong Boy Scouts provide a hint as to his reluctance. In his book on the world tour, *Boy Scouts beyond the Seas*, which was published in 1913, he noted that he had met in the colony "the Boys'

---

1   *HKDP*, April 22, 1912.

2   Charlotte Vesey (comp.), *Celebrating St. Andrew's Church: 100 Years of History, Life and Personal Faith* (Hong Kong: St Andrew's Church, 2004), 16.

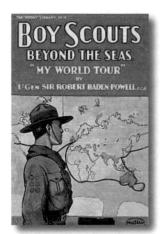

B-P's *Boy Scouts Beyond the Seas*, 1913.

Brigade [boys]...trained and dressed as Scouts," and that he "was very glad to inspect them at a review …in the beautiful grounds of Government House."[1] It is significant that he identified the Hong Kong boys as brigade boys "trained and dressed as Scouts," and not simply as "Boy Scouts." In the *Headquarters Gazette*, the magazine of the British Boy Scouts Association, a similar report was filed, confirming that "the Rev. J. [*sic*] Spink has a company of Boys' Brigade whom he also trains and dresses as Scouts, forty in number."[2]

The likely reason for Baden-Powell's hesitation was the formal association of the St. Andrew's Church with the Boys' Brigade. By this time, in the empire (and even in Shanghai), many Boy Scout Troops were registered with the Imperial Headquarters of the Boy Scouts Association. The company in Hong Kong, however, was part of the Boys' Brigade organization. Baden-Powell was no longer intimately linked to the brigade, and might feel uncomfortable about being associated with a brigade unit in a highly visible manner. More importantly, this company had only adopted the earliest version of Scouting, as a training method for an existing boys' organization, and not its latest form, as a distinct and separate movement led by Baden-Powell. In the interest of growing Scouting, it is quite understandable that B-P did not want to embrace this earlier variant of his movement too enthusiastically.

With the disappointment of a lukewarm reception by Baden-Powell still keenly felt, the fledgling local Scout movement faced a serious challenge from an alternative form of institutionalized training for young men. During this time, growing interest in the militaristic Cadet Corps had a significant influence upon Scouting in the empire, since the corps targeted boys of the same ages as the Scout Troops. In Hong Kong, a Cadet Corps attached to the Volunteers was formed in the 1890s with school boys of many nationalities.[3] In 1907, it received official recognition when Lugard noted his interest in "the Semaphore class of Cadets." By 1908, the cadets had their own bugle band. In 1909, many cadet boys were reported to have "made excellent shooting."[4]

1   Baden-Powell, *Boy Scouts beyond the Seas,* Chapter 5.
2   The *Headquarters Gazette*, August 1912. Spink's full name was Hubert Octavius Spink.
3   *Hong Kong Administrative Report, 1894,* 165.
4   *CM,* November 8, 1907; *HKT,* July 30, 1908; the *Hongkong Weekly Press and China Overland Trade Report,* July 5, 1909.

Baden-Powell had tried to position Scouting as complementary or even superior to the Cadet Corps. In an internal report, he argued that "although the aim of our Movement is citizenship, it gives at the same time, the manliness, keenness and sense of duty which form the essential ground work for training a Cadet."[1] In 1913 the British association declared that "it is gradually being realized that the Cadet and Scout systems can exist side by side."[2] As the specter of war loomed large, there was more pressure to prepare boys militarily, and the debate heated up. In 1915 Baden-Powell wrote a piece entitled "Cadet or Scout Training," which argued that "mere drill and rifle practice" were inadequate for "a soldier for modern war," that character training was more important, and that education authorities in the empire had shown increased interest in Scouting, implying that Scouting was not merely complementary to, but better than, cadet training.[3]

It is significant that in Hong Kong the cadets disappeared from newspaper reports in 1910, coincidental with the founding of the "Boys' Brigade and Scouts." It seems likely that membership of the two organizations overlapped, or that many boys who joined the brigade had been cadets before. In December 1912, after Spink returned to England, Crowther Smith became captain of the brigade.[4] After this, it seems to have disappeared from the press. The brigade was not even mentioned in newspaper articles on a fund-raising bazaar at St. Andrew's in October 1913. This may be considered unusual as the funds raised were to furnish a new church hall to replace the old mat-shed hall, often used by the boys for meetings in the previous two years.[5]

Sir Francis May came back from Fiji in July 1912 to become the new governor. At the start of 1913, around the same time that the Boys' Brigade became inactive, the Cadet Corps was revived, probably absorbing many if not most of the brigade boys. Regulations for its re-establishment for boys aged between ten and eighteen were issued in March 1913.[6] Unlike his predecessors, Governor May had a narrow view on the corps' nationality requirement: a cadet must be attending a

---

1   Baden-Powell, *Report on Boy Scouts Overseas,* August 28, 1912.
2   The *Annual Report, 1913* (London: The Boy Scouts Association, 1913), 9.
3   The *Annual Report, 1916* (London: The Boy Scouts Association, 1916), 18.
4   The *Boys' Brigade Gazette*, December 1, 1912, 63.
5   *CM,* October 6, 1913; *HKT*, October 6, 1913.
6   *HKT*, March 1, 1913.

government British school or, if attending another school, be of British parentage. In effect, this meant that cadet boys must be "ethnically" British, a term which was often used loosely in those days (and will be used in this book) to mean British nationals who were ethnically English, Scottish, Irish and Welsh; or people who "originally" came from Britain. The term "ethnic British" should not be treated as equivalent to, say, European or white. Some comments on race and ethnicity in the context of Hong Kong may be helpful. In the case of the Chinese people in Hong Kong, these two socially constructed terms could be and are often used interchangeably in this study. Most local Chinese were racially *Han* Chinese, and the few non-*Han* Chinese who lived in the colony would be sinicized and would identify themselves as ethnic Chinese. However, the ethnic British in Hong Kong are not the same as the Europeans. Excluded from the former were Europeans who were not British nationals, such as the French. More importantly, just as "both Jews and the Irish... have been perceived as non-Whites at one time or another in the United States," the Portuguese in Hong Kong, though no doubt Europeans, would often not be considered as ethnic British, even though most of them were British nationals.[1]

Aside from drills, inspections, parades, and camps, the cadet boys were required to attend the obligatory firing and musketry training. Significantly, May appointed Smith as the Lieutenant of the Cadet Company. Given the latter's close links with the brigade and the over-lapping age ranges of the two groups, it is likely that most, if not all, brigade boys or "Boy Scouts" were conveniently converted back into cadets. Therefore, shortly after Baden-Powell's visit, the first "Boys' Brigade and Scouts" had disappeared, and the colony was left again without any Boy Scouts, formal or informal.

The motivations which lay behind Hong Kong's decision to revert back to the cadets so soon after informal Scouting was introduced should be considered. A possible reason could be the disappointment experienced by Crowther Smith and the St. Andrew's boys during Baden-Powell's visit. As much as the Chief Scout may have had good reasons not to treat these boys in the same way as Boy Scouts elsewhere, it is

Sir Francis Henry May.

1   Stephen E. Cornell and Douglas Hartman, "Mapping the Terrain: Definitions," in Harry Goulbourne (ed.), *Race and Ethnicity: Critical Concepts in Sociology* (London: Routledge, 2001), 85.

likely that in delaying his meeting with them, he did not endear himself or Scouting to local brigade leaders and the boys. This by itself may not have resulted in the disbanding of the brigade, if the colonial authorities had continued to support Scouting. However, as already noted, there was also a change in official attitudes in favor of the cadets after May's arrival, which was at least partly motivated by the perception that the empire might soon be at war and that military preparedness would be a sound policy. The evidence suggests that May had apparently made up his own mind in the on-going debate about the relative merits of the Cadet Movement and Scouting. In a letter dated June 1913, it was disclosed that Baden-Powell had written earlier to the governor, "urging the formation of Boy Scouts in the Colony."[1] Governor May had responded politely that he would consider the matter, but had also indicated that "it was feared it might interfere with the Cadet Corps."[2] In other words, perceiving a need for stronger colonial defense, May was in favor of the latter as the preferred boys' training program, with its military orientation. In short, by early 1913, both the brigade boys headed by Crowther Smith and the ruling elite under May had good reasons to reconsider the desirability of the Scout Movement. Less than a year after the founder's visit, instead of moving from informal to formal Scouting, Hong Kong abandoned the former in preference for the Cadet Movement.

Crowther Smith.
Jenny Hounsell.

First Hong Kong Troop

Subsequent to Baden-Powell's visit, several efforts were made by the British association to jump-start formal Scouting in Hong Kong, mainly through appeals to the colonial ruling elite and an elitist government school in the colony. An unexpected breakthrough on this front occurred in late 1913 from within the Catholic Church, an institution not originally targeted by either the initial promoters of Scouting or Baden-Powell.

After Baden-Powell's visit, Col. H. S. Brownrigg, the Commissioner for Overseas Dominions and Colonies at the British Scout association, had written to Henry Keswick, the second-generation head

---

1   Letter, Brownrigg to Keswick, June 18, 1913, the Gilwell Archives.
2   Ibid.

OGDEN'S CIGARETTES.

GENERAL
SIR R.S.S
BADEN-POWELL,K.C.V.O.

General Sir Baden-
Powell.

of Jardine, Matheson & Co. and a member of the Legislative Council, soliciting his support for Scouting in Hong Kong, informing him that "there is already a flourishing body at Shanghai and troops of Boy Scouts in China at Tiensin [*sic*] and Wei hai wei."[1] Keswick, who had returned to England for the coronation of King George V in 1911, was either too busy or not interested, and nothing came of this approach. Aside from writing to May, Baden-Powell had also written to Queen's College to appeal for the creation of a troop. In his letter, he emphasized the attractiveness of "Hongkong as a place where boys could have a wonderfully good time 'Scouting,'" and expressed the hope that "Queen's College, like so many other great schools" would soon join "the Brotherhood of Boy Scouts," one that has extended to "every part of the British Empire," and was the embodiment of "the ideal of Confucius that 'all within the Four Seas are brethren.'"[2]

It is interesting that of all the schools, the Chief Scout should decide to single out Queen's. In the 1910s, the school had around five hundred boys, with district feeder schools in Saiyingpun, Wantsai (Wanchai), and Yaumati.[3] In 1911, Cecil Clementi, then acting colonial secretary, noted that while there were sixty-seven government and grant schools, Queen's College was the most important.[4] But it was also a secular school with a predominantly Chinese student body. As Hong Kong was 98% Chinese, and 97% of the Chinese in the colony were Confucians or animists, Baden-Powell was clearly aiming at a sector that would give Scouting the biggest potential growth. However, he was not simply aiming at any and all local boys. There was a class angle. Chinese boys in the Queen's College were considered the *crème de la crème* of the education system, akin to students of the great English public schools like Eton and Charterhouse (Baden-Powell was an old Carthusian himself). They were likely to become future elites in Hong Kong, and perhaps even in China. As David Cannadine might put it, Baden-Powell was, in effect, subscribing to the view that the empire was indeed "one vast interconnected world," and Scouting as a young movement

1   Ibid.
2   The *Straits Times*, 4th July, 1912.
3   *Imperial Education Conference Papers, III.—Educational Systems of the Chief Colonies not possessing of Responsible Government: Hong Kong* (London, 1915), 20.
4   *Colonial Reports—Annual, No. 723, Hong Kong: Report for 1911* (London, 1912), 14.

could be promoted by latching onto the class structure of the imperial periphery, replicating that of the metropolitan society.[1] In hindsight, this tactic could be described as sound. If he had been successful in penetrating the elite secular schools, early history of Hong Kong Scouting might have been different. The young movement could have grown more rapidly, and would certainly not have been bogged down by the sectarian concerns which, as shall be seen later, plagued it during this period.

Queen's College, Hong Kong, c1900.

Though Queen's College had expressed initial interest, it did not introduce Scouting until much later. In June 1912, perhaps in response to Baden-Powell's appeal, B. James of the College wrote to the British association for information. The headquarters responded in August, and followed up again in April 1913.[2] Unfortunately, nothing came of these efforts, and Queen's College did not have a troop until after the Great War. It is unclear as to why this was the case. Doubtless, Queen's, of all schools, would have been most qualified to introduce this innovation in education. Maybe some leaders of this "citadel" of secular education were suspicious of a movement which promoted duty to God. It is also possible that this proud school which had produced prominent Chinese graduates, including Dr. Sun Yat-sen, was wary of the imperialistic nature of Scouting. Perhaps it was discouraged by the colonial authorities who were not interested in promoting Chinese Scouting at this time. At any rate, it is certain that the school was not against militaristic training *per se*: it soon established a St. John's Ambulance Corps, and many boys signed up for the special Police Reserve. In fact, on the speech day in 1916, these uniformed boys formed a guard of honor to welcome Gover-

---

1   David Cannadine, *Ornamentalism: How the British Saw Their Empire* (Oxford Univ. Press, 2002), 3-5.
2   Letter, Brownrigg to James, April 23, 1913, the Gilwell Archives.

nor May as the guest of honor.[1]

There was also a fleeting expression of interest from within military circles. In August 1913 Sergeant Smith from the Royal Garrison Artillery at Victoria Barracks wrote to Britain, indicating that he wanted to start "a troop of Boy Scouts…first among the garrison boys, 50 (30?) of which [*sic*] I have just taken to camp for ten days."[2] Smith noted that "the G.O.C. is anxious for to see [*sic*] a troop formed" and that he would continue until he received "the necessary authority" and information on prices of uniform.[3] In September Brownrigg responded and urged Smith to ask the general officer commanding to be the president, and the governor to be the Chief Scout of the local association.[4] It is possible that interest soon waned, or that Smith was transferred away from the colony shortly after. At any rate, this troop was never registered in Britain, and no contemporary report on its activities, if any, could be found in local newspapers, despite the latter's interest in any news relating to Scouting during these early years.

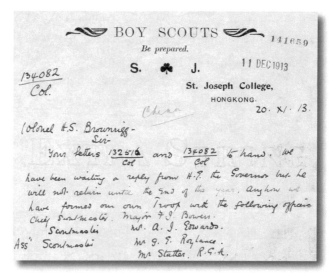

Edwards' letter to the British Scout association, late 1913.

Gilwell Archives.

Eventually, the breakthrough in formal Scouting came from unexpected quarters: the St. Joseph's College. St. Joseph's, pride of Catholic education in those days, was managed by the La Salle Brothers, and

1   Gwenneth and John Stokes, *Queen's College: Its History, 1862-1987* (Hong Kong: Queen's College Old Boys' Association, 1987), 81-82; *HKT*, June 13, 1916.
2   Letter, Smith to the Boy Scouts Association, August 18, 1913, the Gilwell Archives.
3   Ibid.
4   Letter, Brownrigg to Smith, September 22, 1913, the Gilwell Archives.

enrolled Portuguese, Chinese and other non-Chinese boys, regardless of their religious beliefs. In September 1913, Albert Edwards, who had recently left the Royal Navy to become the ward-master at the Gaol Hospital, wrote to the British association about setting up "a troop of Baden-Powell's Boy Scouts" sponsored by St. Joseph's.[1] In October, he wrote a second letter to the British headquarters, requesting "a catalogue of all necessary requirements."[2] In fact, by the time of his first letter, he had already started a troop unofficially, as reported in the local *Bulletin of Catholic Ladies Union*:

> *Boy Scouts: ...The new Director, Br. Adrian, ...has started among the boys a Corps of Boy Scouts, and has secured the co-operation of four keen workers—Major Bowen; Mr. J. A. Edwards, late of the Royal Navy, a newcomer to Hongkong; Mr. Roylance, late of the West Kent Regiment, and Gunner Statter, of the Royal Garrison Artillery. Over 60 boys having submitted applications to join the Corps, they were formally enrolled on the 11th inst....thus St. Joseph's College has given one more proof of its determination not to be behindhand in all that appertains to the well-being of the Catholic youth of the Colony. Another Corps of Scouts is already in existence in Kowloon. It remains for the boys of St. Joseph's College to prove themselves if not first in the field at least first in efficency.[3]*

As this report was originally dated October 10, the St. Joseph's troop's founding on ""the 11 inst." was probably September 11, 1913. The troop enjoyed a promising start, with sixty boys and at least four leaders, all with British military backgrounds, including a member of the artillery, who may or may not have been involved in the earlier efforts led by Smith. Major Bowen was styled the "Chief Scout Master," while Edwards the "Scoutmaster." The comments "another corps of Scouts is already in existence in Kowloon" clearly indicate that, at the time, some believed that the St. Andrew's Boy Scouts were still active. The St. Jo-

1   Letter, Edwards to the Boy Scouts Association, September 13, 1913, the Gilwell Archives.
2   Letter, Edwards to the Boy Scouts Association, October 4, 1913, the Gilwell Archives.
3   *Bulletin of Catholic Ladies Union* (Hong Kong), October 10, 1913. 48-49.

The Scouts Oath.

Each Scout promises in the presence of the Chief Scoutmaster saying with right hand uplifted I promise:—

To be loyal to God and the King.
To help others at all times at all costs.
To obey the "Scout Law".

The Scout Law.

1. A Scout's honour is to be trusted.
2. A Scout is loyal to his King, to his officers and to those in authority.
3. A Scout's duty is to be useful and to help others.
4. A Scout is a friend to all. A brother to every Scout no matter what social class he may belong to.
5. A Scout is courteous.
6. A Scout is a friend to animals.
7. A Scout obeys the orders of his parents, patrol leaders without any question.
8. A Scout smiles and whistles under all circumstances and never uses bad language.
9. A Scout is thrifty.

St. Joseph's enrollment card, 1910s, with Scout Oath and Scout Law.

Gilwell Archives.

seph's boys were, therefore, urged to be "first in efficiency," though they could not be "first in the field."

The Boy Scouts from the St. Joseph's troop were all given an enrollment card, and all took a "Scout Oath" in which they promised "to be loyal to God and the King, to help others at all times and at all costs, to obey the 'Scout Law.'"[1] Note this older version of the Scout Law had nine clauses, including several that were subsequently modified, deleted or merged into others.

The first members of this Troop included many Portuguese and some Chinese as well as boys from other nations, generally reflecting the ethnic backgrounds of students of this Catholic school in Hong Kong. "In a few years until it (Scouting) lapsed during the Great War...the three eldest Braga boys" of José Pedro Braga, viz., 16-year-old José Maria [Jack], 13-year-old Delfino [Chappie] and 11-year-old Clemente Alberto [Clement], were all in the St. Joseph's Troop.[2] J. P. Braga's ancestors came to Macau in early 1700s, and some of them moved to Hong Kong in 1840s, once the British colony was established. He himself was a prominent member of the Portuguese community in Hong Kong, and was to become a Legislative Councillor and chairman of China Light and Power Company in the postwar years. Braga Circuit in Kowloon Tong was named after him.

The St. Joseph's troop prospered in its first months of existence, and even introduced innovative activities such as Scouting for older boys and Sea Scouting. In October 1913, Brownrigg responded to Edwards' letter, happy that a troop was being started, and noted that Hong Kong was "one of the few colonies which have, as yet, not joined the Movement."[3] He advised that a powerful local association should be formed with the governor as the Chief Scout, as was the case in "almost every...Overseas Dependencies."[4]

Baden-Powell also sent the new troop a few words of encouragement, pointing out that "pioneer work is sometimes difficult and the

---

1   Enrollment card, St. Josephs' Boy Scout Troop, c.1913, the Gilwell Archives.
2   Stuart Braga, "Making Impressions: The Adaptation of a Portuguese family to Hong Kong, 1700-1950," Ph. D. thesis, Australian National Univ., Oct. 2012, 233, 248-50, 317-8.
3   Letter, Brownrigg to Edwards, October 14, 1913, the Gilwell Archives.
4   Ibid.

boys may have to put up with a certain amount of chaffing when they first begin."[1] In the same month, Edwards informed Britain that he had already secured the patronage of the Catholic bishop, and was awaiting a reply from the governor, who was out of town.[2] By then, Edwards realized that the St. Joseph's troop would be the first officially registered Boy Scout Troop in Hong Kong, and assured Brownrigg that "the 1st Hong Kong Troop [would]...leave no stone unturned to keep up the reputation of the Association."[3] At prize-giving in December, Brother Adrian noted that the Boy Scouts had been inaugurated and that he was sure that "the Scouts will 'stick it', and be a credit to the College and the Colony."[4] Severn, the guest of honor, was met by an honor guard of fifty Boy Scouts and presented a Life-Saving Medal to Scout F. Coscolluela for rescuing another Scout, Si Kiong-lam, in Deep Water Bay.[5] Severn noted his approval, but regretted that the troop was not started in time for Baden-Powell's visit.[6]

St. Joseph's troop in front of the college, c. 1913.

H. K. Scout Archives.

By the end of 1913, the troop had a magazine called the *Scouts Gazette*, which initially was no more than just "a bright little sheet."[7] Around the same time, Scouting for old boys of the college between

---

1   Letter, Baden-Powell to Edwards, November 20, 1913, the Gilwell Archives.
2   Letter, Edwards to Brownrigg, November 20, 1913, the Gilwell Archives.
3   Ibid.
4   *HKT*, December 20, 1913.
5   *HKT*, December 20, 1913; the *Headquarters Gazette*, March, 1914, 94. Note the names in the latter differed slightly from those in the former, showing F. Coscolluela and Si Kiong-lam vs. Coscollenela and Sikiong Lam.
6   The *Headquarters Gazette*, March, 1914, 94.
7   *HKT*, January 5, 1914.

A card illustrating the Sea Scouts.

eighteen and twenty-five was introduced. The formation of the "St. Joseph's Bodyguards," as these boys were called, presaged the Senior Scouts introduced in Britain in 1917.[1] The community viewed this favorably, and the *HKT* praised it for giving "young men, who have reached the age when character is rapidly being formed, an agreeable occupation for their spare time."[2] In December, Captain Phillip Streatfeild of HMS *Triumph*, a former commissioner for Sea Scouts at Plymouth, gave a talk on sea Scouting.[3] By January 1914, a troop of Sea Scouts attached to the college had been started with thirty-six boys.[4] This was a significant initiative, as Sea Scouting was relatively new even in Britain. Warrington, Baden-Powell's brother and an accomplished amateur sailor, had only written the first official manual for the Sea Scouts in 1912.

"Form B," the registration form for local Boy Scouts' Associations, was signed by Bowen on April 2, 1914, and the official warrant for the St. Joseph's College local association was issued in Britain on May 1st.[5] At the time, St. George, patron saint of England, was being adopted as the patron saint of Scouting, and Baden-Powell was inviting Scouts everywhere to celebrate St. George's Day with a parade. Later in April 1914, the first St. George's Day Rally was held by the St. Joseph's troop in the college square, marking the start of a long tradition of rallies on this day. Christian and imperial symbolism abounded, seemingly confirming that local Scouting's citizenship training was aimed at preparing boys both for God's kingdom and the British Empire. Bowen gave a speech on the slaying of the dragon by St. George, comparing that to the slaying of "the dragon of unrighteousness" by young Christians. A Union Jack flew proudly in the center of the parade ground, and the rally ended with three cheers for the king.[6] With registration completed and the St. George's Day rally held, the St. Joseph's troop finally became the official representative organization of formal Scouting in Hong Kong.

Whereas the Union Church had failed to establish a Scout Troop for English Protestant boys, St. Joseph's College succeeded in setting it up for boys regardless of creed or color. That the college was able to

1   Hillcourt, *Two Lives of a Hero*, 373.
2   *HKT*, January 15, 1914.
3   *HKT*, December 30, 1913.
4   *HKT*, January 15, 1914.
5   Registration Form "B", the St. Joseph's College Troop, the Gilwell Archives.
6   *HKT*, April 24, 1914.

Top part of Form B for the St. Joseph's troop.

Gilwell Archives.

secure official recognition for the first Boy Scout Troop in this British colony can be viewed as a Catholic coup. This is especially remarkable given that initial efforts and official encouragement were all aimed at Protestant or government institutions, and also because the Catholic Church was, generally speaking, not particularly enthusiastic about this movement until after the war. In France, early Scouting was not viewed favorably by the Catholic Church. As Philippe Laneyrie suggests, "early Scouting...found from the prewar years its most energetic detractors within the Catholic Church (*Le scoutisme naissant...trouvera dès les années d'avant guerre ses plus vigoureux contempteurs au sein de l'Église catholique*)."[1] French Canadians also generally shied away from Scouting before the 1930s. Similarly, Catholic parishes in America sponsored very few troops before the Great War, as "many priests saw Boy Scouting as 'Episcopalianism or Presbyterianism transfigured.'"[2] However, the success of the Catholic Church in initiating formal Scouting in Hong Kong, as will be seen later, turned out to be a mixed blessing, since it led to mistrust of the young movement by at least some British Protestants.

The decision of the Catholic Church in Hong Kong to create a racially-inclusive Boy Scout Troop as opposed to the more exclusive ones proposed earlier by the Protestants must be seen in context. It might appear that racial prejudices of the Anglican (or, more generally, Protestant) British in Hong Kong were stronger than those of the Catholic Europeans. The latter's more accepting attitudes may have been informed by the established global missionary traditions of Catholic Europe, as opposed to the more recent ones of Protestant and especially Anglican Britain. James Johnson observed in 1915 that the Catholic Church in

---

1   Laneyrie, *Les Scouts de France*, 54-55.
2   Macleod, *Building Character*, 197.

New York had registered impressive growth because it was "that religious body in which wealth, social distinction, class and race count for least," and that it was "almost impossible to think of a Catholic priest preaching race discrimination."[1]

But the different racial attitudes of the Protestant and the Catholic authorities might also have had something to do with their social positions in Hong Kong. The former's relative intolerance was to be expected from privileged members of the established church of a ruling race. The latter's relative tolerance was at least partly motivated by the fact that in its ranks were many Irish soldiers, Portuguese natives, and Chinese converts who perceived themselves to be "minorities," outside the privileged racial group. In other words, the Catholic Church's more inclusive attitudes were driven partly by the ideology of the church and partly by necessity due to its "outsider" status in the British colony.

The introduction of an inclusive Boy Scout Troop was also a pragmatic alternative for the mixed student body of the college, after the revival of the racially exclusive Cadet Corps. The driving force behind Scouting in the college appears to have been Brother Adrian, the new Irish director. Adrian had been the principal of the Christian Brothers' school in Kuala Lumpur, and would have been aware of early Scouting in the Straits Settlements.[2] He would also have been exposed to the publicity on Scouting surrounding Baden-Powell's visit.

More importantly, restrictions in the revived local cadets introduced in early 1913 might have forced him to look at other options. In the past, the cadets had been popular with many school boys, regardless of their nationality. In fact, the Cadet Corps of 1893 had more third-country Europeans (including twelve Portuguese) than ethnic British boys.[3] Even drills without links to the cadets were in demand. At the 1908 prize-giving day of the college, it was reported that "physical drill has a great attraction for [our boys], especially for the seniors."[4] The educational philosophy of the day seemed to endorse military drills. The *SCMP* commented that "it is a patent fact that the well-drilled school

1   James Weldon Johnson, *The Selected Writings of James Weldon Johnson: The New York age editorials (1914-1923)* (New York: Oxford Univ. Press, 1995), 139.
2   *HKT,* September 9, 1913.
3   *Hong Kong Administrative Report, 1894*, 165.
4   *CM*, January 3, 1908.

cadet is more active, more attentive and responsive to instruction, than the boy without military training."[1]

But when May re-established the cadets, he had restricted enrollment to the ethnic British boys. Most Portuguese, Chinese and non-Chinese students of the college would not have been able to join, as many were not British nationals, and most were not children of British parents, the stated entry requirements of the Cadet Corps. Setting up a Boy Scout Troop, a fashionable thing to do throughout the empire, would have appeared to be a very good (or at least a second-best) solution, as it would allow the St. Joseph's boys to receive character and drill training available to ethnic British boys in the Cadet Corps.

For British boys only

The inclusive racial character of early formal Scouting in Hong Kong was short-lived. At the onset of the the Great War, a colonial decree implemented locally in the name of war-preparedness (but motivated by British and Chinese political considerations) produced a new nationality-based policy for the young movement which effectively excluded most Chinese boys and many Portuguese ones.

Though war clouds had loomed large in Europe for some time, war was declared only in August 1914. The immediate impact on Hong Kong was to precipitate the involuntary departure of all German women and children, the internment of German men of military age, and the taking over of German businesses (much to the joy of the British competitors).[2] The formal start of the war also provided an opportunity for the imposition of restrictive new requirements for membership in local Scouting. The troop's annual report in late 1914 elaborated on the two interrelated policy changes, and its response to it:

> *In August the Troop was entirely re-organised. The charter incorporating the local troop with the London Association made it imperative that the Scouts should be British*

1   *SCMP*, April 19, 1909.
2   Norman Miners, *Hong Kong under Imperial Rule, 1912-1941* (Hong Kong: Oxford Univ., 1987), 7.

*subjects. This naturally weakened us numerically but by
no means diminished the enthusiasm of the boys. At the
present time there are 48 boys in the Senior Troop and 30
in the Junior Troop making 75 in all [numbers do not add
up]. The troop is open to any British subject and, in ac-
cordance with the expressed desire of His Excellency the
Governor, any English boy on application for enrolment
is requested to join the Cadet Corps.*[1]

In short, "English" (a term which was used loosely in the troop report
and often in the contemporary press to mean all ethnically British) boys
should be encouraged to become a cadet, and only British nationals who
were non-ethnically British or, effectively, the British Portuguese and the
British Chinese, could become Boy Scouts.[2]

The *Administrative Report* of the colonial goverment for 1914
confirmed that the St. Joseph's troop's membership had declined due to
the introduction of the rule that "'Baden-Powell' troops should consist
of British subjects only."[3] The new policies relating to uniformed youth
work in Hong Kong can be summarized in the table below:

Ethnicity/Nationality	Uniformed Groups
Ethnic British ("English")	Cadet Corps
"Non-ethnic" British nationals	Boy Scouts
Non-British nationals	None

Uniformed Groups, August 1914

The implied racial hierarchy of the new policies was obvious. The most
desirable youth group, in the eyes of the colonial authorities, was the Cadet Corps, open only to ethnically British boys. Boy Scouts were down-
graded to second-class status, available to British subjects who were not

---

1   *CM*, October 30, 1914; *SCMP*, October 31, 1914. Note both reports contained
the same inconsistent numbers of 48, 30 and 75, which would suggest that the mistake
was in the original annual report.
2   One possible reason why the term "English" was and still is often used loosely
in Hong Kong to refer to all British is because in the Chinese language, while there is
a term for Great Britain (大不列顛), when referring to the *British people*, the Chinese
term is still *yingguoren* (英國人, literally people from England), which is equivalent to
the term for the *English* people.
3   *Hong Kong Administrative Reports, 1915*, Appendix N, 15.

fortunate enough to be ethnically British. Non-British nationals were not to be given training through either the Cadet Corps or Scouting.

This exclusive policy contrasted with open enrollment in British Scouting. Baden-Powell believed that Britain was in danger of a war in Europe which she was not ready to fight and that active intercession through Scouting could help prepare British youngsters. Though Scouting had managed to attract mostly boys from middle or lower middle class backgrounds, it was meant to be all-inclusive from day one. Early Scouting was partly motivated by concerns with perceived negative influences of urban living, leading to the racial degeneration of lower-class British youth living in the crowded inner cities. David Pomfret suggests that it was around this time that "a new discursive construct, the 'town-bred boy', identifiable by his physical appearance," had begun to emerge, as opposed to the healthy country lad.[1] Robert MacDonald argues that the early movement was "a scheme to save the Empire" aimed at transforming urban "slum children" into real men and patriotic citizens who could fight the coming war.[2]

On the other hand, when the movement was transplanted into the colonial setting of Hong Kong, it needed to resolve the additional complication of how to deal with the existence of a large native population (the "ruled" race), most of whom were not British nationals. To fully appreciate the "British subject" requirements, one must understand British nationality in the context of Hong Kong in those days. As in the Orwellian society, some British subjects were "more equal than others." British nationals who were "naturalized" were second-class. For example, the Governor in Council had the right to banish a naturalized British from Hong Kong in the interest of "peace, order and good government," and cancel "his status as a British subject."[3] Not even all natural-born British subjects were equal. For example, only "a British subject of *European descent*, and at the time of his birth his father must have been a British subject, either natural-born or naturalized in the United Kingdom," could become a Police Probationer.[4]

---

1   Pomfret, *Young People and the European City,* 119.
2   MacDonald, *Sons of the Empire*, 3-4.
3   *Hong Kong Hansard*, March 28, 1904.
4   Secretary of State for the Colonies, "Police Probationers: Hong Kong, Straits Settlements, and Federated Malay States," 8th April, 1904.

Similarly, not all British subjects could enter the 1913 Cadet Corps—interested boys had to be ethnically British, either attending a government British school or be of British parentage. Most if not all British Portuguese and British Chinese boys could not enroll. More importantly, only Biritsh subjects (who were not ethnically British) could become Boy Scouts. Estimates based on the 1911 census suggest that at least 40% of the Portuguese and 80% of the urban Chinese boys would be excluded from Scouting based on this restriction.[1] The new policy ostensibly involved only discrimination based on nationality. But in practical terms, the "non-racist" decree had strong racial implications: most Chinese boys and many Portuguese and other non-Chinese boys were excluded from the youth movement.

In response to these new strictures, Bowen had dissolved the old troops, then set up a reconstituted senior troop for young people age seventeen and above and a junior troop for boys at the college, both consisting of only British subjects who were non-ethnic British.[2] The resulting decline in membership was significant. Total enrollment, excluding the older Bodyguards, had grown from sixty in September 1913 to one hundred and twenty in April 1914.[3] An enrollment in the junior troop of thirty in August suggests a loss of ninety boys, even assuming no further growth since April. It would appear that many Portuguese and other nationals and most Chinese boys must have left.

A *de facto* race-based exclusion policy ran counter to Scouting ideals. The original Fourth Scout Law stated that "A Scout is...a brother to every other Scout, no matter to what social class the other belongs."[4] Though this version only mentioned class, Baden-Powell noted that Kim, the Boy Scout, was the "little friend of *all the world*," and all Scouts should aspire to the same.[5] He also pointed out that "almost every race, every kind of man, black, white, or yellow, in the world

1   Locally-born persons could claim British nationality, though in practice many did not. There was a process of naturalization, but this was also very rarely done. The 1911 Census shows that 60% of the 2,558 Portuguese had been born locally, and only 21% of the 314,627 urban Chinese. The *Report of the Census of the Colony for 1911* (Hong Kong, 1911), Tables 6, 7.
2   The *Headquarters Gazette*, November, 1914, 343.
3   Registration Form "B," St. Joseph's College Troop, the Gilwell Archives.
4   Baden-Powell, *Scouting for Boys: the Original 1908 Edition*, Elleke Boehmer (ed.) (Oxford: Oxford Univ. Press, 2004), 45, italics added.
5   Ibid.

furnishes subjects of King Edward VII," again ruling out race-based, though not necessarily nationality-based, exclusion.[1]

Nevertheless, in early Scouting, racial exclusion was common in some colonies. South African Scouting only enrolled white boys for many years. Despite efforts by forward-looking individuals like Canon W. A. Palmer from as early as 1911, natives were barred. Four years after Scouting was introduced to the Cape, Baden-Powell gave a vague response to a challenge from a black clergyman: "I can only refer you to the Fourth Scout Law *but local conditions must govern.*"[2] In 1916, he wrote that he was inclined to agree with "exclusion of coloured boys from the Scout Movement in the Cape."[3] A year later, he condoned Johannesburg's approach, which was to let natives use some ideas in Scouting but not admit them into the brotherhood. This pragmatic attitude was characteristic of the founder in the early years, when it was arguably necessary to ensure the acceptance of Scouting in parts of the empire, where racial problems were acute. The implied racial equality of the Fourth Law was deemed unacceptable by the South African Scout authorities, given their desire to attract white Afrikaner boys. In this context, the nationality (as opposed to race) based exclusion policy in Hong Kong appears milder, at least in theory.

An artist rendition of the Fourth Law, showing brotherhood between two Europeans.

The British nationality requirement would not mean much in practice if the excluded boys were not interested in Scouting to begin with. However, it would be difficult to argue that the Portuguese boys were not interested. Many of them had signed up when the St. Joseph's troop was founded. There were only slightly more Portuguese boys than British boys at the time, but their subsequent response to Scouting was considerably more enthusiastic, judging by the enrollment statistics of the St. Andrew's company versus that of the St. Joseph's troop. The requirement did in fact discriminate against many non-British Portuguese boys, who saw Hong Kong as their permanent home.

On the other hand, some might conjecture that perhaps Chinese boys were indifferent. Few Chinese became Boy Scouts in this period. The St. Andrew's brigade enrolled only British Protestant boys. The

---

1   Ibid., 26.

2   As quoted in Parsons, *Race, Resistance, and the Boy Scout Movement*, 77, italics added.

3   As quoted in Rosenthal, *The Character Factory*, 261.

unregistered garrison troop, if it had existed, would have been comprised only of the boys of British servicemen. St. Joseph's troop was initially open to all. However, Si Kiong-lam was the only Chinese ever specifically mentioned. One could claim that the government's *de facto* racist policy had little impact on the Chinese boys, because they simply were not interested. This hypothesis may be tested against the experience of early Chinese Scouting in China and elsewhere.

An advertisement for Scouting ("Boys' Righteous and Courageous Corps") in China, 1910s.

The evidence from China, to the contrary, indicates strong early Chinese interest. The first Chinese Scout Troop was inaugurated at Wenhua College (文華書院) in Wuchang by Rev. Benjamin C. L. Yen (嚴家麟) in February 1912, under the name of *Tongzi Yiyong Dui* (童子義勇隊), or "Boys' Righteous and Courageous Corps."[1] Some Chinese students in Shanghai became interested and convinced G. S. F. Kemp to start the first Chinese troop there in 1913. In April 1914, another troop was set up in Shanghai at St. John's University.[2] Scouting was introduced in Peking in early 1910s, when residents there became "accustomed to the sight of Boy Scouts parading the main thoroughfares."[3] Stanley V. Boxer started the 1st Hankow Troop for Chinese boys at the Griffith John College (博學書院) in 1915, named after a well-known British missionary who had lived for many years in Hankow.[4] In the same year, a troop was set up at the Canton Christian College, and Edwards from St. Joseph's reported that "it was a splendid sight to see over 150 young Chinese lads so keen and enthusiastic."[5]

In April 1915, the Far Eastern Games in Shanghai featured hundreds of Chinese Boy Scouts in a display in front of youth representatives from many provinces.[6] Soon, local associations were launched in Canton, Soochow, Tientsin, Peking, and Nanking. By 1916, there were eleven Chinese troops in Shanghai alone, with over five hundred boys. In 1916 and 1917, *La Jeunesse* (新青年 *New Youth*), a reformist magazine started by Chen Du-xiu (陳獨秀), later a prominent Chinese

1   Fan, *Zhong Guo Tong Zi Jun Shi.*
2   *HKDP*, April 8, 1914.
3   *HKDP*, July 22, 1915.
4   Griffith John College Papers, the LMS Collection, the SOAS Archive, London. Griffith John was a Welsh missionary attached to the London Missionary Society. He was also involved in the efforts to translate the Bible into Chinese.
5   The *Headquarters Gazette*, April, 1916, 110.
6   Andrew D. Morris, *Marrow of the Nation: A History of Sport and Physical Culture in Republican China* (Berkeley: Univ. of California Press, 2004), 29.

Communist, had published many articles on Scouting using the term *Shao Nian Tuan* (少年團 Youth Corps).[1] In short, the movement quickly gained wide acceptance among Chinese boys in the young republic.

This early interest in China illustrated Scouting's inherent attractiveness for the boys. But Xu Guoqi suggests another possible motive for the adults. At the time, it was widely believed that *tiyu* (體育 physical education) held "the possibility and mission of nation-strengthening," or that "sports could be used to save China," then labeled by some as the "sick man of East Asia" (東亞病夫).[2] This would explain why modern educators, the YMCA, and reformist magazines such as *La Jeunesse* all became interested. Coincidentally, as already noted, similar worries about weak urban youth in the empire had partially motivated Baden-Powell to found Scouting earlier on.

Evidence outside China also indicates strong interest among overseas Chinese boys. Scouting started in 1908 in Singapore with no color bar. In 1910, Frank Cooper Sands headed up the YMCA troop, which was open to boys of all races. In 1916, the two troops catered to European, Eurasian and Chinese boys. In the same year, the Singapore government had decided to fund the practically moribund Cadet Corps. However, unlike Hong Kong, it did not attempt to suppress Scouting, but took "a benevolent, but not a controlling interest in the movement."[3] A Chinese businessman, Seow Poh Leng, became the secretary and treasurer of the local Scout association, another indication of its open ethnic attitudes.[4] Chinese boys in the United States were also keenly interested in the movement in its early years. In 1914, Chingwah Lee and seven other Chinese American boys in a Chinese church in San Francisco read a Boy Scout Handbook, and formed the first Chinese troop in America.[5] In short, when given an opportunity, Chinese boys in China and elsewhere were just as fascinated by Scouting as European boys in Britain,

A commemorative medal of an early Shanghai Scout gathering.
Author's collection.

---

1   *La Jeunesse* 新青年, January 1, 1917; January, 1916; February 15, 1916..

2   Xu Guoqi, *Olympic Dreams: China and Sports, 1895-2008* (Cambridge, MA: Harvard Univ. Press, 2008), 12-20.

3   The *Annual Departmental Reports of the Straits Settlements for the Year 1917*, 236.

4   Kua, "Boys' Brigade, YMCA, and early Scouting in Hong Kong and Singapore," 22.

5   Kevin Starr, *The Dream Endures: California Enters the 1940s* (Oxford: Oxford Univ. Press, 2002), 138; Iris Chang, *The Chinese in America: A Narrative History* (New York: Penguin, 2004), 184; Benson Tong (ed.), *Asian American Children: A Historical Handbook and Guide* (Westport: Greenwood, 2004), 193-194.

Canada, Australia and America.

How, then, can May's exclusionary policies be understood? It is tempting to simply blame British prejudice, and label these as clear cases of racial discrimination. Few could argue against such an assertion, and of course racism was integral to the whole idea of imperial rule. As Joseph Conrad's Marlow puts it in the novel *Heart of Darkness*, "the conquest of the earth, which mostly means the taking it away from those who have a different complexion or slightly flatter nose than ourselves, is not a pretty thing when you look into it too much. What redeems it is the idea only. An idea at the back of it…and an unselfish belief in the idea… "[1] This idea depends on faith in the superiority of the conquering races and the helplessness of the conquered peoples. Marlow was, of course, a fictitious character. But John Stoddard, the American who visited Hong Kong in the late 1800s, would likely subscribe to the veiw that British colonial rule was indeed beneficial to the local Chinese.[2]

Indeed, racist attitudes may well have motivated some of the Britons who supported exclusion. There were many incidences of discrimination pursued at the level of colonial government in early twentieth century Hong Kong. For example, in 1904, May pushed through an ordinance to reserve an area in the Hill District (the Peak) for "all persons of European birth," based on health reasons.[3] In 1918, he championed an amendment to exclude also the Eurasians, justifying it, as David Pomfret points out, "on cultural grounds, focusing…upon white children's vulnerability to their 'degenerate' Eurasian counterparts," many of whom had moved to the Peak.[4] Discrimination was also practiced in education. However, while there were schools that catered to the British youngsters, the government also supported many schools which served Chinese, Portuguese, Indian and other children. If racism was the driving force, the government could easily have introduced segregated Scouting for British and non-British boys, instead of *de facto* racial exclusion.

Another possible concern was the Catholic and Irish links of the St. Joseph's troop. In June 1914, the editor of the *HKT* argued that Boy

1   Robert Kimbrough (ed.), Joseph Conrad, *Heart of Darkness: An authoritative Text, Backgrounds and Sources Criticism*, 3rd edition (New York: Norton, 1988), 10.
2   J. Stoddard, *John L. Stoddard's Lectures, Vol 3* (Chicago, 1909), 227-59
3   *Hong Kong Hansard*, April 19, 1904.
4   David Pomfret, "Raising Eurasia: Race, Class, and Age in French and British Colonies," *Comparative Studies in Society and History*, 2009, 324.

Scouts "make…better material for a cadet" and Scouting for non-British boys would result in "a few good citizens to spread the seed amongst our neighbours"[1] In other words, training good citizens for China could be a side benefit of Scouting, much as educating future leaders of China was an objective of the Hong Kong University, founded in 1911. That this debate was inflected by sectarian concerns was confirmed by a response by "an Irish Unionist," who noted dryly that if a Scout would make a good recruit for the cadets, he would also surely make a good recruit for the National Volunteers in Ireland, since "the Scout movement in Hongkong has been gathered almost exclusively into the hands of the Roman Catholics."[2] To be fair, this observation, while seemingly valid, ignored the fact that Scouting had been encouraged among British Protestant and secular circles even before the Catholics became interested, though without success. "One of the Scouts" responded the next day, by noting that many Scouts were non-Catholics, and declaring indignantly that comments about the National Volunteers were "an insult to the English Scoutmasters, who will tell him that there are no boys in the Colony more loyal than the Boy Scouts."[3]

> Sir,—You seem to me to contradict yourself. You deny that the Boy Scout receives any military training and yet you assert that a trained Scout makes a good recruit for a military organization —the Cadet Corps. Presumably, therefore, he would also make a good recruit for the Nationalist Volunteers. You surely cannot have failed to notice that the Scout movement in Hongkong has been gathered almost exclusively into the hands of the Roman Catholics. In the present political situation cannot you bring yourself to entertain any sympathy for the views of
>
> Yours etc.,
> " AN IRISH UNIONIST."

A letter from "An Irish Unionist."

HKT, June 1914.

---

1   *HKT*, June 9, 1914.
2   *HKT*, June 11, 1914.
3   *HKT*, June 12, 1914.

At any rate, the feelings of "Irish Unionist" were probably shared by some British citizens. The "militaristic" label was difficult to deny given the military background of the troop's leaders and its emphasis on drills, field days, attacks, and maneuvers. The "Irish Catholic" label was hard to avoid as St. Joseph's was a Catholic college, Brother Adrian was Irish, and the enrollment card of the Boy Scout Troop even had a green shamrock on its cover. Nor was this a purely imagined threat. The *Fianna Éireann* had been founded in 1909 along the lines of Scouting, though it emphasized Irish nationalism. The third Irish Home Rule Act had been passed in 1912, and Hobson's Irish Volunteers had grown from just 3,000 in 1913 to 100,000 a year later.[1] From 1915 to 1919, Irish policies in Britian were driven by "three successive Coalition Cabinets of a steadily increasing Unionist...content."[2] A few days after this open political debate in the newspaper columns, Edwards announced publicly the postponement of a planned rally as the time was deemed "unsuitable."[3] After this, intriguingly, local Scouting seemed to have gone into a short period of hibernation.

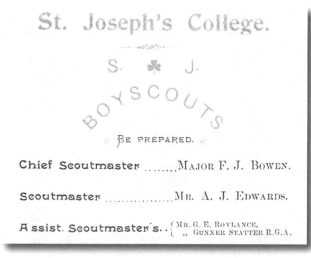

Partial view of the St. Joseph's enrollment card, depicting a shamrock.

Gilwell Archives.

Yet another motivation, held in tension with anxieties over race, concerns a different set of nationals, the Chinese. There was always the

---

1   Thomas P. Dooley, *Irishmen or English Soldiers?* (Liverpool: Liverpool Univ. Press, 1995), 76; J. Bowyer Bell, *The Dynamics of the Armed Struggle* (London: Frank Cass, 1998), 57-61; M. J. Kelly, *The Fenian Ideal and Irish Nationalism, 1882-1916* (Woodbridge, Suffolk: Boydell Press, 2006), 225.

2   Diana Mansergh, *Nationalism and Independence: Selected Irish Papers* (Cork, Ireland: Cork Univ. Press, 1997), 65.

3   *HKT*, June 19, 1914.

troubling question concerning "subject races" across the empire: "Could you in fact trust a loyalty which was superficial rather than spontaneous, a loyalty imposed upon them from above?"[1] Though the Irish Catholic links of local Boy Scouts might have worried some Englishmen, few would seriously believe that Portuguese or Chinese Scouts from St. Joseph's would become involved with the Irish independence movement. China provided a more immediate cause of concern. The situation was perhaps analogous to that of India, where the authorities had been wary of extending Scouting to Indian boys, as it was feared that "organizing them in any way was potentially dangerous, opening up the possibility of infiltration by revolutionary elements."[2] Such fears were accentuated by troubles in 1905-8, when young Indian *swayamsevaks* (volunteers) became involved in anti-British and nationalistic agitations.[3]

Baden-Powell was eager to admit Indian boys, but agreed that "natives imbibing Western ideas [may] seek for an outlet through revolutionary societies, etc."[4] The first Indian troop, organized by missionary Rev. Wood in 1908, had to be disbanded in 1910 due to opposition to having Indian boys as Scouts. Troops for British boys were started in 1909 and soon grew in number. By 1911, the Indian educational authorities' policy was one of non-encouragement: it did not interfere with Scouting for British or Eurasian boys, but would not promote the movement "lest by doing so they should stimulate emulation in schools for Indian boys," which could degenerate into "seditious *samitis*."[5]

Hong Kong played an important role in the efforts to overthrow the Qing Dynasty, though this hardly pleased the colonial authorities. From 1895 to 1911, eight campaigns were organized in the colony, which served "as the centre for intense plotting and preparation, as collection and distribution centre of funds and firearms, as gathering ground and recruitment centre for comrades from overseas and China, and as a haven for disbanded revolutionary members escaping from the Manchu vengeance."[6] The success of the 1911 revolution, as observed by Lu-

---

1   James Pope-Hennessy, *Half-Crown Colony: A Historical Profile of Hong Kong* (Boston: Little, Brown and Co., 1969), 86.

2   Rosenthal, *The Character Factory*, 265.

3   Watt, "The Promise of 'Character'," 42.

4   As quoted in Rosenthal, *The Character Factory*, 265.

5   Watt, "The Promise of 'Character'," 44, 48.

6   K. C. Fok, "The Hong Kong Connection: A Study of Hong Kong's Role in the

gard, "was the occasion of the most amazing outburst [of fire-crackers] which has ever been seen and heard in the history of this Colony...The cracker-firing was contrary to law but...it would have been impossible to check it."[1] Large sums of money were raised for the revolutionaries. Dr. Ho Kai and Wei Yuk, Legislative Councilors, played key roles as "comprador patriots."[2] May was concerned about the revolution, and later terminated Ho's role as a legislator because he "was intimately involved with the...first revolution in Kwantung, and has been intimately connected with the Canton Government ever since."[3]

Scouting was supposed to transform boys into patriotic citizens and obedient soldiers, both of which would be problematic for native boys in a colonial setting. The authorities in Hong Kong and India shared similar worries about revolutionary ideas among their youth. May had a good understanding of the "Chinese mentality" and Chinese politics. Given his concern with Chinese nationalism, he would conceivably object to admitting Chinese into Scouting. The government was clearly opposed to any military training for local Chinese boys. In 1915, May only gave his blessing to a straightforward application for permission to use a rural lot for exercises by Chinese school children after he was assured that the "alleged *military* drill" was totally unfounded, and that "the drill proposed is simply physical and nothing else whatever."[4] Scouting's patriotism and militarism could indeed be seen as dangerous among Chinese boys, at a time when the Chinese Republic had just been established, and a heightened sense of nationalism had been awakened in many impressionable young minds. This pragmatic concern with Chinese nationalism, over and above the somewhat simplistic binaries of colonial racial prejudices or worries about Irish Catholic influence, was probably the immediate motivation for the adoption of a racially-exclusive policy for Hong Kong Scouting.

1911 revolution," *Lectures on Hong Kong History: Hong Kong's Role in Modern Chinese History* (Hong Kong: The Commercial Press, 1990), 53.

1   Fung Chi Ming, "Governorship of Lugard and May: Fears of Double Allegiance and Perceived Disloyalty," in Lee Pui-tak (ed.,) *Colonial Hong Kong and Modern China: Interaction and Reintegration* (Hong Kong: Hong Kong Univ. Press, 2005), 73.

2   Tsai Jung-fang, "The Predicament of the Compradore Ideologists," *Modern China*, 1981, 204-209.

3   CO 129/403, May to Harcourt, August 18, 1913, quoted in Fung, "Governorship of Lugard and May," 81-82.

4   "Application for permission to use land at DD 453, Lot No. 727," CSO No. 1856/1915, HKRS 58-1-75-191, the Public Records Office, Hong Kong, italics added.

High hopes and rapid decline

In early 1915, the inclusion of younger ethnically British boys and for-mation of a colony Scout association supported by the ruling elite gave rise to hopes of expansion of the movement, despite the departure of some members for war services. These hopes, however, were quickly dashed in 1916, when the younger boys were also diverted to the Cadet Corps, the local association was wound up, and the troops at St. Joseph's became inactive.

In spite of the exclusion of non-British boys, the decimated St. Joseph's troop quickly recovered and took active part in the war efforts. In late September 1914, sixty members gathered at the cathedral for a blessing of the troop colors, when the bishop reminded all to be good citizens and good Christians. Two days later, Major General Kelly of-ficiated at an investiture ceremony during which all boys took the Scout Promise and were admitted as Boy Scouts of the newly-reconstituted troop, many probably for the second time. The event betrayed a mili-taristic bias, despite repeated denials of any such links. In attendance were Colonel Irwin, Colonel Watson, Major McHardy and Major Bow-en, whose presence was said "almost to lend a *military importance* to so singular an event."[1] The editor of the *HKT*, consistently an enthusiast, took the opportunity to issue another supportive editorial.[2]

H.R.H. THE PRINCE OF WALES
Chief Scout of Wales

Boy Scouts eagerly served in war preparations.[3] They helped the Volunteers on field days by distributing ammunition and acting as messengers, signalers and orderlies. Lieutenant-Colonel Chapman, the commanding officer, noted that the boys had performed well, though "when distributing ammunitions to the firing line they were apt to be rather too enthusiastic and keen, consequently they occasionally exposed themselves on the sky line too much."[4] In November, Boy Scouts hosted a concert for the Prince of Wales Fund for the War, in the presence of Commodore Anstruther and Major Bowen.[5] In a mobilization exercise

---

1	*HKT*, September 24, 1914
2	*HKT*, September 26, 1914.
3	The *Headquarters Gazette*, November, 1914, 343.
4	*Hong Kong Administrative Report*, 1914, Appendix N, N15.
5	*HKT*, November 16, 1914.

The Prince of Wales, also the Chief Scout of Wales.

in August, thirty-six Scouts were trained in stretcher bearing and ambulance work at the military hospital.[1] In the *Administrative Report* for 1914, Severn confirmed that Boy Scouts "rendered useful service as messengers."[2] In April 1915, in a report to the Secretary of State for the Colonies, the governor praised "the public spirit exhibited by the Boys [*sic*] Scouts in placing their services at the disposal of the Military Authorities and rendering much valuable assistance."[3]

The Peak Pack, 1915, with Bowen (seated, center), Skinner (right).

Scout Assn. Heritage Service

Soon after Scouting began, there were many calls for the inclusion of younger boys. In response, the Wolf Cubs, "a junior branch consisting of boys between 9 and 11 [with]…a modified course of training" was proposed in early 1914.[4] Within months, younger ethnically British boys in Hong Kong also became involved. In late 1914, a Wolf Cub Pack was founded at the Peak School by Miss Skinner, who had just arrived from England.[5] In February 1915, Skinner hosted a reception at the Peak Hotel "to interest parents in the movement," in the presence of fifty ladies, including Lady May and Mrs. Anstruther.[6] Given the governor's interest in training ethnic British boys as cadets, Mr. Ralphs, the Inspector of Schools, hastened to add that Wolf Cubs would be restricted to boys of British parentage who were too young to be cadets, and that they would be enrolled as cadets when they become older. Soon after, a pack was started at the garrison school at the Victoria Barracks.

On March 20, 1915, the two packs and the St. Joseph's troops held a joint parade at St. Joseph's College, presided over by Commodore

Early Wolf Cub Pack leader's hat badge.

Author's collection.

1	*CM*, October 30, 1913; The *Headquarters Gazette*, November, 1914, 343.
2	*Hong Kong Administrative Report, 1914*, 35.
3	*SCMP*, May, 15, 1915; *HKT*, May 14, 1915; *HKDP*, May 14, 1915.
4	*Annual Report, 1914* (London: The Boy Scouts Association, 1914), 27.
5	*HKDP*, April 10, 1915.
6	*HKDP*, February 20, 1915.

Anstruther and Lady May.[1] To the extent that this gathering involved both Wolf Cub Packs and Boy Scout Troops sponsored by three separate schools, it was the first colony-wide Scout parade of the expanded Hong Kong Boy Scouts' Association. Photographs from this period indiciate that while the St. Joseph's troops had several patrols of Boy Scouts and Sea Scouts, the two Cub Packs were smaller, each with, say, ten to fifteen boys. Still, according to an eyewitness report, the ethnic British boys from the packs were the favorites, having "claimed the greater part of the interest as they were for the most part very small boys [and had]… performed…in a very commendable manner."[2]

First joint Scouts & Cubs parade at St. Joseph's College, March 20, 1915.
H. K. Scout Archives.

The introduction of the Wolf Cubs led to a revised structure of uniformed youth groups in the colony, as the following table indicates:

Ethnicity/Nationality	Younger Boys	Older Boys
Ethnic British	Wolf Cubs	Cadet Corps
"Non-ethnic" British nationals	None	Boy Scouts
Non-British nationals	None	None

Uniformed Groups, early 1915

The internal inconsistencies of this structure are obvious. Most Chinese and other non-British were still excluded, regardless of their age. Younger non-ethnic British boys could not join a Wolf Cub Pack though,

---

1   *CM,* March 20, 1915; *HKT*, April 24, 1915.
2   *SCMP*, March 22, 1915.

ANSTIE'S CIGARETTES

WOLF CUB

A Wolf Cub.

to be fair, there appears to be no rule preventing one from being set up. Older non-ethnic British boys could enroll in a Boy Scout Troop, if they were at the St. Joseph's College. Young ethnic British boys could enroll in a Wolf Cub Pack at the Peak or in the garrison but, when they became older, were urged to enroll in the Cadet Corps, even though Cub training was supposed to be followed by Scout training. This highly impractical structure for the uniformed groups was not to last for very long. Still, the structure, however impractical, had the distinct advantage of including some ethnic British boys, which lent an air of respectability to the movement and permitted official sponsorship and community support. By April 1915, the local association had appointed Lady May as its president and Commodore Anstruther as the commissioner.[1] Hong Kong Scouting had finally shaken off its "Catholic" label and acquired colony-wide recognition.

In a meeting in the same month, Bowen touted the necessity of a central Boy Scouts hall, and noted Sir Paul Chater's agreement to fund the project under Lady May's patronage.[2] An appeal for subscriptions noted that it had become "imperative that a central hall should be available for all scouts irrespective of denomination or creed."[3] It appears that the training of ethnically British Protestant boys in a Catholic school was deemed inappropriate by some, in spite of the fact that, in practical terms, the need for a new hall was somewhat questionable, since all of the troops were from St. Joseph's, and the two packs belonged to the Peak and the Garrison schools, both of which had their own facilities. By the month of May, the building fund had a subscription of over two thousand dollars, with contributions from sixty people or organizations. Sir Henry May and Chater headed the list, while Anstruther, Severn, French Consul General Liebert, and local luminaries like Lau Chu-pak, S. D. Dodwell, Robert Ho Tung, Ho Fook, Ho Kom-tong, and Ellis Kadoorie were included. For a movement with few Chinese or Eurasian boys, there were at least a dozen Chinese or Eurasian donors.[4]

On Empire Day in May 1915, Hong Kong British Scouts were given visible symbolic duties which reflected the interest and expecta-

1   *HKT*, April 28, 1915.
2   *HKDP*, April 10, 1915.
3   *HKT*, April 28, 1915.
4   *SCMP*, May 18, 1915.

tions of the colonial community in them, as youth of the empire. St. Joseph's students and Boy Scouts started the day with addresses on the empire movement. They then attended the Empire Day service at the Catholic Cathedral, with a sermon by Bishop Pozzoni on the meaning of duty to the empire and the King, and "a life in obedience to God's tenets."[1] May, Severn, and others attended an Empire Day service for children, including the cadets and Wolf Cubs, at St. John's Cathedral, where Bishop Lander preached on the empire and national service, and also emphasized the central role of God. The two British packs and the St. Joseph's troops then appeared in an Empire Day parade on the Cricket Ground, after a stop at the Queen Victoria Statue, where a Wolf Cub laid a wreath in honor of the Queen. The rally started with a large crowd of spectators in the presence of Lady May, Anstruther, Kelly, Bishop Pozzoni, Bowen, Taylour, and Ralphs. In his speech, Anstruther reminded all that they were parading on Queen Victoria's birthday, and that "the principal lesson one gathers is the glorious 'Unity of the Empire.'"[2] The *SCMP* expressed these lofty expectations of the community:

> *Some of our future men of Britain, in whose hands lie the glory of our nation, sons of men who are giving of their best, and who, if called upon, would be willing to lay down their lives for their country, these boys, of all ages, are learning to be honourable, brave, and capable men, not necessarily in the future to become active defenders of their country, but in whatever sphere of life they find themselves, to bring credit to that Flag, which represents the honour and glory of Great Britain.*[3]

By October 1915, enthusiasm for Scouting had become so pronounced that a meeting was held to discuss its enlargement. Anstruther, by this time a Rear-Admiral, and Lady May were both present. A proposal to form the Hongkong Baden-Powell Boy Scouts Association (as opposed to the St. Joseph's Boy Scouts Association) was unanimously carried. The governor was acknowledged as the Chief Scout, and the Catholic contribution was recognized with the appointment of the broth-

Queen Victoria Statue.

1   *CM*, May 24, 1915.
2   *HKT*, May 25, 1915.
3   *SCM P*, May 22, 1915.

er director of St. Joseph's as one of the two vice-presidents.[1] The *HKT*, an ardent champion of the Catholic cause, could not resist adding that the college should not lose "one atom of the permanent credit that is due to it for having persevered in its 'Scouting' during a trying time when many people were ready to throw cold water on the whole movement in this Colony."[2] The formation of the association was officially confirmed in November 1915, when the Executive Council duly exempted it from registration under the Societies Ordinance of 1911.[3] In many ways, the year 1915 ended for Scouting with high hopes for a bright future.

Even as Scouting took on new levels of symbolic significance for those of the British elite who remained in the colony, the movement felt the impact of departures for war service. Scouts from all over the empire eagerly signed up for duty when the war started. At this juncture, the "senior ranks of the militaristic youth organizations," Scouting included, were "an obvious source of volunteers for the army."[4] Baden-Powell estimated in 1914 that in Britain alone, over 10,000 ex-Scouts and Scoutmasters had entered military services, some 1,300 became coast guard Scouts, and 50,000 were employed in support roles.[5]

The onset of war also precipitated departures which weakened the Hong Kong movement's leadership. In December 1914, Streatfeild left with HMS *Triumph*, which saw action in Tsing Tao against the Germans. In early 1915, Bowen was transferred out.[6] In June, Mrs. Rayner, a Cubmistress, left with her husband Lieutenant Colonel Rayner.[7] Brooks, who was with the St. Joseph's troop, left for the front by the end of 1914, and Basil Taylour was gone in 1915. Spink, who had returned to England, volunteered for the front with the Liverpool Regiment, and was killed by shrapnel in August 1916 in France, when he, as chaplain, was on his way to bury his fallen comrades. The late Captain Rev. Hubert Octavius Spink was thirty-eight at the time, and was buried near Albert.[8]

Capt. Rev. H. O. Spink.

1   *SCMP*, October 2, 1915.
2   *HKT*, October 4, 1915.
3   *Hongkong Government Gazette*, November 26, 1915, 536, No. 511.
4   Michael Snape, *God and the British Soldier: Religion and the British Army in the First and Second World Wars* (Abingdon: Routledge, 2005), 160.
5   Baden-Powell, *Boy Scouts in the Year of the War, 1914, by the Chief Scout* (London: Boy Scouts Association, 1914), x-xv.
6   *HKT*, March 30, 1915.
7   *SCMP*, May 25, 1915.
8   "H. Spink, 1914-1922," WO 339/69095, the National Archives, London; *CM,*

In taking his duties so courageously, he was apparently an atypical army chaplain. Chaplains were under orders from the church not to risk their lives. Robert Graves declared that "no soldier could have any respect for a chaplain who obeyed these orders, and yet there was not in our experience one chaplain in fifty who was not glad to obey them."[1]

Active military service was not limited to Scoutmasters. In April 1915 it was noted that Patrol Leader F. Prouchandy of St. Joseph's was to join the French army.[2] In his Empire Day sermon, Bishop Pozzoni held out Prouchandy as an example, and reminded the young audience that their schoolmate was going to the front, doing his duty to his country.[3] Another French Boy Scout, Adolphe F. Demée, also enlisted. In August 1916, he wrote from the front to his Scoutmaster Jack Braga, indicating that he had been in Verdun, where his unit had suffered from bad weather and food shortages for days. He was still in good spirits though, and asked for "old books and Scout text books" to be sent, and "big Prouchandy's address."[4] In July 1917, Private Demée modestly mentioned that he was decorated with the *Croix de Guerre* for bravery, which was "a rather nice bronze cross, attached to a green and red ribbon."[5]

Demée and Prouchandy were still quite young when they enlisted, which was by no means unusual in the Great War, as many soldiers on both sides were merely young boys in their teens.[6] More significantly, both were French nationals and would presumably have been excluded from Scouting had they remained in Hong Kong. It must have been somewhat embarrassing that the only public examples of local Boy Scouts joining the allied war efforts were those of boys who would have been excluded under the British nationality requirements imposed at the start of the war, ostensibly in the interest of the allied cause.

Contemporaneous developments in Scouting, or rather Guiding, for girls, provide some insight into the difference that gender made to the experience of citizenship training. According to official histo-

A WWI French *Croix de Guerre.*

Author's collection.

---

11 June, 1917.

1   As quoted in Snape, *God and the British Soldier*, 81.

2   *HKT*, April 24, 1915.

3   *CM*, May 24, 1915.

4   *HKT*, 29 September, 1916.

5   *CM*, 28 July, 1917.

6   Richard Van Emden, *Boy Soldiers of the Great War: Their Own Stories for the First Time* (London: Headline, 2005).

ries, Baden-Powell met some girls with Scout hats, scarves and staves who claimed to be "Girl Scouts" at the Crystal Palace rally in 1909, and decided to devise a separate organization for girls called Girl Guides.[1] Primary evidence reveals that the development of Guiding was an evolutionary process which was more complicated and had in fact started earlier.[2] At any rate, the Girl Guides Association was founded in 1910 in Britain, initially with Baden-Powell's sister Agnes as its president.

By January 1916, Guiding had come to Hong Kong, when the upper girls of the Victoria British School formed "a corps of Girl Guides and parade for drill and instruction once a week under Miss Day."[3] (As an aside, it is interesting to note that Scouting for girls actually came to nearby Portuguese Macau several years earlier.[4]) Duncan Tollan, who had four young daughters, was a keen supporter and had apparently performed the first enrollment for the girls in Hong Kong.[5] In February 1916, Day appeared as the captain of both "the Hong Kong Company and the Kowloon Y. W. C. A. Company" in a promotion meeting.[6] In the presence of Anstruther and Governor May's daughters, Day explained that Guiding supplemented rather than replaced training at home by mothers, and that Girl Guides, unlike Boy Scouts, would not be "running wild over the country at all hours," but "were supposed to be in at respectable times," assurances which highlighted the gendered expectations which were probably commonly held in the metropole as well as

Girl Guides.

1   Hillcourt, *Two Lives of a Hero,* 294-296. .

2   "Girls' Guildry," a girls' version of the Boys' Brigade, had existed years before. See the *Boys' Brigade Gazette*, March 1, 1909, 110. In 1908, Baden-Powell observed that: "to ladies interested in the care and education of girls…this [Scout] scheme might supply a suggestion for an attractive organisation and valuable training." An experimental camp for factory girls, lesser-known than Brownsea, had also been a success, leading Baden-Powell to conclude that "scouting camps might...be employed for…girls as well as boys." See Baden-Powell, "Boy Scout Scheme," (London, 1908), 14. In May 1908, he stated that "girls can get just as much healthy fun out of Scouting as boys can." See Baden-Powell, "Can Girls be Scouts?" *The Scout*, May 16, 1908.

3   *HKT,* January 25, 1916.

4   As noted in an April 1912 report, "[a] company of Portuguese girl scouts had been formed in the Colony [of Macau]. The number enrolled…is about two dozen. They are to have their first field day at Calowan, the lair of the bad bold pirates." It would be interesting if one could find out what sort of adventures the girls had, given the frequent visitations of pirates in those days. See *HKDP*, April 13, 1912.

5   *Guiding in Hong Kong* 香港女童軍運動 (Hong Kong: Hong Kong Girl Guides Association, 1986), 21-4. Though not cited in the book, information on Tollan's involvement apparently came from newsletters issued by the local Guide association in 1966. It is not known whether this was, in turn, based on some first-hand documents.

6   *HKT*, February 17, 1916.

the periphery.[1] One is left to wonder if any of the four daugthers of May had also signed up.

Sir Henry, Lady May, and their daughters.

PRO 8-19A-28.

The expanded Boy Scouts Association maintained a high profile through to the first half of 1916. St. Joseph's Boy Scouts formed a guard of honor for May at a Catholic fund-raising fête in November 1915.[2] In April 1916, children of the Peak produced a play at the Mount Austin Theatre, with nursery rhyme characters and several "Boy Scouts," presumably played by members of the Peak Pack.[3] On Empire Day, the usual patriotic rally was held, with Braga and Garcia leading the St. Joseph's troops, Cooper the Garrison Pack, Day the Guide Companies, Crowther Smith the Cadet Corps, and Lau Tai-chai the Chinese troop of the Canton Christian College (嶺南學校).[4] The governor acknowledged this as the first occasion he had to inspect the boys as their Chief Scout and urged them all to "Be Prepared," noting that "the present war is an object lesson of unpreparedness."[5] As in the past, both cathedrals held Empire Day services for children. Over six hundred children, including cadet boys and Girl Guides, were at the Protestant service.[6] Similarly, at the service at the Catholic Cathedral were two thousand children, including Boy Scouts. Bishop Pozzoni talked about the responsibilities that came with living under the protection of the British flag, and urged all to follow the will of God and obey "those whom God has appointed to rule over the temporal affairs of the glorious Empire."[7]

May's first public appearance as the Chief Scout at the rally was to be his last. In August 1916, in an extraordinary meeting chaired by Anstruther, a surprising revelation was made by A. M. Preston, the honorary secretary of the association, who informed the audience of "the complete failure of this Association," indicating that it had "lacked from the very outset that co-operation on the part of members which is essential to such a venture."[8] Preston went on to enumerate a number of "difficulties," the most important of which was the fact that the young ethnic

1	Ibid.
2	*CM*, November 15, 1915; *Headquarters Gazette*, March, 1916, 82.
3	*SCMP*, April 8, 1916.
4	*CM*, May 24, 1916; *SCMP*, May 25, 1916.
5	*CM*, May 24, 1916.
6	*SCMP*, May 25, 1916.
7	*HKT*, May 24, 1916.
8	*HKDP*, August 3, 1916.

ESS, THURSDAY AUGUST 3RD 1916

HONGKONG BOY SCOUTS.

THE ASSOCIATION A "COMPLETE FAILURE."

PRINCIPAL OBJECT FAILS.

Dissolution of the Boy Scouts Association.

HKDP, August 1916.

British boys had been withdrawn from Scouting due to another policy change in the Cadet Corps. Smith had proposed "with the full approbation of His Excellency the Governor" enrolling the younger English boys who were Wolf Cubs into a "junior Cadet Corps," the training of which would be "much the same as Boy Scout training, with the addition of military work suitable to boys of that age."[1]

Smith might have felt a bit out of place in the Empire Day rally in 1916, leading the one Cadet Corps unit, being surrounded by six Scout Troops and Cub Packs, in the presence of May as the Chief Scout. Converting the Wolf Cub Packs into a new junior section of the Cadet Corps would possibly represent a welcome move from his perspective. But this proposal could not have been realised if it did not have May's "full approbation." With this change, ethnically British boys of all ages would be trained through the more militaristic and (as far as May was concerned) preferred Cadet organization instead of Scouting.

As if to distance themselves from this failed venture, neither Governor May nor Lady May showed up for the meeting. Anstruther presided, and a resolution was passed unanimously to wind up the association. The headlines of different press reports are revealing: while the *HKDP* declared that "Hongkong Boy Scouts: The Association a 'Complete Failure,' Principal Object fails," the ever-hopeful and supportive *HKT* reported: "Baden-Powell Boy Scouts: Hongkong Association Wound Up, May be Revived after the War."[2]

The failure of Scouting drew open criticism from some supporters. Mrs. Eva A. S. Rayner, formerly Cubmistress in Hong Kong, wrote on October 1, 1916 from London to the Hong Kong Scouts. This letter

---

1   Ibid.

2   *HKDP*, August 3, 1916; *HKT*, August 3, 1916.

was forwarded by Jack Braga to the local press, which then published excerpts of it in November. Mrs. Rayner, by then leading a Scout Troop and a Wolf Cub Pack in London, remarked that "when I left Hong Kong a little more than a year ago, the Boy Scouts of Hong Kong was in a flourishing condition" and "everywhere interest and enthusiasm was the key note."[1] She asked why the association could not continue, when its principle objective, "the making of the boys of our Colonies into honest men and worthy citizens," was so obviously needed.[2]

The editor of the *HKT* chimed in, noting that what had happened would "surprise no one who [had] marked, learned, and inwardly digested the manners and customs of the Britisher of this delectable Colony," and asked: "Why was this smash not foreseen by those who gave their countenance in the meeting a year ago? Or else: Why need the smash have come at all?"[3] The editor observed that "nothing but the traditional prejudice of Hongkong stood in the way of a successful career for the Wolf Cubs," and lamented that, despite "generous socialistic intentions of General Baden Powell, Hongkong decided that it would rather not be mixed up in the movement; and Hongkong's word on any social matter is, needless to say, final."[4] The finger was clearly pointed at the colonial government under May which had approved the extension of the Cadet Corps to absorb the Wolf Cubs.

In contrast, Guiding remained active. In September 1916, the Helena May Institute for Women, opened by Governor and Lady May, had "a small recreation ground which the Girl Guides will use as their headquarters."[5] By 1917, Guiding became available to Eurasian and other non-ethnic British girls at the Diocesan Girls' School.[6] In 1918, in the Empire Day children's service at the Anglican Cathedral, the "Girl Scouts" were in the congregation.[7] The fact that the Girl Guides survived the war years whereas the Boy Scouts did not provides insights on what was "wrong" with Hong Kong Scouting in the eyes of the ruling

---

1   Rayner to Boy Scouts of Hong Kong, October 1, 1916, scanned copy in Braga collection, the Hong Kong Scout Archives.
2   Ibid., also *HKDP*, November 17, 1916.
3   *HKT*, November 17, 1916.
4   Ibid.
5   *CM*, September 11, 1916.
6   *Guiding in Hong Kong*, 4.
7   *HKDP,* May 25, 1918.

Opening of the Helena
May Institute, Sept. 1916.

PRO 8-19C-284.

elite. Guiding during this time did not have any Catholic links, as it was only available through British government and Protestant schools and the Young Women's Christian Association (YWCA). Most Girl Guides from the existing companies were ethnic British or Eurasians, rather than Chinese, Portuguese or other nationals, and therefore would not trigger concerns with nationalism of the wrong sort. Finally, gender prejudices in those days had meant that girls, unlike boys, were not expected to become prepared militarily to defend the empire. There was simply no female version of the Cadet Corps to replace the Girl Guides. In short, whether in terms of religion, politics, or war, Guiding for girls could be left alone, while Scouting for boys could not.

No evidence of Scout activity can be found in the remaining war years. In 1918, St. George's Day was celebrated without any report of Scout involvement.[1] On Empire Day, St. Joseph's had its usual ceremony, but there was no mention of the Scouts. Bishop Pozzoni again led the children's service at the Catholic Cathedral, and names of all schools were cited, but the St. Joseph's troops were curiously missing. In view of their prominent roles in past St. George's Days and Empire Days, it would appear that the two remaining troops were also inactive. May, Severn, the cadets, and the Girl Guides attended the Protestant Empire Day's service, but the Wolf Cubs were absent, having been replaced by the junior cadets.[2] The Archdeacon's message described in great detail the heroic acts of the naval boy Jack Cornwell, who was killed in action in 1916, and hailed him as a shining example for all boys to emulate.

---

1   *CM*, April 16, 1918, April 27, 1918; *HKT*, April 23, 1918, April 24, 1918.
2   *HKDP*, May 25, 1918.

The sermon failed to mention the inconvenient fact that Cornwell was a Boy Scout, not a Cadet.

Concluding remarks

Scouting in Hong Kong in this period consisted of several years of informal Scouting for ethnic British boys and an equally short period of formal Scouting for non-ethnic British boys and younger ethnic British boys. Citizenship training was aimed at preparing youngsters as citizens of God's kingdom and the British Empire, under the influence of the Church and with a military orientation. The key motives for this effort were "to convert" boys and to prepare them "to fight." But, ironically, religious considerations retarded the start of formal Scouting and hastened its end, while militarism inspired initial calls for Scouting but contributed to the eventual exclusion of most boys. Governance ("to rule") also mattered, but only as a reason for excluding Chinese boys. Race was the key identity along which the Scouting experience of youth diverged, though this was effected through a nationality requirement. However, age played a role through the limited availability of the Wolf Cubs, and gender also mattered by way of the later start and differentiated treatment of the Girl Guides.

In these early years, Hong Kong Scouting was no more than a niche interest for a hundred or so mostly European boys, vying for attention with two other youth movements, the more religious Boys' Brigade and the more militaristic Cadet Corps. However, it generated a fair amount of interest in the newspapers and the expatriate community, as well as high-level sponsorship and government intervention, informed by the metropolitan growth and imperial spread of British youth movements and concerns about the future roles of youth in the British Empire. The early history of the Scout Movement in the colonial outpost of Hong Kong helps to confirm the importance of age as a category underpinning the conceptualization and control of the imperial periphery.

Chapter 2

Relaunch and Racial Inclusiveness

1919-1930

Chapter 2
Relaunch and Racial Inclusiveness
1919-1930

Jack Cornwell and his two gallantry medals.

Previous Page:

Boy Scouts from mostly Chinese troops on a bridge built in the first Boy Scout Jamboree/exhibition at the City Hall, April 1923.

H. K. Scout Archives.

The First World War brought about unprecedented destruction and claimed ten million lives, though Hong Kong was largely spared. When the war ended with the signing of the Treaty of Versailles in June 1919, celebrations ensued in the colony with mile-long processions along brightly-decorated streets marked by impressive triumphal arches. One float featured a ship with a boy playing the role of the teenage hero, Jack Cornwell, and a banner urging all youth to "Follow Jack's Example."[1] Cornwell, a sixteen year old Boy Scout, had served on HMS *Chester*, remaining faithfully at his exposed post despite heavy wounds, and had died in the Battle of Jutland in May 1916. Admiral Jellicoe recommended special recognition, and Cornwell received a Victoria Cross posthumously.[2] Jack also received a Scout gallantry cross, and inspired the creation of the "Cornwell Scout" Badge, awarded for "pre-eminently high character and devotion to duty."[3] The celebrations ushered in a new period in the history of Scouting on this colonial frontier, in which important challenges to governance by way of two major strikes were to stimulate a dramatic reconfiguration of the role of the movement, ensuring that it became entangled with Hong Kong's political fortunes. This development was influenced strongly by the actions of two British governors, who approached the task of ruling with rather different styles.

Sir Reginald Stubbs, who served from 1919 till 1925, was an

---

1   Paul Gillingham, *At the Peak: Hong Kong Between the Wars* (Hong Kong: Macmillan, 1983), 1-4.

2   F. Haydn Dimmock (ed.), *The Scouts' Book of Heroes: A Record of Scouts Work in The Great War* (London: Arthur Pearson, 1919), 128-146. John Travers Cornwell, V.C., was a Boy Scout at the St. Mary's Mission (Manor Park) Troop before he joined the Navy at the outbreak of war.

3   The *POR, 1933* (London: the Boy Scouts Association, 1933), 64.

Oxford graduate, the youngest son of a Bishop, and had previously been Colonial Secretary in Ceylon.[1] He was "a caustic and sometimes ferocious autocrat who spoke no Chinese and believed in corporal punishment for the natives."[2] Sir Cecil Clementi, governor from 1925 to 1930, a fellow Oxonian and son of an Indian army officer, had started locally as a government cadet. In contrast to Stubbs, he was "a regular China-lover, a speaker of Mandarin and Cantonese, a skilled Chinese calligrapher… [and] a bold critic of racial prejudice."[3] Concerned with strengthening colonial rule, both took a keen interest in expanding Scouting. At a time when anti-British feelings among Chinese reached their interwar zenith, Stubbs engineered a quick re-launch of the movement and began to include a few Chinese boys. Keenly aware of the need to cultivate among the local populace respect for British interests, Clementi took Chinese Scouting one step further by adapting the Scout Promise to enable the integration of non-British Chinese boys, who constituted the majority of the colony's youth population, by far.

A new start

Stubbs, who was consistently enthusiastic about Scouting, skillfully marshaled support from key stakeholders and re-started the movement on a politically-informed basis by 1920. Appropriately, the first four Boy Scout Troops were all for British boys; and they represented, respectively, the Protestant, Catholic, civilian and military interests of the British colonial society.

The earliest postwar "Scout" activity was a lecture given by Lieutenant G. J. Ranneft to some British boys. In early 1920, when A. G. M. Weyman was leading a parade of the Cadet Corps, a postman handed him a letter from Ranneft, an old Scout aboard the visiting Dutch warship *Tromp*, addressed to the leader of the Hong Kong Boy Scouts. As there was no Scouting then, the resourceful postman decided that Weyman, heading the only uniformed boys' organization, was the right-

Sir Reginald Stubbs.

---

1   *HKDP*, February 26, 1919, 3.
2   Jan Morris, *Hong Kong: Epilogue to an Empire* (London: Penguin Books, 1988), 193.
3   Ibid., 194.

5th World Jamboree Comm. Stamp, 1937, Dutch West Indies.

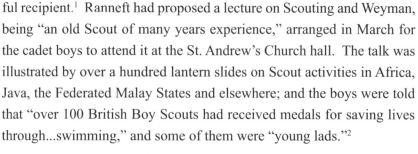

ful recipient.[1] Ranneft had proposed a lecture on Scouting and Weyman, being "an old Scout of many years experience," arranged in March for the cadet boys to attend it at the St. Andrew's Church hall. The talk was illustrated by over a hundred lantern slides on Scout activities in Africa, Java, the Federated Malay States and elsewhere; and the boys were told that "over 100 British Boy Scouts had received medals for saving lives through...swimming," and some of them were "young lads."[2]

(Ranneft's passion for Scouting was to continue. He retired from the navy in 1927, and later became Chief Commissioner (Hoofd-commissaris) of Vereeniging Nederlandsch Indische Padvinders (NIPV), the official national Scout organization of Dutch West Indies (now Indonesia). In 1937, he led a contingent of NIPV Scouts of various ethnic backgrounds to attend the 5th World Jamboree in Netherlands.[3])

Scout publicity in Hong Kong was maintained by reports on the Imperial and International Jamboree (later known as the 1st World Jamboree), the most visible Scout event after the war, held in London in July 1920.[4] At the closing ceremony, a boyish voice had proclaimed B-P "Chief Scout of the World," a title "which no king or government could confer," and one that he most cherished for the rest of his life.[5] The King declared that he was "fully alive to the great benefits, both moral and spiritual, which the Boy Scouts' training assures."[6] The *SCMP* echoed: "a message of this kind should go far to assist the revival of the Boy Scout movement in this intensely loyal British Colony."[7]

In August 1920, Stubbs called for the revival of Scouting, noting that he had accepted an earlier invitation from B-P to become the local Chief Scout. Bowen, who had returned, was appointed the commissioner; P. H. Holyoak, a businessman and a Legislative Councilor, the president; and Weyman, secretary. Though the British nationality requirement was retained, gone was the stipulation, out of step with pre-

Poster, 1st World Jamboree, London, 1920.

1   *CM*, April 26, 1924.
2   *Hong Kong Administrative Report, 1921,* O26-27; *HKT*, Mar. 29, 1920, 1.
3   Email, Jan van der Steen to Kua, May 18, 31, 2012, the Hong Kong Scout Archives, *The Straits Times*, Jun. 19, 1937; *Het Padvindersblad* (official organ of NIPV), Jan. 20, 1930, in which he is listed as the "Hoofdcommissaris" (back of front cover).
4   *HKT*, June 22 and August 5, 1920; *HKDP*, August 6, 1920; *SCMP*, September 17, 1920.
5   Reynolds, *The Scout Movement*, 116.
6   *SCMP*, September 17, 1920.
7   Ibid.

vailing sensibility in a period when memories of the destruction of the Great War were still vivid, that ethnic British boys must join the Cadet Corps.[1] As in the pre-war era, the nationality requirement had implications for the racial profile of those who could join. 35,700 Chinese boys between the ages of six and fifteen were living in urban areas, making them "reachable." However, only a much smaller subset, a little over one thousand urban Chinese boys, were estimated to be British nationals who could legally gain admittance to the revived Boy Scout Movement.[2]

The continued exclusion of most Chinese boys should be viewed in context. Stubbs had served in Ceylon and was probably aware of the developments relating to Scouting in India. At the time, British Scout authorities in India still refused to admit local boys, despite the proliferation of unofficial Indian troops such as those organized by Dr. Annie Besant of the Home Rule League and her followers who had, interestingly enough, "undergone Scout training in Ceylon."[3] Besant and others had even started rival Indian Scout associations, and a conference between them and the British association was called in August 1920. Given the exclusive policy adopted in India, where there was strong demand for native Scouting, it was not surprising that Stubbs would opt to perpetuate exclusion in Hong Kong, where there was no demonstrated need among most non-British Chinese boys.

In the wake of Stubbs' intervention, two troops were quickly formed. Perhaps due to Rannelf's talk, the St. Andrew's Church was first to respond. In September 1920, the *CM* urged all Kowloon boys to attend St. Andrew's recruiting meeting to demonstrate their "British spirit…and show the Colony the stuff that Kowloon's made of."[4] The *SCMP* expressed the hope that soon "every Church Sunday School and every day School should have its own patrol," and that Hong Kong should "lead the East in this important educative training of its youth."[5] This vision was, of course, an impossible one even if the schools were will-

BOY SCOUTS.

PROPOSED RESURRECTION OF HONGKONG CORPS.

When Lieutenant General Baden-Powell paid his visit to

Resurrection of Scouting in Hong Kong.

HKT, August, 1920.

---

1   *HKT*, August 17, 1920; September 1, 1920. Note the press report in August stated that B-P's visit to Hong Kong was in 1911, which was incorrect.

2   The *Hong Kong: Report on the Census of the Colony for 1921* (Hong Kong, 1921), Tables 19-20. British nationals among Chinese boys estimated based on % of British nationals among urban Chinese population.

3   Rau, *Scouting in India*, 28.

4   *CM*, September 20, 1920.

5   *SCMP*, September 20, 1920.

ing to participate, given the nationality rule. At any rate, the rally at St. Andrew's went well, with twenty-six boys enrolled. Captains Fogg and Bourdillon, the leaders, emphasized that "no obstacle is put in the way of Scouts joining the Cadet Corps if they desire to do so."[1] But given the postwar distrust of many parents towards militaristic organizations, they could not resist adding that "the Scout movement is not a military body whereas the Cadet Corps is."[2]

With its strong pre-war profile and after a personal appeal by Bowen, the recruitment at St. Joseph's was even more successful. In late September, some ninety boys of the reformed 1st Hong Kong Troop gathered in the college, with L. A. Gutierrez as Scoutmaster, and J. Rodrigues, L. M. Alarakia, J. Guimguam and senior Patrol Leader L. Baptista as assistants. Ten patrols were formed, and an ambitious plan of having all Scouts complete Tenderfoot Badges by October, and Second Class Badges a month later, was proposed.[3] By the end of 1920, Boy Scout Troops had also been raised at the Murray Garrison School and the Wanchai Wesleyan (Naval and Military) Church, and total enrollment of the four troops was over one-hundred-and-forty boys.[4] The troop at St. Andrew's had mostly ethnic British boys, some from the military base in Kowloon. The Murray troop was attached to the garrison school and had exclusively ethnic British military boys. The Wesleyan troop had ethnic British boys mostly of army or naval background. Only the St. Joseph's troop had Portuguese, Chinese and boys of other races.

Tenderfoot (above) and Second Class (right) Badges, 1909-1927.

Author's collection.

In January 1921, the first postwar rally was held at the Murray Barracks. Stubbs was welcomed by a guard of honor consisting of two Scouts from each troop, then St. Joseph's boys, representing American

---

1   *SCMP,* September 23, 1920.
2   Ibid.
3   *HKT*, September 30, 1920.
4   *Hong Kong Administrative Report, 1920,* Appendix O, O10.

Indians, and boys of the other three troops, representing English settlers, scouted out each other, attacked, communicated to arrange a truce, retrieved their wounded, and performed first aid. Though perhaps unintentional, the racial composition of the two groups was interesting: the "American Indians" were played mostly by Portuguese, Chinese, and other non-ethnic British boys; while the "English settlers" were indeed mostly English boys. Among the guests were Vice-Admiral Duff, Major-General Kirkpatrick, Commodore Smith, Lieutenant Colonel Bowen and Lieutenant Weyman.[1] Judging from the parade ground chosen, the program and the list of guests, one would be hard-pressed to claim that local Scouting had entirely divested itself of its militaristic inflection.

Scouts preparing an ambush.

Why did Stubbs, who had many things to worry about as the first postwar governor, bother to re-start Scouting soon after his arrival? There are several possible reasons. Unlike May, who had no experience with Scouting, Stubbs was "a prominent figure in the Ceylon organization," which was represented at the 1st World Jamboree.[2] His positive experience there might have convinced him of Scouting's usefulness and predisposed him to support it. Baden-Powell's personal appeal was also likely to have influenced his decision. Finally, as shall be seen, it is possible that the expected visit of the Prince of Wales in 1922, if known by late 1920, might have pushed him to take some action to revive a movement that was clearly viewed favorably by the King.

Three features distinguished the postwar movement from its prewar counterpart and ensured that the former would be relatively more successful. Firstly, whereas May's Scout association had distinct sectarian and ethnic biases in favor of Catholic and non-ethnic British (and Irish) interests, Stubbs's reconstituted association had politically-correct ethnic and sectarian orientations in favor of the Protestants and the English ruling elite. Three of the four troops, St. Andrew's, Murray and Wesleyan, were for ethnic British boys of Anglican or non-conformist Protestant and military or civilian backgrounds, living on the island and in Kowloon. Only the fourth, that of St. Joseph's, had non-ethnic British members and was under the guidance of the Catholic Church. Secondly, ethnically British boys could only become cadets in the prewar days, but

1   *CM*, January 10, 1921.
2   The *Headquarters Gazette*, August, 1920, 176.

Early local association secretary hat badge.

Author's collection.

in the postwar years, they had a choice. This change in policy in just a few years was understandable. After the war, support for the militaristic cadets declined sharply. Many had been appalled by the Great War, with its large number of casualties. Even the old soldier Baden-Powell had referred to it as "this reversion to primitive savagery" and "a great disgrace."[1] A 1923 press report clearly revealed its preference between the two organizations: "The outstanding difference is that of principle... The Cadet training imposes collective instruction upon the boys from without; while the Scout movement encourages self-development on the part of the individual from within."[2] Finally, the people involved had changed. Smith, a supporter of the cadets, was replaced by Bowen and Weyman, experienced Scouts, who became the commissioner and secretary. May, who had no exposure to Scouting before and was convinced of the military value of the cadets, was replaced by Stubbs, who had been associated with the successful Scout movement in Ceylon.

Shifting towards racial inclusiveness

Soon after the movement's re-launch, it acquired greater diversity: troops were formed for Scottish, Eurasian, non-ethnic British, and Chinese boys; supporters were drawn from non-British, Eurasian and Chinese elites; and sponsors included government and mission schools, a Chinese church, individuals, a Chinese athletic club, and British commercial enterprises. Important questions therefore arise as to what conditions permitted this diversification of the bases of colonial Scouting and how it played out in the Hong Kong context.

In May 1919, even before Stubbs' arrival, some Chinese had shown an early postwar interest in Scouting. Ng Tin Bo, president of the Chinese YMCA, had apparently invited some pastors of Chinese churches and leaders of Sunday schools to a conference to discuss the organization of a Boy Scout Troop and had sent its European secretary to obtain necessary permission from the government, hence "making pioneering history in Hong Kong Scouting (實開香港童子軍先河)," at

---

1   Quoted in Jeal, *Baden-Powell*, 454.
2   *HKDP*, April 6, 1923.

least in terms of Chinese interest.[1] The local initiative was consistent with the YMCA's strong partnership with early Scouting in other parts of the world. The YMCA in Singapore, for example, played a key role in the nurturing of Chinese Scouting from as early as 1910.

Chinese YMCA, Hong Kong Island.

Ng's meeting, however, did not lead immediately to the formation of a Chinese troop. No evidence can be found of Scout activities in YMCA's magazine, the *Hong Kong Youth* (香港青年), in this year, no YMCA troop was registered with the association formed by Stubbs in 1920, and none appeared in the early rallies. Given the instruction to the European secretary, it is clear that Ng's intention was to start a troop authorized by the Hong Kong branch of the British association, not one affiliated with the Boy Scouts of China. But the timing of the enquiry would have been premature, as the local association was only revived a year later. Nevertheless, this early interest might have inspired other Chinese Christians and could have been partially responsible for some early troops from Chinese churches and Christian schools, soon after the local Scout association was revived.

The Diocesan Boys' School, which served predominantly Eurasian and Chinese boys, had also indicated early interest. In January 1921, the school noted that Scouting "could very well be encouraged," but was concerned with "a certain clause in local Scout rules," and declared that it might start a troop privately, with a link to the movement.[2] Lady Stubbs expressed her support, hoping that a troop could be formed

1   The *Hong Kong Chinese YMCA 50th Anniversary Commemorative Bulletin, 1901-1951*香港中華基督教青年會五十周年紀念特刊, 1901-1951 (Hong Kong: the Chinese YMCA, 1951), 59.
2   *HKT*, January 28, 1921.

Lau Chu-pak.

soon, after "all difficulties had been removed." There is no elaboration on this reference to the "certain clause." The local association had never imposed a formal color bar, but it had a British nationality requirement. Unlike St. Joseph's, which had a large British Portuguese population, Diocesan Boys' School had many non-British Chinese who would not have been allowed to join. Though not expressly mentioned, it is possible that a clause that would exclude most students from a school activity would likely be viewed unfavorably by the principal.

By March, Scouting had secured support from many prominent citizens, including some Chinese and Eurasians. Sir Paul Chater and Sir Robert Ho Tung headed a list of contributors, followed by notables like Ho Fook, Lau Chu-pak, Ho Kom-tong, and Sir Ellis Kadoorie, many of whom had also supported the Boy Scouts' Building Fund before the war. Lau Chu-pak (劉鑄伯), a Legislative Councilor and an acknowledged leader of the Chinese community, was appointed treasurer of the association, becoming the first Chinese to assume a top Scout position.[1]

In November, after Bowen left, Rev. George Turner Waldegrave, chaplain of the Seamen's Institute, became the commissioner. Waldegrave had served in the Royal Navy, and was, like other early supporters of Scouting such as Chater, Southorn, C. H. Blason, and Holyoak, a member of the Masonic Order.[2] As shall be seen, this close link between Scouting and Masonry is notable. Besides him, at least four other Colony/Chief Commissioners in Hong Kong were also Masons.

The Seamen's Institute.

---

1   *SCMP*, March 9, 1921; *Hongkong Government Gazette*, March 5, 1920, 114, No. 123.

2   Christopher Haffner, *The Craft in the East* (District Grand Lodge of Hong Kong and the Far East, 1977), 143, 146, 147-148, 211, 268; Thomas W. Carr, *The Victoria Lodge of Hong Kong: A Century of Fellowship* (Hong Kong: Victoria Lodge of Hong Kong, 1981), 40, 56, 58, 59.

One of the first non-British troops was the Eurasian 5th Hong Kong. It started training in 1921, and was inaugurated in April 1922, in the presence of Sir William Brunyate, Vice-Chancellor of the University of Hong Kong, the Hon. Lau Chu-pak and Waldegrave. The open troop, commonly known as the "Roving Fifth," served mainly Anglo-Chinese and other Eurasian boys.[1]

Eurasians, claimed by some to belong to "a marginalized and isolated colonial category that straddled racial, ethnic and sometimes national boundaries," were literally "the living embodiment of colonial encounters."[2] Though sometimes subtly or even blatantly discriminated against by the British, as they threatened "the fragile boundaries of white identity," they moved easily among British and Chinese elites, and often played important roles as middlemen, especially in times when "imperial stability [was] under threat."[3] It is, therefore, not surprising that they should be among the first outside the ethnic British circle to adopt this latest innovation in education.

The troop's sponsor was Robert Hormus Kotewall (羅旭龢), a Parsee-Chinese who was a Legislative Councilor representing the Chinese, and the troop met at the spacious home of Lau Tak-po.[4] In August 1923, Scoutmaster Barney awarded badges to Patrol Leaders Edward Shea, Lau Chan-kwok, and others. Sixer D. Anderson accepted a shield on behalf of his Cub Pack, and the gathering ended with Anderson and Patrol Leader J. Kotewall presenting Thanks Badges to R. H. Kotewall and Lau Tak-po.[5] Many of these Eurasian boys were students at Diocesan Boys' School or Queen's College, which did not yet have a Scout Troop or Cub Pack.

The first three Chinese troops were all formed in 1921. The first, 6th Hong Kong of Ellis Kadoorie School (育才書院), started to operate in 1921, and was at the Empire Day service at St. John's Cathedral in May.[6] The 7th Hong Kong, Saiyingpun School (西營盤官立學堂),

---

1   *HKT*, April 5, 1922.
2   Vicky Lee, *Being Eurasian: Memories Across Racial Divides* (Hong Kong, Hong Kong Univ. Press, 2004), 8.
3   Pomfret, "Raising Eurasia," 341.
4   *Hongkong Government Gazette*, March 23, 1923, 90; October 5, 1923, 374.
5   *HKT*, August 27, 1923.
6   *SCMP*, May 25, 1921. Note there were two Ellis Kadoorie schools, one serving Chinese boys, and another Indian ones.

Boys of 7th Hong Kong displayed initials of their school, October 1921.

H. K. Scout Archives.

under Leung Yuk-tong (梁玉堂), had its inauguration in October on the grounds of the University of Hong Kong.[1] This troop was supported by Ho Kom-tong (何甘棠), younger brother of Ho Tung, a banker with a long record of public service.[2] While a rendition of "God Save the King" concluded the ceremony and the Union Jack took central position, the five-color flag of the early Chinese Republic was also on display.[3]

By colonial standards, these were early troops for local boys. "The first indigenous scout troops" were started in French Morocco, Tangier, and Madagascar in 1923, in Syria in 1925, and in Equatorial Africa and Brazzaville in 1929, all with Catholic encouragement.[4] That the first two Chinese troops started in elitist government schools is suggestive of the fact that Scouting among the "right" sort of Chinese boys had received official encouragement.

The Chinese Methodist Church also sponsored a troop early on. In 1921, T. K. Chak (翟大光), son of a founding member of this church, formed the 8th Hong Kong with thirty Chinese boys.[5] This troop was linked to a Sunday school. Just as British and Chinese Wesleyans worshipped in separate churches, British and Chinese Wesleyan boys joined segregated troops, a phenomenon which could be interpreted either as race-inspired or language-based. However, racial segregation should be viewed in context. In the interwar years, most school children in Hong Kong would be in segregated schools: the ethnic British in the British

T. K. Chak.

1   *CM*, October 31, 1921; *HKT*, October 29, 1921.
2   *CM*, June 3, 1927, 7; Frances Tse Liu, *Ho Kom-tong: A Man for All Seasons* (Hong Kong: Compradore House, 2003), chronology.
3   *CM*, October 31, 1921; *the Wah Tze Daily* 華字日報, November 1, 1921.
4   Raffin, *Youth Mobilization in Vichy Indochina,* 40.
5   *The Chinese Methodist Church: Commemorative Issue of the 100th Anniversary in Hong Kong 1884-1984* 循道衛理教會:香港開基一百週年紀念特刊, 1884-1984 (Hong Kong: the Chinese Methodist Church, 1985), 9.

government schools, Eurasians in the two diocesan schools, Portuguese and others in St. Joseph's, Chinese in government, mission or private schools, and Indians in a second Ellis Kadoorie school.

When the Prince of Wales visited Hong Kong in April 1922, he was carried around the colony by a party of eight on a Chinese sedan chair decorated on both sides with a beautifully embroidered vermillion silk panel bearing his heraldic badge, the "Prince of Wales' Feathers" with the motto "*Ich Dien* (I serve)."[1] A highlight of his visit was the Scout inspection at Government House. When he arrived, the Cubs and Brownies honored him with a "grand howl," after which "there was a sudden blast of a whistle, and out of the shrubberies sprang a horde of boy scouts and girl guides...all yelling...shrilly."[2] They then gave a loud rendition of the Chinese cordial welcome, *Kung Ying* (恭迎).[3] The following troops and packs were inspected by the prince:

Ostrich Feather Badge of the Prince of Wales.
Wikimedia: Sodocan.

Type	Troops (+ Packs)
British	St. Andrew's, Wesleyan, Murray *(3 Troops + 2 Pack)*
Mixed	St. Joseph's, Roving 5th *(2 Troops + 1 Pack)*
Chinese	Ellis Kadoorie, Saiyingpun, Chinese Wesleyan *(3 Troops)*

Troops and Packs at the Prince of Wales Inspection, 1922

Source: The *Hongkong Telegraph*, April 6, 1922

This royal visit, the highlight for the imperial outpost in the year, would explain the flurry of activity in 1921 related to new troops, if not the start of Scouting in late 1920. The line-up at the inspection would appear satisfactory to the prince, with ethnic British boys forming three troops, Portuguese, Eurasian and other nationals two, and Chinese another three. Whatever the motivations, by 1922, there were troops for some of the most prominent racial groups in the colony.

---

1   The phrase is also a near homophone for "Eich Dyn," or "your man" in Wlesh. Prince Edward was to become King Edward VIII for 325 days in 1936, before abdicating in favor of his younger brother Albert who chose the regnal name George VI.
2   Morris, *Hong Kong: Epilogue to an Empire*, 190.
3   *HKT*, April 6, 1922.

Prince of Wales met the Boy Scouts at Government House, April 1922.

H. K. Scout Archives.

Stubbs continued to devote considerable attention to the minutiae of Scouting, and to the need to tie the work of the troops more closely to the British colonial governorship. In December, he met with the troops at Government House and presented representatives of these troops with a Prince of Wales Banner, made with a silk panel taken from the chair which carried the prince around. Earlier on, Stubbs had apparently suggested to the prince that the two panels from the sedan chair be turned into banners for Boy Scouts and Girl Guides, to be used in their annual competitions, whose winning troops would be called "the Governor's Troop."[1] The Prince of Wales Banner competition and the designation of the Governor's Troop, symbolic of colonial endorsement of Scouting, were to remain *the* competitive event and the coveted honor for Hong Kong Scouts for decades to come.

In the summer of 1921, before the prince's visit, temporary Sea Scout training was re-started by Lieutenant Beauchamp of the H. M. S. *Tamar* for twenty-four "best recruits" from several local troops, when these were inactive due to hot weather.[2] In October, training stopped as planned so as not to deprive the regular land troops of their smartest Scouts. However, Waldegrave had a strong interest in Sea Scouting, and quickly announced a plan "to organize a permanent Sea Scout troop…as soon as a suitable scoutmaster has been discovered."[3] In May 1922, he made good on the promise personally by becoming its first Scoutmaster.

The Prince of Wales Banner presented to the Boy Scouts at Government House, Dec. 1922.

H. K. Scout Archives.

---

1   *HKT*, December 18, 1922.
2   *HKT*, June 16, 1921.
3   *Hong Kong Administrative Report, 1921*, Appendix O, O27.

Photographic evidence from these early years confirmed that most members of the troop were Chinese, although there were a few Eurasians.

The Sea Scouts made impressive progress within a short time, producing in 1923 the colony's first King's (Sea) Scout, Henry Choa, its Eurasian Patrol Leader; and sharing the honor of being the first troops to win the Prince of Wales Banner with 6th Hong Kong (Kadoorie), another Chinese troop.[1] It would only be fair to note that Sea Scouting was apparently favored at the time. Its members were the best boys chosen from other land troops. Waldegrave was doubling as its Scoutmaster. The governor and others had donated a yacht, a rowing boat and a dinghy for their use. The troop's mostly Chinese members were even permitted to participate in races of the usually racially-exclusive Royal Hong Kong Yacht Club, with only a few restrictions.[2] In October 1922, perhaps in line with the heightened interest in water-based activities, the first annual aquatic meeting of the Hong Kong Boy Scouts' Association was held in the swimming pool of the Victoria Recreation Club. The list of winners was racially mixed, including A. May, Tong Tan Chiu, F. Zimmern, W. Shea, J. Kotewall, Ng Wai Man, G. Chu, R. Patheyjohns, Leung Han Li, Ng Hong Sang, and D. Leonard.[3]

Henry Choa, Hong Kong's first King's Scout.

H. K. Scout Archives.

In April 1923, Stubbs presided over the opening ceremony of the first-ever Scout "Jamboree," patterned after the first World Jamboree held earlier in London. Over a two-day period, Hong Kong Scouts put on a rather impressive display in all the rooms on the first floor of the City Hall. As illustrated in the photograph on the cover spread of this chapter, items exhibited included a 24-feet trestle bridge built by a squad of Scouts drawn from various troops, mostly Chinese. Other skills being demonstrated were sick nursing, tailoring, basket-weaving, book-binding, carpentry, metal work, telegraphy, Swedish drill, Chinese exercises, stretcher drills, life-saving, etc. In the evening of the first day, they also hosted a "Scout Campfire Concert" at the Theatre Royal.[4]

In the general meeting at the end of 1923, after presenting the Prince of Wales Banner to the two winning Troops, Stubbs gave a Thanks

1   *HKDP*, January 26, 1924; *CM*, September 25, 1924. By the late 1920s, there were many King's Scouts, including Chan Wai-chit of 6th Hong Kong, C. Y. Liu and C.T. Ng of 18th Hong Kong, and another eleven, mostly Chinese, from the Sea Scout Troop,
2   *HKDP*, October 31, 1923.
3   *HKDP*, October 23, 1922.
4   *HKT*, April 13, 1923.

King's Scout Badge on felt, used in the 1920s.

Author's collection.

Scout Thanks Badge with a Swastika, used till 1935.

Author's collection.

13th Hong Kong (Ying Wa College), founded in 1924.

H. K. Scout Archives.

Badge with a Swastika to B. Wylie, General Manager of the *SCMP*, for services in the Jamboree.[1] Wylie continued a supportive tradition started by the founder of *SCMP* Tse Tsan Tai in the pre-WWI days. (By 1935, however, the British Scout association had to re-design the early versions of both the Thanks Badge and the Medal of Merit, removing the swastika-like cross, to disassociate itself from the Nazis, who had successfully "usurped" this ancient symbol as uniquely their own.) In 1924, Waldegrave, Blason and two Chinese Boy Scouts represented Hong Kong at the Imperial Jamboree in Wembley, Britain.[2]

Chinese Scouting also came to Protestant schools in the 1920s. In March 1924, the 10th Hong Kong had been formed at the Anglican St. Paul's College.[3] A later source suggests that it was started by Wong Shiu Pun, a former Rover Scout from Cambridge who was a teacher at the school.[4] Ying Wa College (英華書院), "the first Protestant school in Asia" founded in Malacca in 1818 by Robert Morrison and moved to Hong Kong in 1843 by James Legge,[5] joined in soon with the 13th Hong Kong. The July 1924 issue of the school magazine *Ying Wa Echo* (英華青年) noted "the forming of a Boys' Scout Troop," which was making promising progress under Scoutmaster B. T. Lewis and Patrol Leaders Kan Man Hon and Tam Kim Hing.[6] Though Lewis returned to England

---

1   *HKDP*, October 31, 1923; Hutcheon, Robin, *SCMP: The First Eighty Years* (Hong Kong: *SCMP*, 1983), 64, photograph of Wylie wearing the Thanks Badge.
2   *The Imperial Jamboree, 1924* (London: Boy Scouts Association, 1924),118.
3   *SCMP*, March 4, 1924.
4   Tse Ping Fui, "The College Scout Troop," the *Wayfarer*, 1957-58, 58. .
5   For early history of this school see Paul Kua, "Students of the Anglo-Chinese College of Malacca, 1818-1843: Fruits of the First Protestant School in Asia," *Monumenta Serica*, Dec. 2023, 453-488.
6   The *Ying Wa Echo*英華青年, July, 1924, Vol. 1, No.1, 1-2.

in early 1925, the troop remained active under the Chinese deputy head-master Lo Kwun Yuen (盧冠元), who led it in the banner competition in March 1926.[1] St. Paul's and Ying Wa had mostly Chinese boys, many of whom were not British nationals, and would have had even more dif-ficulties than the Diocesan Boys' School with the British nationality re-quirement. It is possible that the nationality restriction might have been quietly dropped by this time, or, if it still existed, that it was not adhered to strictly in all Chinese troops.

Inauguration of SCAA troops, officiated by Wal-degrave, Chow Shou-son, April 1925.

H. K. Scout Archives.

As demonstrated by the featuring of Scout exercises in the Far Eastern Games in Shanghai in 1915, many in China had linked Scout training to *tiyu,* or physical education.

In this spirit, the South China Athletic Association (SCAA 南華 體育會) in Hong Kong sponsored the 14th and 15th Hong Kong, which appeared in the 1924 banner rally, and later also took over the 8th Hong Kong, originally with the Chinese Wesleyan Church. Together they had over one hundred boys, making the SCAA a large sponsor of Scouting. In April 1925, these three troops, all under T. K. Chak, had a joint inau-guration in the presence of their patrons Chow Shou-son, Li Yuk-tong and Liang Chi-hoo.[2] Years later, two Boy Scouts from the SCAA troops, Wong Gay Leung (黃紀良) and Yip Buk Wah (葉北華), were to repre-sent Nationalist China in the 11th Olympics in Berlin.[3]

From 1923 to 1925, Scouting for Scottish boys was introduced

---

1   *HKDP,* March 15, 1926.

2   *HKT,* April 20, 1925.

3   Wong and Yip were the goalie and a forward. See *The Special Bulletin Com-memorating the 60th Anniversary of the SCAA, 1910-1970* 南華體育會六十週年會慶特刊 (Hong Kong: SCAA, 1970); *Hong Kong Scouting,* June 2009, 19.

A Scottish Scout.

The kilted Scottish Boy Scouts doing a Scottish dance, 1926.

H. K. Scout Archives.

by the two dockyards, extending its reach to commercial firms. Taikoo Dockyard (太古船塢), the leading shipbuilding company in Hong Kong, and its parent company, Butterfield and Swire, employed a large number of Britons, including many ex-servicemen and Scots.[1] By late 1923, the 9th Hong Kong (Taikoo) had been formed. J. G. P. Foulds, its Cubmaster, assisted in a fund-raising concert in April 1924. R. M. Dyer, the sponsor, provided kilts and sporrans, and funded instruction in bagpipes, Scottish dances and Highland games. In February 1925, these kilted Scouts generated much interest in an evening of fund-raising at the Taikoo Club. In the same year, Kowloon Dockyard founded the 11th Hong Kong (Kowloon Scottish).[2] Kilted Scouts and Scout bagpipe bands were to become a Hong Kong tradition, one eventually even taken up enthusiastically by a few Chinese troops, creating something of an anomaly, perhaps unique among Chinese Scout Troops around the world.

Taikoo soon decided to also sponsor troops for Chinese boys. In June 1925, Waldegrave reported that the 16th, 17th and 18th were "three divisions of one troop formed from boys of the Chinese employees at the Taikoo Dockyard."[3] One might think that Chinese dockyard employees were blue-collar workers who could not afford Scouting for their boys. After all, most Chinese Boy Scouts at this time were from better-off families, the best schools, or leading churches or clubs. In reality, Taikoo and Swire employed many better-paid Chinese, led by its Comprador, Mok Cho-chuen and then Mok Kon-sang. Skilled dockyard workers had

---

1   See Charles Drage, *Taikoo* (London, Constable, 1970), photo facing 144, photo of ex-servicemen dinner menu facing 209, 21; *Hongkong Jurors List for 1925.*

2   *HKDP*, October 31, 1923, February 3, 1925, October 19, 1925; *HKT*, April 17, 1924, February 19, 1925; *CM*, February 19, 1925.

3   Letter, Waldegrave to Butterworth, June 23, 1925, the Gilwell Archives.

also gone on strike in 1920 and 1922 and obtained better wages.[1] According to an interwar survey, many of the dockyard Chinese employees were in fact middle-class people who could afford to have their children attend private schools and participate in Scouting.[2]

Japanese Scouting also came to the colony in 1925. In the early interwar years, Japanese commercial interests grew rapidly, as "the place of the Germans seems to have been filled by the increased number of Japanese, American and Dutch firms."[3] Japanese "displaced Europeans in …the middle levels" and "the number of married women and children [was] largely increased."[4] By 1921, there were 1,600 Japanese, with close to eighty boys between five and fifteen. In 1925 and then again in 1926, the Japanese troop joined the Hong Kong rallies. It had mostly very small boys who were, nonetheless, "very good" and took to the event "inordinately seriously," as a somewhat patronizing reporter observed.[5] Though this is interesting it should strictly speaking not be considered as evidence of inclusiveness in local Scouting. The troop never appeared in any list of local troops, as it was only an associate unit which was presumably registered with the association in Japan.

A Japanese Scout.

Japanese Scoutmasters performing Jujitsu, 1926.

H. K. Scout Archives.

Indeed, inclusion did not extend to all. There was no dedicated Irish troop, perhaps because such a unit would have been considered too politically sensitive, though a few interested Irish boys could have

1   Drage, *Taikoo*, 180-1, 214, 230-231.
2   R. H. Butters, *Report on Labour and Labour Conditions in Hong Kong* (Hong Kong, Noronha & Co., 1939), 161-162
3   The *Hong Kong Census Report*, 1921, 157.
4   Ibid., 158.
5   *HKDP*, January 15, 1924.

been catered to in the military or Catholic troops. A significant racial group without its own troop was the Indians. There were two thousand Indian civilians, many employed in the police or as watchmen, plus a large number in the military. Though many were single men, some did have families, and censuses suggested that there were more Indian boys than Japanese boys.[1] However, Indian boys were not served, aside from the few of them who attended the elite schools with troops.

The exclusively British Peak Cub Pack, late 1920s.

H. K. Scout Archives.

Younger Wolf Cub Packs remained largely reserves of ethnically British and Eurasian boys. When the prince visited, there were two Wolf Cub Packs exclusively for the ethnic British boys and one for the Eurasians. By late 1925, there were five packs, four for the British (including one for Scottish) boys, and one for the Eurasians. It appears that this junior section, built around *The Jungle Book* by Rudyard Kipling which was very popular with British boys throughout the empire, did not catch on with the younger Chinese in the colony.[2]

Similarly, the older Rover Scouts also did not take off. This section, though often plagued with different views about its service targets, organization, and program, grew strongly in Britain in the early interwar years, partly driven by the large number of young men who had been Boy Scouts.[3] Baden-Powell's *Rovering to Success* (more about "an approach to life" than "a clearly articulated structure of organisation and

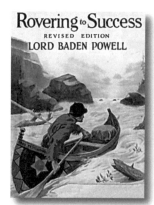

B-P's *Rovering to Success.*

---

1   The *Hong Kong Census Report of 1911* and *1921.*

2   William Dillingham, *Being Kipling* (New York: Palgrave Macmillan, 2008), 3-13.

3   Allen Warren, "Popular Manliness: Baden-Powell, Scouting, and the Development of Manly Character," in J. A. Mangan and James Walvin (eds.), *Manliness and Morality: Middle Class Masculinity in Britain and America, 1800-1940* (Manchester: Manchester Univ. Press, 1987), 199-219.

training"), had sold some 170,000 copies by 1930.[1] But the situation in Hong Kong was rather different. *Rovering to Success* was not available in Chinese, making it unlikely to be widely read. Given the movement's weak existence pre-war, there were few former Boy Scouts whom were old enough to become Rovers. While there were some British Rovers in 1922, these soon drifted away due to their departure from the colony or loss of interest. Later, a few British service people formed a Rover Patrol, and they served often as examiners or instructors. But there was no Chinese Rover Scout at this time.[2]

Revival of "Scouting" for girls came soon after Scouting for boys. Though Guiding was not discouraged by the authorities, it also became inactive later in the war years. Interest was expressed in late 1920, though confirmed activities only began in 1921.[3] The education report for 1920 indicated that "preliminary steps were taken to organize this movement, of which Lady Stubbs has kindly accepted the Commissionership."[4] In early 1921, Miss Rachel Irving, daughter of the Director of Education, became the secretary.[5] By the end of the year, there were "about 130 members, 100 Guides enrolled in five Companies, and one Pack of 30 Brownies," all serving ethnic British and Eurasian girls.[6] Jean and Grace Ho Tung, Sir Robert's daughters, were at the Diocesan Girls' School and had joined the school's company in 1921, with Miss Irving as its Captain.[7] Years later, Jean recalled fondly their regular encounters with Miss Irving on the peak tram, when they would invariably embarrass her by standing up and giving her the three-fingered salute. Unlike in Scouting, there was no Chinese company in this period, though the Diocesan Girls' company might have a few Chinese.

A card illustating a Girl Guide in uniform.

Stubbs and Severn were both scheduled to leave in late 1925, and the Scouts gave both a proper send-off on the same day in October. In the swimming competition in the morning, Severn received a Thanks

---

1   Ibid., 204.

2   Report, Waldegrave on Rovering in Hong Kong, 1930; the Gilwell Archives.

3   In November 1920, Mrs. M. Cater, claimed that she had started a company, but no further report could be located on this initiative. See *SCMP*, November 29, 1920.

4   *Hong Kong Administrative Report, 1920,* Appendix O, O10.

5   *HKT*, February 22, 1921.

6   *Hong Kong Administrative Report, 1921,* Appendix O, O8.

7   Jean Gittins, *Eastern Windows—Western Skies* (Hong Kong: SCMP, 1969), 37-41. Jean became her company's captain in 1929, and also ended up marrying Billy Gittins, an Eurasian Scoutmaster of the 5th Hong Kong.

Badge from the youngest member, Colin Ironside of the Peak Pack. He recounted Baden-Powell's inspection of the St. Andrew's boys in 1912 when he was acting governor, and offered to have photographs of this event presented to the association for their new headquarters on Lower Albert Road, provided by the government only a month previously, so that they could have a record of "the first and only time their Chief Scout visited Hongkong."[1] (As it turned out, Baden-Powell never had the opportunity to visit again in his long life: the visit in 1912 was indeed his only one.) After this event, the boys marched back to their new headquarters, a modest facility with only four rooms, and attended its formal opening ceremony, officiated by Stubbs, just before his departure to become governor of Jamaica. Boys and leaders from the following troops and packs were at the opening ceremony:

Type	Troops (+ Packs)
British	St. Andrew's (+ Pack), Wesleyan, Murray (+ Pack), Taikoo Scottish (+ Pack), Kowloon Scottish, (+ Peak Pack) *(5 Troops + 4 Packs)*
Mixed	St. Joseph's, Roving 5th (Eurasian, + Pack) *(2 Troops + 1 Pack)*
Chinese	Kadoorie, Saiyingpun, 1st to 3rd SCAA, St. Paul's, Ying Wa, 1st to 3rd Taikoo Chinese, Yaumati, Caine Road, the Sea Scouts *(13 Troops)*

Troops and Packs by Ethnic Background, October 1925

Source: *HKDP*, October 19, 1925, 4. Note the Bulldog Cub Pack was attached to the Roving Fifth Scout Troop, as reported later in the *CM*, May 13, 1926.

Included in the above were two new troops not yet mentioned: Yaumati and Caine Road, both dedicated to Chinese school boys, resulting in a total of twenty troops and five packs. There were only four troops in 1920, eight troops and three packs in 1922 and, as recorded in *Silver Wolf*, thirteen troops and six packs in early 1925.[2] The growth was impressive even from the start of 1925, not to mention 1922 or 1920. Bulk of the increase occurred among Chinese boys, with the addition of government

---

1   *HKT*, October 19, 1925; letter, Waldegrave to Butterworth, June 23 and September 29, 1925, the Gilwell Archives.

2   *The Silver Wolf*, IV, 5 (early 1925).

Scouts entering head-
quarters to be opened by
Stubbs, October 1925.

H. K. Scout Archives.

and mission schools, the SCAA, the dockyards, and the Sea Scouts.

Stubbs had been a consistent supporter of Scouting who, as Waldegrave put it, had "done all he could…when approached."[1] By 1925,
local Scouting was broadly-based, with English, Scottish, Portuguese,
Eurasian and Chinese troops which had church, school, commercial and
community backgrounds. However, the clear winners were the Chinese.
While there was no Chinese troop in 1920, there were a total of thirteen
by October 1925. It was appropriate that in the farewell rally, Waldegrave presented Stubbs with a silver figure of a *Chinese* Scout, to which
"every Scout had contributed."[2] Racial inclusiveness, especially the integration of the Chinese, had indeed been achieved under him. However,
less than a decade earlier, the government had imposed a British nationality requirement which effectively prohibited Chinese Scouting. What
could have motivated a change of heart of the Hong Kong colonial state
under Stubbs (and, as shall be seen, Clementi and later governors) to
facilitate the inclusion of Chinese boys from the 1920s onward?

To educate, convert and rule

*While different stakeholders had different motives in wanting to admit
Chinese boys into Scouting, the key ones from the early 1920s to the mid-
1930s were to educate, to convert, and, most importantly, to rule. As tensions increased in Hong Kong, and Chinese nationalism became more
influential, Scouting held out the promise of transforming Chinese boys
into "good" citizens supportive of or at least sympathetic towards colo-*

---

1   Letter, Waldegrave to Butterworth, June 19, 1925; June 23, 1925, the Gilwell
Archives.
2   *HKT*, October 19, 1925.

nial rule. The efforts to make Scouting more inclusive were galvanized by the strikes of 1922 and 1925-6, which convinced Hong Kong's elites, British and Chinese, that the movement was worthy of their support.

Though Scouting in its ideal form was an international brother-hood, the Fourth Law, which demanded inclusion of boys of all creeds, colors and classes, had been studiously ignored in the pre-war context. Leaders in Scouting between the wars, however, were no longer hard pressed to justify a racially exclusive policy. Significantly, the government was increasingly convinced that Scouting could help defend what they saw as their interests. In a society in which the ruling and the ruled were rigidly divided, the movement offered a common space in which British and non-British youth could jointly participate in holistic educational practices, reinforce their religious affiliations, and share in life-affirming experiences. Meanwhile, in the eyes of those concerned with effective colonial governance, what may be the loss due to the dismantling of racial barriers was more than compensated for by the gain in the number of young Chinese committing to serve God and the King, and to help other people.

Admittedly, demographics in Hong Kong, recruiting policies in Scouting in other colonies, and the royal visit of April 1922 were external considerations which favored the development of Chinese Scouting. The demographics were compelling. Without the inclusion of the Chinese, local Scouting could not hope to grow much at all. Enrollment policies in other colonies might have offered useful lessons. Singapore, which had a large Chinese population, had relatively open ethnic enrollment policies from day one. The latest development in India, arguably the most important non-white British colony, was instructive. The amalgamation of independent Indian "Boy Scout" organizations in 1921, partly with the help of a visit from Baden-Powell himself, meant that Indian boys had begun to be admitted. With the inclusion of native boys, Indian Scouting grew impressively, reaching 23,000 members in 1923, and offering powerful lessons to Hong Kong.[1] The expected visit from the Prince of Wales might also have provided some impetus for the first

---

1   Watt, "The Promise of 'Character'," 45-54; *The Scouter*, June 1934, 181. And over 200,000 in 1933, "over half the number of those in the British Commonwealth outside British Isles."

Chinese troops. After all, it would be somewhat disappointing if the prince were to be welcomed only by a few ethnic British Boy Scouts, with the Chinese entirely unrepresented. That initial progress in Chinese Scouting was in two government schools betrayed the fact that this was largely a development inspired by the colonial government.

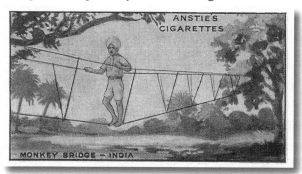

An Indian Boy Scout walking on a "Monkey Bridge" (a bridge made out of three main ropes).

But these external reasons alone would have been inadequate to drive the reformation of the recruitment parameters. If the colonial authorities perceived dangers in including Chinese boys, they could easily have chosen to have a small movement for Europeans boys only, regardless of the inclusiveness evident in India; or to have just a few token Chinese troops for the royal visit. In short, these were necessary but not sufficient conditions. For Chinese Scouting to grow substantially there would have to be other, more fundamental, reasons.

In considering why this shift in approach occurred it is important to look to the successive crises which hit the colonial government from the early 1920s. As will be shown, "to rule" was the most important motivation for extending Scouting to Chinese boys. From the perspective of the ruling elite and the British community, Scout training was highly valuable in this time of crisis, since it held out the promise that Chinese youth, instead of being radicalized, might become "good citizens," thereby permitting British governance to persist in Hong Kong.

Fulfilling one's "duty to the King" was essential to the movement, as conceived by Baden-Powell, who argued that Scouting would instill among the boys "a sense of Imperial Citizenship."[1] Winston Churchill had echoed such views in claiming that "the value of the Boy Scout Movement...[has] been abundantly demonstrated...here and over-

---

1   Baden-Powell's letter to the Secretary of State for the Colonies, November 18, 1921; in "Supply of Uniforms to the Boy Scout Movement in Colonies and Protectorates, 1921-23," CO 323/882/60, the National Archives, London.

seas," and that he had "received representations from Governors testifying to the direct and indirect value of the Boy Scouts organization."[1] The idea of "helping others" was encapsulated within the third Scout Law, which declared that "a Scout's duty is to be useful and to help others," that he should be "prepared at any time to save life, or to help injured persons," and to do "a good turn to somebody every day."[2]

Most demonstrations of "duty to the King" were simple or symbolic: services on the Empire Day, rallies on St. George's Day, respect for the Union Jack, singing of the National Anthem and so on. Likewise, many acts of helpfulness were often not spectacular or risky. B-P explained that "a good turn need only be a very small one," such as putting a coin into a poor box, helping someone cross the street, giving up one's seat to other, or removing a bit of banana skin off the street.[3]

Sometimes, however, fulfilling one's duty to the King and helping others required sacrifices or even risks. B-P had created the Scout's own awards for just this reason. The Bronze Cross was for "special heroism or extraordinary risk," the Silver Cross for "gallantry with considerable risk," and the Gilt Cross for "gallantry with moderate risk."[4] The Imperial Headquarters made much of heroic acts, and decorated boys throughout the empire who had fought in wars, saved lives in dangerous situations or plunged into other disasters for a good cause.

Gilt Cross, Type 1.
Author's collection.

There were some young heroes in Hong Kong. Patrol Leader Lo Kwok-chung of Saiyingpun swam out a considerable distance against strong currents to save a drowning boy at the Kennedy Town beach in August 1921, and was awarded a Gilt Cross. Scouts Li Hok-wai and Chan Hung-yun of Kadoorie found a Chinese man with a gunshot wound on the street one evening in May 1922, and carried him to a police station, when adults nearby had run away in fear, and were both presented Gilt Crosses. Scoutmaster Hugh Braga of 1st Hong Kong risked his life to save a girl from a house which had collapsed due to a landslide in Po Hing Fong in July 1925, and received a Silver Cross.[5]

---

1   Churchill's dispatch, December 29, 1921; in CO 323/882/60.

2   Baden-Powell, *Scouting for Boys*, 1908 edition, 45.

3   Ibid., 23.

4   The *POR, 1933*, 65. This was in line with the fact that the Victoria Cross, made with bronze from a captured Chinese-made cannon used by the Russians during the Crimea war, was the highest gallantry award in the British military.

5   *HKT*, January 16, 1922; March 28, 1922; HKDP; May 22, 1922; December 18,

Readers might recall that three Braga brothers had joined St. Joseph's troop before WWI. Their siblings Hugh and his two younger brothers Tony and Paul had also joined 1st Hong Kong after the war. Hugh entered Hong Kong University in 1922, and became a Scoutmaster. A Scout could earn progressive and proficiency badges based on tests. Hugh insisted that "every Scout in my troop is fully entitled to each badge he possesses", shunning "badge-hunting," common with some. In the 1925 Prince of Wales Banner competition his troop won the competitive events, but when the badges earned by troop were considered, they lost to another, in which some boys "had gone from recruit to King's Scout in 6 months." The Braga brothers were a Hong Kong Scout legend: They came from a large family of nine brothers; six were members of the same Troop, Jack and Hugh had been Scoutmasters, while Chappie and Tony had been Patrol Leaders.[1]

First Gilt Cross awardees, Lo Kwok-chung (center), Li Hok-wai (left) and Chan Hung-yun (right), 1921-22.

H. K. Scout Archives.

In 1923, Hong Kong was ravaged by a deadly outbreak of smallpox, which cost over thirteen hundred lives. In November, a colony-wide vaccination campaign was launched, and Boy Scouts from several troops were mobilized to assist. By mid-December, they had vaccinated many people, in a spirit of "true and effective citizenship."[2] The 6th Hong Kong, under Lam Kwan Shan, took charge of two stations, and vaccinated over two thousands in several months.[3] The relatively small vaccination team of the 1st Hong Kong Sea Scouts, led by Waldegrave, using their expertise at sea, visited people on ships and Chinese living on boats, and vaccinated seven thousand people.[4] Though more people died in 1924, the epidemic was under control by July. In total, the Boy Scouts had vaccinated some fourteen thousand, a record of public service to be proud of, considering its small membership.[5] Official recognition came soon after in the form of a letter from Severn, extending "the Governor's thanks to the various divisions [of the Scout Association] for their energetic work in connection with the campaign."[6]

1922; February 6, 1926; May 13, 1926.

1   *HKT*, April 28, 1924; *CM*, February, 1925; *The Silver Wolf*, IV, 5, 173; Braga, "Making Impressions," 233, 248-50, 334-338, 345; Letters, Waldegrave to Butterworth, June 23, September 29, 1925, the Gilwell Archives.

2   *CM*, December 12, 1923.

3   *HKDP*, January 26, 1924.

4   Photograph albums, Waldegrave, the Hong Kong Scout Archives.

5   *Hong Kong Administrative Report, 1923,* Appendix O, O25.

6   *HKDP*, January 26, 1924.

Hugh Braga wearing his Silver Cross, c. 1925.

Stuart Braga.

The vaccination team of the Sea Scouts with Waldegrave, 1923.

H. K. Scout Archives.

The response of Scouting to two major crises of governance in the 1920s which severely strained the relationship between rulers and ruled further affirmed the value of the movement in the eyes of the authorities. Hong Kong was never immune to political struggles in China, but these were much worse in this period. For most of the 1920s, China had two competing governments, the "warlords" in Peking and the Nationalists in Canton. Worse yet, Britain had chosen to recognize distant Peking instead of nearby Canton, and Canton was heavily influenced by Soviet advisers. Not surprisingly, the early interwar years were marked by strikes and boycotts, two of which were especially damaging in Hong Kong's history, driven as they were both by poor local labor conditions and tense Sino-British (or Canton-Hong Kong) relations.

The 1922 strike, involving over one hundred thousand Chinese, crippled the colony. An earlier demand for a pay rise by engineers had developed into a walkout by nine thousand workers, backed by a Canton labor union. Stubbs responded by enacting an ordinance requiring the registration of all unions, and by prohibiting even peaceful celebrations when Sun Yat-sen was elected president in 1921.[1] Later that year, the Chinese Seamen's Union, with strong Canton links, demanded a wage hike. In January 1922, when their request was ignored, they went on strike, and soon convinced twelve other unions to declare sympathy work stoppages. Over time, around 120,000 workers left for Canton. E. R. Hallifax, secretary for Chinese affairs, Lau Chu-pak and Chow Shou-son all tried to broker a deal with the strike leaders, but without

---

1   *SCMP*, May 13, 1921.

success.[1] Stubbs resorted to a hard-line approach, outlawing the union, declaring martial law, setting up armed posts, and allowing troops and policemen to fire on Chinese civilians crossing the border, killing five. Such repressive measures were censured by the Labor Party in Britain and played into the hands of leftist propagandists who controlled the Nationalist government in Canton. Stubbs and the employers, however, eventually had to give in, and the fifty-two day strike ended in March, with the union reinstated and strikers' demands largely met, in a settlement described by the local press as "deeply humiliating to the Government and the foreign community."[2]

The Boy Scouts played a minor role in supporting the community at the height of the strike. Close to forty boys, all Europeans or Eurasians, responded to calls for help, and were put to work in a variety of posts during the mass walkouts of Chinese workers.[3] Significantly, Waldegrave reported no involvement of Chinese boys. It is also notable that Scout membership peaked at the end of 1921 at 374, and then dropped substantially during the next two years, to reach just 218 by end of 1923. Membership crept up again the following year, but it only exceeded that of 1921 by the end of 1925.[4] These numbers suggest that substantial declines were registered in some troops during 1922 and 1923. For instance, St. Joseph's in late 1923 reported that "20 boys in all had been in the troop, 5 of whom had resigned," leaving it with two patrols, a shadow of its former self.[5] As most ethnic British troops were small or enrolled only Cub-age boys, much of the decline would have had to have come from the Chinese or mixed troops. This may have been due to natural attrition after the initial enthusiasm had worn off, but it is more likely that the 1922 strike had an impact, whether through parents concerned with safety and sending boys away from Hong Kong or keeping them at home, or boys sympathetic of the strikers leaving on their own accord. That would also explain why no Chinese Boy Scout came forward at all during this strike, despite the fact that they would have constituted the majority of the membership at the time.

A European Boy Scout manning an elevator during the 1922 Strike.

H. K. Scout Archives.

1	*CM*, January 16, 1922; February 23, 1922; February 25, 1922.
2	Gillingham, *At the Peak*, 32.
3	Letter, Waldegrave to Butterworth, June 23, 1925, the Gilwell Archives.
4	*Annual Reports, 1921-25* (London: the Boy Scouts Association, 1922-26).
5	*CM*, October 30, 1923.

Stubbs' difficulties with industrial relations in Hong Kong did not end with the settlement of the 1922 strike. A far worse strike and boycott took place from 1925 to 1926. In 1923, when Canton failed to secure aid from Britain or America, Sun Yat-sen turned to the Russians, and signed the Sun-Joffe Agreement, bringing in Russian agents led by Mikhail Borodin, who promptly set about "bolshevizing" Canton. By March 1925, Sun had died, and the government fell into the hands of Russian-dominated leftists.

In May 1925, British policemen in the Shanghai international settlement fired into a crowd of student demonstrators and killed several. This "massacre" by British "imperialists" prompted the Hong Kong Seamen's Union to call for a strike in June, which was followed by strikes in many in other trades, and even walkouts by students in government and missionary schools, partly encouraged by the leftist unions in Canton. In June, British troops fired at demonstrators marching towards Shameen in Canton, and killed fifty-two, adding further fuel to an already raging fire. In July, the Hong Kong-Canton Strike Committee called for a general boycott against Hong Kong and British goods. All told, around 250,000 workers struck, the colony was paralyzed, trade came to a standstill, food prices soared, and bank runs escalated. As Jan Morris puts it, "it was very nearly the rising that the British had feared, on and off, ever since the Indian Mutiny."[1]

Chinese commemorative medal, 1925 Hong Kong-Canton Strike.

Again, Stubbs, who had to delay his planned departure from the colony, reacted sternly. He promptly declared a state of emergency, authorized censorship of mail and the press and sweeping search-and-seize power for the police, appointed food, transport, and labor controllers, and called up the Volunteers.[2] Both sides engaged in excesses, violence, strong-arm tactics, and blatant propaganda. The Chinese *Kung Sheung Yat Po* (工商日報) was started at this time as a pro-government newspaper, when other Chinese papers were silenced or shut down out of fear.[3]

In the midst of this crisis, the Boy Scouts, European and Chinese, played a useful role in supporting the government and those with a stake in preventing the collapse of British rule. The first call for as-

---

1   Morris, *Hong Kong: Epilogue to an Empire*, 197.
2   *CM*, June 23, 1925; HKT, June 22, 1925.
3   R. H. Kotewall, confidential memorandum on the 1925 Strike, October 24, 1925, in "Sir Robert Kotewall, 1945," CO 968/120/1, the National Archives, London.

sistance came from a hospital in June 1925. The Rover Mate of the Sea Scout troop, a Eurasian, "speedily routed out four…Sea Rovers and Sea Scouts and several more Scouts as well…and supplied all immediate needs."[1] Several days later, the *CM* confirmed that some "qualified Scouts" were attached to the hospitals and "many others are holding themselves in readiness for all sorts of other work, down to working in lifts if necessary."[2] Scouts assisted the Labour Controller in registering volunteers, and took over the duties of Chinese ward attendants and other absent Chinese workers at the Peak Hospital and the Matilda Hospital.[3]

A parade that was to take place at Government House was cancelled, and all Scouts were asked to report to the headquarters instead. Waldegrave announced that in handling "applications for services," hospitals and public services would have preference.[4] However, the range and extent of demands on the movement grew considerably within a short time, and in a week close to sixty Boy Scouts were helping three hospitals, the Labour Control Offices, Hong Kong Club, the Central Police Station, and the offices of the Asiatic Petroleum Company, the P. and O. Company, the Hong Kong Canton and Macao Steamboat Company, and the Northern Telegraph Company.

HONGKONG STRIKE GRADUALLY GROWING.

EUROPEAN COMMUNITY WORKING SPLENDIDLY TO COPE WITH THE SITUATION.

WHAT WILL THE DRAGON FESTIVAL BRING?

BOY SCOUTS' LOYAL ASSISTANCE.

"Boy Scouts' Loyal Assistance" in the strike. *HKDP, June 1925.*

While Europeans and Eurasians continued to come forth in good numbers Waldegrave also noted that "actually some pure Chinese [came] forward of whom we had none at all last time."[5] By June 30, at least twenty-four Chinese Scouts had volunteered. By July, the strike was still on, and Boy Scouts were still helping, though some had changed jobs.

---

1   Letter, Waldegrave to Butterworth, June 23, 1925, the Gilwell Archives.
2   *CM*, June 22, 1925.
3   *HKDP*, June 24.
4   *HKT*, June 22, 1925.
5   Letter, Waldegrave to Butterworth, June 23, 1925, the Gilwell Archives.

The English press was impressed, and ran subtitles like "Boy Scouts' Loyal Assistance" and "Boy Scouts' Good Work."[1] The racial angle was sometimes emphasized, when a feature article mentioned that "Chinese Boy Scouts [were] maintaining the prestige of their organization by performing much useful work for the public good."[2] Two Sea Scouts were even assigned as second coxswain and officer's cabin boy in an armed anti-piracy launch.[3] These jobs were a far cry from day-long Empire Day rallies or a few evenings vaccinating the boat people: The Scouts were on board the launch for six weeks, and had to live, along with rest of the crew, on tinned food and in temperatures as high as 110 degrees.[4]

The government pulled out all stops to respond to the strike, which eventually ended in July, only to be followed by a general boycott of British goods.[5] Hong Kong Chinese and Eurasian elites such as Chow Shou-son and Robert Kotewall offered staunch support to government-led efforts to end the agitation. This is in line with the long tradition of collaboration between the local elites and the colonial authorities. But, just as importantly, it demonstrated how class interests had overpowered racial solidarity: strikes engineered by Chinese proletariats in Canton hurt Chinese businesses and the interests of the Chinese and Eurasian bourgeoisie in Hong Kong. Both Kotewall and Chow were concerned with the role of the secondary school students during the unrests, and the former suggested that local education needed to be reformed.[6]

It would take the Chinese-speaking Clementi, who became governor in November 1925, to mend relations with Canton. Like Stubbs, he insisted that the strike had little to do with local conditions, but was driven, as he declared in the Legislative Council in February 1926, by the "unlawful activities of the Canton Strike Committee, instigated by the Bolshevik intrigue."[7] When leftist influence was reduced after Chiang Kai-shek won the upper hand in a military coup in March, Clementi

Sir Cecil Clementi.

---

1   *HKDP*, June 24, 1925.
2   *HKDP*, July 8, 1925.
3   Letter, Waldegrave to Butterworth, June 23, 1925, the Gilwell Archives.
4   Letter, Waldegrave to Butterworth, September 29, 1925, the Gilwell Archives.
5   Frank Welsh, *A Borrowed Place: the History of Hong Kong* (New York: Kodansha Int'l, 1993), 369-373.
6   John M. Carroll, *Edge of Empires: Chinese Elites and British Colonials in Hong Kong* (Hong Kong: Hong Kong Univ. Press, 2007), 139-143; Pomfret, "Raising Eurasia," 328-333.
7   *Hong Kong Hansard*, February 4, 1926.

resumed communication with the Canton government. In the ensuing months there were more negotiations, boycotts, suppressions, and even threats of military action. Finally, on October 10, when for the first time since 1911 Hong Kong Chinese were allowed to celebrate the Chinese national day as a holiday, Canton officially ended the boycott, and Hong Kong was returned to a state of relative normalcy.[1]

Chinese flags decorated Queen's Road, in celebration of October 10th, ROC's independence day.

During the strikes, Stubbs or Clementi had not explicitly opposed the Communists on ideological grounds. They merely attempted to protect British interests. In fact, the government could be just as antipathetic toward Nationalist activities if they were believed to threaten British control. In a secret dispatch from Clementi in 1929, he noted that the Malayan government had refused registration and favored total suppression of the Nationalist Party, arguing that "it may so strengthen its hold on the Chinese population as to become in effect an *imperium in imperio*."[2] In the same dispatch, he then indicated that he also disliked registration but realized that, as long as Britain recognized the Nationalist government, it would be unwise to declare the party unlawful, and advised resolute actions against offending individuals instead.

Hong Kong Scouting's response to the 1922 strike and the 1925-26 strike and boycott inspired a powerful sense of the value of the movement as a social cohesive in times of crisis. *The Silver Wolf*, the first

---

1   Gillingham, *At the Peak*; Earl Motz, "Great Britain, Hong Kong, and Canton: The Canton—Hong Kong Strike and Boycott of 1925-26," Ph. D. dissertation, Michigan State Univ., 1972.
2   Secret dispatch from Clementi to Lord Passfield, December 12, 1929, in folder on "Kuomintang Acts in Hong Kong and Malaya," CO 273/561/13; the National Archives, London.

The Third Law: "A Scout Helps Others."

official organ of the local association, was launched in July 1921. Waldegrave, writing in *The Silver Wolf* in late 1925 and as cited in *China Mail*, declared that "the splendid number of Scouts who volunteered from the very commencement of the trouble for special services was an inspiration in itself, especially in view of the fact that very many scouts were sent away by their parents at once, in anticipation of dangers."[1] Local Scouts had indeed lived up to the Third Law ("A Scout's duty is to be useful and to help others"), and the Commissioner lauded them for having "proved true to the great reputation and tradition of the Brotherhood."[2] The editor of the *CM* seemed to agree:

> *When the records of the Hong Kong crisis of 1925 come to be written, the historian will undoubtedly ascribe to the Boy Scouts of the Colony their rightful place. Keen, alert, intelligent and active, not only in the emergency work which they undertook at the outset of last year's troubles, but also in the countless minor tasks which the later exigencies of the strike offered to their willing hands. It almost seemed that, whatever the work might be, the Scout could perform it as completely and readily as though it were the special kind of work for which he had always been trained. This, indeed, is the result of that particular system of manhood training that owes its inception to the genius of Sir Robert Baden-Powell. Trained and animated by the Scout spirit of service, these many hundreds of boys...could hardly fail to be a valuable asset...and undoubtedly those who were actually employed in public services during the strike exerted a stabilizing influence upon the life of the Colony.*[3]

This unequivocal endorsement of Scouting from the newspaper, declaring it to be "a valuable asset" to the community and "a stabilizing influence upon the life of the Colony," was perhaps only one view. Nonetheless, it was suggestive of the extent to which those who had risked

---

1   *CM*, December 8, 1925. This citation from *The Silver Wolf* comes indirectly from a press report, since all copies of this magazine held by the Scout Assoiation of Hong Kong were destroyed during Japanaese occupation. In 2018, a copy of this rare magazine (vol. IV, no. 1, early 1925) was donated to the H. K. Scout Archives by Sheila Potter, daugther of Hugh Braga.

2   Ibid.

3   *CM*, December 15, 1926.

extending the sponsorship of the colonial state to the fledgling movement may have felt their actions to be vindicated.

While it may be easy to understand why this more inclusive variant of Scouting might have appealed to the crisis-hit colonial elite, we must wonder why others in the community were tempted to participate, building the movement from the ground up. It would appear that "to educate" was a key motive. Many educationalists, who were a vociferous presence in Hong Kong and the metropole, believed in the value of Scouting for students. The British Scout association picked up on this and noted in 1923 that "a great number of the *better* schools, beginning with Eton, had taken up Scout training."[1] Lord Rosebery opined that "Schoolmasters ought to be interested…If they can get the influence that the Boy Scout movement gives the Scoutmaster…in playtime, that at present some of them only have in school time, surely they will have an incalculable reward in the formation of the character of their pupils."[2]

Professor Lancelot Forster, an educationalist from the University of Hong Kong, was an early convert and had actively promoted Scouting.[3] In the May 1926 issue of the *Education Journal*, published by the University's Education Society, an article by "Scoutmaster" declared that "the aim of education is good citizenship." To him, modern educationalists agreed that besides "book-work," "the most important part of education [was] training in character," and that "the conscientious teacher will find the solution…in the methods employed by the Boy Scouts' Association."[4]

In the 1920s, leading schools for Chinese included Queen's, Saiyingpun, Kadoorie, St. Joseph's, Diocesan Boys', St. Paul's, Ying Wa, and the newly-added Wah Yan.[5] King's was started in 1926, Wah Yan would add a Kowloon branch, and St. Joseph's would also start a Kowloon branch, which became La Salle in 1931.[6] By end of 1925, four government schools (Saiyingpun, Kadoorie, Yaumati and Caine Road)

---

1   *HKT*, March 10, 1923, italics added.
2   *HKT*, April 4, 1923.
3   Letter, Waldegrave to Butterworth, May 31, 1926, the Gilwell Archives.
4   The *Education Journal* (Hong Kong: the Hongkong Univ. Education Society, 1926), May 1926, vol.1, no. 1, 32, 37. It is possible though not certain that this person may be Forster.
5   *Hong Kong Administrative Report, 1923,* Appendix O, O4.
6   *Hong Kong Administrative Report, 1931,* Appendix O, O9.

The Silver Wolf, vol. IV, no. 1, early 1925.

H. K. Scout Archives/ Sheila Potter.

and three mission schools (St. Joseph's, St. Paul's and Ying Wa) had Scout Troops. Between 1926 and 1929, schools like Munsang, government schools in Tai Po and Yuen Long, Queen's, Yuek Chee, Shu Man, and Kin Bong would also introduce Scouting. As shall be seen in the next chapter, many other schools, including King's, Diocesan Boys', Wah Yan and La Salle, would eventually sign on later in the interwar years. These schools no doubt entered Scouting with official encouragement, but also because they shared the same enthusiasm of many earlier educationalists about the budding movement and the so-called Scout Method.

The efforts of the colonial elite to stimulate Scouting also dovetailed with the interests of grass-roots supporters in exploiting the movement's potential as an outreach mechanism for securing religious converts. Among missionaries in China, "to convert" was perceived to be a key motive for introducing Scouting from early on. S. V. Boxer from Hankow wrote glowingly on Scouting's value in inspiring among boys reverence to God, obedience, truthfulness and helpfulness. To him, "Scouting is practical Christianity."[1] Baden-Powell was pleased that his hope was "corroborated by [Boxer's] experience—namely, that scouting has proved a spiritual force."[2] Similar feelings in Hong Kong would explain why St. Joseph's, Chinese Wesleyan, St. Paul's and Ying Wa were among the first to introduce Chinese Scouting.

Nevertheless, due to its indirect approach, Scout training as a conversion tool did not gain much currency in the 1920s. By 1925, out of twenty-one troops, only five had Christian sponsors. Even for these, it was doubtful if "duty to God," other than in the form of occasional ceremonies and social "Christianity," was emphasized much. St. Joseph's, the only Catholic troop, had "Protestants, Parsees, Mahomedans [*sic*], non-R.C. Chinese and others."[3] Brother Aimar, director of the college, though supportive, was astounded that there were so few Catholics in the troop and that there was "no trace of R.C. Scouts" in any other troop.[4]

1   Letters from Boxer, "Report for 1914" and "Report for 1915," Griffith John College Papers, the LMS Coll., the SOAS Archive, London.
2   "Scout Honour in China: A Letter from Sir. R. Baden Powell," *The Chronicle of the London Missionary Society*, October, 1916, 196-197.
3   Report, Waldegrave on Roman Catholic Troops and Scouts, c.1926/27; the Gilwell Archives.
4   Ibid.

Scout training usually only promoted spiritual development indirectly. This approach worked reasonably well in countries where the bulk of the population share the same faith, and direct spiritual growth was nurtured by the religious institutions. The Hong Kong Deep Sea Scouts, all members of the Royal Navy, had a successful Rover Crew with a shared vision of service, partly due to their members' common Christian background. The same could not be said of Chinese Rovers. The lack of a common religion among boys in Hong Kong made it difficult to meaningfully fulfill this portion of the promise. In 1930, Waldegrave explained this obstacle in the context of Rover Scouting: "One of the great difficulties in Hong Kong Rovering is the impossibility, owing

A Deep Sea Scout Insignia.

to the many and varied religions of the Rovers, of holding a Moot which can be inspired with a definitely Christian spirit, such as have been held at home. A number of the Rovers are of course Christians, but it is the unanimity which carries weight, all inspired with the same Spirit for Service under the same God, and that cannot be attained under present H. K. conditions."[1] As would be expected, this same limitation applied to other, younger, sections of local Scouting, when the movement began to penetrate the non-Christian Chinese majority.

Hong Kong British Deep Sea Scouts repaired a church in Waihaiwei, China, 1920s.

H. K. Scout Archives.

Demographics, racial inclusion in other parts of the empire, and the visit of the Prince of Wales might all have provided some incentives for including Chinese boys in Scouting. More important was the desire of educators to adopt Scouting as part of their education program, the keenness of evangelizers to use it to facilitate religious conversion, and, especially, the enthusiasm of the colonial authorities to employ it

---

1   Report, Waldegrave on Rovering in Hong Kong, the Gilwell Archives.

to nurture future citizens prone to public-spirited acts and supportive of the established order. These motivations, apparently vindicated by the mid-1920s, stayed valid throughout the remainder of the 1920s and the 1930s. That it had been proven that Chinese Boy Scouts' support could be counted upon not only for the fulfillment of minor public duties but also during the 1925-6 strike and boycott suggested that in other troublesome incidents in the future similar responses could be expected. This served as an important "push-factor" stimulating further efforts toward making Scouting more racially inclusive, especially among non-British Chinese boys. These are discussed in more details in the next two sections, dealing with the adaptation of the Scout Promise and the progress of Chinese Scouting in the second half of the 1920s.

An equivocal Scout Promise

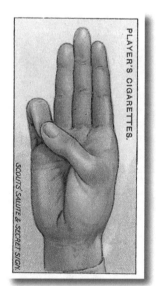

The "Scout Sign", used in saluting and making the Scout Promise.

A key challenge faced by those seeking to recruit Scouts in the early interwar years was that of reaching non-British Chinese boys, including those in the elite schools, who were likely to become useful members in the society in the future. There were two, somewhat interrelated, barriers: British nationality as required by the authorities and allegiance to the King as required by the Scout Promise. Both barriers were to be removed in the 1920s, though the latter had required a creative rephrasing of the Scout promise in Chinese, endorsed by Clementi.

By the end of Stubbs' time in office and the beginning of Clementi's, British nationality as an entry requirement had been removed, if discreetly without any formal announcement in the beginning. This was in line with the treatment of the nationality issue in the colonial community itself. By 1927, the nationality restriction was relaxed even for the military service, when the Volunteer Ordinance authorizing service of "any persons" was interpreted as allowing the enrollment of non-British aliens into existing companies, and a non-British Portuguese company was formed, whose members did not have to renounce their Portuguese nationality.[1] Though later, in 1932, this interpretation was challenged,

---

1   *Hong Kong Government Gazette*, June 29, 1928, 254, No. 366.

the War Office in the end accepted a compromise solution and recommended that enlistment of aliens should be allowed in Hong Kong, up to 50% of the strength of the companies.[1]

The removal of the British loyalty commitment, on the other hand, would require a creative re-think of the Scout Promise used throughout the empire. The first version of the Scout's Oath (as it was called originally) was: "On My Honour I promise that—1. I will do my duty to God and the King, 2. I will do my best to help others, whatever it costs me, 3. I know the scout law, and will obey it." When Scouting was introduced in other Christian parts of the empire, the oath posed no particular problem. However, when it spread to the rest of the world, changes became necessary, and many countries adapted it according to their needs. Still, during this time, most British colonies had remained faithful to the original promise. Clementi, motivated by a perceived need to provide an acceptable oath for the many non-British Chinese boys, finally decided to opt for a clever adaptation of the promise in Chinese in 1926, which was to remain in force in the interwar years.

Examples of adaptations of the Scout Promise in some major countries provide useful comparative insights. The American Scout Oath was: "On my honor I will do my best, 1. To do my duty to God and my country, and to obey the Scout Law; 2. To help other people at all times; 3. To keep myself physically strong, mentally awake, and morally straight."[2] Substitution of "my country" for "the King" was expected, given the republican form of government in the United States of America. The addition of "to keep myself physically strong, mentally awake, and morally straight," a rendition of YMCA's emphasis on all-round development of "body, mind, spirit," reflected the important influence of the YMCA in American Scouting.[3]

Old logo of the YMCA, stressing development of "body, mind and spirit."

La Promesse (the oath) according to *la Fédération des Scouts de France* (the (Catholic) Federation of the Scouts of France), founded in 1920, was: "*Sur mon honneur, avec la grâce de Dieu, Je m'engage à*

---

1   "Hong Kong Volunteer Corps: Enlistment of Foreign Subjects," CO129/54/1, the National Archives, London.

2   Macleod, *Building Character*, 148-149.

3   Clifford Putney, *Muscular Christianity: Manhood and Sports in Protestant America, 1880-1920* (Cambridge; Harvard Univ. Press, 2001) , 70. This phrase and the related inverted red triangle were incorporated into the YMCA official seal in 1891.

Old logo of *Scouts de France*, featuring a large *croix potencée*.

Japanese Scout logo, featuring the sacred mirror.

servir de mon mieux Dieu, l'Eglise, ma patrie, à aider mon prochain en toutes circonstances, et à observer la loi scoute ("on my honor, with the grace of God, I commit myself to serve my God, *the Church*, my fatherland, to help my neighbor in all circumstances, and to obey the Scout Law)."[1] The substitution of "the King" with "my fatherland" was again understandable. The insertion of "the Church," even before "my fatherland," was interesting, and demonstrated the key role played by the Roman Catholic Church in this particular federation. The old logo of the French Scout association incorporated a large *croix potencée* (T-shape cross), again signifying the strong influence of the church.

In Japan, difficulties lay elsewhere. Japanese Scouting could easily substitute the British King with its own "Heavenly Emperor" (天皇). However, God with a capitalized "G" was problematic as Christianity was, at best, a fashionable western religion allowed to co-exist with Shintoism and Buddhism. The Japanese Scout Oath in the 14th Year of the reign of Taisho, or 1925, was "私は神聖なる信仰に基き名誉にかけて次の三条を誓います。 1. 神明を尊び、皇室を敬います。2. 人の為、世の為、国の為に尽くします。 3. 少年団のおきてを守ります。("in the name of sacred faith and honor, I pledge the following three articles. 1: I will respect god (or goodness) and honor the Imperial Family, 2: I will work for the good of the public and the country, 3: I will obey the Scout Law.)"[2] The "imperial family (皇室)" replaced "the King," as would be expected. To this day, the logo of the Japanese Scout association features a sacred mirror (*yata no kagami* 八咫鏡), one of the three sacred treasures of the Japanese emperor. More interestingly, the generic term for deity, *jinmei* "god(s)/goodness (神明)" replaced the specific term "God." The use of *jinmei* was ingenious, as it would be quite acceptable to most Japanese Shintoists and Buddhists, and somewhat acceptable to Japanese Christians.[3]

Early Scouting in China went further than Japan as far as "God" was concerned. In 1917, the Jiangsu Province Federation of Boy Scouts adopted this promise: "某某誠心立願,盡國民之責任,隨時隨地扶助他人,遵守童子軍規律. (I, so-and-so, sincerely promise to fulfill my duty

1   Carine Chabrier, "Scoutisme et Christianisme," http://www.deficulturel.net/modules/news/ article.php?storyid=67591 (accessed May 24, 2010).
2   Scout Association of Japan, *History of Scout Movement in Japan*, vol. I, 31.,
3   Strictly speaking, only the term *Kami* 神 should mean one God, more appropriate in the Christian context.

as a national, to help others at all times and at all places, and to obey the Scout Law.)"[1] Though other parts of this promise were reasonably faithful to the original version, the absence of any reference to God or even "gods," perhaps due to a perceived lack of a strong national religion or even general religiousness among most Chinese, was conspicuous. Similar "godless" versions appeared to have persisted in most parts of China. Since its early years, the logo of the Boy Scouts of China had also incorporated the three Confucian virtues of "wisdom, benevolence, and courage (智仁勇)."

Early Chinese Scout logo with 3 Confucian virtues, and Scout Promise with no mention of God/gods.

Even before Scouting was revived in Hong Kong, the British promise had been amended to become: "I Promise, on my honour, 1. To do my duty to God and the King, 2. To help other people at all times, 3. To obey the Scout Law."[2] Though the sentence structure was simplified, and the qualifier for the second part of the oath, "whatever it costs me," viewed as quite a "tall order" by some, was replaced by the more nebulous phrase "at all times," the essential features of the original promise were maintained. This was the *English* version used throughout the British Empire and in Hong Kong in the interwar period.

With Chinese Scouting, however, came the need to translate

---

1   Fan, *Zhong Guo Tong Zi Jun Shi*, 15.

2   Baden-Powell, *Scouting for Boys* (London: C. Arthur Pearson, 1916), 48.

the promise into Chinese. How could this promise, uncontroversial in Britain, where God and the King were rarely questioned, be rendered in Chinese for Hong Kong, where most people were not religious or were believers of a variety of gods other than the Christian one, and loyalty to the King was, at best, partial and divided? Rendering "God" into Chinese was resolved more or less satisfactorily early on. The Chinese promise for Hong Kong adopted the term for deity *shen* (神), commonly used for the Christian God, instead of *shenming* (神明, god(s), or *jinmei* in Japanese), associated with generic god(s).[1] A contemporary dictionary published in 1909 defined *shen* as "used by many for the true God," but also "the gods, the divinities, a god, in the usage of the pagans."[2] It also defined *shenming* unequivocally as "the gods," with no reference to the Christian God. By using *shen*, the Chinese promise was acceptable to Christians, and also somewhat acceptable to non-Christians. While the Japanese promise had a non-Christian bias, the Hong Kong promise for the interwar years had a Christian bias.

Rendering "the King" into Chinese was more difficult. Given Stubbs' dispositions, nothing could be done to modify the oath as far as this was concerned in his time. But this created some problems for many if not most of the Chinese boys who were being targeted by the movement. Performing one's duty to the King was what all Boy Scouts in the colony had promised to do. But local sentiments regarding loyalty to one's country were complicated in Hong Kong. A few examples serve to illustrate their complexity. The Kadoorie troop hosted a concert in 1923 in front of a large and almost all-Chinese audience. This event ended with the singing of *both* the Chinese National Anthem and "God Save the King," reflecting dual loyalties which were probably typical among many Chinese boys then.[3] In 1922 and 1925-6, many Chinese had gone on strike, and some Chinese boys in elite schools had participated in demonstrations, walk-outs and boycotts in support.[4] The strikes

---

1   As an aside, a great debate in the 19th century in China centered on whether "God" should be translated into *shangdi* (上帝) or *shen*. The intricate complexities of this "Terms Controversy," which actually had originated in the 17th century when the Jesuits first entered China, are beyond our scope. Suffice it to say that some experts had agreed that *shen* was appropriate for the Christian God (but others insisted on *shangdi*), although it could also mean other gods.

2   S. Wells Williams, *A Syllabic Dictionary of the Chinese Language* (Tung Chou, North China Union College, 1909), 692.

3   *HKT*, February 5, 1923.

4   *HKT*, June 22, 1925.

essentially developed along the following lines: the Chinese protested, walked out and went on strike, and the Europeans coped as best they could. The call-out for Boy Scouts might therefore have caused mental struggles for some. Indeed, as noted earlier, Scout membership had declined for two consecutive years after the 1922 strike.

Waldegrave was keenly aware of these feelings among the boys. In June 1925, amidst the anti-British crises, he noted that the 10th Hong Kong was "on strike," then he hastened to qualify the statement by saying "or rather like the other Chinese Troops out of action pro. tem."[1]

In September 1925, Waldegrave complained about an American professor from Canton Christian College who had claimed in a "lying anti-British sermon" that "Boy Scouts [in Hong Kong], rather than swear allegiance to King George, had left the Movement." He suggested that while a few Chinese boys might have walked out as part of the anti-British exodus, "many scouts were sent out of the Colony by their parents when trouble began, and intimidators threatened terrible calamities for Hongkong, and many were not allowed by their parents to volunteer." To him, the boys would not be Boy Scouts if they had not taken the Scout Promise (a valid argument logically if we ignore the possibility that a Chinese boy might simply refuse to join to being with), though he admitted that "possibly there <u>may</u> be one or two boys who left from a mistaken Nationalist idea." He also argued that making the promise did not amount to "swearing allegiance" to the King, a subtle difference which was probably hard for young Chinese boys to perceive.[2]

In short, some Chinese troops had become inactive during the strikes (whether in support of their compatriots or not was subject to interpretation); and the Scout Promise as it related to declaring one's "duty to the King" was for an issue for some Chinese.

Clementi, like Stubbs, was in favor of encouraging Scouting for the Chinese boys. More importantly, with his good understanding of the Chinese language, culture and politics, he was able to address the obstacle of the Scout Promise.

Around this time, Professor Forster of the University of Hong Kong had informed Waldegrave that "the difficulty with *most* of them

---

1   Letter, Waldegrave to Butterworth, June 23, 1925, the Gilwell Archives.

2   Letter, Waldegrave to Butterworth, September 29, 1925, the Gilwell Archives.

[Chinese students] is the promise of 'duty to the King,'" thus confirm-ing the American professor's claim to some extent.[1] It is interesting to note that Waldegrave's "one or two boys" had become Forster's "most" Chinese, when the boys who *might* join are included.

At any rate, it would seem that the problem was serious enough for Waldegrave to take the trouble to speak with Clementi. The Chief Scout was sympathetic, and agreed to an important adaptation, a com-promise solution. As reported in May 1926 by Waldegrave: "Clementi is fully in favor of our using in Chinese the words "the Head of the Nation" for "King," as he feels as we do the great importance of the movement in combating Bolshevism which is making another attack on the schools here, and I have been instructed to pass the word quietly to the Chinese S.M.s [Scoutmasters] to allow that form of promise to be taken. *Noth-ing on the matter is being put in writing*."[2] On the surface of it, there is nothing out of the ordinary with this proposed amendment. After all, the "King" was indeed the "the head of the nation" in Britain. However, given the unique situation in Hong Kong, use of the generic description "the head of the nation (國家元首)" in the Chinese promise served an-other purpose: it allowed Chinese boys to declare dual loyalty or loyalty only to China by interpreting it to mean the president of the ROC as well as or instead of the British King.

camp during their next vacation. He tells me that the difficulty with most of them is the promise of "duty to the King." You will re-member my talking that over with you and the Chief etc. Clementi is fully in favour of our using in Chinese the words "the Head of the Nation" for "King", as he feels as we do the great importance of the

Waldegrave's letter on Clementi's agreement to modify the promise in Chinese, May 1926.

Gilwell Archives.

In this matter, Hong Kong was arguably more "progressive" than many other colonies. In British Nigeria, the promise in local lan-guage was not even commonly known to exist. Many interwar Nigerian Scoutmasters actually thought that "to be able to speak English was a condition of membership, since otherwise a Scout could not…make the

1   Letter, Waldegrave to Butterworth, May 31, 1926, the Gilwell Archives, italics added.

2   Ibid.

Promise!"[1] It was largely the unwillingness of Scouts in British South Africa "to abandon the Union Jack or to omit the reference to the King" which led to the creation of an alternative Afrikaans language youth movement called the *Voortrekkers* in 1931, whose members vowed to do their duty to God, his "Volk" and his country.[2] Years later, Indian Boy Scouts still had to commit to do their duties to the King. K. N. Kadam was a Boy Scout in India in late 1930s, and recalled that in those days, Indian boys had to take this oath: "On my word of honor, I promise to do my duty to God, King, and Country."[3] It is significant that though "country" was added, no doubt meaning India for most Indian boys, it did not replace, but was rather preceded by, the British King.

Not only was a Chinese version of the promise allowed in Hong Kong, it was substantively altered to cater for the political sensitivities of the local boys. Three points need to be made. Firstly, the English version of the promise had remained the same, meaning that any boy taking the promise in English would still have had to commit to do his duty to the King, regardless of his nationality. A non-British Portuguese or French boy would not have the option of using the words "the head of the nation," unless he could take the promise in Chinese.

Secondly, it was clear that while Clementi had supported this modification he had done so not because of his belief in the international brotherhood of Scouting as an ideal *per se*, but largely due to his more pragmatic concern with the growing influence of Bolshevism or nationalism among Chinese school boys. In other words, he felt this adaptation would help colonial authorities to entrench their influence among non-British Chinese boys. The dichotomous treatment of the promise in English and in Chinese by language rather than nationality of the Scout defied logic, but is more easily understandable in light of Clementi's intention, which was primarily to reach Chinese boys.

Finally, Clementi had instructed that the revised Chinese prom-

---

1   Arthur Brown, "The Development of the Scout Movement in Nigeria," *African Affairs*, 46/182, January, 1947, 39.
2   Sheila Patterson, *The Last Trek: A Study of the Boer People and the Afrikaner Nation* (London: Routledge, 2004), 265; Tom Lodge, *Mandela: A Critical Life* (Oxford: Oxford Univ. Press, 2006), 41. "Volk" in Afrikaans = (Afrikaner) people/nation
3   K. N. Kadam, "The Birth of a Rationalist," Eleanor Zelliot and Maxine Bernsten, *The Experience of Hinduism: Essays on Religion in Maharashtra* (SUNY, 1988), 288.

ise should be implemented unofficially, without putting anything on paper. This suggested that he was aware that this treatment could potentially be politically sensitive in Britain or other parts of the empire, and therefore wanted to avoid unnecessary negative publicity.

Waldegrave predicted that, with this pragmatic step in recognition of sentiments of the local majority, "you may now see a very big increase in our numbers very soon."[1] His optimism about the future growth in the movement with the newly adapted Scout Promise appears to betray the perceived seriousness of the problem with the original version. If the original promise was only problematic for "one or two boys," there would clearly not be a significant increase in membership among the Chinese when it was modified to accommodate their burgeoning nationalistic feelings.

The bi-lingual booklet on the Scout Promise and the Scout Law, 1931.

H. K. Scout Archives.

By late 1920s and early 1930s this discreet pragmatism was openly acknowledged. A 1931 official Boy Scouts Association booklet written by Rev. E. A. Armstrong, District Commissioner for Kowloon, and translated into Chinese by Ng Wai Kay (吳瑋璣) contains the following Scout Promise in Chinese: "我願竭盡忠誠, 對於神及國家元首盡我責任, 隨時扶助他人, 遵守童子軍規則. (literally "I will loyally do my best, to do my duty to God and to *the head of the nation*, to help others at all times, to obey the Scout Law.") The adaptation relating to "duty to the King" in this book formally confirmed in writing what was allowed verbally by Clementi in 1926.

The related original Second Law was: "A Scout is loyal to the King, his country, his officers, his parents, and his employers and those under him." The 1931 Chinese version of this law likewise substituted "the King" with "the head of state (元首)." The paragraph elaborating on the law refrained from mentioning the King at all in both the Chinese and the English texts, and merely pointed out that a Scout "realises the blessings which come from having orderly government and therefore he is loyal to it and he does all in his power to help the government to improve its laws and administration so that contentedness may increase."[2] But it also noted that a Scout "loves his country and helps to preserve its

---

1   Letter, Waldegrave to Butterworth, May 31, 1926, the Gilwell Archives.

2   E. A. Armstrong, *The Scout Law* 童子軍規律 (Hong Kong: the Boy Scouts Association, 1931), italics added in the first citation. Armstrong was a Wood Badge holder who came to Hong Kong in 1929 and returned to Ireland in 1932.

learning, arts, and good customs so that it may contribute its share to the knowledge of mankind and the beauty of the world."[1] One could again easily interpret this short paragraph as condoning dual or divided loyalty, loyalty to British Hong Kong, and loyalty to China, especially Chinese culture.

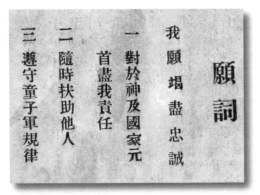

The 1931 version of the Scout Promise in Chinese for Hong Kong.

H. K. Scout Archives.

In contrast to places with a single religion and national identity, the Scout Promise in Chinese adopted in Hong Kong in 1926 was intentionally ambivalent in stipulating both "duty to God" and "duty to the King," largely reflecting awareness among the colonial elites of a pragmatic need to reach out to non-British Chinese boys. This concession made the Chinese promise acceptable as a sincere oath to be taken by the Chinese boys, mostly non-British nationals and non-Christians, and enabled many more of them to be included in Scouting, perceived to be beneficial to colonial governance.

Some non-British Chinese boys

While some non-British Chinese boys might have been admitted to Scouting in the early 1920s, serious efforts to include them started only after the strikes and the adaptation of the Chinese promise to accommodate the nationalistic feelings of the local populace. Considerable progress was made in the second half of the 1920s, as first the membership losses in 1922 and 1923 were recovered, and then healthy gains resumed. By the end of the first postwar decade, Scouting was no longer confined exclusively to British nationals, but was also available at least to a selection of elite non-British Chinese boys from more comfortable families.

1   Ibid.

A Scout Esperanto language badge.

In March 1926, over a hundred British, Chinese and Japanese Scouts attended a campfire, at which Holyoak and Waldegrave spoke about Scout brotherhood and referred to Clementi's plan for a local Concord Club, with Scouts playing lead roles.[1] Clementi called the club a bridge between nations, classes, creeds and races. Clearly with the recent strikes in mind, he suggested that such clubs among Chinese students would prevent them from becoming "victims of lying propaganda" and causing troubles.[2] Unfortunately, like the proposed international Esperanto language to which Baden-Powell himself had lent his support, the Concord movement did not take off in the colony or elsewhere.[3] Still, it is revealing of Clementi's motives for encouraging Chinese Scouting, in the aftermath of the ethnically-constructed crises of the 1920s, in which "misguided" young people were seen to have played a part.

Scout display at the VDC Headquarters, the 1920s.

H. K. Scout Archives.

Clementi met the Scouts for the first time as their Chief Scout in a rally held at the headquarters of the Volunteer Defence Corps in May 1926, attended by twenty troops and three packs (including Clementi's son as a member of a Cub Pack).[4] As already noted, the performances demonstrated the growing ethnic diversity of Scouting, with first aid by Chinese Scouts from Ying Wa, Jujitsu and Japanese fencing by the Japanese Scouts, and Highland dancing by boys from the Taikoo Scottish.[5]

In July 1926, after Holyoak had passed away, Clementi ap-

---

1   *CM*, March 29, 1926.
2   *HKDP*, February 23, 1928.
3   *HKT*, March 7, and April 8, 1929. B-P had suggested that Esperanto be used as a secret language among Scouts of all nations. See *Scouting for Boys,* 1908 edition, 177. To this day, there is still a *Skolta Esperanto-Ligo* (Scout Esperanto League).
4   Letter, Waldegrave to Butterworth, May 31, 1926, the Gilwell Archives.
5   *HKDP*, May 13, 1926.

proved Waldegrave's recommendation to appoint Robert Kotewall, arguably the most loyal and helpful leading "Chinese" during the Strike-Boycott of 1925-26, as president of the association, in view of his stature within the Chinese community. The commissioner argued privately that "considering the great number of Chinese Scouts we have it would, especially at the present time, make a very good impression to have him."[1] Later, Clementi expressed a similar rationale openly:

> *To succeed, the movement had to have the goodwill and support of the Chinese community who formed by far the largest part of the Association in Hongkong. It was...a very great pleasure...to welcome...as president... Dr. Kotewall, who enjoyed the very highest degree of respect of the Chinese community whom he very worthily represented on the Legislative Council...The fact that Dr. Kotewall had...accept[ed] the office showed that although the Scout movement originated in Great Britain, it was capable of being acclimatized in this Colony.*[2]

Robert Kotewall.

Kotewall, a Eurasian, was the next best thing to a pure Chinese, being the official representative of the Chinese community. At a time when Chinese endorsement was perceived to be critical, Waldegrave and Clementi went to great lengths to reach out to Hong Kong's Chinese youth by appointing a "Chinese" president, when public and private organizations in the colony typically had British leadership.

In December 1927, an ordinance was passed to make the local association a protected institution, much like a similar ordinance had done for its counterpart in the Straits Settlements in 1926.[3] It prohibited any organization or individual other than the Hong Kong Branch of the British Scout association from distributing badges with the word "Scout" or the equivalent Chinese characters *tongzijun* (童子軍), unauthorized possession of such badges or closely-resembling ones, or the formation of a Boy Scouts association without prior authorization.[4] While the Attorney-General had simply noted that the objective of the ordinance was

---

1   Letter, Waldegrave to Butterworth, May 31, 1926, the Gilwell Archives.
2   *SCMP*, December 15, 1926.
3   *Hong Kong Hansard,* December 1, 1927.
4   *HKT*, October 29, 1927

The Silver Wolf.

Author's collection.

Waldegrave wearing
the Silver Wolf.

H. K. Scout Archives.

to protect local Scouting from undesirable imitations which "might be used for political and militaristic purposes," it was likely that the colonial authorities had learned their lesson from other parts of the empire.[1] Lacking such an ordinance, parallel Scout associations had emerged in India which formed troops for native boys. In fact, even after the amalgamated Boy Scouts Association of India had started to admit native boys, the *Seva Samiti* Scouts Association stayed independent, and became "a parallel All-India Scout Association" with a nationalistic bias.[2] Though not explicitly mentioned, it is clear that the ordinance was aimed at protecting the colony from interference by the Boy Scouts of China. The last thing the authorities wanted was a Hong Kong equivalent of the *Seva Samiti*. In 1928, Waldegrave was awarded a Silver Wolf, the highest merit award for leaders in British Scouting, in recognition of his many years of selfless service to the Hong Kong Boy Scout Movement. He was the first person in Hong Kong to receive this award.

Queen's College, the leading government school which Baden-Powell himself had targeted in a personal letter in 1913, formed a troop much later than the other important schools, with some "encouragement" from the authorities. Waldegrave noted in May 1926 that "the principal Government School for Chinese…has long refused to have anything to do with us, but now under pressure from above is willing to have a troop, provided we get the right man."[3] A troop was formed in early 1928, and *the Yellow Dragon*, the school magazine, reported that the Scouts were allowed to use a school room for meetings, that there was only one

1   *HKDP*, November 11, 1927.
2   Rau, *Scouting in India*, 36.
3   Letter, Waldegrave to Butterworth, May 31, 1926, the Gilwell Archives.

patrol with Patrol Leader Li Kai-ying, and that they had their first camp in Saiwan, led by Y. F. Fenton.[1]   Shortly after, an editorial lauded the benefits of "the Boy Scout camps" and expressed the wish that "every schoolboy had the opportunity of going to a good camp."[2]

21st & 22nd Hong Kong, the first rural troops.

H. K. Scout Archives.

A significant milestone in Chinese Scouting was the progress made in non-elitist rural and private schools in the late 1920s. Scouting became available to a few rural Chinese boys when Justice J. A. Fraser, District Officer for Northern New Territories, started the 21st Hong Kong at Tai Po (大埔) in 1927. Soon, W. G. Routley, Land Bailiff, set up the 22nd Hong Kong at Un Long (Yuen Long 元朗).[3] As both places had a government school, it is likely that many if not most boys came from these schools. These two troops were significant in that while many rural boys were born locally and therefore British subjects, they were often disadvantaged in terms of access to educational and recreational opportunities. They were exceptions to the rule, as even the most basic western education was available to only few rural boys. A study of the well-established Liao (廖) lineage village in Sheung Shui (上水) indicated that education at the time was mostly conducted in old-style Confucian schools, and the first western Fung Kai Primary School (鳳溪學校) was only set up in there in 1932.[4]

Soon Scout troops also appeared in a few private unaided (i. e., not helped by public funds) schools. In 1927, the 25th Hong Kong was

1   The *Yellow Dragon* 黃龍報 (Hong Kong: Queen's College), March 1928, 54.
2   Ibid., August and September, 1928, 185.
3   The *Hong Kong Scouting Gazette*, Vol. VII, No. 2, Feb., 1941, 21.
4   Huge D. R. Baker, *A Chinese Lineage Village: Sheung Shui* (Frank Cass, 1968), 24, 72-74.

founded in Yuek Chee College which, with nine hundred students, was the largest of hundreds of private vernacular schools.[1] In 1928, a troop was formed by Edward Shea, former member of the Roving 5th, in Mun-sang College (民生書院), a new school in Kowloon founded two years earlier.[2] Soon after, the 26th Hong Kong was started at Kin Bong English School (建邦英文中學), a private school in Shamshuipo. In 1929, Waldegrave inaugurated the 24th Hong Kong at Shu Man Chinese School (樹民學校), another vernacular school in Yaumati.[3]

Inauguration of the 26th Hong Kong (Kin Bong School), 1928.

H. K. Scout Archives.

Guiding for Chinese came later. The first company, 2nd Hong Kong (St. Paul's School), started only in November 1926. 3rd Hong Kong (Belilios School) came a few months later. In May 1928, colors of both companies were presented, and Mrs. Bella Southorn, the Guide commissioner, expressed her pleasure "in the formation of the first Chinese Company in the Colony."[4] Others followed, including that of the Chinese Mei Fang Girls' School (梅芳女學校) in July 1929, and that of the SCAA, the first open Girl Guide company.[5]

Local Guiding's policy regarding uniforms provides another interesting insight into gendered differentiation. During this time, Chinese Guides wore Chinese-inspired uniforms instead of the western-style

---

1   The *Kung Sheung Yat Po* 工商日報 (KSYP), September 20, 1928.
2   *HKT*, June 30, 1928, 2.
3   *HKT*, January 30, 1929, 13.
4   *HKDP*, May 25, 1928, 5.
5   *KSYP*, July 17, 1929.

ones of the Europeans. When these attires first appeared in a ceremonial occasion, they were described as "becoming" uniforms which had received "many [presumably positive] comments…from the [presumably European] ladies present."[1] Photographic evidence from the late 1920s shows that, instead of a blouse with long stocking, a scarf (or tie) and a hat, the Chinese uniform was a Chinese-style pant suit, with color trim for the top, and with no scarf or hat, though the latter were the most easily-recognizable trademarks of Scouting and Guiding around the world. White fabrics were used in the summer, while darker ones in winter. This Chinese uniform might have been adopted later also by the Diocesan Girls' School company, which served Eurasian and Chinese girls. Gertie Choa, who joined this company in the late 1929, recalled that the "uniform used to be trousers and coats trimmed with Company colours, not at all like what we have now."[2] This would appear to be the Chinese Guides uniform.

Hong Kong Chinese girls in Chinese Guides uniforms, the 1920s.

H. K. Scout Archives.

The uniform question is not a trivial one. In an interesting analysis of the use and misuse of the Boy Scout uniforms in Colonial Kenya, Timothy Parsons concludes that "Scout uniforms…were tangible but malleable archives of social reality that enable their wearers to imagine, if not recreate, new identities and realities," especially in a colonial context.[3] No reason was provided for this ethnic emphasis in the design of uniforms worn by the Chinese girls in Hong Kong. The Boy Scout uniform also appeared very western, but a more Chinese-looking version was never created for Chinese boys in the colony.

---

1   *HKDP*, May 25, 1928, 5.

2   *Diamond Jubilee, 1916-1976* (Hong Kong, the Hong Kong Girl Guides Association, 1976).

3   Timothy H. Parsons, "The Consequences of Uniformity: The Struggle for the Boy Scout Uniform in Colonial Kenya," *Journal of Social History*, Winter 2006, 377.

There were some precedents in China for such "discriminatory" adoption of western clothing. Regulations issued in 1912 on formal clothing for the new Chinese republic allowed both Chinese and European options for men, but only Chinese style for women.[1] On the other hand, studies revealed that uniforms for Chinese girls in modern schools in those days often took the form of fully-pleated skirts which finished just below the knee, with "stockinged calves" exposed and "feet clad in leather shoes," instead of embroidered cloth shoes.[2] Similar clothing was also adopted by politically-active Chinese women in the republic, in the hope that they would be perceived as educated and progressive.

In this context, Girl Guide skirts (which had similar hemlines), stockings, shoes, and especially the distinctive scarves and hats, would not have seemed out-of-place for Chinese girls being educated in western schools in the colony. The elimination of these items from the dress code applied to the Chinese Girl Guides in Hong Kong could easily be construed as a form of racial discrimination, not unlike in South Africa, where native and colored girls (and boys) were enrolled in a separate movement, also with different, less-Scout-like, uniforms.

Pinewood, a campsite leased from the British military, 1923-25.
H. K. Scout Archives.

The Clementi years ended in 1930 with the opening of the first permanent Scout campsite in Hong Kong.[3] Pinewood Battery, the first campsite, temporarily leased from the military in 1923, had to be given up in 1925.[4] In the same year, efforts were made to find alternatives at

1   The *Shen Bao* 申報, August 20, 1912, 2.
2   Mina Roces and Louise Edwards (ed.), *The Politics of Dress in Asia and Americas* (Brighton: Sussex Academic Press, 2007), 49.
3   *CM*, March 8, 1930, 14.
4   *Hong Kong Administrative Report, 1923,* Appendix O, O25.

Rennie's Mill in Junk Bay and Saiwan (Chaiwan) on Hong Kong Island, and the latter was eventually secured.[1]

The development of Saiwan campsite was truly a team effort shared by all members of the young association. The so-called Barker's Bungalow was first acquired, and then application was submitted to the Government for the adjoining ground. Many Scouts and Rover Scouts voluntarily helped to clear the site of the tangled masses of cactuses, old stumps, stones, etc., and turned it into a campground. The few buildings had to be repaired, and water supply, sanitary facilities, flagpoles and a suitable campfire area had to be installed. Much of this work was done by the Scouts themsevles, under the guidance of the honorary architect, A. J. Lane. A report noted that "it will of course take us rather longer than it would a contractor, but it will take 50 per cent off the cost, be excellent experience for us, and give many scouts a chance to win Mason and Carpenter Badges."[2] Such was the spirit of the early Scouts in Hong Kong. In line with this approach, in these early years, each troop was assigned the use and care of a designated campsite.

The "Mason" Badge.

Saiwan, first permanent campsite for Hong Kong Scouts, opened in 1930.

H. K. Scout Archives.

Waldegrave declared that Saiwan had "quite good scouting country around" and was easily accessible.[3] In her speech at the open-

---

1 "Application from the Commissioner of Hongkong Boys [*sic*] Scouts Association for an area of land at Rennie's Mills for training purposes," CSO 1441/1925, HKRS 58-1-135-85, "Boy Scout Training Camp—Sai Wan," HKRS 156-1-3331, the Public Records Office, Hong Kong.

2 *CM*, November 2, 1929.

3 Letter, Waldegrave to Butterworth, June 23, 1925, the Gilwell Archives.

A Chinese troop camping at Saiwan, c. 1930.

H. K. Scout Archives.

ing ceremony in January 1930, Mrs. Southorn emphasized the benefits of outdoor living, quoting a poetess who showered a "thousand pities" on "the poor folks in the cities," and urging all to spend their time outdoors, "nowhere so well as in a camp like this"—a message which was informed by the anti-urban and pro-rural discourse of the time.[1] Finally, by way of Saiwan, local Scouting was able to join in the modern health movement "to extricate adolescents, youths and…children from the urban core" and to "resituate the young in 'spaces of nature.'"[2]

Membership trends in this decade were notable for their unevenness, as illustrated in the graph on the next page. Growth in the Stubbs years had been erratic, with initial jump in 1921 followed by decline in 1922-23, due to the negative impacts of the 1922 strikes, and then growth again in 1924-1925. Growth was steadier in the Clementi years, though it also flattened out later. By 1930, the penetration of Scouting was still relatively low in comparison to Britain and even nearby Singapore. In that year, Singapore, which had a smaller population, had 711 Scouts versus 621 for Hong Kong. Hong Kong reported 0.7 Scout per thousand persons, versus 1.3 in Singapore, and 9.8 in Britain.[3] Looking at youth population alone, while the take up of Scouting was good

---

1 *CM*, January 13, 1930, 10; the *Hong Kong Sunday Herald* (*HKSH)*, January 12, 1930, 1.

2 David M. Pomfret, "The City of Evil and the Great Outdoors: the Modern Health Movement and the Urban Young, 1918-1940," *Urban History*, 28, 3, 2001, 405.

3 Appendix D, "Membership Statistics."

among non-Chinese youth, it was still very low among the Chinese boys. The penetration of non-Chinese youngsters is estimated at around 15-20%, while that of the Chinese boys only around 0.5%, based on census numbers and membership statistics.[1]

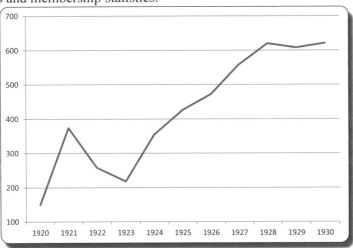

Membership Trends, Hong Kong, 1920-1930

Source: Appendix D, "Membership statistics."

In other words, by the time Clementi left to become the High Commissioner of Malaya, though Scouting had become available to many European and some middle-class Chinese boys, it was still largely out-of-reach for most Chinese. Even if all designated troops were active, there were less than thirty troops as of 1930. An official report in 1926 indicated that, besides the elite schools, there were 545 private urban vernacular schools, and 191 rural ones.[2] In the first interwar decade, Scouting was not available to practically all the boys from these schools. There were also many children outside the school system. F. B. L. Bowley estimated that only around 15% of young persons of school age were enrolled in a school.[3] Even official figures would put the ratio of Chinese

Scouts at camp.

---

1   There were 1,000 non-Chinese boys and 73,000 Chinese boys aged 6 to 15 in 1931. There were 551 Scouts in 1930 (including 118 Cubs and 56 Rovers). As most Cubs, many Rovers and some Scouts were non-Chinese, it can be assumed that roughly 150 to 200 boys were non-Chinese. This would mean that 15-20% of the non-Chinese boys, but only around 0.5% of the Chinese boys were in Scouting. See *Hong Kong: Report on the Census of the Colony for 1931* (Hong Kong: Census Office, 1931); *Annual Report, 1930* (London: the Boy Scouts Association, 1931).

2   *Hong Kong Administrative Report, 1926,* Appendix O, 4.

3   *SCMP*, October 12, 1911.

children attending schools or otherwise being educated at only 25%.[1] The others would roam the streets unsupervised or be employed as child laborers. A commission under Stubbs had looked into child labor in thirteen factories, and concluded that children employed in all of them had to work hours which were "universally excessive."[2] Among these boys and girls, Scouting or Guiding would have been a leisure activity which they had neither the energy nor the time for, even if troops and companies had been made available to them.

Concluding remarks

Scouting was first re-launched in the postwar decade for ethnically British boys, though its sponsors quickly adopted a more inclusive approach to membership, resulting in the movement becoming available to a small number of other ethnic groups and eventually also non-British Chinese boys. Citizenship education was increasingly organized with a view to training British boys and a small number of Chinese elites to become public-spirited participants in community services and active supporters of the colonial government. For the leaders and supporters, "to educate," "to convert," and especially "to rule" were important motives. But religion tended to become less relevant over time, as the number of secular sponsors grew and more non-Christian Chinese boys were enrolled; while governance became the dominant motivation especially after the Chinese strikes in 1922 and 1925-6, driven by the colonial elite's perception of Scouting's value to their efforts to sustain British rule.

Chinese nationalism mattered, but unlike in the pre-war years, it prompted the authorities to seek new ways of including non-British Chinese boys, first by eliminating the nationality requirement and then by adopting an equivocal Scout Promise in Chinese. Race as a barrier to membership became less important, as Chinese, Portuguese, Eurasians, Scottish and Japanese were included. Gender played a role, as both eth-

---

1   16,937 Chinese children "attending schools or being otherwise educated," divided by 68,450 children between the ages of 5 and 14. See *Hong Kong: Report on the Census of the Colony for 1911* (Hong Kong: Census Office, 1911), 6.

2   *Report of the Commission Appointed to Enquire into the Conditions of the Industrial Employment of Children in Hongkong, and the Desirability and Feasibility of Legislation for the Regulation of Such Employment* (Hong Kong: Hong Kong Government, October 1921), 122-124.

nic British girls and Chinese girls were slower to enter Guiding, and Chinese girls were required to conform to certain ethnic related notions when it came to attire. Class was a barrier, as Scouting had only reached the privileged few by 1930 and remained unavailable to most Chinese boys in most private vernacular schools and outside the school system.

In this period, Hong Kong Scouting was readily available to the European boys though it remained a niche movement reserved for only a few hundred Chinese boys. It was perceived to serve specific political ends, and as such was made available to many ethnic groups from a variety of institutions, including British schools, government, mission and private schools for the Chinese, churches, a sports club and commercial firms. Through patronage of the governors, support of the ruling and business elites, visibility in the community, occasional gallant acts and public services in the colony's times of need, it had in a short time acquired symbolic importance considerably beyond its small numbers.

Chapter 3

Dual Loyalty and Indigenization

1930-1945

Chapter 3
Dual Loyalty and Indigenization
1930-1945

In a confidential report on the strikes and boycotts, Robert Kotewall had noted the significant part played by students "corrupted" by outside political influences, and advised watchfulness in the schools, especially the vernacular schools.[1] When he became president of the local Boy Scouts Association, he declared that Scouting "trains our youth to become good citizens...who...will...constitute the strongest bulwark against Bolshevism and Communism."[2] In other words, Scouting for the Chinese school boys offered a solution to Chinese nationalism and political propaganda, which was understood to be increasingly filtering into Hong Kong. This vision of Scouting, shared by the ruling elite, was largely achieved under Sir William Peel, who became the governor in May 1930, and Sir Andrew Caldecott, who arrived in Hong Kong in late 1935 and left in 1937.

By the late 1930s, Japan's intensified territorial ambitions in China increasingly threatened British interests in Asia and raised the possibility of war in Hong Kong. British Conservatives had initially favored the appeasement of Japan, even after the latter's invasion of Manchuria, where British interests were minimal, despite the outrage expressed by many countries and condemnation by the League of Nations. However, in 1937, when Japan bombed Shanghai and Canton, and British lives and property were affected, the British, whether left, right or center, became one, and finally realized that their old Asian ally, Japan (the "Britain" of Asia), was increasingly a common enemy of China and the United Kingdom.[3] Sir Geoffry Northcote arrived as governor in October 1937, as the

Previous Page:

Hong Kong Scouts gathered at Government House to greet the Duke of Gloucester in April 1929. These boys, mostly Chinese, were to become increasingly identified with China in the 1930s.

H. K. Scout Archives.

1   Kotewall, confidential memorandum on the 1925 Strike, in "Sir Robert Kotewall, 1945," CO 968/120/1.
2   *HKDP*, December 15, 1926.
3   Kingsley Martin, "British Opinion and the Proposed Boycott of Japan;" and H. Hessell Tiltman, "Japan's 'Anti-British' Drive," both from *Japan's Aggression and*

war clouds darkened, and openly condoned dual loyalty towards Britain and China in Scouting, given the pressing needs to motivate Chinese boys to fight for the colony. Chinese nationalism suddenly became more acceptable. This new attitude, coupled with the evacuation of ethnic British boys in 1940, enabled local Scouting to grow impressively and become fully indigenized by the time Sir Mark Young started his short-lived term in September 1941.

In the later interwar years, then, Scouting in Hong Kong had to respond to multiple pressures, notably political extremism in China and the threat of war in Hong Kong. Yet, through the successful negotiation of the manifold difficulties and the pragmatic adoption of apparently contradictory policies along the way, it gradually took native roots and acquired local characteristics, to become a vibrant, if profoundly altered, indigenized youth movement, just before the fall of Hong Kong.

Nationalistic and politicized Chinese Scouting

During this period, many youth movements in Europe were influenced by Baden-Powell's Scouts, but some were dedicated to extremist political ideologies, and proliferated in the service of anti-democratic forces. In the context of growing Chinese nationalism, what happened to youth movements in Nazi Germany, Fascist Italy, and Communist Russia had a substantial impact upon the youth movements in China from the mid-1920s to the 1930s, and therefore also influenced or at least threatened to influence that of nearby Hong Kong.

German Nazis formed a youth league in 1920 and renamed it *Hitler Jugend*, or Hitler Youth, in 1926, then one of a plethora of politicized youth groups, including the Christian *Jungschar*, "a boy scout movement with...strong patriotic nationalistic undercurrents."[1] After Hitler's rise to power, the Hitler Youth simply absorbed the *Jungschar* and other groups. Hitler Youth, though to some extent "Scout-like," had near-compulsory membership, intense Nazi indoctrination and serious

A *Hitler Jugend* poster, urging youth to serve Hitler.

Public Opinion (Kunming: National Southwest Associated Univ. Library, 1938), 474-5 and 484.

1   Henry Metelmann, *A Hitler Youth: Growing Up in Germany in the 1930s* (London: Caliban Books, 1997), 39.

military training. The recruitment poster of the Hitler Youth appealed to young people to serve Hitler personally. The boys' oath was centered on the *Führer*: "I swear to devote all my energies, all my strength, to the savior of our country, Adolf Hitler. I am willing and ready to give up my life, so help me God. One People, One nation, One Führer."[1] Many independent-thinking Germans were against Nazism, but few dared to fight it openly, as the Nazis could and did resort to using the power of the state to persecute those who opposed them.

MOSCHETTO REGOLAMENTARE
"BALILLA"
FABBRICA NAZIONALE D'ARMI·S·A·BRESCIA

A *Balilla* poster, emphasizing its militarism.

Usurpation of Scouting by extreme nationalism also occurred in Italy under Mussolini. The *Balilla*, the Fascist version of Boy Scouts, was constituted in 1926. Fascist journals such as *La Fiamma* would argue that children trained in the international brotherhood of Scouting did not love Italy or were not patriotic.[2] Two years later, Mussolini stated that "given the fullness of the Balilla and Avanguardisti movement [for older boys], and given its State character, other movements lose their 'raisons d'être'," ending Scouting, up to then tolerated as a friendly gesture towards the Catholic Church.[3] Like the Hitler Youth, this movement was very militaristic, very political, and centered on its leader, as revealed by some of their commandments: 1. The Fascist…should not believe in perpetual peace…, 5. Your musket and ammunition belt…must be kept in good condition for wartime…, 8. Mussolini is always right…, 10. …the life of the Duce should be dearer to you than everything else.[4]

Similarly, the Communists were also inclined to involve youth in adult politics. The "Reds" in Russia were not always against Scouting. In fact, despite Russian Boy Scouts' tendencies to side with the "Whites", and Communist's suspicion that Scouting was an instrument of the bourgeoisie, Russian Communists had tried to work with the Boy Scouts up to the early 1920s. Later official disassociations notwithstanding, the Young Pioneers set up in 1922 were patterned on "a reorganized Scouting system," imbued with Communist ideologies, and used the motto Будь готов (*Bud'gotov*, Be Prepared), the same as that of Baden-

1   Anna Rauschning, *No Retreat* (1939), in http://www.spartacus.schoolnet.co.uk/GERyouth.htm (accessed October 23, 2006)

2   *La Fiamma*, October 3, 1926, in Enrico Biagioli, *Origini e nascita dello Scautismo in Umbria*, 122, 131. "*Balilla: non "scout..!...80,000 fanciulli educati alla fratellanza universaale non li vogliamo in Italia: questo e chiaro e pacifico.*"

3   *HKT*, April 28, 1928.

4   *CM*, October 1, 1929.

Powell's Boy Scout Movement.[1] But instead of wearing scarves with individual troop's own colors, all Young Pioneers wore red scarves, signifying their links to the Communist party. As Bertrand Russell pointed out, they were "a copy of the Boy Scouts," but took a class- and ideology-driven oath to defend "the cause of the working class" and to carry out "the covenants of Lenin."[2] Just like in Germany and Italy, Scouting was banned once the Young Pioneers were set up.

These Fascist or Communist examples would be of little relevance to Hong Kong if they were not consciously copied in China. In the interwar years, the Nationalists struggled for and eventually won control of China. Their efforts were first directed against the northern warlords and then against the Chinese Communists, the latter through alternating periods of toleration and harassment. Chinese leaders, Nationalists and Communists, looked to Europe for ideas as to how to nurture nationalism and build the young republic.

A Young Pioneer, with the Communist red scarf.

Soviet advisors had strong influence early on in the Nationalist government in Canton under Sun and among the Chinese Communists, whether they were part of the Nationalist government or independently running the Soviet districts in China.[3] Chiang Kai-shek was enthusiastic about both Scouting and Fascism. His son, Jiang (Chiang) Wei Guo (蔣緯國), was a Boy Scout in China in the late 1920s, and was sent to Germany for military training in 1936, when he was twenty.[4] Many military advisors in the Nationalist army were German, as was much of its military equipment. The influence of the more extreme forms of European youth movement was evident in the "Blue Shirt Society" and the "New Life Movement" in the 1930s. Some in the Nationalist establishment even went so far as to call for Chiang to become "China's Hitler."[5]

These influences and the turbulent political context largely

1   Jim Riordan, "The Russian Boy Scouts," October 1988, *History Today*, 51-2.
2   Bertrand Russell, *Education and the Social Order* (London: George Allen & Unwin, 1932), 116-7.
3   Maurice Parmelee, *Bolshevism Fascism and the Liberal Democratic State* (New York: Wiley, 1934), 173-176.
4   Gao Si-yin 高仕隱, *Jiang Wei Guo Jin Hu Tui Hu* 蔣緯國: 進乎? 退乎? (Jiang Weiguo: Going Forward or Backward?) (Taipei: Chang Ge Chu Ban Shi, 1990), 126-130. Jiang Wei Guo acknowledged the long-lasting influence of Scouting on him as a person and as a citizen ("童子軍信條對他的人格有很深遠的影響...讓[他]成為一個...頂天立地,忠貞不貳的國民").
5   William C. Kirby, *Germany and Republican China* (Stanford: Stanford Univ. Press, 1984), 145-185.

Chiang Wei Guo in Scout uniform with his father.

The modified Chinese Scout logo, incorporating the Nationalist emblem.

shaped the fate of Scouting in China. Even in parts outside the control of the Nationalists, the movement tended to be politicized. In 1928, Xiao Hong (蕭紅), the Chinese writer who was attending a girls' school in the northeastern city of Harbin then, described how some Boy Scouts, armed with long staves, came into her school and "forced" her principal to allow the girls to join an anti-Japanese protest.[1]

In parts of China controlled by the Nationalist Party, Scouting was pushed into a more extreme form of nationalism, akin to those which appeared in parts of Europe. In 1926, the Nationalist Party decided to *dang-hua* (黨化) or "partyize" Chinese Scouting, making it virtually a party organ. A new Scout logo incorporated the "Blue Sky and White Sun" emblem of the Chinese Nationalist. The Chinese Nationalist Party Boy Scout Committee (中國國民黨童子軍委員會) took over Scouting "to ensure that our Party's ideologies will be adopted in the hearts [of the Boy Scouts] and demonstrated in the enterprises [of Scouting]."[2] The Scout Promise was accordingly modified: Chinese Nationalist Party Boy Scout "X" swears that he will try his best with his comrades to: 1) Obey the last will of the *Tsung-li*, believe in the *San-min-chu-yi*, and complete the Nationalist revolution; 2) Help farmers, workers and all oppressed people; and 3) Obey discipline/order.[3] The *Tsung-li* was a title reserved for Sun Yat-sen, and *San-min-chu-yi* (Three Peoples' Principles) were the Nationalist ideologies of *min-tzu* (民族 nationalism), *min-quan* (民權 democracy), and *min-sheng* (民生 people's livelihood, or socialism). This promise was a far-cry from the Scout Promise crafted by Baden-Powell. God was not mentioned. The prominence of the founder of the party and Nationalist ideologies would remind one of the oath of the Hitler Youth or the commandments of the *Balilla*.

The Nationalists recognized that Scouting could play an im-

1   Xiao Hong (*née* Zhang Naiying 張乃瑩), "Yi Tiao Tie Lu De Wan Cheng一條鐵路的完成(The Completion of a Railroad)," in Zhang, Yumao, and Zhihong Yan (eds.), *Xiao Hong Wenji* 蕭紅文集 (the Collected Works of Xiao Hong) (Anhwei: Anhwei Wenyi Chubanshi, 1996), Vol. 3, 208-209. "拿長棒的童子軍... 沖進了校長室...'你們跟着去吧...,' 她好像被鷹類捉拿到的雞似的軟弱, 她是被拖在兩個戴大帽子的童子軍的臂膀上. (Boy Scouts carrying starves...rushed into the principal's room...'You go with them...'[said the principal,] she was weak like a hen caught by some eagles, she was dragged on the arms of two Boy Scouts wearing large hats.)"
2   "務使其將本黨主義訥諸內心而形諸事業," see Fan, *Zhong Guo Tong Zi Jun Shi*, 42-43.
3   "中國國民黨童子軍某某誓必盡力與各同志: 一, 遵奉總理遺囑, 信仰三民主義, 完成國民革命. 二, 扶助農工及一切被壓迫民眾. 三, 服從紀律.

portant role in their attempt to prepare the rising generation for their revolution. In 1927, they relocated the capital to Nanking (Nanjing), ushering in the so-called Nanking Decade (南京十年). In 1928, when the Communists were outlawed by Chiang Kai-shek, Boy Scouts worked with the military police to "prevent any distribution of 'Red' or seditious literature."[1] When Chiang addressed national Boy Scout representatives in Nanking in 1930, he linked Scouting to the "Three People's Principles" and the Nationalist revolution.[2] In 1932, the central executive committee of the *Kuomintang* (*KMT* 國民黨), or the Chinese Nationalist Party, passed a new resolution to re-organize Scouting. Party and government control was ensured, with Chiang as the chairman, and the minister of education as the director-general of the Chinese Scout National Supervisory Committee.[3] A top level organization chart of the Chinese Boy Scouts Association published in 1934 clearly defined the direct hierarchical relationship between the association and the Central Committee of the Chinese Nationalist Party.[4]

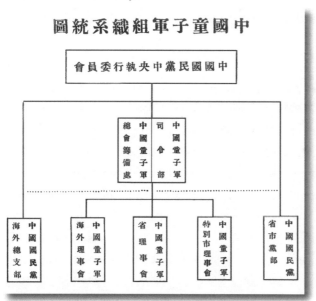

Organization chart of Boy Scouts of China, reporting into the Nationalist Party Central Committee, 1934.

The highly secretive *Lixingshe* (力行社 Society for Vigorous Practice), dubbed by some "Chiang's Freemasonry," existed between

1   *HKDP*, March 30, 1928.
2   *KSYP*, April 25, 1930.
3   Hsu Long-hsuen and Chang Ming-Kai, *History of the Sino-Japanese War, 1937-1945* (Chung Wu Publishing Co., 1971), 132.
4   Work Report of the Preparatory Bureau of the Boy Scouts Association of China 中國童子軍總會籌備處工作報告 (Nanking, 1934), 166.

1932 and 1937. At its peak, it controlled half a million members, and secretly orchestrated the mass mobilization of millions. It set up a satellite operation called the *Lijinshe* (力進社 Society for Vigorous Advancement) charged with penetrating Scouting. By April 1933, *Lijinshe* had around three hundred members, all occupying key offices of Boy Scouts of China, giving the Nationalists practically total control of the movement.[1] From 1934, Scouting expanded even more dramatically, when it became a required course in all lower middle schools.

However, despite tight controls by the *KMT*, Robert Culp concludes that Chinese Scouting during the Nanking decade was neither entirely militaristic nor wholly fascist. In fact, the movement provided an eclectic range of activities, enabling the Scouts to develop a sense of individuality based on a wide range of interests, as opposed to purely military training.[2] This phenomenon serves to confirm again the negotiated nature of Scouting, dependent on the interactions between the adults and the youth participants. Many schools were also offering the same broad spectrum of activities to both boys and girls, distinguishing it from the more gendered fascist military programs in Europe.

Similar efforts were taken by the Chinese Communists to organize youth under their control. When Madame Sun Yat-sen (Soong Ching Ling 宋慶齡) was in Moscow in 1927, she was most impressed with the Communist Youth in the Soviet Union, declaring that upon her return to China, "one of [her] first tasks will be to start a movement similar to this great movement."[3] Early Chinese Communists had followed the Soviet examples and created their own politically-indoctrinated Young Vanguards who, at one time, numbered some forty thousands in the northwest Soviet districts of China. These youngsters wore uniforms with red starred peak caps and served as "orderlies, mess-boys, buglers, spies, radio-operators, water-carriers, propagandists, actors, *mafoos*, nurses, secretaries, and even teachers," typical wartime roles for Boy Scouts.[4] Edgar Snow praised these Young Vanguards as any enthusiast

Madam Sun Yat-sen (Soong Ching Ling).

1   Frederic E. Wakeman, *Spymaster: Dai Li and the Chinese Secret Service* (California: Univ. of California Press, 2003), 46, 76-77.

2   Robert Culp, "Rethinking Governmentality: Training, Cultivation, and Cultural Citizenship in Nationalist China," *The Journal of Asian Studies*, August 2006, 529-554.

3   Soong Ching Ling, *The Struggle for New China* (Peking: Foreign Languages Press, 1953),24.

4   Edgar Snow, *Red Star over China* (London: Victor Gollancz, 1937), 341. *Ma-*

of Scouting would the best Boy Scouts. According to him, "they were invariably cheerful and optimistic, and they had a ready '*hao!*' [great!] for every how-are-you, regardless of the weariness of the day's march. They were patient, hard-working, bright, and eager to learn…Here in the Vanguards was the future of China…"[1]

Palle Huld with some Boy Scouts in Korea.

Instead of acting like brothers, Chinese Scouts drawn into politics became enemies—vindicating the wisdom of Baden-Powell's counsel that politics should be kept out of Scouting. The reputation of Chinese Scouting suffered as a result. In 1928, Palle Huld, a lucky 15-year-old Danish Boy Scout who won a sponsored world tour, met Boy Scouts from many countries, including those from Korea, but was advised by the Danish consul in Harbin to stay away from the Chinese Scouts "as there were two kinds of Scouts— 'red' or Bolshevik Scouts and 'white'—and whenever the two were…together the meeting ended in a fight."[2] Sure enough, in 1930, at a Chinese national Jamboree held in Nanjing, clashes broke out between hundreds of Boy Scouts from Tsinan and Hankow, resulting in many being wounded and suppression by garrison forces. According to the Nationalist officials, "Communist propaganda [was] the direct cause."[3] As shall be seen in the next section, viewed from Hong Kong, these developments throughout China appeared especially problematic.

---

*foos*馬伕 attend to and take care of the horses.

1 Ibid., 56-57, 345. *Hao* 好 means "great!" or "fine!"

2 Palle Huld, *A Boy Scout Around the World* (New York: Coward-McCann, 1929), 141. The free tour was offered by a Danish newspaper in commemoration of Jules Verne, the author of *Around the World in Eighty Days*. Huld, said to have been the inspiration for the globe-trotting cartoon character *Tintin*, went on to become an accomplished actor, and only passed away in November 2010, at the age of 98.

3 *HKT,* April 24, 1930.

A commemorative stamp of a national Jamboree in the 1930s in Nanjing.

Indigenizing yet avoiding Chinese politics

The impact upon China of youth movements affiliated with political parties which subscribed to extremist ideologies in Europe posed an indirect yet potent threat to the British model of Scouting in Hong Kong. Kotewall's vision of Scouting as an "antidote" to the spread of extremist anti-colonial ideology among youth appeared to be in jeopardy. This threat was profoundly felt as it emerged at a time when the efforts to indigenize Scouting in Hong Kong had achieved, at least in terms of membership, steady success. One strategy through which the colonial authorities might meet this challenge was to re-negotiate the Chineseness of local Scouting by distancing it from extreme expressions of Chinese nationalism, typically labeled in Hong Kong as Chinese "politics."

If Scouting was to have any real influence on the youth of the colony it had to become an indigenized movement. Indigenization means different things to different people. In a study on the indigenization of Christianity in China, Yamamoto Sumiko defined it as consisting of two basic elements, namely "ethnicity," or the taking on of particular ethnic characteristics, and "embeddedness," or "putting down roots" and becoming "closely attached to the hearts, lifestyles and societies of its adherents."[1] In the second interwar decade, Hong Kong Scouting had indeed acquired both increasing Chinese ethnicity and embeddedness among the Hong Kong Chinese, though it at the same time had managed to steer clear of the more politicized and extremist form of Chineseness which had plagued Scouting in China for much of this period.

Under Peel, who "always took a deep interest in the work of the [Scout] movement," Scouting became more "embedded," growing strongly among the Chinese schools, as opposed to just the British and Christian ones.[2] From 1921 to 1931, the number of Chinese boys between the ages of six to fifteen in urban areas grew 55% to fifty-five thousand, mostly in Kowloon; and school children almost doubled, 75% of whom in vernacular schools.[3] Significant progress was achieved in nur-

Sir William Peel.

1   Yamamoto Sumiko, *History of Protestantism in China: The Indigenization of Christianity* (Tokyo: The Toho Gakkai, 2000), 2-3, 5.
2   *HKSH*, May 31, 1931.
3   *Hong Kong: Report on the Census of the Colony for 1931* (Hong Kong: Census

turing urban Chinese troops, especially in Kowloon and in the (vernacular) schools. The principals of vernacular schools might have viewed Scouting as a way to associate their schools with the elite schools, which all seemed to have Scout Troops. But the motive for the ruling elite was related to governance. Waldegrave expressed this motivation well, when he claimed in 1932 that non-British Chinese Boy Scouts would learn "to stick to the rules of the Scouting Movement" and, while "guests in a British Colony," "be obedient and loyal."[1]

Before returning to Ireland in early 1932, Armstrong started the 7th Kowloon at Ling Tung College (嶺東中學).[2] Later in the same year, Chung Nan College (中南書院) formed the 17th Hong Kong with Rev. N. V. Halward's help, and the Diocesan Boys' School the 6th Kowloon under C. B. Sargent, its headmaster.[3] In 1934, Peel gave warrants to leaders from troops at the outlying island of Cheung Chau (長洲), and the vernacular Ching Hua College (清華書院) and Cheuk Yin College (卓然學校). Soon St. Stephen's College, then a private school for Chinese, also started a troop "which [gave] immense delight, and valuable training."[4] Except for the Diocesan school, all six were Chinese schools, and five had no Christian links, suggesting increased embeddedness of Scouting in Hong Kong.

Armstrong with Chinese Scouts at 7th Kowloon (Ling Tung College).

H. K. Scout Archives.

The indigenization of Scouting was also exhibited in its growing Chinese "ethnicity." Aside from the sinicized Scout Promise already noted, increased ethnicity could be seen in Scout honors, Scoutmasters, supporters, membership, and Chinese national symbolisms, etc.

Office, 1931), tables 11, 17-8; *Hong Kong Administrative Report, 1921,* O3; *1931,* O30, table 2.

1   *CM*, September 16, 1932.

2   *CM*, May 28, 1932.

3   *CM*, September 10, 1932; the *Steps*, December 1947, 6.

4   *HKDP*, November 8, 1934.

Peel met Boy Scouts at Goverment House, 1931.

H. K. Scout Archives.

In May 1931, Peel met Hong Kong Scouts at Goverment House and presented the cherished banner to the Central Chinese troop.[1] In December, he gave the banner to the largely Chinese Sea Scouts, and warrants to four Chinese Scoutmasters, while Chinese lay supporters Chau Tsun-nin and Tang Shiu-kin raised funds for Saiwan.[2] On Empire Day in 1932, over four hundred Scouts gathered at Flagstaff House, and Major-General Sandilands noted that many of them were not British subjects, and presented all three Scoutmaster's warrants to Chinese leaders.[3] A journalist observed that "one has only to attend a mass parade…and one will see the large number of Chinese wearing the Boy Scout uniform."[4] In April 1934, St. Paul's, a Chinese troop, won the banner. Quah Cheow-cheong (柯昭章) became a District Scouter in 1935 and then the first Chinese District Commissioner in 1937.[5]

Given the growing "Chineseness" of local Scouting, it is not surprising that occasionally symbols of Chinese nationalism would emerge. As illustrated by a photograph taken by the Sea Scouts who helped at a fund-raising garden fete organized by the St. Peter's Church, both the Union Jack and the Chinese Nationalist flag were prominently displayed

Sea Scouts at a fete where British and Chinese flags were featured.

H. K. Scout Archives.

1   *HKSH*, May 31, 1931.
2   *HKDP*, December 17, 1931; *CM*, December 23, 1931.
3   *HKT*, May 25, 1932; *CM*, May 28, 1932.
4   *CM,* September 17, 1932.
5   *HKDP*, April 5, 1934; *HKT*, February 28, 1935; Novemver 30, 1937..

at the venue.[1] It shall be seen in this chapter that this manifestation of "dual loyalty" to Britain and China would become much more common-place towards the end of the 1930s.

The Governor's Mountain Lodge at the Peak.
PRO 1-16-426.

Chinese Scouts occasionally participated in gatherings unimaginable for any Chinese in those days, suggestive of the racial inclusiveness of local Scouting. In September 1933, the Peels entertained nearly five hundred Scouts and Guides, including boys from the vernacular schools Chung Nan and Ling Tung, at the Mountain Lodge, their residence on the Peak. Peel spoke only briefly, noting that his good turn of the day was not imposing a long speech upon the youngsters. For most if not all these Chinese boys, this probably was their first trip up to the exclusive Peak, not to mention the governor's summer home. Over six hundred Scouts and Guides gathered at the lodge again in August 1934 for a farewell party for Waldegrave, who was leaving the colony shortly, to be succeeded by Rev. N. V. Halward, an Anglican Pastor and the Scoutmaster of St. Paul's College.[2]

Though Chinese Scouts and troops tended to dominate the movement, there was still an element of elitism among them. Winners of the banner in these years were invariably prestigious troops mostly from elite schools. In fact, even participation in this event was elitist. In 1934, eleven troops, including 1st Hong Kong Sea, St. Joseph's, Catholic Cathedral, Murray, King's, St. Paul's, Wah Yan, St. Andrew's, Wah Yan Kowloon, Roving Fifth, and Diocesan Boys', took part in the banner competition; but Chinese vernacular school such as Yuek Chee, Shu Man, Chung Nan and Ling Tung were all absent.[3]

Rev. N.V. Halward.
H. K. Scout Archives.

---

1   *HKDP*, February 2, 1931.
2   *CM,* October 2, 1933; *HKDP*, August 27, 1934. Nelson Victor Halward, M. C., M. A. was awarded the Military Cross for gallantry in WWI.
3   *HKDP*, April 30, 1934.

Peel ended his term fittingly with a joint Scouts and Guides Jamborally in May 1935, held in commemoration of King George V's silver jubilee, in which eight hundred Scouts, including some from Canton and Macau, participated. It was impressive, as "never before in the history of the Colony has a youth movement held a demonstration like this on such a vast scale."[1] Out of the twenty-two local troops present, thirteen were Chinese, and five were mixed with Chinese members.

During Caldecott's short time as Chief Scout progress in Chinese Scouting continued. He met the Scouts for the first time in November in a fund-raising campfire.[2] In the annual meeting held shortly after, the arrests of two burglars by Chinese Scouts from the 7th and 8th Kowloon, troops in lower-income Shamshuipo and Kowloon City, were noted, again as evidence confirming the value of Chinese Scouting. Caldecott attended a banner competition in which two British, two mixed, and seven Chinese troops competed. That the only detailed report of this Scout event came from the Chinese newspaper *Kung Sheung* was perhaps indicative of the growing indigenized nature of the movement. Of all the English papers, only one briefly reported the event, and much later, despite the governor's presence.[3]

Camping competition at Chaiwan, November 1936.

KSYP, Nov. 29, 1936.

The continued growth of Chinese Scouting had fundamentally transformed the movement by the mid-1930s. With economic and so-

1   *CM*, May 9, 1935.
2   *HKSH*, November 8, 1936.
3   *KSYP*, November 17, 1936, November 29, 1936, November 30, 1936; *HKT*, December 7, 1936.

cial development in the interwar years came an expanding urban Chinese middle class, whose members could afford to send their children to the growing number of public or private schools in Hong Kong.[1] As with Scouting in America and elsewhere, somewhat earlier in time, this emerging middle class became the main source for new members.[2] However, the expanded base also posed certain risks. If Scouting, with its closer links to many vernacular schools, was to serve the purpose that the colonial authorities had in mind, infiltration by Chinese politics and Chinese nationalism had to be prevented.

Initially, the response to this threat barely extended beyond limp rhetorical interventions. From time to time, the local association would warn Scouts against unwelcome "Chinese influences." In 1929, under the pen name of "Uncle Charles," a contributor to a *China Mail* column dedicated to Scouting contrasted the failure of an earlier French youth program established by M. Ballue de Bellinglise, which had a political and militaristic tone, with the success of Scouting. He concluded that: "our Chinese brother Scouts in the Colony...must not fall into the pit that the Chinese Scouts in other parts of China...have fallen, and that is to meddle with politics which they know nothing about."[3]

Admonitions such as this should be viewed in context of the worldwide movement's established policy regarding partisan politics. Early in the movement's history, a non-political philosophy had been explicitly adopted. It was decreed that Boy Scouts should be above party politics, though, as individuals, they were free to participate in political activities. This ideal had partly originated from Baden-Powell's strong dislike of politicians, with whom he once famously said he would not trust his grandmother's toothbrush.[4] The British *POR* of 1933 declared that the Scout Association was not linked to "any political body" and that

POLITICS.

Politics Movement Non-political	13. The Boy Scouts Association is not connected with any political body. Members of the Association, in uniform, or acting as representatives of the Movement, must not take part in political meetings or activities.

The British *POR* of 1933, stating the non-political nature of Scouting.

1   Steve Tsang, *A Modern History of Hong Kong* (Hong Kong: Hong Kong Univ. Press, 2004), 62-65, 106-114.
2   Macleod, *Building Character*, 15.
3   *CM*, September 7, 1929.
4   Hillcourt, *Two Lives of a Hero*, 385.

"members of the Association, in uniform, or acting as representatives of the Movement, must not take part in political meetings and activities."[1] This philosophy, which could easily be interpreted as implying that all Hong Kong Boy Scouts should stay out of party politics, was conveniently latched onto by the colonial ruling elite and informed their antipathy to the influence of Chinese politics upon local youth.

While political domination of Scouting was frowned upon by the Scout Movement in general, Hong Kong's objection was motivated by fundamental concerns about the colony's own governance. More generally, the authorities had encouraged a school curriculum "characterized by a depoliticized, backward-looking culturalism that would prove an effective antidote to xenophobic nationalism."[2] In 1930, the Colonial Office admitted that "special local conditions justified more attention being paid to ancient civilizations than to current events," and that "it is not considered desirable to interest Hong Kong students too much in political and administrative questions."[3] In the early 1930s, civics was introduced in schools to combat the influence of new and unwelcome political currents in China, including the emerging New Life Movement.[4]

Later on, and in light of the flagrant political coloring of Chinese Scouting, the grandees of the Hong Kong association opted for a policy of non-recognition of their counterparts in China. In January 1931, Waldegrave announced that "as the Chinese Scout Association in Canton has not yet complied with the requirements of the International Scout Bureau...we are not able to officially recognise its members," and that cooperation would be impossible until "Political Party and Military influences are divorced from Scouting in China."[5] In June 1932, the association reiterated that "one of the biggest troops of Scouts in Canton is managed by the City Kuomintang," and because of that "the Canton Scouts have not been officially recognized by the local Boy Scout

---

1   The *POR, 1933*.

2   Edward Vickers, Flora Kan, Paul Morris, "Colonialism and the Politics of 'Chinese History' in Hong Kong's Schools," *Oxford Review of Education*, Vol. 29, No. 1, March 2003, 99.

3   A. E. Sweeting, "Politics and the art of teaching history in Hong Kong," *Teaching History*, 64, 30-37.

4   W. O. Lee and Anthony Sweeting, "Controversies in Hong Kong's Political Transition: Nationalism versus Liberalism," in Mark Bray & W. O. Lee, *Education and Political Transition: Themes and Experience in East Asia* (Hong Kong: the Univ. of Hong Kong, 1997), 103.

5   *SCMP*, January 14, 1931.

authorities."[1] When fifty Boy Scouts from Canton in their brown fascist-looking shirts marched down Chatham Road in Kowloon, Waldegrave again declared that they were not recognized, and the local association had nothing to do with them.[2] The logic was clear: Hong Kong Boy Scouts were to be distanced from the "unrecognized" Boy Scouts in China, and thus divorced from Chinese politics.

The assumptions that undergirded this approach were not always entirely sound. Political neutrality was feasible and perhaps even wise in countries like Britain and the United States, where the transfer of power from government to government was regularly achieved through elections, political leaders did not demand total commitment from party members or citizens at large, and party members and citizens alike were unwilling to give their unquestioned devotion to the parties. Even in mature democracies, there were times when strict separation was not easy.[3] Adopting a politically neutral position proved especially difficult in a country where democracy was not well-established, revolution rather than peaceful change of power was openly pursued, and political parties were imbued with ideological fervor, and, when in power, demanded total dedication to the party not only from members but also from all citizens. Such was the case in China under the Nationalist Party.

The problem of politicized Chinese Scouting was attenuated somewhat in 1933 when the desire of the ROC for international recognition prompted efforts to align practices in China with those of world Scouting. In 1933, China issued an "improved" version of the promise, one that emphasized, besides the Scout Law, "the teachings of the late Director-General (總理遺教)," and called for being "a loyal citizen of the Republic of China," "helpfulness and service," and "own intellectual, moral and physical development," with no reference to duty to God.[4] Except for the continued absence of any reference to God/gods, understandable given a lack of consensus among Chinese regarding religion,

Dr. Sun Yat-sen.

1   *HKT*, June 12, 1931.
2   *CM*, June 4, 1932.
3   In the 1920s, the Executive Board of BSA had a distinct conservative and partisan bias: except for a couple southern Democrats, its members were practically all Republicans, many with links to late President Theodore Roosevelt, and had become "an agency of aggressive Americanism." See Macleod, *Building Character*, 182, 185.
4   "誓遵奉 總理遺教, 確守中國童子軍之規律, 終生奉行下列三事, 一, 勵行忠孝仁愛信義和平之教訓, 為中華民國忠誠之國民. 二, 隨時隨地, 扶助他人, 服務公眾 三, 力求自己智識道德體格之健全. Fan, *Zhong Guo Tong Zi Jun Shi*, 68.

this was better aligned with the generic Scout Promise. The conspicuous presence of Sun Yat-sen ("the late Director-General") confirmed the dominance of the Nationalists, but at least loyalty was no longer explicitly to the party, but to the republic itself.

Even after the 1933 reorganization, the Chinese Boy Scouts were hardly rendered apolitical, and in Hong Kong concerns about government dominance, compulsory enrollment, militarism, and links with Fascist youth movements persisted. In July 1934, three years' of Scout training became mandatory in junior secondary schools.[1] Photographic evidence confirms that this policy continued throughout the remaining interwar years: a class photograph taken in 1937 for a Shanghai girls' middle school shows all graduating students wearing Girl Scout uniforms, and another taken in 1941 shows the whole primary six class in a school in Guangzhou in Boy Scout uniforms.[2] This situation prompted H. S. Redfern, a contemporary, to lament in 1941 in a missionary magazine that "the Scout movement in China has ceased to be a voluntary agency, but has been enlisted in the service of the state."[3]

The budget for the National Jamboree in 1935 was a "Party Affairs Temporary Expenditure."[4] Key leaders after the re-organization remained military men: Generals Chiang Kai Shek, Ho Ying Chin and Chang Chih Chung.[5] President Wang Ching-wei declared that "an excellent army comes from a complete Scout [organization] (有完整童軍始有良好軍隊)," and that Scouting was the "'Nursery' for the Army."[6] In 1937, Boy Scouts of China sent a delegation to the Italian substitute Jamboree for the *Balilla*, and a contingent to the 5th World Jamboree, reflecting its "dual personality" at the time.[7] In fact, the World Jamboree contingent from the ROC also stopped at Berlin, where they were hosted by the Hitler Youth, before they went to Amsterdam.[8]

The 1937 Jamboree Badge.

1   *KSYP*, July 4, 1934, June 6, 1934.
2   Graduation class photograph, Shanghai Girls' Middle School (上海女子中學), 1937, Author's collection; *Guangzhou Pui Ching Middle School: 1947 Class of "Hung" List of Classmates* 廣州私立培正中學校：一九四七年級虹社同學錄 (Guangzhou, 1947).
3   *The Kingdom Overseas*, March, 1941, 33.
4   *KSYP*, July 10, 1935.
5   *HKDP*, February 7, 1933.
6   *KSYP*, July 31, 1934; *HKDP*, August 11, 1934.
7   *HKDP*, June 28, 1937.
8   *CM*, July 23, 1937, July 27, 1937.

A graduating class of a Shanghai school, with students all in Girl Scout uniform, 1937.

Author's collection.

Chinese politics from the mid-1920s to the mid-1930s gave colonial authorities real cause for concern and a legitimate excuse for embarking on de-politicizing programs for schoolboys inside and outside Scouting. In Scouting, the local association's moral force was strengthened by the worldwide movement's declared non-political position and the International Scout Bureau's censure of Boy Scouts of China.

After the re-organization of Chinese Scouting in 1933, however, a rapprochement between the two Scout associations was slowly brokered. In March 1934, Waldegrave observed that "Scouting in China is gradually taking a turn in the right direction which will eventually bring it into line with the Scout policy held by…the International Scout Bureau."[1] A month later, he indicated that there were "great possibilities opening up" for British advisers in Scouting in Canton, and introductions for visiting Chinese Scouts.[2] Halward began to devote three nights a week for six months to his efforts "to teach the Canton Scout Masters the right way to carry on the Scouting movement."[3] Clearly, the policy had shifted to one of cautious engagement. Finally, in 1937, China was

---

1   *HKDP*, March 23, 1934.

2   *SCMP*, April 5, 1934.

3   *HKDP*, April 30, 1934.

admitted to the world Scout body at the 9th World Scout Conference. Scouts from China were again officially brothers to Scouts around the world, including those in Hong Kong. By this time, staying out of Chinese politics appeared to be difficult. Both the Japanese and the Chinese World Jamboree contingents passed through Hong Kong on their way to Europe. While the Chinese contingent was warmly anticipated by most Hong Kong newspapers and similarly received by local Boy Scouts; there was only a single, very brief, report on the Japanese contingent appearing in front of the cenotaph, apparently not accompanied by any Scouts in Hong Kong, perhaps suggestive of the prevailing sentiments among the Chinese boys in Hong Kong at the time.[1]

Leveraging the ideal of brotherhood

Given the fact that the Chinese government was closely, if not wholly, identified with the Nationalist Party in the 1930s, it was increasingly difficult to draw a clear demarcation between nationalistic feeling for China, which Chinese Boy Scouts in Hong Kong could legitimately aspire to, and Chinese party politics, which they were supposed to rise above. This brought into focus the question of how Chineseness could be reconciled with British imperialism within expanded and indigenized Scouting. Before 1937, the answer to this conundrum seems to have been that the Chineseness of Hong Kong Scouts should be rendered as diffused as possible, first by identifying it with ancient culture and language rather than modern nationalism and politics, and then by subjugating it beneath a wider sense of being a member of a supranational Scout "brotherhood."

Brotherliness, in practical terms, could take different forms according to the Fourth Scout Law. The 1908 version stated that: "a Scout is a friend to all, and a brother to every other Scout, no matter to what social class the other belongs," and that "a Scout must never be a snob… who looks down upon another because he is poorer, or who is poor and resents another because he is rich…'Kim,' the boy scout, was called by

The Fourth Law: "A Scout is a friend to all."

---

1   *HKDP*, June 18 & 28, 1937; *CM*, June 28, 1937; *KSYP*, June 22, 23, 24, 27, and 28, 1937, etc. All on the Chinese contingent except one report in *HKDP*, June 18.

the Indians 'Little friend of all the world,' and that is the name that every scout should earn for himself."[1] As noted in Chapter 1, this version of the law, on the one hand, seemed to espouse brotherhood across social classes only and, on the other, imply friendship among people of all races, an ambiguity that was to cause different interpretations over time.

Brotherly acts could be bestowed upon a visiting Scout, temporarily, or upon a Scout in the same country, more or less permanently. The interacting brother Scouts could be from similar races, classes or religions, or they could be from totally different backgrounds. In the interwar years, many Boy Scouts in Hong Kong, nearby cities and further afield put the ideal to test. Most instances of interaction involved short-term contacts between boys of similar ethnic, class or religious backgrounds, such as visits between Portuguese and Chinese boys in Catholic troops and their counterparts in Macau or Chinese Boy Scouts in Hong Kong and their counterparts in China. These were simple and easy to implement, requiring no further elaboration.[2]

Hong Kong Portuguese Scouts visited Portuguese Macau in the 1940s.

Author's collection.

There were also occasional short visits to distant land or from afar. The Pan-Pacific Jamboree in Melbourne in December 1934 was an ethnic experiment of sort, as Baden-Powell had wondered "how Far Eastern races have grasped the ideals of scouting, and how far they mix with the European and Australian elements."[3] A Chinese Rover Scout, Tsoi Mang-suen (蔡孟蓀), of 10th Hong Kong, and two Scoutmasters, R.

Tsoi Mang-suen (right) at the Pan-Pacific Jamboree in Melbourne, 1934.

Author's collection.

1   Baden-Powell, *Scouting for Boys: the Original 1908 Edition*, 45.
2   *CM*, February 12, 1925, July 27, 1931; *KSYP*, July 28, 1928, November 8, 1930, February 26, 1934, March 8, 1934, March 13, 1934, May 28, 19363.
3   Hillcourt, *Two Lives of a Hero*, 395.

Dormer and R. H. Wong, from 1st Kowloon, represented Hong Kong and participated in this experiment, along with other Asians. One of them, possibly Tsoi, acted as one of Baden-Powell's honorary bodyguards as he rode around the campsite.[1] In a meeting of the Rovers held at the Jamboree, Rovers of all colors and creeds reaffirmed their solidarity. Tsoi was deeply moved, and said that "I feel like crying. Here we are all friends, and China is divided. I wish we could have more and more Scouts in my nation."[2] (It should be noted that he referred to China, not Hong Kong or Britain, as "my nation.") In a subsequent report, Baden-Powell declared the racial mixing an unqualified success, where "East and West certainly met on equal footing and on good terms as brother Scouts."[3]

Press reports of Scouts who visited Hong Kong in the 1920s to 1930s.

Also, a few bona fide young globe-trotters came to Hong Kong, and they were often welcomed. These included Scouts from Latvia, Greece, Germany, Hungary, and India.[4] They came by boat, on land, on foot, and on bicycles. All had traveled long distances, some for several years, determined to see the world up close against all odds, and had accumulated adventurous tales to last several lifetimes. One was on his way to locate his parents in war-torn Shanghai. These were appropri-

1   The *Courier-Mail* (Brisbane, Queensland), January 1, 1935; *Western Australian* (Perth, Western Australia), December 18, 1934.
2   The *Argus*, January 4, 1935.
3   *HKT,* November 26, 1934; *CM,* December 1, 1934, December 28, 1934; *HKDP*, December 31, 1934.
4   *CM*, December 7, 1926, April 27, 1933, September 5, 1935, December 21, 1935; *HKT*, December 19, 1930, May 10, 1934; *SCMP*, April 28, 1933, April 6, 1938; *HKDP*, May 11, 1934, September 24, 1935, April 6, 1938.

ately received by brother Scouts and the community, in Hong Kong as elsewhere. They hosted talks, displays, concerts, and radio broadcasts; and were met by dignitaries ranging from Baden-Powell in Hungary, President Hoover in America, General Chang Hsueh-liang in Manchuria, Governor Clementi in Singapore, and Southorn in Hong Kong.

Brotherliness expressed in temporary visits was relatively easy. The real litmus test of brotherhood was whether boys from different class, race or religious backgrounds could get along on a permanent basis. The Fourth Law was not just a good, Christian, ideal. A key "selling point" was its potential value to the British Empire, through a brotherhood of boys of all races. The British Empire, like most great colonial enterprises, was founded on discriminatory thinking. However, in certain contexts, and notably within the confines of the youth movement, a kind of bridging between races could be brokered. Baden-Powell had claimed in 1921 that "the Boy Scout Brotherhood provides a strong and natural solvent for racial differences."[1] His optimism disguised some problems in practice within the empire.

The example of Africa is informative. Ashantee on the Gold Coast of Africa had native Boy Scouts by the late 1910s.[2] On the other hand, throughout the interwar years, Scout associations in South Africa steadfastly refused to admit native African, Indian or other colored boys, who then signed up for alternatives such as the Braves, the Pathfinders, the Paladins, and Indian Scouts, which could not use the Scout logo, uniform, and even the seemingly innocent staves. Similarly, native girls joined the Girl Wayfarers' instead of the Girl Guides.[3] There were other, subtler, forms of discrimination: the Wayfarers' Law was simpler than the Guide Law, with only four clauses.[4] In 1929, Major Mawe noted "the pathetic faces of those little black boys trying to look like Scouts," and lamented that the police had "locked them up for the night for carrying staves without permission."[5] The problem continued in the 1930s,

A native African Boy Scout from Ashantee.

---

1   Baden-Powell's letter, November 18, 1921, in "Supply of Uniforms to the Boy Scout Movement in Colonies and Protectorates, 1921-23," CO 323/882/60, the National Archives, London.

2   *Boy's Life, the Boy Scouts' Magazine, May 1917* (New York: Boy Scouts of America, 1917), 47.

3   Parsons, *Race, Resistance, and the Boy Scout Movement*, 72-77.

4   *CM*, November 9, 1929.

5   Proctor, "A Separate Path," 616.

as "European prejudice prevented native children from joining the Scout and Guide movements."[1] In late 1933, the outgoing governor had decided to admit natives, but his successor was unsure, and had not done so by 1935.

In 1936, Baden-Powell noted that blacks could not be admitted because "white parents would never allow their children to consort with black," and predicted that any attempt to force this issue would only result in boycotts by the white people in South Africa.[2] Racial difficulties were complex among white settlers (Boers and British), white colonizers, native Africans, and minorities of other (Asian) races. This blatant disregard of the Fourth Law was only more or less resolved when B-P helped to secure a compromise in 1936 with a federation of separate Scout organizations for native, Indian and white boys.[3] Finally, the Chief Scout could take pride in the fact that, through Scouting, noticeable everywhere "was the good will of the white people to the Old Country and the universal sense of loyalty to the King on the part of the natives," evidence of the eventual success of the Scout brotherhood.[4]

A Malay Scout and a head-hunting Dyak.

The British Straits Settlements provided easier victories. Scouting for native boys began in the 1910s in the Federated Malay States.[5] In 1929, Sir Hugh Clifford, the Chief Scout of Malaya, noted that "boys belonging to all the many nationalities…of the Malay Peninsula parade side by side…Only for the Malay boy are there troops reserved for one nationality and these only in the rural districts."[6] Other sources confirmed that Scouting was indeed available to all races, though racially-integrated and segregated troops were both common, reflecting the ethnic make-up of their sponsors. In the early 1920s, some of the eleven troops in Singapore were exclusively for Chinese boys (Fort Canning Chinese, Chinese High School, and Tao Nan School), one was for Malay boys (5th Headquarters Malay), and some were integrated (Raffles Institute and St. Joseph's).[7] A 1930s photograph of the Raffles Institute troop in which

---

1   "The Pathfinder and Wayfarer Movements, Northern Rhodesia, 1934-35," CO 795/72/7, the National Archives, London.
2   Rosenthal, *The Character Factory*, 261.
3   The *Times*, June 6, 1936.
4   *HKDP*, June 11, 1936.
5   *Boy's Life, the Boy Scouts' Magazine, May 1917*, 47.
6   *CM*, August 10, 1929.
7   Tan and Wan, *Scouting in Singapore*, 32, 34, 48, 50-51.

Lee Kuan Yew, later prime minister of Singapore, was present as a young Boy Scout clearly shows that the troop was racially-integrated, though Chinese boys constituted the majority.[1]

In Hong Kong, with sensitivity to nationalist infiltration of the movement heightened, the need to dampen down nationalistic feeling and to give credence to notions of international brotherhood was particularly strong. Here Baden-Powell's own gaffes and his racial insensitivity were distinctly unhelpful. In 1937, after his return from India, Baden-Powell observed in London that Indian Scouts had to fight against India's three faults: "lack of character, lack of health, and lack of unity."[2] This speech, intended for a British audience, caused an indignant uproar when it was reported back in India. Many were insulted, and some even threatened to sever official links with British Scouting.

A Sentry at Canton.

"A Sentry in Canton," a caricature by B-P.
The Scouter, 1929.

Earlier, in 1929, when a critique of the Chinese military appeared in *The Scouter*, the founder chimed in by contributing a rather uncomplimentary caricature of a Chinese solider drawn by him and added his personal observation that the "description of the Chinese soldier exactly tallies with him as I found him [in] 1912. A nondescript figure, armed to the teeth, not very certain for whom he was fighting, or for what."[3]

---

1 Ibid., 68-69; Alex Josey, *Lee Kuan Yew* (Singapore: Asian Pacific Press, 1968), 223.
2 *HKSH*, June 17, 1937.
3 The *Scouter*, July, 1929, 250. Baden-Powell supplied many illustrations for his

Given Clementi's desire to promote racial harmony through Scouting and the Concord movement, Waldegrave reacted strongly to these undiplomatic utterances. He noted that the "sketch and few words on the subject, however true they may be, will not be of nay help to us here who are trying to emphasize international brotherhood, and who see in Scouting a way to accomplish that end…and I for one am amazed at the Chief sending it in, considering the knowledge which he must have of the Oriental mind."[1] He also expressed concerns with possible negative reactions from "race-touchy" Chinese Scout Troops, and urged that no further "criticism of national things…as regards China" appears in the magazine.[2] Fortunately, in striking contrast to India, there was no widespread protest in local Scouting circles.

That the caricature was received differently in Hong Kong may have owed something to the fact that the roots of a notion of a Hong Kong identity separate from the Chineseness of China were contemporaneously being set down, with reference to negative images of militarism across the border, and glowing portrayals of Hong Kong's cosmopolitanism. The "Old Scout" noted in the *CM* that "the Scout Movement in Hong Kong [was] a cosmopolitan one", with "British, Chinese, Portuguese, Indians, and other nationalities," suggesting growing pride in the hybrid local Scouting.[3] During this period, Hong Kong Scouts were taught largely cultural and de-politicized associations with China. At any rate, many of them were probably not wholly sympathetic with the Chinese military, in particular, the armies of the northern "warlords," which relied heavily on mercenaries and illiterate farmers.

This Hong Kong Chinese identity was sometimes also tacitly expressed through symbolic gestures. In 1936, the association created its first Hong Kong Scout emblem, which featured the Victoria Peak, a British tea clipper anchored in the harbor next to a Chinese Junk, and "a Chinese merchant dressed in white with his coolie in attendance," shaking hands with a British trader, near chests of merchandise.[4] The

---

own books.
1   Letter, Waldegrave to Butterworth, August 26, 1929, the Gilwell Archives.
2   Ibid., 2.
3   *CM*, October 26, 1929.
4   *Annual Report, 1935-1936* (London: Boy Scouts Association, 1937), 78. This detailed description clearly distinguished the pre-war emblem illustrated here from the postwar ones (to be described in the next chapter), which did not depict any coolie, and

graphical representation was similar to the one used on the colonial seal of Hong Kong at the time, and depicted the colonial outpost as a trading port made successful through Sino-British cooperation.[1] Significantly, despite the British colonial imagery, the only words on the emblem were the Chinese characters "香港" (Hong Kong) on top and "童子軍" (Boy Scouts) below, highlighting the hybrid nature of the movement.

The Hong Kong Boy Scout emblem, Pre-WWII Issue.

Yau Yu Kai's collection.

How far did the idealized brotherhood of the Hong Kong movement actually extend? Kotewall had confidently declared that "Scouting…breaks down all national, racial, religious and class barriers."[2] A local association booklet in 1931 urged all Boy Scouts in Hong Kong to embrace the brotherhood, to neither "look down on others because they are of a different race or nationality or religion" nor "despise or resent those who are richer or poorer."[3] The racial make-up of the local Scout Movement by the 1930s did indeed reflect the ethnic diversity of the population of the colonial society, if mostly through racially segregated troops. But this should be judged in contemporary contexts, when subtle racial segregation or even blatant racial discrimination abounded, in Hong Kong and elsewhere, inside and outside Scouting. A few examples are illustrative. During this time, the Hong Kong colonial government employed many Europeans in the police force, often on more preferential terms than their Chinese colleagues. In 1921, "there were more than 180 Europeans in the police force [of Hong Kong], compared with 40 in

---

did not show the merchant dressed in white.

1   Geoffrey Cadzow Hamilton, *Flag Badges Seals and Arms of Hong Kong* (Hong Kong: Government Press, 1963), plate VII, 16, 29.

2   *SCMP*, November 17, 1927.

3   *The Scout Law* (Hong Kong: The Boy Scout Headquarters, 1931), 2.

Singapore and 23 in Ceylon (whose population was more than six times that of Hong Kong)."[1] In 1939, the lowest-ranking European policeman was paid nearly eight times more than his Chinese counterpart of the same rank. A Chinese policeman could only be promoted to the rank of subinspector just before the Second World War, and even then, he would be supervised by more junior British officers.

The segregation of Scouting for boys of the ruling and the ruled races or along color lines was quite common. In French Indochina, French-Vietnamese Pierre Brocheux recalled that he was "*le seul non-Européen, non «Français pur»* (the only non-European, non-pure-French)" in his *Scouts de France* Troop in Saigon in early 1940s, though there was another Eurasian, from a prominent family, in another troop, and no *Pondicherien* or French Indian at all.[2] In America, Percy Sutton, a black boy from Texas who had earned his Eagle Scout (the highest Scout award in the BSA) in 1936, noted that his all-black troop was never invited to Jamborees and other Scout events. But then again that only mirrored the wider currents of prejudice alive in the American society. Before the Supreme Court ruling in *Brown v. Board of Education of Topeka* of 1954, many states had laws providing for separate schools for black and white children. On their way to a camp outside San Antonio in the 1930s, Percy and his brother had to ride on the back of a public bus, as all blacks were required to do so then.[3]

Furthermore, in Hong Kong, there were at least a few exceptions to the rule of segregated Scouting. Some were expected, as they reflected racial mixing of their sponsors. The St. Joseph's troop and the Catholic Cathedral troop had members of different ethnic backgrounds, just like the college and the cathedral. As far as one can tell, the boys mixed well. In a campfire of the cathedral troop at Saiwan, a spontaneous singing contest broke out, with the Portuguese singing Portu-

The Eagle Scout Award, BSA's highest award for boys.

---

1   John M. Carroll, *A Concise History of Hong Kong* (Hong Kong: Hong Kong Univ. Press, 2007), 113.

2   There were Vietnamese Boy Scouts in Da Nang, if not in Saigon. In a chance meeting between the French and Vietnamese troops, they attended a campfire together. But, according to Pierre, "*on est restés séparés pendant le feu de camp. Nous étions assis à côté les uns des autres, mais il n'y a pas eu d'échange, sauf entre les chefs* (We stay separated during the campfire. We sat side-by-side to each other, but there was no exchange, except between the leaders.)" See "Une adolescence indochinoise," entretien avec Pierre Brocheux réalisé par Agathe Larcher-Gosha et Daniel Denis, in Nicholas Bancel, et al, *de l'Indochine à l'Algérie*, 39, 42.

3   Townley, *Legacy of Honor*, 48-50.

guese songs and the Chinese the latest Chinese hits, though it ended appropriately with all joining in to sing "God Save the King."[1] Members of the Eurasian Wong family in the English St. Andrew's troop were fully accepted, served as leaders, and represented the troop in an international Jamboree. A photograph taken in 1929 clearly illustrated that the group was ethnically mixed, with Chinese, Eurasian and European leaders (including Patrol Leaders) and members. Similarly, 6th Kowloon had Eurasian, third-country nationals, and Chinese boys, reflecting the ethnically-mixed student body of the Diocesan Boys' School. Members mentioned in 1935 included Dudley, Matthews, Rapley, Dodd, Fisher, Harris, McCormick, Knight, Hulse, Jarrett, Lay, and Crary; but also Chang, Chung, Cheung, Kan, Tan, Hui, Ko, and Poon.[2] However, it is worth noting that these Scouts, though ethnically different, had common bonds besides their troop membership: the same Catholic college, Catholic Cathedral, Protestant church or Protestant college, and probably similar middle-class backgrounds.

The ethnically-mixed St. Andrew's Troop, 1929.

H. K. Scout Archives.

There was another exception, that of the Sea Scout Troop, which is more unique: it was an open unit with no link to any institutional sponsor, but it also had a racially mixed membership. Waldegrave started this troop in 1922, with mostly Chinese and a few Eurasian boys, at least some from less well-to-do families. Then in 1926, two British boys from good middle-class families wanted to join. Waldegrave "watched with fear and trembling to see how they would mix" in the first evening

---

1 *CM,* August 31, 1929.
2 The *Steps,* July 1935, 50-53; December 1935, 39-41.

which was "a strain, as both 'sides' were taking stock," until the younger British boy "took a liking to the smallest Chinese who [was] a most cheery little soul," "the liking was reciprocated," and the older British boy brought along three of his classmates, and the experiment in mixed Scouting was successfully launched.[1]

Inter-racial interaction became more interesting when it came to the task of forming patrols: "One Chinese tentatively suggested a Chinese and a British patrol. I let it stand for a minute or two and went on with another point, but brought up the suggestion later. I was delighted when both Chinese and British howled it down, and insisted on both patrols being 'mixed.'"[2] Members of a patrol had a much more intimate relationship with each other than members of a troop. The Patrol Leader was frequently in charge of teaching, caring for, and helping the newer patrol members. A patrol competed with other patrols, and planned and executed patrol hikes and camps as a team. In outings and camping trips, patrol members had to share work, cook for each other, live together and sleep in the same tent.

The racially-integrated 1st Hong Kong Sea Scout Troop, 1928.

H. K. Scout Archives.

This sort of integration despite differences in color, creed and class among the boys certainly went beyond the norms of the colonial society, where quiet discrimination was common, segregation was the rule, and peaceful coexistence was only practiced occasionally when other common bonds dictated. While the Sea Scouts Troop was not the only troop to be mixed, it was the first open troop to be organized thus. It won the banner in 1927, 1928, and 1931, proving that racially mixed troops could function well. As can be seen from Waldegrave's own comments,

---

1   Letter, Waldegrave to Butterworth, May 31, 1926, the Gilwell Archives.
2   Ibid.

integration was not an easy process. Had it not been for the fact that this was the only Sea Scout Troop, and Waldegrave was skillful in handling the mixing, it probably would not have happened. But the wider contextual pressures lent significance to such an experiment.

This ideal did not always work out in practice, as a less seasoned Sea Scout leader soon discovered. In 1934, Maurice Scott, son of a missionary, educated at Oxford, and employed by Butterfield and Swire, became the new Scoutmaster of the Sea Scouts. From the beginning, he was concerned with the troop's "mixed nationality."[1] He started with thirty boys, got rid of one troublesome European, the most troublesome Chinese, and then most other Chinese, leaving the decimated troop with five European and three Chinese boys. Then, in a meeting in December 1934 he "found...only the Europeans there, five in number," as "the Chinese it appears have decided to boycott [him]."[2] Scott surmised that something like this went deeper, and reflected the mistrust between the two races and their respective superiority complexes, and expressed regret that "through [his] mishandling of a difficult, an almost impossible situation, [he had] helped to keep alive this feeling."[3]

In February 1935, he met with Halward and the "defected" Chinese Sea Scouts in a long-awaited hearing, and observed that it was "going to be the world's stiffest job to get the decent Chinese element back without letting 'em feel they have lost too much face, and at the same time keep the loyal European element happy," but if that could be done, it would be "a good job for scouting, for the Colony, and for racial goodwill."[4] At any rate, the meeting cleared the air somewhat, so that at the gang show a week later, there was a hornpipe dance by two Chinese Sea Scouts and a one-act farce by the five European boys. Scott left shortly after for Shanghai, with the awkward situation partly resolved. This little crisis in his time highlighted how fragile racial harmony in the Scout brotherhood could be, even in the most integrated troop.

Despite this unhappy episode, 1st Hong Kong Sea Scouts recovered and remained a strong mixed troop. Sammy Chiu Suk-ming

---

1   Scott Family Papers (PP MS 49), Scott's letter, September 13, 1934, the SOAS Archive, London.
2   Ibid., Scott's Letter, December 22, 1934.
3   Ibid., Scott's Letter, January 17, 1935.
4   Ibid., Scott's letter, February 21, 1935.

joined in 1935. Several years later, he became a King's Scout and the Patrol leader of Buffalo Patrol, which had ethnically British boys. In an interview conducted in 2005, when prompted, he confirmed that the Scoutmaster was English, but could not name him. However, he fondly recalled many details of his experience with this troop, and spontaneously sang aloud the old Scout favorite "By the Blazing Council Fire's Light," remembering the lyrics perfectly, suggestive of how much he had enjoyed his Scouting days (and perhaps the relative (un) importance of some details of that experience.)[1] Winning was not everything, but the troop did win the banner again in 1936 and then in 1940 though, by then, its members were mostly Chinese boys, partly due to the evacuation of European boys in 1940.

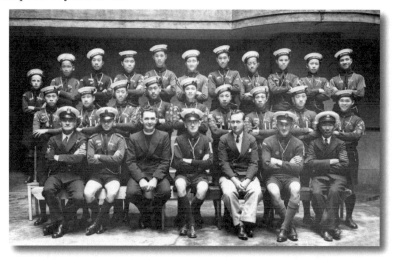

1ˢᵗ Hong Kong Sea Scouts in 1938, when most boys were Chinese.

H. K. Scout Archives.

Even if their lived experience did suggest that the realization of the brotherhood was fragile, at best, Hong Kong Scouts in the later part of the interwar years were at least aware of the importance of transnational racial harmony to official notions of what it meant to be part of Scouting. For some, the de-politicizing programs and nurturing of a uniquely Hong Kong version of Chineseness for the boys of the local movement might be judged somewhat successful. Significantly, they seemed to have had no problem reconciling their ethnic identity with a British imperial orientation, justifying to some extent the colonial authorities' willingness to promote Chinese Scouting. The big event for 1937 was the coronation rally in May, which occurred just after Caldecott left to become gover-

1   Interview, Sammy Chiu Suk-ming, November 8, 2005, the Hong Kong Scout Archives.

nor of Ceylon. Though most of the youth present were Chinese, imperial symbolisms abounded, including a pageant with Scouts and Guides representing parts of the empire congregating around a platform where "St. George sat motionless on his horse" and a rally with "Britannia" surrounded by youthful participants in a wheel formation which evolved as the band played and all sang "God Save the King."[1]

    The particular contextual pressures faced by the leaders in Hong Kong Scouting stimulated a creative response to the challenge of Chinese nationalism. It also led to the Fourth Law being applied more conscientiously and successfully in Hong Kong than in some other colonies. Still, one must remember that Scouting for the non-white boys in, say, South Africa was controversial because fundamental racial issues between the British, the Afrikaners, the black Africans and the other colored people (mostly Asians) were deep-seated and unresolved during this period. Though the ethnic policies of the Hong Kong Scout association were relatively progressive, they could only be so since the underlying racial relationship of the Hong Kong colonial community was such that these policies were accepted. While it might be simplistic to claim that such methods employed by local Scouting were successful it is worth noting that, in this period, strikes and boycotts of British interests had again occurred in Shanghai, Tangshan, Shandong, and Zhejiang, mostly driven by labor disputes, but at least one by the New Life Movement targeting Chinese youth. But, unlike in the 1920s, Hong Kong students were not drawn in.[2] Though a profound economic depression hit much of Europe, America and China and had affected the colony in the 1930s, there was no further community-wide strike or boycott on the scale of that of 1925-1926, in which local students had played a part.

Sammy Chiu Suk-ming.
H. K. Scout Archives.

Preparing local boys to fight

By late 1930s, as open conflict between British Hong Kong and the advancing Japanese troops became increasingly likely, Chinese nationalism and politics suddenly seemed more palatable. Though Hong Kong

---

1   *SCMP*, May 15, 1937; CM, May 5, 1937; *HKDP*, May 15, 1937.
2   Jurgen Osterhammel, "Imperialism in Transition: British Business and the Chinese Authorities, 1931-1937," *The China Quarterly*, No. 98, June 1984, 277-279.

OGDEN'S CIGARETTES.

DISPATCH RIDING.

Despatch riding, a common Scout skill.

was not officially at war, the threat of imminent hostility was clear, as the colony was flooded with half a million refugees, and more parts of China fell under the control of the Japanese. Members of the local Scout movement were increasingly prepared "to fight," and were encouraged to sign up for the Volunteers Corps, the Air Raid Precaution (ARP) Despatch Corps, and other auxiliary services in large numbers, inspired by heroic Scout war services in China, and the official endorsement of dual loyalty to Britain and China against their common enemy, Japan.

At the time, Japan's advance into China appeared unstoppable. For years, the former had developed a seemingly unquenchable thirst for territorial growth, annexing Taiwan, Korea, Tsingtao, and then Manchuria. The Second Sino-Japanese War broke out in July 1937, when the Japanese besieged and took over Peking in twenty days. Hitler chose Japan as his ally to counter the Soviet Union, and, in turn, the Nationalist Chinese signed the Sino-Soviet Non-aggression Pack in August 1937, and formed a united front with the Chinese Communists. In the same month, hostilities erupted in Shanghai, which fell in November, after a heroic and costly resistance. Following another bloody fight, Nanking was lost in December, and the Nanking Massacre ("a story of such crime and horror as to be almost unbelievable") took place, in which up to three hundred thousand Chinese were killed.[1]

Despite a few stunning setbacks, such as the 1937 Ping-xing Pass campaign led by Communist Lin Biao and the 1938 Tai-er-zhuang campaign led by Nationalist Li Tsung-jen, Japanese troops continued to push forward. Soon the Sino-Japanese war was brought much closer to home, as far as Hong Kong was concerned. By October 1938, Canton and Hankow had both been taken. Chinese refugees, with or without means, flooded the colony. From 1937 to 1939, hundreds of thousands came, and soon there were "over half-a-million people sleeping in the streets."[2] The government was forced to build temporary camps, and as-

---

1   H.J. Timperley (comp.), *Japanese Terror in China* (New York, Modern Age Books, 1938), 20-21; For estimates of casualties see Mark Eykholt, "Aggression, Victimization, and Chinese Historiography of the Nanjing Massacre," in Joshua A. Fogel (ed.), *Nanjing Massacre in History and Historiography* (Berkeley: Univ. of California Press, 2000), 47.

2   The *Hong Kong Annual Report* (Hong Kong: the Hong Kong Government, 1961), 315.

sorted voluntary agencies opened up their facilities. War was no longer a distant reality but would sooner or later come to British Hong Kong. This had far-reaching consequences for local Scouting.

With pressing defense needs and supportive attitudes of local Chinese, Scouting penetrated many more schools and membership doubled from 1936 to 1941, despite loss of all ethnic British boys.[1] Steady growth was registered in 1937-39. In a rally in 1939, six hundred Scouts, including those from vernacular and rural schools of Yiu Yeung (耀揚), Nam Yuet (南粵), Yeurk Chi (鑰智), Yiu Ying (耀英), Pui Ching(培清), Tak Ming (德明) and Tai Po Tsai (大埔仔), showed up.[2] Sargent reorganized the DBS Troop in 1938, with Graham S. P. Heywood from the Royal Observatory and St. Andrew's Troop as his Assistant. By end of the year, membership topped the one thousand mark, with youth members in school troops constituting 60% of total, versus only 40% the previous year.[3] International Scout brotherhood broke down somewhat. In 1938, when some Japanese Boy Scouts stopped over on their way to Europe, an official of the local association declared coldly that "no local arrangements have yet been made to welcome" them.[4]

A joint camp for twenty three groups from Kowloon and the New Territories was held in August 1939. As some Boy Scouts from the Island were also invited, this, in a sense, was the first-ever "colony-wide" Jamboree. Some two to three hundred Boy Scouts camped on the slopes between Beacon Hill and the Lion Rock. On the first day, all gathered around and saluted the Union Jack and the Chinese national flag as they were being hoisted. Chan Fook-hong spoke of the Fourth Scout Law and suggested that if this were obeyed by peoples of all nations, there would be fewer prejudices, misunderstanding and false sense of superiority on the part of one class or nation over the other, and perhaps more happiness and peace in the world. Halward was not present due to his work among refugees in Kunming, and Chan urged all to be as selfless as their commissioner if and when an emergency arises.[5]

Membership stayed flat in 1940, due to the loss of the British

1   Total membership was 713 (youth 605) in 1935, 1,542 (youth 1,344) in 1941.
2   *HKT*, April 24, 1939; *KSYP*, April 23, 19391.
3   *Hong Kong Administrative Report, 1938*, O17, *1939*, O21. Youth members: 820 in 1938, 1,034 in 1939; school members: 330 and 620.
4   *HKT*, June 2, 1938.
5   *HKT,* September 2, 1939.

boys. In June 1940, secret communications referred to a scheme to evacuate European women and children.[1] While, with hindsight, it was timely, there was no shortage of critics at the time, including leading citizens like Stanley Dodwell and Henry Pollock.[2] Its racist nature was criticized by the Legislative Council and many others.[3] *The Economist* called it "a grave blunder" as it implied that "the Colony was in peril from attack or starvation, in which case a few thousand individuals of British parentage should not have been given an advantage over some 600,000 or 700,000 of Chinese or mixed race in finding sanctuary."[4] Despite all of the protests, the evacuation went as planned, and all ethnic British boys left Hong Kong. Gains from revived groups at St. Stephen's and Munsang and new groupst at Min Kiu, Chiu Chow, St. Louis, etc. were just enough to offset losses from troops at Murray, the Cathedral, Stanley and the Garrison. Halward reported a total which remained "exactly the same as last year."[5] The only British formation left seemed to be the Rover Scouts with the military and the navy, including Rev. L. Sherley-Price, their fleet commissioner.[6]

Chinese Troop at Munsang College, revived in 1940.

H. K. Scout Archives.

1   "Evacuation of British Families from Hong Kong," CO 323/1808/6, the National Archives, London. Later on, some "wives and children of Chinese residents… thought to justify exceptional treatment" were evacuated.

2   Ibid., the *Birmingham Post*, July 27, 1940.

3   *Hong Kong Hansard*, July 25, 1940, 100-103.

4   The *Economist*, September 7, 1940, 310.

5   *HKT*, July 3, 1941.

6   The *Hong Kong Scouting Gazette*, February 1941. Rev. L. Sherley-Price was listed as representative of the Deep Sea Scouts on the local Scout Council.

On January 8, 1941, Scouts around the world were deeply grieved by the sad news of the passing away of their beloved founder, Baden-Powell, at Nyeri Kenya. Despite his advanced age, he had remained remarkably active until the last, and had built himself a bungalow on the slope of Mount Kenya where he and Lady Baden-Powell had stayed for the past few years. The next day, he was buried in Nyeri, according to his last wish.[1] Lord Somers, his deputy since 1935, became the new Chief Scout.[2]

On Sunday, January 19, memorial services in his honor were held at both the St. John's Cathedral and the Catholic Cathedral in Hong Kong. Acting Governor Norton, the Hon. Sir Robert Kotewall, and C. Champkin, the Deputy Commissioner, among many others, were present in the former, while most Scouts from the Catholic Troops attended the latter. The messages in both services were hopeful and upbeat, one predicting that the "movement…will go on and on" despite the death of the founder, while the other praised the Chief Scout as a man who "impressed himself on the absent as if he was present."[3]

B-P in 1939.

The optimistic messages seemed justified. In 1941, the movement grew strongly again. In May the New Territories was separated out as a third district, headed by Chan Fook-hong.[4] In November, the association held its last prewar annual meeting, in Chief Scout Mark Young's first appearance, when it was noted that membership grew 34% to reach 1,542.[5] New or revived groups included two churches (St. Paul's and Rosary), vernacular schools such as Kwong Wah (光華), Chung Wah (中華), Kiu Kwong (九江), Fong Lam (仿林), Man Fan (民範), South China (南華), Ming Sang (明新), Wah Nam (華南), Tai Tung (大同), Canton University Middle School (廣大附中), Ling Tung (嶺東), and the renumbered rural ones at Shun Tat (崇德), Cheung Chau (長洲), Kwong Pui (廣培) at Tai Po Tsai, Fanling (粉嶺), Fung Kai (鳳溪) at Sheung Shui, Pok Man (博文), Wing On (永安) at Yuen Long, Yeurk Ying (育英), and Yeurk Yin (育賢).[6] This long list is significant:

---

1   *HKDP*, January 9, 1941; *CM*, January 10, 1941.
2   6th Baron Somers (Arthur Somers-Cocks) was the deputy Chief Scout from 1935 to 1941, and served as the Chief Scout from 1941 until his death in 1944.
3   *HKDP*, January 20, 1941.
4   The *Hong Kong Scouting Gazette*, June 1941, 67.
5   *HKSH*, November 21, 1941.
6   The *Hong Kong Scouting Gazette*, June 1941, 20-21, 68; interview, Liu Cheuk-

A Scout enrollment card
signed by Somers, the new
Chief Scout.

most new groups were from Chinese vernacular and rural schools. Just before the war, Hong Kong Scouting became fully indigenized, and had substantively broken the indirect "class" barrier of the few elitist government and mission schools.

By this time, with their common enemy and large influxes of Nationalist schools from China, dual loyalty in Scouting was tolerated if not embraced. In the St. George's Day rally in 1939, Northcote's arrival was followed by the hoisting of the Union Jack and the Chinese "Blue Sky and White Sun (青天白日)" flag and the renewal of the Scout Promise in Chinese.[1] Deputy Commissioner Champkin was in charge, as Halward was in Canton and could not attend. Tse Ping-fui (謝炳奎), who was a Boy Scout in the St. Paul's troop then, noted later that they were permitted to raise British and Chinese national flags on alternate weekly meetings.[2]

With the protection afforded by an ordinance, Scout Troops could not be set up without the local association's approval. But many "Overseas Chinese schools (僑校)" maintained dual registrations of

wing, March 4, 2004, the Hong Kong Scout Archives. The rural troops were renumbered 1st New Territories to 9th New Territories, respectively.
1   *HKSH*, April 23, 1939; *HKT*, April 24, 1939.
2   Interview, Tse Ping-fui, October 26, 2004, the Hong Kong Scout Archives.

the schools and their Scout Troops with both Chinese and Hong Kong authorities. In another context, even Clementi, a staunch supporter of Scouting for the Chinese, was opposed to colonial Scout Troops linked to Boy Scouts of China.[1] In a sense, dual registration was conceptually analogous to dual citizenship, and could be viewed as "a measure of convenience rather than commitment that debases and undermines the very currency of belonging."[2] However, just as dual citizenship was to become grudgingly accepted years later in some countries, dual registration of troops was pragmatically permitted in Hong Kong at this time, given the need to mobilize Chinese boys for the defense.[3]

Many schools in China migrated south to the relative safety of Hong Kong, and private secondary schools soared from six in 1936 to eighty-two in 1937, and over one hundred in 1938.[4] Many of these had Scout Troops registered in China. Simultaneously, colonial attitudes softened. Dual registration became officially accepted if not openly encouraged. Many Scouts in the Nationalist schools maintained links with both Scout associations, a practice that was confirmed by Halward after the war, when he acknowledged that there were troops which were "registered both with the Chinese Government and with the British Scout Headquarters, H.K. before the war."[5]

Champkin, the Deputy Commissioner.

Gilwell Archives.

Tak Ming Middle School (德明書院), founded in the 1930s, is illustrative. Just as the school was registered both with the Committee on Overseas Chinese Affairs (僑務委員會) in China and the Hong Kong Education Department, its Scout Group was recognized by both Scout associations. Like other activities in the school, Scouting was subjected to the same "partyization," with emphasis on anti-communism and loyalty to the Nationalist Party. But Tak Ming troops also participated in

---

1   "Charter: Boy Scouts Association, 1930" PC 8/1275, the National Archives, London. In July 1930, Clementi, as the new Chief Scout in Malaya, wrote to B-P about his intention to prevent the formation of Chinese Boy Scout units in Malaya linked to the Boy Scouts of China.

2   Valerie Preston, Myer Siemiatycki, and Audrey Kobayashi, "Dual Citizenship among Hong Kong Canadians: Convenience or Commitment?" in Thomas Faist et al. (eds.), *Dual Citizenship in Global Perspective: From Unitary to Multiple Citizenship* (New York, Palgrave, 2007), 203.

3   See, for example, Thomas Faist, "The Fixed and Porous Boundaries of Dual Citizenship," 6.

4   *Hong Kong Administrative Reports for 1936, 1937 and 1938,* App. O.

5   Meeting minutes, Kowloon Scouters' meeting, 1947, the Hong Kong Scout Archives.

colonial Scout gatherings such as the St. George's Day rally in 1939. By 1941, Tak Ming had three troops, making it one of the largest school sponsors in the colony.[1]

Despite tolerant attitudes towards dual registration, some Chinese schools still opted for a Scout-like corps (labeled euphemistically *Shao Nian Tuan*, or youth corps 少年團), not linked to the local association, providing Scout training for boys and girls. In March 1938, on the day of the Nationalist Chinese Scout Festival (童子軍節), members of the *Shao Nian Tuan* of Lai Chak Girls' Middle School (麗澤) were sworn in, and all sang the Nationalist Chinese Scout song (童軍歌).[2] In June 1939, the inauguration of the *Shao Nian Tuan* of Yeung Chung Girls' Middle School (養中) was officiated over by a leader of the Nationalist Chinese Wartime Boy Scout Service Corps (中國童軍戰時服務團), in the presence of *Shao Nian Tuan* from other schools, including those of Lai Chak and Ling Tung.[3] Ling Tung had a Scout Troop in early 1930s but, for some reason, it was considered "unsatisfactory" and was shut down by the Hong Kong association in 1940.[4] A Yeung Chung school magazine in 1939 noted that all first and second year students were required to join the *Shao Nian Tuan*, "its training program was equivalent to that of Scouting (其訓練大綱,均與童軍等)," and its mottos were "Be Prepared (準備)," "Do a Good Turn Everyday (日行一善)," and "Life's Purpose is to Serve (人生以服務為目的)."[5]

Investiture of the "youth corps" at Lai Chak school.
Ta Kung Pao, March 1938.

---

1   *HKDP*, April 12, 1939; *KSYP*, April 23, 1939; *HKT*, July 3, 1941.

2   The *Ta Kung Pao* 大公報, March 16, 1938.

3   Ibid., June 23, 1939.

4   *HKT*, July 3, 1941.

5   *Yang Zhong Zhong Xue Shi Wu Zhou Nian Ji NianTe Kan* 養中中學十五週年紀念特刊(15th Anniversary Commemorative Magazine of the Yeung Chung Middle School, in Chinese) (Hong Kong: Yeung Chung Middle School, 1939), 9, 58.

These Scout-like corps, probably registered in China, were apparently rather widespread. In March 1940, boys and girls from "more than thirty (數十)" *Shao Nian Tuan* sponsored by the many overseas Chinese schools located in Hong Kong gathered for an inspection by a member of the Nationalist Chinese Central Education Committee. In this gathering there was no display of dual loyalty or British colonial symbols. It featured only the Nationalist Party and the Chinese Republic flags, along with the portrait of Dr. Sun Yat-sen.[1]

Rules for the "Boy Scout War Service Corps," to be set up in all provinces to assist in transportation, security, propaganda, entertainment, pioneering, logistics, scouting, first-aid, and fire fighting, were promulgated by the Nationalist government in 1937. Two years later, over 19,000 Boy and Girl Scouts were involved, working with the Red Cross, medical service corps, refugees, wounded soldiers, children's education, and publicity and fund-raising drives. At times, war service could be quite dangerous. In Shanghai alone, more than three hundred Scouts were serving at the front by 1939, and twelve had died from the time that war had broken out two years earlier. Some examples are illustrative. Japanese planes machine gunned forty Chinese Scouts on their way to perform first aid in Shanghai. Twelve-year-old Scout Chao Chia-ting lost his life saving others at an air raid in Sungkiang (松江 Songjiang).[2] In 1938, reporters observed that, after ten days of heavy bombing of Canton by Japanese planes, "a number of Boy Scouts and Girl Guides... were killed while attending wounded," and that "in the pile of slaughtered humans could be discerned the uniforms of...Boy Scouts."[3]

Some who served in these corps were Chinese Boy Scouts and Girl Scouts from overseas. The Singapore Chinese Scout War Front Service Corps, with nine boys and seven girls, arrived in late 1937, and went immediately to the frontline in Shanghai, Soochow, Nanking, and Shansi. A year later, only two were left: Ng Chee-keng (吳志強), 19, with bullet wounds and a fractured skull, and Miss Chong Yeng-tack (鍾英德), whose right leg had to be amputated due to machine-gun wounds. As one observer noted, these were sacrifices in the "highest traditions of

---

1   The *Ta Kung Pao* 大公報, March 30, 1940.
2   *KSYP*, August 4, 1937; *HKDP*, September 11, 1939, June 6, 1938; *HKSH*, November 7, 1937.
3   *HKDP*, May 31, 1938, June 7, 1938.

「模範童軍」
吳志強傷愈抵湘
將來粵轉道返星洲
積極從事對外宣傳

中央社長沙電　星洲切、於滬戰時組織中國青
華僑男女童軍馬少貞、吳年童子軍星洲華僑戰地服
志強等十六人、愛國心務團決死隊、於去歲九月

Report on the "Model Scout," Ng Chee-keng.
KSYP, August 1938.

Chinese Girl Scout Yang Hui-min.

the Movement."[1] In April 1939, over seventy Annamese-Chinese Scouts went to China, following an earlier corps of over fifty who had served in Dongjiang and Huizhou, with twenty lives lost.[2] These Boy Scouts were most likely members of Chinese troops attached to pro-Nationalist schools in British Singapore and French Annam.

Through reporting in the press or propaganda visits, Scout war services in China greatly impressed the Hong Kong Scouts, and could explain why so many of them would later serve in local defense or return to China to join the resistance war. In January 1938, Shanghai Scout leaders came to Hong Kong to mobilize support and raise funding. Films on war services, one featuring the famous Girl Scout, Yang Hui-min (楊惠敏), who had risked her life to deliver a Chinese national flag to soldiers defending Shanghai, were shown to thousands of young people at many schools. The local association hosted a tea party for the Shanghai Scouts, and organized a viewing of the films at St. Paul Girls' College. Halward praised their efforts, and urged local Scouts to follow their examples, some of which, he emphasized, meant great sacrifices.[3] Later in the same year, local press printed a detailed article entitled "1,000 Scouts Doing Relief Work in Canton," and quoted a Belgian Catholic priest who had served there, speaking highly of the impressive discipline and courage of the Scouts involved. A little over a week later, the same newspaper featured a front-page photograph showing Cantonese Boy Scouts rescuing wounded Chinese.[4]

Though officially Hong Kong was still neutral, war preparation had begun, if discreetly at the beginning. Nationalistic sentiments grew among Hong Kong Chinese, expressed in terms of anti-Japanese activities, assistance for war refugees, and support for the war efforts. *The Chimes* (鐘聲報), school magazine of St. Stephen's College, declared that "1937-8 will ever be remembered as the year of the outbreak of the war in China," and reported that many students had signed up for the military in China or contributed to war charities, partly in response to Halward's briefings on China.[5] On October 10, 1937, the Chinese national

1   *HKDP*, July 20, 1938; *KSYP*, August 2, 1938.
2   *KSYP*, April 8, 1939, April 15, 1939.
3   *KSYP*, January 1, 1938, January 10, 1938, January 14, 1938.
4   *HKDP*, June 8, 1938, June 16, 1938.
5   *The Chimes* 鐘聲報, 1939.

day, students of Diocesan Boys School organized a fund-raising concert, with Scouts from 6th Kowloon in charge of a program.[1] An article in the school's magazine *Steps* in February 1939 spoke of the responsibilities of a student, which included participation in Scouting.[2] Local Chinese, including many Scoutmasters and Rover Scouts, enlisted in the Volunteers for "the Chinese [in Hong Kong] felt that a joint defense with the motherland [China] against the enemy [Japan] was equivalent to protecting our homeland."[3] Nor were these limited to Chinese nationals—both the Portuguese and the Eurasian companies of the Volunteer Corps had many Scouters and Rovers. By 1938, the reorganized Diocesan Boys' School troop under Scoutmaster Sargent had mostly Eurasian or European members.[4] Many, including Fisher, Crary, Read, and the two Matthews brothers, had all joined the Volunteers Corps.

Besides serving as volunteer soldiers, many Scouts signed up for other defense-related duties. By November 1937, at the request of T. H. King, Inspector General of the police, one hundred and fifty Boy Scouts had offered their services as public messengers.[5] In early 1938, A. H. Steele-Perkins, the newly-appointed ARP Officer, incorporated these messengers into the overall ARP organization.[6] Scouts between fourteen and twenty who were able to ride a bicycle were trained as ARP Communications Wardens who would be posted to depots often supervised by Scouters.[7] Later in the year, an official emphasized the importance of Boy Scouts in air defense, as exemplified in Canton, and urged young people who had yet to join Scouting to sign up.[8] In April 1939, "five hundred Boy Scouts…have been placed at the disposal of Wing-Commander Steele-Perkins" and "formed into different groups, for…conveying necessary information from bombed areas to the nearest Air-Raid Warden Station."[9]

Six hundred members of the ARP Despatch Corps, as these units

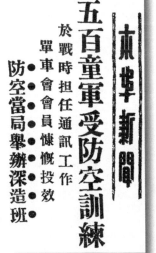

東華新聞

五百童軍受防空訓練

於戰時担任通訊工作
單車會會員慷慨投效
防空當局舉辦深造班

Report on 500 Hong Kong Scouts in ARP work. *KSYP, April 1939.*

---

1   The *Steps*, January 1938, 60-61.
2   The *Steps*, February 1939, 12.
3   *The Memorial Booklet* 香港義勇軍光榮史 (Hong Kong: Hong Kong Volunteer Defence Corps (Chinese) Club, 1949), "華人以與祖國聯防抗敵不啻保衛桑梓."
4   The *Steps*, January 1938, 58, July 1938, 27.
5   The *Hong Kong Scouting Gazette*, June 1941, 73.
6   *Hong Kong Administrative Report, 1938*, P (1).
7   The *Hong Kong Scouting Gazette*, June 1941, 73.
8   *KSYP*, August 16, 1938.
9   *HKSH*, April 16, 1939.

became known, took part in their first public parade in June 1941. B. H. Puckle, Deputy Director of the ARP, inspected the gathering, accompanied by Scouters Champkin, Chan Fook-hong, and Sin Ka Wing. As reported in a 1941 issue of the *Hong Kong Scouting Gazette*, Puckle noted that the corps was but one-third of its desired full strength, but expressed confidence that it would serve gallantly and "worthily uphold the traditions of the Boy Scouts' Movement."[1] Out of nineteen members promoted Senior Communications Wardens, eighteen were Chinese, and most if not all were Scouters. In September, a black-out of the New Territories was held, with Royal Air Force planes staging mimic air raids, and members of the Despatch Corps on duty at all stations.[2] By end of the year, the corps had eight reserve depots, manned largely by trained Scouts, and "the Commissioner…has been supplied with details as to where the Scouts should report in time of emergency."[3] In November 1941, its ranks had swelled to 1,155, not counting 300 recent recruits, yet to be trained. Later in the month, another civil defense test was held, and trial messages were carried between the ARP posts by the Boy Scouts.[4]

Cover of *Hong Kong Scouting Gazette* in 1941, featuring the parade of the ARP Despatch Corps in June.

1   The *Hong Kong Scouting Gazette*, June 1941, 70-72.
2   Ibid.; *HKSH*, June 15, 1941, September 17, 1939.
3   *Hong Kong Administrative Report, 1939*, P (1) A.R.P., "General Statement on A.R.P. during the period 1st January, 1939, to 31st December, 1939," 3.
4   *KSYP*, November 20, 1941, November 21, 1941; *HKSH*, November 21, 1941; *SCMP*, November 20, 1941, December 1, 1941.

The experience of Guiding again provides useful insights into the gendered nature of local Scouting at this time. Generally, the girls also served, but typically in more limited roles. Guides helped refugees in the Happy Valley camp, the Central British School, and the Yaumati shelter for street sleepers. They were often engaged in duties such as making beds, supervising linen-cupboards in refugee camps, knitting patchwork blankets, rolling bandages and making swabs for hospitals. In 1939, the first New Territories Company was founded at the Taipo Rural Home for underprivileged girls, and a company was set up at the Sze-Sze College, which had relocated from Canton. Aside from Sze-Sze, no other new company in schools from China had been noted, though there were many *Shao Nian Tuan*'s in Chinese girls' schools.

ARP Corps badge, Hong Kong.

Guiding slowed considerably after the evacuation of British women and children, including Mrs. T. H. King, the commissioner, in July 1940.[1] Despite urgent needs of the Despatch Corps, Guides were not trained for this wartime work. The relatively low level of activities in Guiding in the last pre-war years in contrast to the rapid growth in Scouting is intriguing. Possible reasons include the paucity of dual registered Guide Companies, absence of senior leaders after the evacuation, lack of encouragement from the authorities as there was no plan to include Guides in defense efforts, and unattractiveness of the roles available in local Guiding versus those offered to Girl Scouts in China, who took up frontline and life-threatening duties like the Boy Scouts.

A graph of membership growth in the period, as shown in the next page, is instructive. While membership growth in Scouting was modest in the early part of the period under review, it became significantly stronger towards the late 1930s, as the colony geared up for war and defense. By 1939, the number of Hong Kong Boy Scouts surpassed the one thousand mark. Though there was no growth during 1940 due to the evacuation of British boys, discussed earlier in this section, membership number jumped substantially again in 1941, to reach 1,542. These increases in the last prewar years, though very significant, must be viewed in context. Singapore, a smaller colony, for instance, reported over two thousand members in both 1938 and 1939.[2]

---

1   *Guiding in Hong Kong*, 14-16.
2   Appendix D, "Membership Statistics;" Tan and Wan, *Scouting in Singapore*, 271.

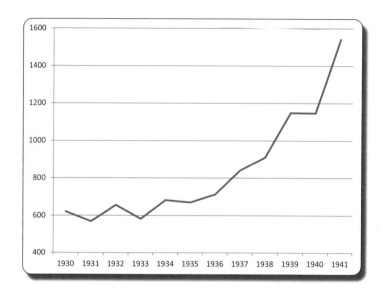

Membership Trends, Hong Kong, 1930-1941

Source: Appendix D, "Membership Statistics."

At any rate, by late 1941, many Hong Kong Boy Scouts, young and old, were prepared to defend Hong Kong, typically as Volunteers or in the Despatch Corps. In the face of a possible war, citizenship training in the form of Scouting now meant largely preparing youngsters to fight. Membership grew very rapidly in these years even without including those in the Scout-like *Shao Nian Tuan*, thanks to strong official encouragement, but, just as importantly, growing nationalism among local Chinese and closer identification with the anti-Japanese war efforts. Whether in India, Algeria, Ireland, or Indochina, native Boy Scouts involved in military actions typically came out on the side of the ruled races fighting against the ruling race for home rule or independence. Members of the *Fianna Éireann*, for instance, were involved in the 1916 uprising against British rule in Ireland, and some of its young leaders were executed afterward.[1] Hong Kong Scouting is unique in that its military efforts during this time were solidly behind the colonial British authorities in their struggle against Japan, the common enemy of British Hong Kong and Nationalist China, the country of origin of most Hong Kong Chinese Boy Scouts.

---

1   Rona M. Fields, *Northern Ireland: Society Under Seige* (New Brunswick: Transaction, 1980), 11-12.

Scouting in war and occupation

Though the attack on Hong Kong had been expected, its defensive forces were hopelessly inadequate for the task at hand. Many older Scouts fought as Volunteers, and over one thousand Scouts served in the Despatch Corps in the brief Battle for Hong Kong. After the fall of the colony, Scouting was prohibited, though it existed on a small scale clandestinely in the Stanley camp. By and large, Hong Kong Scouts acquitted themselves well in war and occupation, some with supreme sacrifices, re-affirming the value of this type of citizenship training.

Many books have been written on Hong Kong's defense, fall, and occupation. These feature tales of courage, gallantry, loyalty, selflessness, generosity, and sacrifice; and those of cowardice, selfishness, duplicity, betrayal, cruelty and even wanton inhumanity (most of which will not be repeated here), confirming the old adage that war often brought out the best and the worst in people. Readers of these stories may be amazed at both the strength and frailty of human nature, which enabled people to fall so far beneath or rise so high above their situations; and perhaps grateful that they are not put through similar tests.

Given the amount of Japanese intelligence intercepted before the attack, some through a listening and code-breaking post set up in Hong Kong in 1935, it could not be said that Hong Kong was taken by surprise when the Japanese attack commenced.[1] But many had refused to take the threat of war seriously, or were confident that Hong Kong could withstand a sustained siege. In June 1941, Northcote asked that shipping capacity be maintained for a four-month food reserve, noting that a reduction in this shipping (no mention was made of the defense) capacity "must automatically bring down the period for which we could

---

1   It was John Tiltman from this post in Hong Kong who had cracked the Japanese code JN25, making much intelligence accessible to the Allies. In November 1941, the Americans deciphered the infamous Japanese "winds" codes, which was to communicate a state of war in the form of weather forecasts. Finally, on Sunday, December 7, Hong Kong intercepted the coded "winds" message: *higashi no kaze, ame; nishi no kaze, hare* (Easterly wind, rain; Westerly wind, fine), signaling that Japan was to declare war on Britain and America immediately. See David Kahn, *The Codebreakers: the Story of Secret Writing* (New York: Scribner, 1996), 31-32; Michael Smith, *The Emperor's Codes: the Breaking of Japan's Secret Ciphers* (New York: Arcade Publishing, 2000), 4-5, 36, 56-57, 60-61, 100.

A Hong Kong war poster.

stand a siege."[1]

In September 1941, Sir Mark Young arrived in Hong Kong as the new governor. On December 1, the government again urged non-defense personnel to "remove themselves and their families," but few were interested, and ships departed with many spaces on board.[2] Interestingly, forty Japanese left the day before, leaving behind less than one hundred businessmen. On December 4, the governor and others attended Sir Robert Ho Tung's golden wedding anniversary celebration. Two nights later, the colonial elites gathered for a China Relief Ball.[3] Two missionaries wrote on December 5 about air-raid drills at their school: "our students think it a great joke to be practicing when there is no real need," as, after all, "everyone says that the Japanese will not dare to attack," and, even if they did, "Hong Kong is impregnable."[4]

Young inspected the defense line with military leaders, late 1941.

PRO 7-4-100.

Actually, the defense forces were woefully insufficient. The garrison of some fourteen thousand men consisted of six infantry battalions, the Volunteer Corps, an artillery contingent, and small naval and air units. The British battalions were the Royal Scots and the Middlesex; the Indian ones the martial races of Rajputs, Punjabi Muslims, and Sikhs; the Volunteers had British, Portuguese, Eurasian and Chinese units (all with some Scouters and Rover Scouts); and the Canadian battalions consisted of newly-recruited volunteers who had arrived in November.[5] In

1   "Semi-official and personal correspondence between Secretary of State and Governors Sir Geoffry Northcote and Sir Mark Young,1941-45," CO 967/70, the National Archives, London.
2   *SCMP*, December 2, 1941.
3   Jan Henrik Marsman, *I Escaped from Hong Kong* (Sydney: Angus and Robertson, 1943), 7-8.
4   Alice Y. Lan and Betty M. Hu, *We Flee from Hong Kong* (Grand Rapids, Mich.: Zondervan, [1944]), 18.
5   Tony Banham, *Not the Slightest Chance: The Defence of Hong Kong, 1941*

a secret imperial conference in Tokyo in December 1941, the Japanese Army Chief of Staff noted the Canadian reinforcements, but stated dryly that "an increase of this magnitude will be of no consequence."[1] His nonchalant attitude was quite understandable, given the plan to send sixty thousand battle-hardened Japanese soldiers from China.[2] The multiracial forces also had issues which the enemy did not hesitate to play up. Many Sikh soldiers and policemen were in a mutinous mood at the time.[3] Japanese propaganda labeled the war as one against white supremacy and for the oppressed Asiatic races, with slogans like "Asiatic people should…drive the Americans and British out of Asia," and "Come, Indian soldiers, we treat you especially good!"[4] Some Chinese and Indians bought this propaganda, as evidenced by damaging Fifth Column activities and Indian collaboration. Nor was defense helped by many last-minute changes in colonial and military leaders, some of whom hardly had time to fully understand the situation in the colony.[5]

On December 6 to 7, many Rover Scouts, including over thirty from the La Salle crew, attended the 2nd Rover Moot on a hill off Clearwater Bay Road amid constant alarms.[6] In the morning of December 8, Japanese forces poured over the border between China and Hong Kong, and over thirty fighters attacked Kai Tak airfield, quickly destroying the small Royal Air Force unit. The Royal Scots, the Rajputs and Punjabis tried with some difficulty to hold the Japanese back at the so-called "Gin Drinkers' Line" in Kowloon. On the same day, the Royal Navy left for Singapore, leaving only five motor torpedo boats (MTBs).

By the time the Rovers returned home from the Moot, the Volunteers had been mobilized. (Former) Scoutmasters Bill Gittins, a Sergeant

---

(Toronto: UBC Press, 2003), 11-12; Lèo Paul Bèrard, *17 Days Until Christmas* (Canada, 1997), iii, 177-178; Wenzell Brown, *Hong Kong Aftermath* (New York: Smith & Durrell, 1943), 34-35.

1   Nobutaka Ike (trans.), *Japan's Decision for War: Records of the 1941 Policy Conferences* (Stanford: Stanford Univ. Press, 1967), 280-281.

2   Tim Carew, *Fall of Hong Kong* (London: Anthony Blond, 1960), 37.

3   Gerald Horne, *Race War: White Supremacy and the Japanese Attack on the British Empire* (New York: New York Univ. Press, 2004), 69-71.

4   Horne, *Race War*, 69.

5   G.B. Endacott, *Hong Kong Eclipse* (Hong Kong: Oxford Univ. Press, 1978), 55-9. Norton acted as governor till March 1941, Northcote returned and left in September, replaced by Young, Fraser became defense secretary in April, Grasett handed over the garrison to Maltby in July, Colonial Secretary Smith was succeeded by Gimson on December 7, the night before the attack.

6   Folder, Henry Ma Papers, 1940s-1960s, the Hong Kong Scout Archives.

2nd Rover Moot on Dec. 6-7, 1941, just before the Japanese attack started.

H. K. Scout Archives.

in the 4th Battery, and G. R. Ross, a Gunner with the 2nd Battery, went to their respective stations.[1] Rovers and Scouters John Chong, Francis Lim, Richard Ma, Henry Ma, Quah, Clifford Matthews, Eric Matthews, and Joseph Read from the Eurasian No. 3 Company were under Major Evan George Stewart, a Group Scoutmaster and the principal of St. Paul's College.[2] This company, heavily manned by Scouts, was posted to Stonecutters Island, where they, as H. Ma later recalled, "enjoyed being shelled by Jap guns."[3] Four men were wounded, including Quah, who was hit in the leg. By December 11, with no naval or air support and a broken defense line, Major-General Christopher Maltby reluctantly ordered withdrawal from the mainland. No. 3 Company was ferried by MTB 08 to the Island, and posted to Wongneichong Gap.[4] G. B. Longman, a crew member of MTB 08, would know some of the Scouters, as he was with the Deep Sea Scouts.[5]

The Despatch Corps, mobilized on December 8, was promptly shelled out of its headquarters, and had to re-establish itself at the St. John's Cathedral Hall. It issued government stores, rationed food, dis-

---

1 Jean Gittins, *Stanley: Behind Barbed Wire* (Hong Kong: Hong Kong Univ. Press, 1982), 21; Evan Stewart, *Hong Kong Volunteers in Battle: A Record of the Actions of the Hongkong Volunteer Defence Corps in the Batter for Hong Kong, December, 1941* (Hong Kong: RHKR (The Volunteers) Association, 2005), 6.
2 *HKDP*, December 4, 1939; Clifford Matthews, "Life Experiences: From Star Ferry to Stardust," in Clifford Matthews and Oswald Cheung (eds.), *Dispersal and Renewal: Hong Kong University During the War Years* (Hong Kong: Hong Kong Univ. Press, 1998), 227-246; the *Steps*, July 1947, 47-49.
3 Folder, Henry Ma Papers, the Hong Kong Scout Archives.
4 Lt. Kilbee, "Diary of Lt. Kilbee," http://www.mwadui.com/HongKong/Fleet_C.htm#Kilbee (accessed February 20, 2008)
5 *The Fulcrum: the Magazine of the China Fleet Deep Sea Scouts*, May 1939.

tributed bicycles, transmitted messages, enrolled recruits and settled personnel from occupied districts. John Pau, Scoutmaster of the King's College group, was in charge.[1] As the Kowloon peninsula was lost quickly, Kowloon Scouts only saw action for a few days. Ambrose Wong (王昌雄) from the 17th Kowloon served in the Shamshuipo Station, and when the corps was disbanded, went home and threw away his uniform.[2] A Rover from the 21st Kowloon, Yeung Chun-man (楊俊文), served with the motor-cycle messenger team in Kowloon, and then returned to his home on the Island.[3] Despite growing confusion and mounting pressure after the mainland was lost, the boys stayed "very keen and did everything possible to help put things in order," and worked "deep into the night by kerosene light."[4]

Lieutenant-General Sakai's letter demanding the surrender of troops defending Hong Kong was issued even as the last British soldiers were just crossing the harbor. Young turned it down flatly, given the expectation of a long siege. In reality, British attitudes about the defense of Hong Kong had wavered over time. As late as January 1941, Winston Churchill had been opposed to reinforcing Hong Kong, believing that "if Japan goes to war…there is not the slightest chance of holding Hong Kong or relieving it."[5] He later changed his mind and approved the reinforcements. On December 13, Churchill sent a telegram in which he declared that in Britain all were "watching day by day and hour by hour your stubborn defence of the port and fortress of Hong Kong," and that every day of the resistance would bring Britain "nearer our certain final victory."[6] A botched crossing on December 15 suggested there might be some grounds for optimism. On December 17, Young again declined "most absolutely" another "peace mission" from the Japanese.

Bombardment of the Hong Kong Island, Dec. 1941.

PRO 1-22-674.

At the time, No. 3 Company continued to hold Wongneichong gap. Lieutenant Donald James Anderson, a former Cub Sixer of the 5th Hong Kong, an outstanding cricketer, the first local magistrate, and

1   Hilary St. George Saunders, *The Left Handshake: The Boy Scout Movement during the War, 1939-1945* (London: Collins, 1949), 169-170.
2   Interview, Ambrose Wong, December 14, 2004, the Hong Kong Scout Archives.
3   Interview, Yeung Chun-man, November 2004, the Hong Kong Scout Archives.
4   Saunders, *The Left Handshake*, 169.
5   Winston S. Churchill, *The Second World War, Volume III: The Grand Alliance* (London: Cassell & Co., 1966), 4th ed., 157.
6   CO 967/70, "Semi-official and personal correspondence...," 1941-45.

youngest of four officers of No. 3, wrote to his younger sister Catherine, who was a Girl Guide, with foreboding: "So far we have had no shelling or dive bombing but I feel certain our time will come soon."[1]

In the nights that followed, three regiments totaling some 7,500 Japanese made three landings on the Island, and fierce fighting ensued. No. 3 Company fought heroically to defend Wongneichong, until overwhelmed by much-superior forces by December 19.[2] R. Ma's section of nine men held its post until five were killed and three wounded, and the post was finally overcome with a bayonet charge.[3] All told, "the company suffered 80 per cent casualties…and it virtually ceased to exist as a formation after paying thus heavily for its heroic stand."[4] Anderson was among the casualties. H. Ma was shot on the chest and arrested, but later escaped, rejoined British forces, and was transferred to Queen Mary Hospital, where he met up with Quah, who "could not take food."[5] The Eurasian Company had proved itself a tough unit to beat, despite much larger enemy forces. After the Japanese took Wongneichong, Colonel Shooji felt compelled to send a message of apology to his commander due to the large number of casualties on his side.[6] Given the losses suffered by their company, both Quah and Ma could count themselves fortunate indeed. Major Stewart was later decorated with the Distinguished

A Japanese postcard depicting the battle of the Wongneichong Gap.

1   Catherine Joyce Symons, *Looking at the Stars* (Hong Kong: Pegasus, 1996), 25.

2   Robert L. Gandt, *Season of Storms: The Siege of Hong Kong, 1941* (Hong Kong, South China Morning Post, 1982), 118-121.

3   Stewart, *Hong Kong Volunteers in Battle*, 27.

4   Endacott, *Hong Kong Eclipse,* 90.

5   Folder, Henry Ma Papers, the Hong Kong Scout Archives.

6   Gandt, *Season of Storms*, 222.

Service Order for his gallant leadership.[1]

By December 20, Japanese forces were strongly established on the Island, with an almost inexhaustible pool of reserves. On December 21, Churchill sent yet another telegram, urging that "there must… be no thought of surrender. Every part of the island must be fought and the enemy resisted with the utmost stubbornness" and that "there must be vigorous fighting in the inner defences, and, if need be, from house to house."[2] A number of gallant counterattacks were organized but all failed. Some ARP stations continued to function during the seige. Even after December 17, "daily reports were received from District headquarters and a daily inspection was made."[3] Tse Ping-fui of the 10th Hong Kong was attached to St Paul's first-aid station, and led men to bombed sites and assisted with rescuing wounded people.[4]

In the morning of Christmas Day, Young urged all the soldiers to "fight on" and "hold on, for King and Empire." Maltby declared that "the order of the day is 'Hold Fast.'"[5] However, as disclosed later, both had been aware for days that "the question before us was not whether but when the enemy would be able to occupy the whole of the Colony," and the Colonial Secretary in Britain had authorized Young "to exercise the discretion…when further resistance ceased to be possible."[6] Therefore, not surprisingly, later that day, Maltby advised Young that the military situation was hopeless. They then informed the Japanese about the decision to cease fire. The Japanese insisted that unless they go immediately to the Japanese local headquarters in Kowloon, an attack would be launched. Finally the two reluctantly crossed the harbor and surrendered to General Sakai at the Peninsula Hotel.[7] Just before and even after the surrender, widespread and ruthless looting, raping, and killing (of Chinese and non-Chinese, civilians and soldiers) by Japanese soldiers were reported by many shocked and incredulous eyewitnesses.[8]

PLAYER'S CIGARETTES

DISTINGUISHED SERVICE ORDER, GT BRITAIN.

A card depicting the Distinguished Service Order.

---

1   Stewart, *Hong Kong Volunteers in Battle*, 102.
2   Churchill, *The Second World War, Volume III*, 563.
3   Saunders, *Left-hand Shake*, 169.
4   Interview, Tse Ping Fui, December 14, 2004, the Hong Kong Scout Archives.
5   John Luff, *The Hidden Years* (Hong Kong: *SCMP*, 1967), 146.
6   Young's despatch, 28th December, 1941, *Third Supplement to The London Gazette*, published in 1946, HKRS 264-1-19, the Public Records Office, Hong Kong.
7   Marsman, *I Escaped from Hong Kong*, 84-85.
8   Ibid., 125-132; Charles G. Roland, *Long Night's Journey into Day: Prisoners of War in Hong Kong and Japan, 1941-1945* (Waterloo: Wilfrid Laurier Univ. Press,

The Boy Scout National Service Badge.

Many Hong Kong Scouts attached to the Despatch Corps on the Island served till the last day. Among them was Tse, who saw Stewart, who was by that time wounded, at the morning service on Christmas day. In the afternoon, when he heard over the radio that Hong Kong had surrendered, he went home, and hid his uniform.[1] Later, D. A. Pockson, assistant commissioner, reported that "our A. R. P. Despatch Corps did very well."[2] M. L. Bevan, Deputy Director of ARP, confirmed that within a short time, all ARP centers had an adequate complement of messengers and in some, "quite extensive use was made of them," and "the boys worked with keenness and efficiency…for long hours both by day and by night."[3] Thomas F. Ryan, a Jesuit priest, saw some of these "official messenger boys in uniforms" and noted that "the courage of the boys sometimes seemed to Fr. Kelly very close to reckless."[4] These boys would all qualify for the red Boy Scout National Service badge.

Heywood, a VDC gunner, was not captured in battle, but as a civilian, on his way back to Royal Observatory after dismantling some of its instruments in the New Territories on December 8.[5]

Unlike Shameen in Canton, which upon being captured was handed over to the puppet Chinese government in Nanking, the "Captured Territory of Hong Kong (香港占領地)" came directly under a Japanese governor, partly because of the desire to eventually separate it from China, so that it could become a Japanese colony. General Rensuke Isogai (矶谷廉介) became governor from February 1942, and stayed to the end of 1944. He spoke of Hong Kong's new role in "the Greater East Asia War" and of "the Kingly Way" to which all subjects of the occupied territory must aspire.[6] Hundreds of Japanese experts were brought in to head up various government bureaus.

Chinese civilians and Europeans from countries not at war with

2001), 29-43.

1   Interview, Tse Ping Fui, December 14, 2004, the Hong Kong Scout Archives.

2   Letter, Pockson to Butterworth, October 18, 1945, the Gilwell Archives.

3   Letter, Bevan to the Boy Scouts Association, October 8, 1945, reprinted in the *Hong Kong Scouting Gazette*, January 1946, 3.

4   Thomas F. Ryan, S. J., *Jesuits Under Fire in the Siege of Hong Kong, 1941* (London: Burns Oates & Washbourne, 1944), 155-156.

5   Graham Heywood, *It Won't be Long Now: The Diary of a Hong Kong Prisoner of War* (Hong Kong: Blacksmith Books, 2015), 22. But he was still interned as a POW.

6   Robert Ward, *Asia for the Asiatics: The Techniques of Japanese Occupation* (Chicago: Univ. of Chicago Press, 1945), 57-58.

Japan were officially "free." Under pressure and *de facto* house arrests, leading Chinese residents were forced to co-operate, and many did. A Chinese Representative Council was set up, chaired by Sir Robert Kotewall. It, together with the governor, selected members for a larger Chinese Co-operative Council, chaired by Sir Shouson Chow. Much has been written about Chinese collaboration, but it should be noted that Chinese leaders represented by Kotewall and Chow had been advised on December 26 by three senior colonial officials, R. A. C. North, J. A. Fraser and C. G. Alabaster, to co-operate with the Japanese in order to save Chinese civilians and restore public order.[1] By mid-1942, Hong Kong had returned to some semblance of normality. Around 75% of former civil servants had returned to work, and the police force had two thousand men, 80% former policemen, supplemented by Japanese military patrols, which took over during curfew. But food was scarce and was rationed, necessitating a drastic reduction of the population through the systematic repatriation of Chinese back to the mainland. The census in October 1943 counted a population of 855,888, or roughly half of that before the war, reflecting the magnitude of the program.[2]

Though Japanese authorities had banned Scouting for Chinese boys in occupied Peiping (Peking) in as early as 1937, it had encouraged Japanese-style Scouting (*Syonendan*少年團) in some occupied territories.[3] Zhang Peng Yuan (張鵬雲), in school in Manchukuo in 1938, had to join the "Concord *Syonendan* (協和少年團)." Li Lian-ju (李連舉) noted that membership in the Manchukuo *Syonendan* was compulsory.[4] A Manchukuo Boy Scout belt buckle as illustrated here shows that it was once also styled the Manchukuo Boys Corps (滿州國童子團), and retained the Chinese Boy Scout slogan of "wisdom, benevolence, and courage (智仁勇)," suggesting a desire to keep a perceived link to Chinese as opposed to Japanese heritage, despite Japanese dominance in Manchukuo. Japanese military had also collaborated with the Chinese puppet government in Qingdao in 1938 to set up a Chinese Youth Corps

A Manchukuo Scout belt buckle, with the original Chinese Boy Scout slogan.

Andrew Lai's collection.

---

1   "Sir Robert Kotewall," CO 968/120/1.
2   Saito Koji 齋藤幸治, 軍政下の香港 (*Hong Kong under Military Rule*) (香港: 香港占領地總督監修, 東洋經濟新報社編, 昭和十九年, 1944), Appendix.
3   *CM*, October 22, 1937.
4   Li Lian-ju 李連舉, "Wan Guo Ri Ji 亡國日記 (Diary during the Fall of the Country)"; Zhang Peng-yuan 張鵬雲, "Wo Zai Dong Bei Lun Xian Qu Qin Li De Ri Ben Nu Hua Jiao Yu 我在東北淪陷區親歷的日本奴化教育(My Experience with Japanese Slavish Education in the Occupied Northeast Region)".

Taiwanese boys in an anti-Japanese *Shaoniantuan*.

(青島中國少年團) to "remove Chinese boys from harmful influences of Nationalist Party education…and transform them into pioneers of Sino-Japanese friendliness and peace."[1]

Japanese interest in Taiwan had a long history. A Formosan tribal head had reportedly offered "tribute" to a Tokugawa shogun in 1627, when the Dutch had already colonized part of the island.[2] Decades after wresting control of Taiwan from Qing China in 1895, an assimilation movement (*huangminhua yundong* 皇民化運動) ensued, and Taiwan *Syonendan* had also been introduced.[3] Ironically, from 1939 onward, some Taiwanese boys were enrolled in a pro-China Scout-like corps called *Taiwan Shaoniantuan* (臺灣少年團) which had assisted in resisting the Japanese, proving again that teaching boys of a ruled race about patriotism did not always bring the desired result.[4]

Young Formosans in a Japanese assimilation program.

In French Indochina, where Japanese control over the peninsula was secured late in the war, native Vietnamese Scouting was also permitted. Brocheux, a Eurasian French Scout in Saigon, recalled that after Bao Dai was installed as a puppet ruler in 1945, the Japanese would use Vietnamese Boy Scouts to control the French population.[5] British Scouting did not always end with Japanese occupation either. In Shanghai, A.

---

1   "使中國少年階級者脫離國民黨教育之弊害,…而為中日敦睦之先驅." See Wang Xiang-uan 王向远, *Ri Ben Dui Hua Jiao Yu Qin Lue* 日本对华教育侵略 (Japanese Invasion of Chinese Education) (China, 2005), Chapter 28, 4,

2   Paul Kua, *Europe meets Formosa, 1510-1662: Two historical studies* (London: Propius Press, 2023), esp. 108-9,

3   Wang Jin-que 王錦雀, *Tai Wan Gong Min Jiao Yu Yu Gong Min Te Xing* 台灣公民教育與公民特性 (Taiwan's Citizenship Education and Citizenship Characteristics) (Taipei: 台灣古籍出版公司, 2005), 109.

4   Di Yu 翟钰 (ed.), "Tai Wan Wang Shi—Hui Guo Fu Jiang 台湾往事《挥戈复疆》(Taiwan reminiscences)"

5   "*Ils ont pénétré dans les quartiers où habitaient les Français. Au bout de ma rue, ils avaient fait un cordon sanitaire…et un scout vietnamien en faisait partie* (they penetrated the districts where the French lived. At the end of my street, they had made a "sanitary" cordon…and a Vietnamese Scout was part of it)." See "Une adolescence indochinoise," in Nicholas Bancel, et al, *de l'Indochine à l'Algérie*, 46.

H. Gordon negotiated with the Japanese to allow Scouting for boys of various nationalities (presumably excluding Chinese) to continue in early 1942, though they were involved mainly in efforts at self sufficiency through raising vegetables and keeping livestock in the Hungjao Scout camp, rather than in more politically sensitive roles.[1]

The Japanese encouraged schooling in Hong Kong, but passive resistance and evasion among the local Chinese people were prevalent. In early 1943, there were only 3,200 students, compared to 110,000 before the war. The Education Department adopted measures to boost attendance, ranging from providing scholarships to inserting lottery-tickets into textbooks, with little success.[2] The authorities revealed plans to organize a Hong Kong Youth Corps.[3] However, perhaps because of poor responses to schooling, more pressing demands, or an increasingly difficult military situation, Japanese-style Scouting was never introduced, as it had been elsewhere. The former headquarters of the local Scout association was taken over by the Japanese for other purposes, and eventually "stripped of everything," including even the floor itself.[4]

A British Scout badge for service during occupation of the Shanghai International Settlement.

Allied military personnel and non-Chinese civilians were interned. The North Point Camp housed British naval personnel and Canadian soldiers, including the Deep Sea Scouts and Rovers in the navy and perhaps former Scouts from Canada.[5] The Shamshuipo Camp at first housed both British army officers and men, but officers were later transferred to the Argyle Street Camp, and Indians to Ma Tau Chung. While Portuguese, Eurasian and other non-Chinese Volunteers were interned, most Chinese did not enter the camps or were released soon after. Scoutmasters Stewart, Ross, Heywood, Hill and Gittins were all interned and all except Stewart were later transferred to Japan. Some older Scouts who fought as Volunteers, including Denham Crary, Clifford Matthews, Eric Matthews and Joseph Read, all from the 6th Kowloon, were also interned at Shamshuipo and then in Japan.[6] Halward, who was serving

---

1   *The Scouter*, July 1942, 115.
2   Philip Snow, *the Fall of Hong Kong: Britain, China and the Japanese Occupation* (New Haven, Yale Univ. Press, 2003), 174-179.
3   Koji, *Hong Kong under Military Rule*, 283.
4   Letter, Pockson to Butterworth, October 18, 1945, the Gilwell Archives.
5   Some Canadians were transferred to Shamshuipo Camp later, and then, in 1943, to Japan. See Bèrard, *17 Days Until Christmas*, 101-111.
6   The *Steps*, July 1947, 47, 49.

Chinese refugees in Canton when it fell, was interned there.[1] European civilians from Allied countries and some Eurasians and Chinese married to Europeans were interned, initially at the Kowloon Hotel, and then at the Stanley Camp from January 1942.[2] This was the only camp where children were present. Many suffered great deprivations in internment, most were undernourished, and quite a few had died.

Some internees at the Stanley camp, 1945.

PRO 6-2-48.

Scouting continued in some internment camps. J. W. Cockburn, a key player in postwar Hong Kong Scouting, called a Scout troop for British internees in China "the most successful Troop," if success was measured "by the value and worth of Scout training to the boys."[3]

Scout leaders like Champkin, Pockson, Wylie, Fraser and Forster, as well as some Guiders, were interned in Stanley.[4] Both Scouting and Guiding existed inside this camp, though uniforms were not allowed and meetings had to be held in secret.[5] Scout Edward Read and Patrol Leader Ronald Whitfield from 6th Kowloon were both enrolled.[6] After the war, Whitfield went to Scotland and produced proof that he had passed tests in Stanley for his handyman, swimmer, ambulance man, public health man, and missioner badges, "in spite of daily slappings and beatings from the Japanese, of air-raids, of an operation for appendicitis, and of school lessons from Hong Kong University professors." His handyman badge had been well-earned, as he had helped a blacksmith and doctors at the camp hospital, worked as a carpenter's apprentice, and "buried garbage of all kinds."[7] Postwar, he became a King's Scout,

1   The *Kong Yuet Diocesan Echo* 港粵教聲, November 15, 1946, 5.

2   Marsman, *I Escaped from Hong Kong*, 83, 87, 109.

3   The *Scout Bulletin*, No. 5, Sept.-Oct., 1962, 2-3.

4   Report, Muffett to International Relief Service, December 2, 1945, the Gilwell Archives.

5   *Guiding in Hong Kong*, 21-22.

6   The *Steps*, July 1947, 47.

7   Saunders, *Left-hand Shake*, 170-1. It is interesting that Whitfield should lump "lessons from Hong Kong University professors" with "air raids," "daily slappings and

and was recognized by the Chief Scout with a Medal of Meritorious Conduct.[1] Charles and Fred Wong from 1st Kowloon kept a Rover Crew going during their internment.[2] Miss B. M. Moses and Mrs. J. Skinner led Girl Guide meetings while being interned, using a new venue each week. An attendance sheet signed by fifteen Guides in Stanley and dated May 1942 survived the war.[3] Forster, besides supporting Scouting, organized the school and edited *the Church Review*.[4] Jean Gittins, daugther of Sir Robert Ho Tung and wife of Bill Gittins, helped with the school, and claimed that from Guiding she had learned to be resourceful and self-reliant, lessons which had helped her tremendously "throughout internment."[5]

A printed King's Scout Badge, used 1939-45, when materials were scarce.

Author's collection.

Some Scouting activities took place in Macau. In 1943, under constant Japanese pressure to collaborate, Tsun-Nin Chau, a Scout supporter, moved with his family to Macau, a Portuguese colony which remained neutral. His son Cham-son, who was later to play key roles in the postwar movement, had his first taste of Scouting there by joining Troop 531, a Nationalist Chinese Troop registered with Boy Scouts of China.[6] J. A. Ozorio, a Scout from La Salle College, likewise took refuge in Macau. As food was scarce, he and his friends "used scouting skills to survive." They would "take a sampan to Taipa and then swim to Coloane and stay for a week, catching fish and camping." He had also "made a catapult carved with a dragon, and used it to catch birds when they had nothing else to eat."[7]

There were also some courageous acts involving great risks and/ or sacrifices worthy of highest Scouting ideals in these trying times. In December 1941, Sea Scout Wong Kai-chung (黃啟忠) swan out a great distance in the shark-infested Waglan Sea (橫瀾海峽) to save a fisherman who was drowning after his sampan had been sunk by the Japa-

For his gallant act in 1941, Wong Kai-chung received a Silver Cross from Mark Young in 1946.

H. K. Scout Archives.

beatings from the Japanese," and "an operation for appendicitis."

1   The *Steps*, July 1947, 51.
2   The (Scout) *Bulletin*, July-August, 1966, 3.
3   *Guiding in Hong Kong*, 21-22; Moses and Skinner were recognized for Guiding work at Stanley after the war, see *Annual Report, 1945-47* (Hong Kong: the Girl Guides Association,1947), 6.
4   The *Church Review*, Stanley, July 1942, 1, 14; "Educational Work in Stanley Internment Camp," Secretariat 1/179/1946, HKRS 41-1-1157, the Public Records Office, Hong Kong.
5   Gittins, *Eastern Windows—Western Skies*, 39.
6   Interview, Chau Cham-son, April 27, 2010, the Hong Kong Scout Archives.
7   Email, Anne Ozorio to Kua, February 2, 2013, the Hong Kong Scout Archives.

Ride, Lee and two others after their escape to China, 1942.

nese.[1] He was to receive a Silver Cross from Mark Young after the war. Internee Bill Gittins, by then in his mid-forties, was drafted to go to Japan for hard labour, though most others included were much younger. He steadfastly rejected his friends' suggestions that he try to excuse himself on the grounds of his age, as he believed that "if he did not go someone else would have to fill in to make up the number they wanted."[2] At Stanley, there were many incidences of unfairness, private gain, manipulation, and betrayal. However, Wylie was respected and trusted by most, and had chaired the initial Temporary Committee, the Billeting Appeal Tribunal and the Camp Relief Fund.[3] Fraser, who had started the first troop in the New Territories, organized escape plans and a secret wireless service, exchanging important information with the outside world. When arrested, he refused to betray his companions despite prolonged torture, and was finally shot in October 1943. He was awarded a George Cross posthumously in 1946.[4]

Francis Lee Yiu-piu (李耀標), a former Scout from Kowloon, had served in Field Ambulance under Col. Lindsay Ride. Like all Chinese servicemen, he could simply return home after the war. But he chose to follow his commander and was also interned in Shamshuipo. In January 1942, he helped Ride and two British naval officers escape over the hills of Kowloon to Sai Kung where, aided by the East River Column (東江縱隊), they sailed across Dapeng Bay (大鵬灣) and trekked overland to Huizhou (惠州) in Free China. Ride then organized the British Army Aid Group (BAAG), under which Lee soon returned to Hong Kong for secret missions, was arrested and tortured (but not identified) by the Kempatei, escaped again and came back months later to set up liaison posts. Ride's son Edwin confirms that "Francis...played an outstanding part not only in Ride's escape from Shamshuipo but in the establishment and operation of the BAAG in which he rose to the rank of captain."[5] For his "courage and devotion to duty of the highest order...knowing full well that his recognition by the Japanese would mean certain death," Lee

The BAAG logo.

1   *CM*, August 17, 1946; *KSYP*, August 17, 1946.

2   Gittins, *Stanley: Behind Barbed Wire*, 152.

3   John Streicker, *Captive Colony: The Story of Stanley Camp, Hong Kong* (S.l.: s.n., 1945), typed manuscript, the Hong Kong Univ. Library. Ch. IV, 1; Ch. V, 17.

4   *3rd Supplement to the London Gazette*, Issue 37771, October 25, 1946, 1.

5   Edwin Ride, *BAAG: Hong Kong Resistance, 1942-45* (Hong Kong, Oxford Univ. Press, 1981), ch. 1; David Bellis, Lawrence Tsui, et al "Francis Yiu-piu LEE," https://gwulo.com/node/17846 (accessed April 2, 2024).

was awarded the Military Medal and a military MBE after the war.[1]

Both Quah and Henry Ma also joined BAAG in China. Ma became a security agent in Kweilin in August 1942, was transferred to Macau and then to Kwangchowan as a field agent in 1943.[2] Quah trained Hong Kong escapees in India and then served in the "Chindits" in Burma under British Brig. Gen. Wingate.[3] Quah, Ma and other Scouts who fought for Hong Kong were awarded British WWII Stars (incl. the Pacific Star), Defence Medal and War Medal. Tse Ping-fui was an interpreter with the American air force and later in intelligence in Guangdong.[4]

James Dudley, former Patrol Leader of 6th Hong Kong, had served in the Royal Air Force in North Africa and had died in Libya in 1942. He was awarded the Distinguished Flying Cross.[5] According to Col. (later General) Robert L. Scott, who commanded the Flying Tigers, a common denominator of his squadron commanders was that "they were all Boy Scouts."[6] Scott himself was an Eagle Scout from Troop 23 in the state of Georgia, and had won the first Boy Scout Aviation merit badge from that part of the country. In October 1942, he did his best as a true Scout would, when he led a team of seven P-40s which escorted ten bombers in the first Allied bombing of occupied Hong Kong, and personally shot down four Japanese Zeros and Messerschmitts.[7]

Many Scouts survived war and occupation and went on to better lives. Maurice Sully trekked through enemy territory to reach Chungking.[8] Henry Ma and Matthew Young went to Kwangsi and then Chungking. Ho Hak Hoy stayed in Swatow. Marcus Ng lived in his village in Toishan. Young Yuen Chow and Hung Mun Chiu joined the Chinese Air Force and later became head of weather stations in airfields in China. Jimmy Wong became a pilot in China.[9] Ross survived Shamshuipo

The George Cross.

The WWII Pacific Star.

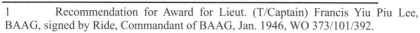

1   Recommendation for Award for Lieut. (T/Captain) Francis Yiu Piu Lee, BAAG, signed by Ride, Commandant of BAAG, Jan. 1946, WO 373/101/392.

2   Stewart, *Hong Kong Volunteers in Battle*, 93; folder, Henry Ma Papers, the Hong Kong Scout Archives.

3   *SCMP*, August 27, 1965.

4   Vincent H. Y. Fung (ed.), *From Devotion to Plurality: A Full History of St. Paul's College, 1851-2001* (Hong Kong: St. Paul's College, c2002).

5   *The Steps*, December 1935; July 1948.

6   Townley, *Legacy of Honor*, 27.

7   Robert L. Scott, Jr., *God is My Co-Pilot* (Garden City: Blue Ribbon Books, 1943), 2, 221-233.

8   *The Steps*, July 1947, 49.

9   Folder, Henry Ma Papers, the Hong Kong Scout Archives.

A tombstone in Stanley for an unnamed soldier who died on Dec. 24, 1941 Words at the bottom: "KNOWN UNTO GOD".

and Japan, and had a successful business career after the war. Clifford Matthews later became a professor in America until he retired in early 1990s.[1] Oxonian Heywood became Director of Royal Observatory between 1946-55 and stayed active in Scouting in Hong Kong and after his return to England, receiving a Silver Acorn in 1969.[2] Postwar, Quah, Ross and Ma would, respectively, become the first Chinese commissioner, its longest-serving president, and the commissioner who oversaw Hong Kong's transition to an independent Scout association.

But many Scouts had died in the war. A full list is not available, given the postwar chaos, large number of unidentified bodies, lack of information during occupation, and the fact that many returned to China to fates unknown. Lim Kim Huan, John Yew Mun Chong, Francis Seang Teik Lim, Enrique Lee, Yeung Man On, Donald James Anderson, James Dudley, William Minto Gittins, John Alexander Fraser, Arthur Ernest Job, Robert Ashton Hill, Leung Xiu Yuen, Henry Wong, David Lee, Chiu Kam Lam, E. D. Fisher, E. Rapley, and Preston Wong Shiu-pun, among others, paid the ultimate price.[3] Anderson, the two Lims, Chong (Chung), Fisher, and Job appear in the official list of Volunteers "killed in action or died of wounds."[4] Anderson, who died in battle, and Preston Wong and Fraser, who served with the BAAG and were executed by the Japanese, were buried in Stanley.[5] The two Lims and Job were buried in Saiwan. Hill and Gittins, who died in Japan, are listed as Volunteers who "died whilst prisoner of war," and were buried in Yokohama.[6] Many more were not even remembered by name, still less by a marked grave. This long list of names, albeit incomplete, suggests that the community's faith in this small youth movement had not been misplaced.

Concluding remarks

"To rule" continued to be the dominant motive for the expansion of Scouting among Chinese boys in Hong Kong until the late 1930s. Mean-

---

1 Matthews, "Life Experiences," 227.
2 Heywood, *It Won't be Long Now*, 21-32. BA, BSc. and MA from Oxford.
3 The *Hong Kong Scouting Gazette*, Feb. 1946, 2-3; the *Steps*, July 1947, 42, 50.
4 Stewart, *Hong Kong Volunteers in Battle*, 87-88.
5 Edwin Ride, *BAAG: Hong Kong Resistance, 1942-1945* (Hong Kong: Hong Kong Univ. Press, 1981), 331-332.
6 Stewart, *Hong Kong Volunteers in Battle*, 90.

while, Chinese nationalism was discouraged owing to fears that local Scouting might become politicized, partly through emphasizing the movement's non-political ideals. The increasingly indigenized movement navigated carefully between a vague patriotism for China and a politicized Chinese nationalism. The Fourth Law on brotherhood of all Scouts, problematic in a colonial context, was useful in countering the more extreme forms of nationalistic expressions. From the late 1920s to the 1930s, unlike in many parts of China, Chinese schoolboys in Hong Kong were not involved in any major strikes, boycotts or uprisings.

Citizenship training by way of Scouting had taken on an entirely different meaning by 1937, when "to fight" became the over-riding motive for expanding the organization. As the colony geared up for war, a lot more boys were needed for its defense, and dual loyalty became increasingly acceptable. Rapid growth of both formal Scouting and unregistered Chinese Scouting occurred in the late 1930s, and more than compensated for the loss of ethnic British boys who were evacuated. Troops were started in numerous schools, including many Chinese vernacular and rural ones, some only recently relocated to the colony. Many Scouts served in various capacities in the brief Battle for Hong Kong, in the front-line or elsewhere, and their performance appeared to vindicate the value of citizenship training through Scouting. After the fall, all were prevented from overt participation in the movement in occupied Hong Kong, though Scouting persisted clandestinely for a small number of non-Chinese in the context of the internment camp.

By end of 1941, just before the war, Hong Kong Scouting had acquired substantial Chinese "ethnicity," or characteristics closely attuned to the Chinese majority, and "embeddedness," or penetration of the Chinese youth population. It had, in effect, become an "indigenized" youth movement, through gaining both Chinese participation and a form of "Chineseness" particular to Hong Kong, as expressed in practices such as the adapted Chinese Scout Promise, presence of both Chinese and British national symbols in gatherings, predominance of Chinese boys and leaders, prominence of Chinese troops in competitions and rallies, tolerance of dual registrations, and rapidly growing levels of local participation across different school types both urban and rural.

Chapter 4

Reconstruction and Reaching Out

1945-1964

Chapter 4
Reconstruction and Reaching Out
1945-1964

Japan announced its surrender on August 15, 1945, shortly after the nuclear bombs "Little Boy" and "Fat Man" were dropped on Hiroshima and Nagasaki, respectively, devastating these cities and killing hundreds of thousands. The *SCMP* printed on August 30 an official announcement of the arrival of Rear Admiral Cecil H. J. Harcourt and his fleet to take over the territory, the first communiqué from the Hong Kong Government since December 1941.[1] Hong Kong was formally restored as a British colony when military administration under Harcourt was proclaimed on September 1.[2] The Pacific war had caused tremendous losses in Asia and enormous suffering among Asian people. But the Japanese challenge to white supremacy and rhetoric of "an Asia for Asians" had also resulted in a changed mentality among the ruling and the ruled races. Nationalist movements grew and demands for local representation in many Asian colonies followed. Hong Kong Scouting and the colonial community were not immune to these developments.[3]

When Sir Mark Young was reinstated as governor of Hong Kong in May 1946, the most pressing priority was reconstruction of all aspects of colonial life, including Scouting, which was quickly re-launched in its pro-China form. When Sir Alexander Grantham took over as governor in July 1947, he initially continued to tolerate dual loyalty and even experimented with Chinese leadership in the Scout Movement. However, the founding of the PRC in 1949 elicited major shifts in policy. In the interest of stable governance and buttressed by economic prosperity, constitu-

Previous page:

Hong Kong Scouts on the way to the Botanical Garden for the first postwar parade in April 1946, attracting a crowd of young onlookers.

Official Photograph, U. S. Navy.

---

1   *SCMP*, August 30, 1945.
2   Endacott, *Hong Kong Eclipse*, 232-233, 261.
3   Joyce C. Lebra, "the Significance of the Japanese Military Model for Southeast Asia," in Wolf Mendl, *Japan and South East Asia: Vol. 1, From the Meiji Restoration to 1945* (London: Routledge, 2001), 256-269.

tional development was indefinitely postponed. Education and Scouting alike went through a gradual process of denationalization, while efforts were made to break down class divides to reach out to many underprivileged youngsters. These policies were continued by Sir Robert Black, who became governor in January 1958 and stayed till early 1964. By this time, with extensive penetration within the Chinese middle class and significant breakthroughs beyond it, Hong Kong Scouting could finally lay claim to being a mass movement with a broadly-based membership which was representative of the postwar colonial community.

Revival of nationalistic Scouting

Sir Mark Young.
PRO 7-3-66.

In late 1945, soon after the British reoccupied Hong Kong, Scouting was revived and resumed its late interwar form as an indigenized movement with a strong pro-Nationalist Chinese orientation. Most of the troops in the restarted movement were from elite or vernacular schools. Some of these were registered also (or solely) with the Scout authorities in China. Indeed, the influence of the Nationalist-dominated ROC was even stronger than it had been in the late 1930s. In these early postwar years, the colonial government again found it politically expedient to condone, if not encourage, dual loyalty to Britain and China in the contested space of citizenship training through Scouting.

Upon resuming control of Hong Kong, the British took a generally tolerant attitude towards Japanese "quislings" and collaborators, in view of the apparent British authorization to cooperate just after the fall, the large number of Chinese community leaders involved, and the pragmatic need for continued cooperation from the Chinese. This attitude largely reflected that of the community: there was apparently little resentment towards the two Chinese councils formed during Japanese occupation, suggesting that most Chinese understood that their leaders had no choice but to cooperate. As John Carroll suggests, in the final analysis, when the Chinese bourgeoisie in Hong Kong collaborated (with the British colonists or the Japanese occupiers), "they were acting not simply out of economic interest but out of a need to preserve *their* Hong Kong in a turbulent era," an approach which often also benefited the lo-

Sir Tsun-nin Chau.

Chau Cham-son's collection.

cal populace in general.[1] These were, to some extent, win-win arrangements for all.

Sir Robert Kotewall, former president of the association, was the leading "Chinese" who collaborated with the Japanese regime. North, by this time the colonial secretary, defended Kotewall as having acted under authorization and in the interest of the local community. In the end, Kotewall, though not tried for his actions during the occupation, was considered to have been "guilty of an error of judgment" and had to withdraw completely from public life.[2] On the other hand, Tsun-nin Chau (周埈年), former vice-president and treasurer of the Boy Scouts Association, was probably the only ranking Chinese "to have entirely clean hands," as he had slipped away to Macau after the Japanese arrived.[3] Chau continued to serve the community in the postwar era, and remained a vice president of the association in this period. He became the senior Chinese unofficial member of the Executive Council in 1953, and was knighted in 1956.

The experience of wartime occupation and the emergence of China as one of the five victorious powers at the end of the war prompted a shift in the mindset of the rulers and the ruled alike. Tolerance of Chinese nationalism and dual loyalty persisted, as well as calls for a larger official role for the Hong Kong Chinese. As Franklin D. Roosevelt and Chiang Kai-shek had wanted to restore Hong Kong to China and even the Colonial Office had admitted that retrocession might form part of a postwar settlement, British authorities doubtless considered themselves fortunate to have recovered the colony.[4]

Chinese Nationalism was riding high. Chiang, allied commander-in-chief of the China Theatre (which included Hong Kong), had initially opposed the British proposal to receive the Japanese surrender. A diplomatic impasse was only resolved after Harcourt agreed to sign the Instrument of Surrender twice, once on behalf of Chiang. The victory parade in September 1945 featured the Union Jack and the Nationalist Chinese flag. Sir Man-Kam Lo appealed for a government that would

1   Carroll, *Edge of Empires*, 188.
2   "Sir Robert Kotewall, 1945," CO 968/120/1, the National Archives, London.
3   Ibid.
4   Wm. Roger Louis, "Hong Kong: the Critical Phase, 1945-1949," *The American Historical Review*, 102/4, Oct., 1997, 1052-1084; John M. Carroll, *A Concise History of Hong Kong* (Hong Kong: Hong Kong Univ. Press, 2007), 126-129.

uphold "the interests of the Colony as a whole and not those of any particular section of the community."[1] Harcourt felt that Europeans needed to adopt "a 1946 outlook," "imbued with a spirit of national pride in China," and that the "colour bar problem" should be addressed by putting "Chinese in positions of responsibility."[2]

Soon after Young took over, he proposed the "Young Plan," aimed at giving Hong Kong a measure of democracy with an elected municipal council. The Nationalist Chinese government was also allowed to appoint a special commissioner for Hong Kong. Though Grantham effectively delayed and finally jettisoned the Young plan, he understood the need for more prominent roles for the Chinese. To him, "the mental arrogance on the part of some Europeans towards Asians" had resulted in "as much, if not more resentment than... the establishment of colonies and territoriality."[3]

from D.A. Pockson, Esq. Asst Colony Comr. Hong Kong & Hong

H.Q. ASA. H.K.

1 - NOV 1945

No. 17773

Arms Office, Central Police Station Hong Kong.

18. 10. 45.

Dear Mr Buttemont,

My last letter to you was written on Dec. 7th. 1941 but war broke out here during the night & it was never posted. Both my home and also our Headqrs. were taken over by the Japanese a few weeks later & when I returned to Hong Kong from Stanley last month I found both places stripped of everything – Headqrs. had also had the floor removed! I'm afraid all our records are gone but we are fortunate in having many of our Scouters still here and have already, with the help of the

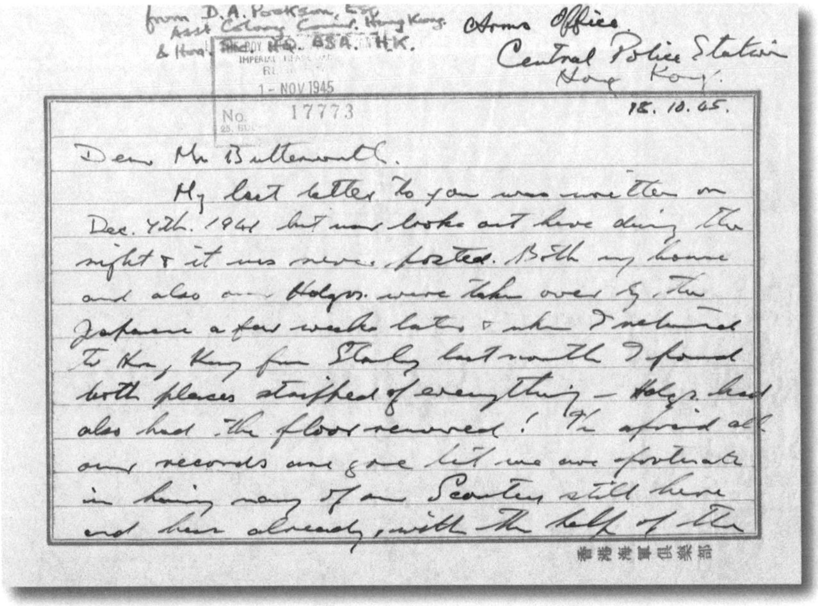

Pockson's report on Hong Kong Scouting, Oct. 1945.

Gilwell Archives.

Scouting activities restarted soon after the British regained control, despite the absence of most senior Scout leaders. Key players like Champkin, Heywood, and Mrs. Booker had all gone home. Pockson, who had filed the first postwar report to Britain on Hong Kong Scouting, was the only expatriate leader who attended the first two gatherings called in late 1945. But he was preoccupied with police work, and de-

1 Welsh, *A Borrowed Place*, 434.
2 Horne, *Race War*, 283.
3 Ibid.

parted in April 1946.[1] Halward, the pre-war commissioner, was at a third meeting held in October, though he also left for America and Britain in December. Quah, a pre-war District Commissioner, came back from China and was promptly appointed the acting Deputy Colony Commissioner, and John Pau, an acting District Commissioner.[2]

Among the earliest groups to be re-established were the 13th Hong Kong (Central Chinese), the 7th Hong Kong (King's College) and the 16th Hong Kong (St. Louis School), all revived in late 1945. By February 1946, thirteen groups, mostly Chinese, were reactivated. By September, twenty-two troops were registered, including those of the elite schools like St. Joseph's, St. Paul's, Queen's, Wah Yan, and La Salle; churches like the Catholic Cathedral, St. Margaret's, Christ, and Rosary; but also Chinese schools like Tak Ming, Pui Ying, King Sun, and Fong Lam.[3] Almost all these had Chinese or at least mixed membership. In December, one thousand Scouts gathered at the La Salle College in a grand campfire to welcome back Halward, who had just returned from Britain, where he was consecrated as an assistant Bishop.[4]

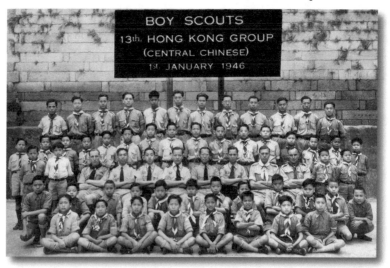

Members of 13th Hong Kong, mostly without any Scout badge, 1946.

Gilwell Archives.

Facilities and materials were in short supply in the immediate postwar years. The 7th Hong Kong met at a Wanchai school, as King's College had been completely demolished. The St. Joseph's boys met at

---

1   Letter, Pockson to Butterworth, October 18, 1945, the Gilwell Archives.

2   Reports, Muffet to International Relief Service, December 2 and 15, 1945, the Gilwell Archives.

3   The *Hong Kong Scouting Gazette*, April 1947, 4.

4   *CM*, December 9, 1946.

their Scoutmasters' homes, as the college had not re-opened. The 21st Kowloon met at the Chinese YMCA on the Island, as their headquarters in Kowloon was yet to be de-requisitioned. Two Tak Ming groups met at the Kowloon school as the Island branch was not yet revived.[1] The 10th Hong Kong "struggled cheerily with practically no training equipment."[2] The first formal meeting of the Rovers of the 17th Kowloon (La Salle) in April 1946 took place at the Kadoorie School, as La Salle's premises, requisitioned since the war started, were not returned until the summer. The Sea Scouts appeared in khaki instead of white as the latter could not be purchased cheaply. No Scout badge was available in the beginning. Later on, when the Hong Kong Badge was re-introduced, it was a printed version which faded easily, and then a rather coarse hand-embroidered version, each slightly different from the others. The *Scouting Gazette* revived in January 1946 was a modest publication. There was one exception. At the investiture of the St. Louis School troop, all Scouts were in full uniforms: a priest at the school, a national of a neutral country, was not interned, and had hidden all the uniforms and equipment in his room throughout the Japanese occupation.[3]

An early postwar hand-embroidered Hong Kong Scout Badge.

Author's collection.

Members of 15th Hong Kong (Wah Yan), wearing only the Tenderfoot Badge and no H.K. Badge, 1947.

William Kwan's collection.

Some help came from Scouters in the military and the Scout International Relief Service. The latter was formed in Britain in 1942 to provide services to civilians after the war. Following a request from Hong Kong, Team VIII, consisting of five Scouters led by L. A. Muffet, was withdrawn from Germany and sent to the colony from November

1   The *Hong Kong Scouting Gazette*, January 1946, 9; February 1946, 4.
2   Tse Ping Fui, "The College Scout Troop," the *Wayfarer*, 1957-58, 59.
3   *Scouts International Relief Service: A Record of Work Done, 1944-1946* (London: Reprinted from Jamboree, 1946), 6; the *Piokelde Post,* February 1946, 5-6.

An early postwar machine-stitched Hong Kong Scout Badge.

Yau Yu Kai's collection.

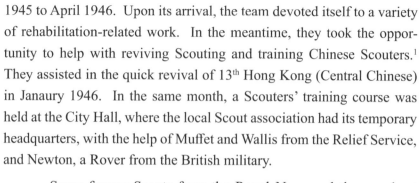

1945 to April 1946. Upon its arrival, the team devoted itself to a variety of rehabilitation-related work. In the meantime, they took the opportunity to help with reviving Scouting and training Chinese Scouters.[1] They assisted in the quick revival of 13th Hong Kong (Central Chinese) in Janaury 1946. In the same month, a Scouters' training course was held at the City Hall, where the local Scout association had its temporary headquarters, with the help of Muffet and Wallis from the Relief Service, and Newton, a Rover from the British military.

Some former Scouts from the Royal Navy and the merchant service revived the China Fleet Deep Sea Scouts.[2] In October 1945, the Deep Sea Scouts from HMS *Pioneer* and HMS *Kelantan* had outings with local Scouts, from which "lasting friendship with our Chinese Brother Scouts" grew.[3] Soon more signed up as Rovers, including many from the army and the Royal Air Force, making this a joint-service venture. They celebrated their first peacetime Christmas since 1941 by inviting twenty-five needy Chinese boys as guests, selected from among those considered "*ho pang yow* (Cantonese Romanization of 好朋友, or good friends)" of the crew.[4] At the opening of the crew's den in February, "the Union Jack was…unfurled and the British National Anthem sung," as would be expected. However, reflecting local sentiments of the day, immediately after this, "two young Chinese boys sang the Chinese National Anthem."[5] The Rovers, in line with tradition, quickly got involved in service projects, including the Scouters' training course already mentioned, regular visits to the Central Chinese troop, a building job at the King's Park orphanage, and running a boys' club at the Chinese YMCA.[6]

Chinese nationalism and dual loyalty were tolerated and quite visible in Scouting. In February 1946, the *Scouting Gazette* featured an article on the history of the Chinese national flag.[7] In April, six hundred

A hand-embroidered Services Crew Badge.

Roger Yu's collection.

---

1   Reports, Muffet to the International Relief Service, December 2 and 15, 1945, the Gilwell Archives; the *Hong Kong Scouting Gazette*, January 1946, 7.
2   The *Piokelde Post*, May 1946, 8.
3   A. J. Clarke, "History of the 1st HMS Kelantan Deep-Sea Rover Scout Crew: First Outing with 'Pioneer' and Hong Kong Scouters ," http://www.scrich.co.uk/deepsea/index.html (access March 10, 2008).
4   The *Piokelde Post*, June and July, 1946, 4-5.
5   Clarke, "History of the 1st HMS Kelantan Deep-Sea Rover Scout Crew..."
6   The *Piokelde Post*, April, 1946, 2; June and July, 1946, 5-6.
7   The *Hong Kong Scouting Gazette*, February 1946, 6 (Chinese).

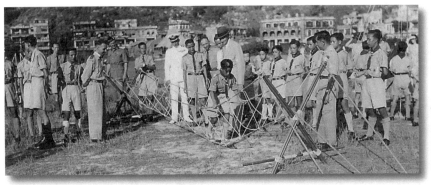

Young reviewed a display at the rally in August 1946.

H. K. Scout Archives.

Scouts turned out in the first postwar parade at the Botanical Garden, in the presence of General Festing, accompanied by Quah. As the Boy Scouts marched past the streets on their way to the parade, they attracted the attention of many curious on-lookers, including many youngsters who had not seen Boy Scouts for almost four years, when Hong Kong was under Japanese occupation. The St. Louis School's band played the national anthem as the "national flags" (both the British and the Chinese ones) were hoisted.[1] The Cub Promise and the Scout Promise were both repeated in English *and* Chinese.

In August 1946, Young met eight hundred Hong Kong Scouts in Causeway Bay, a belated welcome for him, as he had not met them officially in 1941, and "the Chinese and the British flags [were] raised immediately after [his arrival] (中英國旗隨之上升)."[2] As already noted in the last chapter, he also presented a Silver Cross to Wong Kai-chung during this gathering.

The Scout Promise in Chinese still took its prewar compromised form, requiring loyalty to "the nation" instead of "the King," but without specifying whether this meant Britain or China.[3] A troop document on the requirements for the Tenderfoot Badge specified that a boy should learn about "the Union Jack," or, for Chinese boys, "the Chinese National flag."[4] In April 1947, Young attended the St. George's Day parade (which was both his first and last), when national anthems of both China and Britain were played as the two national flags were being hoisted.[5]

一到，港督蒞場，童軍界理副總監柯照章出場歡迎，中英國旗隨之上升，小狼團即

The British and Chinese flags welcomed Young to the rally in August 1946.

KSYP, Aug. 17, 1946.

1   *CM*, April 29, 1946.
2   *KSYP*, August 17, 1946.
3   Circular, questions and answers during an investiture, 1946, the Hong Kong Scout Archives.
4   Circular, the Tenderfoot test, 18th April 1946, the Hong Kong Scout Archives.
5   *CM*, April 15, 1947; *KSYP*, April 18, 1947, April 20, 1947.

A soft drink advertisement depicting a Chinese Girl Scout and a small Chinese Nationalist Flag, 1948.

H. K. Scouting Gazette, 1948.

The indigenized nature of local Scouting was quite evident. In the same year, five Chinese boys from 13th Hong Kong became King's Scouts.[1] In a 1948 issue of the *Hong Kong Scouting Gazette*, an advertisement of a soft drink tellingly featured a Chinese Girl Scout and only the Chinese national flag in the distant background.[2] In April 1949, Grantham and Arthur Morse, chief manager of Hong Kong and Shanghai Bank and new president of the association, inspected 1,500 Scouts at a parade. Again, as in other early postwar rallies, "all scouts were called to the 'alert' as the Chinese and British flags were hoisted."[3]

The Nationalist influence in Scouting went beyond the symbolic level and extended to administrative structure and training. Chinese Nationalist Boy Scout training materials were used in some Hong Kong schools. The Kai Ming bookstore advertised in a school brochure in 1946 for a Scout textbook from China entitled *Beginning course for Boy Scouts* (童子軍初級課程), available from its outlet on Nathan Road.[4] In September 1946, at a meeting of principals of the overseas Chinese schools in the colony, it was agreed that a China-linked Scout council for Hong Kong would be set up.[5] Shi An-fu (施安甫), the Hong Kong and

Arthur Morse.

---

1   The *Hong Kong Scouting Gazette*, August 1947, 7. They were Li Sze Pok, Yuen Pak Ying, Leung Yu Tung, Chan Chok Leung, and Sin Ka Yin.
2   The *Hong Kong Scouting Gazette*, no. 3, 1948, 25.
3   *HKSH*, April 24, 1949.
4   The *Hong Kong Scouting Gazette*, 3rd issue,1949, inside cover page.
5   *Gang Jiu Qiao Xiao Shi Lue* 港九僑校史畧(Brief Histories of the Overseas Chinese Schools in Hong Kong and Kowloon, in Chinese) (Hong Kong, 1946), 42. "童

Kowloon Chinese Boy Scouts Liaison Commissioner (港九中國童子軍聯絡專員) from the ROC, visited in December 1947. On this occasion, a conference for all leaders was held to discuss overseas Scouting and elect members to the "Committee for the General Registration of China's Overseas Boy Scout Leaders Resident in Hong Kong (中國童子軍僑港服務員總報到委員會)." In January 1948, Scouters were asked to report to Ling Dao Middle School (領島中學) or Tak Ming Middle School (德明中學), where "current Scout Leaders in Hong Kong's Overseas Chinese schools" should register.[1] In May, a national conference of the Boy Scouts of China was held in Nanjing, and the association's constitution was amended to allow for overseas subsidiary branches. In the meeting, it was noted that Macau had already set up such a branch, and Hong Kong would soon also organize one.[2]

By the late 1940s, there were apparently many pro-Nationalist Scout troops which belonged to both the Boy Scouts Association of Hong Kong and the Boy Scouts of China. In May 1949, boys of the Chinese Boy Scout Troops from Chung Hwa (中華), Tak Ming (德明), Chun Wan (振寰), Ling Tung (嶺東), Suen Nam (選南), Yuet Nam (粵南), Hing Yan (興仁), and Ying Choi (英才) participated in two colonial Scout competitions.[3] As these schools had maintained dual registrations with both the Hong Kong and one or more of the Chinese educational authorities, their troops, besides being registered locally, would also have to be registered with the Boy Scouts of China.

Though dual loyalty and Chinese nationalism were generally accepted, it soon became apparent that the association was somewhat less tolerant of troops which were perceived to lean too much towards China, including some which were not registered in Hong Kong at all. In 1946, for example, Nam Wah Middle School (南華附中) started a troop which did not appear on the local association's list of troops, and had Boy Scouts sporting American-style Chinese Scout uniforms instead of British-style Hong Kong uniforms.[4] Rev. Canon Sorby-Adams, the commissioner of Singapore, identified a similar problem there, and re-

Registration of Chinese Troops in Hong Kong with Boy Scouts of China, 1946.

KSYP, Jan. 9, 1948.

軍訓練方面與中央童軍理事會取得聯絡後, 設港九童軍理事會."

1   *KSYP*, January 9, 1948.
2   *KSYP*, May 24 and 30, 1948.
3   *KSYP*, May 5 and 29, 1949.
4   *Nam Hua Fu Zhong Te Kan* 南華附中特刊 (Magazine of the Nam Wah Middle School) (Hong Kong, 1946), 4, 13.

marked in 1947 upon the "politically sponsored Chinese bodies aping the BP Movement."[1] To coax these troops to sign up locally, the Singapore association offered various privileges and the use of its facilities. The Hong Kong association also strove to "convert" these unofficial troops into official ones, often by relying on the force of law. In October 1946, it announced in the Chinese press that, based on a local ordinance (i.e., the Boy Scouts Association Ordinance), any organization wanting to form a troop in Hong Kong must obtain registration from the local Scout association.[2] In January 1948, the Director of Education informed all schools that any Scout Group must be officially registered in Hong Kong, and that unregistered ones would be dealt with severely.

At times, local leaders also took steps to discourage what was seen as an "excessive" identification with the Boy Scouts of China. In April 1947, Halward chaired a Scouters' meeting in Kowloon and argued for an hour with leaders of some (pro-Nationalist) Chinese troops on the point that Scout members registered with both the Chinese and the Hong Kong associations should not wear any Chinese Scout badge except for one (presumably the Chinese Scout association or group identification badge). He also went on to criticize compulsory membership in China.[3] Objections regarding the non-voluntary nature of Chinese Scouting were not new. But Halward failed to explain the link between these objections and his insistence that Chinese Scout badges earned should not be worn. After all, boys had enrolled in the dual-registered Chinese troops in Hong Kong voluntarily, just like boys in all the other local troops, and had presumably gained these Chinese badges by passing their requisite tests. Outward displays of dual loyalty, though accepted given the prevailing political realities in the colony, clearly had their limits.

Chinese leadership on a trial basis

From 1950 to 1954, in the spirit of the "1946 outlook," two senior Chinese Scouters were appointed in quick succession as the top leaders of local Scouting, in a colony which had up to then generally preferred

---

1   Tan and Wan, *Scouting in Singapore*, 107.
2   *KSYP*, October 15, 1946. "凡在香港九龍及新界各學校及社團等, 欲組織童軍團者, 必須向香港童軍總會接洽, 正式登記, 以符法規."
3   Minutes, Kowloon Scouters meeting, 1948, the Hong Kong Scout Archives.

expatriate leadership. Considerable progress was made in the move-
ment under Quah, the first Chinese commissioner and, to a lesser extent,
under his successor Luke. Yet, in 1954, this policy of localization at the
top was reversed. A Briton was again appointed to the highest position
in Hong Kong Scouting, which did not see another Chinese at the helm
until a decade later.

In the interwar years, an increasing number of Chinese boys had joined the movement, but the top leadership remained European. Conventionally, aside from the Chief Scout (primarily a symbolic position, invariably filled by the governor), leaders were classified into "lay supporters" headed by the president, and "uniformed leaders" led by the commissioner. Out of the four presidents, Holyoak, Kotewall, Cock, and Sollis, only Kotewall, appointed right after the 1926 strike and boycott, when goodwill among the Chinese was perceived as essential, could be considered a "Chinese" (though he was Eurasian), as he did represent the Chinese community. The Colony Commissioners, arguably the most important leaders besides the Chief Scouts, were Bowen, Waldegrave, and Halward. The Deputy Commissioner for a long time was Champkin. Assistant Commissioners were Champkin, Christian, Sweet, Pockson, Booker, Grad, Halward and Heywood. The most "junior" commissioners were the District Commissioners. Even these leaders were all Europeans, namely Armstrong, Sweet, and Dormer, until Quah was appointed in 1937 and Chan in 1940.

However, in the immediate postwar years, as the pressure for more substantial Chinese representation grew and given the paucity of European leaders, fundamental changes in leadership started to occur. While Morse became the president, and Halward returned as the commissioner, Quah became the first Chinese Deputy Colony Commissioner in 1946. From 1946 to 1950, Quah often acted on behalf of Halward, whose many missionary responsibilities in Southern China meant that he was rarely available in Hong Kong.[1]

By 1950, Quah was for all intents and purposes the *de facto* commissioner. A few examples may illustrate this development. Morse

F. E. C. C. Quah.
Steven Quah's collection.

1   The *Kong Yuet Diocesan Echo* 港粵教聲, November 15, 1946, 5; February 15, 1947, 8; March 15, 1947, 12; June 15, 1947, 4; July 15, 1947, 4.

A Scout wedding: J. A.
Ozorio, July 1950.

H. K. Scout Archives.

and Quah officiated at a bazaar in January to raise funds for a new association headquarters.[1] Quah opened a district camp in early April and was the commissioner-in-charge in the St. George's Day rally at the Botanical Garden, in the presence of Grantham.[2] Morse and Quah were also present when Grantham conferred King's Scout certificates in June upon twelve Scouts, among whom there were eleven Chinese.[3]

In July, Quah attended three events: a farewell party for Lieutenant Beaglehole, member of the Services Rover Crew, the wedding of District Scoutmaster J. A. Ozorio (Bino) and his wife Pat, with La Salle Scouts forming a key part of the wedding party, and the funeral for Patrol Second Joseph Yue Chung-kwong (余仲光).[4] Yue, a member of 15th Hong Kong (Wah Yan), persevered with Scouting despite a long duration of illness and hospitalization, and received the first posthumous award of the Cornwell Scout Badge in Hong Kong. Besides Quah, Scoutmasters Chau Cham-lam and Chau Cham-son were both present, and Scouts from Wah Yan and St. Joseph's were the pall bearers. Halward was absent from all these events and, in fact, had decided that since he could no longer visit Hong Kong regularly, he should resign.[5]

It is not known whether Halward was inspired by Bishop R. O. Hall's example to recommend Quah as his successor. Hall was a great supporter of Chinese causes and had ordained the first woman, Florence

1   *KSYP*, January 10, 1950, January 29.
2   *CM*, April 7, 1950; *KSYP*, April 4 and 8, 1950; *SH*, April 23, 1950.
3   *CM*, June 2, 1950.
4   *CM*, July 7, 1950, August 4, 1950, August 7, 1950; Logbook, C. C. Quah, 1950s, the Hong Kong Scout Archives.
5   The *Hong Kong Scouting Gazette*, no.1, 1951, 2, 36.

Li Tim-oi, to the priesthood in the Anglican Church in 1945, albeit in the unusual circumstances of war.[1] At any rate, sensitive to Chinese expectations in the postwar community, Grantham agreed to the recommendation. In August 1950, Rowallan, the Chief Scout of Commonwealth and Empire, approved Quah's appointment as the Colony Commissioner, making him the first Chinese to assume the post.[2] This move was in line with the fault lines of political change of the time. In 1946, the Peak ordinances were repealed, allowing wealthy Chinese to reside on the Peak if they so desired. In the same year, Young declared that locally recruited persons would be given opportunities "to rise in the service of the public up to the highest posts and to fulfill the highest responsibilities of which they are capable or can be assisted to become capable."[3]

A Cornwell Scout Badge.
Author's collection.

A Scout funeral: J. Yue, Hong Kong's first Cornwell Scout, July 1950.

H. K. Scout Archives.

If Hong Kong Scouting was to have a Chinese leader, Quah appeared to be an ideal choice, from both the perspective of the movement and that of the colonial authorities. He had joined Scouting in the 1920s as a Wolf Cub and then a Boy Scout at the St. Xavier's Institution in Penang. When he came to Hong Kong in the 1930s as a teacher at St. Joseph's College, he immediately became involved in local Scouting. Since then, he had served as a Scoutmaster, the first Chinese District Commissioner, and the first Chinese Deputy Colony Commissioner. Significantly, he had also demonstrated his loyalty to Britain and the

---

1   Ian T. Douglas and Pui-lan Kwok, *Beyond Colonial Anglicanism: the Anglican Communion in the Twenty-first Century* (New York: Church Publications, c2001), 59.

2   *KSYP*, November 22, 1950. The 2nd Baron Rowallan (Thomas Corbett) was the Chief Scout of the British Commonwealth and Empire from 1945 to 1959.

3   Quoted in Lau Siu-kai, *Society and Politics in Hong Kong* (Hong Kong: Chinese Univ. Press, 1984), 52.

colony, having fought and been injured in the battle for Hong Kong as a Volunteer, and having been involved with resistance and intelligence efforts led by the BAAG in China during the Japanese occupation.[1] As a gesture in recognition of his war contributions, he was chosen to represent the Royal Hong Kong Defence Force at the coronation parade in England in 1953.[2]

In a sense, Quah was an example of the successful localization of Hong Kong Scouting, just as Paul Tsui Ka-cheung (徐家祥), an early senior Chinese civil servant, was an example of the successful localization of the administrative service in colonial Hong Kong.[3] Yet, as shall be seen later, Quah's appointment as the first Chinese commissioner was to test the limits of both Scouting's ideological advocacy of racial equality and the Hong Kong colonial administration's newly-found sense of respect for Chinese people.

There were few complaints from stakeholders as to the progress made by Scouting under Quah's leadership. In 1950, he mobilized the movement to perform two "Gang Shows" for the benefit of the anti-tuberculosis fund and the Society for the Protection of Children, events which he hoped would become "a yearly affair…to help some worthy Charitable Organization."[4] The Scout magazine, inactive since 1950, was re-launched in 1951. As suggested by F. H. J. Dahl, the Travelling Commissioner from Britain, and in the interest of growth through decentralization, he subdivided the colony into five districts.[5]

The first Chinese members of the leaders' training team were appointed in 1951. In August, Hong Kong sent its first-ever official contingent to the World Jamboree in Austria, an all-Chinese team of seven boys led by Hon Chi-hoy (韓志海). Documents provided by Lai Yuk-shu (黎玉書), one of the lucky boys chosen to participate in this once-of-a-

Hong Kong Scouting Gazette, 1951.

1   The *Hong Kong Scouting Gazette*, no.1, 1951, 2, 6.

2   P. C. Lee (comp.), the *Hongkong Album* 香港時賢, 1st. ed., (Hong Kong, 1960), 223.

3   Paul Tsui, like Quah, served in the BAAG. He joined the administrative service in 1946, became the first Chinese cadet in 1948, and eventually reached the top administrative grade, despite the racial "glass ceiling" in the colonial services. Steve Tsang, *Governing Hong Kong: Administrative Officers from the Nineteenth Century to the Handover to China, 1862-1997* (Hong Kong: Hong Kong Univ. Press, 2007), 115-120.

4   *CM*, September 22, 1950; *KSYP*, October 23, 1950; the *Hong Kong Scouting Gazette*, no.1, 1951, 3.

5   Report, Dahl's visit, c. January 1950; the Hong Kong Scout Archives.

lifetime event, indicates that the whole trip to England and Austria took around four months, and all the boys' expenses were fully paid for by the Boy Scouts Association, supported by a series of fund-raising activities.[1] Quah met the contingent in England for various visits and then went with it to the Jamboree.

Hong Kong contingent to the 1951 World Jamboree, August 1951,

H. K. Scout Archives.

A troop for delinquent boys at the Stanley Correctional Centre was formed in September 1951.[2] The coverage of annual competitions was expanded in the same year: The Prince of Wales Banner was re-classified as an award reserved for Senior Scouts over fifteen years old, while a new Carlton Trophy, named after Capt. Carlton Tinn, then the Deputy Camp Chief in Hong Kong, was created for Boy Scouts up to fifteen. The Boy Scouts of 8th Kowloon became the first winners of the Carlton Trophy, while the Senior Scouts of 17th Kowloon were the first winners of the Prince of Wales Banner *as a Senior Scouts event*.[3] Following the practice in some British colonies and as recommended by the British Scout association, Grantham indicated in December that the government would pay for an "Organising Commissioner," starting a tradition of public funding for paid staffing in Scouting.[4]

In May 1951, when a tragic fire broke out among cottages on the mountainside of Causeway Bay, Senior Scout Chan Kwok-chak (陳

The 1951 Jamboree Badge.

---

1 Folder, Lai Yuk-shu, 1950s, Hong Konh Scout Archives.

2 *KSYP*, July 15, 1951, August 20, 1951, November 2, 1953.

3 This change was made in the second half of 1951. *KSYP*, April 29, 1951, August 31, 1951, May 3, 1952; *The Hong Kong Scout*, January 1952, 3-4; 57.

4 "Boy Scout and Girl Guide Movement in the High Commissioner Territories, 1936," DO 35/487/3, the National Archives, London; letter, Grantham to Heywood, December 15, 1951, Hong Kong Scout Archives.

Chan Kwok-chak (top) and Ho Siu-hay, first postwar Gilt Cross awardees, 1951.

Gilwell Archives.

國澤) and Patrol Leader Ho Siu-hay (何兆熙), both of 15th Hong Kong, fought the fire gallantly. Chan single-handed destroyed two huts to prevent the fire from spreading, and Ho risked his life to enter a cottage to save a young child. They became the first recipients of gallantry awards for *postwar* acts, and were presented Gilt Crosses by Grantham.[1]

In May 1952, Quah organized the 5th Rover Moot in Macau with a record participation of close to ninety Rovers.[2] Ten Scouts, including four from the vernacular Man Wah School, attended the Far East Jamboree at Kuala Lumpur in August, demonstrating that not all overseas opportunities went to better-off boys from elite schools.[3] During this period, training courses were often held for leaders at the Morse Hut on Garden Road on Hong Kong Island, completed in 1950. In November, Jim A. Hudson arrived from Britain to become the first Organising Commissioner. He played a large role in the 1950s, though his effectiveness was at times hampered by his lack of knowledge of Chinese, and the full expatriate costs for his family was difficult to justify long-term.

A month later, twenty-six Scouts, led by Raymond Yue (余子洲), left for the Pan-Pacific Jamboree in Australia. In those days, although jet planes were already available, most long journeys were still made by sea. A trip by sea to Australia was time-consuming and demanding. According to Solomon Kui-nang Lee (李鉅能), a youthful Senior Scout from 35th Hong Kong (Ling Ying), the journey aboard the small ship *Changsha* took many days and was rather rough, and "only one Sea Scout was not totally sea sick."[4] Upon their arrival, however, they enjoyed warm and hospitable home stays with Australian families and then a wonderful Jamboree with brother Scouts from all over.

On St. George's Day in 1953, Grantham inspected over two thousands Boy Scouts.[5] As local Scouting continued to expand under Quah, a new headquarters became necessary. A new building on Cox's Road, in the heart of Kowloon, was proposed. In early 1953, the Executive Council of Hong Kong approved the granting of the site to the Scout

1   *KSYP*, Ocotber 7, 1951; *The Hong Kong Scout*, January 1952, 29.
2   Letter, Ma to Gover, May 21, 1952, the Hong Kong Scout Archives.
3   *KSYP*, August 3, 1952.
4   Interview, Solomon Kui-nang Lee, October 30, 2010, the Hong Kong Scout Archives; *KSYP*, November 28, 1952.
5   *KSYP*, April 26, 1953.

association on a private treaty lease.[1] Plans for the building, to be named the Morse House, "one of the most modernized Boy Scout Headquarters around the world," funded largely by the Jockey Club, were approved in August.[2] In the same month, Quah, having completed his term, retired and became an honorary commissioner.

Leaders in training at Morse House, 1956.

H. K. Scout Archives.

D. W. Luke, another Chinese, succeeded Quah as the commissioner. Luke, then the secretary of the association, was also the Scoutmaster of the Catholic Cathedral troop and, therefore, like Quah, was perceived as a "Catholic" Scouter. Unfortunately, some of his first acts did little to allay possible suspicions. In September 1953, when the president of the Philippines Scout association visited, Luke and Hudson welcomed him at the airport, with Boy Scouts from the Wah Yan college, a prominent Catholic school. In the same month, Catholic Scouts organized a big party to celebrate Luke's promotion at the cathedral hall, with Scouts from Wah Yan, La Salle, Rosary Church and St. Margaret's Church; and Luke urged Catholic Scouts to strengthen their unity. In November, he showed up for a Kowloon District rally, held at Wah Yan. Nevertheless, progress continued under Luke. He oversaw the revival of the Stanley Correctional Centre troop and started Scouting for "shoeshine" boys and also poor boys at the St. Peter's Welfare Centre. He also urged that Sea and Air Scouting be introduced for rural boys.[3]

The Scout Gilt Cross, Type II.

Author's collection.

1   "Boy Scouts Association Headquarters (K.I. L. 6248), Application for site at Cox's Road, Kowloon…," ENV 8/576/52, HKRS 156-1-3444, the Public Records Office, Hong Kong.

2   *KSYP*, August 19, 1953.

3   *KSYP*, September 18, 23 and 27, 1953, November 2, and 15, 1953. By this

Scouts using the jumping sheet to save people from a fire.

When another devastating fire broke out in Shep Kip Mei on Christmas night 1953, Luke led one hundred Scouts to help fight it, relay messages, evacuate residents, and salvage their property. Fire-fighting was, of course, one of those "citizenship" skills which had always been emphasized in Scout training. Its continued relevance in the postwar years was demonstrated by the gallant acts of Chan and Ho, already described, and also in this particular disaster. Afterwards, "order in the Relief Camps was maintained by the Police, boyscouts [*sic*] and members of the C.A.S."[1] On St. George's Day in 1954, Grantham noted the 30% growth in membership, and presented Queen's Scout certificates to thirty-two boys, both new records. Morse House, the modern headquarters, was opened in June by the governor. This was followed by a Colony Scouters' Conference in July, a Scouters' training course in August, district camps in November, and a charity ball in December.[2] Rowallan visited in October and remarked that "the Chinese Scouts were in good shape" in the colony.[3] Given all these pleasing developments, Luke's resignation on Christmas day in 1954 might appear somewhat surprising.[4] The official announcement stated simply that the governor had accepted Luke's resignation "due to pressure of business…with regret."[5]

The Shep Kip Mei fire on Christmas Day, 1953.

PRO 183-1.

time, the association had three Sea Scout Groups and only one Air Scout Group, all located in the urban areas of Kowloon and Hong Kong

1   *Report of Sham Shui Po Shek Kip Mei Six Villages Fire Relief Committee* (Hong Kong: the Fire Relief Committee, 1954), I.

2   *KSYP*, April 24, 1954, June 23, 1954, June 25, 1954, August 27, 1954, October 8, 1954, November 5, 1954, December 7, 1954.

3   Lord Rowallan, *Rowallan: the Autobiography of Lord Rowallan, K.T.* (Edinburgh: Paul Harris Publishing, 1976), 160.

4   *KSYP*, December 25, 1954.

5   *Headquarters Bulletin*, No. 3, January 11, 1955.

The tentativeness of Hong Kong Scouting's experiment with Chinese leadership in the early 1950s should not surprise many. Making Scouting available to Chinese boys was an entirely different matter to making its top leadership Chinese. With a Chinese at the helm, it was no longer true that the Europeans were perceived as "giving" and the Chinese as "receiving." The expected roles of the ruling and ruled races became somewhat complicated. In appointing a Chinese leader in 1950, the local movement was a pioneer of sorts. It is worth noting that despite reforms aiming at eventual political independence of Singapore, Europeans remained in charge of Singapore Scouting till 1957, when a Singapore-born Eurasian and then an Indian served. Chu Chui Lum, the first Chinese commissioner, was only appointed in 1969.[1] The Hong Kong Girl Guides retained mostly European leadership throughout this period. It had only appointed its first Chinese *assistant* commissioner, G. Choa, more than a decade later, in 1966/67.[2]

Rowallan with Luke and the Hong Kong Scouts, Oct. 1954.

H. K. Scout Archives.

Quah's relatively short tenure and Luke's even shorter term should be viewed in a broader context. Here the experience within the YMCA in China or the civil service in colonial Hong Kong is instructive. Earlier, the YMCA's effort to localize its professional secretaries in China had "tested their ideals of racial equality."[3] G. A. Fitch, a secretary in China, observed that a "persistent feeling of Anglo-Saxon race superiority" had made it difficult "to be absolutely democratic in relation to other countries."[4] The localization of senior civil service positions

1   Tan and Wan, *Scouting in Singapore*, 116, 146, 269.

2   *Annual Report, 1966-67* (Hong Kong: the Girl Guides Association, 1967), 12.

3   Jun Xing, *Baptized in the Fire of Revolution: the American Social Gospel and the YMCA in China: 1919-1937*, Ph. D. dissertation, Univ. of Michigan, 1995, 21.

4   George A. Fitch, *My Eighty Years in China* (Taipei, Taiwan: Mei Ya, 1967),

did not make much progress in Hong Kong, despite a few highly visible appointments such as that of Paul Tsui. In the civil service of British Hong Kong, a truly color-blind merit system took a very long time to implement. By 1956, only three out of 57 Administrative Officers, a mere 5%, were local; and even by 1962, local officers only constituted 15% of the total.[1]

It is important to note that by the early 1950s, the so-called "1946 outlook" had also faded somewhat. After 1949, as Goodstadt has suggested, the "Chinese were viewed as more susceptible to ideological conversions than English" and hence were considered less trustworthy.[2] Even Grantham's much watered-down constitutional reforms in May 1952 were rejected by the unofficial members of both councils. Similarly, "as Chinese refugees flooded in…local demands for reforms subsided," and the British became "more confident in retaining Hong Kong without making any significant changes."[3] It could be argued that just as democratic reforms were put on hold on the pretext that Communist China might view these unfavorably, so Chinese leadership in various capacities in the colony was delayed on the premise that this might be perceived as undesirable in the eyes of the Communist Chinese and, therefore, as inviting trouble. After all, most Hong Kong Chinese at the time were likely to be pro-Nationalist rather than pro-Communist.

Even within Scouting circles, there were concerns over having a Chinese (with Catholic links) at the top post. Rev. T. E. Gover revealed in a confidential letter to Dahl in October 1951 that when Quah was away in Europe, Grantham had asked him, then the acting commissioner, whom he thought might be the best choice to succeed Quah, and that he had recommended "a strong and independent leader" who was "apart from all the local 'factions,'" possibly "one…of the prominent Europeans in the Colony."[4] According to him, "it will NEVER DO to let the whole set-up fall into the hands of the Chinese; nor, for that matter, to allow it to become a department of the Roman Catholic Church."[5] In a growing movement with members from many religious, ethnic or so-

F. H. J. Dahl.

H. K. Scout Archives.

307, as quoted in Jun Xing, *Baptized in the Fire of Revolution*, 21.

1   Lau, *Society and Politics in Hong Kong*, 53.
2   Quoted in Carroll, *A Concise History of Hong Kong*, 134.
3   Ibid.
4   Letter, Gover to Dahl, October 20, 1951, the Gilwell Archives.
5   Ibid., capital letters by Gover himself.

cial backgrounds, mistrust based on perceived differences could not be avoided. But Gover's comments, hardly befitting the high ideals of the Scout brotherhood, suggest that even a senior Scout leader could not rise above racial prejudice or factional politics. They also seemed somewhat unfair. Scouting had become largely a Chinese movement since the interwar years, and yet Chinese Scouters only became commissioners in significant numbers after the war. Catholic influences were strong in Scouting because Catholic institutions had been supportive from the earliest years. Finally, despite the fact that very few members were British or Protestant boys, two British Protestant clergymen had been in charge in the interwar years and the early postwar ones.

At any rate, perception is often reality, and it would appear that Chinese leadership of the Hong Kong Scout Movement in the early 1950s was indeed ahead of its time. The Quah years, and, to a lesser extent, the Luke year, were marked by significant progress. Quah could have been appointed to a second term, much like Waldegrave or Halward before him. It was probably not easy to be fully effective as the first Chinese commissioner, at a time when heads of most colonial organizations were expected to be Europeans. One could reasonably expect more significant results in Quah's second term, after he had gained some experience and become more established. Luke might indeed have his problems, business or personal, which prevented him from being allowed to complete his three-year term. But, in theory at least, this in itself should not necessarily have prevented the Chief Scout from appointing another Chinese. Yet the practice of having Chinese leaders was discontinued in 1955, and it would be nearly a decade later, in 1963, before Hong Kong saw another Chinese at the top.

Denationalizing the Scout Movement

Throughout the 1950s, local Scouting adopted measures aiming at "denationalizing" and yet at the same time "colonializing" and "sinicizing" (or "Hongkongizing") the movement, removing Chinese nationalistic symbols and content from training and reducing contact with the Boy Scouts of China in Taiwan; while adding Chinese cultural and linguistic elements and keeping colonial and local features. Such actions

were often taken with a careful balancing of British colonial, Chinese
Communist and Chinese Nationalist interests in mind; and were only
possible with the tacit agreement of both the nearby PRC government
and the majority Chinese populace in Hong Kong.

By the late 1940s, British Hong Kong's future again appeared precarious. In China, the Nationalists were rapidly losing ground. The colonial authorities predicted "a large influx of refugees—either alone or with bodies of defeated Nationalist troops."[1] Sure enough, the population grew from 600,000 in 1945 to over 2.2 million by 1950, with illegal squatters claiming large portions of urban space.[2] By October 1949, the People's Liberation Army (PLA) was in Guangzhou, menacingly close to Hong Kong. The British Foreign Secretary Ernest Bevin had committed to transforming the colony into another Berlin if necessary by putting in place a strengthened garrison, while the Communist general Peng Zhen advised against attacking Hong Kong "rashly and without preparation."[3] Soon after, however, the existing borders were accepted, and a reasonably amicable relationship ensued, partly helped by the British Labour Government's early recognition of the PRC.[4] That colonialism in Hong Kong did not end in the era of decolonization owed much to "the acquiescence of both...the People's Republic of China...and...the local Chinese population," the former saw its economic value, the latter its political expediency.[5]

From the late 1940s, the government embarked upon a systematic process of denationalizing local education, in an effort to reduce the influence of both the Nationalists and the Communists. This was often done utilizing regulations and guidelines on school registration, syllabi, textbooks, and examinations.[6] Soon after the war, left-wing schools such as Heung To (香島), Hon Wah (漢華), and Pui Kiu (培僑) were (re-)

1   "Hong Kong Defence: Refugee Nationalist Troops etc. attempting to enter the Colony, 1949," CO 537/5024, the National Archives, London.
2   *Hong Kong Statistics, 1947-1967* (Hong Kong: Census and Statistics Department, 1969), Table 2.2.
3   Quoted in Welsh, *A Borrowed Place*, 443.
4   William Roger Louis, *Ends of British Imperialism: the Scramble for Empire, Suez and Decolonization, Collected Essays* (London: Tauris, 2006), 376.
5   Vickers, Kan, and Morris, "Colonialism and the Politics of 'Chinese History' in Hong Kong's Schools," 98.
6   Amy Tsui, James W. Tollefson (ed.), *Language Policy, Culture, and Identity in Asian Contexts* (London: Lawrence Erlbaum Associates, 2007), 123.

started, partly due to the colonial authorities' desire to offset the dominance of the Chinese Nationalists in local education. However, in 1950, the principal of Heung To, Lu Dong (盧動), was extradited; while Hon Wah's registration was revoked based on fire safety rules.[1] In 1951, the education authority recommended that public examinations and textbooks be cleansed of "Communist and the Nationalist mythology," so as to discourage "a strong pro-Beijing, pro-Taiwan, or Chinese national identity."[2] A 1953 report decreed that local history textbooks should emphasize "Social and Cultural History rather than Political History."[3] As H. K. Luk concludes, the objective of these measures was to produce students who identified themselves as Chinese, "but relate that Chineseness" to "a Chinese identity in the abstract, a patriotism of the émigré… not connected to tangible reality."[4]

A similar denationalizing process also took place in Scouting, starting with the removal of Chinese nationalist icons from official ceremonies. Significantly, on St. George's Day in April 1950, only the

Union Jack became the only national flag featured in gatherings since 1950.

H. K. Scout Archives.

1   Wong Chung Leung, "School Leadership in the Context of Change: A Case Study of 'Patriotic Schools' in Hong Kong," thesis, the Chinese Univ. of Hong Kong, 2006, 81; Wong Ting-hong, State Formation and Chinese School Politics in Singapore and Hong Kong, 1945 to 1965, Ph. D. dissertation, Univ. of Wisconsin—Madison, 1999, 131-140.

2   Wong Ting-hong, *Hegemonies Compared: State Formation and Chinese School Politics in Postwar Singapore and Hong Kong* (Routledge, 2002), 215-216.

3   Education Department, *The Report of the Chinese Studies Committee* (Hong Kong: Hong Kong Government Printer, 1953), 31.

4   H. K. Luk, "Chinese Culture in the Hong Kong Curriculum: Heritage and Colonialism," *Comparative Education Review*, Vol. 35, No. 4, November 1991, 668.

Union Jack and the British national anthem were present.[1] From then on, the Chinese Nationalist flag was rarely seen in public Scout gatherings. Photographic evidence from these years suggests that in official Scout events, if a national flag was present, it would be the Union Jack or, less frequently, the Hong Kong colonial blue ensign flag.[2] The practice continued into the 1960s. Circulars on St. George's Day parades from this period typically noted that "as H. E. reaches the dais, the Union Flag will be broken, and the Band will play 'The Queen.'"[3]

This shift in policy did not lead to widespread protests largely because local Scouts and their supporters tended to be pragmatic in the face of the political reality which followed the founding of the PRC. At the time, most Hong Kong Chinese would still identify with the Chinese Nationalists, many having recently escaped from Communist controlled parts of China, some incurring great economic losses in the process. Martin Booth, who grew up in the colony, observed that, in the 1950s, many buildings were decked out with huge portraits of Chiang Kai-shek and Nationalist flags in October at the time of Chinese national day, though there were also a few "defiant Communist Chinese flags and a picture of Chairman Mao."[4]

Like their parents, most local Scouts would probably have preferred to see the Chinese national icons in Scout gatherings. But after 1949, even if the British authorities were willing to permit public displays of symbols of Chinese nationalism, they would have been at a loss as to which ones to choose. The continued use of Nationalist symbols would have been politically embarrassing given Britain's recognition of the PRC, and would probably have elicited protests from the latter. However, to switch to the "Five-Star Red Flag (五星紅旗)" of the Communist Chinese and the "March of the Volunteers (義勇軍進行曲)" would have been quite unacceptable to the Hong Kong community, given the prevailing pro-Nationalist sentiments. It appears that the least politically tendentious option was simply to remove any Chinese nation-

1   *KSYP,* April 23, 1950.
2   See the *Scout Bulletin,* March-April, 1963, photograph next to P.16 (Chinese edition); the *Scout Bulletin,* July-August, 1958, photograph next to P.11; photographs in photograph albums, C. C. Quah, H. Ma and C. H. Wong, 1950s-1960s, the Hong Kong Scout Archives.
3   Circular, St. George's Day Rally, 1960, 1961, the Hong Kong Scout Archives.
4   Martin Booth, *Gweilo: A Memoir of a Hong Kong Childhood* (London: Bantam Books, 2004), 350.

alistic icons, Nationalist or Communist.

If absence of Chinese national icons could be explained away by the pragmatism necessary to avoid political confrontation with the PRC, new changes to the Scout Promise and the Scout Law could not. In January 1951, Dahl indicated that the promise in Chinese could be adapted to local conditions. As there was no king in China and not all Scouts were Christians, they should be permitted to substitute "the country (國家)" for "the King (英皇)" and "the head of one's religion (所信仰之教主)" for "God (上帝)." However, he emphasized that, as good citizens, Scouts must also do their duty to "the government of the place in which they live (當地政府)."[1]

But the amended promise for non-British Scouts in the local *POR* of 1952 was considerably more pro-church and pro-Britain than Dahl's proposed version: "To do my duty to God, *the King* and my country." Queen Elizabeth II succeeded King George VI in 1952, and in the local *POR* of 1954 this phrase became "to do my duty to God, *the Queen*, and the country in which I am living."[2] "God" is retained, and while "my country" and "the country in which I am living" could both still be interpreted to mean China or Hong Kong by the Scouts, unlike the Chinese promise in the interwar years, loyalty to the British sovereign had been added back as a requirement for non-British boys.

James Wilfred Cockburn was a British educationalist involved in Scouting in China before the war and had continued postwar as a staff and Scoutmaster of the Central British School and Queen's College. He became the Deputy Colony Commissioner in 1951 and the Colony Commissioner in January 1955.[3] Unlike Waldegrave or Halward, Cockburn was not a clergyman, but an educator who later became a senior official in the education department.[4] His dual roles in education and Scouting were significant, in view of the denationalization policy being implemented in the schools at the time. Further steps toward denationalizing Scouting occurred soon after he took over.

J.W. Cockburn.

H. K. Scout Archives.

---

1   *KSYP*, January 7, 1951.
2   *Local amendments to Rule 3 of the POR, 1952, 1954* (Hong Kong: the Boy Scouts Association, Hong Kong Branch, 1952, 1954). Italics added.
3   *KSYP*, December 25, 1954; the *Hong Kong Scouting Gazette*, no.1, 1951, 16.
4   But like Waldegrave and Halward, he was a Mason. See Carr, *The Victoria Lodge of Hong Kong*, 60, 62, 70; Haffner, *The Craft in the East*, 211.

The old Second Law on loyalty to the King/Queen.

In July 1955, "the Queen" was taken out from the optional promise for non-British subjects, which became "the country in which I am now living." But, more significantly, this promise for non-British subjects, when rendered into Chinese, the version that was used by most local boys, was denationalized further, as "the country in which I am now living" was officially translated as *juliudi* (居留地, place of residence)." Similarly, the Chinese rendition of the second Scout Law, which stated that "A Scout is loyal to the Queen," became "A Scout is loyal to his place of residence."[1] During this period, the Scout Promise was reaffirmed in both languages by all participants of the annual St. George's Day parades. In circulars from 1960 through to 1964, the English promise would always call for loyalty to "the Queen," and the Chinese promise would refer to loyalty to the "place of residence," presumably because British subjects would take the promise in English, and non-British would take it in Chinese.[2] In other words, the expression of loyalty to China, however vague, was no longer allowed. It is also interesting to note that Hong Kong was referred to as only "the place of residence," reaffirming the transitory nature of the colony, as perceived by most residents at the time, many of whom new immigrants.

Another aspect of denationalization involved efforts to reduce the influence of the Nationalists in Scouting and the cooling of relationship with the Boy Scouts of China in Taiwan. In 1950, the association forbade all troops from participating in group activities and parades in Scout uniforms on October 10th, the national day recognized in the ROC.[3] When Hsu Guan-yu (徐觀餘), the Chinese delegate to the International Scout Conference in 1953, passed through the colony, only the Overseas Chinese Boy Scout Service Corps (僑港中國童子軍服務隊) hosted an official welcome dinner.[4] In the same year, Hong Kong decided against sending a delegation to the 3rd National Jamboree in Taiwan. Cockburn explained later in a confidential letter that Grantham had approved a policy of private contact only: "we have never sent any Scouts officially to Taiwan, and when Scout officials have visited here e.g., Mr. Hsu, we

---

1   *Local Amendments to POR, 1958* (Hong Kong: the Boy Scouts Association, Hong Kong Branch, 1958), 1.

2   Circulars, St. George's Day Rally, 1960-1964, the Hong Kong Scout Archives.

3   *KSYP*, September 30, 1949.

4   *KSYP*, October 3, 1953, October 6, 1953.

have entertained them privately, without any public Scout honours."[1]

In June 1950, a day after the outbreak of the Korean war, the colonial authorities resettled many Chinese refugees at the abandoned Rennie's Mill (Tiu Keng Leng 調景嶺).[2] This camp, which once housed over twenty thousand refugees (including eight hundred youngsters), mostly former Nationalist soldiers, supporters and their family members, naturally became a pro-Nationalist enclave. At the time, there were three schools in the enclave, one Catholic, one Protestant, and the Tiu Keng Leng Secondary School (調景嶺中學), funded by the Taiwan Nationalists. In 1957, when a Taiwanese Scout troop was started in the Nationalist school, the local association demanded that it be registered in Hong Kong or be disbanded. It was never registered, and its members stopped wearing Scout uniforms, though Cockburn suspected that Nationalist Scouting continued.[3] The commissioner did not respond by forming a British-style troop at, say, the mission schools or the mission-supported Tiu Keng Leng Students Aid Project (調景嶺學生輔助社), whose European sponsors might be interested.[4] Perhaps, given the background of most parents and boys there, it was felt that the denationalized colonial Scout program would have little appeal anyway.

Taiwanese Boy Scouts, being the only official Boy Scouts from China, understandably took every opportunity to seek visibility at international Scout events, sometimes to the embarrassment of the British authorities. Boy Scouts from Taiwan were to attend the 9th World Jamboree in England in 1957, which would include a march past on August 3, with the Queen as the guest of honor. As the British Boy Scouts Association had declared that they were not able to exclude the Formosan Scouts from the event, a potentially embarrassing situation was at hand.

我願以信譽為誓竭盡所能，對神及居留地盡我責任，隨時隨地扶助他人，導守童子軍規律，

The Scout Promise in Chinese as of July 1955, stressing duty to "place of residence."

A Nationalist Scout badge for "overseas Chinese."

---

1   Letter, Cockburn to Cooke, August 14, 1958, the Hong Kong Scout Archives.
2   Edvard Hambro, *The Problem of Chinese Refugees in Hong Kong: Report Submitted to the United Nations High Commission for Refugees* (Leyden: Sijthoff, 1955), 53. The name of the place requires some explanations. Canadian businessman A. H. Rennie had set up a milling company at Junk Bay on the eastern part of Kowloon. His business failed, and he drowned himself there in 1908, although he was mistakenly reported to have hanged himself on the slope, giving the site the Chinese nickname of Tiu Keng Leng (吊頸嶺, literally "hang-neck mountain"). These Chinese characters, considered inauspicious, were later replaced by similar sounding ones, 調景嶺, which could be roughly translated as "adjusting-scene mountain," a somewhat appropriate name given its use as a camp for refugees from China.
3   Letter, Cockburn to Cooke, August 14, 1958, the Hong Kong Scout Archives.
4   The *Ming Pao Monthly* 明報月刊, 512, August 2008, 61-66.

The 1957 Jamborette Badge.

The Foreign Office confidentially instructed the consulate in Taiwan to delay the granting of visas so that the boys would arrive after August 3. However, they flew to Paris and applied for visas there, and the Free China Information Service followed up with enquiries about the delay, forcing through the processing of the visas in order to avoid still greater embarrassment and negative publicity. When informed, Ormsby-Gore, the Minister of State, noted dryly that "the Chinese Nationalist Scouts seem to have embraced the Scout teaching on the showing of initiative all too freely."[1] The Chinese contingent, armed with the Chinese Nationalist flag, eventually marched past the Queen.[2]

In October 1957, a Colony Jamborette was held at the Kam Chin Village (金錢村) in Sheung Shui, where 1,300 Boy Scouts camped out in celebration of the Golden Jubilee of world Scouting and the centenary of the birth of B-P, with the Chinese saying "all are brothers inside the four seas (四海之內皆兄弟)" as the theme.[3] Cockburn personally took charge of the Jamborette, with Hudson as his deputy. This four-day event was a sort of "join-in" camp, held in the same year as the 9th World Jamboree, which will be described later in this section. The Golden Jubilee Jamboree Song ("March, march, march, on the road with me...") and the Hong Kong Scout Song ("Here's to all the happy hours...") were featured in the Jamborette handbook, and were to become favorites among Hong Kong Scouts for many decades to come.

In 1961, the year 1911 was "chosen" as the founding year of Hong Kong Scouting, though it was admitted then that "*early records are so shrouded in mystery that it would be difficult to say whether or not the selection of the year is historically correct.*"[4] But "early records" need not be "shrouded in mystery" if one looks in the right places. As shown in Chapter 1, first Scout training in a Boys' Brigade Corps started in 1910, *not* 1911, at St. Andrew's; and first official Boy Scout Troop was founded in 1913, *not* 1911, at St. Joseph's. Both facts are amply supported by reliable primary sources.

A recent study in *Hong Kong Scouting* reviewed contemporary

1   "Visit of the Formosan Boy Scouts to attend the World Jamboree, 1957," FO 371/127519, the National Archives, London.
2   *KSYP*, August 5, 1957.
3   *KSYP*, October 19, 1957, October 21, 1957.
4   The *Annual Report*, 1961 (H. K.: Boy Scouts Association, 1961). Italics added.

sources from before WWI, in the interwar years, and after WWII, especially in 1961 and post-1961, and concluded that "[t]he legends within the association related to both the first Scouting activities in 1909 and in 1911 were created in late 1950s to early 1960s and *not substantiated by contemporary evidence*."[1] There was *no* Scouting activities in Hong Kong in 1909, and what happened in 1911 were all activities related to the St. Andrew's Boys' Brigade Corps formed in 1910.

Regardless, in 1961, several events commemorated local Scouting's "50th" anniversary. For the 2,400 Cub Scouts, a Jubilee Cub Rally with games and competitions was organized. In December, the Golden Jubilee Jamborette was held at the Kowloon Tsai Park. It featured the theme of "One World (天下一家)" and the same Jamboree song (this time celebrating Hong Kong's own "Golden Jubilee"); and gathered over three thousand Scouts, including some from America, Korea, Japan, Singapore, Australia, Malaysia, Thailand, Ceylon and Brunei.[2] This major camping event was the largest of its kind postwar, as illustrated by a panoramic view of it on the next spread, and was easily the most memorable for Hong Kong Scouts from this period.

(As it turned out, the choice of the historically incorrect 1911 as the starting year of Hong Kong Scouting in 1961 was somewhat unfortunate. It was followed by other celebrations such as the Diamond Jubilee Jamborees in 1971 and again in December 1986 to January 1987,[3] the 90th Anniversary Jamboree in December 2001, etc. These have created a tradition of its own and generations of Hong Kong Scouts, this author included, who only (erroneously) remember 1911 as the founding year. Sadly, falsehood, when repeated over and over again, could be perceived as truth; and history could thus be re-written. In 2010, a compromise solution between history and tradition was adopted by the Scout Association of Hong Kong, when the Centenary Jamboree was held a year earlier, between December 2010 and January 2011.)

The earlier initiative on the part of the Taiwanese Scouts in Britain apparently had repercussions in British Hong Kong. Despite the

1   Paul Kua, "The Founding Year Myth: 1910 or 1911?", *Hong Kong Scouting*, vols. 286-9, Feburary-May, 2008, 18, 20, 14, 22. Italics added. See also Paul Kua 柯保羅, *A Century of Hong Kong Scouting* 香港童軍百年圖史, 27-9.
2   Folder, the Golden Jubilee Jamboree, the Hong Kong Scout Archives.
3   Note both 60th and 75th anniversaries are customarily referred to as the Diamond Jubilee.

Golden Jubilee Jamborette Badge, Dec. 1961.

theme, brother Scouts from Taiwan were deleted from the list of invitees at the last minute as Governor Black informed the association that he would not declare the Jamborette open if the Taiwanese Scouts were

present.[1] This incident caused some public embarrassment for the association. A press release stating that Taiwan had been invited was inadvertently passed on (or intentionally leaked) to the Chinese press even after the decision not to do so had been taken.[2]

As befitting the largest youth organization supportive of and supported by the colonial authorities, Black came to the Jamborette as the Colony's Chief Scout in full Scout Uniform and opened the camp. Lord Maclean, who succeeded Rowallan as the Chief Scout in Britain since 1959, also visited and toured the campsite extensively.

Black inspected Scouts at the Jamborette, December 1961.

H. K. Scout Archives.

1   Memo, Law to Ma, September 1, 1960, the Hong Kong Scout Archives.
2   Memo, Ma to Cockburn, November 23, 1960, the Hong Kong Scout Archives.

Nevertheless, Nationalists continued to exert some influence in local Scouting. In Tak Ming Middle School, the most prominent pro-Nationalist school, denationalization saw Scouting become inactive by the

A panoramic view of the Golden Jubilee Jamborette, December 1961.

H. K. Scout Archives.

early 1950s.[1] But in 1958, it was resumed under the new designation of the 35th Kowloon.[2] A 1965 graduate of Tak Ming proudly listed his Scout experience in Hong Kong, and declared that he was to go to Taiwan to attend the Nationalist military academy.[3] As shown in the group photograph on the next page, in the inauguration ceremony of the 41st Kowloon, sponsored by the Kwong Tai Middle School (廣大中學), both the Union Jack and the Chinese Nationalist flag were prominently displayed, suggestive of the group's founders' political sympathies. In the early 1950s, some local youngsters joined the China Youth Anti-Communist National Salvation Corps (中國青年反共救國團), billed as a continuation of Scout training, which had at one time seven "battalions" in Hong Kong.[4] While membership was kept confidential, it was likely that some older Boy Scouts or Scouters were involved. Hong Kong did not send an

1   The *Hong Kong Scouting Gazette*, April 1947; the *Scout Bulletin*, May 1955.
2   The *Scout Bulletin*, May-June 1958.
3   *Xiang Gang De Ming Zhong Ying Wen Zhong Xue Bi Yeh Tong Xue Lu* 香港德明中英文中學畢業同學錄 (List of Graduating Students of the Hong Kong Tak Ming Chinese and English Middle School) (Hong Kong: Tak Ming School, 1965), 3-5, 36, 51.
4   "Deportation of Members of the China Youth Anti-Communist National Salvation Corps from Hong Kong, 1953," FO 371/105352, the National Archives, London. A brochure noted that junior high students need not join because "they have been subject to boyscout [*sic*] training."

The 41st Kowloon at Kwong Tai School, c. 1958.

H. K. Scout Archives.

official contingent to the 1956 National Jamboree in Taiwan, but it was "represented" in the "Overseas Chinese" sub-camp, probably by Scouts from Nationalist Chinese schools.[1] Cockburn's suspicion about continued Nationalist Scout activities at the Rennie's Mill was later confirmed. In July 1959, two members from the supposedly disbanded Scout Troop there, Cheung Choi (張才) and Tsang Fan Tsun (曾繁俊), left for Taiwan to join the official Boy Scouts of China's contingent to the 10th World Scout Jamboree to be held in the Philippines.[2]

The authorities in nearby Macau were not nearly as determined or as successful in suppressing expressions of Nationalist Chinese sentiments in Scouting. In 1957, a Chinese Scout rally with over six hundred Scouts from "Free Overseas Chinese Schools (自由僑校)" in Macau celebrated October 10th, though no such event was held in Hong Kong, where there was a much larger population of Chinese Scouts. In 1958, eight hundred Macanese Chinese Scouts celebrated the Chinese Scout Festival, recognized only in the ROC, with the Chinese national flags and portraits of Dr. Sun Yat-sen and President Chiang Kai-shek. In this gathering, the boys were urged to be loyal to the (Nationalist) party and to love the country (忠黨愛國).[3] In 1959, they again celebrated the Scout Festival, and were told that, under Chiang, "anti-Communism will win, and national restoration will be accomplished (反共必勝, 復國必成)."[4] The only visible public event in Hong Kong was the Colony Youth Rally held a day later, in honor of the Duke of Edinburgh, when thousands of school children sang "God Save the Queen" in Chinese,

1   *KSYP*, September 11, 1956, November 2, 1956.
2   *KSYP*, July 7, 1959.
3   *KSYP*, October 7, 1957, March 6, 1958.
4   *KSYP*, March 6, 1959.

and the Boy Scouts built a bridge and performed a lion dance on it.[1] In March 1961, the Chinese Scout Committee in Macau (澳門中國童子軍理事會) again celebrated the Scout Festival.[2]

The different treatment of pro-Nationalist Scouting in the two colonies is intriguing. Macanese schools at the time were "an uncoordinated collection of institutions based on models in Portugal, the PRC, Taiwan, and Hong Kong."[3] It is possible that, without a unified education system or extensive public funding of schools, the colonial government in Macau exerted relatively weak control, and the Nationalists were given considerable freedom to influence local Scouting.

Denationalization was, of course, a negative act—that of taking something out of Scouting. Positive efforts were also needed to add content. As in the schools, there were measures aimed at buttressing the colonial aspects and the local and Chinese cultural and linguistic features of the increasingly indigenized movement. The denationalizing theme thus proceeded alongside what might be referred to as "colonializing," "sinicizing" or "Hongkongizing" sub-themes. Some efforts were made to retain or reinforce colonial symbolism. To pass the Tenderfoot Badge, a Boy Scout had to "know the composition of the Union Flag, and how to hoist, break and fly it."[4] Therefore, from the 1950s onward, the Hong Kong Chinese Boy Scouts would be taught and tested only on their knowledge of the Union Jack. Unlike in the interwar and early postwar years, no further reference in Scout training would be made to

How to hoist the Union Jack (top), and its component crosses (left).

---

1 "Youth Rally at the Hong Kong Stadium," Secretariat GR 1/761/59, HKRS 41-2-274, the Public Records Office, Hong Kong; the *Scout Bulletin*, January-February 1959, 4.

2 *KSYP*, February 26, 1961.

3 Mark Bray, "Colonialism, Scale, and Politics: Divergence and Convergence of Education Development in Hong Kong and Macau," *Comparative Education Review*, August 1992, 328.

4 The *POR* (London: Boy Scouts Association, 1964), 93.

either of the two competing Chinese national flags. To pass the One Star test, a Wolf Cub had to learn three component crosses of St. George, St. Andrew and St. Patrick of the Union Jack and stories of the three patron saints, and "recite God Save the Queen."[1] In May 1953, Boy Scouts sold official coronation programs on behalf of the government, and the Scout Groups were offered a free colored portrait of the Queen which, Hudson declared, "would make a splendid addition to any group's Headquarters."[2] The Scouts marched along with the military men in the coronation parade (a "pageant of imperial militarism") which took place along Queen's Road.[3]

Lord Maclean.

Against the advice of the British headquarters, colonial terminology was retained. In May 1960, the British Scout association suggested that the title "Chief Commissioner" would be "more in keeping with present ideas" than "Colony Commissioner."[4] A year later, under the new leadership of Maclean, it asked that the "Imperial Headquarters" be called simply the "Headquarters," and again that the descriptor "colony" be taken out of the local titles.[5] But Governor Black was adamant about keeping the word "colony." He claimed that conditions in Hong Kong were different, that he was "proud to be called the Colony Chief Scout and greatly prefers this for Hong Kong to Local Chief Scout," although he left it to Cockburn to decide whether he wanted to become the "Chief Commissioner."[6] Understandably, given Black's preference, Cockburn also decided to remain the "Colony Commissioner."[7]

There were also efforts to sinicize and Hongkongize the movement. Upon Hudson's departure in 1958, Law Kwan Fook (羅君福) became the first Chinese Executive Commissioner, starting a tradition of having paid local staff at a senior level.[8]

B-P "romanticised the Zulu's discipline and courage, and he

---

1   *Golden Jubilee Cub Rally* 金禧年全港小狼大會 (Hong Kong: the Boy Scouts Association, Hong Kong Branch, 1961), 30.
2   Circular, Hudson, May 20, 1953, the Hong Kong Scout Archives.
3   Booth, *Gweilo*, 185-186.
4   Letter, Cockburn to Ma, May 17, 1960, the Hong Kong Scout Archives.
5   Letter, Cooke to Cockburn, May 1, 1961, the Hong Kong Scout Archives.
6   Letter, Ingles (secretary to Black) to Cockburn, May 6, 1961, the Hong Kong Scout Archives. .
7   Letter, Cockburn to Cooke, May 8, 1961, the Hong Kong Scout Archives.
8   Folder, the Organising Commissioner, 1952-1958, the Hong Kong Scout Archives.

adapted many of their cultural institutions to Scouting", including the Zulu praise song "Een-Gonyama", Nguni age tests for the solo journey required for the First Class Badge and beads from a twelve-foot-long Zulu necklace (supposedly captured from King Dinizulu/Dinuzulu during the Zulu Wars) as a centerpiece of the Wood Badge, awarded to leaders after they completed the prescribed training.[1]

The Hong Kong Scout emblem introduced in 1959.

Wood Badge training for leaders in Hong Kong was led by the Training Commissioner who was also called the Deputy Camp Chief, in relation to the Camp Chief, the guru of training in the Gilwell Park in Britain.[2] Local Training Commissioners were first appointed in the later part of the interwar years, starting with Alan Grad as the Assistant Commissioner for Training and a Deputy Camp Chief in mid-1930s. Halward succeeded Grad as the Assistant Commissioner for Training. The first postwar Deputy Camp Chiefs were Muffet, Dahl, Tinn, and Hudson. In 1951, Loo Mang Hoon (盧孟煊) became the first Chinese appointed to this post. By 1959, the training team had almost forty members, led by six Deputy Camp Chiefs, all of whom were Chinese.[3]

In the same year, a new Hong Kong Scout emblem based on the shield of the new coat of arms for Hong Kong was introduced. The association's Publication Board (later known as the Publicity Branch) had by 1959 published twenty-two booklets, all except one of which was in Chinese.[4] Local sentiments were considered as Scout terms were rendered into Chinese. The Queen's Scout became known as the less-colonial-sounding "Honorable Boy Scout (榮譽童子軍)." The Colony Commissioner became the "Commissioner for Hong Kong (全港總監)" in Chinese, and the Colony Chief Scout was simply "Hong Kong's Chief Leader of the Boy Scouts (本港童子軍總領袖)," with no mention of the colony (*zhimindi* 殖民地).[5] The 1958 amendments to local rules for

Gilwell Reunion for Wood Badge holders in Hong Kong at Junk Bay, 1957.

H. K. Scout Archives.

---

1   Parsons, *Race, Resistance, and the Boy Scout Movement*, 58. Note B-P's biographer Tim Jeal argues that the necklace was taken from a dying Zulu girl instead. See, for example, William Atkins' *Exiles: Three Island Journeys* (London: Faber, 2022) for a fuller story of Dinuzulu, including his exile by the British to the St. Helena Island in 1890-1897, and imprisonment in 1908.

2   The Scout Association, "The Origins of the Wood Badge," http://www.scout-base.org.uk/ library/hqdocs/facts/pdfs/fs145001.pdf (accessed August 1, 2008).

3   They were Henry Ma, Wong Yick Hong, Wong King Hong, Wu Wen Wei, Chan Po Chi and Jerome Yeung; see the *Scout Bulletin*, May-June, 1959, 6-7 (Chinese edition).

4   The *Scout Bulletin*, November-December, 1959, 5 (Chinese edition).

5   *Scouting in Hong Kong* 童子軍運動在香港 (Hong Kong: Boy Scouts Asso-

test requirements for badges provide other interesting examples of sini-cization: "papaya seed" replaced "acorn," "congee" replaced "porridge," "acidic and alkaline poisoning" replaced "ice breaking," and "Chinese Calligraphy" replaced "lettering."[1]

Hong Kong contingent to the 1957 World Jamboree visiting Royal Doulton.

H. K. Scout Archives.

Hong Kong Scouts' representation in World Jamborees contin-ued. In 1957, Law Kwan-fook led a group of twelve Chinese, including nine Senior and Boy Scouts, to the 9th World Jamboree at Sutton Park in England.[2] According to Robert Chow, one of the participants, all the boys were chosen by a committee, and all attended the Jamboree with full funding.[3] This was apparently possible due to an association-wide fund-raising campaign. The youngest boy, So Nam, whose "big broad grin and keenness in taking part always struck the right cord," was pre-sented with Law to the Queen after the march past.[4] In 1959, Tse Ping-fui led sixty-two Scouts to the 10th World Jamboree in the Philippines, Hong Kong's largest-ever World Jamboree contingent, though in this case, only a small percentage of the participants were fully-funded by the association.[5] In 1963, Chau Cham-son headed a contingent of eight Chinese which attended the 11th World Jamboree in Greece.[6] The rela-tively small size of the 1963 Greek contingent could be explained by the expenses involved with traveling to Europe.

The 1957 World Jamboree Badge.

ciation, 1957), 4, 5.

1   *Local Amendments to POR, 1958*, 1, 2.

2   *CM*, June 26, 1957, 10; *KSYP*, July 18, 1957, 6; folder, the Jubilee Jamboree, 1957, Hong Kong Scout Archives.

3   Interview, Robert Chow, April 7, 2010, the Hong Kong Scout Archives.

4   Folder, the Jubilee Jamboree, 1957, the Hong Kong Scout Archives.

5   *CM*, July 14, 1959; *KSYP*, July 15, 1959, April 8, 1960.

6   *KSYP*, July 25, 1963.

Hong Kong Contingent to the 1959 World Jamboree.

H. K. Scout Archives.

In fact, given the generally high costs related to sending boys to any World Jamboree, there were some internal discussions on the wisdom of such a move. In 1959, in the context of the 10th World Jamboree, Cockburn presented both sides of the arguments, using pseudonyms from made-up groups:

> *"A complete waste of time and a greater waste of money," thought Sam Leggatt of the 102nd. "Think what we could have done with the $80,000 we spent sending boys to the Jubilee Jamboree. We could have set up a complete new campsite, and in this way have done something for all the Scouts of the Colony..." "But think what a wonderful practical demonstration of the fourth Scout law a Jamboree provides," interposed Bill Logan. "We in the 101st have sent a Scout to the last two Jamborees, and we are sending one to the Philippines this year. Each time the whole troop has worked to raise funds to send one boy..."[1]*

This, of course, is a somewhat complicated, if familiar, argument facing many organizations and involving tradeoffs between quantity, quality, efficiency, cost-effectiveness, access, equity, and so on. It would continue to plague stakeholders and policymakers in the association. Nevertheless, Hong Kong's representation in this world event was to become an established practice during this period.

To stay away from entanglement in the Nationalist-Communist conflict and to avoid displeasure of the PRC government were the obvi-

The 1959 World Jamboree Badge.

---

1   The *Scout Bulletin*, May-Jun 1959, 1.

The 1963 World Jamboree Badge.

ous excuses given for pursuing denationalization. Given the long association of the movement in China with the Nationalists, it was unlikely that the Communists could exert much influence on Scouting at this time. This implied that if Scouting was to remain "patriotic," it would be likely to do so in a pro-Nationalist mode. It was plausible to suggest that the PRC might not sit quietly on the side and watch the colonial authorities educate local Chinese boys to grow up as Nationalist sympathizers through Scouting. Some in Hong Kong, including members of the ruling elite, believed that Scouting could not expand unhampered without an active denationalization program, since the Communist Chinese would simply not tolerate it.

But there was another possible motivation for denationalization: nationalist Scouting could be detrimental to colonial governance. Native Muslim Scouting in French Algeria from the 1930s onward provides an example of how this danger might play out.[1] Many troops formed by militant reformists with experience in French Scouting emphasized patriotism which, in colonial Algeria, "implied observation of the principles of Islam and loyalty to the fatherland, therefore to nationalism and the Algerian colors."[2] *Scouts musulmans algériens* (*SMA*, Muslim Scouts in Algeria) had frequent clashes with French Algerian authorities in the war years, as the latter demanded loyalty to France as the "fatherland," while the former asserted that "by fatherland they understood to mean the country of their birth, therefore Algeria."[3] Muslim Scouts played a key role in the war of liberation in November 1954: of the twenty-two men involved in the initial decision, six were former Scouts, and the historic meeting was held in the home of another *SMA* leader.

Similarly, postwar Scouting in Vietnam eventually became highly politicized. Ann Raffin concludes that "Scouts were active participants in the August [1945] Revolution" and contributed "hundreds of healthy, motivated, disciplined cadres to the Viet Minh."[4] The Vietnamese Scout association became so partisan that in April 1946 Ho Chi Minh

---

1   Derouiche, *Scoutisme école du patriotisme*, 21.
2   «impliquait l'observation des principes de l'islam et la fidélité à la patrie, donc au nationalisme et aux couleurs algériennes», Mahfoud Kaddache, "'Les soldats de l'avenir' Les Scouts musulmans algériens, 1930-1962, " in Bancel et al., *de l'Indochine à l'Algérie*, 68.
3   «par patrie ils entendaient le pays de leur naissance, donc l'Algérie», ibid., 72.
4   Raffin, *Youth Mobilization in Vichy Indochina*, 197.

was asked to be its president. By this time, "French officials character-ized the scout association of Tonkin as a Viet Minh organization whose committees breathed into it their "violent patriotic spirit."[1]

Though in many colonies, French or British, "patriotic practices and discourses sponsored by the colonial state" had ended up serving "indigenous nationalism," to the dismay of the colonial rulers;[2] Chi-nese nationalism, prominent in Hong Kong Scouting in the 1940s, was successfully purged postwar. The denationalization of Hong Kong's youth movement was pursued evidently with some success. By the early 1960s, it had re-emerged from the shadow of Scouting in China, and had become predominantly a means of training local youth for the colony, not for both Hong Kong and China, or even for China only.

But Hong Kong succeeded where other colonies failed not be-cause the local authorities were particularly skillful in their maneuver-ing. The denationalization of Scouting proceeded relatively smoothly in the Hong Kong context because China tolerated it, and the local Chinese people accepted it. Given the visibility of Nationalist Scouting in nearby Macau, it could be argued that even if some Hong Kong Scouts had continued to exhibit such sentiments, China might have turned a blind eye. Still, the PRC did loom large over the colony and occasionally threatened its very existence. This provided a convincing excuse for the authorities to denationalize Scouting and rejuvenate in it certain colonial aspects, with a touch of sinicization.

Crossing class divides

From the 1950s through to the 1960s, Hong Kong Scouting gradually crossed the colonial community's class divides and began to include many underprivileged boys, a development which occurred relatively late in comparison with Britain and some other colonies, but which nev-ertheless took off in earnest in this period. Many youngsters from the disadvantaged classes, boys who were poor, orphaned, institutionalized or disabled, became Boy Scouts. This initiative brought momentum and dynamism to a movement which had seen its energy somewhat sapped by

---

1   Ibid.
2   Ibid, 3.

the denationalizing efforts dictated by the authorities and political reality of the British colony.

Scouting was in theory inclusive of all classes, though there was a gap between ideal and practice, and inclusion was not always embraced unconditionally. B-P declared that "the Indian boy and the British boy, the public school boy and the slum boy and boys of every religion" were all "equal partners in this wonderful brotherhood."[1] But the inclusion of lower class boys was not common even in more prosperous countries. David Pomfret observes that while it might have been the aim of Scouting to include the poorest boy, quite often, "the expense involved in membership of the Scouts largely prevented its achievement."[2] Robert MacDonald concludes that experience in Britain demonstrated that "the majority of the boys themselves belonged to the middle or lower middle classes."[3] Similarly, David MacLeod points out that "sponsorship patterns and residential clustering kept roughnecks out of most troops" in America, and BSA officials were careful in describing the Scout training program as "formative rather than reformatory."[4]

Still, the Scout Movement in a number of countries had attempted to reach out to at least some underprivileged boys from the earliest years. Scouting for disabled boys in Britain started with the 1st Gosforth Troop in a "crippled home" in 1908. By 1912, there was a commissioner for special (physically disabled) schools in London. The Disabled Scouts Branch was created in 1926, with "115 troops or patrols of physically defective, epileptic, deaf and dumb [*sic*], blind and mentally defective boys." This branch was renamed the Special Tests Branch two years later, and then the Handicapped Scouts Branch in 1936.[5] Moreover, British Scouting was relatively progressive in the interwar years, promoting full integration of disabled boys, when the community itself frequently resorted to segregation and discriminatory practices.[6] In 1930, a leader

---

1   Baden-Powell, *Aims, Methods and Needs* (London: Boy Scouts Association: [1929]), no page number.
2   Pomfret, "The City of Evil and the Great Outdoors," 420.
3   MacDonald, *Sons of the Empire*, 153-154.
4   Macleod, *Building Character*, 216.
5   Letter, August 4, 1926, the Gilwell Archives, quoted in A. Stevens, "Changing Attitudes to Disabled People in the Scout Association in Britain (1908-1962): a contribution to a history of disability," *Disability & Society*, September 1995, 283.
6   Stevens, "Changing Attitudes...," 281-294.

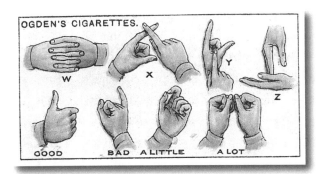

Sign language, often taught to Scouts.

of the branch defended these boys' access to the highest Scout awards, despite concerns expressed by B-P.[1] In 1936, a group of Scouters had proposed that disabled Scouts should be segregated, a proposal which again was met with indignation from Scouters who were serving these boys.[2] Similarly, from early on, Scout supporters in America "gloried in rough brands plucked from the burning, such as Antonio Draginetti of Chicago's stockyards district, who had once attacked a teacher with an axe but then found a place in Scouting and rose to be a patrol leader."[3] The BSA took in at least some "promising" juvenile delinquents in a few towns, and also recruited actively in some slums, though it generally only "skimm[ed] the cream" in these areas.[4]

Scouting for the underprivileged was much less common in the colonies in the earlier years. Compared to boys of the ruling race in many European colonies, most indigenous boys could be considered to some degree "underprivileged," though not necessarily disenfranchised. In this sense, extending Scouting from European boys to the locals in itself was akin to reaching out to a "lower" stratum, in the context of the racially-driven class hierarchy of the colonies. Nevertheless, in the early years, if Scouting was available to local boys, it tended to be relatively elitist. Most boys included were among the privileged few attending the highly-selective mission or government schools, and they often came from relatively comfortable families.

---

1 B-P wrote to Sir Stephen Burrows, chairman of the Special Test Branch Committee that "it hardly seems fair on the other Scouts and more especially the general public, that these boys should rank as First Class and especially King's Scouts." Burrows seemed adamant, and responded "I am afraid I do not quite understand the question. Why should they not become First Class Scouts and who are the people who object." See Stevens, "Changing Attitudes...," 286-288.

2 C. W. Durward, "Handicapped Scouts," *The Scouter*, December 1936, 430.

3 Macleod, *Building Character*, 216.

4 Ibid.

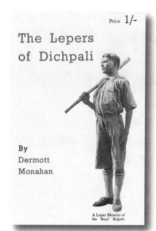

Monahan's *The Lepers of Dichpali*, with story of the brigade boys there.

There were a few isolated efforts to reach out to the truly disadvantaged boys in the colonies in the interwar years. Notably, boys afflicted with the dreadful "Hansen's disease," or leprosy, were among the earliest underprivileged boys to be included. At this time, leprosy was still common in parts of Asia and Africa although it had become rare in Britain.[1] By the early 1930s, there were Boy Scout troops in leper settlements in Malaya, West Africa, and Ceylon. For their daily good turns, boys in the West African leper troop charted the temperatures of thousands of lepers in the camp.[2] To be fair, one should not be misled by a sense of Scouting exceptionalism. Other youth organizations had also tried to reach out to these unfortunate youngsters in some of the colonies. There were successful Boys' Brigade Companies and, indeed, the first Girls' Life Brigade in India from as early as the late 1920s for children afflicted with leprosy in Dichpali, India. The brigade boys who were "Hindus, Moslems, Outcasters, and Christians" broke entrenched traditions and ate and served together.[3]

The involvement of Hong Kong Scouts with underprivileged boys in the service tradition of Scouting (as opposed to the enrollment of underprivileged boys as Scouts) started in the interwar years. Aside from one-off service projects during holidays or on occasions of special needs such as during war time, there was evidence of longer-term commitments. The first boys' club, known then by its descriptive Chinese name of *pin er hui* (貧兒會 poor children's club), was opened in 1936 on Bonham Road with the help of Deep Sea Scouts from the Royal Navy. In 1938, the St. Andrew's Rover Crew, led by R. Dormer and G. S. P. Heywood, started a boys' club on Argyle Street in Kowloon. Though these poor boys were not part of any Boy Scout Troop, they were taught first aid and personal hygiene, Swedish drill, simple gymnastics, community singing and games of all sorts. Twenty of them enjoyed a bathing picnic at North Point, forty had games and "a magnificent 'high tea'" on the grounds of St. Andrew's Church on the New Year day. Chinese Boy Scouts were involved later. Yip Wing Hong and Scouts of the 7th Hong Kong led a boys' club in Wanchai in 1950, whose members' par-

---

1   Michael Worboys, "The Colonial World as Mission and Mandate: Leprosy and Empire, 1900-1940," *Osiris*, 2nd Series, 15, 2000, 207-208.
2   *The Scouter*, March, 1931; *CM*, May 23, 1931, January 16, 1932.
3   Monahan Dermott, *The Lepers of Dichpali* (London: Cargate Press, 1938), 73.

ents were hawkers, laborers, coolies, workmen or unemployed.[1] In the early 1950s, some Boy Scouts from Kowloon and the Maryknoll Convent School Girl Guides also served poor youngsters of the King's Park Social Welfare Center, founded by the Maryknoll Sisters in 1952.[2] These were all commendable gestures, but were made more in the spirit of service than of inclusiveness, as the underprivileged boys served did not become Boy Scouts.

Aside from a few efforts to reach out to rural boys in the interwar years, significant efforts to include the underprivileged only began in the 1950s under Quah and Luk. Quah divided the New Territories into two districts. A large tract of land was soon put aside for a multi-purpose headquarters, opened by Morse in November 1952. Scouters from Kowloon were sent. When dignitaries visited, their attention was directed to these budding rural districts.[3] In 1954, when Rowallan visited, he made a special trip to meet the Boy Scouts in the New Territories.

Rowallan visited rural Scouts, 1954.

H. K. Scout Archives.

In 1952, the 3rd Hong Kong sponsored by the Social Welfare Office and the 24th Hong Kong for the Wah Yan Poor Boys' Club were started.[4] Scouting soon became available to boys considered to be "delinquent." As noted, in 1951, the 8th Hong Kong was started in the Stanley Reformatory School (赤柱兒童感化院). J. T. Burdett, the commissioner of prisons, in a memorandum to the colonial secretary, proudly

---

1   *Annual Report, 1936, 1938, 1950* (Hong Kong: The Boys' and Girls' Clubs Association).
2   Cindy Yik-Yi Chu, *The Maryknoll Sisters in Hong Kong, 1921-1969: in Love with the Chinese* (New York: Palgrave Macmillan, 2004), 73-75.
3   *KSYP*, November 2, 1952, December 3, 1952.
4   *Census Reports, 1952*, the Hong Kong Scout Archives.

A bronze Yuan Dynasty Nestorian Cross, similar to that featured on scarf of 1st Hay Ling Chau.

Author's collection.

labeled this as "a big event in the short history of this school, and… proof…of the great progress made in training these boys to become useful citizens."[1] In early 1953, boys from the school were moved to the new Castle Peak Boys' Home managed by the Salvation Army.[2] In November, boys inside the Stanley prison were invested into a re-organized 8th Hong Kong by Scoutmaster Cheng Ji-chiu (鄭子超).[3]

The drive to reach disadvantaged boys became a systematic focus in Cockburn's time, as Scouting "branch[ed] out into different segments of the population" which it had "not touched before."[4] It is as if Cockburn, being a European leader taking leadership back from previous Chinese incumbents, and being responsible for implementing a systematic denationalizing program in the movement, had to try twice as hard to live up to the brotherhood ideal of Scouting by reaching out to the underprivileged Chinese boys in the colony.

The 1st Hay Ling Chau, inaugurated in 1955.

H. K. Scout Archives.

There was considerable progress in Scouting for disabled boys. In these early postwar years, with the influx of migrants from China, the number of leprosy patients increased substantially. In the early 1950s, the government and the Leprosy Mission in London jointly built a leprosarium on an uninhabited island which was renamed Hay Ling Chau

1 "Stanley Reformatory School," Secretariat 10/33711, 1951, HKRS 41-1-6799, the Public Records Office, Hong Kong.
2 "Boys in Stanley Reformatory School," Secretariat 2/289/52, HKRS 41-1-7360, 1952, the Public Records Office, Hong Kong.
3 *KSYP*, November 2, 1953.
4 Letter, Ma to Steele, December 13, 1955, the Hong Kong Scout Archives.

(the Healing Island or, in Chinese, the Island of Joyful Souls). In 1954, Grantham opened the Hay Ling Chau Leprosarium (喜靈洲痲瘋院), which had a strong Christian influence. In November 1955, after months of exploratory efforts, Cockburn founded a leper group there.[1] Donald Barton and Ip Kam Fat (葉錦發) became Scoutmasters of 1st Hay Ling Chau, Hong Kong's first "handicapped" group, with ten Rover Squires and twelve Scouts.[2] Like the logo of the leprosarium, the scarves of this group also featured a Nestorian cross, probably the only Scout unit in the world to have adopted this ancient symbol, often considered proof of early Nestorian Christian presence in China.[3]

The "Handicapped [*sic*] Auxiliaries" were formed in 1956, to better support activities in this area. A troop for boys at the School for the Deaf (真鐸啟喑學校) in Diamond Hill began in January 1957.[4] Within months, groups for blind boys in North Point and the Children's Convalescent Home (大口環兒童康院) were started. In May, the recently-formed "Handicapped Branch" (弱能童子軍支部, or, literally, the "Weak-capabilities Scout Branch," both terms which could be considered inappropriate by modern standards) held a colony-wide conference for interested Scouters, which then became an annual event. Over the years, the branch was the focal point for Scouters in support of various activities to reach out to physically challenged youngsters.

In November 1957, Cockburn invested disabled boys from Lai Chi Kok Hospital's crippled children's ward (荔枝角殘廢兒童病院) into a Wolf Cub Pack.[5] By end of 1958, groups at the Hong Kong Overseas Chinese School for the Dumb and Deaf (香港華僑聾啞學校), the old Tsan Yok Hospital (社會署贊育盲人福利會), and the Ebenezer Home for the Blind (心光盲人院) were registered.

Further progress was seen in the inclusion of institutionalized boys. In July 1955, a Sea Scout Group was founded at the Tung Tau Wan

Handicapped Auxiliaries Badge, with the Chinese charaters for "weak capabilities."

---

1 *SCMP*, November 28, 1955.

2 Letter, Ma to the Junior Chamber of Commerce, October 18, 1955, the Hong Kong Scout Archives.

3 These bronze cruciform relics from the Yuan Dynasty were typically found in the Ordos region in China. See James Menzies's articles on Nestorian bronze crosses (青銅十字架) in *Qi Da Ji Kan* 齊大季刊 (Shandong, Jinan: Qi Lu Univ., 1934), No. 3, 1-168.

4 *Hong Kong School for the Deaf 25th Anniversary* (Hong Kong School for the Deaf, 1960), 4-9.

5 *KSYP*, November 11, 1957.

Cockburn with Cubs (and Brownies?) of the Lai Chi Kok children's ward, 1957.

H. K. Scout Archives.

Training Centre at Stanley (赤柱中童教導所).[1] In December 1957, Ma inaugurated a group for inmates of Children Detention Centre (社會局兒童羈留所).[2] In Britain many believed that the war had contributed to the postwar increases in juvenile crime ("the expression of a particularly disturbed generation, a delayed effect of the war").[3] Similar worries were not apparent in Hong Kong at this time. In fact, in the mid-1950s, incidents of juvenile delinquency were at an all-time postwar low, suggesting that the efforts to include so-called delinquent youth in local Scouting largely presaged communal or official concerns.[4]

In Cockburn's time, many groups were also started for disadvantaged boys in rural areas, squatter huts, resettlement estates, orphan homes, or on the streets. In 1956, Scouting penetrated the island of Lantau, with the start of the 1st Lantau at the Tai O School (大澳學校).[5] Two years later, the island of Cheung Chau started groups for rural boys at Kwok Man School (國民學校) and Chi Kwong School (慈光學校).[6] Poor boys from squatter families in King's Park, Chuk Yuen Resettlement Estate, Shek Kip Mei Resettlement Estate, and Tsuen Wan Children's Club were enrolled in troops sponsored by the Boys' and Girls' Clubs and the Salvation Army. By 1959, the Boys' and Girls' Clubs were

1   *KSYP*, June 29, 1955, July 4, 1955.
2   *KSYP*, December 21, 1957.
3   T. R. Fyvel, *The Insecure Offenders; rebellious Youth in the Welfare State* (Harmondsworth: Pelican, 1963), 51.
4   The Hong Kong government only issued its first-ever official report on juvenile delinquency in 1965. See John Winterdyk, *Juvenile Justice Systems: International Perspectives* (Canadian Scholars' Press, 2002), 212-213.
5   The *Headquarters Bulletin*, May 1956.
6   *KSYP*, January 16, 1958, June 6, 1958.

running six troops and two packs.[1] In this period, Scouting also became available to orphan boys in Faith Love Christian Herald Home (信愛兒童院) in Fanling, Hong Kong Juvenile Care Centre (香港兒童安置所), Kowloon Children's Centre (九龍兒童習藝所), and Children's Garden (兒童新村) in Ma On Shan.[2]

The inclusion of disadvantaged boys improved markedly in the 1950s. In 1957, twenty "Special Scout Groups" (特殊童子軍旅), including five Boys and Girls Clubs groups, four Salvation Army groups, a squatters group, four groups at Stanley Training Centre, two orphanage groups, and four handicapped groups, held a joint meeting.[3] These units, excluding the rural groups, which were also to some extent disadvantaged, constituted 15% of the total number of groups in the year.[4] When George F. Witchell, the Travelling Commissioner, visited in the same year, five out of his fifteen recommendations dealt with efforts to reach out to the underprivileged, reflecting the strategic importance of this type of Scouting.[5] Growth in this segment continued in the 1960s. By May 1960, for instance, the number of groups considered "handicapped" had grown to a total of eight.[6] By 1962, there were eleven active handicapped groups, including five for deaf boys, three for blind ones, two for physically handicapped ones, and the leper group.[7]

Progress in the densely populated resettlement estates, another area of focus in this segment, is illustrative. The association worked closely with the government to promote this work, receiving first-hand information on new resettlement estates being developed and special subsidies dedicated to penetrating these areas. In 1961, a government subvention was provided for Scouting in the resettlement estates, covering a full-time professional, and subsidies for uniforms, gear, and lead-

---

1   The *Headquarters Bulletin*, November 1955, 3; *Annual Report, 1957-58, 1958-59* (Hong Kong: The Boys' & Girls' Clubs Association,); the *Bulletin,* November 1958, 4; *KSYP*, May 9, 1959.

2   *Children's Voice* 童聲 (Hong Kong: the Christian Children's Fund, 1955), December 1955; May 1958, 29; November 1960, 41; *Annual Report, 1957* (Hong Kong: Boy Scouts Association, 1957), 3-4; *KSYP*, July 11, 1960.

3   Circular, Underprivileged Groups, June 17, 1957, the Hong Kong Scout Archives.

4   *Census Reports, 1957*, the Hong Kong Scout Archives.

5   Report, George Witchell, June 18, 1960, the Hong Kong Scout Archives.

6   Folder, Handicapped Scouting, 1957/63, the Hong Kong Scout Archives.

7   *Ruo Neng Tong Zi Jun Huo Dong* 弱能童子軍活動 (Activities of the Handicapped Boy Scouts) (Hong Kong: the Boy Scouts Association, c.1962), 10.

LI CHENG UK

ers' training. Within a short time, the association also partnered with community centers, schools, the Boys and Girls Clubs, and the Salvation Army to establish new groups in the resettlement estates of Wong Tai Sin, Chuk Yuen, Pak Tin, Shek Kip Mei, Tai Wai, Ho Man Tin, Li Cheng Uk, Lo Fu Ngam, Tsuen Wan, and Kwun Tong. By 1963, twenty-four "Resettlement Estate" groups were registered, and by 1966, the number had increased to thirty-six.[1] These totals, though impressive, did not include open groups located near the estates but nonetheless served the boys there. The 159th Kowloon, started by the Anglican St. Barnabas Church (聖公會聖巴拿巴堂) in 1966, is illustrative. Though the church was situated centrally in the new town of Kwun Tong, the group's early recruits came largely from the affiliated St. Barnabas Primary School, located in the Kwun Tong Resettlement Estate, and Lam Pak Sau (林柏秀), the primary school's principal, was a member of the executive committee of the Kwun Tong Scout District .[2]

Badge for Li Cheng Uk District (top), and the district's inauguration.

H. K. Scout Archives.

Though disadvantaged Boy Scouts became increasingly common, they did not always participate as fully as other boys, especially in the 1950s. Among the sixty-plus Scouts who attended the 1959 Jamboree were seven sponsored by the local bottler for Coca-Cola, proposed by groups, screened by districts, and selected by the headquarters. None of these fortunate boys belonged to elite troops, three lived in the New Territories, and one each came from two orphanage groups, 23rd Kowloon and 25th Hong Kong. But, aside from these, not one of the other Boy Scouts came from the New Territories or the underprivileged

1   Report, K. F. Law, "Resettlement Scouting," April 28, 1966, the Hong Kong Scout Archives.
2   *Inauguration Ceremony* 成立典禮專刊 (Hong Kong: Kwun Tong District Local Association, 1967); Scout Association of Hong Kong, "the 159th East Kowloon Group," http://www.159.bravehost.com/ page3.html (accessed July 1, 2009).

groups, only two of the fifteen Senior Scouts came from rural groups in Yuen Long, and none of the seven Rover Scouts. On the other hand, ethnic British boys from the Shek Kong group contributed four of the fourteen Boy Scouts, and boys from 1st Hong Kong six of the fifteen Senior Scouts.[1]

A Queen's Scout Badge, in use till 1967.

Rural boys constituted 20% of total members in the mid-1950s, but, from 1954 to 1959, their share of the Queen's Scout awards, a reasonable proxy for achievement, was only 7%. Nevertheless, marked improvements were achieved in the 1960s. From 1960 to 1966, the rural groups boasted of having 17% of the Queen's Scout awards, close to their share of membership. Disadvantaged boys besides the rural ones were still more under-represented. The underprivileged groups, as noted earlier, made up 15% of the total number of Scout Groups in 1957, but they produced less than 1% of the top awards between 1954 and 1959.[2] These groups also made good progress in the 1960s, at least partly attributable to one glaring exception among them—the 3rd Hong Kong Sea Scouts at the Hong Kong Sea School, which trained orphans, poor children, and some boys with minor offences for a career at sea.[3] Its first Queen's Scout, "boy no. M13" (Lam Chi-chiu 林志超), who won this coveted award in 1963, clearly inspired his group mates.[4] From 1964 to 1968, the group produced seventeen Queen's Scouts, demonstrating that, with the right kind of motivation, disadvantaged boys could participate just as fully as boys in more fortunate circumstances.

The Girl Guides were not left behind in efforts to reach the underprivileged. A Salvation Army unit, the 3rd Kowloon Company, was started in 1947, and remained active in the 1950s.[5] In 1950, the first deaf company began at the School for the Deaf under Kong Uen Laan.[6] Lady Grantham officiated at its inauguration in 1952, earlier than the first

---

1   *KSYP*, June 25, 1959; the *Scout Bulletin*, May-June 1959, 13-14.

2   Lo Wai-shing (ed.), *Directory of Recipients of the King's Scout Award, the Queen's Scout Award, and the Hong Kong Special Administrative Region Scout Award*榮譽童軍獎章持有人名錄 (Hong Kong: the Scout Association, 2000), 21-39.

3   Peter Wood, "Training for a New Life," in HKRS 365-1-86-1-10, the Public Records Office, Hong Kong; *The Hong Kong Sea School: Scout Report, March 1962*.

4   The *School Magazine, March 1962* (Hong Kong Sea School, 1962).

5   *Report of the Girl Guides Association of Hong Kong , 1947-48, 1948-49, 1954-55* (Hong Kong: Girl Guides Association of Hong Kong), 9-10, 15-16, 29, respectively.

6   Hong Kong School for the Deaf, the *Principal's Report, 1950-1951* (Hong Kong: Hong Kong School for the Deaf, 1951).

handicapped Boy Scout Troop.[1] In 1954, two companies were founded for girls from the Boys' and Girls' Club.[2] A rural company started in Cheung Chau in 1955.[3] By 1956, there were companies in four rural schools.[4] In 1958, Lady Baden-Powell took advantage of her visit to open the Guides headquarters for the Hay Ling Chau leprosy village.[5] By 1959, the Boys' and Girls' Clubs were running three Guide Companies and two Brownie Packs.[6] In 1960, orphan girls in the Children's Garden were invested, two years after a Scout Group was formed there. In the same month, Fung Hao-chen (馮巧珍) became the first Hong Kong girl to receive a Girl Guide Gallantry Cross for having courageously chased a robber. Fung did not come from an elite company: She belonged to the 3rd Kowloon, sponsored by the Salvation Army.[7] Lady B-P re-visited in November 1962. A joint campfire was held for over 2,500 Scouts, Cubs, Guides and Brownies, but she also made a point of seeing the Girl Guides at Hay Ling Chau again.[8]

Lady B-P met Scouts, Cubs, Guides and Brownies in a campfire in 1962.

Roger Yu's collection.

Why had Scouting not already reached the underprivileged before the war, as it had in Britain? After all, the Salvation Army had started operations in the colony in 1930.[9] The first boys' club and the first school for the deaf had both been founded in the mid-1930s.[10] Lep-

---

1   *KSYP*, May 22, 1952, May 24, 1952.

2   Minutes, the Council Meeting, the Girl Guides Association, January 6, 1955.

3   *KSYP*, March 6, 1955, September 4, 1955.

4   *KSYP*, September 21, 1956.

5   *KSYP*, March 29, 1958.

6   *Annual Report, 1958-59* (Hong Kong: The Boys' & Girls' Clubs Association, 1959), 5.

7   *KSYP*, July 11, 1960, July 23, 1960.

8   *Annual Report, 1962-63* (Hong Kong: The Girl Guides Association, 1963), 12. Lady B-P's stay was extended as her planned visit to India was canceled last minute.

9   *What is the Salvation Army?* (Hong Kong: the Salvation Army: 1994), 18-19.

10   Bao Rui-mei 鲍瑞美, "Hong Kong's School for the Deaf (香港真铎启音学

ers had been treated at the Tung Wah Hospital in the same decade.[1] In the interwar years, Hong Kong had many coolies and squatters living in Wanchai, Sheung Wan, Yaumati and Mongkok, where "raising children and shaping them into decent and good citizens [was] very difficult."[2] But Scouting in the early interwar years remained elitist, reserved for expatriate children and Chinese boys from select schools and churches. Even by the later interwar years, the indigenized movement was still largely for better-off and middle-class Chinese boys.

Possible reasons for the lack of development in Scouting for disadvantaged boys in the interwar years may include the fact that the movement was still drawing recruits mainly from among upper and middle class boys, and had simply not evolved to such a stage that it needed to reach out to the lower classes. Furthermore, from the authorities' perspective, when governance was a major motive, the key targets at this stage were the elite Chinese boys who were likely to become future leaders. Also, prejudices towards disabled and disadvantaged persons were common, perhaps more so in Hong Kong than in some other western communities. Finally, in the last interwar years, the colony had been preoccupied with preparing for war, and Halward was in China much of the time. Major policy shifts were not likely to have been considered and, even if deemed desirable, would have had to be put aside.

The situation changed dramatically postwar, especially after 1949. Much has been written about the Chinese diaspora, or the international migration or dispersion of the Chinese people over the centuries.[3] Since its founding as a colony, Hong Kong formed part of the Chinese diasporic network, and was often perceived as a stepping-stone rather than a final destination. No other social group personifies the colony's diasporic experience better than the refugees who flooded Hong Kong from the late 1930s to the early 1950s, fleeing war and revolution in China. This problem significantly worsened around the time when the Nationalists lost control of most parts of China to the Communists. As

校)," http://www. etabc.com/html/article-22573.html (accessed July 28, 2008).

1   *HKDP*, June 17, 1938.

2   Otto J. Golger, "An Environmental Study of Squatter and Resettlement Housing in Hong Kong," Ph. D. dissertation, Univ. of Hong Kong, 1968, 133-137.

3   Laurence J. C. Ma and Carolyn L. Cartier, *The Chinese Diaspora: Space, Place, Mobility and Identity* (Lanham, Md.: Rowman & Littlefield, c2003); Wang Ling-chi and Wang Gungwu, *The Chinese Diaspora: Selected Essays* (Singapore: Times Academic Press, 1998.)

Han Suyin puts it, with large influx of refugees, Hong Kong in 1949 was a city of "transients...refugee camp...[or a] squatters' colony...where people come and go and know themselves more impermanent than anywhere else on earth."[1] In the same year, Ch'ien Mu (錢穆), a prominent historian from China, arrived and founded the New Asia College. The song he wrote for the college included these words: "empty hands, without a thing, long journeys, without an end (手空空, 無一物, 路遙遙, 無止境)," which perhaps expressed well the predicaments and sentiments of these transients in Hong Kong.[2]

Yet, most transients were not able to move on. Huge number of squatters occupying much of Hong Kong's precious urban space, coupled with a number of devastating fires (e.g. in the Kowloon walled city in 1950, Tung Tau in 1951, and Shek Kip Mei in 1953), forced Grantham to adopt a massive resettlement program.[3] Impressive progress was made, but great needs still remained. By 1959, there were still 500,000 illegal squatters and only 190,000 resettled tenants. By 1964, there were over 540,000 people in resettlement estates, though a similar number still lived in squatter areas.[4] Dealing with the large number of underprivileged boys, especially those living in the crowded and substandard urban housing areas, became a priority in these decades largely because the community, the government and the Scout association all perceived the potential political and social dangers of neglecting them. As it turned out, these youngsters would play a significant role in the agitations in 1966 and 1967, to be discussed in the next chapter.

Scouting had been successful in penetrating the middle class, but the underprivileged segment provided opportunities hitherto unexplored. For the government devoting an ever-larger budget to welfare, education and housing, Scouting was a natural partner for outreach efforts targeting disadvantaged boys, many of whom were not attending school. A survey in 1957 indicated that less than half of the children in

---

1   Han Suyin, *A Many-Splendoured Thing* (Harmondsworth: Penguin Books, 1961), 29. Han, or Dr. Elizabeth Tang, was an Eurasian born in China to a Chinese father and a Belgian mother.
2   Long Ying-tai 龍應台, *Da Jiang Da Hai: Yi Jiu Shi Jiu* 大江大海: 一九四九 (Our 1949) (Hong Kong: Cosmos Books, 2009), 148.
3   Alan Smart, *the Shek Kip Mei Myth: Squatters, Fires and Colonial Rule in Hong Kong, 1950-1963* (Hong Kong, Hong Kong Univ. Press, 2006).
4   Sue Palmer, *Living and Partly Living: The Problem of Youth in Hong Kong* (Hong Kong, 1975), 43.

the resettlement estates were in schools, suggesting a great need to reach out to them through informal channels such as the Scout Movement.[1] For other social service providers, most of which were rapidly expanding their programs to meet "the needs of the children crowding our city streets," Scouting complemented their efforts.[2]

Macleod suggests that the effectiveness of American Scouting was doubtful as a character-building agency since "most recruits were probably fairly decent before they joined."[3] In the earlier years, stakeholders involved in Hong Kong Scouting, much like elsewhere, had shied away from making claims to provide character and citizenship training to the lower class boys who needed it the most. In the postwar years, however, the movement took on precisely this task, as those involved in Hong Kong Scouting rose to the challenge of its inclusive ideals, and made extensive and systematic efforts to reach out to underprivileged boys, including the rural, the poor, the orphaned, the physically-challenged, and even the institutionalized.

Boys from a blind troop enjoyed camping.

H. K. Scout Archives.

In a sense, to borrow Han Suyin's words, the movement helped to reconstruct for these boys some of the "many worlds" on this "beautiful island…in the arms of the sea."[4] It could be said that in the immediate postwar decades, Scouting had found a new mission in this city of transients: to transform the colony for some from "a *non-place*—…a passage that only serves as an access to somewhere else" into "a *multi-*

---

1   C. S. Hui, W. F. Maunder & J. Tsao, *Hong Kong's Resettled Squatters: the Final Report on the 1957 Sample Survey of Resettlement Estates* (Hong Kong: the Univ. of Hong Kong: 1959), 49-50.
2   *Annual Reports, 1949-50; 1960-61* (Hong Kong: Boys' and Girls' Clubs Association, 1950, 1961). The association grew from 41 clubs in 1950 to 208 clubs in 1961.
3   Macleod, *Building Character*, 305.
4   Han, *A Many-Splendoured Thing*, 29.

place which conditions the spacing of many other places," especially for those who could not or chose not to run further.[1] Youth membership in local Scouting was no longer reserved mainly for decent boys from the middle class, but was available to all, including many boys from the large disadvantaged classes.

Substantial growth was achieved in the first two postwar decades, despite some initial hiccups, as the red line in the graph below illustrates. The movement grew slowly in the 1940s, and even declined in the later part of the decade, as pro-Nationalist troops disappeared due to Nationalists' setbacks in China and the colonial authorities' denationalization efforts. By 1952, total membership stood at 2,300, the level it had already achieved in 1946. However, from then on, with active encouragement in both the elite and vernacular schools and systematic programs to reach out to the underprivileged sectors of the community through close partnership with other voluntary organizations and government authorities, Scouting in Hong Kong took off impressively.

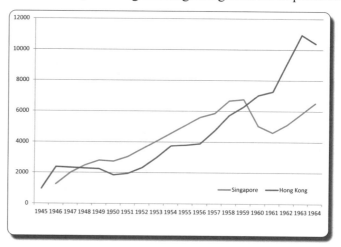

Membership Trends, Hong Kong and Singapore, 1945-1964

Sources: Appendix D, "Membership Statistics;" Tan and Wan, *Scouting in Singapore*, 271. Note Singapore data points for 1952-55 and 1963 are not available, and are shown on the graph above as "smoothed out" data points.

Comparative statistics from nearby Singapore, depicted by the blue line in the graph, are also instructive. Throughout the 1950s, Scout membership in Hong Kong had consistently trailed that in Singapore,

1   Juanita C. But, "The Other Race: Settler, Exile, Transient and Sojourner in the Literary Diaspora," Ph. D. dissertation, Univ. of New York at Buffalo, 1999, 122-123.

despite the latter's smaller population. In 1960, Singapore suffered a sudden drop in membership and, for the first time in history, there were more Scouts in Hong Kong than in Singapore. By the end of 1964, the Hong Kong movement had a population penetration three times that in 1941, and had over 10,000 members, or close to 60% more than that of Singapore.[1] It seems that local Scouting had finally shaken off its niche label and gained critical mass, despite its denationalized nature.

Concluding Remarks

These years under review saw the quick re-launch of Scouting, flavored with strong Chinese Nationalist influence; a short period of Chinese leadership, inspired by the postwar preference for larger roles for the Chinese; and a decade of renewed European leadership, marked by de-nationalization efforts, the inclusion of underprivileged boys, and the transformation of Scouting into an emerging mass movement. "To rule" (sometimes executed with the more palatable label "to educate"), was the key motive, as the government struggled to buttress fragile governance in the face of a powerful and somewhat belligerent Chinese neighbor which could over-run the colony by force if it chose to.

Comic series "Boy Scouts," produced by Ng Gei-ping in the early 1960s.

Perhaps the most flattering if unintentional recognition of Hong Kong Scouting as a mass movement came from outside, by way of commercial media intended for mass consumption. Comic books, or *man-hua* (漫畫), became popular after the war, reflecting life in the colony

---

1   See Appendix D, "Membership Statistics."

and expressing the Hong Kong identity. A popular series entitled the *Boy Scouts* (童子軍) was produced by Ng Gei-ping (伍寄萍) in 1960, featuring two gun-touting Boy Scouts, Siu-ming and Siu Sam-ji, young war heroes who fought the Japanese in various adventures, with series titles like "Surprise Attack by Parachute," "Counter-attack of the Death Island," and "The Destruction of Enemy Battleship."[1] The "Scout Master (童軍教練)," the first and only commercial film made in Hong Kong solely about Scouting, featuring the Cantonese movie stars Leung Sing-bor (梁醒波) and Chan Bo-chu (陳寶珠), was simultaneously released in 1959 in Mandarin and dubbed Cantonese.[2] Details in the film, including the Scout uniforms, were not always correct. But one review assured all that this "educational comedy (富教育性的喜劇片)" was guaranteed to make one "laugh until one's stomach aches (笑到肚皮刺痛)."[3] Commercial firms were driven by profit motives and would only invest in projects which had adequate popular appeal. "The Scout Master" and the *Boy Scouts* may or may not have accurately portrayed the ideals of Scouting. But the fact that two commercial concerns had chosen to invest in a movie and a comic series with a Scout theme reaffirmed the

Pictorial booklet promoting the film "The Scout Master," 1959.

Author's collection.

1   The association eventually sued to have the title removed, using protection of the official name Boy Scout (童子軍) afforded by local ordinance, and the series continued for a period of time under the new title *Siu-ming* (小明.) See Wendy Siu-yi Wong, *Hong Kong Comics: A History of Manhua* (New York, Princeton Architectural Press, 2002); 108-109; Frenchy Lunning, *Emerging Worlds of Anime and Manga* (Minnesota: Univ. of Minnesota Press, 2006), 30.
2   Law Kar, Frank Bren, and Sam Ho, *Hong Kong Cinema: A Cross-cultural View* (Oxford: Scarecrow Press, 2004) , 167.
3   *KSYP*, November 21, 1959.

growing popularity and social acceptance of the youth movement.

Race and class became less significant obstacles to involvement as Scouting was fully indigenized. By the mid-1960s, Hong Kong Scouting was no longer a niche movement for a small number of elites, but a budding if not yet fully-developed mass youth movement, as evidenced by its aligned (albeit denationalized) ideologies, inclusiveness, rapid growth, professional support, and capacity to host major events and participate in international Scouting.

During the immediate postwar decades, the colonial authorities were successful in transforming a strongly nationalistic Scouting into a denationalized and Hong Kong-focused movement, while driving its growth. This phenomenon is intriguing. In countries where there was (perceived or real) subjugation of the native group(s) by those from outside, native nationalism typically underpinned the transformation of Scouting into a mass movement. For example, when the nationalistic *Fédération du scoutism musulman algérien* was founded in 1939 by Mohamed Bouras, it grew rapidly and absorbed other Scout Groups in French Algeria.[1] It appears that this pairing of native nationalism and Scouting did not apply to Hong Kong in quite the same way.

In fact, it could be argued that, denationalization was perhaps necessary for the growth of local Scouting. In this unique colonial context, one may suggest that even if Chinese nationalism could be encouraged in Scouting without PRC's interference, the movement might have become too divisive because of it. By inculcating in the boys of Hong Kong a sense of loyalty to their place of residence, coupled with a vague sense of respect for Chinese culture and language instead of commitment to any Chinese political entity, Scouting was able to extend its appeal to a broader audience, and to steer clear of diplomatic wrangling with its watchful neighbor up north. In doing so, Hong Kong Scouting developed into a budding mass movement with its own characteristics, both Chinese and British, but at the same time not fully consonant with either Britain or China (whether Communist or Nationalist).

---

1   Jacques Cantier, «Un enjeu essentiel: Vichy et les jeunes dans l'Empire Français,» in Jacques Cantier and Éric Jennings (ed.), *L'Empire colonial sous Vichy* (Paris: Édition Odile Jacob, 2004), 111-112.

Reforms and Independence

1964-1977

Chapter 5
Reforms and Independence
1964-1977

Sir David Trench succeeded Sir Robert Black in April 1964. A few years later, Trench was faced with the 1967 riots, in which many youngsters participated. In one incident, when a bomb placed by the rioters blew up on a crowded street, Boy Scouts voluntarily helped with both crowd control before and first aid after, and some of them were injured. While this unfortunate incident drew different comments from newspapers with diverging political biases, it highlighted the value of citizenship training provided by Scouting, and heralded in decades of government- and community-sponsored expansion of the movement.

During this time, Hong Kong came out of postwar recovery into a period of impressive economic growth. From 1961 to 1971, when Sir John Cowperthwaite, personification of Hong Kong's *laissez-faire* or positive non-intervention economic policies, was the financial secretary, real wages rose 50%, households with monthly income of less than $400 dropped from over 50% to less than 16%, and the government consistently reported large budgetary surpluses and accumulated impressive sterling reserves.[1] Hong Kong's economy was in the process of transitioning from a traditional trade and manufacturing driven mode to a modern finance and service based one. This was, of course, a gradual process which continued in the following decades, eventually transforming Hong Kong into a more prosperous economy, with per capita income which was to exceed that in Britain. But on the political and social fronts, Hong Kong was faced with serious challenges which drove home the need for fundamental re-thinking on governance, educational policies, social welfare and, more particularly, the role of Scouting.

The years covered in this chapter could be characterized as a

Previous Page:

MacLehose met Scouts, incl. female Venture Scouts in modernized uniforms, at Police Football Ground, Kowloon, April 1979, two years after local Scouting became independent. *H. K. Scout Archives.*

---

1   Welsh, *A Borrowed Place*, 459-465.

period of reforms and independence for local Scouting. These two processes started hand-in-hand with the successive installations of Chinese
Scouters as top leaders of the movement. Unlike their compatriots in the
early 1950s, they stayed on longer and were able to implement necessary
management reforms to deliver healthy expansion of the movement despite sluggish growth in population. After the unrests in 1966 and 1967,
and in response to the perceived needs of youngsters living in densely-
populated urban areas and encouragement from the government and the
community, the association expanded its scope beyond its traditional
boundaries to serve many non-Scout youth. By the late 1960s and early
1970s, both the looks and the programs of local Scouting were "modernized" based on recommendations of the British association, though a few
of these metropolitan-centric and top-down reforms were not appropriate and had negative impacts on the movement's growth. Sir Murray
MacLehose took over from Trench in November 1971 and stayed till
May 1982, making him the longest-serving governor, exceeding the record of Grantham by one month. In 1977, with blessings from both the
British Scout Association and MacLehose, the Hong Kong branch was
"decolonized," and became a standalone "National" Scout Organization
(NSO) of the worldwide Scout community, making Hong Kong equal
to Scout Associations of independent nations in the British Commonwealth, despite her colonial status.

Planned growth under Chinese leaders

*A fresh attempt to localize leadership in the 1960s, unlike the earlier
one, proved more lasting. Kenneth Lo succeeded Cockburn in late 1963,
followed by Henry Ma; and both had relatively longer tenure and were
effective in utilizing modern management techniques such as multiple-
year plans, project management, organizational reforms, and improved
communication to drive impressive growth of local Scouting from mid-
1960s to late 1970s, despite modest increases in youth population during
the same period.*

In Cockburn's later years, when Hong Kong Scouting's localization was almost complete, the appointment of a Chinese to the top

post seemed overdue. Kenneth Ching-kan Lo (羅徵勤) took over in September 1963, just months before Trench replaced Black as the Chief Scout and G. R. Ross replaced Benson as the president. Lo had joined the movement as a boy, served since 1954 in various lay posts, and as the Deputy Colony Commissioner since March.[1] By this time, the "Chineseness" of the movement was evident. Trench attended his first parade in April 1964, and met twenty-three Queen's Scouts, all but two were Chinese.[2] A year later, Sir David gave certificates to forty-eight Queen's Scouts, only one a non-Chinese boy, and a gallantry cross to Scoutmaster Lau Tat-chuen (劉達銓) for saving the lives of two drowning Chinese boys in Cheung Chau.[3] Chinese Scouters dominated the whole leadership team, not just the top position. In 1966, Lo, Henry Ma, Edmond Woo and Hans Leung were the Colony Commissioner, the deputy, and the two assistants, respectively. Of the forty-seven commissioners, only four had non-Chinese last names. By 1970, only one European (Barton) appeared in the long list of commissioners. By 1976, localization was complete: all thirty senior commissioners were Chinese.[4]

Trench, accompanied by Lo, met the Scouts.

H. K. Scout Archives.

1   Influence of the Masons continued—though Lo was not a Mason at the time of his appointment, he was initiated into the Foochow Lodge in 1968, and became its second Chinese master in 1977. See Kenneth Cox, *The First Hundred Years: The History of Foochow Lodge* (Hong Kong: Foochow Lodge, 1982), 8-9, 48, 51.
2   *KSYP*, April 26, 1964.
3   The *Bulletin*, May-June 1965, 4-6 (Chinese), *KSYP*, April 24 and 25, 1965.
4   The *Annual Report* (Hong Kong: the Boy Scouts Association/the Scout Association), 1965/66, 1979/70, and 1975/76.

In contrast, leadership in local Guiding remained in European hands in the 1960s and 1970s, again suggesting gendered differences between the two movements. In 1966, the Colony Commissioner, the deputy and the assistant were all Europeans, and only fourteen of the other twenty-four commissioners had Chinese last names. In 1970, the Colony Commissioner and the deputy were Europeans, though the two assistants were Chinese. By 1976, the Colony Commissioner and one of her two deputies were still Europeans. Sally Leung (梁王培芳), the first Chinese Chief Commissioner, assumed her post in 1980, but was replaced three years later by Jane Akers-Jones.[1] Perhaps expatriate wives were more available and willing to serve, or there were cultured and gendered perceptions which had discouraged Chinese women from leadership roles in the movement. At any rate, Hong Kong Guiding continued to be led by non-Chinese long after the leadership of Hong Kong Scouting had become localized.

Lau Tat-chuen.
Gilwell Archives.

Efforts to reach out to underprivileged segments continued. When Maclean, the kilted Chief Scout, visited again in October 1964, he attended a rally, a reception hosted by Trench, and a campfire; but also met Chinese troops in resettlement estates and the rural areas. The association also initiated efforts to penetrate the manufacturing sector through a Factory Auxiliary Group (工廠輔助團) in Sham Shui Po, bringing citizenship training to young people who were excluded from the somewhat elitist school system. In November, Ross opened a New Territories area headquarters in Sheung Shui, with the generous support of a local village elder, Liu Ren Sum (廖潤琛). This new facility signified another milestone in rural Scouting, which had grown ten-fold in a decade to over three thousand members. In July 1965, Lo officiated at the opening of a training center in the rural township of Yuen Long, on a site loaned by another rural leader, Tang Kin-sun (鄧乾新).[2]

Lo also brought in new disciplines of multi-year planning and managed expansion, partly driven by concerns with slackened momentum in the movement. The Golden Jubilee year in 1961 was celebrated in a grand fashion, culminating in the Jubilee Jamborette in December.

1   The *Annual Report* (Hong Kong: the Girl Guides Association), 1964/65, 1969/70, 1975/76, 1982/83, 1986/87.
2   *KSYP*, October 8, 9, and 13, and November 28, 1964; the *Wah Kiu Yat Po* 華僑日報 (*WKYP*), October 10, 25 and November 30, 1964.

However, by 1964, youth membership registered a slight drop, something that had not happened since 1950. Lo declared that only by planning ahead could the movement succeed in reforming and renewing itself continuously, and appointed Ma to the newly-created post of Assistant Colony Commissioner (Planning) in 1965.[1] Efforts were soon taken to develop a five year plan, "designed to give better Scouting to more boys," covering 1967/68 to 1971/72.[2]

THE BOY SCOUTS ASSOCIATION

HONG KONG BRANCH

5 Year Plan of Development

1967/68 —

1971/72

Hong Kong Scouting's first
5 Year Plan, 1967-1972.

When the association adopted this plan, multiple-year strategic planning was still at the fore-front of modern management techniques. A study by Denning and Lehr of three hundred British companies in 1967 indicated that only 22% had corporate planning system, and in many industries, less than a quarter of the firms had long-range plans of three years or more.[3] The plan was a substantial document of over fifty pages, with five-year financial projections and eleven appendices on key initiatives.[4] Trench called it "a most commendable attempt to keep up with the needs of the community."[5]

---

1   The *Annual Report* (Hong Kong: the Boy Scouts Association), 1964-65, 4; the *Bulletin*, July-August 1965, 2.
2   The *Bulletin*, September-October 1966, 3.
3   W. Denning and M. E. Lehr, "The Extent and Nature of Corporate Long Range Planning in the U.K.: Part 1," *Journal of Management Studies*, May 1971.
4   *5-Year Plan of Development, 1967/68—1971/72* (Hong Kong: the Boy Scouts Association, 1966), 1.
5   The *Hong Kong Standard*, April 23, 1967.

The plan aimed at growth through the Scout and Cub sections, strengthened district support, improved campsites, new leaders, Scouting in a satellite town, and additional support staff. During the plan years, large donations were obtained for new or improved facilities in many Scout campsites or activities centers. Impressive growth came from geographical reorganization, decentralization in all regions, and innovative programs such as the Cadet Groups (見習領袖旅), consisting of trainee male and female leaders who would eventually be transferred to the Scout Groups or Districts, and the village Scout Groups (鄉村童軍旅), sponsored by larger villages and hamlets.[1] By end of 1967, after intensive recruitment, there were fourteen Cadet Groups, typically attached to districts, areas or the headquarters, including three in the New Territories. True to their slogans, "Forward" and "Service," these trained cadet leaders became instrumental in developing many new Scout Groups and supporting existing ones throughout Hong Kong in the following decade. Air Scouting, started in the 1950s, was revived at Kowloon Wah Yan in 1967 by Father Cunningham.

A mixed Cadet Group in training at the Gilwell Campsite, 1968.

H. K. Scout Archives.

Coinciding with the last year of the plan, 1971, was the official 60th anniversary of Hong Kong Scouting, celebrated with several international Scout events. The most important of these was the Diamond Jubilee Jamboree, held in July at Castle Peak, with almost five thousand participants. The Jamboree was marked by a number of "firsts." Lo succeeded in obtaining the Postmaster General's blessing to issue a set of

1   The *Annual Report* (Hong Kong: the Boy Scouts Association/the Scout Association), *1967/68*, 6-8; *1968/69*, 15-18; *1969/70*, 18-20; *1970/71*, 32-36; the *Bulletin*, October-December 1968, 4 (English), 11-13 (Chinese).

One of a set of three stamps issued on the Diamond Jubiliee, 1971.

commemorative Scout stamps, a first in local postal history, on the opening day of the Jamboree. There was the presence of 1,500 non-Scout youngsters among the participants, a first in a Scout Jamboree. As will be discussed in the next section, the association had by this time been regularly serving large numbers of non-Scouts for several years, and had decided to invite some of them as guests to the Jamboree, in three shifts of three days each, paid for partly by the government. Finally, the Jamboree had the dubious honor of being visited by two typhoons, another first in the history of local Jamborees. These caused a delay of the opening and considerable interruptions during the camp, though also created memorable shared experience for many local Scouts and their young brethrens from nine Asian countries.[1]

Performance on the Jamboree square, 1971.

H. K. Scout Archives.

As in the past, Chinese politics still meant the necessary exclusion of brother Scouts from Taiwan, despite the theme of "World Harmony (大同)." Sir Hugh Norman-Walker, the colonial secretary, noted in a confidential letter that "there would be complications if an organized

1   The Diamond Jubilee Jamboree folder, the Hong Kong Scout Archives.

contingent were to be invited from Tai Wan [*sic*] and if it made use of its own national flag, for example, at an opening ceremony." Ross promptly reassured him that the association had never invited any official contingent from Taiwan, and that it was its standard policy not to do so.[1]

The jubilee year was also marked by the hosting of a regional Scout training course in March, a World Scout Public Relations seminar in July, and the 4th Commonwealth Scout Conference in August. In the same month, the colony participated in the 13th World Jamboree in Japan with a contingent of one hundred, its largest ever, led by Jerome Yeung Yiu-tin (楊堯天). Geographic skew of the sixty-five youth participants, all Chinese boys, suggests significant economic disparities between different regions in Hong Kong: forty-two were from troops on the Hong Kong Island, twenty-one from troops in Kowloon, and only two from troops in the New Territories.[2] The Jamboree was followed by the 23rd World Scout Conference, which Lo attended. The agenda of this meeting would not have surprised Lo: much time was devoted to the "World Scouting Five Year Plan," which stated that "long range planning is as vital to Scouting as it is to other aspects of society."[3]

A participant's badge for the Diamond Jubilee Jamboree, 1971.

The 2nd five-year plan commenced in 1972, when youth membership declined slightly from the year before, suggesting that Scouting was again faced with short-term stagnation, like that seen a decade ago, after the Golden Jubilee. Incidentally, Singapore also had a similarly worrisome trend, as membership peaked in 1969, and then declined for three years, prompting it to adopt its first multi-year plan.

Despite its "non-political" policy, Scouting was occasionally drawn into local political struggles. In 1973, some teachers-cum-Scoutmasters who belonged to the Joint Secretariat of Hong Kong Educational Bodies claimed that the Scout Association had bowed to pressures from the government and reneged on an agreement to allow them to use the Scout hall for a mass meeting to discuss their disputes with the government over pay and conditions, and called for a boycott of the Scout rally in April.[4] By this time, Lo was due to retire. Ma worked with Szeto

1   Ibid.

2   *13th World Jamboree* 第十三屆世界大露營, *August 1971* (Hong Kong: the Scout Association, 1971).

3   *World Scouting* (Geneva: World Scout Bureau, 1973), July-September, 1973, 16.

4   *CM*, April 18, 1973.

Henry Ma in post-*APR*
uniform, 1970s.

H. K. Scout Archives.

Wah (司徒華), the Secretary General of the teacher's organization, and obtained the latter's consent to issue an open letter urging all teachers to support Scouting and attend the rally.[1] This maneuver narrowly averted the threatened boycott, which would have embarrassed both the government and the movement. In September, Henry C. Ma (馬基) took over as the Chief Commissioner. As a Scouter with a distinguished service record within the movement both before and after the war, and being a key player in Cockburn's time and Lo's most important assistant, he needed little introduction in the local Scouting community.

Besides multi-year plans, Ma also used market research, communication sessions, and project management to gather feedbacks, build consensus, disseminate objectives and drive initiatives. He authorized qualitative and quantitative research exercises to identify needs for improvements, including a management survey conducted by J. Plaridel Silvestre of the Asia Pacific office of the World Scout Bureau in 1973 which resulted in reforms aimed at streamlining and enhancing the effectiveness of the association.[2] He also instituted consultative forums at different levels, including the Chief Commissioner's Council (香港總監諮議會), periodic gatherings for Regional and District Commissioners, and a colony-wide Group Leaders' Consultative Council.

Ma was particularly fond of project management, which, according to one expert of the field, was only emerging in the late 1960s "holistically as a management discipline," and created dedicated multi-year projects for many challenges.[3] A list in 1975 contained twenty projects covering facilities, Scout Groups, leaders, youth training, staffing, funding, and even the future status of the Hong Kong Branch.[4] Some of these were quite complicated and multi-faceted. Two illustrations would suffice. Project B covered many real estate sub-projects, the most important of which was that related to the redevelopment of the headquarters, eventually completed in the 1990s, to be discussed in the next chapter. Project W was aimed at doubling membership within four years, and comprised seven sub-projects covering Scout Leaders, support staffing,

1   Letter, Szeto Wah to Ma, April 19, 1973, the Hong Kong Scout Archives.
2   J. Plaridel Silvestre, *A Preliminary Report on the Management/Organisation Audit of the Hong Kong Branch, the Scout Association,* October 1973, the Hong Kong Scout Archives.
3   Dennis Lock, *Project Management*, 9th ed. (Aldershot: Gower, 2007), 3.
4   "List of Projects, October 1975," the Hong Kong Scout Archives.

and properly-equipped premises and training centers.

All these modern management techniques would mean little if they did not positively impact Scouting. Contemporary research from the business world suggested that such techniques often improved organizational performance. Malik and Karger measured performance of 273 American companies from 1964 to 1973, and concluded that those with formal integrated long-range plans significantly out-performed the non-planners across industries using various business performance indicators.[1] Harold Kerzner noted that from mid-1960s onward, formal project management became mandatory especially in organizations facing complex tasks in dynamic environments.[2] Membership and population statistics in Hong Kong in the two plan periods, when similar techniques were extensively adopted in Scouting, are revealing:

	12/66	*12/71*	*%*	*12/76*	*%*
Youth Members	11,155	15,736	41%	21,392	37%
Pop. (male, 5-19)	712,820	746,611	5%	755,850	1%
Rel. Growth Ratio (Youth %/Pop. %)		8.7			30.8

Youth Membership vs. Pop. Growth, 1966-1976

Source: Youth membership statistics from Census Reports, various years, the Hong Kong Scout Archives. Population numbers for 1966, 1971 and 1976 from *Hong Kong By-Census, 1976: Main Report, Vol. II: Tables*, Table III 1, 12.

Scout youth membership grew over 40% from over 11,000 in 1966 to almost 16,000 in 1971 and another 37% to over 21,000 in 1976.[3] Such increases, though impressive, may not seem outstanding when compared with growth rates logged in the immediate postwar decades. But when they are put side-by-side with population growth rates, a very different picture emerges: growth in youth membership was close to nine times

1   Z. A. Malik and D. W. Karger, "Does Long Range Planning Improve Company Performance?" *Management Review*, September 1975. One could argue that this could be due to the fact that better performing companies tend to do planning, not vice versa.
2   Harold Kerzner, *Project Management: A Systems Approach to Planning, Scheduling, and Controlling*, 10th ed. (New Jersey: John Wiley, 2009), 39-40.
3   The *Annual Report* (Hong Kong: the Boy Scouts Association/the Scout Association), 1966/67, 4; 1972/73, 2; 1976/77, 2.

that of target population growth in the first plan period, and over thirty times in the second, using male population between the ages of five and nineteen as a proxy. Clearly, such impressive growth of the movement from mid-1960s to mid-1970s had to be underpinned by an increase in demand in the community, but modern management techniques under Lo and Ma had apparently also paid off, at least to some extent.

Inclusion of non-Scout youngsters

In the 1960s, much of the youthful population in Hong Kong resided in highly-concentrated urban areas and overcrowded resettlement estates. The 1966 disturbances and the 1967 riots, besides being part of a world-wide phenomenon of youth activism, served to remind all that youth problems in Hong Kong were daunting and urgent revamping of social policies was required. Scouting had demonstrated its capacity to exert a calming influence on young people during the unrest. More significantly, it transformed itself thereafter, as it responded to the calls from the community and the authorities to reach out to many more youngsters, in terms of both reforms in and expansion of its existing Scout program, to be discussed later in this chapter, and the introduction of new programs for non-Scout youth, which will be addressed in this section.

In the postwar decades, disillusioned youth and juvenile delinquents were frequently involved in disturbances in Britain, France, Japan, Singapore and many other places.[1] In these incidents, youthful players with different ethnic, economic, political, and cultural backgrounds and motivations participated, suggesting that the adolescence experience around the world, as Bradford Brown and Reed Larson point out, was more differentiated ("kaleidoscopic") than similar ("kinescopic").[2]

---

1   See Bill Osgerby, *Youth in Britain Since 1945* (Oxford: Blackwell Publishers, 1998), 121, 150-2, 162-7; Richard Jobs, *Riding the New Wave: Youth and the Rejuvenation of France After Second World War* (Stanford: Stanford Univ. Press, 2007), 130; Huang Jianli, "The Youth Pathfinders: Portrayal of Student Political Activism," in Michael D. Barr and Carl A. Trocki, *Paths Not Taken: Political Pluralism in Post-War Singapore* (Singapore: NUS Press, 2008), 188-205; and Duncan McCargo, *Contemporary Japan* (Hampshire: Palgrave, 2000), 154.

2   B. Bradford Brown and Reed W. Larson, "The Kaleidoscope of Adolescence: Experiences of the World's Youth at the Beginning of the 21st Century," in B. Bradford Brown, Reed W. Larson, T.S. Saraswathi (eds.), *The World's Youth: Adolescence in Eight Regions of the Globe* (Cambridge: Cambridge Univ. Press, 2002), 1-19.

Youth activism was likewise common in Hong Kong in the 1960s. But, as shall be shown, these were typically driven more by causes unique to Hong Kong and China than common to all.

In Britain and other countries, Scouting, like other youth services, was often perceived as an effective citizenship training program which would discourage juvenile delinquency and youth participation in agitations.[1] Some argue that youth service was not merely to keep youth "off the streets," but to give those not in schools "a means of combating the effects of 'disadvantage.'"[2] Others contend that "not poverty but unaccustomed riches seems an equally dangerous inducement to wild behaviour, or even crime."[3] Whether delinquency and agitations among youth were due to "disadvantage" or "unaccustomed riches," "the postwar youth service was intended to function not simply as a palliative to delinquency, but as a fully integrated component within Britain's revamped education system," aimed at "monitoring and orchestrating [young people's] leisure time" and socializing them "into the disciplines of the workplace."[4] As such, Bill Osgerby concludes, postwar youth services in Britain had become "an integral part of the national scheme for further education," not allowed to develop in isolation.[5]

Faced with the challenges presented by the two riots in Hong Kong in the 1960s in which many youngsters participated, the perceived roles of Scouting as a youth service and a citizenship program were likewise redefined. These unrests shocked the colony and challenged many to re-think how best to deal with its youngsters. Afterward, with the full support of the government and the community, Scouting became an integral part of Hong Kong's educational and social programs.

The 1966 disturbances were ostensibly triggered by a proposed

---

1   Two examples are illustrative. Walter Daniel concludes that Scouting helped to prevent juvenile delinquency among Negro youth in America in the 1950s. In 1958, a Parisian judge estimated that the juvenile delinquent probation program *liberté surveillée*, which substituted incarceration with character reeducation (including Scouting), had a success rate of 71%. See Walter G. Daniel, "The Role of Youth Character-Building Organizations in Juvenile Delinquency Prevention," *The Journal of Negro Education*, 28/3, Juvenile Delinquency Among Negroes in the United States, Summer 1959, 301-317; and Jobs, *Riding the New Wave*, 157-158.

2   Mica Nava, *Changing Cultures: Feminism, Youth and Consumerism* (London: SAGE publications, 1992), 75.

3   Osgerby, *Youth in Britain Since 1945*, 140.

4   Ibid., 140-141.

5   Ibid., 140.

fare increase by the Star Ferry in 1965, which met with a lot of negative press, partly fanned by mass signature campaigns against it initiated by Mrs. Elsie Elliot, an Urban Councilor. In response, the government-appointed advisory committee recommended in March 1966 no increase in fares except those for first-class passengers. This was unfortunately followed by independent increases of some government fees and rents, confirming the public's worst fears of general inflation. In April, twenty-seven-year-old So Sau-chung staged a hunger strike at the Star Ferry, and was arrested for obstruction. A demonstration march followed, went past two resettlement estates and gathered a group of several hundred young people, which was eventually dispersed by force. Disturbances, destruction of property, and clashes occurred in the following evenings in congested parts of Kowloon despite a curfew imposed by the police. Many demonstrators were youngsters wearing school uniforms or slippers, and some were of primary school age. Of the 1,500 people arrested, 5% were under fifteen, and 30% under twenty.[1]

Commissioner Lo was appointed to a governor's task force investigating the 1966 disturbances. The task force concluded that overcrowded housing, shortages of open space, inadequate school places, lack of character training, and absence of community spirit were the primary causes for youngsters' involvement in the agitation, and suggested "moral training and character building" programs and "more facilities for healthy recreation."[2] These proposals aligned well with the purpose and approach of Scouting. An implied response was to expand Scouting, a cost-effective alternative to reaching out to disadvantaged youth who fell outside the elitist education system. The events in the next two years would re-affirm the need for a larger role for the movement.

The next serious challenge to colonial governance, the riots of 1967-68, was driven as much by developments in China as by those in the colony. In May 1966, Mao Zedong inaugurated the Great Proletarian Cultural Revolution (無產階級文化大革命), a struggle for succession aimed at ridding the country of its liberal bourgeois elements and perpetuating revolutionary class struggles through China's youth, who became the "Red Guards (紅衛兵)." The troubles in Hong Kong were conceived

---

1   *Kowloon Disturbances 1966: Report of Commissioner of Inquiry* (Hong Kong: the Government Press, 1966), 8-60, 155-159.

2   Ibid., 136, 138, 141-142, 147.

in this Chinese context. What started as May Day labor celebrations and isolated labor disputes soon developed into a small-scale local "Cultural Revolution," complete with strikes, riots, property damage, bombs, violence, deaths, and negotiations between the colonial, British, and Chinese governments. Initially, the "Anti-British Struggle Committee" enjoyed strong support from China. On May 17, one million protesters in Beijing marched past the British mission, demanding that the British leave Hong Kong. Next day, one hundred thousand people attended an anti-British mass rally, in the presence of Premier Zhou Enlai.[1]

Governor Trench proposed strong countermeasures (as opposed to the more accommodating approaches advocated by the British mission in Beijing), and his line was approved by London. It was reasoned that Hong Kong, China's window for foreign trade and source of hard currencies, had important economic value. If Hong Kong could contain the riots, then Beijing would not be pushed into supporting the local Communists, which it might if things got out of hand.[2] A typical British reading was that: "the campaign...had proved an expensive failure... The leftists [in Hong Kong] had believed that they would ultimately be successful...When it was obvious...that the campaign was doomed, Peking had unreservedly withdrawn its assistance...[and] the campaign

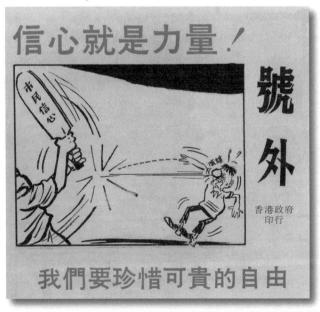

An anti-riot poster issued by the government, 1967.
PRO PO000331(A).

---

1   Carroll, *A Concise History of Hong Kong*, 153.
2   Ray Yep, "The 1967 Riots in Hong Kong: The Diplomatic and Domestic Fronts of the Colonial Governor," *The China Quarterly*, 2008, volume 193, 122-139.

had begun to peter out even more quickly."[1] However valid this interpretation was, Trench's gamble worked. The PLA never crossed the border. As far as the ruling elite in Beijing was concerned, the colonial status of Hong Kong, though undesirable, could still be tolerated as a necessary evil for the time being.

Youth again played an important role in the riots. Students were in the labor protests in May, and student struggle committees (鬥委會) grew from June, leading to school raids and closures throughout 1967.[2] Most of the students arrested came from pro-PRC schools such as Heung To and Pui Kiu.[3] But elite schools were not immune. A girl was expelled from the Belilios School for political agitation, and a struggle committee was formed in Queen's College.[4] Tsang Tak-sing, a Boy Scout and student from the St. Paul's College, was jailed for distributing anti-government and leftist leaflets.[5] Hoax bombs marked in Chinese "compatriots stay clear (同胞勿近)" were placed in students' toilets in Ying Wa College, and large characters in red denouncing "slavish education (奴化教育)" were painted on the floor of its assembly hall.[6]

George Wong, a former Boy Scout who became the personal assistant of the Commissioner of Police, confirms that at the peak of the disorder hundreds of bombs and hoax bombs (nicknamed collectively in Cantonese "home-made pineapples (土製菠蘿)") were planted often in crowded public places each day, causing much disruption to daily lives.[7] Some youngsters were involved in making bombs, and at least

1   John Cooper, *Colony in Conflict: The Hong Kong Disturbances May 1967—January 1968* (Hong Kong, Swindon Book Co., 1970), 284.

2   Stephen Waldron, "Fire on the Rim: A Study in Contradictions in Left-wing Political Mobilization in Hong Kong, 1967," Ph. D. dissertation, Syracuse Univ., 1976, 41-43, 161-169.

3   Wong Cheuk Yin, "The Communist-inspired Riots in Hong Kong, 1967: A Multi-Actors Approach," Master's thesis, the Univ. of Hong Kong, August 2000, 147.

4   Cooper, *Colony in Conflict*, 242; Ma Ming (ed.), *The Riot in Hong Kong, 1967* 香港動亂画史 (Hong Kong: Sky Horse Book Co., 1967), 64.

5   Chi Kuen Lau, *Hong Kong's Colonial Legacy: A Hong Kong Chinese's View of the British Heritage* (Hong Kong: the Chinese Univ. of Hong Kong, 1997), 10; Paul Kua (ed.), *21st World Jamboree: Hong Kong Contingent, England, 2007* (Hong Kong: the Scout Association of Hong Kong, 2007), 43.

6   These incidences were witnessed by the author as a junior former. The boys had morning assembly in the hall and all saw the painted message. Terence Ivor Iles, the British principal, refrained from discussing the message, but did refer briefly to a school regulation which prohibited defacing school premises.

7   George Wong 黃奇仁, *The Lighter Side of a Hong Kong Police Inspector's Career in the 1960s* 警官手記: 六十年代香港警隊的日子 (Hong Kong: Joint Publishing, 2008), 182.

two boys were jailed for handling bombs. All in all, over one hundred and fifty young people dubbed "juvenile delinquents" were estimated to have been involved in the riots, including nine charged with possession, planting or throwing of explosive substances.[1]

Peace-loving People Appeal For Quick End To Unrest
Bishop's Call For Prayers For Peace

Newspaper headlines reflecting the sentiments of some about the riots. *SCMP, May 22, 1967.*

Widespread violence, wanton destruction of property, and indiscriminate planting of bombs did not win hearts and minds, especially in a community comprised of many who had escaped recently from Communist China and harbored distrust of anything Communist. Literally hundreds of civic groups, communal and trade organizations, voluntary agencies and even the student bodies came out on the side of restraint, peace, and, implicitly, the colonial authorities. The Hong Kong University Students' Union advised "youth and fellow students…NOT TO… participate in any activities that may result in disturbing civic peace."[2] The Federation of Students and the Girl Guides Association issued similar statements calling for peace.[3] In a statement in *Sing Tao*, *Wah Kiu*, and the *SCMP* in May 1967, the Scout association appealed "to the youth of Hong Kong to be law abiding and to avoid any disturbances," and urged them "to co-operate with the government in its efforts to maintain peace and good order so that the present difficulties may soon be overcome."[4] In June, it received both a thank-you letter from Paul Tsui, the acting Secretary for Chinese Affairs, and a threatening letter from an organization styled "Hong Kong's Traitors-eliminating Regiment, the Ever-victorious Brigade (香港鋤奸團全無敵大隊)."[5]

In supporting the authorities the association was perhaps doing

1   Cooper, *Colony in Conflict*, 310; Wong, "The Communist-inspired Riots in Hong Kong," Table 6.3, 146-147.
2   Ma, *The Riot in Hong Kong* 香港動亂画史, 30.
3   Cooper, *Colony in Conflict*, 98.
4   Folder, the 1967 Riots, 1967, the Hong Kong Scout Archives. See also the *Hong Kong Standard*, May 22, 1967; *Ming Pao* 明報, May 22, 1967.
5   Folder, the 1967 Riots, 1967, the Hong Kong Scout Archives.

what the government had expected it to do. Nor was this sort of expectation only to be found in Hong Kong. In 1964, Lee Kuan Yew contended that Scouting could help fight two "anti-democratic" forces in Malaysia, that of "the Communists" and the "the communal bigots."[1] One could easily draw the analogy: "communal bigots" and "Communists" were responsible for the troubles in Hong Kong in 1966-67 and Scouts could help counter them. But it must be noted that the leaders in Scouting were also acting according to the sentiments of their members and the community, which had little sympathy for the aims of the rioters, not to mention their violent tactics. The leftists' cause became even less popular when, in August, Lam Bun (林彬), a radio announcer who spoke out against the riots, was burned to death in his car by a leftist group.[2]

In November 1967, some Boy Scouts were involved and injured in a bombing incident. Members of the 80th Hong Kong, on their way home from duties at the Hong Kong Week, passed a suspicious-looking travelling bag in the middle of two tramway tracks on Yee Wo Street in Causeway Bay. Led by their Scouter, they voluntarily helped to divert traffic and keep the crowd from the object, until the arrival of Senior Inspector McEwen, who thanked them and proceeded to draw the suspected object with a string to the curb. Unfortunately, an explosion occurred, killing McEwen and injuring four Boy Scouts, the Scouter, and sixteen others. After the explosion, uninjured Scouts on the scene assisted in crowd control and applied first aid to the many wounded until a large party of policemen and ambulance staff arrived. First aid and crowd control, both useful "citizenship" skills which the Boy Scouts had

Boy Scouts engaged in a "scrum" to keep the crowd back.

1   Alex Josey, *Lee Kuan Yew: the Struggle for Singapore* (London: Angus and Robertson, 1980), 223-225.
2   The *Ta Kung Pao* 大公報, August 25, 1967; *KSYP*, August 25, 1967. The former, a leftist paper, detailed Lam's anti-leftists "crimes" and reported that the "Underground Anti-traitors Guerilla Brigade (地下鋤奸突擊隊)" claimed responsibility.

traditionally been taught, apparently became handy in this emergency situation. The selfless acts of the boys were praised by both Trench, the Chief Scout, and F. C. Eates, the Commissioner of Police.[1]

Newspaper headlines on this incident are revealing of their respective political biases. The more "neutral" newspapers like the *Hong Kong Tiger Standard*, the *SCMP*, and *Ming Pao* simply noted that a police officer was killed (警官殉職) "in blast" or when "moving a bomb." Right-leaning papers such as the *Hong Kong Times* (香港時報), *Wah Kiu*, and *Sing Po* (成報) branded leftists as thugs of "ten-thousand evils" (萬惡暴徒) who had gone mad (瘋狂), and committed shocking, cruel and bloody crimes (驚人罪行, 殘酷血腥罪行). On the other hand, left-leaning newspapers such as *Jing Bao* (晶報), *Zheng Wu Bao* (正午報), and *Ta Kung* claimed that the colonial government, lacking sufficient manpower, had pushed Boy Scouts into the front line (兵力不足, 驅童子軍上陣), or that the British in Hong Kong had forced Boy Scouts to die for them (港英迫童軍替死).[2]

Boy Scouts performing first aid.

No doubt, "juvenile delinquents", often referred to as *Ah Fei* 阿飛 or *Fei Tsai* 飛仔 in Cantonese ("young hooligans and criminals"), were involved in the riots.[3] But most youngsters drawn into the disturbances were not *Fei Tsai*'s, but simply restless youth. After all, as of 1966, 50% of the population, or almost 1.9 million people, were under the age of twenty.[4] In contrast, in 1961, there were only five hundred youngsters on probation in the whole colony. Unlike in many western societies in the sixties, where restlessness was stirred up by increasingly affluent youth, there is evidence that in Hong Kong many of the rioters were underprivileged youngsters from congested urban areas. Frank Welsh attributes the 1966 disturbance to "relative deprivation and endemic boredom," as "a young man who lived in a shared cubicle in an overcrowded tenement would find it very difficult to stay out of any excitement on the streets."[5] The fact that the protest march only picked up

---

1   Folder, Yee Wo St. Incident, Nov. 1967, the Hong Kong Scout Archives.
2   The *Hong Kong Tiger Standard*, *SCMP*, the *Ming Pao* 明報, the *Jing Bao* 晶報, the *Zheng Wu Bao* 正午報, the *Ta Kung Bao* 大公報, the *Hong Kong Times* 香港時報, *WKYP*, and the *Sing Po* 成報, November 6, 1967.
3   Harold Traver, "Juvenile Delinquency in Hong Kong," in John Winterdyk (ed.), *Juvenile Justice Systems: Int'l Perspectives*, 2nd ed. (Toronto: Canadian Scholars' Press, 2002), 213. Traver's translation of the Cantonese term.
4   The *Hong Kong By-Census, 1976, Main Report,* Vol. II, Table III.1.
5   Welsh, *A Borrowed Place*, 466.

steam after it went through two resettlement estates suggests that this conclusion is at least partially valid. Similarly, John Cooper points out that youth drawn into the 1967 unrests were mostly not "content to slave away in poor conditions as did their fathers."[1] Some were in low-paying jobs. Others were in left-leaning schools discriminated against by the education system. Many were unemployed and not in any school at all. For these people, who had no access to a "system allowing everyone the best opportunity," it was natural that "political ideals [would] replace academic ones."[2] The riots were at least partially driven by youth disappointed with their prospects of securing a larger share of the growing economic pie of the colony.

The colonial government was criticized by some for its inaction in the wake of the disturbances. The *Far Eastern Economic Review* maintained that Trench had failed to implement needed social reforms and "had done little to widen [his] traditionally narrow circle of friends and advisers."[3] Lord Rhodes declared that the greatest danger faced by the colony was the "old, dead hand of an outdated administration."[4] Such perceptions were hardly expelled when Trench insisted on taking his vacation in the summer of 1967 (possibly also to deliberate with officials in London), an absence that could be interpreted as shying away from taking charge at a time of need. To prevent a recurrence of youth-inspired unrests, the government had to devise better ways of reaching out to the small but growing number of youth prone to be categorized as juvenile delinquents and the large number of underprivileged young people, many living in crowded public housing with minimal facilities. The Sir David Trench Fund for Recreation was set up in 1970 with a private donation, partly as a response to this perceived need.[5]

When he became the governor, MacLehose acknowledged that "young people…[had] the time to spare to help other people in their complaints" and had given "encouragement to violent protest."[6] Later on, he

1   Cooper, *Colony in Conflict*, 312.
2   Ibid., 314.
3   Quoted in Cooper, *Colony in Conflict*, 297.
4   Ibid., 296-7.
5   "The Governor's Fund for recreation, donations to,1970-71," HKRS 163-9-622, the Public Records Office, Hong Kong.
6   The *Hong Kong Annual Review*, 1971 (Hong Kong: the Hong Kong Government, 1971).

noted that "facilities for recreation...are no longer luxuries but essential parts of our social infrastructure."[1] More fundamentally, MacLehose's first annual review was "a manifesto for change."[2] Keenly aware of the need to win public acceptance, he replaced the half-hearted social policies of the 1960s with what Tang Kwong-leung labels as the "big bang" ones in the 1970s, aiming at housing, education, and health.[3] In 1972, a ten-year program was launched to re-house over one million people in public estates, many in new towns like Kwun Tong, Tsuen Wan and Sha-tin. While the program was considered a success, it also exposed many social issues and conflicts related to urban development, and heightened the perceived need for social and youth services.[4]

Lo with youngsters in a congested resettlement estate, 1967.

H. K. Scout Archives.

The Scout association quickly rose to the challenge to reach out to the large number of youngsters in the congested housing areas. To some extent, this is to be expected, for, as in other places, Scouting was seen as an effective remedy for young trouble makers. In 1964, a troop chairman quoted a common saying "One more Boy Scout, One less *Fei Tsai* (多一個童軍, 少一個飛仔)," highlighting this belief.[5] The chair-

---

1   *Hong Kong Hansard*, October 17, 1973. MacLehose's speech on the set up of a Council for Recreation and Sport.
2   Welsh, *A Borrowed Place*, 477.
3   Tang Kwong-leung, *Colonial State and Social Policy: Social Welfare Development in Hong Kong, 1842—1997* (Lanham: Univ. Press America, 1998), 51-53, 61-64.
4   A study claims that about 18% of the social conflicts in the late 1970s were related to housing problems, and 33% to urban development. See Denny Kwok Leung Ho, "The Rise and Fall of Community Mobilization: the Housing Movement in Hong Kong," in Stephen Wing Kai Chiu and Tai Lok Lui (eds.), *The Dynamics of Social Movement in Hong Kong* (Hong Kong, Hong Kong Univ. Press, 2000), 187.
5   *WKYP*, September 28, 1964.

man of a Scout District noted in 1970 that "young people join groups by nature. So rather than having children join hoodlum gangs, it would be better if they joined the Scouts."[1] But such eagerness to respond to the community's needs must also be understood in the context of challenges within Scouting everywhere. Ian Craib notes that it was losing relevance, and its ideals were "dated by very rapid social changes."[2] In the early 1960s, membership numbers had been declining in British Scouting. Coincidentally, there was also a slight decline in membership in Hong Kong in 1964, the first recorded since the early 1950s, suggesting a slackened momentum, paralleling that of the metropole.[3]

Summer camp for non-Scout youngsters, 1967.

H. K. Scout Archives.

In this context, the association was understandably also receptive to calls to serve new targets outside Scouting. In July 1967, it deliberated on expanding service to non-Scout youth, partly in response to requests from neighborhood community groups (*Kaifong* associations 街坊團體).[4] With encouragement and funding from the government and the Jockey Club, it soon organized summer camps for a thousand underprivileged youngsters, activities which were praised by Charles Maclean, the Chief Scout of the Commonwealth, as having helped to ease "the tension which so unhappily besets the Colony."[5] To support the outreach efforts, Service Scout Units (SSUs) staffed with young men and women were formed in many districts.[6] As part of the efforts to improve

1   The *Star,* December 17, 1970.
2   Ian Craib, *The Importance of Disappointment* (London: Routledge, 1994), 153.
3   *Census Reports, 1963, 1964*, the Hong Kong Scout Archives.
4   Meeting minutes, the Chief Commissioner's Council, July 8, 1967, the Hong Kong Scout Archives.
5   *The Scout Bulletin,* Jul-Sep. 1967, 3.
6   Meeting minutes, the Chief Commissioner's Council, December 7, 1967, the

community awareness of the movement, a marching brass band was set up as the 3rd SSU. In September, the associaton launched "Operation Brotherhood," and "Operation Campfire," both aimed at non-Scout youngsters. In late 1967, year-long programs for underprivileged youth were proposed, and a grant of $500,000 was approved by the Jockey Club to fund it for five years.[1]

Operation Brotherhood, September 1967.

H. K. Scout Archives.

In a joint Scouts and Guides seminar held in March 1968, one asked rhetorically: "should we continue to devote our efforts only to the... Scouts? Can we afford to?"[2] In the summer, the association went further with its outreach efforts, and organized camps, holidays, campfires, movie nights, friendship days, and concerts for sixty thousand youth, several times that of its membership, suggesting that there was indeed large unfilled demand in overcrowded urban areas.[3] This assessment was re-affirmed by the government when G. T. Rowe, the Director of Social Welfare, urged that the programs be expanded since Hong Kong's "increasingly youthful population" living in congested urban spaces needed "outlets for their pent-up energies, especially in the open air"[4]

In 1969, eighty events held outside the summer reached ninety thousand people.[5] As Ma observed, Hong Kong seemed to become convinced that "scouting was for the community rather than just for boys,

Hong Kong Scout Archives.

1   Folder, the Friends of Scouting, 1968-77, the Hong Kong Scout Archives.

2   Folder, Guides and Scouts Joint Seminar, March-April 1968, the Hong Kong Scout Archives.

3   The (Scout) *Bulletin*, July-September 1968, 6 (Chinese).

4   The *South China Sunday Post-Herald*, November 24, 1968.

5   *Annual Report, 1968-69* (Hong Kong: the Scout Association, 1969), 29.

A campfire for youth out-side Scouting.

H. K. Scout Archives.

The FOS logo, with the Chinese character for "friends" at the bottom.

and that scouting was a service rather than a game."[1] However, these programs quickly became a heavy drain on the limited resources of the association, and it was obvious that a separate organization with its own dedicated management would be needed, if support for the traditional Scout program were to be maintained.

A new subsidiary, the "Friends of Scouting (FOS 童軍知友社)," was created in December 1969 to assume full responsibility for programs for "young people [boys or girls] who are not members of the Scout Association," whether because they could not afford the related expenses or were simply unwilling to subject themselves to the discipline of the uniformed movement, so that they, too, "may take a constructive place in society."[2] This organization had high-level patronage: the Hon. Sir Hugh Norman-Walker and the Hon. Sir Denys Roberts, both colonial secretaries, were its first presidents. This "new scouting movement," as the FOS was called by the English press at the time, was judged to be "a big success."[3] Highly visible fund raising events also suggest strong community support. In 1971, for example, Lt. General Sir Richard Ward was the patron of an FOS fund raising program featuring the gala pre-miere of the movie *The Big Boss* (唐山大兄), in the presence of Bruce Lee (李小龍), the star of the movie.[4]

1   *SCMP*, July 7, 1967.
2   Folder, the Friends of Scouting, 1968-1977, the Hong Kong Scout Archives.
3   The *Hong Kong Standard*, June 11, 1971.
4   Bruce Thomas, *Bruce Lee: Fighting Spirit* (Berkeley, CA: Frog, 1994), 129-139.

Scouts marched along Nathan Road during the Festival of Hong Kong, 1971.

H. K. Gov't Info. Service.

The first "Festival of Hong Kong (香港節)," an ambitious program to bring week-long entertainment, sports, music, variety shows and exhibitions to young and old in Hong Kong, was launched in the same month in which the FOS was set up. Featured events included a large-scale float parade and an evening open-air dance fiesta. Unlike the Hong Kong Week of 1967, which had a commercial overtone and had emphasized the use of Hong Kong products, this festival focused more on cultural activities for young people.[1] Perhaps representative of the views within the Chinese community, the Chinese newspaper *Wah Kiu Yat Po* issued editorials in support of the festival, claiming that it would enhance the sense of belonging of all citizens, especially the young people, and urging that it be turned into an annual event.[2] True to its mission, FOS took an active part and organized over forty events for the festival office, reaching out to a large number of non-Scout youngsters. The Scout Association and, in particular, the FOS subsidiary, was also very supportive of both the 2nd and the 3rd Festival of Hong Kong, which took place in 1971 and 1973.

Poster of the Festival of Hong Kong, 1973.

PRO PO00095.

---

1   The *Hong Kong Standard*, May 4, 1969; *WKYP*, May 4, 1969.
2   *WKYP*, May 5, 1969, July 2, 1969.

During the 1970s, Hong Kong Scouting continued steadfastly to execute programs both year-long and in the summer, on its own as well as in partnership with other organizations, including government departments, for non-Scouts. In the early 1970s, for instance, it joined hands with the Urban Council to organize a series of "Neighbourhood Evenings," entertainment activities which were typically held in congested public housing areas, providing healthy distractions free-of-charge for large numbers of youngsters.

Scouts served in a "Neighbourhood Evening," 1970s.
H. K. Scout Archives.

In February 1972, the Scout Association further developed the Service Scouting concept and created a Community Services Organization (CSO) with some eight hundred members belonging to ten co-educational CSO units. These CSO members, many of whom former non-Scout youth, played key roles in supporting numerous FOS programs throughout the years. When the CSO was set up, the band was transferred to this organization, and it was further developed, with the addition of a Scottish bagpipe band, a fife band and a bugle corps. As the unit continued to grow, it was detached again in 1973 from the CSO, and placed directly under the association headquarters. The band was invited frequently to appear in many government or non-governmental community events, reaching out to many citizens, including thousands of youngsters, every year. Later on, in line with the tradition of many British military bands, the Scout Band also hosted an annual "Beating the Retreat (鳴金收兵)," a public musical performance event which typical-

ly attracted a large crowd and, in the process, had become a well-known goodwill ambassador of the Scout Movement.[1]

Consistent with colonial social welfare policies and in order to better manage the on-going programs throughout the year, FOS eventually also established a number of permanent youth centers. By 1972, it had centers in the So Uk Resettlement Estate, the Wo Lok Estate in Kwun Tong, and the Helena May Annex on Garden Road; as well as the Cockburn Youth Centre based in the Morse House.[2] In 1973, the Cockburn Centre relocated to Ma Tau Wai Estate in Tokwawan. In the same year, the FOS organization was honored by the Asia-Pacific Scout Conference with the Ala-ala Award, in recognition of outstanding community services provided by it to the youth of Hong Kong.

The Scout Band performed at a rally, 1970s.

H. K. Scout Archives.

Such efforts were clearly in line with the desire of the authorities to better serve the youthful population. In the rally in 1974, MacLehose observed that "what boys need most is group activities which they can enjoy...and which often take them outside the crowded urban areas in which they live to the mountains and the beaches," and urged Scouts to take the lead to invite non-Scouts as their guests in all sorts of outdoor activities and to allow them to use the Scout campsites.[3] In the same

---

1   The band also took goodwill trips overseas, including one to Macau, and one to the Philippines, to participate in the 1st Asia Pacific Scout Jamboree in December 1973. Interview, Tsin Chi-ming, March 14, 2011, the Hong Kong Scout Archives.

2   *2nd Annual Report of the Friends of Scouting*, April 1971/March 1972.

3   The *Hong Kong Standard*, April 21, 1974.

year, the association launched "Project T," aimed at subtantially expanding recreational programs in the summer and throughout the year. Typical summer programs would include camps, campfires, picnics, carnivals, barbecues, singing contests, film shows, fun fairs, concerts, variety shows, table tennis and chess competitions. Typical year-long programs would include some of these, but also a large variety of outdoor and indoor training courses and interest groups related to such pursuits as singing, football, folkdance, guitar, first aid, sewing, English, Cantonese opera, knitting, table tennis, karate, and the like. Many of these activities were funded by government subventions, the Jockey Club, and many other sources of donations.

Scouts entertained a large crowd of non-Scout youngsters.

H. K. Scout Archives.

A snapshot of activities organized by the FOS in 1971/72, its second full year of operations, and 1976/1977, just before the Hong Kong Scout Association became independent, is shown in the table on the next page. In the 1970s, Hong Kong Scouting had around twenty to thirty thousand members. As indicated, FOS would often serve more boys and girls annually than the number of Scouts, even excluding the big boost in number from the Festival of Hong Kong programs.

Event Type	1971/72		1976/77	
	No. of events	*People*	*No. of Events*	*People*
Summer Programs	26	25,790	196	35,426
Year-long Programs	61	18,604	35	6,249
Fest. of HK Programs	38	40,230	N/A	N/A
Total	125	84,624	231	41,675

FOS Programs and Attendance, 1971-1977

Sources: *Annual Report of the Friends of Scouting, 1971/72 and 1976/77.*

Amidst concerns over the movement's relevance, and in response to the post-riot desire of the community for its citizenship training "to reach out to youth not heretofore served," Scouting launched its non-Scout extension in 1967.[1] By the late 1970s, unlike other NSOs, the Scout association of Hong Kong had become more than just a uniformed youth group. It was a fully-fledged youth service provider, bringing outdoor activities, informal training, interest groups and other social interactions to many non-Scouts in crowded urban spaces, and helping to mold them into better citizens. In meeting the needs of the growing population of hyper-urban Hong Kong, it had redefined itself as a movement for all youngsters, male and female, including many who could not afford or were not interested in traditional Scouting.

Opening of the FOS's Cockburn Centre. *WKYP, Mar. 28, 1972.*

British-centric modernity

Right around the time when Hong Kong Scouting launched its first five-year development plan, the British association also made a comprehensive attempt at modernity, largely top-down and almost entirety British-centered, which eventually swept through the commonwealth. Some reforms met with strong resistance even in British Scouting, though most were adopted wholesale by Hong Kong. Many modernizing changes

---

1   Irving A. Spergel, *Planning for Youth Development: the Hong Kong Experience* (New York: UN Commissioner for Technical Co-operation, 1972), iii, 21-22.

were beneficial and/or necessary. However, a few did not cater to real needs in Hong Kong and were either not implemented fully or were implemented but had negative impacts on local Scouting for years.

Though Scouting started as a modernizing educational movement itself, genuine concerns in the 1960s that it was losing relevance among British youth led to the appointment of a task force named the "Advance Party" in 1963 by the Chief Scout "to study all aspects of the future of Scouting and to make recommendations...as to the development of the Movement, both in the immediate future and for the 1970's."[1] In a later analysis, Reuven Kahane argues that although Scouting had been successful in constructing "an authentic, meaningful model of life" for the "postmodern youth" based on "a code of informality," it was losing ground to newer postmodern variants of informality, including postwar youth subcultures "marked by freedom, spontaneity, some rebellious trends, 'disordered leisure,'...and even deviancy to an extent and in forms previously unknown."[2] This prognosis seems to have been borne out by developments at the time. British Scout membership had peaked in 1960, and then declined throughout the decade.[3]

In June 1966, the task force issued the *Advance Party Report* (*APR*), a large tome with twenty chapters and over five hundred single-spaced pages, containing many modernizing proposals.[4] The first seventeen chapters covered proposed changes on all aspects of Scouting, chapter eighteen dealt with implementation, nineteen listed participants, and twenty summarized the 409 proposed reforms. It was unfortunate that this last chapter, which listed proposals without explanations, justifications or background, was the only one widely disseminated, as such partial information often caused misunderstanding and unnecessary resistance for many proposed changes, regardless of their intrinsic value.

---

1   *The Chief Scout's Advance Party Report* (London: The Boy Scouts Association, 1966), 8.
2   Reuven Kahane, *The Origins of Postmodern Youth: Informal Youth Movements in a Comparative Perspective* (Berlin: Walter de Gruyter, 1997), 1-2, 23.
3   British Scout membership peaked at 588,396 in 1960, then declined year-on-year until it reached 540,128 in 1964. See *Annual Reports, 1951-1964*, (London: the Boy Scouts Association); Steven Harris, *Legalised Mischief* (London: Lewarne Publishing, 2003), Vol. 2, 142.
4   *The Scout Association, Annual Report, 1966-67* (London: the Scout Association, 1967), 4, 8.

The local association adopted most *APR* recommendations within in a few years. In 1966, the proposed new uniforms and a short report on the *APR* (entitled in Chinese rather clumsily as 英總會未來動態調查委員會報告書) appeared in the local *Bulletin*.[1] In 1967, the new Scout emblem was adopted, the headquarters went through a substantial reorganization, partly in response to the proposals of the *APR*, and details of the new Cub Scout program were issued.[2] In 1968, the new Scout program was announced.[3] Lo attended the 6th Far East Scout Conference in September in full post-*APR* uniform, with long trousers, a green tie instead of a scarf, a simple metal head badge instead of the colorful leader's plume, and new Scout insignia.

The *APR*, 1966; the *Bulletin* of 1966, featuring the post-*APR* uniforms.

In 1969, the new promise, law, names of ranks, and badges and uniforms for leaders, Cub Scouts, and Scouts were promulgated, and post-*APR* training was conducted for many leaders.[4] By October, post-*APR* leaders' training became obligatory for all newly-appointed leaders and those changing their appointments.[5] The post-*APR* Venture Scout training scheme was implemented in early 1970. Even the Chief Scouts dutifully followed these changes. In the rally in 1969, Sir David came

1   The *Bulletin*, September 1966.
2   Ibid., January, May, July, and October 1967,
3   Ibid., January 1968.
4   *Annual Report, 1968/69* (Hong Kong: the Scout Association, 1969), 25-27.
5   The *Bulletin*, January 1970.

in the new uniform. Likewise, in 1972, MacLehose appeared in his first rally in full post-*APR* uniform, and met Venture Scouts who wore the new green ties instead of the traditional scarves.

MacLehose met Venture Scouts in post-*APR* uniforms, April 1972.

H. K. Scout Archives.

Naming conventions reflect cultural values and norms. Some modernizing name changes perhaps helped to make the aging movement more appealing to its modern targets. The word "boy" was dropped from the title of the movement, henceforth to be called the Scout Movement, to avoid the image of being juvenile. Similarly, Boy Scout Troops became Scout Troops, and the Boy Scouts Association, the Scout Association. Though the name change was readily adopted locally, its Chinese rendition remained problematic. In the past, Boy Scout was rendered in Chinese somewhat unsatisfactorily as *tong zi jun* (童子軍, literally "Boy Soldiers/Boy Army"). Post-*APR*, the term *tong jun* (童軍) was used, taking out the middle character *zi* (子), which removed the boy connotation, but keeping both the juvenile (*tong* 童) and the military (*jun* 軍) allusions.[1] The Wolf Cubs, or *xiaolang* (小狼 little wolf), with dated association with Kipling's stories in colonial settings, became Cub Scouts,

---

1   The phrase *Tong zi* 童子 usually means boy(s), while the character *Tong* 童 simply means child(ren) or juvenile, and *Jun* 軍 means army or military. The term *Tongzijun* 童子軍 was still used in an article on the three new *APR* sections in May/June 1967. Couple months later, *zi* 子 was taken out. See the *Bulletin* (Hong Kong: the Boy Scouts Association), May and July 1967,.

or, in Chinese, *youtongjun* (幼童軍, younger Scout or younger juvenile soldier), which had no link to the animal at all, in early 1968.[1]

The new diamond shape membership badge, with six background colors representing different training sections or branches, was supposedly a modernizing improvement over the dated Tenderpads for the Wolf Cubs and Tenderfoot Badges for the Scouts. However, this reform proved short-lived. In the early 1970s, these badges were further simplified and replaced by the same world Scout membership badge for all, with the *fleur-de-lis* surrounded by a rope tied with a reef/square knot.[2] This badge, also known as the World Crest in America, became increasingly *the* membership badge adopted by NSOs around the world.

The proposed new aim and promises were clear modernizing improvements. The new aim, "to encourage the physical, mental and spiritual development of young people so that they may take a constructive place in society," was considerably simpler and clearer than the old one.[3] The new promise for both Scouts and Cub Scouts, "I promise that I will do my best—to do my duty to God and the Queen, to help other people, and to keep the (Cub) Scout Law," eliminated superfluous minor differences of the previous versions.[4] These were quickly adopted in Hong Kong, and the Chinese versions were issued in January 1969. Significantly, the new promise in Chinese replaced the specific term *shen* (神 gods or God) with the term *shenming* (神明 deity), following the earlier usage of the term *Jinmei* (神明) in Japan. The promise also replaced the pre-*APR juliudi* (居留地, place of residence) with *bentu* (本

The post-*APR* membership badge for Venture Scouts in red.

---

1   The *Bulletin,* July 1967. In 1968, the Cub Scout Committee (幼童軍小組委員會) was inaugurated, and basic Cub Scouter training (幼童軍基本訓練) was offered, confirming the official adoption of the new name for the section, though there was still a regional (Wolf) Cub Pack Holiday course (小狼渡假技訓班) and the inauguration of a (Wolf) Cub Pack (小狼團) at the YMCA, both still employing the old term. See the *Bulletin,* January and April 1968.

2   *The Chief Scout's Advance Party Report, 1966,* 502; The *POR, Part Four: Training Badges and Awards* (London: The Scout Association, 1972), 6, 29.

3   *The Chief Scout's Advance Party Report, 1966,* 16; the old aim was "to develop good citizenship among boys by forming their character—training them in habits of observation, obedience and self-reliance—inculcating loyalty and thoughtfulness for others—teaching them services useful to the public, and handicrafts useful to themselves—promoting their physical, mental, and spiritual development." See The *POR, 1964 Reprint* (London: the Boy Scouts Association, 1964), 5.

4   The old Boy Scout Promise was "On my honour, I promise that I will do my best—to do my duty to God, and the Queen, to help other people at all times, to obey the Scout Law." The old Wolf Cub Promise was "I promise to do my best—to do my duty to God, and the Queen, to keep the Law of the Wolf Cub Pack, and to do a good turn to somebody every day." See The *POR, 1964 Reprint,* 5.

The world Scout membership badge, aka the World Crest.

土, this/native territory). This change strengthened the parallelism of the Chinese promise, with the two-character phrase *bentu* matching the two-character phrase *shenming*.[1]

More importantly, there were subtle differences between this promise in Chinese and the one promulgated in the 1950s. Hong Kong finally opted for the middle ground of a generic deity, more closely aligned with the religious orientation of the Chinese majority, instead of the "godless" version used in China, or the Christian "God" from Britain and used locally until this time. Even more significantly, it chose "native territory," meaning Hong Kong, over "my country" for China or "the Queen" for Britain. This was the next logical step, in the further Hongkongization of Scouting, following the move away from the equivocal "the head of the nation" used in the nationalistic interwar years, and then the awkward and more transient "place of residence" endorsed in the early postwar years. By the late 1960s, this less transient term for Hong Kong appeared more appropriate. After all, whereas many youngsters in the 1940s and the 1950s were born in China, most in the 1960s were born locally and took pride in calling Hong Kong their home.

John Carroll argues that in the 1960s and the 1970s "many local people became proud of Hong Kong's hybrid status," and adopted "a distinctively Hong Kong identity," one that blends Chinese, British, local and cosmopolitan elements.[2] This sense of belonging was shaped by, among other things, Hong Kong's economic prosperity, growing ties with China, the authorities' efforts to nurture a local identity and, later on, the realization that Hong Kong would be returned to China.

Local adaptations of the Scout promise in Chinese can be seen as a specific manifestation of this process of "becoming Hongkongese."[3] The adventure of Francis Chin Yiu-cheong (錢耀昌), Queen's Scout from 14th Tsuen Wan West Group in 1968, perhaps also personified well this growing pride and confidence in the hybrid Hong Kong Chinese identity. In December 1971, Francis, at the age of 22, and his older brother, Dominic Chin Yiu-chong, took off from London in a single-

Francis Chin in Senior Scout uniform, 1960s.

Francis Chin's collection.

1   *Cub Scout Training: Hong Kong, the Official Handbook of the Scout Association, Hong Kong Branch* (Hong Kong: the Scout Association, 1969), 2-3. The full *APR* Promise in Chinese was: 我願以信譽為誓, 竭盡所能, 對神明,對本土, 盡責任, 對別人, 要幫助, 對規律, 必遵行.

2   Carroll, *A Concise History of Hong Kong*, 167-169.

3   Ibid., 167.

Dominic and Francis Chin (right) landed at Kai Tak Airpot after their historic flight, January 1972.

Francis Chin's collection.

engine Bugle "pup," a small two-seater airplane, and embarked on a historic marathon 129-hour flight to Hong Kong. Most experts had advised against this journey, because the plane was not designed for such a long flight. Both the Chins had logged relatively few flight hours, but other pilots approached would not participate, as the trip was considered highly riskly, if not suicidal. During the journey, they ran into many people who, impressed with their courage and adventurous spirit, had been very helpful. But there were also airports in various countries which could not be contacted due to their weak wireless equipment, or refused landings or takeoffs for one reason or another. They were even forced to take a riskier route directly from Calcutta to Bangkok, and had to fly on empty gas tank on their last miles to the airport there. Nevertheless, against all odds, the brothers continued, broke two flight records along the way, and landed safely on the Kai Tak Airport on January 8, 1972.[1] Chin was promptly appointed Hong Kong's Air Scout Commissioner, though this section never really took off, perhaps due to the difficulty in and cost of obtaining flying experience for youngsters locally.

The post-*APR* Scout Law had eight (which was soon reduced to seven) instead of ten clauses, and was an improvement in terms of clarity and simplicity of language and alignment with modern thinking and educational philosophy. A few illustrations would suffice. The old law "A Scout is loyal to the Queen, his country, his Scouters, his parents, his employers, and to those under him" was replaced by "A Scout is loyal," which, while not providing a laundry list of to whom loyalty was due,

---

1   *KSYP*, January 9, 1972; *Asia Weekly*, February 6, 1972; *Readers Digest,* February 1973, 27-39.

ANSTIE'S CIGARETTES

SEVENTH SCOUT LAW

The Seventh Law on obedience was eliminated by the *APR*.

covers loyalty to all (including other family members and friends), and is less limiting. The new law, "A Scout is friendly and considerate," is an ingenious effort to combine several old laws covering helpfulness, courteousness, friendliness to others and to animals, and could be interpreted broadly to cover, say, friendliness toward nature and the environment—modern requirements which were becoming fashionable then. The new law, "A Scout is a brother to all Scouts," unlike the old one, could not be interpreted to exclude boys of other races. The new Scout Law did not contain a clause equivalent to the old law, "A Scout obeys orders of his parents, Patrol Leader, or Scoutmaster without question," much criticized by thoughtful persons due to its emphasis on blind obedience and on only leaders inside Scouting.[1] Similarly, good editing was done to the Wolf Cub Law. The old law, based on Kipling's *Jungle Story*, was nebulous at best, and downright incomprehensible at worst: "1, The Cub gives in to the Old Wolf; 2, The Cub does not give in to himself."[2] The *APR* recommended that the Cub Law be rewritten as follows: "A Cub Scout always does his best, thinks of others before himself, and does a good turn every day."[3]

The Chinese version, issued in January 1969, used simple, easy to remember, and balanced seven-character phrases, each starting with the two-character name "a Scout" (童軍), with the next five characters taking on one of two forms. The first, which applies to the First, Second, Fourth and Fifth Law, starts with a two-character noun followed by a three-character adjective or description. For example, the First Law starts with a two-character noun "trustworthiness (信用)" followed by a three-character description "respected by others (為人敬)," resulting in "A Scout's trustworthiness [is] respected by others." The second form, which applies to the Third, Sixth and Seventh Law, starts with a two-character noun followed by another two-character noun at the end, with a single-character conjunction in between. For example, the Seventh Law states that a Scout "respects himself (自重)" and "also (又)" "respects others (重人)." The *APR* Cub Scout Law, being new, required a fresh translation.[4] A good gauge of whether reforms are sound is whether they

1   For the new Law see *The Chief Scout's Advance Party Report, 1966*, 17-18; for the old Law see The *POR, 1964 Reprint*, 5-6.
2   The *POR, 1964 Reprint*, 6.
3   *The Chief Scout's Advance Party Report, 1966*, 19.
4   The Scout Law in Chinese: 童軍信用為人敬, 童軍待人要忠誠, 童軍友善兼

survive the test of time. The post-*APR* movement and section names, promises, laws, together with their generally well-done Chinese translations, are largely still in use today, some forty years later, despite the fact that the local association has been independent for decades and could, in theory at least, revise these anytime at will.

Several *APR* reforms did not address real needs due to British biases or top-down orientations and were either not implemented or were implemented only years after, when local conditions were rife. The proposed revision to the religious policy, reflecting British-centric conservatism, was clearly unsuitable and was not implemented. As Scouting became a worldwide movement, it increasingly came into contact with countries where religion(s) other than Christianity dominated or where religion did not figure strongly in people's lives, so much so that the World Scout Conference of 1949 had adopted this liberal statement: "The man who sincerely finds it impossible to accept one creed, or to join any one church, yet at the same time continue his search for the truth, can in all honour take the Scout Promise."[1]

In contrast, the *APR* proposed that all "Commissioners, Group Scout Leaders and Leaders of Training Sections" must be "active members of some religious body" before they could be appointed, so that they could set "a good example" for others.[2] In the 1960s, this requirement was alright in the British context, where 96% of the Scouters attended church services at least once in a while, and almost 50% of all Scout Groups were sponsored by churches.[3] Nevertheless, it was oddly strict given the tolerant attitude of the world Scout body. More pertinently, this rule would clearly be unacceptable locally, where Christianity had a modest penetration of the Chinese majority, and most Scouters could not be said to be active members of any religious body. This impractical restriction, which would most likely disqualify many if not most Chinese Scouters in the colony, was simply ignored.

Some *APR* proposals for handicapped Scouting were likewise impractical in the Hong Kong context. The *APR* had recognized that with

The Sixth Law on friendliness to animals was combined in the *APR* with other laws to cover friendliness to all.

親切, 童軍相處如手足, 童軍勇敢不怕難, 童軍愛物更惜陰, 童軍自重又重人; and the Cub Scout Law: 幼童軍，盡所能，先顧別人才顧己，日行一善富精神.

1   *The Chief Scout's Advance Party Report, 1966*, 19.
2   Ibid., 19-20.
3   Ibid., 292, 343. Based on surveys of joining Scouters in 1963, and of sponsoring authorities in 1961.

MacLehose met some Extension Scouts, 1970s.

H. K. Scout Archives.

medical advances, the word "handicapped" might be inappropriate, and had proposed that Scouting copy from Guiding and use the word "extension," a euphemistic term which avoided labeling the boys.[1] Superficial name change was easy. The local Handicapped Branch quickly became the Extension Scout Branch, and the Chinese name went from *ruoneng* (弱能, "weak capabilities") to *teneng* (特能, "special capabilities").[2]

Fundamental reforms were more difficult. The *APR* had recommended "the integration of members of the [Extension] Branch into ordinary Scout Groups," and Scouting for the "educationally sub-normal boys" and "the maladjusted."[3] Evidence for Hong Kong suggests that Extension Scouts were not integrated. In 1969, Scouts from ten Extension Scout Groups participated in the 3rd Extension Scout Camp. While eighty-two disabled Scouts attended the 1971 Jamboree, they stayed in their own branch camp inside the Somers Sub-Camp, indicating that, unlike in Britain, Extension Scouts in Hong Kong were generally not "mainstreamed," but remained segregated.[4]

By the 1970s, Scouting also reached educationally challenged boys, including the 157th Hong Kong, sponsored by a school (晨崗學校) in Causeway Bay for children with IQ between 50 and 75, founded in 1975.[5] A report in the same year indicated that Extension Scouts be-

1   Ibid., 233.
2   The *Bulletin*, January-February 1968, 11 (Chinese).
3   *The Chief Scout's Advance Party Report, 1966*, 235-236.
4   The *Bulletin*, July-August 1971, 9.
5   *Hong Kong Scouting*, May 1979, 6.

longed to seven groups for deaf boys, one for physically disabled boys, and six for mentally-challenged boys, reflecting the segregated nature of local special schools, again illustrating that Scouting often mirrored the biases and practices of the community in which it operated.[1]

Large increase in full-time paid Scouters, another *APR* recommendations, was not carried out in Hong Kong. At the time, British Scouting had substantially fewer paid staff than, say, American Scouting. But it had become increasingly difficult to find "volunteers of the calibre required who have the necessary time," perhaps reflecting the fact that gentlemen of leisure were becoming a rare breed and full employment a common reality in postwar Britain.[2] The *APR* proposed that paid Executive Commissioners be appointed to all headquarter branches, and that paid Field Commissioners, county secretaries, and even Assistant District Commissioners for training be hired, declaring that "up to one thousand [paid staff] could be used without upsetting the all important voluntary balance of the Movement."[3]

While the Hong Kong association did re-organize its headquarters in 1967 with the appointment of many new commissioners, these were all volunteers, not paid staff.[4] Realistically, it could not afford to hire many full-time Scouters, even if it had wanted to, without a big jump in public funding. In 1968 it added two paid Assistant Field Commissioners and in 1969 it added one, funded publicly and partly to handle the large amount of non-Scout youth outreach work encouraged by the government.[5] By 1970, Yeung Yiu-tin was appointed full-time Administrative Commissioner, the only paid staff at a senior level.[6] During the period under review (and indeed after), local Scouting remained largely volunteer-driven, and branches, regions and districts were all headed up by part-time volunteers.

Last but not least, sweeping modernizing reforms in the older Rover and Senior Scout sections (merged and renamed the Venture Scout

The modernized Venture Scout uniform proposed by the *APR*, 1966.

---

1   Ibid., 2-3.
2   *The Chief Scout's Advance Party Report, 1966*, 273, 384. While in Britain there was one full-time paid Scouter for every 25,000 members, in the United States the number was one for every 1,000.
3   Ibid., 273, 396-399.
4   The *Bulletin*, March-April 1967, 3-4, May-June 1967, 3-5.
5   Ibid., October-December 1968, 2, April-June 1969, 3.
6   Ibid., July-August 1970, 2.

section), mostly related to their symbolic system, led to resistance from many Scouts and Scouters, controversies and years of declines in Scouting for older youth. The *APR* had declared that "Scouts in [the existing] uniform…present a picture of a juvenile organization," and that its reforms would make Scouting "much more attractive to boys, young men and adults," optimistic predictions which were, as it turned out, not always borne out by facts.[1]

A main reason for the failure of these changes seemed to be their departure from traditions. While updated uniforms and modernized badges had apparently worked in some cases, they did not seem to appeal to older British or Hong Kong Scouts who had been exposed to the traditional symbolic system. In one fell swoop, the trademark and cherished "lemon squeezer" hats, shorts, Senior Scout badges, chords, epaulettes, hat plumes, Wood Badge, and the scarves were replaced by berets, long pants, standard hat badges, simple badges for Venture Scouts, and a tie. The elimination or drastic redesign of these hallowed symbols, many created by B-P himself, were controversial.

Wood Badge, hat plumes, chords, epaulettes, Senior Scout badges, and other traditional symbols abolished by the *APR*.

In 1969, the Scout Action Group was formed in Britain, demanding that groups be allowed to continue with the traditional approach. In 1970, it issued the Black Report as a rejoinder to the *APR*, and set up the Baden-Powell Scouts' Association, which operated groups along pre-*APR* lines. This organization eventually had counterparts in Ireland, Australia, Canada, Denmark, Ghana, and the United States. In 1996, they formed their own World Federation of Independent Scouts (WFIS), and in 2002, held their first World Jamboree.[2] Though the splinter organiza-

1   Ibid., 300.
2   "Baden-Powell Scouts Association," https://en.wikipedia.org/wiki/Baden-Powell_Scouts; "World Federation of Independent Scouts," http://en.wikipedia.org/wiki/

tion did not siphon away many members, the main association did suffer significant losses. There were over 55,000 Senior and Rover Scouts in Britain in 1966, but less than 22,000 Venture Scouts three years later. Its ranks only gradually crept up to 39,000 by 1989, including girls, admitted since 1976.[1] While there may be other reasons, such serious losses right after the modernizing efforts must at least be partially attributed to the *APR* reforms. There was some truth to the criticism that the senior section suffered losses "due to the disregard of traditions," as these were "sacrificed on the altar of modernity."[2]

Hong Kong also had a tough time implementing the reforms for older boys, and had suffered declines for a number of years. The Venture Scout training scheme went on trial in 1970, and was fully implemented in 1972.[3] If acceptance by youth members was the litmus test, then these reforms had clearly failed, as demonstrated by the pre-*APR* and Post-*APR* membership and Queen's Scout statistics:

Years	Senior/Venture Scouts	Queen's Scouts	% of members
1966-1970	10,646	523	4.9%
1971-1975	8,880	30	0.3%

Cum. Totals of Senior/Venture Scouts & Queen's Scouts, 1966-1975

Sources: Youth membership statistics from Censuses, various years, the Hong Kong Scout Archives; No. of Queen's Scout awards from *Directory of Recipients of the King's Scout Award...*, 37-58.

In the last five pre-*APR* years, Senior Scouts totaled more than 10,600 cumulatively. But, in the first five post-*APR* years, Venture Scouts totaled less than 8,900. The number of these older Scouts peaked in 1967 at 2,336, then declined year-on-year until 1972, when it reached a low of 1,586. Though it grew again from 1973, it only exceeded its 1967 peak in 1976. The contrast was greater in terms of Queen's Scout awards earned.

World_Federation_of_Independent_Scouts (accessed April 20, 2010).

1   Michael Foster, "The Growing Crisis in the Scout Movement," http://www.netpages.free-online.co.uk/sha/crisis.htm (accessed September 20, 2009). Note this was also partly due to the introduction of a maximum age for the Rover Scouts.

2   Ibid.

3   The *Bulletin*, May-June 1970, 8; September-December 1972, 5-8 (Chinese edition).

In the five pre-*APR* years, over five hundred such awards were given out, constituting 4.9% of membership. In the five post-*APR* years, only thirty were presented, constituting 0.3% of membership. The evidence clearly suggests that there was a "rush" to gain the pre-*APR* Queen's Scout Awards before the rules changed, followed by a considerable waning of interest post-*APR*, when membership dropped and Queen's Scout awardees declined even further.

In short, from the late 1960s onward, sweeping British-centric modernizing reform proposals were largely adopted within local Scouting. While most of these were reasonable and helped in keeping the movement relevant to a modern audience, several were impractical in the local context and were either not adopted or adopted and caused considerable short-term difficulties in the next decade.

"Decolonizing" Hong Kong Scouting

From 1970 on, the British Scout association became interested in facilitating the Hong Kong branch's independence, out of enlightened or selfish reasons and perhaps recognizing the eventual inevitability of this transition. The local association, initially hesitant, warmed to the idea and took steps to achieve independence by 1977. It was another milestone in the long process of "Hongkongizing" the local Scout Movement which had started in the interwar years, and added impetus to reinforce the hybrid nature of this movement with British, Chinese, Hong Kong and cosmopolitan features.

While the "decolonization" of Hong Kong Scouting occurred late relative to most other parts of the British Empire, its uniqueness must be emphasized. The table on the next page compares the years in which Commonwealth countries became independent and the years in which they joined WOSM:[1]

---

[1]   Year of independence is not always straightforward. Australia became "independent" in 1901, but Britain retained considerable power in foreign affairs and legislation. The Statute of Westminster in 1931 formally ended most constitutional links between the UK and South Africa, Canada, Australia and New Zealand, etc. South Africa and Canada became independent immediately, and Australia and New Zealand upon ratification of the statue in their own legislatures, which took place in 1942 and 1947, respectively. In 1997, Hong Kong did not gain independence, it was returned to China.

Country/Colony	Independence	WOSM Member	Gap
South Africa	1931(note 1)	1937	+6
Canada	1931(note 1)	1946	+15
Australia	1942(note 1)	1953	+11
New Zealand	1947(note 1)	1953	+6
Malaysia	1957	1957	0
Malta	1964	1966	+2
Singapore	1965	1966	+1
Gambia	1965	1984	+19
Guyana	1966	1967	+1
Botswana	1966	1967	+1
Barbados	1966	1969	+3
Swaziland	1968	1968	0
Mauritius	1968	1971	+3
Fiji	1970	1971	+1
Bahamas	1973	1974	+1
HONG KONG	**1997**(note 1)	**1977**	**-20**

Independence & World Scout Membership Years, 1931-1997

Sources: Tony Smith, *The End of the European Empire: Decolonization after World War II* (Lexington: D.C. Heath, 1975); list of National Scout Organizations, WOSM's website, http://www.scout.org/ (accessed May 10, 2010).

In short, it is possible to discern how, as the political decolonization of British colonies started in late interwar years and picked up momentum after the war, WOSM membership followed. Sometimes, such as in the case of Singapore, the latter would occur either in the same year or only a few years later. Sometimes, such as in the case of Canada, the gap could be more than ten years. But invariably, former colonial Scout associations would only become independent NSOs after their countries gained sovereign status. In contrast, the Hong Kong branch became a standalone NSO and WOSM member in 1977, two decades before Hong Kong's retrocession of sovereignty.

In fact, the topic of independence had been on the agenda since

1970, when it was raised by the British association. A confidential note to Lo in late 1970 referred to an earlier discussion and encouraged Hong Kong to consider independent membership at the WOSM, arguing that: "of all the Overseas Branches …Hong Kong is well able to stand on its own feet; there is, moreover, no reason why such an application should be deferred merely because the territory remains a Crown Colony."[1] Discreet discussions followed in January 1971 at the Commissioner's Advisory Board.[2] In the next two years, the association gradually became more receptive toward the idea. In 1971, due to Sir David's opposition, Lo vetoed suggestions to discuss the matter with G. F. Witchell, the Travelling Commissioner.[3] In confidential correspondences, it was noted that Trench feared that "the Chinese might take offence" with the independence of the colonial branch, and that it "might become more prone to infiltration."[4] When Dymoke Green, the Commonwealth Commissioner, visited for the Diamond Jubilee celebrations, he again confirmed that Britain would assist, if the local branch so desired.

By late 1972, as indicated by a letter from Ross, the branch became interested in at least a status upgrade, if not full independence.[5] But this compromise solution was shown to be impractical as Sir Marc Noble noted that "our Royal Charter and the Constitution of the World Scout Conference do not cater for a 'half-way house'…There are only two legal courses…either you are a Branch or an Independent Member of the World Scout Conference."[6]

Around this time, the colonial authorities' attitude shifted. In early 1973, when local Guiding raised the issue of independence through the Foreign and Commonwealth Office, the Hong Kong government again confidentially expressed concerns about possible objections from

1   Letter, Green to Lo, December 1, 1970, the Hong Kong Scout Archives.
2   Report, the Future Status of the Hong Kong Branch, Jan. 1971, the Hong Kong Scout Archives.
3   Folder, Witchell's visits, the 1970s, the Hong Kong Scout Archives. As Witchell could "give some verbal assistance in the right quarters, e.g., H.E. and Sir Charles [the Chief Scout]."
4   "Girl Guides in Hong Kong, Constitution," HKRS 163-10-70, the Public Records Office, Hong Kong. Despite the title, this record deals with confidential correspondences on the independence of both the Guide and the Scout Associations issued in 1973-76.
5   Letter, Ross to the British association, November 8, 1972, the Hong Kong Scout Archives.
6   Letter, Noble to MacLehose, December 14, 1972, the Hong Kong Scout Archives.

the PRC or Taiwan and risks of infiltration, though it judged these to be unlikely. In June, MacLehose asked Ross to speak with Mrs. Gordon, the Guide commissioner, so that the two could "move in parallel," but indicating that he had "no view on all this—except perhaps a doubt as to whether the subject is anything like as complicated as it has been made to appear."[1] Sir Marc Noble, the new Commonwealth Commissioner, later confirmed this attitude change, noting that "whereas the previous governor [Trench]...was completely opposed to the idea, the present one [MacLehose] doesn't appear to give a damn either way."[2]

After Henry Ma became the commissioner, he began to pursue the matter enthusiastically. In October, Witchell visited and suggested that the branch should "seek advice...from H. E. as Chief Scout."[3] In March 1974, a panel appointed by Ma proposed a multi-year timetable towards independence. In June, a consultation was conducted, and an overwhelming majority of members consulted were in favor of the move. This was taken into consideration in a meeting of the executive committee of the Colony Scout Council in December, when all except one voted for independence.[4] Soon after, Sir Murray's blessing was obtained, and the association was set on a definite path to independence.

In the 1970s, earlier proposals by the British Association to "decolonize" some local titles were also adopted. As noted earlier, suggestions to remove the word "colony" from the titles of the local chief scout and commissioner by the British association in 1961 had met with resistance, as Black felt then that this was unnecessary. In 1967, Green from Britain again suggested the need to "update" local titles from "the now outmoded term 'Colony Commissioner'" to the "Chief Commissioner."[5] But this proposed reform was still ahead of its time. Chinese, native language of 98% of the people in the colony, was only recognized as an official language alongside English in 1974. Even then, the latter was still "more equal": Chinese versions of existing legislation were not required until more than a decade later. In 1973, after expensive corporate re-

---

1 "Girl Guides in Hong Kong...," HKRS 163-10-70.

2 Letter, Siebold of the World Scout Bureau, July 19, 1974, the Hong Kong Scout Archives.

3 Folder, Witchell's visits, the 1970s, the Hong Kong Scout Archives.

4 Letter, Ma to Aide-de-camp of the governor, c. Dec. 1974, the Hong Kong Scout Archives.

5 Letter, Green to Lo, September 18, 1967, Hong Kong Scout Archives.

organization studies by McKinsey, the Secretary for Chinese Affairs (華民政務司, as if the Chinese were a minority to be dealt with exclusively through one government department) was finally renamed the Secretary for Home Affairs. Two years later, the Colonial Secretary became the Chief Secretary.[1] Given the prevailing communal sentiments, it was not surprising that the association finally decided by early 1974 to take out its own colonial labels, and the Colony Scout Council, Colony Chief Scout and Colony Commissioner became, respectively, Scout Council, Chief Scout, and Chief Commissioner, more than a decade after the initial appeals for changes from Britain. In October, the corresponding titles in the local Girl Guides Association were likewise "decolonized."[2]

Noble, accompanied by Ma, opened the Tung Tsz Campsite, 1975.

H. K. Scout Archives.

In 1975, after another visit from Noble, a working party took charge of all preparatory work for independence.[3] By 1976, a draft of the new constitution was ready.[4] In April 1977, Hong Kong's application for full membership in WOSM was accepted, and the association became a "National" Scout organization, despite its colonial status. The formal membership certificate of "The Scout Association of Hong Kong" issued by the World Scout Bureau was dated April 16, 1977. A month later, the Scout Association (Amendment) Bill of 1977 came into effect in Hong Kong, incorporating the necessary changes.[5] Sir Murray MacLehose became the first Chief Scout and G. R. Ross the first president of the newly-

1   "General Correspondence Files relating to Community Organisations," HKRS 894, the Public Records Office, Hong Kong; Frank Welsh, *A Borrowed Place*, 485-7.

2   *Annual Report, 1974-75* (Hong Kong: Girl Guides Association, 1975), 8.

3   Folder, Project Y, 1975-76, the Hong Kong Scout Archives.

4   The *Hong Kong Standard*, December 17, 1975.

5   *SCMP*, April 1, 1977; *Hong Kong Hansard*, May 4, 1977.

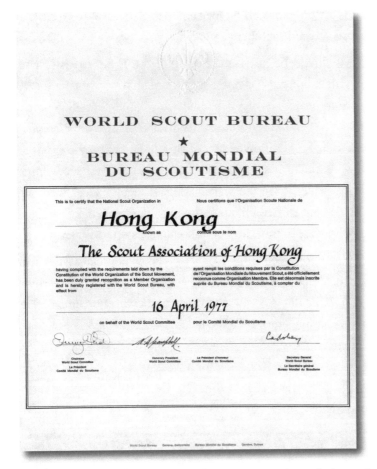

Hong Kong Scout Association's WOSM membership certificate, 1977.

H. K. Scout Archives.

independent Scout Association of Hong Kong. Scouting's independence was celebrated with a goodwill visit to Malaysia, Singapore, Indonesia and Thailand by the association band, complete with kilted Chinese bag-pipe playing Scouts, led by Ma. As this was done outside the colony, it was in line with MacLehose's earlier caution that the Scouts should not "make their new status a cause for...exaggerated celebration," to avoid possibly upsetting the local Chinese cadres.[1]

MacLehose had also warned Gordon that "if against all expecta-tions Peking makes some fuss about the change in status of the Scouts they might have to go into reverse."[2] China, on the verge of economic reforms and the open-door policy, did not react. In 1978, Lady MacLe-hose signed the "Deed of Transfer," making local Guiding also indepen-dent from Britain. Months later, it became an associate member of the

---

1   "Girl Guides in Hong Kong,,,," HKRS 163-10-70.
2   Ibid.

World Association of Girl Guides and Girl Scouts (WAGGGS). In 1981, it was granted full membership.

It should be noted that, up until 1977, the British Scout Association still exercised considerable formal control over the local branch, though Europeans had by that time constituted a small minority of its membership. The latter adhered to the *POR* issued in Britain, its programs and insignia followed that of British Scouting, the appointment of the local commissioner and the awards to its members were approved by the headquarters, even the warrants of all local leaders were signed by the Chief Scout in Britain, sometimes countersigned by the local Chief Scout, who was, in turn, invited to assume that post by Britain.

In 1976, given Hong Kong's expected new status in world Scouting, the local Scout Association bid against Australia for the right to host the 11th Asia Pacific Scout Conference and won. In August 1978, Hong Kong association's new independence was celebrated with Scout leaders from nineteen Asia Pacific members of the WOSM, when they gathered in the Holiday Inn in Kowloon for a week to deliberate on "Scouting for the 80s." This was the first time the Hong Kong association hosted a regional Scout conference.

The 11th Asia Pacific Scout Conference held in Hong Kong, August 1978.

H. K. Scout Archives.

If "decolonization" is defined as "the taking of measures by indigenous peoples and/or their white overlords intended eventually to end external control...and the attempt to replace formal political rule by some kind of new relationship" then the independence of the Hong Kong branch from the British Scout Association can to some extent be viewed as the "decolonization" of Hong Kong Scouting.[1] In this sense, John Springhall's three reasons for decolonization, namely the nationalist or peripheral explanation (emphasizing indigenous upheavals), the international explanation (stressing international politics), and the metropolitan or domestic explanation (focusing on political choices taken by the center based on domestic concerns) provide a useful framework for analyzing local Scouting's independence in 1977 (though, as shall be seen later, not necessarily for understanding the handover of Hong Kong to China two decades later).[2]

There were metropolitan or British considerations. With the disintegration of the empire, the British Scout Association had by the 1960s lost most of its overseas branches. In fact, the *APR* had recommended the elimination of the commonwealth department as "the countries of the Commonwealth are rapidly moving towards independent membership of the World Conference."[3] By the 1960s, Hong Kong was a significant branch, and her interest had to be represented. In 1965, Lo was selected as one of the six members of the British Scout delegation to the 20th World Scout Conference, the first time a Hong Kong commissioner was to attend this forum. Green, Witchell, and Noble had all appeared neutral about the branch's possible independence, and at times even encouraged it, perhaps motivated to different extents by concerns about limited resources to support overseas branches, lessons learned from break-away branches in newly-independent countries, difficulties encountered in implementing the British-centric *APR* reforms, enlightened views about Hong Kong's eventual political decolonization, or even a naiveté about Hong Kong's colonial realities. In fact, Ma later admitted that Noble's role was "instrumental."[4] Perhaps such an attitude in British Scouting was indicative of the "post-colonializing" mentality in the metropolitan culture, which may have begun to emerge in the 1950s, though some suggest "the fifties," so to speak, largely "only happened in the 1970s."[5]

1   John Springhall, *Decolonization since 1945: the Collapse of European Overseas Empires* (Basingstoke, Hampshire: Palgrave, 2001), 2.
2   Ibid., 4-17.
3   *The Chief Scout's Advance Party Report, 1966*, 330.
4   Ma noted that Noble "was mainly instrumental in persuading" the Hong Kong leadership "into agreeing to take the first steps towards effecting a change in status of the Branch." See Ma's letter to the Aide-de-Camp of the governor, October 21, 1982, "The Scout Association, 1978-82," HKRS 921-1-95, the Public Records Office, Hong Kong.
5   Stephen Howe, "When (if ever) did Empire End? 'Internal Decolonisation' in British Culture since the 1950s," in Martin Lynn (ed.), *The British Empire in the 1950s:*

At any rate, as far as British Scouting was concerned, it was clear that "the 'will to rule' gradually slackened" by the 1970s, and this worked in favor of the Hong Kong branch, creating an atmosphere conducive to a change in status.[1]

There were also international factors to consider. The flexible policy at the world Scout body played an important role. In earlier years, WOSM had allowed multiple Scout associations from the same country to join, but usually as a single NSO through a federation of constituent associations. For example, the German *Ring Deutscher Pfadfinderverbände* had three member associations, and the French *Scoutisme Francais* had five, but they both had a single membership in WOSM.[2] However, correspondence from the World Scout Bureau in 1973 indicated that it was willing to consider admitting Hong Kong as a standalone NSO, as long as the application was sent through the British association.[3] This suggests that its position had softened by this time. The fact that Britain, a founding and leading member of WOSM, was supportive of the change in status was, no doubt, an important consideration. That the Hong Kong association would be larger and better resourced than many other independent members in WOSM, being in reality a loose federation of NSOs dependent on subscription fees from its members, may also have been a relevant factor.

Most importantly, there were "nationalist" or colony-based motives. Local attitude towards independence went from being opposed to or at best neutral about it to being lukewarm and then very supportive. The key person here was the Chief Scout. It is intriguing to consider why MacLehose would have entertained such liberal ideas about the future status of the branch, when Hong Kong itself was still not on a definite path towards decolonization. It is unlikely that this was due to any apathy as far as he was concerned. MacLehose had been quite supportive of Scouting, as part of his overall social and youth programs. He praised local Scouting for taking young people "outside the crowded ur-

---

Retreat or Revival? (Basingstoke, Hampshire: Palgrave, 2006), 233.

1   Springhall, *Decolonization since 1945*, 13.

2   Belgium, Denmark, France, Germany, Israel, Luxembourg and Italy all had multiple associations, often of different religion/denomination, which joined WOSM through a federation. See list of NSOs in WOSM's website, http://scout.org/ (accessed May 10, 2010).

3   Letter, Siebold of the World Scout Bureau, November 16, 1973, the Hong Kong Scout Archives.

ban areas...to the mountains and the beaches," and considered its efforts to include boys who could not be Boy Scouts as "making a very practical contribution to [the] community."[1] He would typically edit speeches prepared for him for Scout functions with his own hand. Despite his busy schedule, he had a consistent policy of attending three Scout functions every year, "one evening function, one outside function, and one annual review."[2] He once wrote a personal check for the Scout Fund.[3]

As indicated in confidential correspondences between 1973 and 1976, MacLehose was fully informed about the possible (though unlikely) political risks involved in the branch's change in status. Still, he decided to "withdraw the government's objection," based on what he viewed as "the improved relationship with China and the totally non-political nature of the Movement."[4] He saw it as no more than "an administrative adjustment."[5] But then he also asked both the Scouts and the Guides to go about the matter "in a low key" manner, with "a minimum of publicity," and even the Guides to prepare to go in reverse, if there were "any difficulty caused by the action of the Scouts."[6]

MacLehose did not reveal in these letters why he had even bothered to allow independence to happen, despite the potential political risks. It is possible that he was simply yielding to the demands of local Scouting. But his attitude might also have been partly motivated by what he saw as the inevitable political decolonization of Hong Kong. By this time, Britain had been contemplating the future of the colony for many years, given the known deadline of 1997 for the leased portion. In fact, Sino-British talks on the political future of Hong Kong followed soon after MacLehose's visit to Beijing in 1978, at the invitation of the Chinese Minister of Foreign Trade.[7] The governor may also have perceived in decolonized Scouting, with its public disassociation from Britain, the

1   The *Hong Kong Standard*, April 21, 1974.
2   "The Scout Association of Hong Kong (Chief Scout)," 1971-1977, GH/GP/SYO/8I, HKRS 921-1-94, the Public Records Office, Hong Kong. Note from Cartland, October 23, 1975.
3   Ibid.
4   "Girl Guides in Hong Kong,,,," HKRS 163-10-70.
5   Ibid.
6   Ibid.
7   Welsh, *A Borrowed Place*, 503-4. Official talks started in September 1982, when Prime Minister Margaret Thatcher visited Beijing.

potential of reaching out to more Chinese youngsters, especially the disadvantaged ones who might view British links negatively. Giving up British affiliation might allow local Scouting to expand further, which was consistent with his approach to the local youth problem. In some sense, this move would be analogous to Clementi's concession regarding the Scout Promise in Chinese, or Young's agreement to include Chinese national icons in Scout functions earlier on. They were all tradeoffs: giving up symbolic British control of Scouting in the interest of improved colonial governance through Scouting.

Of course, Ma took many steps to build consensus among members of the association and to plan for its change in status, and the Scouting community at large was eventually overwhelmingly supportive. Without Ma's personal leadership, the governor's permissive attitude would not have been adequate. Without the members' endorsements, Ma's proposals would not likely receive the blessings of the colonial authority. In a sense, growing sympathy towards the idea of going it alone was part of local Scouting's on-going process of adjusting to its unique identity as a Hong Kong movement.

It was just as well that Hong Kong Scouting, by this time largely indigenized, should also become independent. Ethnic British members were a minority, and expatriate leadership was not evident, except for figureheads like the Chief Scout and the president. Scouting had been "cleansed" of Nationalist Chinese influences. Some of the changes implemented at the same time as the *APR* reforms, especially those related to the Scout Promise in Chinese, already discussed in the last section, also reflected further Hongkongization. In this context, decolonization of the Hong Kong branch can be interpreted as another affirmation of the gradual but sure distancing of local Scouting from both the British and the Chinese Scout movements.

With its newly-acquired freedom, the Hong Kong association adopted a hybrid approach in moving forward as an independent organization. While it freely retained the more desirable components of British Scouting and links with Britian which were considered useful, it also readily introduced appropriate new policies and symbols and revived popular traditional elements as it saw fit to ensure the movement's continued acceptance in the local community.

The Hong Kong association kept many features which reaffirmed ties with the metropole. 1977 was the 25th anniversary of the Queen's accession to the throne. In April 1977, a grand ball with MacLehose as the guest of honor celebrated at the same time "HER MAJESTY THE QUEEN'S SILVER JUBILEE and the Association becoming a Member of the World Scout Conference," held at the Hong Kong Convention Centre. The annual Scout rally continued to be held on St. George's Day. The Queen's Scout award, cherished by many Chinese boys, was retained, after a petition sent to the Queen through the British association had been granted.[1] In the first editions of the *POR* of the independent movement, issued in 1979-80, the promise in English still required commitment "to God and to the Queen," though the promise in Chinese called for commitment to "deity" and the "native territory."[2] Effectively, however, since most boys took the promise in Chinese, few would have committed to do their duty "to God and to the Queen."

Hong Kong Scouts celebrated the Queen's Jubilee in 1977, and retained the Queen's Scout Badge after.

On the other hand, Hong Kong Scouting also adopted features which it considered appropriate for the periphery, just as it did with the post-*APR* Scout promise in Chinese. It created a more elaborate set of local awards, judged to be necessary to recognize the large number of leaders and supporters. The Gold, Silver, and Bronze Lions and Dragons and several lower merit awards replaced the Silver Wolf, Silver Acorn and the Medal of Merit. The Gold Lion (Type I), the highest award for uniformed leaders and commissioners, was in the form of a Chinese bronze seal (a traditional symbol of authority and power) with a seated lion handle, rather than a more dynamic running lion, as would be expected for a Scout award. Perhaps even more interestingly, the Gold Dragon, the highest award for lay supporters, was in the form of a tradi-

---

1   Letter, Ross to Noble, February 2, 1977, the Hong Kong Scout Archives.
2   The *Policies, Organisation, and Rules*, 1979, 8; the Chinese edition, 1980, 5.

The Gold Lion (Type I) and the Gold Dragon awards, introduced in 1977.

tional Chinese mythical dragon, symbolic of power, strength and good fortune, often used by the emperors and other members of the imperial families in Chinese dynasties in the past. This dragon was clearly not the same evil animal that was slain by St. George, the patron saint of Britain and also of British Scouting.

On St. George's Day in 1977, immediately after the independence of the local Scout Association, the first Gold Lions were awarded to Ma, without question the most important architect of the decolonization of Hong Kong Scouting; and J. Plaridel Silvestre, the Asia Pacific regional executive commissioner of the World Scout Bureau. In 1978, the Tang Shiu-kin Building in Wanchai was officially opened as the regional headquarters for the Hong Kong Island Region. In the same year, the first Gold Dragon was given to Sir Shiu-kin Tang, a long-time lay supporter of Hong Kong Scouting.

MacLehose and Tang at the opening of the Tang Shiu-kin Building, 1978.

H. K. Scout Archives.

In line with local needs, Scouting continued to drive growth in the rural areas through a five-year development plan and a substantial development fund, encouraged by David Akers-Jones, then the Secretary for the New Territories and president of the New Territories Regional Scout Council.[1] Also, as shall be discussed in the next chapter, it soon began to introduce coeducation and a pre-Cub section aggressively, even ahead of Britain. It also revived the Rover Scout section and many other pre-*APR* traditions and symbols, such as the epaulettes, the plumes, the Wood Badge, and scarves for older boys and leaders, considered attractive by many locally and in other Asian countries.

Unlike in other commonwealth countries, Hong Kong Scouting broke away from the British movement fully twenty years before Hong Kong's retrocession of sovereignty to China through a combination of favorable metropolitan, international and especially local factors. On the other hand, the "decolonized" movement continued to develop as a hybrid which comfortably combined British, colonial, Chinese and local features, highlighting its Hongkongness and cosmopolitanism (or some may say lingering vestiges of colonialism).

During this period under review, healthy growth was registered. As illustrated in the graph on the next page, membership trends from 1964 to 1977 were relatively smooth, and did not exhibit the major ups and downs which had characterized those of the previous periods. Nevertheless, total membership grew more robustly in the second half of the 1960s, when major programs were introduced to reach out to more youngsters both as Boy Scouts and outside the youth movement; and slowed down a bit in the early 1970s, coinciding with the implementation of the *APR* reforms, partly driven by the loss in members in the older Venture Scouts section.

By the time the Hong Kong Scout Association became independent of the British Scout Association in 1977, it had close to 33,000 members, and boasted of a population penetration ratio of 7.3 per thousand, substantially ahead of that in Singapore, which stood at 5.6 per thousand, though still behind that in Britain, the "standard of excellence" in the world of Scouting, at 11.2 per thousand.[2]

---

1   "Future Expansion of Scouting in the N. T., 1978-93," HKRS 684-5-40, the Public Records Office, Hong Kong.

2   See Appendix D., "Membership Statistics."

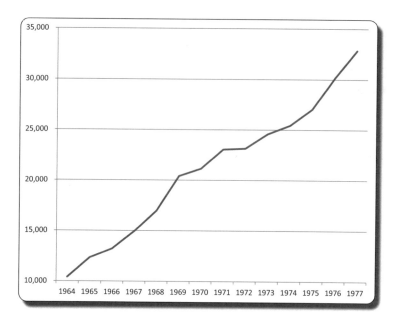

Membership Trends, Hong Kong, 1964-1977

Sources: Appendix D, "Membership Statistics."

Concluding remarks

From the mid-1960s through to 1977, Hong Kong Scouting had modernized its programming, appearance, service targets, scope, management
methods, and organization structure. "To rule" was again a key motive
early on, at least from the perspective of the colonial elites who had gone
through two disturbances in the 1960s which had seriously challenged
governance. Race re-emerged as a relevant issue as the increasingly Chinese youth movement's top leadership was once again indigenized, this
time permanently, with a succession of Chinese senior commissioners,
considerably earlier than in, say, local Guiding. In response to perceived
needs of the community subsequent to the riots in the 1960s, the movement reached out to non-Scout youngsters, including girls, and eventually formed a dedicated subsidiary to serve many young people outside
Scouting. At around the same time, the local movement also adopted a
large number of modernizing reforms proposed by British Scouting. Finally, at the end of the period under review, Hong Kong Scouting broke

away from the British parent, fully two decades ahead of the political de-colonization of Hong Kong, in a move that was unique among territories in the British Commonwealth.

In constantly adapting to new challenges of the modern society of both the center and the periphery, the local Scout association demon-strated its ability to continuously transform and improve. In this sense, it was worthy of being labeled a growing movement (which B-P had repeated emphasized as the appropriate nature of Scouting) rather than a static organization. It also exhibited essential characteristics of a modern learning organization, even before that term was to be popularized in management literature.[1] In a later study, when this term became fash-ionable, Mac W. M. Mak would argue that the Scout Association was indeed a good example of a learning organization.[2] By 1977, the local youth movement was an independent member of the world Scout body with a brand new program, a brand new image, and even a large subsid-iary which served non-Scout youth. With a fast growing and impressive population penetration ratio, it was very much part of life in the Hong Kong community, and part of growing up for many of her youth.

---

1   This term became fashionable in management literature in the late 1980s and early 1990s. See Mike Pedler, John Burgoyne, Tom Boydell, *The Learning Company: A Strategy for Sustainable Development* (London: McGraw Hill, 1991); Peter Senge, "The Leader's New Work: Building Learning Organization," *Sloan Management Review*, Fall 1990, 7-23; Peter M. Senge, T*he Fifth Discipline: the Art and Practice of the Learning Organization* (London: Century Business, 1992); David A. Garvin, "Building a Learning Organization," *Harvard Business Review*, July-August 1993, 78-91.

2   Mac W. M. Mak, "The Scout Association as a Learning Company," in G. Welshman, T. Boydell, J. Burgoyne, and M. Pedler, *Learning Company Conference 1994: Collected Papers* (Sheffield: 1994).

Chapter 6

Expansion and Realignment

1977-2010

Chapter 6
Expansion and Realignment
1977-2010

Shortly after Hong Kong Scouting became independent of the British youth movement, MacLehose and the British government also initiated talks with the government of PRC on the political future of Hong Kong. Sir Edward Youde succeeded MacLehose as governor in 1982 and was involved in the talks started by his predecessor, culminating in the Joint Declaration of December 1984, confirming Hong Kong's eventual return to China. Sir David Wilson, who arrived in 1987, and the Hon. Christopher Patten, who came in 1992, both governed Hong Kong as it counted down its last years as a British colony. They were also the last Chief Scouts before Hong Kong became a Chinese Special Administrative Region (SAR). The Hon. Tung Chee Hwa (董建華), the first Chief Executive (行政長官) of the SAR, followed the tradition of governors before him and became the Chief Scout in late 1997. In June 2005, The Hon. Sir Donald Tsang Yam-kuen (曾蔭權) became the second Chief Executive and also the new Chief Scout of Hong Kong. Tsang's second term as the Chief Executive ended in June 2012.

In 1985, several years after Youde replaced MacLehose as the Chief Scout, Chau Cham-son (周湛燊), son of Sir Tsun-nin, became the Chief Commissioner. He was to become the longest-serving commissioner, and stayed on till December 1996, except for a short break in 1993. In July 1988, soon after Wilson became the Chief Scout, Sir Ti Liang Yang (楊鐵樑), the Chief Justice, succeeded Sir Denys Roberts as the president. The appointment of the first Chinese (Kotewall was an Eurasian) to this largely honorary post signified another milestone in the decolonization of Scouting. In January 1997, John Hui (許招賢) succeeded Chau. In 1998, shortly after Tung became the Chief Scout, the Hon. Mr. Justice Patrick Chan (陳兆愷), Chief Judge of the High Court,

Previous Page:

Hong Kong Scouts, including Cub Scouts and female youth members, went on a cross-country trip with Mainland Chinese youngsters, culminating in a visit to the Tiananmen Square in Beijing, July 2010.

H. K. Scout Archives.

became the second Chinese president. In January 2004, Pau Shiu-hung (鮑紹雄) became the second post-handover commissioner, followed by Anthony Chan (陳傑柱) in November 2007, whose term ended in late 2011. In August 2008, the Hon. Mr. Justice Geoffrey Ma (馬道立) took over the presidency. In September 2010, Ma became the Chief Justice of the Court of Final Appeal, the most senior member of the Hong Kong judiciary, and stayed on as the president until 2018.[1] In these decades, coeducation, a pre-Cub section, and other initiatives helped local Scouting to stay relevant and underpinned its continued expansion. These developments will be discussed in separate sections of this chapter.

After Hong Kong's political fate was sealed by the Sino-British Accord, all aspects of the Hong Kong society, including Scouting, underwent a sure if somewhat hesitant process of decolonization. Indigenized or "Hongkongized" Scouting continued to grow despite a shrinking local youth population and declining Scout membership levels in many countries, but it nevertheless had to deal with some challenges longer term. By 2010, citizenship training à la Scouting, like citizenship education in Hong Kong, was only being slowly reconstructed, with a modest renationalizing theme, reflecting the interactions of multiple underlying social forces and tensions. More than a decade after Hong Kong's handover to China, not withstanding its apparent robustness, the post-colonial youth movement is faced with considerable uncertainties as to its future role(s) in Hong Kong, as part of China.

Breaking gender barriers

Throughout the study, it has from time to time been beneficial to make reference to Scouting (Guiding) for girls in Hong Kong in order to provide some insights into the gendered nature of the movement, broadly defined. From before World War I to the years just before Hong Kong Scouting broke away from the British parent, girls and boys continued to be trained in segregated Scouting and Guiding with gendered programs and differentiated experiences. However, as shall be seen in this section, shortly after local Scouting became a standalone movement, it plunged

---

1   See Appendix C for names and tenures of key leaders of the Scout Association of Hong Kong after 2010, the cut-off year of this study.

resolutely into coeducation, and girls became an increasingly common sight in the traditionally all-male movement, though Hong Kong Guiding was to remain largely reserved for female members.

It has been noted that before the First World War, Scouting for girls came later than that for boys, but was, on the other hand, allowed to continue after Scouting for boys was discouraged in favor of the militaristic Cadet Corps. Though Guiding was revived postwar soon after Scouting, Chinese Guiding didn't begin until late 1926, and, unlike Scouting for boys, came with a race-based uniform reserved for the Chinese girls. During the Sino-Japanese war period, the heavy and equal utilization of Boy and Girl Scouts in China in war time and frontline roles contrasted with the differentiated treatment which they experienced in Hong Kong, where the Boy Scouts were used in limited defense-related duties, and the Girl Guides only in support work of a more genteel nature. It has also been observed that, in the first decades after Second World War, top leadership in Guiding continued to be monopolized by Europeans, unlike that in Scouting, though both movements were equally enthusiastic in their respective efforts to cross the class barriers and to reach out to disadvantaged youngsters. By the 1960s, there were occasional mixed activities for Scouts and Guides, such as the 1967 Joint Patrol Leaders' camp at the Gilwell campsite. In the mid-1970s, even experimental mixed units had emerged, mainly through the enthusiasm among some leaders in the Scout organization.

Joint Boy Scout and Girl Guide Patrol Leaders' Camp at Gilwell, 1967.

H. K. Scout Archives.

To the extent that Scouting was a non-formal educational movement, breaking gender barriers and admitting members of the opposite sex represent a special case of coeducation. By the late 1970s, Hong Kong Guiding and Scouting, freed from the controls of Britain, again chose to deal with another contemporary challenge, in this case coeducation, quite differently. Despite resistance from the Girl Guide organization, coeducation was introduced in the older Scout sections in the late 1970s, and in all age groups by the mid-1980s. By the 2000s, there were more girls than boys involved in combined Scouting and Guiding, though there were more boys than girls in the underlying population, prompting questions about the reasons for this trend and concerns as to what should be done for the boys in a movement that was originally conceived of as integral to the fashioning of masculine behaviors.

Coeducation often meant different things to different people. In a narrow sense, it could just mean having both sexes learning in the same institution, and did not even have to imply desegregation within it. Booker T. Washington's Tuskegee Institute of the nineteenth century was "coeducational," but men and women had "sex-segregated learning, sex-specific teachers, and sex-determined curriculum."[1] By this definition, Scouting and Guiding had been coeducational from day one, as boys and girls were both admitted from the earliest years. But much more could be implied by the word. Plato argued that "if we are going to use men and women for the same purposes, we must teach them the same things…and treat them in the same way."[2] Mary Wollstonecraft, hailed as the "philosophical mother of coeducation," suggested that education should cultivate students' character regardless of sex instead of students' behavior as men and women, and that this could only be done by "mixing…children [of both sexes] together, and making them jointly pursue the same objects."[3] Based on these ideals, Scouting and Guiding were not coeducational up to the late 1970s: boys and girls trained in single-sex units, and were often taught gendered topics.[4]

1   Susan Laird, "Rethinking 'Coeducation'," in Jim Garrison (ed.), *the New Scholarship on Dewey* (Dordrecht: Kluwer Academic Publishers, 1995), 198.
2   Plato, the *Republic*, trans. by Desmond Lee (Penguin Classics, 2003), 161.
3   Susan Laird, *Mary Wollstonecraft: Philosophical Mother of Coeducation* (London: Continuum Int'l, 2008), 124-125.
4   Popular Girl Guides' badges included such "domestic" badges as Hostess, Child Nurse, Laundress, Homemaker, and Needlewoman, all unavailable to Boy Scouts. See *Annual Report, 1969-70* (Hong Kong: the Girl Guides Association).

Girl Guides Patrol Emblems used flowers, and Proficiency Badges included "Hostess" and "Child Nursing," all unavailable to Boy Scouts.

By the 1960s and the early 1970s, coeducation was becoming fashionable in many countries. In America, the principle on racial segregation in the Supreme Court case of *Brown v. Board of Education* was applied by feminists to open up public all-boys schools for girls. Coeducation was welcomed in many American women's colleges.[1] Similarly, some established single-sex secondary schools in Hong Kong also experimented with coeducation, typically in their upper Forms. Joint Scout and Guide activities also became popular, forcing the issue upon leaders of the two organizations in Britain. In 1970, John Beresford questioned whether the Victorian decision to keep girls in Guiding was still valid in a modern society which emphasized sexual equality, coeducation, and the removal of gendered labels from pursuits. He recommended continued experiments with joint activities, re-alignment of county boundaries and policy coordination, and asked if the two associations should not soon work together "as one united Movement."[2]

Motivated by perceived needs of the time both in Britain and locally, a Scout and Guide Coordinating Board was formed in Hong Kong in 1970. In its first meeting, it was agreed that joint training activities should be held, and the feasibility of an experimental unit of Venture Scouts and Ranger Guides would be examined. In 1971, joint Scouts and Guides fund-raising "Jamboree cookies" were introduced.[3] In 1972, three thousand Scouts and Guides served in the "Keep Hong Kong Clean" campaign, though with gendered division of labor.[4] In 1974, the board agreed that the boundaries of Scout and Guide Districts should be aligned.[5] However, two years later, the Guides still had nine districts on the Island, twelve in Kowloon, and eight in the New Territories; while the Scouts had six, sixteen, and eleven districts, suggesting little progress had been made in this direction.[6]

At the time, the world Scout bodies were relatively open-minded

Joint Scouts and Guides Jamboree cookies, 1971.

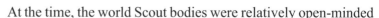

1   Leslie Miller-Bernal and Susan L. Poulson (eds.), *Challenged by Coeducation: Women's Colleges Since 1960s* (Nashville: Vanderbilt Univ. Press, 2006), xi.

2   John Beresford, "Crossfire," *The Scouter*, August 1970.

3   *Annual Report, 1971-72* (Hong Kong: Girl Guides Association).

4   The 2,200 Scouts were in charge of cleaning public areas, and the 700 Guides provided refreshment and issued promotional materials.

5   Folder, the Scout and Guide Coordinating Board, 1970-1975, the Hong Kong Scout Archives.

6   *Annual Report, 1975/76* (Hong Kong: Girl Guides Association, 1976), 6-7; Leung et al., *75 Years of Hong Kong Scouting*, 109.

about coeducation. In 1973, the two world committees issued a joint statement, declaring that Guide and Scout organizations could be consti-tuted as "a joint organization (with separate Scout and Guide sections)" or "a merged organization (where there is no separate structured body for either Guides or Scouts)," if they wish to "collaborate on a permanent basis."[1] Still, divergent attitudes were also revealed in the document. The Scout committee believed that "the Scout Movement is destined mainly for boys…[but] Scout national organizations are not precluded from enrolling girls."[2] On the other hand, the Guide committee believed that coeducation should be done through joint activities or joint units comprising of Scouts and Guides, but membership of Guide national organizations should not be open to boys. Clearly, the former's stance was more inclusive than the latter's.

A poster for the "Keep Hong Kong Clean" campaign.
PRO PO000106.

This difference in attitude mirrored those of the leaders of the two movements in Hong Kong. In a joint meeting in 1974, it was re-vealed that there were one or two "purely experimental" Venture Scout units with girls. When the Guide commissioner indicated that some "Guiders have strong views on this topic" and asked whether they would be kept informed of developments in this direction, Ma responded non-committally that the Girl Guides Association would "more than likely" be consulted again before the final decision to go ahead.[3]

In April 1975, the Scout association authorized two types of ex-periments, joint units (混合團) with Venture Scouts and Ranger Guides and Venture Scout Development Units (深資童軍拓展團) with girls re-cruited into Venture Units.[4] The rationale offered was that "young peo-ple of that age like to do things together, and we'd rather have supervised mixed activities than let them run wild."[5] Two joint units and one devel-opment unit were approved. In August 1975, the Island Development Unit (IDU) was formed at the coeducational Matteo Ricci College, and swore in eleven young men and fifteen young women, the latter being the first official female Venture Scouts.[6]

---

1   Folder, the Scout and Guide Coordinating Board, 1970-1975, the Hong Kong Scout Archives.
2   Ibid.
3   Ibid.
4   The *Hong Kong Scouting*, November 11, 1975, 23.
5   *SCMP*, June 16, 1975.
6   The *Hong Kong Scouting*, March 1979, 9.

When Noble visited in 1975 he counseled caution. To him, the issue was "highly explosive" in Britain, with concerns expressed by the Guide organization and even the Queen, and asked that Hong Kong "follow official policy—at least until such time as you are an Independent Association."[1] Official policy was elaborated in a joint statement by the two British associations in June, which called for a coordinated approach, given the potential risks of divergent approaches on membership.

Soon after, a joint secretariat was set up in Britain to encourage and regulate convergence and hopefully to work towards a common section for older members. For the time being, it was promulgated that Venture Units must pursue coeducation through a joint unit with the Guide body.[2] Ma suggested that a joint secretariat be set up locally to study the British scheme with a view to its possible adoption. Mrs. Gordon responded that there was no need for this, until the outcome of the British secretariat was known.[3] One party was evidently more eager to pursue coeducation than the other. In 1976, only a year after Noble's call for restraint, the British Scout association made the controversial decision of allowing Venture Units to admit girls, suggesting that the Scout associations in Britain and Hong Kong were both more ready to include girls then their respective counterparts were to admit boys.[4]

The local Scout association plunged fully into coeducation soon after independence. In May 1978, Mrs. Gordon expressed her concern with the Scout Movement's plan to admit girls in a letter to C. M. Leung, the chairman of the Executive Committee of the Scout Association, and copied it to MacLehose. Gordon declared that "it is an accepted worldwide opinion that girls of 7 to 16 years of age must be looked after by women;" and Leung replied that constitutionally the Scout association could enroll girls of all ages and that it had over one thousand female leaders (who could presumably look after younger girls), but also noted that at the time only girls sixteen or above were being considered.[5]

---

1   Letter, Noble to Ma, July 6, 1975, the Hong Kong Scout Archives.
2   Jim Hart, "Joint Units," *Scouting*, October 1975.
3   Folder, the Scout and Guide Coordinating Board, the Hong Kong Scout Archives.
4   The Scout Association, "The History of Scouting," http://www.scoutbase.org.uk/library/ history/ (accessed February 10, 2010).
5   Letters, Gordon to Leung, May 3, 1978, Leung to Gordon, May 10, 1978, HKRS 921-1-95.

Hong Kong contingent to the 1983 World Jamboree, with four female Venture Scouts.

H. K. Scout Archives.

Sir Murray, whose wife was the president of the Girl Guides, wisely stayed out of the argument, and responded to Gordon as follows: "I am sure that two such experienced and sensible organisations (and, if I may say so, people) can sort out a difference of this sort between themselves...I hope therefore that you will excuse me from commenting!"[1] By June 1978, a revised *POR* provided for mixed Venture Units and Rover Crews.[2] In July, girls were admitted as Venture Scouts.[3] The IDU became the 176th Hong Kong, the first mixed Venture Unit.[4] By March 1979, twenty mixed Venture Units were registered. Soon, existing units in the CSO, which had both male and female young adults, were also converted into mixed Rover Crews, consequently creating immediately a substantial mixed Rover Scout section. In 1983, four female Venture Scouts, including three Sea Scouts, attended the 15th World Scout Jamboree for the first time as members of the Hong Kong Contingent.

Several years later, girls under sixteen were also included. In March 1982, the Rainbow Project (天虹計劃), which experimented with having girls in the Cub and the Scout sections and studied the feasibility of a pre-Cub section, was launched. Three mixed pre-Cub "Grasshopper Units" were set up, and seven Cub Scout units and six Scout units became mixed.[5] In late 1984, Grasshoppers for boys and girls between the ages of six and eight were formally introduced, and girls were admitted to the Cub Packs.[6] By the mid-1980s, Hong Kong Scouting was fully co-

The *Hong Kong Scouting* in 1982, featuring the Rainbow Project.

1   Letter, MacLehose to Gordon, May 18, 1978, HKRS 921-1-95.
2   The *POR, 1st Edition* (Hong Kong: the Scout Association of Hong Kong, 1979), II. The portions on the two mixed older sections were approved in June 1978.
3   *Annual Report, 1977-78* (Hong Kong: the Scout Association), 8.
4   The *Hong Kong Scouting*, March 1979, 13-14.
5   The *Hong Kong Scouting*, July 1985, 19-33.
6   *Annual Report, 1984-85* (Hong Kong: Scout Association of Hong Kong), 17.

educational in all its sections. At around the same time, the first female District Commissioners were appointed. In 1986, Jane Hansen became the Commissioner of the Silver Jubilee District, which will be referred to again later in this chapter; and in 1988, Grace Chow Oi-chu (周愛珠) became the first Chinese woman to head up a district.[1]

Some first female members admitted under the Rainbow project.

H. K. Scout Archives.

In admitting girls into all youth sections, the local movement was several years ahead of British Scouting, which allowed mixed Venture units in 1976 but mixed Cub Packs and pre-Cub "Beaver Colonies" only in late 1980s. In fact, it was relatively "progressive" in coeducation in the world of Scouting. By 1990, only over thirty NSOs, including those of Britain and Australia, were fully coeducational. Japan, on the other hand, only admitted girls into its Rover section (ローパー部門) in 1990, and into all its youth sections in 1995.[2]

Why was local Scouting eager to pursue coeducation? After all, women's rights in Hong Kong were not particularly advanced. *Mui Tsai*'s, young girls sold into virtual domestic servitude, were still common in the interwar years.[3] Polygamy through concubinage was legal until 1971.[4] Indigenous women could not inherit land in the New Territories until after the 1990s.[5] To this day, only male descendants of native villagers in the New Territories have the legal right to apply to the

---

1   The *Hong Kong Scouting*, August 1988, 3.

2   Scout Association of Japan, *History of Scout Movement in Japan* 日本ボーイスカウト運動史, Vol. II, 119-121.

3   See David Pomfret, "'Child Slavery' in British and French Far-Eastern Colonies, 1880-1945," *Past & Present*, November 2008, 176-213.

4   Athena Nga Chee Liu, *Family Law for the Hong Kong SAR* (Hong Kong: the Hong Kong Univ. Press, 1999), 16 .

5   Irene Lik Kay Tong, "R-inheriting Women in Decolonizing Hong Kong," in Jill M. Bystydzienski and Jotl Sekhon (eds.), *Democratization and Women's Grassroots Movements* (Bloomington: Indiana Univ. Press, 1999), 49-66.

government for land to build a home on concessionary terms.[1]

A number of factors might have contributed to this policy shift. Preference for coeducation in schools at home and overseas, WOSM's open attitudes, and the introduction of mixed Venture Units in Britain would all encourage emulation. But the Hong Kong branch was on a clear path to independence. It could choose to ignore local, metropolitan and global trends in Scouting or education if these were considered inappropriate. Why did it push ahead with coeducation even more aggressively than the parent movement?

There were favorable factors inside local Scouting. Another slowdown in membership growth suggested that something had to be done: growth in youth members had been over 10% in both 1976 and 1977, but had dropped back to 5% in 1978, then 1%, 3%, -1% and 0.1%, respectively, from 1979 to 1982.[2] With FOS, Scout-like activities were already available to many girls. Amongst the SSUs in the CSO, many young women and men in Scout uniforms had been accustomed to working side-by-side. Extending Scouting to girls of all ages was a natural next step, especially as the community had urged the inclusion of more youngsters, regardless of gender. Also, the local experiments with mixed Scouting in all sections were well-received, judging by the rapid growth in the number of mixed units. Finally, the branch's independence from Britain meant freedom, allowing local Scouting to become fully coeducational a few years before the parent movement.

Over time, coeducation proved to be rather successful. As demonstrated by the table in the next page, female participation in Scouting grew steadily, from 4% in 1984 to 32% in 2010, and female share of Scouting and Guiding combined was around 60% in 2010, both of which are significant numbers in the context of gender trends in Scouting elsewhere and in the population in Hong Kong.[3] By 2010, the female share of youth membership in British Scouting was less than 15%.[4] There

1   Fanny M. Cheung (ed.), *EnGendering Hong Kong Society: A Gender Perspective of Women's Status* (Hong Kong: The Chinese Univ. Press, 1997), 393.

2   *Census Reports*, various years, the Hong Kong Scout Archives.

3   There were 51,572 members in Guiding in 2010, including 8,420 in the mixed Bees section. Assuming half the Bees were boys, there would be 65,328 girls in the two movements with 108,445 members, or around 60%. See *Annual Report, 2009/10* (Hong Kong: Hong Kong Girl Guides Association, 2010).

4   In 2009/10, 62,380 of the 405,110 youth members in British Scouting, or 15%, were female. See *The Scout Association's Report and Accounts 2009/10*, 52.

were consistently more boys than girls between the ages of five and nineteen in population censuses taken in Hong Kong from 1981 to 2006.[1] By 2009, female share of children and youth up to the age of fourteen, the key age range for Scouting, was still only 48%, though its share of youth between the ages of fifteen and twenty four was around 50%.[2]

	Boys	Girls	Total	Girls' %
1984	27,357	1,194	28,551	**4%**
1997	28,400	7,760	36,160	**21%**
2010	38,907	17,966	56,873	**32%**

Scout Youth Membership by Gender, 1984-2010

Sources: *Scout Association Annual Reports*, various years, supplemented by census reports, various years, the Hong Kong Scout Archives.

It is possible that local boys became less interested in joining a movement that was originally designed for them partly because the ability to access the many distractions of modern youth was gendered, even in a developed society like Hong Kong. There is some evidence that boys tended to be more interested in youth subcultures such as Internet surfing, electronic or online games, sports and alcohol, tobacco and soft drugs.[3] Their preoccupation with these might have reduced their interest in Scouting. Furthermore, protective attitudes could imply that Scouting, being generally acceptable to even the more conservative Chinese parents, might have been among the few sanctioned extra-curricular activities for some girls. Perhaps more so than in western, more permissive, societies, it is conceivable that some parents would be more comfortable with their girls going on a camping trip with a mixed troop

---

1   See the *Hong Kong Population Census 2001: Main Report, Vol.1*, Table 3.2, 34; *Hong Kong 2006 Population By-census, Main Tables*, Table 1.10.
2   See http://www.gov.hk/en/about/abouthk/factsheets/docs/population.pdf (accessed April 1, 2011).
3   See Kenneth Roberts, *Youth and Leisure* (London: George Allen & Unwin, 1983), 23-31; Kaveri Subrahmanyam, et al., "New Forms of Electronic Media: the Impact of Interactive Games and the Internet on Cognition, Socialization, and Behavior," in Dorothy G. Singer and Ejrome L. Singer (eds.), *Handbook of Children and the Media* (California: Sage Publications, 2001), 73-100; Richard Muscat, et al., *Risk Factors in Adolescent Drug Use: Evidence from School Surveys and Application in Policy* (Strasbourg Cedex: Council of Europe Publishing, 2007), 113-117.

under adult supervision then spending a few nights outside with boys, as an unsupervised and unstructured activity.

A more interesting question to ask is, given that Scouting became coeducational, why Guiding did not, or, indeed, why Scouting and Guiding did not simply merge? These would both seem logical solutions for the two sister movements when gender-segregated training was no longer perceived as necessary. Why was single-sex training insisted upon by the Girl Guides?

Some considerations were institutional, both at the metropole and on the periphery. The Scout and Guide organizations in Britain chose to remain separate, though British Scouting also became coeducational. Local Guiding, though smaller, grew healthily despite its single-sex approach. There were personality differences among the leaders of Scouting and Guiding, the former being more eager to pursue coeducation, as personified by Ma and Gordon, the two commissioners. There was institutional resistance and inertia, typical among organizations facing the prospect of being rationalized. Finally, there was the power of the diverging traditions which had developed in the two movements, despite their common roots. Over the years, the Guides and the Scouts in Hong Kong had acquired different policies, cultures, practices, programs and uniforms. The prospects of having to merge all these would have been daunting even for the most enthusiastic of proponents.

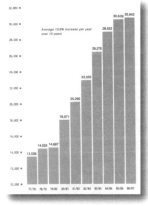

Membership growth in Hong Kong Guiding, 1977-1987.

Annual Report of the H. K. Girl Guides Assn., 1987/8.

There was another institutional influence: the persistence of single-sex schools. Some felt that girls needed their own single-sex institutions, as there was the so-called "chilly climate" in coeducational colleges, which was thought to discourage women from achievement.[1] Whether for this or other reasons, even though most newer schools would be mixed, the established girls' schools in Hong Kong tended to remain single sex. As of today, there are still around thirty all-girl schools, some with both primary and secondary sections. Even though, in theory at least, these girls' schools could have all-girl Venture Scout Units linked to the local Scout association, few would do so. Many of them, including the Diocesan Girls', Belilios, True Light, Maryknoll Convent, St. Paul's Convent, St. Paul's Secondary, and Precious Blood, have Guide

---

1   Leslie Miller-Bernal, "Introduction: Changes in the Status and Functions of Women's Colleges over Time," Leslie Miller-Bernal et al. (eds.), *Challenged by Coeducation*, 9.

Companies or Brownies Packs, some quite well-established.

However, some motivations went deeper and were possibly rooted in the social context of Hong Kong. The language of colonialism, as Helen Carr suggests, often places "non-Europeans" and "women" in "the same symbolic space," or, as Nancy Stephan argues, represents "lower races [as] the 'female' type of the human species, and females the 'lower race' of gender."[1] As we have already observed, women's rights in Hong Kong were often suppressed. It could be said that some local women were indeed treated as if they were the "lower race" of gender. This phenomenon extended to young girls. As of 1971, though there were more boys than girls between the ages of ten and fourteen, 23,380 girls had to work, versus only 12,545 boys.[2] This gender inequality would support the claim that only Guiding could devote the attention necessary to provide equal opportunities to the girls, in or out of the schools.

If Hong Kong was, to some extent, sexually discriminatory, then several feminist rationales for single-sex education could be relevant. Mrs. Gordon declared in 1977 that "Guiding is for the girl and for the women...Guiding will help the girl to become a woman of compassion, who can be relied upon to help her family, and her community."[3] In 1978, she went further and noted that: "the right reasons for having joint activities with the Scouts is when it is better for the education of the Girl Guides, including the development of the power of leadership. The wrong reason is when a joint activity...is introduced because men and boys want it in circumstances which may not be in the best interests of the girls."[4] The "feminist responses to co-education," Madeleine Arnot explains, argue that single-sex education enables breaking away from "myths about women's role in society" ("the liberal reformist perspective"), prepares women "for their uniquely feminine futures" ("the conservative perspective"), or isolates them from mixed schools as "the main means of reproducing the patriarchal relations of [male] domi-

---

1   Helen Carr, "Woman/Indian, the 'American' and his Others," in F. Barker, P. Hulme, M. Iversen and D. Loxley (eds.), *Europe and its Others,* vol. 2 (Colchester: Univ. of Essex Press, 1985), 50; Nancy L. Stephan, "Race and Gender: The Role of Analogy in Science," in Gill Kirkup, et al. (eds.), *The Gendered Cyborg: A Reader* (New York: Routledge, 2000), 39.
2   *Hong Kong Population and Housing Census, 1971, Basic Tables* (Hong Kong: Census and Statistics Department, 1971), Tables 1, 6 and 8.
3   *Annual Report, 1976/77* (Hong Kong: Girl Guides Association, 1977), 19.
4   Letter, Gordon to Leung, May 3, 1978, HKRS 921-1-95.

nation" ("the radical perspective").[1] Though these three perspectives were very different, they could all justify single-sex training. Supporters could argue that, given the discrimination which marked the social context, womanhood (defined according to one of the perspectives) would need to be nurtured in a protected environment such as all-girl Guiding. As implied by Gordon's comments, local Guiding did seem to use all three perspectives to support its *raison-d'être*.

How about the achievement of girls in Scouting? Was there a "chilly climate"? In 1981, Chan Kuen-kuen (陳娟娟), Chan Siu-kam(陳笑琴), Ng Kwai-lai (吳桂麗) and Yeung Kit-ching (楊潔貞) from the 231st East Kowloon and Ma Ngan-yong (馬顏容) from the 14th Yuen Long West became the first female Queen's Scouts in Hong Kong.[2] In 1987, the first "Scout(s) of the Year (模範童軍)" selection was held, and youth members were chosen among entrants who had been recommended by their Scout Leaders, parents, and principals or employers. This event became an annual tradition.[3] Three years later, in 1989, Amy Chong Yuen-yu (莊宛儒) of 211th Hong Kong became the first girl chosen as a Scout of the Year.[4]

First female Queen's Scouts met MacLehose, 1981.

H. K. Scout Archives.

Some attempt at an assessment of whether there was a chilly climate can be made by comparing the ratio of the girls' share of the Queen's Scout awards (or its post-1997 equivalent) as a proxy of achievement to their share of the Venture Scouts. This ratio went from 42% in 1984 to 74% in 1996-99, 86% in 2000-03, 98% in 2004-07, and

1   Madeleine Arnot, "A Cloud over Co-education: An analysis of the forms of transmission of class and gender relations," in *Reproducing Gender? Essays on educational theory and feminist politics* (New York: RoutledgeFalmer, 2002), 94-97.

2   The *Hong Kong Scouting*, June 1981, back inside cover.

3   The *Hong Kong Scouting*, December 1987, 10.

4   Report, List of "Scouts of the Year," 1987-90, the Hong Kong Scout Archives.

123% in 2008-2010.[1] To the extent that the top award was an appropriate index of achievement, girls in Scouting did play a catch-up game for years, suggesting that there might have been a chilly climate, and this might justify having an all-girl Guiding Movement. However, by the mid-2000s, girls in mixed Scouting had achieved an impressive share of the top award, at a level commensurable with and even exceeding their membership share. For example, in 2008-2010, the average female share of the top honor was 36%, while girls only constituted 29% of the Venture Scouts, implying the possible presence of a "chilly climate" for the boys in mixed Scouting. Having said that, it could also be argued that an all-girl movement remained relevant, as long as there were *some* girls who learn and grow more effectively in a single-sex environment. There is some evidence that this was indeed the case, judging from the on-going demand for places in the all-girl schools, mentioned earlier.

Coeducation was successively introduced in Scouting from the 1970s to the 1980s, though single-sex Guiding persisted, for a number of institutional and social reasons. By the 2000s, with combined Scouting and Guiding, boys became a minority in a citizenship training program which had been started exclusively for them, and were possibly "achieving" less than the girls. Some have argued for "all-boys" institutions, as "places where unreconstructed masculinity shines."[2] In some studies in some countries, it has been shown that mixed educational settings may have resulted in perceived underachievement of some boys.[3] It appears that a similar trend might have emerged in Hong Kong Scouting.

Infantilizing a youth movement

After a couple years of experimentation, Hong Kong Scouting launched a pre-Cub Grasshopper section. Cubs and Grasshoppers registered consistently faster growth than older Scouts, Venture Scouts and Rovers, resulting in a continuous lowering of the average age of youth members.

---

1   *Census Reports*, and *List of Awardees*, the Hong Kong Scout Archives.
2   Peg Tyre, *The Trouble with Boys: A Surprising Report Card on Our Sons, Their Problems at School, and What Parents and Educators Must Do* (New York: Crown Publishers, 2008), 203
3   Colin Nobel and Wendy Bradford, *Getting it Right for Boys...and Girls* (London: Routledge, 2000), 3-23; Tyre, *The Trouble with Boys*, 222-224.

This "infantilizing" trend, evident in Scouting, other youth organizations, education, and the community, was driven by forces inside and outside the movement, in Hong Kong and elsewhere. Critics questioned whether this trend is good for Scouting and whether five- or six-year-old children could benefit from its citizenship program, while supporters saw it as new opportunities for growing Scouting and also to effectively impart citizenship training at an early age.

Pre-Cub Grasshoppers, introduced in the 1980s.

H. K. Scout Archives.

In 1982, Hong Kong experimented with a pre-Cub section. Two years later, the Grasshopper Rings were launched for children between the ages of six and eight.[1] In 1996, its lower age limit was extended to five. However, infantilization actually started earlier, before the advent of the Grasshoppers, as revealed by these shares by age group:

	1952	1960	1970	1980	1990	2000	2010
Grasshoppers/Cub Scouts	25%	40%	45%	46%	60%	64%	64%
(Boy) Scouts	49%	47%	42%	37%	33%	28%	27%
Venture/Senior/Rover Scouts	26%	13%	13%	17%	7%	8%	9%

Scout Youth Membership by Age Group, 1952-2010

Sources: Census reports, various years, the Hong Kong Scout Archives. As of 2010, age limits for Grasshoppers were 5 to 8, Cub Scouts 7 ½ to 12, Scouts 11 to 16, Venture Scouts (formerly called Senior Scouts) 15 to 21, and Rover Scouts 18 to 26.

1   *Annual Report, 1984-85* (Hong Kong: Scout Association of Hong Kong), 17.

The combined shares of Grasshoppers and Cub Scouts grew consistently from 25% in 1952 to 64% in 2010. In other words, while the younger section(s) constituted only a quarter of youth membership in the 1950s, they became the majority from the 1980s onward.

Just as importantly, there was a significant decrease in average age even among the two younger sections in the recent decades, as illustrated in the graph below. Cub Scouts' shares peaked at 57% in 1990 and then went back down to around 45%, while shares of the youngest Grasshoppers rose very quickly from 3% in 1990 to over 20% in 2010. By 2010, most Hong Kong Scouts were under the age of twelve, and many were less than eight years old. Scouting was fast becoming a children's movement. To understand this trend, we need to look at developments driven by factors which also underpinned the infantilization of local Scouting. These developments in Scouting elsewhere, in other youth organizations, in early education, and in commerce (especially in products targeting youngsters) will be analyzed in turn.

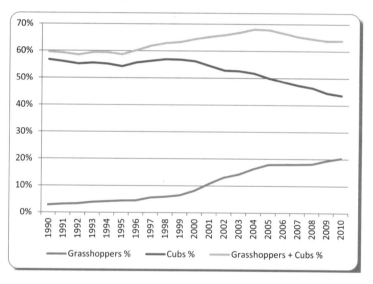

Grasshoppers and Cubs as % of Youth Members, 1990-2010

Source: Census reports, various years, the Hong Kong Scout Archives.

One must not assume that the local Scout Movement was unique. Firstly, Hong Kong Scouting's infantilization closely mirrored that of Scouting elsewhere, Guiding and other youth groups. The pre-Cub Beavers were introduced in 1982 and became an official section in British

Scouting in 1986. By 2010, the Beavers and the Cubs constituted 62% of the youth members, and the beavers alone accounted for 27%, even higher than the share of Grasshoppers in Hong Kong.[1] Infantilizing trends were also observed in American Scouting and among many other WOSM members.[2] Similarly, Brownies' share of local Guiding's youth membership went from 39% in 1967 to over 50% in the 1990s. In 2001, Guiding stretched its lower age limit with the Happy Bees (快樂小蜜蜂, later simply 小蜜蜂) for girls *and boys*, starting at the even younger age of four.[3] By 2010, the Bees and Brownies made up more than 63% of its youth members, similar to that of Scouting.[4] Infantilization, often with higher shares in kindergarten than Scouting, was also common in other, smaller, youth organizations in Hong Kong, including the Road Safety Association, the Boys' Brigade, and the Girls' Brigade.[5]

Cub Scouts became the largest section.

H. K. Scout Archives.

1   *The Scout Association Annual Report*, 2009/10 (London: the Scout Association, 2010).

2   BSA added the pre-Cub "Tiger Cubs" in the early 1980s. The younger Tiger Cubs, Cubs, and Webelos Scouts constituted less than 50% of youth membership in the 1980s but over 60% in the 1990s and the 2000s. See *Annual Reports*, Boy Scouts of America, various years. In 2001, a WOSM survey revealed that Scouts over the age of fifteen constituted only 9% of membership in the 52 NSOs which had responded. See *Worldwide Survey on Young People Over 15 in Scouting* (Geneva: WOSM, 2001).

3   *Annual Report 2001-02* (Hong Kong: Girl Guides Association., 2002), 32.

4   *Annual Report 2009-10* (Hong Kong: Girl Guides Association., 2010), 32.

5   The Road Safety Association added the Young Children's Patrol (幼兒隊) for kindergartens. By 2009, 35% of its patrols were in kindergartens, and 73% in kindergartens and primary schools, See "學校隊名錄," http://www.rsa.org.hk/rsp/sch_page/schoollist/index.htm (accessed September 14, 2009). The Boys' Brigade introduced a pre-junior section in the late 1990s, the pre-junior and the junior members (for children from 5 to 12) constituted 64% of its members by 2008, and in 2009 it added the Anchor Lambs for children from 3-5, see *Annual Report 1999-2000; 2007-08*; (Hong Kong: The Boys' Brigade, Hong Kong, 2000, 2008) ; *The Boys' Brigade, Hong Kong: 50th Anniversary Journal, 1959-2009* (Hong Kong: The Boys' Brigade, Hong Kong, 2009), 110. In the Girls' Brigade, 79% of its units were for girls between six and twelve, see "分隊網絡," http://www.gbhk.org.hk/chi/coynetwork.html# (accessed September 16, 2009).

The predominance of Cub Scouts was, as would be expected, also reflected in their shares of the highest sectional awards. Traditionally, youngsters who had achieved the highest awards in their respective sections would be publicly recognized in the annual Scout rally. In the rally in November 2009, for instance, 24 Rover Scouts received the B-P awards, 59 Venture Scouts the Dragon Scout (equivalent to the earlier Queen's Scout/SAR Scout) Awards, and 267 Scouts the Chief Scout Awards. On the other hand, 1,245 Cub Scouts were recipients of the Golden Bauhinia Awards. While trying to appropriately recognize the increasing number of youth awardees in all sections in recent years had always been a challenge, the large number of Cub Scout awardees had been especially problematic. Typically, only a small percentage of them would be lucky enough to be chosen to participate in the "grand howl" and be inspected by the guest of honor.

Cub Scout Golden Bauhinia awardees met Geoffrey Ma, 2009.

H. K. Scout Archives.

Brian Harrison suggests that the Beaver Scouts were introduced in Britain to maintain growth in the face of declines due to waning popularity of "war-related and uniformed recreation for children."[1] If so, this strategy seemed to work, at least in the intermediate term. Membership in British Scouting dropped below the 500,000 mark by the mid 1980s. With the growing numbers of Cubs and Beavers, it rose again to reach an all-time peak of 676,988 in 1989.[2]

1   Brian Harrison, *Finding a Role: The United Kingdom 1970-1990* (Oxford: Oxford Univ. Press, 2010), 246-247.
2   The Scout Association, "UK and World Census Figures," http://www.scoutbase.org.uk/ library/history/census.htm (accessed April 1, 2010).

From the late 1970s onward, similar pressures were felt in Hong Kong Scouting. The number of Scouts, Venture Scouts, and Rovers peaked in 1978-80, and then declined in the following years. Scouting received annual subventions and its census numbers were regularly reported to the government. In the post-riot years it is conceivable that there may have been subtle if not open pressure from the authorities or the headquarters to serve more youngsters. Pressure to grow did not necessarily have to come from the top either. Leaders of Scout Groups or Districts experiencing lower enrollments in their senior sections would also tend to seek growth through the Cubs and Grasshoppers. At any rate, youth membership in Hong Kong did register healthy growth from the mid-1980s onward, but only because the number of Cub Scouts and Grasshoppers grew strongly: 66% between 1980 and 1990, and then another 53% between 1990 and 2000.[1]

Secondly, these infantilizing trends mirrored those in local education, as children started school at increasingly younger ages over time. In 1971, only 18% of children aged zero to four, and 93% of those from five to nine were in pre-schools or kindergartens. The corresponding percentages were 42% and practically 100% in 1991. In the 1990s, "85 percent of children between the ages of three and five [were] attending kindergartens," a figure which was "fairly high by international standards."[2] By 2006, enrollment had increased to 89%.[3]

Such high ratios were significant as pre-school education was neither compulsory nor fully subsidized, and many had to pay substantial fees. The rationales, Cheng Tong Yung observes, were simple: "if a child fails to enter a 'good' nursery school, his chances of entering one of the 'good' kindergartens...and later the 'best' secondary schools, are significantly trimmed."[4] Others offer other reasons. Hong Kong parents were relatively well-off and could afford to send their children to pre-schools. There were increasing numbers of working couples who needed early education for their children, which doubled as a baby-sitting service.[5]

Top awards of the four youth sections, from grasshoppers (top) to Rovers (bottom).

1   Ibid. Cub Scouts and Grasshoppers reached 11,864 in 1980, 19,646 in 1990, and 29,971 in 2000.

2   Gerald A. Postiglione, Wing On Lee, *Schooling in Hong Kong: Organization, Teaching and Social Context* (Hong Kong: Hong Kong Univ. Press, 1997) , 31.

3   *Hong Kong 2006 Population By-census, Main Tables*, Table 2.2.

4   Cheng Tong Yung, *The Economy of Hong Kong* (Hong Kong: Far East Pub., 1977), 363.

5   Postiglione, *Schooling in Hong Kong*, 31.

Furthermore, the number of divorces had steadily increased since the early 1980s, resulting in many single-parent families, which had inherently greater needs for pre-school education.[1]

These same reasons would apply to Grasshopper and Cub Scouting, which targeted children of the same age group. Middle-class families which sent their kids to nurseries and kindergartens could also afford the money required for uniforms and activities of the Grasshopper Rings. Dual-career couples and single parents would welcome the weekly breaks when their children would be in Scout meetings, outings or camping trips. Some parents would perceive their children's participation in structured extra-curricular activities like Scouting as advantageous when they apply to "better" schools later.

Finally, similar infantilization apparently also occurred in the commercial sector. Harrison calls this the "commercialization of childhood," when prosperous societies such as Britain and America "push[ed] the market for toys to ever younger age-groups while promoting precociously adult teenage tastes," as witnessed by the rapid growth of "Toys R Us" and the popularity of computerized video games in the 1980s.[2]

Another instance of this phenomenon can be located in trends in the entertainment business. In the 1960s, Hollywood movies were aimed at the "19-year old male" audience based on the "Peter Pan Syndrome."[3] But in the 1970s, similar trends in other markets and new research convinced producers to reconsider their strategy. In this context, George Lucas developed *Star Wars*, "good enough to convince the most skeptical 8-year-old sci-fi buff," which broke all box office records in its 1977 release.[4] It heralded in a new era in the 1980s, when family movies came back strongly, many aimed at children under the age of twelve.[5]

Similarly, products from the music and the games industries also

---

1   Nelson Chow, "Social Welfare," T. L. Tsim and Bernard H.K. Luk (eds.), *The Other Hong Kong Report* (Hong Kong: The Chinese Univ. of Hong Kong, 1989), 216.
2   Harrison, *Finding a Role*, 246.
3   Which says that "a younger child will watch anything an older child will watch;…a girl will watch anything a boy will watch." Peter Krämer, "It's aimed at kids—the kid in everybody," in Yvonne Tasker (ed.), *Action and Adventure Cinema* (Abingdon: Routledge, 2004), 362.
4   Ibid., 365-6.
5   Incidentally, the movies and the toys markets were quite closely linked: by the early 1980s, licensed *Star Wars* toys had grossed more than double the movies themselves. See Susan Gregory Thomas, *Buy, Buy Baby: How Consumer Culture Manipulates Parents and Harms Young Minds* (New York: Houghton Mifflin, 2007), 56.

increasingly aimed at a younger audience. Susan Thomas notes that the targeting of younger audiences in commercial circles had a lot to do with the cultural shifts in work and family life in developed societies, "characterized by single working parents and latchkey children," and the rise of the TV as a "babysitter." In this new culture, the chief point of contact between parents and children was no longer playing together, but buying something for the children to play with.

It is easy to make the connection from this phenomenon to the infantilization of Scouting. The same pressures in family and work life might have motivated the parents who relied on the TV, toys, video games, and movies as "babysitters" to also seek out Scouting for their young children. In fact, given widespread concerns with the potentially harmful impacts of the TV on their latchkey children, it is quite conceivable that some parents would prefer to encourage their offspring to participate in outdoor activities such as Scouting as opposed to home-based entertainment like the TV and video games. This would especially be the case with the many "Baby-boomer" parents who had been Scouts or Guides themselves in the postwar 1950s to the 1970s, when Hong Kong Scouting grew substantially and became a mass movement.

Scouting's efforts to target a younger clientele was not always viewed positively. Some worried that the presence of younger Scouts would encourage the older ones to quit the movement. E. M. Robinson, a founder of American Scouting, believes that three years were "the maximum age span feasible in any one group."[1] MacLeod concludes that "in both Britain and America, Boy Scouting suffered from the Gresham's Law of boys' work: younger boys drive out older ones."[2] Based on these beliefs, the extension of the lower age limits in Scouting, though contributing to near-term growth, would mean eventual losses. Older boys and girls would leave in order to disassociate themselves with the really young children, or because they thought they had done enough "Scouting" after having spent some years in the younger sections.

As far as local Scouting is concerned, the evidence for this hypothesis is mixed. It was true that total number of Venture and Rover Scouts peaked at 4,426 in 1980, and then dropped to a low of 2,299 in

---

1 Ibid.
2 David Macleod, *Building Character*, 282. The Gresham's Law says that "bad money drives out good."

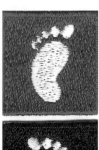

The four Grasshopper "Step" badges.

1990. But since then it grew again to 3,464 in 2000, and then 5,481 in 2010, suggesting that, eventually, the large gains in the younger sections actually helped the older ones slightly.[1]

Some critics argued that gains in younger Scouts would not be useful as they were not ready for citizenship education through Scouting. This concern is more difficult to prove or refute. Children differ in their "readiness," even if this could be clearly defined. Furthermore, "readiness" as a concept in education is complex and linked to both perceived characteristics of the children and socially constructed sets of meanings which could vary from place to place.[2] Raising the issue of "readiness" invariably begs the question of "ready for what?" In other words, whether the children are ready or not depends to some extent on what they are going to be taught. Some believed that younger children of the increasingly precocious society could benefit from Scout training. Pre-Cub training in Hong Kong utilizes games, dances, plays, singing, story-telling, and crafts. Also, unlike the older sections, it only has four simple "Steps" badges for which *no* prescribed test was required.

Robert Fulghum may be right in suggesting that important values and world views are acquired while we are still very young, and all that one really needs to know about "how to live and what to do and how to be" is learned in kindergarten.[3] Gordon Mathews and others argue that "the most effective way to teach national identity, one practiced by countries across the globe, is to teach it uncritically at an early age. Through flag raisings, anthem singings, pledges of allegiance, history told as heroic myth, and other such training, a taken-for-granted love for country can be formed, that serves as a bedrock that subsequent, more critical, training may never shake."[4]

According to these scholars, when training in "love for country" occurs at a very young age, "before one can critically contest that training," young citizens would end up loving their country unquestioningly, after they become adults.[5] It was quite possibly in this spirit that the

1   *Census Reports*, various years, the Hong Kong Scout Archives.
2   M. Elizabeth Graue, *Ready for What: Constructing Meanings of Readiness for Kindergarten* (New York: State Univ. of New York, 1993), 1-18.
3   Robert Fulghum, *All I Really Need to Know I learned in Kindergarten* (New York: Ivy Books, 1986), 4.
4   Mathews et al, *Learning to Belong to a Nation,* 86.
5   Ibid., 154

SAR government implemented in 2005 the "I love China" campaign, targeting kindergarten children.[1]

According to this perception, starting Scouting's citizenship training with the Grasshopper section could be effective. Given appropriate content, the movement could help to instill a stronger sense of national identity among young Hong Kong citizens, something which, as shall be seen in the last section of this chapter, they were perceived to lack in comparison to youngsters from other places.

In the postwar decades and especially since the 1980s, Hong Kong Scouting's membership targets became younger. This infantilizing trend mirrored those observed in Scouting elsewhere, in other youth organizations, local education, and the commercial sector. But, in the final analysis, this shift must largely be explained by the fact that Scouting was attractive to many parents of young children. Grasshopper and Cub Scouting offered a progressive, structured, activities-based, program in a team setting which was considered to be helpful in the emotional and social development of children between the ages of five and eleven, especially by occupied working couples, over-stretched single parents, and eager parents wanting the best preparation for their children for better schools and the workplace. Regardless of pre-Cub and Cub Scouting's perceived effectiveness as a citizenship scheme within Scouting or in the eyes of the authorities, they were increasingly popular because aspirational parents wanted additional opportunities for their children to engage in peer group interactions, early holistic education, alternative (and free) baby-sitting service, or healthy entertainment.

Staying relevant

In the most recent decades, besides responding to the needs of the community by admitting girls and younger children, Hong Kong Scouting also maintained a multi-faceted dynamism which enabled it to continue to grow substantially in the evolving community. Whether in terms of developing its supporting physical facilities and financial resources, reaching out to a variety of target audiences, attracting a broad array of adult volunteers, and upgrading its domestic and international profile,

---

1   Ibid., 86.

the independent movement successfully leveraged its resources to drive expansion both in the last colonial days and after decolonization.

There was significant progress in the development of campsites and other support facilities. In 1960, the government gave a large tract of land around Kowloon Peak (Fei Ngo Shan 飛鵝山) to the association for use as a campsite. The Gilwell Campsite, as the place became known, soon developed into a popluar destination for outdoor camping for many Scouts. By the late 1960s, it was understood that the old Chai Wan campsite would eventually be resumed by the government, and efforts had started to develop a new campsite and a sea activity center at Tai Tam. At the same time, a second sea activity base was being created at Tai Lam Chung. Chai Wan was surrendered in 1970, and the Tai Tam Campsite (大潭營地) opened in 1972. Its sea activity center became a focal point for sea activities and Sea Scout Regattas in the 1970s. In 1975, the Scout Training Centre at Tung Tsz (洞梓童軍中心) near Plover Cove opened. In the early 1980s, new sea activities centers started in Tai Mei Tuk (大尾篤), Pak Sha Wan (白沙灣), and Pak Tso Wan (白鱎灣), in response to growing interest. Pak Sha Wan was expanded over time to become a major sea activities center with camping facilities. In these developments, the government, lottery fund, businesses, individual donors, and even the British military, were often close partners.[1]

Winners of the 1992 Scout Regatta, held at the Pak Sha Wan Sea Activities Centre.

H. K. Scout Archives.

---

1   The *Annual Reports*, 1967/68 to 1974/75, 1981/82, 1983/84.

Utilization of the four main campsites (and sea activities centers) in the last several decades are as follows:

	1981	1991	2001	2010
Gilwell	49,109	4,364	5,430	9,306
Tai Tam	30,811	25,419	63,536	50,563
Tung Tsz	30,771	17,528	28,131	33,717
Pak Sha Wan	4,065	18,912	35,206	27,891

Users of Campsites/Sea Activities Centers, 1981-2010

Source: Annual and quarterly reports of the campsites and sea activity centers, the Hong Kong Scout Association. Total number of users per year, residential camp, day camp and camping combined. Note Tung Tsz figure under the 1991 column was from 1989.

Gilwell only cater for outdoor camping, and had seen a substantial drop in utilization over time, reflecting the declining popularity of outdoor camps among the increasingly younger members. Tung Tsz offers both residential and outdoor camping and has seen relatively stable utilization. Tai Tam and Pak Sha Wan, which offer sea activities and residential and outdoor camping, have both recorded growing demand up to the 2000s, though utilization waned slightly in the most recent years.

By the late 1960s it became increasingly obvious that the association headquarters would need to be redeveloped. As it turned out, this project spanned three commissioners: hatched in Lo's time, nurtured during the Ma years, it only came to fruition in Chau's era, more than two decades later. In 1969, a proposal to build an administrative headquarters cum youth hostel was tabled, aiming at providing in one stroke much-needed office space for a growing movement, more facilities for training, accommodation for budget-conscious travelers and steady revenue to the association.[1] By 1970, specifics related to the proposed Hong Kong Scout Centre, as it then became known, were developed. It was to have a podium block with a basement and several floors of administrative and activity rooms, with a youth hostel with five hundred rooms

Sea activities became increasingly accessible, with the addition of new Sea Activities centers.

H. K. Scout Archives.

---

1   Folder, Project Q, the Hong Kong Scout Archives. This idea, though innovative, was not original, as similar facilities already existed in the form of the Baden-Powell House, the British Scout hostel and conference center in London, donated to the British association and opened in 1961.

on top.[1] Chau, a Scouter and a government urban planning expert, was involved. In 1975, to avoid duplication of efforts, a number of real estate projects, including that of the headquarters, were combined and managed by one working party, convened by Pau Shiu-hung, another Scouter and government architect, with Chau as adviser.

In 1989, the Executive Council advised and Governor Wilson approved the grant of a large tract of land for a new headquarters with a commercial hostel. Gordon Wu (胡應湘), a prominent businessman and a former Scout from the 15th Hong Kong, headed the list of supporters by donating $25 million for the land premium and facilitating a loan guarantee.[2] In 1991, Sir Ti Liang Yang and Chau officiated at a foundation laying ceremony for the center.[3] It was clearly the star in 1994, as it was featured on the cover of *Hong Kong Scouting* three times, with reports on many events, including a "house warming."[4]

The Hong Kong Scout Centre, viewed from the Kowloon Park.

H. K. Scout Archives.

As a bus depot, a telephone exchange complex, and a multi-storied car park were added, the project was a win-win deal, ensuring the association a more spacious headquarters and new sources of income and providing the government with needed public facilities and the old lot of the Morse House, which would yield a considerable sum in land auction due to its desirable location.[5] As it turned out, from the 1990s

1   Memo, "Schedule of Accommodation - Hong Kong Scout Centre," September 1970, the Hong Kong Scout Archives.
2   Folder, Project Q, 1960s-1990s, the Hong Kong Scout Archives.
3   The *Hong Kong Scouting*, February 1991, 2-4.
4   The *Hong Kong Scouting*, June 1994, July 1994, and October 1994.
5   Interview, Chau Chamson, May 3, 2010, the Hong Kong Scout Archives. Chau

onward, the on-going income from the hostel and carpark did indeed support the growth of Scouting above and beyond what could be afforded with the limited annual government subventions.

But, fundamentally, growth in the youth movement had to come from participation of increasingly more youngsters, not from better facilities or more financial resources. There were favorable factors on the demand side. Firstly, though Hong Kong's population was aging and the total number of youngsters had shrunk during this period, more of them were attending schools, as access to educational opportunities improved. There were 886,000 kindergarten, primary and secondary students in 1966, and 963,000 in 2007/8.[1] As chidren in the school sytem were easiest to reach, this meant that the pool of potential primary targets of Scouting actually increased in the most recent decades.

Some considerations could have motivated more parents to encourage their children to join the movement. As already noted, the competitiveness of school places might have convinced some parents to seek out Scouting to enhance their children's chances of entering the better schools. Economic gains in recent decades could have resulted in a sort of "generationalism," whereby parents who could not afford to join Scouting as young people could now make their children "first generation" Scouts. The extreme urbanism which had characterized Hong Kong's development could have persuaded some parents to favor a movement which offered outdoor activities and more interactions with nature for their children. The increasing number of single-parents, families with single-child, and dual-career couples might have created a demand for Scouting as alternative childcare, a source of peer group interaction, and an opportunity for healthy extra-curricular activities.

An important development in this period was the large influx of immigrants. From the 1990s onward, many mainland Chinese wives were allowed to migrate to Hong Kong to join their husbands, often bringing along their children. In 2006, 107,000 local youngsters between the ages of five and fourteen were born in China.[2] There is evidence that

---

later became Director of Buildings and Lands in Hong Kong, until he retired in 1990.
1   Education Bureau, "Kindergarten Education," http://www.edb.gov.hk/index.aspx?langno=1&_nodeid=1037 (accessed April 29, 2010); *Hong Kong Statistics, 1947-1967*,Table 11.2.
2   *2006 Population Bi-Census, Main Tables,* Table 1.6.

The Silver Jubilee District badge, with words in Chinese, English, and Gurkhali.

many new immigrants from China were "wives and children of low-paid workers."[1] For these mothers, a key reason for migrating and suffering much discriminatory treatment was "the belief that life in Hong Kong offered substantially better future opportunities for their children than life on the mainland," after they were integrated into "Hong Kong's westernized lifestyle," which was one of Hong Kong's "legacies as a former British colony."[2] Scouting in a number of countries was perceived as an effective activity for facilitating the integration and assimilation of immigrant children.[3] Some immigrant mothers, especially those in the lower income groups, might perceive Scouting as a means of achieving more rapid social integration and networking with local people for their children, creating a different type of "first-generation" Scouts. The growing number of youngsters who applied for funding through the need-based subsidy schemes of the association in the 2000s provides an indirect evidence of this phenomenon.[4]

In the decades after its independence, Hong Kong Scouting also took special measures to cater for non-Chinese boys (perhaps ironic in view of the fact that it was reserved mostly for these boys when it started), by forming a colony-wide "district" based on non-Chinese languages as the unifying dimension (entitled the Silver Jubilee (銀禧區), to mark its commencement in 1977, the Queen's Jubilee year), which grew to become a region (later named the Brotherhood Region (大同地域), with Hari N. Harilela, a prominent Sindhi businessman and leading member of the Indian community, as the chairman), and then shrank again to become two districts (the Silver Jubilee and the Gurkha Districts) and, finally, one district (when the Gurkha District was disbanded).[5]

---

1   Stewart MacPherson, "Hong Kong," in John Dixon and David Macarov, *Poverty: A Persistent Global Reality* (London: Routledge, 1998), 74.

2   Nicole Dejong Newendorp, *Uneasy Reunions: Immigration, Citizenship, and Family Life in Post-1997 Hong Kong* (Stanford: Stanford Univ. Press, 2008), 188-189.

3   For example, the Americanization programs of the Girl Scouts of America. Tammy M. Proctor, *Scouting for Girls: A Century of Girl Guides and Girl Scouts* (Santa Barbara, CA: ABC-CLIO, LLC, 2009), 64.

4   *Annual Reports, 2006-2010* (Hong Kong: Scout Association of Hong Kong).

5   The *Hong Kong Scouting*, September 1977, 18-19; May 1991, 20; *Annual Reports, the Brotherhood Region*, 1983-84, 1984-85. There was at least one dissenting voice: in a meeting of the non-Chinese groups in 1976, one person regretted that this district was to be created, as he felt that a great opportunity to integrate non-Chinese Scouts with the Chinese majority would be lost by it. Alternative names originally proposed for the Silver Jubilee District included "Commonwealth" and the somewhat tongue-in-cheek "Gwailo" (鬼佬, Cantonese rendition of "foreign devils"). See Folder, the Silver Jubilee District, 1976-80, the Hong Kong Scout Archives.

Traditionally-British units such as the 1st Kowloon soon re-emerged as a constituent group of the Silver Jubilee District, and the boys were proudly sporting the district badge, "unique not only because of its colour [silver], but also because it incorporates...lettering in three languages Chinese, English and Gurkhali."[1] Later on, after the English Troops broke away and formed a standalone Silver Jubilee District, the Gurkhali Troops formed their own district. In the late 1970s and the 1980s, there were seven to eight Gurkhali groups, all with boys from military families. The Gurkha District remained active until 1997, when the local Gurkha soldiers were disbanded or relocated.[2]

Scouts of the Gurkha District at camp, gathering under a Napalese flag.

H. K. Scout Archives.

After the influx of the Vietnamese boat people in the 1970s, the Silver Jubilee District attempted to include their youngsters. The first Group, the 300th East Kowloon, started in 1981 at the Kai Tak refugee camp (啟德難民營).[3] Others followed in the 1980s at, for example, the camp in Chimawan on Lantau Island and the Silver Jubilee Transit Centre. By the 2000s, though there were no more British military groups, and the Nepali and Vietnamese boys had either left or become integrated into the community, the Silver Jubilee District remained active. But, by this time, it would be the smallest of forty-plus Districts, and most of its members would be ethnic Chinese youngsters (many with Canadian, Australian, British or American passports and/or attending English-speaking schools), and the question as to whether it should be re-integrated or "mainstreamed" would be raised periodically.

The Gurkha District badge, featuring the Kukri, the curved knife of the Nepalese soldiers.

1   The *St. Andrew's Church News*, January 1979, 6. While there must be some tri-lingual Scout badges around, this was likely the only Scout district badge in the world to feature these three languages, symbolic of the hybrid nature of Hong Kong Scouting.
2   Folder, the Gurkha District, 1985-1996, the Hong Kong Scout Archives.
3   Report, "大同地域未來動向 (Future Direction of the Brotherhood Region)", May 11, 1985, the Hong Kong Scout Archives.

The growing movement meant needs for adult resources which would largely be met by volunteers, who headed up all the headquarter functional departments, unlike in, say, British or American Scouting. Part-time volunteers also played pivotal roles in the regions and districts, as in most other countries. While local Scouting, like other non-profit organizations, would occasionally complain about not having enough people, it appears that there was no real shortage of volunteers, at least in terms of numbers. In 1977, there were 4,000 voluntary Scouters and 2,600 lay supporters. In 2010, the former had almost tripled to 11,500, and the later had grown to over 6,700. These were supported by a relatively small team of paid staff which numbered fewer than one hundred in the late 1970s, and was less than three hundred in 2010, including staff of the non-Scout programs of the FOS.[1]

Why was it that Scouting could continue to attract adults to serve voluntarily, often committing to much time over many years? What kind of adults chose to join? These people clearly were not all or even mostly upper class "men of leisure" or elitist "high-achievers." After all, by definition, these tended to be a small percentage of any society. Their overall profile reflected that of Hong Kong in terms of education, profession, income, religion and so on. In fact, enabling adults from all walks of life to contribute and gain self-actualization through volunteering as Scouters was very much part of the social value of Scouting, and genius of B-P's scheme for marshaling resources for the movement.

Many people volunteered because they had enjoyed and benefited from Scouting in their younger days. Many perhaps have children and/or friends in the movement. Many felt that they gained satisfaction or grew personally or professionally. These people would often be willing to devote time every week or perform prescribed duties for years. They were committed individuals whom Bill Hybels might consider "professional volunteers" or "lifers."[2] On the other hands, many others were new to Scouting and had joined for the first time as adults simply because they wanted to support a worthwhile cause. They were people whom Jonathan McKee and Thomas Mckee would describe as "the new

---

1   Census reports, 1977, 2010, the Hong Kong Scout Archives.
2   Bill Hybels, *the Volunteer Revolution: Unleashing the Power of Everybody* (Grand Rapids, Michigan: Zondervan, 2004), Ch. 2. Who believed "that volunteers can transform society and at the same time find deep personal satisfaction."

breed of volunteers," who could be experienced professionals, young men, single parents, etc. who have various expertise and could help but were pressed for time and demanded flexibility and customized responsibilities.[1] Many were perhaps in between or a bit of both.

The Scout Association has been successful in recruiting and utilizing many types of volunteers, ranging from the "lifers" to the "new breed." It appears to have adopted most of what McKee would consider as effective ways for recruiting volunteers. Most Scout volunteers were asked to serve by other fellow volunteers, typically someone they knew. As every group, district, region and other Scout units recruited their own volunteers, there was an effective network and a very large recruiting team in which each member would target people based on his/her needs and in his/her own circle of friends. People could often make one-time, short-term, or project-based commitments rather than longer-term or multi-year ones. As practically every leader of Scout units would do his/ her own recruiting, people who said no to someone for a certain task at a point in time were likely to be asked again by someone else in a different capacity at another point in time. Finally, the leaders of specialist branches or committees would often target only the right people with the appropriate professional or vocational skills rather than just "any ol' B.I.C. [Butt in the Chair]," as McKee would call them.[2]

Hong Kong Scouting continued the tradition of publicly recognizing volunteers with awards, which became more elaborate and numerous over time. Besides the Lion (later modified to depict a running as opposed to a seated one) and Dragon, already referred to, the Distinguished Service Cross, the Distinguished Service Medal, the Distinguished Service Award (later renamed Dedicated Service Award) and, since 1994, the Good Service Award were added. Ma also created the Gold, Silver and Bronze Whistles, first awarded in late 1970s, which were combined into a single award called the Chief Commissioner's Whistle in 1987, and later renamed the Chief Commissioner's Commendation, as a Chief Commissioner's *High* Commendation had been added in 2002. Local gallantry crosses replaced the British ones. Long service awards (with up to four stars) featuring side portrait of Baden-Powell for

The Gallantry Cross, with the Chinese characters for "courage."

H. K. Scout Archives.

---

1   Jonathan W. McKee and Thomas W. McKee, *The New Breed: Understanding & Equipping the 21st Century Volunteer* (Loveland, Colorado: 2007), 17-24.

2   McKee and McKee, *The New Breed*, 33-47.

those who had served for 15 to 55 years were introduced. Since 1994, to help finance major projects or events such as the Scout Centre and the centenary activities, special contribution medallions were produced from time to time. Many commemorative medallions were also issued for volunteer workers in several Jamborees and the centennial celebrations. That the award system comfortably combined the Chinese dragon and Chinese characters with Christian crosses and the portrait of Baden-Powell is again perhpas suggestive of the hybrid, cosmopolitan and yet Chinese, nature of the Hong Kong Scouts.

Merit awards given out during this period did not seem to have increased significantly. A total of 319, 215, 274 and 417 "merit" awards were issued in 1981, 1991, 2001 and 2010, respectively, to 3.8%, 2.5%, 1.8% and 2.3% of the adult members.[1] These small percentages suggest that many volunteers were indeed the "new breed," and were not necessarily motivated by tangible awards. Nevertheless, together with the long service awards, the commemorative medallions and the special contribution medallions, the numbers do add up, indicating that, in general, awards do constitute an important component of the overall recognition program for the Scout volunteers.

The Long Service Award, with side portrait of B-P.

It has been noted that in many countries the largest potential adult resources for non-profit organizations in recent years could be the baby boomers, people who were born between 1946 and 1964, and who were either retired or at a stage in life during which they could potentially contribute a lot to volunteer work of their choice. The Scout Association of Hong Kong would clearly need to tap on these people in order to achieve its vision ("To be the best voluntary organisation for the development of young people in Hong Kong for the betterment of society") and mission, introduced in 2000. But these people are not easily satisfied with basic, repetitive work. "They want...service options so they can choose the ones that best fit their interests and their busy lives," "they want to...have an impact on the organization's vision and mission," and to tap them the organization must "transform volunteer management into volunteer engagement."[2] Based on this new paradigm, the key was no longer re-

---

1   Annual honor lists, the Hong Kong Scout Association. Defined as the Lions, Dragons, DSC, DSM, DSA, GSA, and the Whistles/Commendations.

2   Jill Friedman Fixler, Sandie Eichberg and Gail Lorenz, *Boomer Volunteer Engagement: Collaborate Today, Thrive Tomorrow* (Bloomington, Indiana: AuthorHouse, 2008), 9-10..

cruitment but cultivation and networking, not placement but negotiation and agreement, not supervision but support, not performance review but performance measurement, and not recognition but acknowledgement.

Like in many developed economies, Hong Kong has an aging population. The population pyramid of the 1960s with a large base of young people has become the one in the 2000s with a bulging center of people aged forty to sixty. It is predicted that people aged 65 and above will surge from 13% in 2009 to 17% in 2019 and 25% in 2029, and median age would grow from 40.7 in 2009 to 43.4 in 2019 and 45.7 in 2029.[1] The table below provides a reading of how successful the Scout Association has been in attracting older people as volunteers:

	Total	Age >=40 (%)
Senior Commissioners	172	166 (97%)
Junior Commissioners	513	315 (61%)
All other uniformed Leaders	9,093	3,395 (37%)
Lay Supporters	4,068	1,973 (49%)

Age Distribution of Adult Volunteers, 2011

Source: Scout Membership Information System, the Scout Association of Hong Kong (accessed April 11, 2011).

As of early 2011, close to forty percent of all uniformed leaders, over seventy percent of all commissioners, and nearly 97% of all senior commissioners were forty or over in age. Of all the lay supporters at the headquarters, regional, district and group levels, half were forty or over. It is clear that Scouting has done well in tapping into the large pool of mature people, many of whom would be classified as "boomers." .

While the caliber of these volunteers are much harder to quantify, a cursory look at the list of names of recent annual reports of the association would convince one that it appears capable of recruiting accomplished individuals and experienced professionals, many of whom among the who's who in the community, government or industry, to

---

1   "Hong Kong Population Projections, 2010-2039," http://www.censtatd.gov.hk/ (accessed April 13, 2011).

join the Scout Council, its executive committee, and the many advisory committees in areas such as finance, internal audit, estate development, informational and communications technologies, public relations, religion, personnel, training, performing arts, and business operations. On the other hand, all uniformed leaders and commissioners are by policy required to retire when they reach the age of sixty-five. One could question the reasonableness of such a policy given the great need for more volunteer leaders and the aging population in Hong Kong.

Throughout the recent decades, Scouting has maintained a visible profile inside and outside Hong Kong. 1982 was declared "The Year of the Scouts," as Scouts around the world celebrated the 75th anniversary of the movement. Commemoration in Hong Kong culminated with a carnival co-organized with Radio Television Hong Kong (RTHK), the local public broadcaster, and held at the Queen Elizabeth Stadium in Wanchai. Tickets for the 3,500 seats were sold out soon, and the star-studded event boasted of the presence of well-known local singers and movie or TV stars, including Mary Cheung (張瑪莉),Olivia Cheng (鄭文雅),Cheng Dan-shui (鄭丹瑞),Brigitte Lin Ching-Hsia (林青霞),Frances Yip (葉麗儀); and ended with George Lam (林子祥) singing "今天開始 (Starting from Today)," a song he wrote for the Hong Kong Scouts.[1] This being the beginning of the golden age of the "Cantopop" (Cantonese popular music), a hybrid and cosmopolitan Hong Kong genre performed in the local dialect, the song was in Cantonese, unlike most earlier Scout songs,

George Lam (center) and Frances Yip (left) performing at the 1982 carnival.

H. K. Scout Archives.

---

1   *Hong Kong Scouting*, December 1982, 19-22; Programme, "The Year of the Scout Carnival," 1982, the Hong Kong Scout Archives.

typically in English. In December, an International Jamborette, a relatively small event with only two hundred participants, was held at the Tai Tam campsite.

Based on the practice started in 1961, local Scouting celebrated its 75th anniversary in 1986. In April, more than ten thousand Scouts gathered for the anniversary rally, and Youde presented certificates to over twenty Queen's Scouts, including two young ladies. *The* event of the year was the Diamond Jubilee Jamboree held at Tai Po Tsai (大埔仔) in Sai Kung in December. As Youde had just sadly passed away in a fatal heart attack in Beijing, Sir David Akers-Jones, acting governor, officiated at the event. Over five thousand boys and girls, including Scouts from thirteen overseas locations, attended the largest camp ever held in the colony. Three thousand Cub Scouts gathered over 70,000 eggs from all over the campsite to form the numbers "75" on the camp's square, breaking a Guinness World Record set earlier in America. On New Year's eve, "Enjoy Yourselves Tonight (歡樂今宵), " then Hong Kong's most popular TV program on prime time, did a live broadcast at the camp, sharing the event with millions of viewers.

Singer Hacken Lee at the Scout rally in 1998.

H. K. Scout Archives.

In 1991, the 80th anniversary rally was held at the Victoria Park, and 13,000 Scouts marked the occasion by forming a human Scout logo on its grounds, gaining considerable public attention. In 1996, Hacken Lee (李克勤), popular singer and former Boy Scout from 15th Hong Kong (Wah Yan), was appointed the "Vitality Ambassador (活力大使)" of Scouting. In 1999, the "Outstanding Scout Groups" scheme was introduced, encouraging groups to upgrade their standards. Three thousand plus Scouts attended the Millennium Jamboree (跨世紀大露營), which

13,000 Scouts formed a Scout logo to mark the 80th anniversary of local Scouting, 1991.

H. K. Scout Archives.

Guinness World Record, "Most People Performing Flag Signals," 2010.

H. K. Scout Archives.

took place in Sai Kung from December 28th, 1999 to January 2nd, 2000. This was followed by the 90th Anniversary Jamboree (九十周年紀念大露營) held in December 2001, with 3,100 campers and another 1,900 who attended a related Cuboree. In December 2006, over 4,200 Scouts were present at the Metropolitan Jamboree (大都會大露營), which celebrated the 95th anniversay of Hong Kong Scouting, held on a charming waterfront site with great harbor view in West Kowloon, on the verge of being redeveloped. In November 2010, a total of 23,321 participants at the Scout rally at the Hong Kong Stadium used signal flags to send the short message "HKS100," heralding in the centenary, and broke a Guinness World Record for "Most People Performing Flag Signals." From December 27th, 2010 to January 1st, 2011, nearly 5,200 people camped at the Centennial Jamboree (百周年紀念大露營) on Lantau Island, right next to the Disneyland park.[1]

In the 1980s, FOS operated centers in Kwun Tong, Kowloon Bay, Tsuen Wan and Shatin, key new towns with large and growing population levels. In 2005, when it celebrated its 35th anniversary, the FOS had become a diversified service provider involved in integrated youth and children services, school social work, and adult education. Such efforts to include non-Scout youngsters, though not typical among Scouting elsewhere, were not unique to Hong Kong. American Scouting, for example, had also experimented with school-based programs from the late 1970s onward, and launched the Learning for Life subsidiary in 1991, with programs for children and youth of both genders which also did not

Night view of the harbor from the campsite during the Metropolitan Jamboree, December 2006.

Author's collection.

1   The *Hong Kong Scouting,* December 1991, 2-4; January 2000, 1-23; January 2001, 1-19; July 2006, 5-6; December 2006, 1-25; January 2011, 1-28; April 2011, 2.

rely on traditional elements of the movement, such as the Scout Promise, the Scout Law, or the Scout uniforms.[1]

    Hong Kong Scouting was equally enthusiastic in participating in worldwide and regional Scout events. Its representation in the World Scout Jamborees, the Scout event which invariably attracted the most youth and adult participants, is illustrative. The 15th World Jamboree scheduled to be held in Iran in 1979 was cancelled due to political instability in the host country. In 1983 and then 1987, Hong Kong sent a contingent of forty and another of thirty to the 15th World Jamboree in Alberta, Canada and the 16th World Jamboree in Sydney, Australia, despite their distance. In 1991, a record number of 128 Scouts attended the 17th World Jamboree held in the Soraksan National Park in South Korea, near the border of North Korea. Smaller delegations were sent to the next two Jamborees hosted by Netherlands and Chile in 1995 and 1999, respectively. In August, 1995, a join-in Jamboree in four local campsites was also held at the time of the World Jamboree. Hong Kong's record in this area was broken in 2003, when 143 Scouts attended the 20th World Jamboree held in Sattahip, Thailand, the second Jamboree to be hosted by a Southeast Asian country, after that of 1959 in the Philippines.

Hong Kong Scouts broke world record for "Most People Performing Flag Signals" in Nov. 2010.

H. K. Scout Archives.

---

1   Hans Zeiger, *Get Off My Honor!: The Assault on the Boy Scouts of America* (Nashville: Broadman & Holman, 2005), 114-115.

In July 2007, to celebrate the centenary of world Scouting at the place where it all started, Hong Kong sent a contingent of 669 people, its largest contingent to a World Jamboree by far, to the 21st World Jamboree held in Hylands Park, Chelmsford, England. This delegation ranked sixteenth in size among the 160 delegations from WOSM member countries. Of the "national" associations from outside Europe, only the United States, Japan, India, Mexico, and Brazil sent more people, suggesting the healthy state of Scouting in the former British colonial outpost which has become a Chinese SAR.[1] A join-in Jamboree was held locally for 1,400 in Sai Kung. The Hong Kong contingent to the 22nd World Jamboree in Sweden in July 2011 had over five hundred members, which again ranked among the leading delegations from outside Europe.

Some members of the contingent to the 21st World Jamboree in England in 2007.

H. K. Scout Archives.

Hong Kong Scouts were also active in attending regional Jamborees, especially those in Asia. Sometimes they organized unique adventures overseas, such as one involving thirteen Scouters who scaled the Gokyo Peak in Nepal in 1994.[2] Leaders were similarly enthusiastic in participating in Scout conferences and committees. Even before local Scouting's independence in 1977, it had sent observers to regional and world Scout conferences. In 1980, delegates attended the 12th Asia Pacific Scout Conference in Australia, and Henry Ma was elected a member of the regional Scout Committee. In 1981, Hong Kong was represented at the 28th World Scout Conference in Senegal, Africa. Since then, it would send delegations to most regional and world conferences, and its leaders would serve in regional and even world committees.

1   Kua (ed.), *21st World Jamboree: Hong Kong Contingent,* 5-6.
2   The *Hong Kong Scouting*, November 1994, 7-9.

Chau Cham-son sat on the Asia-Pacific Scout Committee from 1986 to 1992, and the World Scout Committee from 1993 to 1999. John Hui served on the regional committee from 2001 to 2007. Another senior commissioner, Herman Hui Chung-shing (許宗盛), was elected to the World Scout Committee in 2002, and served as its Chairman from 2005 till 2008.

Hong Kong Contingent Badge, 21st World Jamboree, 2007.

A recent World Scout Foundation's annual report presented outreach programs targeting underprivileged youth sponsored by Scout associations from around the world. A feature story was about a teenager sentenced to Hong Kong's juvenile detention center after he was caught drug trafficking and, instead of finding the usual horrors of a prison, was given an opportunity to join a Scout Group, taught Scout skills, musical instruments, discipline, and even provided an outside internship arranged by the leaders. The teenager noted: "Through Scouting, I learned how difficult I have been for my parents, I am ashamed of what I have done to them, and want to make it up. In the troop I have learned to respect others and follow the rules. Now I think carefully before acting and I'm better in dealing with peer pressure. Scouting has changed my vision of my life—now I know I'm OK!"[1] He may not know it, but he was among many juvenile offenders who had gone through Scout training in Hong Kong over the years, since the first group for boys in a correctional service center was founded more than fifty years ago.

Scouting in many societies encountered setbacks during this period, as the postwar generations broke away from pre-war conventions, abandoned established institutions and rejected accepted values. The movement struggled to empty itself of its earlier ideological resonances and its links to an essentially late-nineteenth century problematic of how to defend race, nation and empire. British Scout membership peaked at 677,000 in 1989, but was at 482,000 in 2009.[2] Canadian Scouting had 200,000 members in 1990, and only 101,000 in 2010.[3] *Youth* membership in the United States was at 4.7 millions in 1970, but only 2.8 millions in 2009.[4] Membership in Japanese Scouting went from 326,000

---

1   *World Scout Foundation, Annual Report 2005: Peace is not as simple as black and white* (Geneva: World Scout Foundation, 2005), 10.

2   *Annual Reports*, various years (London: (Boy) Scout Association).

3   "Stemming Membership Decline," http://scouteh.ca/resources/ScoutEh-membership.php (accessed Jan. 20, 2009); *Annual Report, 2009-10* (Scouts Canada).

4   "Boy Scouts and Girl Scouts: Membership and Units," http://www.allcoun-

in 1984 to 167,000 in 2008.[1] Scout membership in Singapore peaked at 13,381 in 1986, but was at 10,292 in 2009.[2]

In this context, Hong Kong Scouting, with its initiatives to stay relevant, did comparatively well, as illustrated below:

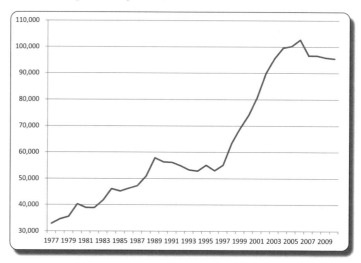

Membership Trends, Hong Kong, 1977-2010

Sources: Appendix D, "Membership Statistics."

While growth in Scout membership was a bit uneven in the 1980s, and setbacks were experienced in the late 1980s and early 1990s, growth resumed and stayed very strong from 1997 through to the early 2000s. Membership peaked in 2005 to 2006 above the 100,00 mark, and declined somewhat year-on-year since then.

As shown in the first table on the next page, total membership grew close to 2.5 times from 1981 to 2010, to over 95,000. More importantly, youth members increased over 2.2 times, despite a decline of 26% of the main target population (using youth between the ages of five and nineteen as a proxy), causing Scouting's penetration of youth population to grow from just 1.8% in 1981 to 5.4% in 2010.

tries.org/uscensus/_443_boy_scouts_and_girl_scouts_membership.html (accessed May 10, 2010); *BSA 2009 Annual Report* (U.S.: BSA, c2010). Note numbers excluded adult leaders and members of Learning for Life, the non-Scout program of the BSA.

1 Scout Association of Japan, *History of Scout Movement in Japan* 日本ボーイスカウト運動史, Vol. II, 294; Scout Association of Japan, 財団法人ボーイスカウト日本連盟平成20度事業報告書 (Anuual Report) (Japan, 2008), 3.

2 Tan and Wan, *Scouting in Singapore,* 271; *Annual Report, 2009* (Singapore: the Singapore Scout Association, 2010).

	1981	1991	2001	2010
Total Members	38,850	56,172	80,923	95,494
Hong Kong Population	4,986,560	5,522,281	6,708,389	7,063,300
% of Population	0.8%	1.0%	1.2%	1.4%
Youth Members	25,619	34,426	53,648	56,873
Youth Population, 5-19	1,412,749	1,224,047	1,280,657	1,045,300
% of Population	1.8%	2.8%	4.2%	5.4%

Population Penetration of Scouting, 1981-2010

Sources: Population from *Hong Kong Censuses,* various years; projections for 2010, http://www.censtatd.gov.hk/hong_kong_statistics/ (accessed March 29, 2011). Membership numbers from annual reports of the Scout Association, various years.

It should be noted that even though absolute total membership numbers declined in the most recent years, youth members' penetration of youth population (using the available census age ranges of 5-14 and 15-24 as proxies) continued to increase, as illustrated in this table:

	2006	2010
Grasshoppers, Cubs, and Scouts	60,134	51,392
Population, 5-14	727,070	612,800
% of Population	8.27%	8.39%
Venture and Rover Scouts	5,079	5,481
Population, 15-24	909,005	892,800
% of Population	0.56%	0.61%

Youth Members as a % of Target Youth Groups, 2006, 2010

Sources: Youth population from *Hong Kong Census, 2006*; *Projection of Population Distribution, 2010-2019*, http://www.censtatd.gov.hk/ (accessed April 5, 2011). Scout membership numbers from annual reports of the Scout Association of Hong Kong. Note the population age ranges from the censuses do not exactly correspond to the age limits of the various Scout sections, though they are very close to each other.

In short, it is fair to say that local Scouting grew strongly in the last three decades, in absolute number and as a percentage of the underlying population. As noted earlier, as of 1977, Hong Kong Scouting's population penetration ratio was slightly ahead of that of Singapore, but still trailed that of Britain. By 2009, there were 13.7 Scouts per thousand people in Hong Kong, while the comparable number for Singapore was 2.1, and for Britain was 8.1.[1]

The fact that local Scouting came to its own just as Hong Kong acquired a new sense of its identity and when decolonization was set in motion helped to secure support from the authorities and the community, both perhaps anxious to maintain the territory's institutions and values, given the prospect of having to rejoin China, with her own institutions and values, many of which were unfamiliar and perhaps viewed with suspicion by some Hong Kong people. That Scouting comfortably combined local preferences with international influences, and maintained a high profile both in Hong Kong and outside, perhaps reflected its indigenized but cosmopolitan nature. With features such as an adapted promise, increasing shares of female and very young members, ample outdoor facilities, adequate financial resources, strong participation of new immigrant and non-Chinese youngsters, and a large pool of volunteers from all walks of life, independent Hong Kong Scouting maintained a reasonable semblance of being an open space for all, living out the inclusive ideals of the movement.

Tentative renationalization

Technically at least, since July 1997, it is no longer correct to claim, as WOSM still does, that "there are 6 countries without Scouting," including the PRC.[2] The decolonization process in local Scouting began before that date, in 1977, when it became independent of British Scouting; or at least by 1984, when the Sino-British accord was signed, sealing the political future of Hong Kong. In this period, it grew steadily despite the prospect of political decolonization and amidst declining member-

---

1   See Appendix D, "Membership Statistics."

2   See WOSM, "Census," http://www.scout.org/en/about_scouting/facts_figures/census (accessed May 1, 2010).These are Andorra, the PRC, Cuba, North Korea, Laos and Myanmar. There are also countries with Scouting which are not WOAM members.

ship levels in Scouting in most developed countries. It also made tentative attempts at re-introducing largely symbolic nationalistic elements into its programs. Yet, by 2010, more than a decade after the handover, Scouting's decolonization remains incomplete. The youth movement and the community in which it operates are still working through the roles of post-colonial Scouting both in the SAR and in the PRC, with reference to the concept of "one country, two systems."

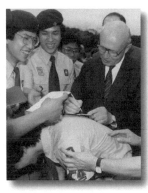

Youde signing autographs for Venture Scouts, 1983. *H. K. Scout Archives.*

In many colonies the local Scout organization formed intimate ties with the authorities. Most Scout Movements in former colonies went through a renationalization process before and after decolonization, quickly realigning with the emerging ruling elites and forging links with the new political regime. In decolonized Kenya, for example, the Scout association "went from condemning Kenyatta as the sinister force behind Mau Mau to pleading with him to become their ceremonial chief Scout once he became prime minister, and later president, of Kenya."[1] This study has demonstrated how native Scouts tended to be nationalistic and supportive of decolonization or separation in contexts as varied as Ireland, British India, French Indochina and Algeria.

Hong Kong Scouting defied tendencies elsewhere by growing much more rapidly than most developed societies in recent years. The movement also bucked international trends by renationalizing considerably more slowly than most former colonies in its last colonial and the first post-colonial decades. Though Youde was very involved with negotiating the Sino-British Joint Declaration, he managed to show up for his first St. George's Day parade in April 1983, when he noted that "the value of [Scouting's] influence on the lives of our young citizens and our society has been incalculable."[2] In late 1985, almost a year after the signing of the Joint Declaration, a cover story in the *Hong Kong Scouting* on citizenship education focused on preparing the citizens for a "democratic 'Hong Kong people rule Hong Kong' government (民主港人治港政府)."[3] There was only one brief reference to educating students about the PRC political system.

---

1   Parsons, *Race, Resistance, and the Boy Scout Movement*, 238.

2   Youde's speech, April 16, 1983, "The Scout Association (Chief Scout), 1983-1986," HKRS 921-1-96, the Public Records Office, Hong Kong.

3   The *Hong Kong Scouting*, September 1985, 27.

Governor Wilson was a sinologist with a doctoral degree in contemporary Chinese history, and had studied Chinese at the University of Hong Kong in the early 1960s. He was possibly more aware of Chinese sensibilities. The association took advantage of his term as the new Chief Scout to schedule the 1987 annual rally in the Fall, hence breaking a long tradition of holding rallies on St. George's Day in April.

It was symbolically significant that this move away from a day named after the patron saint of Britain (and British Scouting) took place a decade before Hong Kong's return to China. The official reason was "to avoid the greater possibility of wet weather in April."[1] One was left to wonder why local Scouting had not thought of adopting this change years ago, if weather had been a serious problem. In reality, eigthy percent of Hong Kong's rainfalls occured between May and September, albeit, to be fair, historic photographs suggest that, at times, rallies were indeed somewhat inconvenienced by rain.

Tung at his first rally as the new Chief Scout, November 1997.

H. K. Scout Archives.

More significantly, another change of a similar nature which could in no way be linked to the weather also took place. In the same year, Hong Kong Scouting finally resolved the dichotomous treatment of the Scout Promise in English and Chinese, and replaced the former's requirement to do one's duty to "the Queen" with loyalty to "the Territory," meaning Hong Kong, hence aligning it with the term *bentu* (this

---

1   Letters, Tam to Collier, Aide-de-camp of Governor Wilson, October 2, 1986; Collier to Tam, October 23, 1986, "The Scout Association, 1982-1988," HKRS 921-1-97, the Public Records Office, Hong Kong.

territory) in the Chinese Promise.[1]

In a sense, both changed timing of the rallies (whether due to local weather or to avoid the perceived British links of St. George's Day) and revised Scout Promise in English could be interpreted as steps to further Hongkongize the movement. Still, one should not assume that all British colonial symbols were purged long before 1997. In Patten's first appearance as the Chief Scout in 1992, the rally still opened with God Save the Queen, and many Queen's Scouts were honored.[2]

Hong Kong Scouting seemed to have adjusted well to the retrocession. In November 1997, Tung Chee Hwa made his first appearance as the new Chief Scout in the annual rally. In 1998, Hong Kong delegation to the 19th World Jamboree received the SAR flag at the former Government House from Tung; he also opened the 19th Asia Pacific Scout Conference, held at the Hong Kong Scout Centre. In the same year, Hong Kong issued its first set of Scout stamps since the 1997 handover, which were marked "HONG KONG, CHINA (中國香港)." In December 1999, Tung visited the Scouts camping at the Millennium Jamboree. In March 2000, the SAR government continued a tradition started by the colonial governors, and hosted an open day at Government House. Members of the public were invited to admire this charming historical building and view the blossoming azalea in the surrounding garden. On this occasion, the Scout Association Band was invited to perform for the public. In November 2001, Tung attended the annual rally commemorating local Scouting's 90th Anniversary.

One of a set of four stamps issued in 1998, marked "Hong Kong, China".

The Scout Band performed at Government House's open day, 2000.

H. K. Scout Archives.

---

1   The *POR,* 1987, 2.
2   The *Hong Kong Scouting*, December 1992, 1.

2009-10 Policy Address

Breaking New Ground Together

Hong Kong must strive for economic growth and wealth creation to address the employment and poverty issues. If we were to maintain welfare-based relief measures on a long-term basis, we would have to overhaul our tax system and increase tax rates. I believe the public would not agree with this approach. The fundamental solution lies in our common efforts in promoting the development of our industries.

The cover of the brochure for the 2009/10 Policy Address featured Tsang with some Scouts.

In 2005, Donald Tsang Yam-kuen became the second post-1997 Chief Scout. In 2007, when Scouts around the world celebrated the movement's centenary, Hongkong Post joined in the celebration by issuing its second set of Scout stamps since handover. The cover of the bilingual brochure which summarized Tsang's official policy address for 2009-2010 entitled "Breaking New Ground Together" contains only one photo. It featured the Chief Executive (and Chief Scout) of the SAR surrounded by smiling Hong Kong Scouts. Local Scouting appeared to have been successfully transformed into an officially-sanctioned youth movement in the Chinese SAR of Hong Kong.

Post-colonial Scouting, as a platform for the reconstruction of citizenship for youth in Hong Kong, made a modest effort at renationalization. Appropriately, like the new SAR flag, the post-colonial Hong Kong Scout emblem featured the de-politicized *Bauhinia blakeana* flower of the SAR, replacing the colonial seal, a key component of the old Scout emblem.[1] In Tung's first rally, he honored the first "Hong Kong

---

1   It is perhaps ironic that this sterile orchid tree was named after Sir Henry Blake,

Special Administrative Region Scouts," which replaced the colonial Queen's Scouts.[1]

Interestingly, the British biased King's or Queen's Scout became the Hong Kong-focused SAR Scout, rather than, say, a more PRC-oriented President's Scout.[2] In 2008, this honor was renamed the Dragon Scout, referring to the legendary Chinese creature which often symbolizes China or the Chinese (as in "descendants of the Dragon 龍的傳人"), echoing the earlier creation of the Gold Dragon as the highest award for lay supporters.[3] While this second renaming of the coveted youth award arguably strengthened the Chinese (as opposed to the Hong Kong) identity of local Scouting, it is clearly more of a cultural than a political identification. It should be noted that the Chinese name of this honor, created in the colonial days and not changed since, was and is still the more generic "Honorable Scout (榮譽童軍)".

Hong Kong Badge, post-1997.

Chinese national icons were rarely seen in Scout functions in the early post-colonial years. In 1999, a Scout Group celebrated the national day by raising the national flag at the top of the Tai Mo Mountain (大帽山), the highest peak in Hong Kong. But this was clearly unofficial: the event was reported in *Hong Kong Scouting* as a letter from readers,

Hong Kong stamps commemorating the centenary of world Scouting, 2007.

the governor of Hong Kong from 1898 to 1903. See Arthur van Langenberg, *Urban Gardening: A Hong Kong Gardener's Journal* (Hong Kong: the Chinese Univ. of Hong Kong, 2006), 39.

1 The *Annual Report, 1997-98* (Hong Kong: Scout Association of Hong Kong, 1998), 16.

2 The head of state of the PRC is known officially as the President (國家主席, literally Chairman of State).

3 The decision to rename the SAR award was made in 2006, but official circular for the name change was issued only in 2008. See meeting minutes, the Chief Commissioner's Council, November 13, 2006; Circular, Programme Branch, July 15, 2008, the Hong Kong Scout Archives.

Badge of the Shenzhen-Hong Kong exchange camp, 2004.

and the photographs featured two Scouts touting what appeared to be toy Carbines, one on each side of the Scout holding the flag, a militaristic imagery that was not likely to be encouraged by the association. In 2000, a district organized a course on how to raise the Chinese national flag at the left-leaning Heung To School, with the help of the latter's teaching staff.[1]

The "supreme authority" of the association, as stipulated in the *POR*, is the Scout Council. As this body only meets once a year, its responsibilities are largely delegated to an executive committee, whose members consisted of senior commissioners and lay advisers.[2] Given the close links to and the funding from the government, representatives from the Home Affairs Bureau, the Education Department and the Social Welfare Department regularly attended meetings of the committee as observers, although they did not vote on decisions. In 1998/99, a staff from the Xinhua News Agency, Hong Kong Branch (新華通訊社香港分社), then the *de facto* diplomatic mission of the PRC in the SAR, became an observer. In 2000, this agency assumed the more appropriate if somewhat verbose name of the Liaison Office of the Central People's Government in the Hong Kong Special Administration Region (中央人民政府駐香港特別行政區聯絡辦公室), and its representation in the committee continued in this new designation.[3]

The final change to align the Scout Promise with Hong Kong's new status was to come later than expected, again suggesting that a certain hesitancy accompanied the renationalizing of Scouting. In January 2001, three-and-a-half years after Hong Kong became part of China, the executive committee approved a new promise. In English, the members were required to commit to do their duty "to God and to my Country," instead of "this Territory." In Chinese, it continued to use *shenming* (deity), but replaced *bentu* (native territory) with *guojia* (國家 country).[4] In short, though the subtly dichotomous treatments in English and Chinese regarding religious duty persisted, members must all commit to do their duty to China, and no longer to Hong Kong. Similar changes were

---

1   The *Hong Kong Scouting*, February 2000, 14; April 2000, 5.
2   The *POR* (Hong Kong: Scout Association of Hong Kong, 1993), 102-104.
3   The *Annual Report, 1999-2000* (Hong Kong: Scout Association of Hong Kong, 2000).
4   Circular, Admin., 01/2001, January 15, 2001, the Hong Kong Scout Archives.

made to the Cub Promise ("my Country" replaced "this Territory") and the Grasshopper Promise ("to love my Country" replaced "to love Hong Kong.")[1] In this matter, Hong Kong Guiding was politically more correct, having already adopted "my country" in their promise in English and Chinese as of July 1, 1997.[2]

In February 2004, a month after he became the commissioner, Pau Shiu-hung and hundreds of Hong Kong Scouts and youngsters from the Chinese city of Shenzhen attended the first large-scale joint camp in the PRC. A participant from Shenzhen observed: "I feel Hong Kong Scouts are 'good people (*hao yang de* 好樣的)'…when lining up for breakfast, the [Chinese] national anthem was suddenly broadcasted. The students [Scouts] from Hong Kong immediately turn to the national flag [which was being hoisted], quickly removed their berets, looking very serious…It is only a raising of the national flag, but how many of our students from the Mainland could do this?"[3] The youthful Chinese participant's observations, while anecdotal, effectively articulated the perceived value of the citizenship training delivered through Scouting.

The Chinese national flag (center) being hoisted in the 2004 rally.

H. K. Scout Archives.

In November 2004, the PRC national flag and national anthem were featured for the first time in the annual rally, as twenty thousand Scouts stood in attention, all urged by the master of ceremony to sing

1   Ibid., Interestingly, the Grasshopper promise still used the term shen (God/ god), not *shenming* (deity). This promise was changed from "愛神愛人愛香港" to "愛 神愛人愛國家"
2   *Annual Report, 1996-97* (Hong Kong: Girl Guides Association., 1997), 12-13. Non-Chinese nationals were required to add "the country in which I live."
3   The *Shenzhen Evening News* 深圳晚報, February 8, 2004, B8. "我覺得香港 的童子軍真是好樣的…吃早飯排隊時, 突然響起了國歌, 來自香港的同學立即轉向 國旗, 迅速脫下帽子, 樣子十分嚴肅…雖然只是升一次國旗, 可是我們內地又有多少 同學能夠做到呢?"

Event (top) and Participant (bottom) Badges, Scout Rally, 2010.

along (though observers noted that not too many people in fact did.) Henry Tang Ying-yen (唐英年), the Financial Secretary, was the guest of honor, as the Chief Scout was not available.[1]

Since then, these two national icons were present at all annual rallies, the largest Scout gatherings. In November 2010, Andrew Li Kwok-nang (李國能), former Chief Justice and former Boy Scout of 36th Hong Kong, officiated at the rally which ushered in the centenary year of local Scouting, celebrated with a series of events from December 2010 to December 2011, including the official Centennial Rally in October 2011, officiated by the then Secretary of Justice and former Cub Scout Wong Yan-lung (黃仁龍).[2] In these two rallies, the color party raising the national flag were youth members who had won territory-wide flag hoisting competitions; and a Scout choir/band led the singing of the national anthem, before the Scout Promise was re-affirmed by all.

In July 2007, it was Tsang Tak-sing (曾德成), the former Boy Scout who had got into trouble with the British colonial authorities in the 1967 riots, who presented the SAR flag to the delegation to the 21st World Jamboree, two days after he assumed the office of the Secretary for Home Affairs. Tsang took the opportunity to comment on the Scout Promise. He told the audience that when he was a Scout in the 1960s, he was not sure which country was being referred to in the promise. Ten years after Hong Kong's retrocession, he observed that he was glad that local Scouts could commit to do their duty to "the country," unequivocally meaning China, as Chinese nationals.[3]

Event (top) and Participant (bottom) Badges, Scout Centennial Rally, 2011.

Still, in contrast to the common sight of the Union Jack in the earlier decades, the Chinese national flag or even the SAR flag rarely featured in Scout events. This was partly due to the fact that the SAR government, perhaps in line with practices in the PRC, does not easily grant permission for Scouts to use the SAR flag. Consistent with the pledge to do their duty to the country, Scouts from many countries, including Britain, America, Australia, Canada, Singapore, Korea, and Japan, would routinely wear cloth emblems of their national flags on their uniforms. Though Hong Kong contingents to international Scout events

---

1   The *Hong Kong Scouting*, November 2004, 1-2.
2   The *Hong Kong Scouting*, December 2010, 2; November 2011, 2-4.
3   Kua, *21st World Jamboree*, 43. In Tsang's days the promise in English for non-British referred to "the country in which I am now living." See Appendix B.

would be permitted to carry the SAR flag (but not the Chinese national flag), their members would not be allowed to wear cloth emblems representing the flag, even if they wish to do so. Instead, if these contingents desire to have a Hong Kong identity, they would be encouraged to adopt the less political albeit quite attractive flying dragon of the so-called "Brand Hong Kong," promoted by the SAR government since 2001, and associated with the slogan "Hong Kong: Asia's World City."[1] The Hong Kong Contingent to the 22nd World Jamboree in Sweden, for example, was only able to obtain permission to use the dragon symbol instead of the SAR flag for its contingent scarf and badge.

H. K. Contingent Badge for the 22nd World Jamboree, with the dragon of "Brand Hong Kong" (bottom).

This relative reluctance to permit the use of the SAR or the national flag on Scout uniforms by Scouts attending international events is interesting. Josep Llobera has noted that "flags are particularly relevant as carriers of national sentiments."[2] If this is ture, it could be argued that not being allowed to use the Chinese national flag or the Hong Kong SAR flag in appropriate situations may weaken youngsters' identification with and sentimental ties to either Hong Kong or China.

Perhaps more significantly, just as in the colonial days with regards to "God Save the Queen," not too many people participated in mass singing of the Chinese national anthem in most Scout rallies. Benedict Anderson has observed that for most peoples around the world the singing of their national anthems may be "an experience of simultaneity" and may provide "occasions for unisonality, for the echoed physical realization of the imagined community."[3] It appears that for the people of Hong Kong, this emotional connection with "the March of the Volunteers," the national anthem of the PRC, has yet to be established.

One aspect of renationalization is the increasingly common exchanges with the Chinese youth in the PRC. There were some pre-handover exchanges and visits, mostly in the 1990s, sometimes with the Young Pioneers (少年先鋒隊). Among the earliest of these was a joint camp with sixty Scouts from Hong Kong and seventy Young Pioneers from Guangdong in August 1990.[4]

---

1   http://www.brandhk.gov.hk/ (accessed May 11, 2011)

2   Josep R. Llobera, *Foundations of National Identity: From Catalonia to Europe* (Berghahn Books, 2004), 36.

3   Anderson, *Imagined Communities*, 145.

4   The *Hong Kong Scouting*, March 1990, 12-13.

The first post-handover visit, a small joint camp in Fujian, was held in the summer of 1997.[1] Others soon followed.[2] Scout leaders attended a national meeting of the Young Pioneers in Beijing in 2000.[3] In the same year, forty Scouts went on a "Chinese History and Cultural Educational Tour" which took them to, among other places, the Great Wall in Beijing. It is interesting to note that this visit again emphasized history and culture, as opposed to aspects of modern China.

In 2001, the association set up a mainland liaison office to strengthen "mutual understanding," and 170 Young Pioneers from Shaanxi (陝西) spent time with local Scouts in the summer.[4] Scouts visited Beijing in the first "10,000 Miles Friendship Trek (同心同根萬里行)" in 2002. This was followed by similar treks to many parts of China subsequently.[5] Hong Kong Scouts hosted numerous camps and service activities, some to remote provinces like Sinkiang, Gansu, Jilin, Qinghai, and Inner Mongolia. In 2007, thirty-two trips for 1,200 Scouts to China and fourteen trips for 800 Mainland youngsters to Hong Kong took place. In 2010, over 1,500 Scouts went to different parts of China.[6] In many exchanges and service visits, the representative from the Liaison Office of the Central People's Government played a key role as an advisor and facilitator.

Hong Kong Scouts at the Tiananmen Square in Beijing, China, 2006.

H. K. Scout Archives.

1   The *Hong Kong Scouting*, October 1997, 8-9.
2   The *Hong Kong Scouting*, May 1998, 13; September 1998, 14-7; December 1998, 17; December 1999, 18-19; May 2000, 18-19; July 2000, 5; October 2000, 19; March 2001, 8, 23; June 2001, 18.
3   The *Hong Kong Scouting Magazine*, August 2000, 3.
4   The *Annual Report, 2000-01* (Hong Kong: the Scout Association, 2001), 12; the *Hong Kong Scouting*, March 2001, 1; September 2001, 1.
5   The *Hong Kong Scouting*, August 2006, 1.
6   Reports, China Exchanges, 2007, 2010, the Hong Kong Scout Association.

A recent project went beyond short-term visits and may portend a more substantial engagement with many youngsters in China. A massive earthquake in Sichuan in May 2008 made millions homeless and damaged 40% of the seventy youth centers in the province. After several exploratory visits, the association committed to reconstruct youth facilities in the cities of Mianyang (綿陽) and Deyang (德陽) and to run a youth training scheme, with support from a Hong Kong government Sichuan Reconstruction Trust Fund. This project, valued at US$5 millions, included a training program based largely on the Scout Method, with the aim of reaching over one hundred thousand children in earthquake-damaged townships in five years. From 2009, before the centers were reconstructed, the association had already organized experimental exchange and service visits to Sichuan.[1] The local partners for these projects were the youth federations of the province of Sichuan and the cities of Mianyang and Deyang, which had close ties to the Young Pioneers and shared leadership with the provincial and city branches of the Communist Youth League of China (中國共青團).

Sichuan exchange/service badge, w/ Chinese characters for Sichuan and Hong Kong as a combined character inside a heart.

The many contacts with the Young Pioneers are interesting. Thomas Jordan suggests that they are but "less acceptable versions—except in their own countries—of the themes embraced and advanced by Robert Baden-Powell."[2] As the only officially-sanctioned youth movement in the PRC, they do have many Scout-like characteristics, down to a patrol system, a scarf, its own salute, a promise and the slogan "always prepared (時刻準備着)."

The movement differs in its ideological coloration: the pioneers' scarves are uniformly red, a Young Pioneer promises to love the party (before the motherland and the people), the slogan is in response to a call to fight for communism, and the pioneers are supervised by the Communist Youth League.[3] China's (or former Soviet Union's) Young Pioneers

1   Report, Reconstruction in Sichuan, July 2009, the Hong Kong Scout Archives. The new Deyang and Mianyang Youth Palaces were completed in 2012-13, and the youth training scheme finished in 2017, with 170,000 person-times (人次) served. See Paul Kua 柯保羅, *Hong Kong Scout Stories* 香港童軍故事, 392-5.

2   Thomas E. Jordan, *Victorian Child Savers and their Culture: A Thematic Evaluation* (Lewiston, N.Y.: Edwin Mellen Press, c1998), 76. Jordan's study focuses on the Victorian Child Savers, including B-P, and his comment on the nature of Young Pioneers (of the Soviet Union, which the Chinese Young Pioneers were patterned on) should be viewed only as a casual observation, not one based on detailed research.

3   "我熱愛中國共產黨,熱愛祖國,熱愛人民..." and "準備着,為共產主義事業而奮鬥". "Zhong Guo Shao Nian Xian Feng Dui Zhang Cheng 中国少年先锋

Hong Kong Scouts with PRC youngsters and Young Pioneers in a campfire and First Aid training in Sichuan, 2010.

H. K. Scout Archives.

Movement has never been a member of WOSM. In fact, WOSM is one of the very few international organizations in which Taiwan still represents China, and the troublesome issue of "one China," "two-China," or "one China, many members," commonly encountered in the United Nations, the International Olympics Committee and other international bodies, is not relevant.[1]

Deng Xiao-ping (鄧小平) proposed the policy of "no change in fifty years (五十年不變)" to ensure smooth transition and the merger of Hong Kong with China in the year 2047. But this policy notwithstanding, changes will and have already started to occur. The inevitable question is how Hong Kong Scouting will evolve in the shadow of the Young Pioneers Movement in China in the future.

Scouting, like the schools, has been organized "to preserve the status quo," with pro-establishment "socialization processes" which helped "to legitimize a society's dominant institutions." But a movement which preserves the status quo may be ill-prepared for the needs of the SAR. Could Scouting "play a transformation role," and help "to harmonize capitalism, socialism and patriotism within a 'one country, two systems' arrangement"?[2] The movement is not, in principle, opposed to patriotic education. In response to a call for "improved teaching of patriotism" in British schools in 1916 B-P had responded that:

队章程 (Articles of the Young Pioneers of China)," http://61.gqt.org.cn/sxd/200905/ t20090512_239909.htm; and website of the Communist Youth League, http://www.ccyl. org.cn/ (accessed May 1, 2010).

1   Steve Tsang (ed.), *In the Shadow of China: Political Development in Taiwan Since 1949* (Hong Kong: Hong Kong Univ., 1993), 1-11; Xu, *Olympic Dreams*, 75-116.

2   Gerard A. Postiglione, "The Decolonization of Hong Kong Education," in Gerald A. Postiglione (ed.), *Education and Society in Hong Kong: Toward One Country and Two Systems* (Armonk, N. Y.: An East Gate Book, 1991), 4.

I am...fully in sympathy with the idea provided that <u>education</u> in patriotism is insisted upon and not mere <u>instruction</u>; also provided that it is not a political step of one party or class against another...[1]

But there is a fine line dividing "education" and "instruction" and, as have been shown in these chapters, patriotism could have very different meanings in Hong Kong for different people and over time.

These recent encounters and exchanges between Scouts from Hong Kong and Young Pioneers and other youngsters from Mainland China either in the SAR or on the Mainland could be perceived as more substantive renationalization efforts, beyond the organizational changes, the new Scout Promise and the presence of national icons such as the flag or the anthem on annual occasions.

Nevertheless, to casual observers the relative hesitancy and tentativeness of the renationalization of local Scouting in the first post-colonial decade might appear puzzling. After all, Hong Kong Scouting had been completely Chinese for decades before 1997. In the interwar and the early postwar years, Chinese influence in Scouting was noteworthy, in the form of dual-registration, Chinese nationalism, a promise which incorporated this nationalism, and the presence of Chinese national icons in official Scout events. While it could be argued that reforms in, say, training programs, take time, this cannot explain why simple and symbolic changes were not made earlier. Why did it take more than three years after July 1997 to replace "this Territory" with "my Country" in the Scout Promise? Why did it take more than seven years to introduce the national anthem in the rally? Why was it that most youngsters still did not join in the singing of the Chinese national anthem? Why was the Chinese national flag or the Hong Kong SAR flag not more commonly featured in Scout gatherings large and small?

To understand these phenomena we must try to see them with reference to the social context of citizenship education in Hong Kong. Citizenship education in many Asian countries had been a relatively recent development, a result of postwar decolonization and independence

---

1   Baden-Powell to T. C. Fry, March 8, 1916 (Founders Papers, Training/Patriotism, 1916-1931), the Gilwell Archives/Scout Association Heritage Service.

of former European colonies. In the special case of Hong Kong, it came even later, and in a greatly modified form. Whether as a British colony or a Chinese SAR, Hong Kong was never an independent nation-state. While a colony, students in Hong Kong were educated largely with a de-nationalized, depoliticized, colonial curriculum, nurturing them as residents of Hong Kong, not citizens of any nation.

After 1984, with the prospects of reintegration with China, *Guidelines on Civic Education* in schools were issued in 1985 and 1996. Then, following handover, the focus of civic education was on nurturing Chinese nationalism and "patriotism," based on a good understanding of the Basic Law, Hong Kong SAR's new mini-constitution, and of the concept of "one country, two systems," invented by Deng for the purpose of re-absorbing former colonies of Hong Kong and Macau.[1]

Herein lays the unique requirements of the SAR's citizenship education. Whereas practically all former colonies going through decolonization eventually became independent, typically "democratic", nation-states; Hong Kong was to reunite with Socialist China, but maintain a high degree of autonomy and its existing, capitalistic, way of life. As Thomas Kwan-choi Tse points out, the citizenship movement in Hong Kong could be viewed as "a complicated interplay of patronage by the colonial government, domestication by the Chinese government and the quest for empowerment by the local civil society."[2]

It is not that Hong Kong politics was not transformed by the prospect of decolonization. In fact, the political climate had started to change from the 1980s. In the last decade of colonialism, Hong Kong became increasingly politicized, a development underpinned by the introduction of direct elections in the Legislative Council, the June 4 incident in Beijing in 1989, and Christopher Patten's confrontational approach.[3] However, the reasons for Hong Kong's retrocession were not the same as those in other colonies.

Unlike even the independence of local Scouting in 1977, the handover of Hong Kong in 1997 was not driven by metropolitan, in-

1   Tse, "Civic education and the making of deformed citizenry...," in Ku et al. (eds.,) *Remaking Citizenship in Hong Kong,* 55.
2   Tse, "Civic education...,", 57.
3   Lee, "Citizenship Education in Hong Kong:...," in Lee, et al. (eds.), *Citizenship Education in Asia and the Pacific,* 59-60.

ternational or local factors, making Springhall's model of decolonization inappropriate. Hong Kong's changed status was not due to Britain's slackening "will to rule." Britain was willing to go to war with Argentina over the Falklands in 1982, and was just as eager to negotiate a permanent solution for Hong Kong with China. Retrocession was not driven by international pressure. America and others were not keen to force Britain to give up Hong Kong. Finally, the local people did not clamor to substitute British rule with that of the Chinese.

The primary motivation was perhaps unique among former colonies. Retrocession was inevitable because China wanted Hong Kong back, and Britain and, more particularly, the people of Hong Kong were not in a position to refuse. In fact, the latter had absolutely no say in this transaction, as China insisted on dealing only with Britain. Even Britain's ability to negotiate was quite limited, as it "was powerless to resist had the Chinese chosen to take Hong Kong by force."[1]

Because of these unique circumstances under which Hong Kong returned to China, the "diasporic consciousness" of her post-colonial people is complicated. Juanita But suggests that the people of Hong Kong resisted being "politically identified with the Mainland Chinese," as "their adopted colonialist cultural ideals of progress, piety, rationality, and order—or their 'Hong Kongness'—give them a sense of pre-eminence over the Chinese who live under the Communist regime." The handover has resulted in a "political and cultural displacement" which required "a necessary rethinking and negotiation of the identity of Hong Kong, or the 'Hong Kongness' of its people."[2] This kind of identity renegotiation often takes a long time. The reorientation of education policies is illustrative. In 1988, a new subject, Government and Public Affairs, was added.[3] In 1991, six leftist "patriotic" schools finally succeeded in becoming fully subsidized, like most local schools.[4] The *Guidelines on Civics Education* promoted "a sense of Chinese national identity, love for the Chinese nation and pride in China."[5] Textbooks for primary and

---

1   Springhall, *Decolonization since 1945*, 192.

2   But, "The Other Race," 6-7.

3   Mark Bray, "Decolonisation and Education: New Paradigms for the Remnants of Empire," *Compare*, Vol. 24, No. 1, 1994, 37-51.

4   Ip Kin Yuen, "Organisational Change: the Case of a 'Leftist School' in Joining the Direct Subsidy Scheme," M. Ed. thesis, Univ. of Hong Kong, 1994, 6-7.

5   Lee, "Citizenship Education in Hong Kong," 62.

secondary schools, though published commercially, increasingly "focus on China much more than in the past" and adopt "a degree of self-censorship in portraying China in a positive light."[1] In 2004, curriculum changes aimed at inculcating national identity in students of all ages, down to kindergarten students, were introduced.

But there was a gap if not a gulf between the ideal and the practice of citizenship education in Hong Kong. The Education and Manpower Bureau often needed to balance the demands of the "pro-China" and the "pro-democratic" camps. Furthermore, many in the community, including teachers, were only lukewarm about the teaching of national identity, largely because they themselves had yet to acquire it, having grown up in a colonial society, and being ambivalent about Communist-controlled China. "While a few schools raise the [national] flag every day, many more do so twice a year;" while some schools emphasized national identity education, "many others do the community-accepted minimum."[2] Just as importantly, local secondary students were typically faced with intense academic pressure, driven by public examinations. National identity, not directly tested in public examinations (as is the case in most liberal societies), was often ignored.

As far as Hong Kong people are concerned, what does it mean to belong to China? "People throughout the world feel that they have a national identity as a matter of common sense; but this has not been true in Hong Kong in recent decades, and remains largely untrue today."[3] In a survey in 2000 in twenty-eight countries, Hong Kong students scored among the lowest in terms of their attitudes towards the nation. Only around half of the respondents considered the national flag and anthem important, though almost all were proud of Hong Kong's achievements.[4] In interviews with university students from the United States, China, and Hong Kong from 2001 to 2005, while the former two groups overwhelmingly professed their love for their county, a large majority of the Hong Kong students offered hesitant responses, such as "I'm not really sure" or "I don't feel much of anything."[5] The community fares no bet-

---

1   Mathews et al, *Learning to belong to a Nation*, 83.
2   Ibid., 87.
3   Ibid., xiii.
4   Lee, "Citizenship Education in Hong Kong," 75.
5   Mathews et al, *Learning to belong to a Nation*, 116-117.

ter. Surveys in 1996 to 2006 revealed that over 20% of the people perceived themselves as "Hongkongese," not "Chinese" or even "Hongkongese and Chinese." In 2006, less than half of the citizens took pride
in the national flag and the national anthem, although these percentages
have been increasing over time.[1]

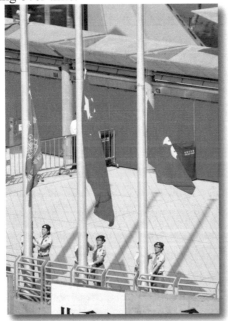

Scouts hoisted the Chinese
national, SAR and Scout
flags in the 2010 rally.

H. K. Scout Archives.

Given the situation in education and in the community in recent
decades, the slow renationalization of Scouting becomes more understandable. As in the past, Scouting emerged from and evolved in relation to the political, social and cultural developments of its underlying
community. In order to maintain its relevance to its target audience,
Hong Kong Scouting's brand of citizenship education had to be aligned
with the perceived needs of its members and the community. The (re)
introduction of the national anthem and the national flag was slow in
Scouting, and only for annual events such as the rallies, largely because
this reflected the sentiments of many "Hong Kongese," who identified
weakly with such symbols. The phrase "my Country" was late in entering Scouting parlance, because many in the community, including many
youth, could not (yet) profess unqualified love for China, though it has
been officially their country for over ten years.

In short, for a variety of reasons, Hong Kong Scouting managed

---

1   Ibid., 97-105.

to remain relevant, in spite of declining target population and sctbacks in the movement in the rest of the world. Having been slow to take off in an earlier colonial context as a racially-restrictive organization, it grappled successively with denationalizing, sinicizing, globalizing, indigenizing and renationalizing trends to become a Hongkongized movement which remained attractive to local youngsters for longer than in many other western or Asian contexts.

But this history of post-colonial Scouting must be viewed in relation to the bigger picture of Hong Kong as part of China. How should local Scouting respond to the territory's new status? What is Hong Kong Scouting's role in the post-colonial society? What could Scouting achieve as an informal educational program for youth and children in the transitional stage of fifty years? How should Scouting as a citizenship training scheme be conducted? Are its modest renationalization efforts adequate, or is the movement still living in its colonial past and imparting denationalized citizenship training, divorced from the needs of the evolving society? Conversely, might the movement be seen as becoming too accommodating of the perceived desires of the SAR and the PRC authorities and imparting politicized citizenship training, disregarding cherished traditions of neutrality in partisan politics? Have the Chief Executives of the SAR, as Chief Scouts, proactively led strategic changes in the largest local youth movement, as colonial governors before them did? Or have they simply been avoiding this "colonial" institution rather than making it a component of an overall plan for citizenship education? How will the relationship between Scouting and the Young Pioneers evolve? This section has attempted to address some of these questions briefly. But the reality is that it is perhaps still too early to fully address most of them. This is so because, more than a decade after the former British colony of Hong Kong became a Chinese SAR, the generalized version of most of these questions remain unresolved in the post-colonial community itself.

Concluding remarks

In the last three decades, the Hong Kong Scout Movement expanded substantially while it was reformed and decolonized. The need "to rule" effectively can again be seen as a key motive in the early part of the period, at least from the perspective of the authorities, although "to educate" quickly emerged as a critical influence, especially for parents, educators and the community more generally. Gender became a defining category, as girls were served through the FOS programs, the Venture Scout section, and then all youth sections. Age parameters, always a relevant consideration in this history of a youth movement, remained a key consideration, and shifted, as a pre-Cub section was created in the 1980s, the rapid growth of which underpinned an infantilizing trend in local Scouting, mirroring similar developments in Scouting in other countries, other youth movements, education, and even in commercial circles. The newly-independent movement also continued to expand its support facilities, reach out to a variety of service targets, draw on a large pool of adult volunteers, and maintain impressive presence both in Hong Kong and in the international arena.

By the end of the period, Hong Kong Scouting, as an independent member of the world Scout body, was a fully indigenized mass movement with its own distinct (and hybrid) identity, a mildly renationalized program, girls in all its sections, and many pre-teen members. It was alive and well as the leading local youth movement, with growing membership and population penetration ratios. However, despite such achievements, post-colonial Scouting, reflecting hesitant trends in citizenship education and the complex and evolving nature of the Hong Kong identity in the post-colonial community, had yet to find a clear strategic direction. It appears that its leaders were still seeking to redefine this brand of citizenship training in the contested symbolic space of youth education and resolve longer-term uncertainties regarding its role in the SAR and as part of the PRC.

Epilogue

Scouting started in 1907, when Baden-Powell organized an experimental camp for twenty-one British boys on the Brownsea Island. It came to Hong Kong several years later, when Spink introduced Scout training to twenty-eight British boys in Kowloon. In 2010, there were thirty million Scouts in 161 countries and territories, including nearly one hundred thousand in Hong Kong. A hundred years after its founding, Scouting is truly international and still retains an important presence in many parts of the world.

According to the latest WOSM statistics, Hong Kong's total Scout membership ranked fifteenth, and this membership as a percentage of total population ranked tenth, among the 161 WOSM members. The apparent robustness of the Hong Kong movement defies simple explanations. Hong Kong has a small population, which ranked 89th among the WOSM members in 2009.[1] Hong Kong's population has been aging in recent decades: children and youth under the age of fourteen as a percentage of her total population was only half that of the world or Asia, below North America, and even Europe.[2] Unlike in Britain, the United States, Canada and Australia, Scouting in Hong Kong was not well-established early on, having only become a mass movement in the postwar years. Nor could one rely on the Asian contexts or the British colonial links to explain local Scouting's relative strength. Taiwan had a population three times larger, but its Scout membership was only over half that of Hong Kong.[3] Though the current and the only two former prime ministers

1   Membership numbers by NSO from the WOSM's "Census," http://www.scout.org/en/about_scouting/facts_figures/census/; population in 2009 from "World Atlas," http://www.worldatlas.com/; http://www.censtatd.gov.hk/ (accessed April 5, 2011).
2   For 2005, the percentages were 14.4% for Hong Kong, 28.4% for the world, 28.2% for Asia, 20.5% for North America, and 15.9% for Europe. See United Nations, Department of Economic and Social Affairs, http://esa.un.org/unpp/p2k0data.asp (accessed May 8, 2010).
3   Taiwan's population was 22.8 million in 2007, and its Scout membership, as reported on WOSM's website, was 57,039.

of Singapore were all former Boy Scouts, Singapore's population and Scout membership were 71% and 11% that of Hong Kong, respectively.[1] One has to look further to identify the reasons behind the continued relevance of Hong Kong Scouting in recent decades.

This study has dealt with the history of the Scout Movement in Hong Kong from its pre-First World War founding in 1910 to its post-handover developments up to 2010, broken into six periods. It is, at the same time, a primary-source based narrative of the history of local Scouting, an analytical review of its social, political and cultural contexts, and a critical study of the forces underpinning the evolution of this citizenship training scheme, including the possible reasons behind its slow early progress and its more rapid recent growth.

It has been shown that Scouting started in Hong Kong in the 1910s as a niche movement for a few British boys. In these early years, the proverbial Hong Kong Scout was a British national who was Christian, non-Chinese, and among the few privileged enough in colonial society to be prepared for God's kingdom and the British Empire through this new and innovative game of Scouting, which had originated in England and was spreading rapidly throughout the empire and beyond.

In the interwar years, race became a less significant barrier to entry, as the indigenization of the movement and the nationalization of its genre of citizenship training were substantially realized. In the 1920s, the typical Hong Kong Scout became a British national who might be English, Scottish, Eurasian, Portuguese or Chinese, but was still part of the colonial elite, and was trained to become better citizen of the colony. In the second interwar decade, the archetypal Scout had become a Chinese middle-class boy who was comfortable in his identity as both a Hong Kong resident and a Chinese national, was being nurtured in a youth movement which tolerated dual loyalty, and was increasingly ready to fight for the British colony and Nationalist China against their common enemy, Japan.

In the first two postwar decades, Scouting grew rapidly, with far greater penetration of lower income groups. Training was also dena-

---

1   Singapore's population was 4.987 million in 2009, and its Scout membership as reported in *Annual Report, 2009* (Singapore: the Singapore Scout Association, 2009) was 10,292. Lee Kuan Yew, Goh Chok Tong, and Lee Hsien Loong were all former Boy Scouts. See the *Straits Times*, February 28, 2010.

tionalized. During this time, the Hong Kong Scout was a Chinese boy who might be from a middle or lower class, urban or rural background, and who might even be from a group considered disadvantaged. Scout training distanced participants from both Communist China and Nationalist Taiwan, and educated them for some useful roles in the increasingly prosperous postwar Hong Kong society.

From the 1960s to the late 1970s, Scouting expanded further and became a true mass youth movement, as it depended on modern planning and management techniques and British-centric reforms to drive healthy growth, and responded to the community's call to serve more youngsters, including a large number of boys and girls outside the movement. Strong support came from the authorities and within the community, informed by a growing sense of Hong Kong's own distinct identity and culture, and a belief that the movement would aid governance and help address the youth problems identified as besetting the colonial society. In this period, the typical member of the Hong Kong Scout Movement was a Chinese boy (or girl) with a growing sense of his (or her) hybridity, which was neither fully Chinese nor British, who had joined Scouting or the FOS outreach program as part of his (or her) Hong Kong-focused educational experience.

Finally, from the late 1970s to 2010, gender-related barriers to entry were fully broken down, age parameters through which membership was defined were broadened, and initiatives were taken to help Scouting remain relevant in an evolving community; while a tentative renationalization of its symbolic framework and training program took place due to the decolonization of Hong Kong. The government and those within Hong Kong society who were anxious to maintain Hong Kong's identity and institutions given the prospect of reunification with China afforded the movement extensive support. The Hong Kong Scout was increasingly a girl and a younger person, mostly a pre-teen, who was enrolled by his or her parents with a view to securing a better education, and who was subjected to modest renationalization by way of a new promise to serve the country, exchange visits to China and occasional exposure to nationalistic symbolism.

In short, over the years, race, class, gender, and age as categories regulating the membership and meaning of Scouting evolved and the power relations through which they operated shifted in the Hong Kong context, impacting upon the inclusivity of Scouting, transforming it into an indigenized and coeducational mass movement for youth and children of a broadened age range. Its growth over the years had been motivated by the desire of the stakeholders "to convert, educate, rule or fight," or, in other words, to achieve religious conversion, to promote secular education, to facilitate colonial and post-colonial governance and military and para-military preparedness.

Scouting had juggled British, Chinese, and Hong Kong influences in the contested space of citizenship training for youth throughout the years. The expanding Hong Kong Scout Movement had produced a negotiated "Chineseness" which increasingly included more Chinese youngsters and a large dose of "Hongkongness," but this might or might not include Chinese nationalism, which was in turn defined differently at different points in time.

In the discourse about patriotism, a key component of the citizenship ideals of the Scout Movement, it is useful to borrow a concept in colonial analysis which distinguishes between the patriotism of the *petit pays* (small homeland, the colonized territory) and that of the *grand pays* (big homeland, the colonizing or the "mother" country).[1] In the case of Hong Kong, there were, so to speak, three possible forms of patriotism in Scouting: that for Hong Kong, the *petit pays*, that for the British Empire and/or China, both of which could legitimately claim to be the *grand pays* at some point in time.

Although the colonial authorities could in theory demand patriotic obeisance for Hong Kong and Britain only; pragmatically, that had rarely been insisted upon in the citizenship program of Scouting in the earlier years, except as a symbolic gesture. In fact, from the interwar years up until the 1950s, Hong Kong Scouting had tolerated a certain amount of patriotism for China, and sometimes (such as just before the Battle for Hong Kong in 1941 and in the postwar 1940s) these demands had been rather more substantial. Since 1949, however, the authorities

---

1   This analytical framework is explained well by a governor of French Indochina: "inside the 'Indochinese Federation' each country had the right...to adhere to a local patriotism...so long as it never forgot that next to and even above the small homeland, the thoughts of all should go constantly to the grand French homeland, the guardian and protector of the Federation." See Anne Raffin, *Youth Mobilization...*, 6.

had successfully denationalized the movement. By the 1970s, local Scouts' patriotism was almost entirely focused on the *petit pays* of Hong Kong, ignoring both Britain and China. However, as decolonization began in the mid-1980s, and especially after 1997, China became increasingly the only *grand pays* of relevance, and patriotism towards China became important again, if not predominant.

Nothing illustrates the evolving nature of the citizenship training provided through local Scouting better than the various versions of the Scout Promise over the years. In the beginning, there was only the Scout Promise in English, the same one used in Britain and many other parts of the British Empire, committing boys to do their duties to God and the King. In the interwar years, when Chinese nationalism became popular, a version of the promise in Chinese became available, first quietly but later openly and officially. This still committed the boys to serve a Christian God, but allowed them to swear allegiance to the equivocal "head of state" which, in the case of many non-British Chinese Scouts, was no doubt taken to mean the president of the Republic of China rather than the King of the British Empire. This compromise version remained in use throughout the last interwar years and the early postwar ones, when Nationalist Chinese influences were quite visible in many areas of the local youth movement.

After the founding of the PRC in 1949, a strong denationalizing current prevailed in the colony. While the Scout promise in English still called for loyalty to the King or, after 1952, the Queen, the promise in Chinese was denationalized, calling for commitment to the "place of residence," referring to neither China nor Britain, but to Hong Kong, and suggesting the transient nature of the latter as perceived by most people in Hong Kong. Then, in the late 1960s, and in a manner indicating the growing recognition of a distinct Hong Kong identity, this promise was further Hongkongized, calling the boys to do their duties to the generic "deity" instead of the Christian God, hence aligning the religious requirement with the sentiments of the non-Christian Chinese majority; and to the "native territory," again meaning Hong Kong, but by then perceived as the permanent home by most youthful members, who, unlike their parents, were largely born locally.

In 2001, several years after the retrocession of sovereignty, an attempt at renationalizing this promise took place, and boys and girls were urged to commit to do their duty to the country, which clearly meant China. More than ninety years after the founding of local Scouting, the movement had finally adopted a Scout Promise which was fully "decolonized" and similar to that of the Scout organizations in most sovereign countries in the world.

But this was likely little more than a perfunctory nod in the direction of what Anderson might label as the "official nationalism" of the PRC.[1] After the Communist revolutionaries took over China in 1949, they effectively employed the power of the state to nurture the "imagining" of the new nation of the PRC and the related official nationalism. As noted in the last chapter, students from China would readily admit love for the country, while those from Hong Kong would be more reserved. Local Scouts' commitment to do their duty to the country is only likely to represent a genuine shift in mindset when this official nationalism has been successfully nurtured in the Hong Kong community more generally, and internalized by the people of the SAR.

The resolution of the differentiating categories over time, the interplay of the varying motivations of the different stakeholders, and the evolving nature of the religious and nationalistic ideals of Hong Kong Scouting have all contributed to the impressive development of the movement, especially in the recent decades, when it bucked downward trends in Scouting in many developed parts of the world, and the trend toward an aging local population. But in all these developments, the social, political and cultural contexts of Hong Kong played key roles. In other words, Hong Kong Scouting and the typical Hong Kong Scout did not develop in a vacuum but had evolved with the perceived needs of the time, largely mirroring (though at times leading or lagging) trends in the wider community.

Why did Scouting, this colonial-era institution, continued to thrive even after Hong Kong shifted into the post-imperial world and reunited with a nascent superpower which did not subscribe to this movement? In certain respects, it could be argued that the recent growth in Hong Kong Scouting was driven by the late twentieth century anxieties of post-colonial Hong Kong society, and that these were in some cases

---

1   Anderson, *Imagined Communities*, 158-159.

similar to those which had originally inspired Baden-Powell to start the Boy Scout Movement in Britain at the beginning of the twentieth century. It has been observed that a distinct Hong Kong identity began to take hold in the community from the 1960s and the 1970s onward.[1] This was constantly being reconstructed. With decolonization, which started in the 1980s, there emerged a need to reconcile this identity with one which is more clearly and closely aligned with China. Uncertainties and anxieties over the fate of Hong Kong and its cultural identity profoundly influenced the society in the run-up to 1997 and even beyond.

Today, the proverbial Hong Kong Scout had essentially become a hybrid, a result of long years of interactions between Britain, China and Hong Kong, a "Eurasian" of sort, a Hongkongized product, having British and Chinese features, but not entirely being one or the other. This, of course, is the kind of "in-betweenness, diasporas, mobility and cross-overs of ideas and identities" typically spawned by colonialism, an intellectual hybridity commonly seen in post-colonial societies.[2] In this regard, the Hong Kong Scout is similar to the typical Hong Konger, proud of who he or she is, but nonetheless still searching for a new definitive identity as a member of the post-colonial Hong Kong community and as a PRC national.

By 2010, China was the world's most populous and, according to many pundits, possibly soon-to-be the world's most powerful and even most prosperous nation. Lee Kuan Yew points out that "between the aspirations of the people of Hong Kong, who wants more democracy to protect their comfortable, prosperous way of life, and the expectations of China's leaders, who want a Hong Kong that will be useful and mischief-free, there is a wide and deep gap indeed."[3] Lee wondered if post-colonial Hong Kong could "learn to work with Chinese officials and understand their different...system and mindset" while retaining "the characteristics that made it an indispensable intermediary between China and the world, as during British rule."[4] To a large extent, the an-

---

1   Carroll, *A Concise History of Hong Kong*, 167-169; Mathews et al, *Learning to Belong to a Nation*, 22-39.
2   Ania Loomba, *Colonialism/Postcolonialism*, 2nd ed. (London: Routledge, 1998), 145.
3   Lee Kuan Yew, *From Third World to First: The Singapore Story, 1965-2000* (New York: HarperCollins Publisher, c2000), 557.
4   Ibid.

swer to this question might determine how well Hong Kong fares as a semi-independent Chinese SAR in the fifty years of transition and, perhaps even beyond.

One could also ask how hybrid local Scouting should be positioned within the context of Hong Kong as a Chinese SAR. In March 2011, Xi Jinping (習近平), the vice president of the PRC who is also in charge of Hong Kong affairs, noted that Hong Kong must try to promote its young people's "sense of identification," "sense of belonging," and "sense of responsibility" towards the country.[1] Few would argue with the need to do so in the context of Hong Kong, after its relatively recent handover to China. Furthermore, those who subscribe to the professed aims of Scout training might suggest that Scouting is indeed one way to promote these three "senses." But whether the approaches taken by the youth movement, or, indeed, by the Hong Kong community, towards nurturing these "senses" would be considered adequate or not depends largely on one's perspective. In recent years, the Education Bureau of the Hong Kong SAR would from time to time stress the need to teach and promote "national education" in the schools. A subtitle of a recent editorial in the daily newspaper *Ming Pao* on this subject perhaps expressed well the mixed sentiments of some Hong Kong people: "The arguments regarding whether to teach or not will not be too great, the arguments about how to teach will not be small."[2] In other words, should Hong Kong's national education focus largely on instilling patriotic feelings and positive identifications with China, or should it allow or even encourage young people to think independently and judge what is good and what is not so good about China?[3]

As Homi Bhabha observes, it is possible that "the paranoid threat from the hybrid is finally uncontainable because it breaks down the symmetry and duality of self/other, inside/outside."[4] In this matter, the Hong Kong youth movement largely shares the fate of the Hong Kong community. If "the display of hybridity" by the Hong Kong Scout

---

1   The *Hong Kong Economic Journal* 信報, March 5, 2011. "增強港澳地區年輕人對國家的認同感,歸屬感和責任感." Xi was speaking to the Hong Kong representatives to the national People's Political Consultative Conference.

2   The *Ming Pao*, May 9, 2011. "教與不教爭議不太大,如何教爭議不會小."

3   Ibid.

4   Homi K. Bhabha, *The Location of Culture* (Oxon: Routledge, 1994, reprinted 2005), 165.

(often reflecting that of the Hong Kong people), including his hesitancy about an unqualified patriotism towards the *grand pays* of China, "terrorizes authority," then he might eventually be marginalized or subsumed by, say, the Chinese Young Pioneer.[1]

On the other hand, there are possibilities that this product of historic "cultural imperialism" might be transformed into a rejuvenated movement in a modern-day context of "cultural globalization," in a Hong Kong which has become the most cosmopolitan city and a useful if not indispensable intermediary of the PRC.[2] If so, then the Hong Kong Scout might play a role in the future of the SAR, and one distinct from that of the Young Pioneer, in the transitional period of fifty years and possibly after. He or she might even have a role in China, as a bridge between youth there and elsewhere, much like the Eurasian in Hong Kong, who served in the past as a link between the East and the West.

Carroll observes in a study issued in 2022 that "Hong Kong and China not only coexisted with but benefited from each other for more than 150 years," as they were able "to use each other economically, politically, socially, and culturally," even after the PRC was established in 1949. But he also suggests that "this is likely to be the end of a relationship...that endured for more than 150 years," based on some events which had taken place in recent years.[3]

The development of local Scouting in the post-colonial era will no doubt continue to reflect the development of Hong Kong society itself, and it will also depend to a great extent on evolution of the Chinese youth movement and, more generally, of China herself. Carroll's prognosis, if correct, will likely impact the future of Hong Kong Scouting as a unique symbolic space for citizenship training for local youngsters, just as it will the future of the Chinese SAR of Hong Kong as a distinct community within China.

---

1   Ibid.

2   Marwan M. Kraidy, *Hybridity, or the Cultural Logic of Globalization* (Philadelphia: Temple Univ. Press, 2005), 38-39; and John Tomlinson, "Cultural Globalization and Cultural Imperialism," 170-190, in Ali Mohammadi (ed.), *International Communication and Globalization* (London: SAGE Publications, 1997),

3   John Carroll, *The Hong Kong-China Nexus: A Brief History* (Cambridge: Cambridge Univ. Press, 2022), 2, 61, 74.

Appendices

Appendix A

Chronology

Hesitant Start and Early Demise, 1910-1919

1910   "1ˢᵗ Company of Boys' Brigade and Scouts" inaugurated at the St. Andrew's Church in Kowloon (May 11ᵗʰ).
1912   Baden-Powell inspected the St. Andrew's brigade boys "trained and dressed as Scouts" at Government House (April 19ᵗʰ).
1913   1ˢᵗ Hong Kong Troop started at St. Joseph's College.
1914   Warrant for the 1ˢᵗ Hong Kong Troop issued (May 1ˢᵗ).
        1ˢᵗ Hong Kong Troop reorganized to exclude non-British nationals.
        Wolf Cub Pack formed at the Peak School.
1915   First joint Boy Scouts and Wolf Cubs parade (March 20ᵗʰ).
        The Hong Kong Boy Scouts Association formed, with May as Chief Scout and Anstruther as Commissioner.
1916   May presided over Empire Day Scouts and Guides Rally.
        The Hong Kong Boy Scouts Association dissolved (August 2ⁿᵈ).

Re-launch and Racial Inclusiveness, 1919-1930

1920   Ranneft's talk on Scouting at St. Andrew's Church.
        Stubbs revived Scouting.
        St. Andrew's Church, St. Joseph's College, Murray Garrison School and Wanchai Wesleyan Church (re)started Boy Scout Troops.
1921   First post-war rally at the Murray Barracks (January 8ᵗʰ).
        First Chinese Troops started at government schools (Kadoorie and Saiyingpun) and Chinese Methodist Church.
        First open Troop for Eurasian boys formed.
        The Silver Wolf magazine launched.
        Lo Kwok-chung awarded Gilt Cross for saving the life of a man.
1922   Prince of Wales inspected the Boy Scouts at Government House.
        1ˢᵗ Hong Kong Sea Scout Troop inaugurated.
        Boy Scouts served in the 1922 strike.
        First Scout Aquatic competition at the Victoria Recreation Club.
        Li Hok-wai and Chan Hung-yun awarded Gilt Crosses.
1923   Henry Choa became the first King's (Sea) Scout.
        First Scout "Jamboree"/exhibition at the City Hall (April 13ᵗʰ -14ᵗʰ).
        Scouters' training camp at Pinewood Hill.

1st Hong Kong Sea Scouts and 6th Hong Kong (Kadoorie) jointly won the first Prince of Wales Banner competition.

First Scottish Troop started at Taikoo Dockyard.

Boy Scouts served in large-scale vaccination campaign.

1924   Chinese Troops at Protestant schools (St. Paul's and Ying Wa) and the South China Athletic Association founded.

Hong Konge Scouts attended the Imperial Jamboree at Wembley.

1925   Boy Scouts served in the general strike and boycott.

First Japanese Troop started.

Association headquarters on Hong Kong Island opened.

Hugh Braga awarded Silver Cross.

1926   Clementi adapted the Scout Promise in Chinese to accommodate Chinese nationalistic feelings.

Kotewall, an Eurasian, became president of the association.

1927   Boy Scouts Ordinance passed to protect local Scouting.

First New Territories Troop started in Taipo.

First Troop in a vernacular school, Yuek Chee College, founded.

1928   Troops started in Queen's College and Munsang College.

1929   Hong Kong divided into two Scout Districts.

The Deep Sea Scout Branch set up.

Duke of Gloucester inspected Boy Scouts at Government House.

1930   Saiwan (Chaiwan) Campsite opened.

Dual Loyalty and Indigenization, 1930-1945

1931   Scout Promise in Chinese with duty to "head of nation" instead of "King" first appeared in an official association publication.

1933   Peel entertained five hundred Scouts and Guides at Mountain Lodge.

1934   Three Scouts attended Pan-Pacific Jamboree in Melbourne.

1935   Eight hundred youngsters attended a Scouts and Guides Jamborally at the Hong Kong Football Club (May 8th).

1936   First Hong Kong Scout cloth emblem adopted.

Fund-raising campfire held at the Cricket Club.

1937   Scouts and Guides Coronation Rally at the Happy Valley (May 14th).

1938   Tea party for Shanghai Scouts and viewing of patriotic Scout films.

Boy Scouts served in a Despatch Corps in preparation for the War.

1939   Joint camp for over twenty Troops on the slopes of Lion Rock.

1940   Membership topped the one thousand mark.

First Rover Moot held on Nicholson Hill.

1941   Memorial service for B-P at the two cathedrals.

The New Territories District created.

Appearance of many nationalistic Scout-like youth corps.

Membership exceeded 1,500.

ARP Despatch Corps had over 1,400 members, mostly Boy Scouts.

Second Rover Moot held just before war broke out (December 6-7th).

Scouts participated in defense of Hong Kong as volunteer soldiers.

1941- Official prohibition of Scouting during Japanese occupation, many Boy Scouts
  1945   and Scoutmasters interned, isolated Scout activities under captivity in Stanley
         internment camp, Scouts involved in Japanese resistance in POW camps and
         outside, some under BAAG.

Reconstruction and Reaching Out, 1945-1964

1945   Scouting revived in Hong Kong.
1946   First postwar St. George's Day Rally at the Botanical Garden.
1947   Young officiated in rally which featured both Chinese and British national anthems
         and flags.
         Wong Kai-chung awarded a Silver Cross.
1948   Prince of Wales Banner competition revived.
1949   Morse Hut on Hong Kong Island opened as headquarters.
1950   Quah became the first Chinese Colony Commissioner.
         Gang Shows raised funds for charities.
1951   Three Scout Districts (Hong Kong, Kowloon, N. T.) set up.
         First Chinese Deputy Camp Chief appointed.
         Carlton Trophy competition started for Boy Scouts, and Prince of Wales Banner
         competition converted to a Senior Scout event.
         Eight Scouts, all Chinese, attended 7th World Jamboree in Austria.
1953   Hong Kong and N.T. each divided into two Districts.
         Boy Scout Week, a colony-wide publicity event, held.
1954   Morse House on Cox's Road in Kowloon opened as headquarters.
         Rowallan visited Hong Kong.
1955   Scout Promise called for doing one's duty to "place of residence."
         Troops started for delinquent boys and boys afflicted with leprosy.
1956   40th Anniversary of Wolf Cubbing celebrated.
         Handicapped Auxiliaries formed to support handicapped Scouting.
1957   1,361 Scouts attended first Colony Jamborette in Kam Chien Village, Sheung Shui
         (October 19th-22nd).
         Twelve Chinese Scouts attended 9th World Jamboree in England.
         Inauguration of Troops for deaf and crippled boys.
1958   Lady Baden-Powell visited Hong Kong.
         First Gilwell Reunion at Junk Bay.
1959   Sixty-two Scouts attended 10th World Jamboree in the Philippines.
         Commercial film "Scout Master" released in Cantonese & Mandarin.
1960   Gilwell Campsite at Fei Ngo Shan in Kowloon set up.
1961   Hong Kong divided into three Areas with eighteen Districts.
         Jubilee Cub rally held.
         Maclean visited Hong Kong.
         1961 "chosen" as the founding year of Hong Kong Scouting
         Three thousand Scouts attended the Golden Jubilee Jamborette in Kowloon Tsai
         (December 27th, 1961-January 2nd, 1962).
1963   Eight Scouts participated in 11th World Jamboree in Greece.

Reforms and Independence, 1964-1977

1964   District Auxiliary Group for factory workers started.
1965   New Territories Area Training Centre opened.
1966   UK published the *APR*, advocating major modernizing reforms.
1967   First year of Hong Kong's own 1st Five-Year Plan.
        Phased implementation of the *APR* reforms began.
        Scout Promise called for doing one's duty to "this territory."
        First Cadet Scout Groups formed.
        Large-scale programs targeting non-Scout youngsters introduced.
        Twelve Scouts participated in 12th World Jamboree in the USA.
1968   Hong Kong divided into three Regions with twenty-four Districts
        Hong Kong became Associate Member of the Far East Scout Conference.
1969   First Service Scout Groups formed.
        Association Scout Band inaugurated.
        "Friends of Scouting" organization inaugurated.
        First Commissioners' Roundtable Conference held.
1970   Chief Commissioner's competition for Cub Scouts introduced.
        The issue of independence of Hong Kong Scouting first raised.
1971   Stamps in commemoration of the 60th anniversary issued.
        Five thousand Scouts participated in the Diamond Jubilee Jamboree at Castle
        Peak (July 22nd-28th).
        Hong Kong hosted the 5th Commonwealth Scout Conference
        Hong Kong hosted the 2nd World Scout Public Relations Seminar.
        One hundred Scouts attended 13th World Jamboree in Japan.
1972   First year of the 2nd Five-Year Plan.
        Community Service Organization formed.
        Tai Tam Campsite opened.
1974   Proposal for independence approved by the Association.
        Colony Commissioner renamed Chief Commissioner.
1975   Experimental mixed Venture units with female members introduced.
        Tung Tsz Training Centre in Tai Po opened.
        Hong Kong International "Camporee" held in Tai Po.
        Six Scouts participated in 14th World Jamboree in Norway.
1976   East Kowloon Region formed as the fourth region.
1977   The Scout Association became 111th full member of WOSM (April 16th).
        The Scout Association (Amendment) Bill came into effect.
        Goodwill visit to South East Asian countries.
        Rover Scout section revived.
        Territory-wide non-Chinese Silver Jubilee District formed.

Expansion and Realignment, 1977-2023

1978   Admission of girls into Venture Scout section.
        Tang Shiu-kin Building opened as Island's regional headquarters.
        Hong Kong hosted 11th Asia-Pacific Scout Conference.

1979   Hong Kong attended the 27th World Scout Conference in England.
1980   TV series on Scouting entitled "Tiger Patrol" broadcasted.
       First commissioners' administration conference held.
       First Troop for Vietnamese boys in a refugee camp started.
       Extension Scouts in "Int'l Year of the Disabled Persons" events.
1981   Policy paper "Blueprint for the 1980s" circulated.
1982   Rainbow project (girls in younger sections) launched experimentally.
       "Year of the Scouts" and 75th anniv. of Scouting celebrated.
       International Jamborette held at Tai Tam.
       Territory-wide non-Chinese Brotherhood Region set up.
1983   Forty Scouts participated in 15th World Jamboree in Canada.
       Pak Sha Wan Sea Activities Centre opened.
1984   Eleven thousand youngsters attended Scout Fun Day.
1985   Gurkha District founded.
       Pre-Cub Grasshopper Section for children 6-8 started.
       Girls admitted to all Scout Troops and Cub Scout Packs.
1986   5,200 campers participated in the Diamond Jubilee Jamboree in Sai Kung
       (December 27th, 1986-January 1st, 1987).
1987   Tang Shiu-kin Scout and Guide Centre in Kwai Chung opened.
       Thirty Scouts participated in the 16th World Jamboree in Australia.
       First "Scouts of the Year" selection held.
1991   Ten-year membership development targets introduced.
       Foundation laying for the new Scout Centre in Kowloon.
       128 Scouts attended the 17th World Jamboree in Korea.
1993   The Scout Centre on Austin Road in Kowloon opened.
1994   Association headquarters moved into the Scout Centre.
1995   Continuous Education Centre founded at the Scout Centre.
       Seventy Scouts attended the 18th World Jamboree in the Netherlands.
       Join-in Jamboree in Tai Tam, Fei Ngon Shan, Pak Sha Wan, and Tung Tze (August
       4th-August 7th).
1996   Fund raising organized on 85th anniv. of Hong Kong Scouting.
1997   Training Branch divided into Training and Programme Branches.
1998   Hong Kong hosted the 19th Asia-Pacific Scout Conference.
       Hongkong Post issued second set of Scout stamps.
       Thirty-nine Scouts attended the 19th World Jamboree in Chile.
1999   The "Outstanding Scout Groups" Scheme introduced.
       Three thousand Scouts attended the Millennium Jamboree in Sai Kung (December
       28th, 1999-January 2nd, 2000).
2000   New Territories East Region created.
       Vision, Mission and Values of the Association launched.
2001   5,800 Scouts attended the 90th Anniv. Jamboree.
       Scout Promise called for doing one's duty to the "country."
2002   The Law Ting Pong Scout Centre for the NT East Region opened.
2003   143 Scouts attended the 20th World Jamboree in Thailand.
2004   Chinese national anthem first sung in the annual rally.
2005   Total membership exceeded one hundred thousand.

2006   "Strategic Planning and Organizational Review" completed.

       4,221 Scouts attended the Metropolitan Jamboree (MetroJam) in West Kowloon (December 27th, 2006-January 1st, 2007).

2007   669 scouts attended the 21st World Jamboree in England.

       1,400 attended Joint-in Jamboree in Sai Kung (July 29th-August 2nd).

       Hongkong Post issued stamps commemorating Scouting's centenary.

       Scout Leadership Institute opened.

2009   Government funding for Sichuan post-earthquake reconstruction projects approved.

2010   23,321 participants in the rally at the Hong Kong Stadium broke a world record for "the most people performing flag signals."

       5,200 Scouts attended the Centennial Jamboree in Lantau (December 27th, 2010-January 1st, 2011).

2011   Scout Association held centennial celebration events in Hong Kong.

       500+ Scouts attended the 22nd World Jamboree in Sweden.

       Sichuan reconstruction: Deyang Youth Palace rebuilt.

2012   Sichuan reconstruction: Mianyang Youth Palace rebuilt.

       "Sichuan Youth Quality Training Project" launched.

       Guizhou Taijiang County's "Hong Kong Scouting Centennial Bala River Bridge" completed.

2013   Scout Association of Hong Kong hosted WOSM's 1st World Scout Education Congress (November 22nd - 24th).

2014   First Aviation Training Centre opened.

2015   600 Scouts attended the 23rd World Jamboree in Japan.

2016   5,500 Scouts attended the 105th Anniversary Jamboree on Lantau (December 23rd - 27th).

2017   "Sichuan Youth Quality Training Project" completed, with many youngsters in Mianyang and Deyang cities served.

2018   Rover Scouting centennial events, Hong Kong Air Scouting Golden Jubilee celebrations.

2019   Hong Kong Scout Centennial Building on Hong Kong Island opened.

       300+ Scouts attended the 24th World Jamboree in USA.

2020   "Hong Kong Scout - Health Guard" programme launched.

       "Hong Kong Scout 110th Anniversary Kick-off Ceremony" (October 30th).

2021   14th World Scout Youth Forum (virtual).

2022   Hong Kong Scout 110th Anniversary celebratory events.

       27th Asia-Pacific Regional Scout Conference (virtual).

2023   460 Scouts attended the 25th World Jamboree in Korea.

       Golden Jubilee of *Hong Kong Scouting*, the local Scout magazine.

Appendix B

The Scout Promise

The Scout Promise commits a Scout to do his or her religious, political, social and "Scout" duties and has evolved over the years. This appendix lists the various versions of the Scout Promise in Hong Kong from the early 1900s to the 2000s, reflecting the contemporary ideals of what a good citizen meant at a particular point in time in Hong Kong, as a British crown colony or as a Special Administrative Region of the People's Republic of China.

Before World War One

1. 1908, *Scouting for Boys*:

On my honour I promise that —
I will do my duty to God and the King.
I will do my best to help others, whatever it costs me.
I know the scout law, and will obey it.

2. 1913, the St. Joseph's Troop enrollment card:

I promise:-
To be loyal to God and the King.
To help others at all times and all costs.
To obey the "Scout Law."

The Interwar Years

3. 1916, *Scouting for Boys*:

I promise, on my honour,
To do my duty to God and the King.
To help other people at all times.
To obey the Scout Law.

4. 1926-31, approved by Clementi, confirmed by Association publication:

In English

On my honour I promise that I will do my best—
To do my duty to God and the King,
To help other people at all times,
To obey the Scout Law.

In Chinese

我願竭盡忠誠 (I will loyally do my best),
對於神及國家元首盡我責任 (to do my duty to God and head of the nation),
隨時扶助他人 (to help others at all times),
遵守童子軍規則 (to obey the Scout Law).

After World War Two

5. 1950-52, local amendments to the *POR*:

For British subjects, regardless of race

On my honour I promise that I will do my best—
To do my duty to God and the King,
To help other people at all times,
To obey the Scout Law.

For non-British subjects

On my honour I promise that I will do my best—
To do my duty to God, the King and my country,
To help other people at all times,
To obey the Scout Law.

6. 1952-54, local amendments to the *POR*:

For British subjects, regardless of race

On my honour I promise that I will do my best—
To do my duty to God and the Queen,
To help other people at all times,
To obey the Scout Law.

For non-British subjects

On my honour I promise that I will do my best—
To do my duty to God, the Queen and the country in which I am living,
To help other people at all times,
To obey the Scout Law.

7. 1955-58, local amendments to the *POR*:

For British subjects, regardless of race

On my honour I promise that I will do my best
To do my duty to God and the Queen,
To help other people at all times,
To obey the Scout Law.

For non-British subjects, in English

On my honour I promise that I will do my best—
To do my duty to God and the country in which I am now living,
To help other people at all times,
To obey the Scout Law.

For non-British subjects, in Chinese

我願以信譽為誓, 竭盡所能 (On my honour, I promise to do my best),
對神及居留地盡我責任 (to do my duty to God and place of residence),
隨時隨地扶助他人 (to help others at all times and in all places),
遵守童子軍規則 (to obey the Scout Law).

8. 1967-1969, post *APR* amendments:

In English

I promise that I will do my best -
To do my duty to God and to the Queen,
To help other people,
and to keep the Scout law.

In Chinese

我願以信譽為誓, 竭盡所能 (On my honour, I promise to do my best),
對神明, 對本土, 盡責任 (to do my duty to deity and my territory),
對別人, 要幫助 (to help other people),
對規律, 必遵行 (to obey the Scout Law).

9. 1979-80, 1st editions of the *POR* of the independent Hong Kong Scout Association:

(Same as the 1967-69 versions)

10. 1987-94, revised editions of the *POR*:

In English

On my honour, I promise that I will do my best -
To do my duty to God and to the Territory,
To help other people,
and to keep the Scout law.

In Chinese

(Same as the 1967-69 version)

11. December 2001, approved by the Executive Committee of the Association:

In English

On my honour, I promise that I will do my best -
To do my duty to God and to my country,
To help other people,
and to keep the Scout law.

In Chinese

我願以信譽為誓, 竭盡所能 (On my honour, I promise to do my best),
對神明, 對國家, 盡責任 (to do my duty to deity and the country),
對別人, 要幫助 (to help other people),
對規律, 必遵行 (to obey the Scout Law).

Appendix C

Key Leaders

The Chief Scout (formerly Colony Chief Scout), figurehead of Hong Kong Scouting, has always been the governor or, since 1997, the Chief Executive of Hong Kong. The president of the Association is typically a prominent member of the community, often a leading member of the judiciary, a member of the Executive or the Legislative Council, a senior government official, or a business leader. The Chief Commissioner (formerly Colony Commissioner), a volunteer appointed by the Chief Scout, is the chief executive of the movement. He is usually assisted by one to several Deputy Chief Commissioner(s) and a number of Assistant Commissioners, all volunteers, and the Chief Scout Executive (formerly Administrative/Executive Commissioner), who is head of the paid staff. The chairman of the executive committee of the Scout Council (formerly chairman of the Scout Council) is a post created after WWII. Two other key officers of the Executive Committee are the Secretary and the Treasurer. This appendix lists some of the key leaders over the years and their terms of office.

(Colony) Chief Scouts:

Sir Francis Henry May (梅含理), 1915 - 1916[1]

Sir Reginald Edward Stubbs (司徒拔), 1920 - 1925[2]

Sir Cecil Clementi (金文泰), 1925 - 1930

Sir William Peel (貝璐), 1930 - 1935

Sir Andrew Caldecott (郝德傑), 1935 - 1937

Sir Geoffrey Northcote (羅富國), 1937 - 1941

Sir Mark Aitchison Young (楊慕琦), 1941 - 1947[3]

Sir Alexander Grantham (葛量洪), 1947 -1957

Sir Robert Brown Black (柏立基), 1958 - 1964

---

1   May was governor of Hong Kong from 1912 to 1918, but he only became the Chief Scout when the Hong Kong Boy Scouts Association was formed in late 1915, and left that post in August 1916, when the association was disbanded.

2   Stubbs was governor from 1919 to 1925, but he only became the Chief Scout when the association was revived by him in August 1920.

3   Young came to Hong Kong in September 1941 and became the Chief Scout. But as he was interned from December 1941 to 1945, and did not return to Hong Kong as the governor again until May 1946, he effectively only resumed his duties as a Chief Scout from that time till May 1947, when he left Hong Kong again.

Sir David Clive Crosbie Trench (戴麟趾), 1964 - 1971

Sir Murray MacLehose (麥理浩), 1971 - 1982

Sir Edward Youde (尤德), 1982 - 1986

Sir David Wilson (衛奕信), 1987 - 1992

The Hon. Christopher Patten (彭定康), 1992 -1997[1]

The Hon. Tung Chee Hwa (董建華), 1997 - 2005[2]

The Hon. Sir Donald Tsang Yam-kuen (曾蔭權), 2005 - 2012 [3]

The Hon. Leung Chun-ying (梁振英), 2012 - 2017

The Hon. Mrs. Carrie Lam Cheng Yuet-ngor (林鄭月娥), 2017 - 2022

The Hon. John Lee Ka-chiu (李家超), 2022 -

Presidents:

Lady May (梅含理夫人), 1915 - 1916

The Hon. P. H. Holyoak, 1920 - 1926

The Hon. Dr. R. H. Kotewall (羅旭龢), 1926 - 1934

Edward Cock, 1934 - 1940

C. G. Sollis (梳利士), 1940 - 1941

The Hon. Sir Arthur D. Morse (摩士), 1947 - 1953[4]

G. E. Marden (馬頓), 1953 - 1959[5]

D. Benson (賓臣), 1959 - 1964

The Hon. G. R. Ross (羅斯), 1964 - 1982

1 Patten was the last governor to assume the post of the Chief Scout, and held that post until July 1, 1997, when Hong Kong was handed over to the PRC.
2 Tung was the first Chief Executive of the Special Administrative Region of Hong Kong to assume the post of the Chief Scout, after Hong Kong's handover to the PRC.
3 Tsang was knighted by Prince Charles in 1997, hours before the handover.
4 Morse was absent in Scout events from 1946 to early 1947, including the farewell rally for Young in April 1947. His first appearance as president of the association was with Grantham in September 1947. He was knighted in June 1949.
5 Marden's name was sometimes translated into Chinese as 馬登. Here the translation used in the annual reports of the association is adopted.

The Hon. Sir Denys Roberts (羅弼時), 1982 -1988

The Hon. Sir Ti Liang Yang (楊鐵樑), 1988 - 1998

The Hon. Mr. Justice Patrick Chan (陳兆愷), 1998 - 2008

The Hon. Chief Justice Geoffrey Ma Tao-li (馬道立), 2008 - 2018[1]

The Hon. Mr. Justice Jeremy Poon Shiu Chor (潘兆初), 2018 –

Chief Commissioners (Colony Commissioners):

Rear Admiral Robert Hamilton Anstruther (安史德), 1915 - 1916[2]

Lieutenant Colonel F. J. Bowen (寶雲), 1920 -1921

Rev. G. T. Waldegrave (華德利), 1921 - 1934

The Rt. Rev. Bishop N. V. Halward (候利華), 1934 - 1950[3]

F. E. C. C. Quah (柯昭璋), 1950 - 53

D. W. Luke (陸榮生), 1953 - 1954

J. W. Cockburn (高本), 1954 - 1963

C. K. Lo (羅徵勤), 1963 - 1973

Henry C. Ma (馬基), 1973 - 1984

Dr. Chau Cham-son (周湛燊), 1985 - 1996[4]

John Hui Chiu Yin (許招賢), 1997 - 2003

Pau Shiu Hung (鮑紹雄), 2004 - 2007

Anthony Chan Kit-chu (陳傑柱), 2007 - 2011

Cheung Chi-sun (張智新), 2011 - 2015

---

1   Ma was Chief Judge of the High Court from 2003 to August 2010, and became the Chief Justice of the Court of Final Appeal in Hong Kong in September 2010.

2   Anstruther became the Commissioner upon the formation of the Hong Kong Boy Scouts Association in 1915. At the time, he was first referred to as a commodore, and then a rear admiral. The association was disbanded in 1916. Also, Anstruther had only served as the senior officer on the coast of China from 1914 to 1916, suggesting that he left the colony in 1916.

3   Halward was interned in China during the Japanese occupation of Hong Kong. He was consecrated an assistant Bishop in late 1946.

4   Chau was Chief Commissioner for two terms until the end of 1992, but after a six-month break as Deputy Chief Commissioner during which Kenneth K. W. Lo (盧觀榮) served as an interim Chief Commissioner, he was re-elected the Chief Commissioner as of July 1, 1993, and served till end of 1996.

Ng Ah-ming (吳亞明), 2015 - 2019

Joseph Lau (劉彥樑), 2019 - 2023

Dr. Wilson Lai Wai-sang (黎偉生), 2023 -

Chairmen (of the Executive Committee) of the Scout Council:

F. C. Clemo (克利模), 1952 - 1958[1]

The Hon. G. R. Ross (羅斯), 1958 - 1964

C. J. G. Lowe (盧家禮), 1964 - 1973

C. M. Leung (梁超文), 1973 - 1983

Dr. Chau Cham-son (周湛燊), 1983 - 1984

Kenneth K. W. Lo (盧觀榮), 1984 - 1990

C. P. Lee (李銓標), 1990 - 1994

Philip Ching (程耀樑), 1994 - 1999

Leung On-fook (梁安福), 1999 - 2009

Dr. Patrick Wu Po Kong (伍步剛), 2009 - 2012

Li Fung-lok (李逢樂), 2012 - 2016

David Yip Wing-shing (葉永成), 2016 -

---

1   The appointment of Clemo (then translated into Chinese as 克里姆) was first noted in a contemporary report in 1953, which indicated that he was still the chairman of the Executive Committee of the Scout Council, suggesting that he had been in that position at least from 1952. Before 1952, reports of annual gatherings typically only mentioned the president (Morse), besides the Commissioner. This position was initially entitled both Chairman of Scout Council and Chairman of the Executive Committee of the Scout Council, but since the late 1970s it became simply the Chairman of the Executive Committee.

Appendix D

Membership Statistics

Membership definitions evolved, generally covering more membership categories over the years. Pre-WWI statistics are from contemporary reports or manual census logbooks in Gilwell Archives. From inter-war years onward till today, statistics are mostly official census numbers in annual reports or census returns in Hong Kong Scout Archives. Membership statistics do not exist from 1916-1919, when Scouting was inactive; and from 1942-1944, when Scouting was prohibited.

Year	Membership	Year	Membership
1910	28	1936	713
1911	N/A	1937	842
1912	30	1938	911
1913	60	1939	1,149
1914	78	1940	1,147
1915	155	1941	1,542
1916	N/A	1942	N/A
1917	N/A	1943	N/A
1918	N/A	1944	N/A
1919	N/A	1945	952
1920	150[5]	1946	2,370
1921	374	1947	N/A
1922	258	1948	2,284
1923	219	1949	2,245
1924	355	1950	1,848
1925	426	1951	1,945
1926	472	1952	2,323
1927	559	1953	2,983
1928	620	1954	3,726
1929	608	1955	3,796
1930	621	1956	3,890
1931	569	1957	4,740
1932	656	1958	5,724
1933	582	1959	6,289
1934	682	1960	7,033
1935	670	1961	7,273

Year	Membership	Year	Membership
1962	9,133	1993	53,328
1963	10,955	1993	52,878
1964	10,398	1995	55,094
1965	12,332	1996	53,049
1966	13,216	1997	55,139
1967	14,967	1998	63,365
1968	17,002	1999	69,121
1969	20,406	2000	74,147
1970	21,137	2001	80,923
1971	23,049	2002	89,925
1972	23,148	2003	95,615
1973	24,573	2004	99,591
1974	25,432	2005	100,223
1975	27,041	2006	102,630
1976	30,137	2007	96,682
1977	32,855	2008	96,648
1978	33,534	2009	95,877
1979	35,514	2010	95,494
1980	40,275	2011	96,296
1981	38,850	2012	95,128
1982	38,813	2013	96,324
1983	41,611	2014	97,190
1984	46,110	2015	98,224
1985	45,221	2016	98,190
1986	46,320	2017	100,829
1987	47,343	2018	102,150
1988	50,978	2019	100,643
1989	57,846	2020	85,904
1990	56,347	2021	84,432
1991	56,172	2022	88,180
1992	54,932		

Membership Statistics by Year, 1910-2022[1]

---

1   Membership number for 1910 was the number of boys present at the inauguration parade with Governor May, as reported in the *SCMP*, May 11, 1910; for 1912 was the number of boys inspected by B-P in April 1912, as reported in the *HKDP*, April 22, 1912; for 1913 was the number of boys enrolled in September 1913, as reported in the *Bulletin of Catholic Ladies Union*, October 10, 1913; and for 1914 and 1915 are numbers from the logbook on censuses in Gilwell Archives. Statistics for 1920 to 1941 are mostly from the annual reports of the British Boy Scouts Association, except for the number for 1920, which came from the logbook at the Gilwell Archives; the numbers for 1922, 1928, 1933 and 1939, which came from *75 Years of Hong Kong Scouting*, App. III; and the number for 1941, which came from *HKSH*, November 21, 1941. Statistics for 1945 to 2022 are from the annual reports of the Hong Kong (Boy) Scout Association, supplemented by the census returns in Hong Kong Scout Archives.

It should be noted that over the years, these membership totals included boys of different age ranges and then also girls, as they became Rover Scouts, Senior/Venture Scouts, Cub Scouts (Wolf Cubs), Grasshoppers (pre-Cubs) Scouts, and Friends of Scouting members. The membership statistics also included leaders, commissioners, and lay supporters and advisers. As membership categories became increasingly varied over the years, it is instructive to look at more detailed breakdowns of the membership statistics in different years. The table on the next page compares membership statistics by category in the years 1957, 1977 and 2010:[1]

Category	1957	1977	2010
Grasshopper Scouts	0	0	11,529
Cub Scouts	1,469	9,984	24,742
Boy Scouts	1,865	9,944	15,121
Senior/Rover/Service/Venture Scouts	965	3,792	5,481
Leaders, Commissioners & Staff	441	4,138	11,522
Lay Supporters	0	2,590	6,759
FOS Members	0	2,407	20,018
Overseas/Associate Members	0	0	322
Total Membership	**4,740**	**32,855**	**95,494**

Membership Statistics by Category, 1957, 1977, 2010

To aid understanding of population penetration of Scouting over time, some comparative figures may be helpful. The table on the next page compares Scout membership per thousand people in the population in Hong Kong, Singapore, and Britain at six different points in time, namely pre-WWI (1915), the mid-interwar period (1930/31), just before the fall of Hong Kong (1939/41), the post-war mid-1960s (1964), the time when Hong Kong Scout Association became independent (1977), and the present day (2009).[2] As can be seen from the table, penetration of Scouting in Britain was way ahead of both Hong Kong and Singapore until the most recent decades, and Singapore had higher penetration ratios than Hong Kong in the first four periods. Scout membership in Hong Kong grew consistently and exceeded that in Singapore in absolute terms in the first postwar period. By the 2000s, Hong Kong Scouting's population penetration ratios exceeded those of both Britain and Singapore.

---

1   Census Reports, 1957, 1977, 2010, the Hong Kong Scout Archives.
2   Scout membership numbers for Hong Kong in 1915, 1930, 1941, 1964, 1977 and 2009 from Appendix D; for Singapore in 1915 from the manual logbook on censuses and warrants, the Gilwell Archives, in 1930, 1939, 1964 and 1977 from Tang and Wan, *Scouting in Singapore*, 271, and in 2009 from the *Annual Report 2009* (Singapore: the Singapore Scout Association, 2010); for Britain in 1915, 1930, 1940, 1964 and 1977 from "UK and World Census Figures," http://www.scoutbase. org.uk/library/history/census.htm, and in 2009/10 from *Annual Report 2009/10* (London: the Scout Association, 2010). Population numbers from Jan Lahmeyer, "Populstat," http://www.populstat.info/, *Hong Kong Statistics, 1947-1967* (Hong Kong: Census and Statistics Department, 1969), http://www.gov.hk/en/about/abouthk/factsheets/docs/population.pdf; http:// www;singstat. gov.sg/stats/themes/people/hist/popn.html; and http://www.statistics.gov.uk/cci/nugget. asp?id=6 (accessed on Nov. 20, 2010).

Location	Scouts	Population	Scouts/1000 People
Pre-WWI (1915)			
Hong Kong	**155**	**509,200**	**0.30**
Singapore	149	349,000	0.43
Britain	152,000	40,129,700	3.79
Mid-interwar (1930/31)			
Hong Kong	**621**	**840,473**	**0.74**
Singapore	711	557,700	1.27
Britain	438,098	44,937,400	9.75
Late-interwar (1939/41)			
Hong Kong	**1,542**	**1,600,000**	**0.96**
Singapore	2,182	727,600	3.00
Britain	343,000	48,220,000	7.11
Early Postwar (1964)			
Hong Kong	**10,398**	**3,594,200**	**2.89**
Singapore	6,525	1,841,600	3.54
Britain	540,128	54,066,000	9.99
Independence (1977)			
Hong Kong	**32,855**	**4,514,000**	**7.28**
Singapore	12,925	2,325,300	5.56
Britain	627,569	55,852,000	11.24
Post-handover (2009)			
Hong Kong	**95,877**	**7,003,700**	**13.69**
Singapore	10,292	4,987,600	2.06
Britain	499,889	61,792,000	8.09

Population Penetration by Country by Year

These comparisons are not strictly "apple-to-apple," as the three Scout associations have different membersip policies. On the other hand, using "apple-to-apple" comparisons, Hong Kong still had significantly higher population penetration ratios in 2009. Taking into consideration only Cub Scouts, Boy Scouts, Venture Scouts and Rover Scouts (Singapore does not have Grasshoppers) would result in penetration ratios of 6.6 for Hong Kong versus 1.8 for Singapore. Taking into consideration only youth members (including Grasshoppers for Hong Kong and Beavers for Britain) would result in penetration ratios of 8.2 for Hong Kong and 6.6 for Britain.[1]

---

1   *Annual Report 2009* (Singapore: the Singapore Scout Association, 2010); *Annual Report 2009-10* (Hong Kong: the Scout Association of Hong Kong, 2010); and *The Scout Association's Annual Report, 2009/10* (London: the Scout Association, 2010).

Bibliography

This bibliography covers primary and secondary sources referred to or cited in this book and useful further reading materials. Unpublished archival materials are grouped under individual archives, and then listed alphabetically or based on the record series numbers provided by the archives, if available. Organizational publications are further broken down into Scout and Guide publications (which include all works by Baden-Powell, but only other works on Scouting if published by a Scout or Guide association), school and other organizational publications, and government publications. Newspapers are listed alphabetically by names only, followed by their names in Chinese and initials, if any. All other primary and secondary sources, including books, journal articles, dissertations/theses and Internet sources, are listed alphabetically in the last section of the bibliography.

A. Archival Materials:

1. *The Hong Kong Scout Archives, the Scout Association of Hong Kong*

Census Reports, 1950-2010.

Circulars, 1946-2008:

> Administrative, No. 01/2001, January 15, 2001.
> Hudson, May 20, 1953.
> Programme Branch, July 15, 2008.
> Questions and answers during an investiture, 1946.
> St. George's Day Rally, 1960-64.
> The Translation Board, July 1955.
> Tenderfoot test, 18th April 1946.
> Underprivileged Groups, June 17, 1957.

Folders, 1940s-1996:

> The 1967 Riots, 1967.
> The Diamond Jubilee Jamboree, 1971.
> The Friends of Scouting, 1968-1977.
> George Witchell's visits, the 1970s.
> The Golden Jubilee Jamboree, 1961.
> Guides and Scouts Joint Seminar, March-April, 1968.
> The Gurkha District folder, 1985-1996.
> Henry Ma Papers, 1940s-1960s.
> Lai Yuk-shu folder, 1950s.
> Handicapped Scouting, 1957/63.
> The Jubilee Jamboree, 1957.
> The Organising Commissioner, 1952-1958.

Project Q, 1960s-1990s.
The Silver Jubilee District, 1976-80.
Project Y, 1975-76.
The Scout and Guide Coordinating Board, 1970-1975.
The Yee Wo Street Incident, November 1967.

Interviews, 2004-2011:

Chau Cham-son, April 27, 2010; May 3, 2010.
Sammy Chiu Suk-ming, November 8, 2005.
Robert Chow, April 7, 2010.
Liu Cheuk-wing, March 4, 2004.
Solomon Kui-nang Lee, October 30, 2010.
Tse Bing-fui, October 26, 2004; December 14, 2004.
Tsin Chi-ming, March 14, 2011.
Ambrose Wong, December 14, 2004.

Yeung Chun-man, November 2004.

Letters, emails and memoranda, 1916-2013:

Braga, Stuart to Kua and Kua to Braga, November 3, 2017 to July 3, 2018 (various).
Cockburn to Cooke, August 14, 1958.
Cockburn to Cooke, May 8, 1961.
Cockburn to Ma, May 17, 1960.
Cooke to Cockburn, May 1, 1961.
Grantham to Heywood, December 15, 1951.
Green to Lo, September 18, 1967.
Green to Lo, December 1, 1970.
Ingles (secretary to Black) to Cockburn, May 6, 1961.
Law Kwan-fook to Ma, September 1, 1960.
Ma to Aide-de-camp of the governor, c. Dec. 1974.
Ma to Cockburn, November 23, 1960.
Ma to Gover, May 21, 1952.
Ma to the Junior Chamber of Commerce, October 18, 1955.
Ma to Steele, December 13, 1955.
Noble to Ma, July 6, 1975.
Noble to MacLehose, December 14, 1972.
Ozorio, Anne to Kua, February 2, 2013
Potter, Sheila to Kua and Kua to Potter, December 19, 2017 to July 9, 2018 (various).
Rayner, Eva R. S. to Boy Scouts of Hong Kong, October 1, 1916 (scanned copy)
Ross to the British association, November 8, 1972.
Ross to Noble, February 2, 1977.
"Schedule of Accommodation - Hong Kong Scout Centre," September 1970.
Siebold of the World Scout Bureau, November 16, 1973.
Siebold of the World Scout Bureau, July 19, 1974.
Steen, Jan van der to Kua, May 18, 31, 2012
Szeto Wah to Ma, April 19, 1973.

Meeting minutes, 1947-2006:

The Chief Commissioner's Council, July 8, 1967.
The Chief Commissioner's Council, December 7, 1967.
The Chief Commissioner's Council, November 13, 2006.
The Council Meeting, the Girl Guides Association, January 6, 1955.

Kowloon Scouters' Meeting, c. January 1947-48.

Photograph albums, 1920s-1960s:

Blason, 1920s-1930s.
Henry Ma, 1950s-1960s.
C. C. Quah, 1950s.
Waldegrave, 1920s-1930s.
C. H. Wong, 1950s-1960s.
(Plus many others, not organized by individual albums.)

Reports, 1950-2010:

China Exchanges, 2007, 2010.
Dahl's visit, c. January 1950.
The Future Status of the Hong Kong Branch, Jan. 1971.
George Witchell, June 18, 1960.
List of Projects, October 1975.
List of Awardees, 1984-2010.
Reconstruction in Sichuan, July 2009.
List of "Scouts of the Year," 1987-90.
Law Kwan-fook, Resettlement Scouting, April 28, 1966.
大同地域未來動向 (Future Direction of the Brotherhood Region), May 11, 1985.

2. *The Gilwell Archives, the British Scout Association, Gilwell, London*

Letters, 1913-1951:

Baden-Powell to Albert Edwards, November 20, 1913.
Baden-Powell to T. C. Fry, March 8, 1916 (Founders Papers, Patriotism, 1916-31).
Brownrigg to Edwards, October 14, 1913.
Brownrigg to James, April 23, 1913.
Brownrigg to Keswick, June 18, 1913.
Brownrigg to Smith, September 22, 1913.
Edwards to the Boy Scouts Association, September 13, 1913.
Edwards to the Boy Scouts Association, October 4, 1913.
Edwards to Brownrigg, November 20, 1913.
Gover to Dahl, October 20, 1951.
Pockson to Butterworth, October 18, 1945.
Smith to the Boy Scouts Association, August 18, 1913.
Waldegrave to Butterworth, June 19, June 23, and September 29, 1925; May 31, 1926; and August 26, 1929.

Reports, 1926-1945:

Muffett to International Relief Service, December 2 and 15, 1945.
Waldegrave on Roman Catholic Troops and Scouts, c.1926/27.
Waldegrave on Rovering in Hong Kong, 1930.

Other documents, 1911-1931:

Enrollment card, St. Josephs' College Troop, c.1913.
Manual logbooks on early censuses and warrants, 1911-1931.
Registration Form ("B"), St. Joseph's College Troop, April 2, 1914.

3. *The SOAS Archive, University of London, London*

Griffith John College Papers, London Missionary Society Collection, now incorporated into the Council for World Mission Collection.
Scott Family Papers (PP MS 49), esp. the papers, correspondences and diaries of M. W. Scott.

4. *The Public Records Office, Hong Kong*

HKRS 41-1-1157, "Educational Work in Stanley Internment Camp," Secretariat 1/179/1946.
HKRS 41-1-6799, "Stanley Reformatory School, Scout Troop Formed by the Boys of the," Secretariat 10/33711, 1951.
HKRS 41-1-7360, "Boys in Stanley Reformatory School," Secretariat 2/289/52, 1952.
HKRS 41-2-274, "Youth Rally at the Hong Kong Stadium," Secretariat GR 1/761/59.
HKRS 58-1-75-191, "Application for permission to use land at DD 453, Lot No. 727," CSO 1856/1915.
HKRS 58-1-135-85, "Application from the Commissioner Hongkong Boys [*sic*] Scouts Association for an area of land at Rennie's Mills for training purposes," CSO 1441/1925.
HKRS 156-1-3331, "Boy Scout Training Camp—Sai Wan (RBL 134 & 171), 1951."
HKRS 156-1-3444, "Boy Scouts Association Headquarters (K.I. L. 6248), Application for site at Cox's Road, Kowloon…, 1952-60," ENV 8/576/52.
HKRS 163-9-622, "The Governor's Fund for Recreation, Donations to, 1970-71."
HKRS 163-10-70, "Girl Guides in Hong Kong, Constitution," CR1/561/73, 1973-1976.
HKRS 264-1-11, "General Correspondence Files (Confidential), 1946-1975," Letter from Grantham, September 15, 1947.
HKRS 264-1-19, "General Correspondence Files (Confidential), 1946-1975," Despatch submitted by Sir Mark Young 28th December, 1941, *Third Supplement to The London Gazette*, published in 1946.
HKRS 365-1-86-1-10, Peter Wood, "Training for a New Life," (the Hong Kong Sea School).
HKRS 684-5-40, "Future Expansion of Scouting in the N. T., 1978-93."
HKRS 894, "General Correspondence Files relating to Community Organisations, 1962-1988."
HKRS 921-1-94, "The Scout Association of Hong Kong (Chief Scout), 1971-1977."
HKRS 921-1-95, "The Scout Association of Hong Kong, 1978-82."
HKRS 921-1-96, "The Scout Association of Hong Kong (Chief Scout), 1983-1986."
HKRS 921-1-97, "The Scout Association of Hong Kong, 1982-1988."

5. *The National Archives, Kew Garden, London*

CO 129/54/1, "Hong Kong Volunteer Corps: Enlistment of Foreign Subjects."
CO 273/561/13, "Kuomintang: Organization and activities in Hong Kong and Malaya, 1929-30."
CO 323/882/60, "Supply of Uniforms to the Boy Scout Movement in Colonies and Protectorates, 1921-23. "
CO 323/1808/6, "Evacuation of British Families from Hong Kong, 1940."
CO 537/5024, "Hong Kong Defence: Refugee Nationalist Troops etc. attempting to enter the Colony, 1949."
CO 795/72/7, "The Pathfinder and Wayfarer Movements, Northern Rhodesia, 1934-35. "
CO 967/70, "Semi-official and personal correspondence between Secretary of State and Governors Sir Geoffry Northcote and Sir Mark Young, 1941-45."
CO 968/120/1, "Sir Robert Kotewall, 1945."
DO 35/487/3, "Boy Scout and Girl Guide Movement in the High Commissioner Territories, 1936."

FO 371/105352, "Deportation of Members of the China Youth Anti-Communist National Salvation Corps from Hong Kong, 1953."

FO 371/127519, "Visit of the Formosan Boy Scouts to attend the World Jamboree, 1957."

PC 8/1275, "Charter: Boy Scouts Association, Power under Charter to form Boy Scout Units in British Protectorates and British Mandated Territories, 1931."

WO 339/69095, "H. Spink, 1914-1922."

B. Organizational publications:

1. *Scout/Guide publications*

5-Year Plan of Development, 1967/68 - 1971/72. Hong Kong: the Boy Scouts Association, 1966.

13th World Jamboree 第十三屆世界大露營, *August 1971.* Hong Kong: the Scout Association, 1971.

Annual Reports. U.S.: Boy Scouts of America.

Annual Reports. Canada: Scouts Canada.

Annual Reports. Hong Kong: Hong Kong Girl Guides Association (the Girl Guides Association, Hong Kong Branch).

Annual Reports. Hong Kong: Scout Association of Hong Kong (The Boy Scouts Association, Hong Kong Branch).

Annual Reports. Hong Kong: The Brotherhood Region, Scout Association of Hong Kong.

Annual Reports. London: The Scout Association (The Boy Scouts Association).

Annual Reports. Singapore: The Singapore Scout Association.

Armstrong, E. A., *The Scout Law* 童子軍規律. Hong Kong: The Boy Scouts Association, Hong Kong Branch, 1931.

Baden-Powell, R. S. S., *Aims, Methods and Needs.* London, Boy Scouts Association: [1929].

Baden-Powell, R. S. S., *Boy Scouts: A Suggestion.* London, 1907.

Baden-Powell, R. S. S., *Boy Scouts beyond the Seas: My World Tour.* London: C Arthur Pearson Ltd., 1913.

Baden-Powell, R. S. S., *Boy Scouts in the Year of the War, 1914, by the Chief Scout.* London: Boy Scouts Association, 1914.

Baden-Powell, R. S. S., "Boy Scout Scheme," London, 1908.

Baden-Powell, R. S. S., *Report on the Boy Scouts, 1910.* London: Headquarters, 1910.

Baden-Powell, R. S. S., *Rovering to Success, 1922.* London: Jenkins, 1963.

Baden-Powell, R. S. S., *Scouting for Boys.* London: C. Arthur Pearson, 1916.

Boy's Life, the Boy Scouts' Magazine, May 1917. New York: Boy Scouts of America, 1917.

"Boy Scouts and Girl Scouts: Membership and Units," http://www.allcountries.org/uscensus/443_boy_scouts_and_girl_scouts_membership.html (accessed May 10, 2010).

The Chief Scout's Advance Party Report (APR). London: The Boy Scouts Association, 1966.

Cub Scout Training: Hong Kong, the Official Handbook of the Scout Association, Hong Kong Branch. Hong Kong: Scout Association of Hong Kong, 1969.

Diamond Jubilee, 1916-1976. Hong Kong: The Girl Guides Association, Hong Kong Branch, 1976.

Fan Xiao-liu 范曉六 (ed.), *Zhong Guo Tong Zi Jun Shi* 中國童子軍史 (History of Scouting in China). Shanghai: 225 Tong Zi Jun Shu Bao Shi, 1935.

The Fulcrum: the Magazine of the China Fleet Deep Sea Scouts. Hong Kong: the China Fleet Deep Sea Scouts, 1939.

Golden Jubilee Cub Rally 金禧年全港小狼大會. Hong Kong: The Boy Scouts Association, Hong Kong Branch, 1961.

Good will Visit to Malaysia, Singapore, Indonesia and Thailand. Hong Kong: the Scout

Association of Hong Kong, 1977.

Guiding in Hong Kong 香港女童軍運動. Hong Kong: Hong Kong Girl Guides Association, 1986.

Headquarters Bulletin. Hong Kong: The Boy Scouts Association, Hong Kong Branch, 1954-56.

Headquarters Gazette. London: The Boy Scouts Association, 1909-1922.

Hong Kong Scouting/Hong Kong Scouting Magazine. Hong Kong: Scout Association of Hong Kong, 1973-2011.

Hong Kong Scouting Gazette, the 香港童軍會刊. Hong Kong: The Boy Scout Association, Hong Kong Branch, 1941, 1946-1956.

The Imperial Jamboree, 1924. London: Boy Scouts Association, 1924.

Inauguration Ceremony 成立典禮專刊. Hong Kong: Kwun Tong District Local Association, 1967.

Kua, Paul (ed.), *21ˢᵗ World Jamboree: Hong Kong Contingent, England, 2007.* Hong Kong: Scout Association of Hong Kong, 2007.

Kua, Paul, "The Founding Year Myth: 1910 or 1911?", *Hong Kong Scouting*, vols. 286-9, Feburary-May, 2008, 18, 20, 14, 22.

Leung Siu-kei 梁肇祺, Leung Wai-fan 梁惠芬, and Wu Po-sau 胡寶秀 (eds.), *75 Years of Hong Kong Scouting, 1911-1986* 香港童軍七十五. Hong Kong: Scout Association of Hong Kong, 1987.

Lo Wai Shing (ed.), *Directory of Recipients of the King's Scout Award, the Queen's Scout Award and the Hong Kong Special Administrative Region Scout Award* 榮譽童軍獎章持有人名錄. Hong Kong: Scout Association of Hong Kong, 2000.

Local Amendments to Rule 3 of the POR, 1952-54, Hong Kong: The Boy Scouts Association, Hong Kong Branch, 1952, 1954.

Local Amendments to Policy Organisation and Rules, 1958. Hong Kong: The Boy Scouts Association, Hong Kong Branch, 1958.

Het Padvindersblad (official organ of NIPV), Bandung: Vereeniging Nederlandsch Indische Padvinders (NIPV), Jan. 20, 1930.

The Piokeld Post, Hong Kong: the Services Rover Crew, 1946, 1951.

The Policy, Organisation, and Rules, 1933. London: The Boy Scouts Association, Imperial Headquarters, 1933.

The Policy, Organisation, and Rules, 1933. London: The Boy Scouts Association, 1959.

The Policy, Organisation, and Rules of the Boy Scouts Association. London: The Boy Scouts Association, 1964.

The Policy, Organisation, and Rules, Part One, 1st edition. Hong Kong: Scout Association of Hong Kong, 1979.

The Policy, Organisation, and Rules, Part One, 1st edition (Chinese) 香港童軍總會政策、組織及規條第一冊(中文版). Hong Kong: Scout Association of Hong Kong, 1980.

The Policy, Organisation, and Rules. Hong Kong: Scout Association of Hong Kong, 1987.

The Policy, Organisation, and Rules, Revised edition. Hong Kong: Scout Association of Hong Kong, 1993.

The Policy, Organisation, and Rules 香港童軍總會政策、組織及規條. Hong Kong: Scout Association of Hong Kong, 1994.

Ruo Neng Tong Zi Jun Huo Dong 弱能童子軍活動 (Activities of the Handicapped Boy Scouts, in Chinese). Hong Kong: The Boy Scouts Association, Hong Kong Branch, c. 1962.

The Scout, London: The Boy Scouts Association, 1908-1910.

The Scout Association, "The History of Scouting," http://www.scoutbase.org.uk/ library/ history/ (accessed February 10, 2010).

The Scout Association, "The Origins of the Wood Badge," http://www.scoutbase.org.uk/ library/hqdocs/facts/pdfs/fs145001.pdf (accessed August 1, 2008).

The Scout Association, "UK and World Census Figures," http://www.scoutbase.org.uk/ library/ history/census.htm (accessed April 1, 2010).

Scout Association of Hong Kong, "159th East Kowloon Group," http://www. 159.bravehost.

com/page3.html (accessed July 1, 2009).

Scout Association of Japan, *History of Scout Movement in Japan* 日本ボーイスカウト運動史. Tokyo: ボーイスカウト日本連盟, 2005.

Scout Association of Japan, 財団法人ボーイスカウト日本連盟平成20度事業報告書 (Annual Report). Japan, 2008.

The Scout Bulletin/Bulletin 月刊. Hong Kong: The Scout Association/The Boy Scouts Association, Hong Kong Branch, 1957-73.

The Scouter, London: The Boy Scout Association, 1923-1970.

Scouting, London: The Scout Association, 1975.

Scouting in Hong Kong 童子軍運動在香港. Hong Kong: Boy Scouts Association, 1957.

Scouts International Relief Service: A Record of Work Done, 1944-1946. London: Reprinted from *Jamboree*, September, 1946.

Scouts Canada Ordinary-member Unity Taskforce Association (Scout *eh*!), "Stemming Membership Decline," http://scouteh.ca/resources/ScoutEh-membership.php (accessed January 20, 2009).

Silvestre, J. Plaridel, *A Preliminary Report on the Management/Organisation Audit of the Hong Kong Branch, the Scout Association,* Hong Kong: the Scout Association, October 1973.

Silver Wolf, The, no. 5, vol. IV, 1925. Hong Kong: The Boy Scout Association, Hong Kong.

"Stemming Membership Decline," http://scouteh.ca/resources/ScoutEh-membership.php (accessed Jan. 20, 2009)

Tan, Kevin Y. L. and Wan Meng-Hao, *Scouting in Singapore, 1910-2000.* Singapore: Singapore Scout Association, 2002.

Vane, Sir Francis, *The Boy Knight: Essays and Addresses on the Evolution of the Boy Scout Movement.* The Council of National Peace Scouts, 1910.

Work Report of the Preparatory Bureau of the Boy Scouts Association of China 中國童子軍總會籌備處工作報告, Nanking, 1934.

World Scout Foundation, Annual Report 2005: Peace is not as simple as black and white. Geneva: World Scout Foundation, 2005.

World Scouting (Geneva: World Scout Bureau, 1973), July-September, 1973.

World Organization of the Scout Movement, website, http://www.scout.org/ (accessed May 10, 2010).

World Organization of the Scout Movement, *The Essential Characteristics of Scouting.* Geneva: World Organization of the Scout Movement, 1998.

Worldwide Survey on Young People Over 15 in Scouting. Geneva: WOSM, 2001.

WOSM, "Census," http://www.scout.org/en/about_scouting/facts_figures/census (accessed May 1, 2010).

2. *School/other organizational publications:*

Annual Reports. Hong Kong: the Boys' Brigade.

Annual Reports, Hong Kong: the Boys' and Girls' Clubs Association.

Bao Rui-mei 鮑瑞美, "Hong Kong's School for the Deaf (香港真铎启音学校)," http://www. etabc.com/html/article-22573.html (accessed July 28, 2008).

The Boys' Brigade, Hong Kong: 50th Anniversary Journal, 1959-2009. Hong Kong: The Boys' Brigade, 2009.

Boys' Brigade Gazette, 1909-12. London: The Boys' Brigade.

Bulletin of Catholic Ladies Union. Hong Kong: the Catholic Church (?), October 10, 1913.

Children's Voice 童聲. Hong Kong: the Christian Children's Fund, 1955.

The Chimes 鐘聲報. Hong Kong: St. Stephens College, 1939.

The Chinese Methodist Church: Commemorative Issue of the 100th Anniversary in Hong Kong 1884-1984 循道衞理教會:香港開基一百週年紀念特刊, 1884-1984. Hong Kong: the Chinese Methodist Church, 1985.

The *Church Review.* Hong Kong: Stanley Interment Camp, July 1942.

Communist Youth League of China, http://www.ccyl.org.cn/ (accessed May 1, 2010).

The *Education Journal*. Hong Kong: the Hongkong University Education Society, 1926.

Fung, Vincent H. Y. (ed.), *From Devotion to Plurality: A Full History of St. Paul's College, 1851-2001*. Hong Kong: St. Paul's College, c2002.

Gangjiu qiaoxiao shilue 港九僑校史畧 (Brief Histories of the Overseas Chinese Schools in Hong Kong and Kowloon, in Chinese). Hong Kong, 1946.

Girls' Brigade, Hong Kong, "分隊網絡(Network of Units)," http://www. gbhk.org.hk/ (accessed September 16, 2009).

Guangzhou Pui Ching Middle School: 1947 Class of "Hung" List of Classmates 廣州私立培正中學校: 一九四七年級虹社同學錄. Guangzhou: Pui Ching Middle School, 1947.

Hong Kong Chinese YMCA 50th Anniversary Commemorative Bulletin, 1901-1951 香港中華基督教青年會五十周年紀念特刊, 1901-1951. Hong Kong: the Chinese YMCA, 1951.

Hong Kong School for the Deaf 25th Anniversary. Hong Kong: Hong Kong School for the Deaf, 1960.

Hong Kong School for the Deaf, the *Principal's Report, 1950-1951*. Hong Kong: Hong Kong School for the Deaf, 1951.

The Kingdom Overseas, March, 1941.

Kong Yuet Diocesan Echo 港粵教聲. Hong Kong, 1946-47.

Lau Siu-lun, *Sanctuary of Excellence: the History of Ying Wa College*. Hong Kong: Ying Wa College Old Boys' Association, 2001.

The Memorial Booklet 香港義勇軍光榮史. Hong Kong: Hong Kong Volunteer Defence Corps (Chinese) Club, 1949.

Nam Hua Fu Zhong Te Kan 南華附中特刊 (Special Magazine of the Nam Wah Middle School, in Chinese). Hong Kong, 1946.

Principal's Report, 1950-1951. Hong Kong: Hong Kong School for the Deaf, 1951.

Road Safety Association, Hong Kong, "學校隊名錄(List of School Patrols)," http://www. rsa.org.hk/ (accessed Sept. 14, 2009).

The *School Magazine, March 1962*. Hong Kong Sea School, 1962.

"Scout Honour in China: A Letter from Sir. R. Baden Powell," *The Chronicle of the London Missionary Society*, October, 1916.

The Special Bulletin Commemorating the 60th Anniversary of the SCAA, 1910-1970 南華體育會六十週年會慶特刊. Hong Kong: the South China Athletics Association, 1970.

The *St. Andrew's Church News*, January 1979.

The *Steps*. Hong Kong: Diocesan Boys' School,1935-47.

Stokes, Gwenneth and John, *Queen's College: Its History, 1862-1987*. Hong Kong: Queen's College Old Boys' Association, 1987.

Vesey, Charlotte (comp.), *Celebrating St. Andrew's Church: 100 Years of History, Life and Personal Faith*. Hong Kong: St Andrew's Church, 2004.

Wayfarer. Hong Kong: St. Paul's College, 1957-59.

What is the Salvation Army? Hong Kong: the Salvation Army, 1994.

Xiang Gang De Ming Zhong Ying Wen Zhong Xue Bi Yeh Tong Xue Lu 香港德明中英文中學畢業同學錄 (List of Graduating Students of the Hong Kong Tak Ming Chinese and English Middle School, in Chinese). Hong Kong: Tak Ming Middle School, 1965.

Yang Zhong Zhong Xue Shi Wu Zhou Nian Ji Nian Te Kan 養中中學十五週年紀念特刊 (15th Anniversary Commemorative Magazine of the Yeung Chung Middle School, in Chinese). Hong Kong: Yeung Chung Middle School, 1939.

The Yellow Dragon 黃龍報. Hong Kong: Queen's College, 1927-61.

Ying Wa Echo 英華青年, Hong Kong: Ying Wa College, 1924.

"Zhong Guo Shao Nian Xian Feng Dui Zhang Cheng 中国少年先锋队章程(Articles of the Young Pioneers of China)," in http://61.gqt.org.cn/sxd/ 200905/t20090512_239909. htm (accessed May 1, 2010).

3. *Government publications:*

Annual Departmental Reports of the Straits Settlements for the Year 1917. Singapore, 1917.

Butters, R. H., *Report on Labour and Labour Conditions in Hong Kong.* Hong Kong, Noronha & Co., 1939.

Colonial Reports—Annual, No. 723, Hong Kong: Report for 1911. London, 1912.

Education Bureau, "Kindergarten Education," http://www.edb.gov.hk/index. aspx?langno=1& nodeid=1037 (accessed April 29, 2010).

Education Department, *The Report of the Chinese Studies Committee.* Hong Kong: Hong Kong Government Printer, 1953.

Education Journal. Hong Kong: the Hongkong University Education Society, 1926.

Hamilton, Geoffrey Cadzow, *Flag Badges Seals and Arms of Hong Kong.* Hong Kong: Government Press, 1963.

Hong Kong Administrative Reports. Hong Kong, 1894-1939.

The *Hong Kong Annual Report.* Hong Kong: Hong Kong Government, 1961.

Hong Kong Census and Bi-Census Reports, Hong Kong: Census and Statistics Department (former Census Office, etc.), 1911-2006 (under a variety of publication titles as listed in the footnotes).

Hong Kong Government Gazette. Hong Kong: Noronha, 1915-2009.

Hong Kong Hansard. Hong Kong: Noronha, 1904-1997.

Hong Kong Jurors List. Hong Kong.

"Hong Kong Population Projections, 2010-2039," hhttp://www.censtatd.gov.hk/. (accessed April 13, 2011).

Hong Kong Statistics, 1947-1967. Hong Kong: Census and Statistics Department, 1969.

"Hong Kong Statistics: Population and Vital Events," http://www.censtatd. gov.hk/hong_ kong_statistics/statistics_by_subject/index.jsp (accessed April 29, 2010).

Imperial Education Conference Papers, III.—Educational Systems of the Chief Colonies not possessing of Responsible Government: Hong Kong. London, 1915.

Kowloon Disturbances 1966: Report of Commissioner of Inquiry. Hong Kong: the Government Press, 1966.

Report of the Commission Appointed to Enquire into the Conditions of the Industrial Employment of Children in Hongkong, and the Desirability and Feasibility of Legislation for the Regulation of Such Employment. Hong Kong: Hong Kong Government, October 1921.

Report of Sham Shui Po Shek Kip Mei Six Villages Fire Relief Committee. Hong Kong: the Sham Shui Po Shek Kip Mei Six Villages Fire Relief Committee, 1954.

Secretary of State for the Colonies, "Police Probationers: Hong Kong, Straits Settlements, and Federated Malay States," 8th April, 1904.

United Nations, Department of Economic and Social Affairs, http://esa.un.org/ unpp/ p2k0data.asp (accessed May 8, 2010).

C. Newspapers/Periodicals:

The *Argus* (Melbourne, Victoria).
The China Mail (*CM*).
The *Courier-Mail* (Brisbane, Queensland).
The *Economist.*
The Hongkong Daily Press (*HKDP*).
The *Hong Kong Economic Journal* 信報.
Hong Kong Standard (the Standard, the Hong Kong Tiger Standard).
Hongkong Sunday Herald (*HKSH*).
(The) Hongkong Telegraph (*HKT*).
Hong Kong Times 香港時報.
The Hongkong Weekly Press and China Overland Trade Report.

Jing Bao 晶報.
Kung Sheung Yat Po 工商日報 (*KSYP*).
La Jeunesse 新青年 (Shanghai, China).
Ming Pao 明報.
The *Ming Pao Monthly* 明報月刊.
Readers Digest.
Shen Bao 申報 (Shanghai, China).
Shenzhen Evening News 深圳晚報 (Shenzhen, China).
Sing Pao Daily News 成報.
Sing Tao Daily News 星島日報.
South China Morning Post (*SCMP*).
The *South China Sunday Post-Herald.*
The *Star.*
The Straits Times (Singapore).
Ta Kung Pao 大公報.
The Times (London, Britain).
Wah Kiu Yat Po 華僑日報 (W*KYP*).
Wah Tze Daily 華字日報.
The *West Australian* (Perth, Western Australia).
Zheng Wu Bao 正午報.

D. All other Primary and Secondary Sources:

Aitken, W. Francis, *Baden-Powell: The Hero of Mafeking.* London: Partridge, 1900.
Aitken, W. Francis, *The Chief Scout: Sir Robert Baden-Powell.* London: S.W. Partridge, 1912.
Atkins, William, *Exiles: Three Island Journeys.* London: Faber, 2022.
Anderson, Benedict, *Imagined Communities.* New York: Verso, 1991.
Ariès, Philippe, Robert Baldick (trans.), *Centuries of Childhood.* Middlesex: Penguin Books, 1962.
Arnot, Madeleine, "A Cloud over Co-education: An analysis of the forms of transmission of class and gender relations," in *Reproducing Gender? Essays on educational theory and feminist politics.* New York: RoutledgeFalmer, 2002.
Baker, Huge D. R., *A Chinese Lineage Village: Sheung Shui.* Frank Cass, 1968.
Bancel, Nicolas, Daniel Denis, and Youssef Fates, *De l'Indochine à l'Algérie: la Jeunesse en mouvements des deux côtés du mirroir colonial, 1940-1962.* Paris: Éditions La Découverte, 2003.
Banham, Tony, *Not the Slightest Chance: The Defence of Hong Kong, 1941.* Toronto: UBC Press, 2003.
Baubérot, Arnaud, *L'invention du Scoutisme Chrétien: Les Eclaireurs Unionistes De 1911 à 1921.* Les Bergers et Les Mages, 1997.
Begbie, Harold, *The Story of Baden-Powell: The Wolf That Never Sleeps.* London: Richards, 1900.
Bell, J. Bowyer, *The Dynamics of the Armed Struggle.* London: Frank Cass, 1998.
Bellis, David, Lawrence Tsui, et al (Gwulo.com), "Francis Yiu-piu LEE," https://gwulo.com/node/17846 (accessed April 2, 2024).
Bèrard, Lèo Paul, *17 Days Until Christmas.* Canada, 1997.
Bernier, Claire, *Histoire du scoutisme et guidisme francophones en Alberta de 1931 à 1988.* Edmonton: Les Éditions Duval, 1995.
Bhabha, Homi K., *The Location of Culture.* Oxon: Routledge, 1994, reprinted 2005.
Biagioli, Enrico, *Origini e nascita dello Scautismo in Umbria, 1910-1928.* Selvazzano: T. Zaramella, 2010.
Biti, Vladimir, "Periodization as a Technique of Cultural Identification," in John Neubauer (ed.), *Cultural History After Foucault.* New York: Aldine de Gruyter, 1999.

Boehmer, Elleke (ed.), *Robert Baden-Powell, Scouting for Boys: The Original 1908 Edition.* Oxford: Oxford Univ. Press, 2004.

Booth, Martin, *Gweilo: A Memoir of a Hong Kong Childhood.* London: Bantam Books, 2004.

Boris, Eileen, and Angélique Janssens (ed.), *Complicating Categories: Gender, Class, Race and Ethnicity.* Cambridge: Univ. of Cambridge, 1999.

Bouchet, H., *Le Scoutisme et L'individualité.* Librairie Felix Alcan, 1933.

Braga, Stuart, "Making Impressions: The Adaptation of a Portuguese family to Hong Kong, 1700-1950," Ph. D. thesis, Australian National Univ., Oct. 2012.

Bragg, Ross Andrew, "The Boy Scout Movement in Canada: Defining Constructs of Masculinity for the Twentieth Century," MA thesis, Dalhousie Univ., 1995.

Bray, Mark, "Colonialism, Scale, and Politics: Divergence and Convergence of Education Development in Hong Kong and Macau," *Comparative Education Review*, 36/3, August 1992.

Bray, Mark, "Decolonisation and Education: New Paradigms for the Remnants of Empire," *Compare*, Vol. 24, No. 1, 1994, 37-51.

Brendon, Piers, *Eminent Edwardians.* New York: Houghton Mifflin, 1979.

Brown, Arthur, "The Development of the Scout Movement in Nigeria," *African Affairs*, 46/182, January, 1947.

Brown, B. Bradford, and Reed W. Larson, "The Kaleidoscope of Adolescence: Experiences of the World's Youth at the Beginning of the 21st Century," in B. Bradford Brown, Reed W. Larson, T.S. Saraswathi (eds.), *The World's Youth: Adolescence in Eight Regions of the Globe.* Cambridge: Cambridge Univ. Press, 2002.

Brown, Wenzell, *Hong Kong Aftermath.* New York: Smith & Durrell, 1943.

Burke, Peter, "History of Events and the Revival of Narrative," in Peter Burke (ed.), *New Perspectives on Historical Writing.* Cambridge: Polity Press, 1991.

But, Juanita C., "The Other Race: Settler, Exile, Transient and Sojourner in the Literary Diaspora," Ph. D. dissertation, Univ. of New York at Buffalo, 1999.

Butler, L. J., and Anthony Gorst (eds.), *Modern British History: A Guide to Study and Research.* London: L. B. Tauris, 1997.

Cannadine, David, *Ornamentalism: How the British Saw Their Empire.* Oxford Univ. Press, 2002.

Cantier, Jacques, "Un enjeu essentiel: Vichy et les jeunes dans l'Empire Francais," in Jacques Cantier and Éric Jennings (ed.), *L'Empire colonial sous Vichy.* Paris: Édition Odile Jacob, 2004, 91-116.

Carew, Tim, *Fall of Hong Kong.* London: Anthony Blond, 1960.

Carr, E. H., *What is History?* Hampshire: Palgrave, 1961.

Carr, Helen, "Woman/Indian, the 'American' and his Others," in F. Barker, P. Hulme, M. Iversen and D. Loxley (eds.), *Europe and its Others,* vol. 2, Colchester: Univ. of Essex Press, 1985.

Carr, Thomas W., *The Victoria Lodge of Hong Kong: A Century of Fellowship.* Hong Kong: Victoria Lodge of Hong Kong, 1981.

Carroll, John M., *A Concise History of Hog Kong.* Hong Kong: Hong Kong Univ. Press, 2007.

Carroll, John M., *Edge of Empires: Chinese Elites and British Colonials in Hong Kong.* Hong Kong: Hong Kong Univ. Press, 2007.

Carroll, John M., *The Hong Kong-China Nexus: A Brief History.* Cambridge: Cambridge Univ. Press, 2022.

Chabrier, Carine, "Scoutisme et Christianisme," http://www.deficulturel.net/ modules/ news/ article.php?storyid=67591 (accessed May 24, 2010).

Chang, Iris, *The Chinese in America: A Narrative History.* New York: Penguin, 2004.

Cheng, Tong Yung, *The Economy of Hong Kong.* Hong Kong: Far East Publications, 1977.

Cheung, Fanny M. (ed.), *EnGendering Hong Kong Society: A Gender Perspective of Women's Status.* Hong Kong: The Chinese Univ. Press, 1997.

Choi, Sze Hang, "The Scouts Movement and the Construction of New Citizenship in

Republican China (1912-1937)," M. Phil. thesis, Lingnan Univ., 2008.

Chow, Nelson, "Social Welfare," T. L. Tsim and Bernard H.K. Luk (eds.), *The Other Hong Kong Report*. Hong Kong: The Chinese Univ. of Hong Kong, 1989.

Chu, Cindy Yik-Yi, *The Maryknoll Sisters in Hong Kong, 1921-1969: in Love with the Chinese*. New York: Palgrave Macmillan, 2004.

Churchill, Winston S., *The Second World War, Volume III: The Grand Alliance*. London: Cassell & Co., 1966.

Clarke, A. J., "History of the 1st HMS Kelantan Deep-Sea Rover Scout Crew: First Outing with 'Pioneer' and Hong Kong Scouters," http://www.scrich.co.uk/deepsea/index.html (accessed March 10, 2008).

Collis, Henry, Fred Hurll, and Rex Hazlewood, *B-P's Scouts: an Official History of the Boy Scouts Association*. London: Collins, 1961.

Cooper, John, *Colony in Conflict: The Hong Kong Disturbances May 1967—January 1968*. Hong Kong, Swindon Book Co., 1970.

Cornell, Stephen E., and Douglas Hartman, "Mapping the Terrain: Definitions," in Harry Goulbourne (ed.), *Race and Ethnicity: Critical Concepts in Sociology*. London: Routledge, 2001, 76-99.

Cox, Kenneth, *The First Hundred Years: The History of Foochow Lodge*. Hong Kong: Foochow Lodge, 1982.

Cox, Roger, *Shaping Childhood: Themes of Uncertainty in the History of Adult-Child Relationships*. London: Routledge, 1996.

Craib, Ian, *The Importance of Disappointment*. London: Routledge, 1994.

Culp, Robert, "Rethinking Governmentality: Training, Cultivation, and Cultural Citizenship in Nationalist China," *The Journal of Asian Studies*, August 2006, 529-554.

Daniel, Walter G., "The Role of Youth Character-Building Organizations in Juvenile Delinquency Prevention," *The Journal of Negro Education*, 28/3, Juvenile Delinquency Among Negroes in the United States, Summer 1959, 301-317.

Dean, John, "Scouting in America, 1910-1990," D. Ed. dissertation, the Univ. of South Carolina, 1992.

Dedman, Martin, "Baden-Powell, Militarism, and the 'Invisible Contributors' to the Boy Scout Scheme, 1904-1920," *Twentieth Century British History*, 1993, Vol. 4, No. 3, 201-233.

Dedman, Martin, "the Boy Scouts and the 'Girl' Question," *Sexualities*, 4/2, 2001, 191-210.

Denning W. and M. E. Lehr, "The Extent and Nature of Corporate Long Range Planning in the U.K.: Part 1," *Journal of Management Studies*, May 1971.

Derouiche, Mohamed, *Scoutisme école du patriotisme*. Alger: Enterprise Nationale du Livre, 1985.

Di, Yu 翟钰(ed.),"Taiwan Wang Shi, Hui Guo Fu Jiang 台湾往事《挥戈复疆》 (Reminiscences on Taiwan)," http://www.cctv.com/lm/523/51/86231.html (accessed May 10, 2010).

Dillingham, William, *Being Kipling*. New York: Palgrave Macmillan, 2008.

Dimmock, F. Haydn (ed.), *The Scouts' Book of Heroes: A Record of Scouts Work in The Great War*. London: Arthur Pearson, 1919.

Dooley, Thomas P., *Irishmen or English Soldiers?* Liverpool: Liverpool Univ. Press, 1995.

Douglas, Ian T., and Pui-lan Kwok, *Beyond Colonial Anglicanism: the Anglican Communion in the Twenty-first Century*. New York: Church Publications, c2001.

Drage, Charles, *Taikoo*. London, Constable, 1970.

Dray, W. H., "Narrative versus analysis in history," in Robert M. Burns (ed.), *Historiography: Critical Concepts in Historical Studies*. Taylor & Francis, 2005.

Emden, Richard van, *Boy Soldiers of the Great War: Their Own Stories for the First Time*. London: Headline, 2005.

Endacott, G. B., *A History of Hong Kong*. Hong Kong: Oxford Univ. Press, 1973.

Endacott, G. B., *Hong Kong Eclipse*. Hong Kong: Oxford Univ. Press, 1978.

Everett, Percy, *The First Ten Years*. Ipswich: The East Anglian Daily Times, 1948.

Eykholt, Mark, "Aggression, Victimization, and Chinese Historiography of the Nanjing Massacre," in Joshua A. Fogel (ed.), *Nanjing Massacre in History and Historiography*.

Berkeley: Univ. of California Press, 2000.

Faist, Thomas, "The Fixed and Porous Boundaries of Dual Citizenship," in Thomas Faist and Peter Kivisot (eds.), *Dual Citizenship in Global Perspective: From Unitary to Multiple Citizenship*. New York: Palgrave, 2007.

Fields, Rona M., *Northern Ireland: Society Under Seige*. New Brunswick: Transaction, 1980.

Fixler, Jill Friedman, Sandie Eichberg and Gail Lorenz, *Boomer Volunteer Engagement: Collaborate Today, Thrive Tomorrow*. Bloomington, Indiana: AuthorHouse, 2008.

Fok, K. C., "The Hong Kong Connection: A Study of Hong Kong's Role in the 1911 revolution," *Lectures on Hong Kong History: Hong Kong's Role in Modern Chinese History*. Hong Kong: The Commercial Press, 1990.

Foster, Michael, "The Growing Crisis in the Scout Movement," http://www.netpages.free-online.co. uk/sha/crisis.htm (accessed September 20, 2009).

Freedman, Russell, *Scouting with Baden Powell*. New York: Holiday House, 1967.

Friedman, Michael J., "The Brown vs. Board of Education Decision—50 Years Later," http://usinfo.state.gov/usa/civilrights/brown/overview.htm (accessed October 18, 2004).

Fulghum, Robert, *All I Really Need to Know I learned in Kindergarten*. New York: Ivy Books, 1986.

Fung, Chi Ming, "Governorship of Lugard and May: Fears of Double Allegiance and Perceived Disloyalty," in Lee Pui-tak (ed.,) *Colonial Hong Kong and Modern China: Interaction and Reintegration*. Hong Kong: Hong Kong Univ. Press, 2005.

Fyvel, T. R., *The Insecure Offenders; rebellious Youth in the Welfare State*. Harmondsworth: Pelican, 1963.

Gandt, Robert L., *Season of Storms: The Siege of Hong Kong, 1941*. Hong Kong, South China Morning Post, 1982.

Gao, Si-yin 高仕隱, *Jiang Wei Guo Jin Hu Tui Hu* 蔣緯國: 進乎? 退乎? (Jian Weiguo: Going Forward or Backward?). Taipei: Chang Ge Chu Ban Shi, 1990.

Gardner, Brian, *Mafeking: A Victorian Legend*. New York: Harcourt, Brace & World, 1967.

Garvin, David A., "Building a Learning Organization," *Harvard Business Review*, July-August 1993, 78-91.

Gillingham, Paul, *At the Peak: Hong Kong Between the Wars*. Hong Kong: Macmillan, 1983.

Gillis, John R., *Youth and History: Tradition and Change in European Age Relations, 1760-the Present*. New York: Academic Press, 1974.

Gittins, Jean, *Eastern Windows—Western Skies*. Hong Kong: SCMP, 1969.

Gittins, Jean, *Stanley: Behind Barbed Wire*. Hong Kong: Hong Kong Univ. Press, 1982.

Golger, Otto J. "An Environmental Study of Squatter and Resettlement Housing in Hong Kong," Ph. D. dissertation, Univ. of Hong Kong, 1968.

Graue, M. Elizabeth, *Ready for What: Constructing Meanings of Readiness for Kindergarten*. New York: State Univ. of New York, 1993.

Guérin, Christian, *L'utopie Scouts de France, 1920-1995: histoire d'une identité collective catholique et sociale*. Fayard, 1997.

Haffner, Christopher, *The Craft in the East*. Hong Kong: District Grand Lodge of Hong Kong and the Far East, 1977.

Hambro, Edvard, *The Problem of Chinese Refugees in Hong Kong: Report Submitted to the United Nations High Commission for Refugees*. Leyden: Sijthoff, 1955.

Hamilton, Angus, *The Siege of Mafeking*. London: Methuen, 1900.

Han, Suyin, *A Many-Splendoured Thing*. Harmondsworth: Penguin Books, 1961.

Harris, Steven, *Legalised Mischief*. London: Lewarne Publishing, 2003.

Harrison, Brian, *Finding a Role: The United Kingdom, 1970-1990*. Oxford: Oxford Univ. Press, 2010.

Heywood, Graham (S. P.), *It Won't be Long Now: The Diary of a Hong Kong Prisoner of War*. Hong Kong: Blacksmith Books, 2015.

Hillcourt, William, *Baden-Powell: the Two Lives of a Hero*. Boy Scouts of America, 1964.

Hiner, N. Ray, and Joseph M. Hawes (eds.), *Growing Up in America: Children in Historical*

Perspective. Urbana: Univ. of Illinois Press, 1985.

Ho, Denny Kwok Leung, "The Rise and Fall of Community Mobilization: the Housing Movement in Hong Kong," in Stephen Wing Kai Chiu and Tai Lok Lui (eds.), *The Dynamics of Social Movement in Hong Kong*. Hong Kong: Hong Kong Univ. Press, 2000, 185-208.

Horne, Gerald, *Race War: White Supremacy and the Japanese Attack on the British Empire*. New York: New York Univ. Press, 2004.

Howe, Stephen, "When (if ever) did Empire End? 'Internal Decolonisation' in British Culture since the 1950s," in Martin Lynn (ed.), *The British Empire in the 1950s: Retreat or Revival?* Basingstoke, Hampshire: Palgrave, 2006.

Hsu, Long-hsuen, and Ming-Kai Chang, *History of the Sino-Japanese War, 1937-1945*. Chung Wu Publishing Co., 1971.

Huang, Jianli, "The Youth Pathfinders: Portrayal of Student Political Activism," in Michael D. Barr and Carl A. Trocki, *Paths Not Taken: Political Pluralism in Post-War Singapore*. Singapore: NUS Press, 2008.

Hui, C. S., W. F. Maunder and J. Tsao, *Hong Kong's Resettled Squatters: the Final Report on the 1957 Sample Survey of Resettlement Estates*. Hong Kong: the Univ. of Hong Kong, 1959.

Huld, Palle, *A Boy Scout Around the World*. New York: Coward-McCann, 1929.

Hutcheon, Robin, *SCMP: The First Eighty Years*, Hong Kong: SCMP, 1983.

Hwang, Jinlin, "Authority over the Body and the Modern Formation of the Body," in Peter Zarrow (ed.), *Creating Chinese Modernity: Knowledge and Everyday Life, 1900-1940*, New York: Peter Lang, 2006, 183-212.

Hybels, Bill, *The Volunteer Revolution: Unleashing the Power of Everybody*. Grand Rapids, Michigan: Zondervan, 2004.

Hynes, Samuel, *The Edwardian Turn of Mind*. Princeton: The Princeton Univ. Press, 1968.

Ike, Nobutaka (trans.), *Japan's Decision for War: Records of the 1941 Policy Conferences*. Stanford: Stanford Univ. Press, 1967.

Ip, Kin Yuen, "Organisational Change: the Case of a 'Leftist School' in Joining the Direct Subsidy Scheme, " M. Ed. thesis, Univ. of Hong Kong, 1994.

Japan's Aggression and Public Opinion. Kunming: National Southwest Associated Univ. Library, 1938.

Jeal, Tim, *Baden-Powell*. London: Hutchinson, 1989.

Jobs, Richard, *Riding the New Wave: Youth and the Rejuvenation of France After Second World War*. Stanford: Stanford Univ. Press, 2007.

Johnson, James Weldon, *The Selected Writings of James Weldon Johnson: The New York age editorials (1914-1923)*. New York: Oxford Univ. Press, 1995.

Jordan, Thomas E., *Victorian Child Savers and their Culture: A Thematic Evaluation* Lewiston, N.Y.: Edwin Mellen Press, c1998.

Josey, Alex, *Lee Kuan Yew*. Singapore: Asian Pacific Press, 1968.

Josey, Alex, *Lee Kuan Yew: the Struggle for Singapore*. London: Angus and Robertson, 1980.

Kadam, K. N., "The Birth of a Rationalist," Eleanor Zelliot and Maxine Bernsten, *The Experience of Hinduism: Essays on Religion in Maharashtra*. SUNY, 1988.

Kahane, Reuven, *The Origins of Postmodern Youth: Informal Youth Movements in a Comparative Perspective*. Berlin: Walter de Gruyter, 1997.

Kahn, David, *The Codebreakers: the Story of Secret Writing*. New York: Scribner, 1996.

Kelly, M. J., *The Fenian Ideal and Irish Nationalism, 1882-1916*. Woodbridge, Suffolk: Boydell Press, 2006.

Kerzner, Harold, *Project Management: A Systems Approach to Planning, Scheduling, and Controlling*, 10th ed. New Jersey: John Wiley, 2009.

Kiernan, R. H., *Baden-Powell*. Philadelphia: David McKay, 1938.

Kilbee, Lt., "Diary of Lt. Kilbee," http://www.mwadui.com/HongKong/Fleet_ C.htm#Kilbee (accessed February 20, 2008.)

Kimbrough, Robert (ed.), Joseph Conrad, *Heart of Darkness: An authoritative Text, Backgrounds and Sources Criticism*, 3rd edition. New York: Norton, 1988.

Kipling, Rudyard, *The Jungle Book*, 1894. London: Macmillan, 1950.
Kirby, William C., *Germany and Republican China*. Stanford: Stanford Univ.Press, 1984.
Kraidy, Marwan M., *Hybridity, or the Cultural Logic of Globalization*. Philadelphia: Temple Univ. Press, 2005.
Krämer, Peter, "It's aimed at kids—the kid in everybody," in Yvonne Tasker (ed.), *Action and Adventure Cinema*. Abingdon: Routledge, 2004.
Ku, Agnes S., and Ngai Pun, "Remaking citizenship in Hong Kong," in Ku, Agnes S., et. al. (eds.), *Remaking Citizenship in Hong Kong: Community, Nation and the Global City*. London: RoutledgeCurzon, 2004.
Kua, Paul 柯保羅, *A Century of Hong Kong Scouting, an Illustrated History* 香港童軍百年圖史. Hong Kong: Scout Association of Hong Kong, 2012.
Kua, Paul, "Boys' Brigade, YMCA, and early Scouting in Hong Kong and Singapore, 1909-1918: Christian Boy's Work in two Non-Christian British Colonies," conference paper, *Christian Youth Movements: Their History and Significance*, Royal Historical Society/YMCA, Univ. of Birmingham, Feb. 17-19, 2006.
Kua, Paul, *Europe meets Formosa, 1510-1662: Two historical studies*. London: Propius Press, 2023.
Kua, Paul 柯保羅, *Hong Kong Scout Stories* 香港童軍故事. Hong Kong: Joint Publishing, 2019.
Kua, Paul,,"Scouting in Hong Kong: Citizenship Training in a Chinese Context, 1910-2007," Ph. D. dissertation, the Univ. of Hong Kong, 2010.
Kua, Paul, "Students of the Anglo-Chinese College of Malacca, 1818-1843: Fruits of the First Protestant School in Asia," *Monumenta Serica: Journal of Oriental Studies*, 71/2 (Dec. 2023), 453-488.
Laird, Susan, *Mary Wollstonecraft: Philosophical Mother of Coeducation*. London: Continuum Int'l, 2008.
Laird, Susan, "Rethinking 'Coeducation'," in Jim Garrison (ed.), *the New Scholarship on Dewey*. Dordrecht: Kluwer Academic Publishers, 1995.
Lambert, Darrell, "How I Got Booted out of the BSA," *The Humanist*, Jan-Feb, 2003, 7-9.
Lan, Alice Y., and Betty M. Hu, *We Flee from Hong Kong*. Grand Rapids, Mich.: Zondervan, [1944].
Laneyrie, Philippe, *Les Scouts de France: L'évolution du Mouvement des origines aux années 80*. Paris: Cerf, 1985.
Langenberg, Arthur van, *Urban Gardening: A Hong Kong Gardener's Journal*. Hong Kong: the Chinese Univ. of Hong Kong, 2006.
Lau, Chi Kuen, *Hong Kong's Colonial Legacy: A Hong Kong Chinese's View of the British Heritage*. Hong Kong: the Chinese Univ. of Hong Kong, 1997.
Lau, Siu-kai, *Society and Politics in Hong Kong*. Hong Kong: Chinese Univ. Press, 1984.
Law, Kar, Frank Bren, and Sam Ho, *Hong Kong Cinema: A Cross-cultural View*. Oxford: Scarecrow Press, 2004.
Lebra, Joyce C., "the Significance of the Japanese Military Model for Southeast Asia," in Wolf Mendl, *Japan and South East Asia: Vol. 1, From the Meiji Restoration to 1945*. London: Routledge, 2001.
Lee, Kuan Yew, *From Third World to First: The Singapore Story, 1965-2000*. New York: HarperCollins Publisher, c2000.
Lee, P. C. (comp.), the *Hongkong Album* 香港時賢, 1st. ed. Hong Kong, 1960.
Lee, Vicky, *Being Eurasian: Memories Across Racial Divides*. Hong Kong: Hong Kong Univ. Press, 2004.
Lee, W. O., "Citizenship Education in Hong Kong: Development and Challenges," in W. O. Lee, et al. (eds.), *Citizenship Education in Asia and the Pacific: Concepts and Issues*. Hong Kong: Kluwer Academic Publishers, 2004.
Lee, W. O., and Anthony Sweeting, "Controversies in Hong Kong's Political Transition: Nationalism versus Liberalism," in Mark Bray and W. O. Lee, *Education and Political Transition: Themes and Experience in East Asia*. Hong Kong: the Univ. of Hong Kong, 1997.
Leung, Hon-chu, "Politics of Incorporation and Exclusion: Immigration and Citizenship

Issues," in Agnes S. Ku et. al. (eds.), *Remaking Citizenship in Hong Kong: Community, Nation and the Global City*. London: RoutledgeCurzon, 2004.

Li, Lian-ju 李連舉, "Wang Guo Ri Ji 亡國日記(Diary During the Fall of the Country)," http://www.southcn.com/weekend/commend/2005090010.html (accessed Sept. 15, 2005).

Liebel, Manfred, "Citizenship from Below: Children's Rights and Social Movements," in Antonella Invernizzi and Jane Williams (eds.), *Children and Citizenship*. London: Sage Publications, 2008.

Liu, Athena Nga Chee, *Family Law for the Hong Kong SAR*. Hong Kong: the Hong Kong Univ. Press, 1999.

Lock, Dennis, *Project Management*, 9th ed. Aldershot: Gower, 2007.

Liu, Frances Tse, *Ho Kom-tong: A Man for All Seasons*. Hong Kong: Compradore House, 2003.

Llobera, Josep R., *Foundations of National Identity: From Catalonia to Europe*. Berghahn Books, 2004.

Lodge, Tom, *Mandela: A Critical Life*. Oxford: Oxford Univ. Press, 2006.

Long, Ying-tai 龍應台, *Da Jiang Da Hai: Yi Jiu Si Jiu* 大江大海: 一九四九. (Our 1949). Hong Kong: Cosmos Books, 2009.

Loomba, Ania, *Colonialism/Postcolonialism*, 2nd ed. London: Routledge, 1998.

Louis, Wm. Roger, *Ends of British Imperialism: the Scramble for Empire, Suez and Decolonization, Collected Essays*. London: Tauris, 2006.

Louis, Wm. Roger, "Hong Kong: the Critical Phase, 1945-1949," *The American Historical Review*, 102/4, Oct., 1997, 1052-1084.

Luff, John, *The Hidden Years*. Hong Kong: South China Moring Post, 1967.

Luk, H. K., "Chinese Culture in the Hong Kong Curriculum: Heritage and Colonialism," *Comparative Education Review*, Vol. 35, No. 4, November 1991.

Lunning, Frenchy, *Emerging Worlds of Anime and Manga*. Minnesota: Univ. of Minnesota Press, 2006.

Ma, Laurence J. C., and Carolyn L. Cartier, *The Chinese Diaspora: Space, Place, Mobility and Identity*. Lanham, Md.: Rowman & Littlefield, c2003.

Ma, Ming (ed.), *The Riot in Hong Kong, 1967* 香港動亂画史. Hong Kong: Sky Horse Book Co., 1967.

MacDonald, Robert H., *Sons of the Empire: The Frontier and the Boy Scout Movement, 1890-1918*. Toronto: Univ. of Toronto Press, 1993.

MacKenzie, John M., "The Imperial Pioneer and the British Masculine Stereotype in Late Victorian and Edwardian Times," in J. A. Mangan and James Walvin (eds.), *Manliness and Morality*. Manchester: Manchester Univ. Press, 1987.

Macleod, David, *Building Character in the American Boy: the Boy Scouts, YMCA, and their Forerunners, 1870-1920*. Wisconsin: Univ. of Wisconsin, 2004.

MacPherson, Stewart, "Hong Kong," in John Dixon and David Macarov, *Poverty: A Persistent Global Reality*. London: Routledge, 1998.

Mak, Mac W. M., "The Scout Association as a Learning Company," in G. Welshman, T. Boydell, J. Burgoyne, and M. Pedler, *Learning Company Conference 1994: Collected Papers*. Sheffield, 1994.

Malik Z. A., and D. W. Karger, "Does Long Range Planning Improve Company Performance?" *Management Review*, September 1975.

Mansergh, Diana, *Nationalism and Independence: Selected Irish Papers*. Cork, Ireland: Cork Univ. Press, 1997.

Marshall, T. H., "Citizenship and Social Class," in Bryan S. Turner and Peter Hamilton (eds.), *Citizenship: Critical Concepts*. New York: Routledge, 1994, Vol. II, 5-43.

Marsman, Jan Henrik, *I Escaped from Hong Kong*. Sydney: Angus and Robertson, 1943.

Martin, Kingsley, "British Opinion and the Proposed Boycott of Japan," from *Japan's Aggression and Public Opinion*. Kunming: National Southwest Associated Univ. Library, 1938.

Marwick, Arthur, *The New Nature of History: Knowledge, Evidence, and Language*. Hampshire: Palgrave, 2001.

Matthews, Clifford, "Life Experiences: From Star Ferry to Stardust," in Clifford Matthews and Oswald Cheung (eds.), *Dispersal and Renewal: Hong Kong University During the War Years*. Hong Kong: Hong Kong Univ. Press, 1998, 227-246.

Mathews, Gordon, Eric Kit-wai Ma, and Tai-lok Lui, *Hong Kong, China: Learning to Belong to a Nation*. London: Routledge, 2008.

Menzies, James, "Nestorian bronze crosses 青銅十字架," *Qi Da Ji Kan* 齊大季刊. Shandong, Jinan: Qi Lu Univ., 1934, No. 3, 1-168.

McCargo, Duncan, *Contemporary Japan*. Hampshire: Palgrave, 2000.

McKee, Jonathan W. and Thomas W. McKee, *The New Breed: Understanding & Equipping the 21st Century Volunteer*. Loveland, Colorado: 2007.

Mechling, Jay, *On My Honor: Boy Scouts and the making of American youth*. Chicago: Univ. of Chicago Press, 2001.

Metelmann, Henry, *A Hitler Youth: Growing Up in Germany in the 1930s*. London: Caliban Books, 1997.

Miller-Bernal, Leslie, "Introduction: Changes in the Status and Functions of Women's Colleges over Time," in Leslie Miller-Bernal et al. (eds.), *Challenged by Coeducation*.

Miller-Bernal, Leslie, and Susan L. Poulson (eds.), *Challenged by Coeducation: Women's Colleges Since 1960s*. Nashville: Vanderbilt University Press, 2006.

Miners, Norman, *Hong Kong Under Imperial Rule, 1912-1941*. Hong Kong: Oxford Univ., 1987.

Mises, Ludwig von, *Theory and History: An Interpretation of Social and Economic Evolution*. Auburn: Ludwig von Mises Institute, 2007.

Monahan, Dermott, *The Lepers of Dichpali*. London: The Cargate Press, c. 1938.

Morris, Andrew D., *Marrow of the Nation: A History of Sport and Physical Culture in Republican China*. Berkeley: Univ. of California Press, 2004.

Morris, Jan, *Hong Kong: Epilogue to an Empire*. London: Penguin Books, 1988.

Motz, Earl, "Great Britain, Hong Kong, and Canton: The Canton—Hong Kong Strike and Boycott of 1925-26," Ph. D. dissertation, Michigan State Univ., 1972.

Murray, William D., *The History of the Boy Scouts of America*. New York: Boy Scouts of America, 1937.

Muscat, Richard, Thóroddur Bjarnasson, François Beck, and Patrick Peretti-Watel, *Risk Factors in Adolescent Drug Use: Evidence from School Surveys and Application in Policy*. Strasbourg Cedex: Council of Europe Publishing, 2007.

Nasson, Bill, *The South African War*. London: Arnold, 1999.

Nava, Mica, *Changing Cultures: Feminism, Youth and Consumerism*. London: SAGE publications, 1992.

Neilly, J. Emerson, *Besieged with B-P: Siege of Mafeking*. London: Pearson's, 1900.

Newendorp, Nicole Dejong, *Uneasy Reunions: Immigration, Citizenship, and Family Life in Post-1997 Hong Kong*. Stanford: Stanford Univ. Press, 2008.

Nicholson, Edwin, *Education and the Boy Scout Movement in America*. New York: Columbia Univ., 1941.

Nobel, Colin, and Wendy Bradford, *Getting it Right for Boys...and Girls*. London: Routledge, 2000.

Noemo, Captain, *The Boy Scout Bubble: A Review of a Great Futility*. London, 1912.

Ong, Aihwa, *Flexible Citizenship: the Cultural Logics of Transnationality*. Durham: Duke Univ. Press, 1999.

O'Quinn, John C., "How Solemn is the Duty of the Mighty Chief: Mediating the Conflict of Rights in Boy Scouts of America v. Dale," *Harvard Journal of Law and Public Policy*, 24/1 (Fall 2000).

Osgerby, Bill, *Youth in Britain Since 1945*. Oxford: Blackwell Publishers, 1998.

Osterhammel, Jurgen, "Imperialism in Transition: British Business and the Chinese Authorities, 1931-1937," *The China Quarterly*, No. 98, June 1984, 260-286.

Pakenham, Thomas, *The Boer War*. London: Weidenfeld, 1979.

Palmer, Sue, *Living and Partly Living: The Problem of Youth in Hong Kong*. Hong Kong, 1975.

Parmelee, Maurice, *Boshevism Fascism and the Liberal Democratic State*. New York:

Wiley, 1934.

Parsons, Timothy H., "The Consequences of Uniformity: The Struggle for the Boy Scout Uniform in Colonial Kenya," *Journal of Social History*, Winter 2006, 361-383.

Parsons, Timothy H., "No More English than the Postal System: the Kenya Boy Scout Movement and the Transfer of Power," *Africa Today*, 61-80.

Parsons, Timothy H., *Race, Resistance, and the Boy Scout Movement in British Colonial Africa*. Athens: Ohio Univ. Press, 2004.

Patterson, Sheila, *The Last Trek: A Study of the Boer People and the Afrikaner Nation*. London: Routledge, 2004.

Pedler, Mike, John Burgoyne and Tom Boydell, *The Learning Company: A Strategy for Sustainable Development*. London: McGraw Hill, 1991.

Peterson, Robert W., *The Boy Scouts: An American Adventure*. Forbes, 1985.

Phillips, Mark, "On Historiography and Narrative," *Univ. of Toronto Quarterly*, 53, 1983-84.

Plato, the *Republic*, translated by Desmond Lee, Penguin Classics, 2003.

Pomfret, David M., "'Child Slavery' in British and French Far-Eastern Colonies, 1880-1945," *Past & Present*, November 2008, 176-213.

Pomfret, David M., "The City of Evil and the Great Outdoors: the Modern Health Movement and the Urban Young, 1918-1940," *Urban History*, 28, 3, 2001, 593-609.

Pomfret, David M., "Raising Eurasia: Race, Class, and Age in French and British Colonies," *Comparative Studies in Society and History*, 2009; 51(2), 314-343.

Pomfret, David M., *Young People and the European City: Age Relations in Nottingham and Saint-Etienne, 1890-1940*. Aldershot: Ashgate, 2004.

Pope-Hennessy, James, *Half-Crown Colony: A Historical Profile of Hong Kong*. Boston: Little, Brown and Co., 1969.

Postiglione, Gerard A., "The Decolonization of Hong Kong Education," in Gerald A. Postiglione (ed.), *Education and Society in Hong Kong: Toward One Country and Two Systems*. Armonk, N. Y.: An East Gate Book, 1991.

Postiglione, Gerald A., and Wing On Lee, *Schooling in Hong Kong: Organization, Teaching and Social Context*. Hong Kong: Hong Kong Univ. Press, 1997.

Preston, Valerie, Myer Siemiatycki, and Audrey Kobayashi, "Dual Citizenship among Hong Kong Canadians: Convenience or Commitment?" in Thomas Faist *et al* (eds.), *Dual Citizenship in Global Perspective: From Unitary to Multiple Citizenship*. New York: Palgrave, 2007.

Proctor, Tammy M., *Scouting for Girls: A Century of Girl Guides and Girl Scouts*. Santa Barbara, CA: ABC-CLIO, LLC, 2009.

Proctor, Tammy M., "'A Separate Path,' Scouting and Guiding in Interwar South Africa," *Comparative Studies in Society and History*, Vol. 42, No. 3, July 2000, 605-631.

Pryke, Sam, "The Popularity of Nationalism in the Early British Boy Scout Movement," *Social History*, 23/3, Oct. 1998, 309-324.

Putney, Clifford, *Muscular Christianity: Manhood and Sports in Protestant America, 1880-1920*. Cambridge, Mass.; Harvard Univ. Press, 2001.

Qin, Suiling 秦穗齡, "Tong Zi Jun Yu Xian Dai Zhong Guo De Qing Shao Nian Xun Lian 童子軍與現代中國的青少年訓練 (1911-1949) (Scouting and Youth Training in Modern China, 1911-1949)," M. Phil. thesis, National Taiwan Normal Univ., 2004.

Raddeker, Hélène Bowen, *Sceptical History: Feminist and Postmodern Approaches in Practice*. London: Routledge, 2007.

Radey, Kerry-Anne, "Young Knights of the Empire: Scouting Ideals of Nation and Empire in Interwar Canada," MA thesis, Laurentian Univ., 2003.

Rae, Murray, *History and Hermeneutics*. New York: T & T Clark, 2005.

Raffin, Anne, *Youth Mobilization in Vichy Indochina and its Legacies, 1940-1970*. Lanham: Lexington Books, 2005.

Rau, C. Subba, *Scouting in India: What It Is and What It Might Be*. Tumkur: the Tumkur District Scout Council, 1933.

Rauschning, Anna, *No Retreat* (1939), in http://www.spartacus.schoolnet.co.uk/ GERyouth. htm (accessed October 23, 2006).

Reynolds, E. E., *Baden-Powell: A Biography of Lord Baden-Powell of Gilwell.* London: Oxford Univ. Press, 1943.

Reynolds, E. E., *The Scout Movement*, London: Oxford University Press, 1950.

Ride, Edwin, *BAAG: Hong Kong Resistance, 1942-1945.* Hong Kong: Hong Kong Univ. Press, 1981.

Riordan, Jim, "The Russian Boy Scouts," October, 1988, *History Today.*

Roberts, Kenneth, *Youth and Leisure.* London: George Allen & Unwin, 1983.

Roces, Mina, and Louise Edwards (ed.), *The Politics of Dress in Asia and Americas.* Brighton: Sussex Academic Press, 2007.

Roland, Charles G., *Long Night's Journey into Day: Prisoners of War in Hong Kong and Japan, 1941-1945.* Waterloo: Wilfrid Laurier Univ. Press, 2001.

Rong, Zihan 榮子菡, "Guang Dong Tong Zi Jun Yan Jiu 廣東童子軍研究: 1915-1938 (A Study on the Boy Scouts of Guangdong: 1915-1938)," M. Phil. thesis, Jinan Univ., 2002.

Rosenthal, Michael, *The Character Factory: Baden-Powell and the Origins of the Boy Scout Movement.* New York: Pantheon Books, 1986.

Rowallan, Lord, *Rowallan: the Autobiography of Lord Rowallan, K.T..* Edinburgh: Paul Harris Publishing, 1976.

Russell, Bertrand, *Education and the Social Order.* London: George Allen & Unwin, 1932.

Ryan, Thomas F., S. J., *Jesuits Under Fire in the Siege of Hong Kong, 1941.* London: Burns Oates & Washbourne, 1944.

Saito, Koji 齋藤幸治, 軍政下の香港: 新生しれ大東亞の中核 (Hong Kong under Military Rule). 香港: 香港占領地總督監修, 東洋經濟新報社編, 昭和十九年, 1944.

Saunders, Hilary St. George, *The Left Handshake: The Boy Scout Movement during the War, 1939-1945.* London: Collins, 1949.

Scott, Joan, "Gender: a useful category of historical analysis," *Gender and the Politics of History.* New York: Columbia Univ. Press, 1988.

Scott, Robert L., Jr., *God is My Co-Pilot.* Garden City: Blue Ribbon Books, 1943.

Searle, G.R., *A New England: Peace and War, 1886-1918.* Oxford: Clarendon, 2003.

Seidelmann, Karl, *Die Pfadfinder in der deutschen Jugendgeschichte.* Hannover: Schroedel Verlag, 1977.

Senge, Peter, *The Fifth Discipline: the Art and Practice of the Learning Organization.* London: Century Business, 1992.

Senge, Peter, "The Leader's New Work: Building Learning Organization," *Sloan Management Review*, Fall 1990, 7-23.

Smart, Alan, *the Shek Kip Mei Myth: Squatters, Fires and Colonial Rule in Hong Kong, 1950-1963.* Hong Kong: Hong Kong Univ. Press, 2006.

Smith, Michael, *The Emperor's Codes: the Breaking of Japan's Secret Ciphers.* New York: Arcade Publishing, 2000.

Smith, Tony, *The End of the European Empire: Decolonization after World War II.* Lexington: D.C. Heath, 1975.

Snape, Michael, *God and the British Soldier: Religion and the British Army in the First and Second World Wars.* Abingdon: Routledge, 2005.

Snow, Edgar, *Red Star over China.* London: Victor Gollancz, 1937.

Snow, Philip, *the Fall of Hong Kong: Britain, China and the Japanese Occupation.* New Haven: Yale Univ. Press, 2003.

Soong, Ching Ling, *The Struggle for New China.* Peking: Foreign Languages Press, 1953.

Spergel, Irving A., *Planning for Youth Development: the Hong Kong Experience.* New York: United Nations Commissioner for Technical Co-operation, 1972.

Springhall, John, "Baden-Powell and the Scout Movement before 1920: Citizen Training or Soldiers of the Future," *The English Historical Review*, 1987.

Springhall, John, "The Boy Scout, Class, and Militarism in Relation to British Youth Movements, 1908-1930," *International Review of Social History*, 16, 1971, 125-58.

Springhall, John, "Building Character in the British Boy: The Attempt to Extend Christian Manliness to Working-class Adolescents, 1880-1914," in J. A. Mangan and James

Walvin (eds.), *Manliness and Morality*. Manchester: Manchester Univ. Press, 1987.

Springhall, John, *Decolonization since 1945: the Collapse of European Overseas Empires*. Basingstoke, Hampshire: Palgrave, 2001.

Springhall, John, *Youth, Empire, and Society: British Youth Movements, 1883-1940*. London: Croom Helm, 1977.

Springhall, J., B. Fraser, and M Hoare, *Sure and Stedfast. A history of the Boys Brigade 1883 to 1983*. London: Collins, 1983.

Starr, Kevin, *The Dream Endures: California Enters the 1940s*. Oxford: Oxford Univ., 2002.

Steen, Jan H. van der, *Padvinders:100 Jaar Scouting in Netherland*. Zutphen: Walburg, 2010.

Stephan, Nancy L., "Race and Gender: The Role of Analogy in Science," in Gill Kirkup, et al (eds.), *The Gendered Cyborg: A Reader*. New York: Routledge, 2000.

Sterne, Wendy C., "The Formation of the Scouting Movement and the Gendering of Citizenship," Ph. D. dissertation, Univ. of Wisconsin-Madison, 1993.

Stevens, A., "Changing Attitudes to Disabled People in the Scout Association in Britain (1908-1962): a contribution to a history of disability," *Disability & Society*, Vol. 10, No. 3, September 1995.

Stewart, Evan, *Hong Kong Volunteers in Battle: A Record of the Actions of the Hongkong Volunteer Defence Corps in the Batter for Hong Kong, December, 1941*. Hong Kong: RHKR (The Volunteers) Association, 2005.

Stoddard, John L., *John L. Stoddard's Lectures, Vol 3*. Chicago: Shuman, 1909.

Streicker, John, *Captive Colony: The Story of Stanley Camp, Hong Kong*. S.I.: s.n., 1945, typed manuscript, the Hong Kong Univ. Library.

Subrahmanyam, Kaveri, Robert Kraut, Patricia Greenfield, and Elisheva Gross, "New Forms of Electronic Media: the Impact of Interactive Games and the Internet on Cognition, Socialization, and Behavior," in Dorothy G. Singer and Ejrome L. Singer (eds.), *Handbook of Children and the Media*. California: Sage Publications, 2001, 73-100.

Summers, Anne, "Scouts, Guides and VADs: A Note in Reply to Allen Warren," *The English Historical Review*, vol. 102, no. 405, Oct. 1987, 943-947.

Sweeting, A. E., "Politics and the art of teaching history in Hong Kong," *Teaching History*, 64, 30-37.

Symons, Catherine Joyce, *Looking at the Stars*. Hong Kong: Pegasus, 1996.

Tang, Kwong-leung, *Colonial State and Social Policy: Social Welfare Development in Hong Kong, 1842—1997*. Lanham: Univ. Press America, 1998.

Thériault, Raphaël, "Former des homes, des Chrétiens, des Citoyens: Le Project d'Éducation des Scouts du Petit Séminaire de Québec, 1933-1970," M.A. thesis, Univ. of Laval, 2000.

Thomas, Bruce, *Bruce Lee: Fighting Spirit*. Berkeley, CA: Frog, 1994.

Thomas, Susan Gregory, *Buy, Buy Baby: How Consumer Culture Manipulates Parents and Harms Young Minds*. New York: Houghton Mifflin, 2007.

Tiltman, H. Hessell, "Japan's 'Anti-British' Drive," from *Japan's Aggression and Public Opinion*. Kunming: National Southwest Associated Univ. Library, 1938.

Timperley, H.J. (comp.), *Japanese Terror in China*. New York, Modern Age Books, 1938.

Tomlinson, John "Cultural Globalization and Cultural Imperialism," 170-190, in Ali Mohammadi (ed.), *International Communication and Globalization*. London: SAGE Publications, 1997.

Tong, Benson (ed.), *Asian American Children: A Historical Handbook and Guide*. Westport: Greenwood, 2004.

Tong, Irene Lik Kay, "R-inheriting Women in Decolonizing Hong Kong," in Jill M. Bystydzienski and Jotl Sekhon (eds.), *Democratization and Women's Grassroots Movements*. Bloomington: Indiana Univ. Press, 1999.

Townley, Alvin, *Legacy of Honor: The Values and Influence of America's Eagle Scouts*. New York: Thomas Dunne, 2007.

Traver, Harold, "Juvenile Delinquency in Hong Kong," in John Winterdyk (ed.), *Juvenile*

Justice Systems: Int'l Perspectives, 2nd ed. Toronto: Canadian Scholars' Press, 2002, 207-234.

Tsai, Jung-fang, "The Predicament of the Compradore Ideologists," *Modern China*, 1981, 204-209.

Tsang, Steve, *Governing Hong Kong: Administrative Officers from the Nineteenth Century to the Handover to China, 1862-1997*. Hong Kong: Hong Kong Univ. Press, 2007.

Tsang, Steve, *A Modern History of Hong Kong*. Hong Kong: Hong Kong Univ. Press, 2004.

Tsang, Steve (ed.), *In the Shadow of China: Political Development in Taiwan since 1949*. Hong Kong: Hong Kong Univ. Press, 1993.

Tse, Thomas Kwan-Choi, "Civic Education and the making of deformed citizenry," in Agnes S. Ku et. al. (eds.), *Remaking Citizenship in Hong Kong: Community, Nation and the Global City*. London: RoutledgeCurzon, 2004.

Tsui, Amy, and James W. Tollefson (ed.), *Language Policy, Culture, and Identity in Asian Contexts*. London: Lawrence Erlbaum Associates, 2007.

Turner, Bryan S., "Making and Unmaking Citizenship in Neo-liberal Times," in Agnes S. Ku *et al* (eds.,) *Remaking Citizenship in Hong Kong: Community, Nation and the Global City*. London: Routledge Curzon, 2004.

Tyre, Peg, *The Trouble with Boys: A Surprising Report Card on Our Sons, Their Problems at School, and What Parents and Educators Must Do*. New York: Crown Publishers, 2008.

United Nations, Department of Economic and Social Affairs, http://esa.un.org/unpp/p2k0data.asp (accessed May 8, 2010).

Vickers, Edward, Flora Kan, and Paul Morris, "Colonialism and the Politics of 'Chinese History' in Hong Kong's Schools," *Oxford Review of Education*, Vol. 29, No. 1, March 2003, 95-111.

Wade, Eileen K., *Twenty-One Years of Scouting: The Official History of the Boy Scout Movement From its Inception*. London: C. Arthur Pearson, 1929.

Wagner, Carolyn Ditte, "The Boy Scouts of America: A Model and a Mirror of American Society," Ph. D. dissertation, Johns Hopkins Univ., 1978.

Wakeman, Frederic E., *Spymaster: Dai Li and the Chinese Secret Service*. California: Univ. of California Press, 2003.

Waldron, Stephen, "Fire on the Rim: A Study in Contradictions in Left-wing Political Mobilization in Hong Kong, 1967," Ph. D. dissertation, Syracuse Univ., 1976.

Waley, Arthur, "A Debt to China," reprinted in Hsiao Ch'ien (ed.,) *A Harp with a Thousand Strings: A Chinese Anthology in Six Parts*. London, 1944.

Wang, Jin-que 王錦雀, *Tai Wan Gong Min Jiao Yu Yu Gong Min Te Xing* 台灣公民教育與公民特性 (Taiwan's Citizenship Education and Citizenship Characteristics.) Taipei: 台灣古籍出版公司, 2005.

Wang, Ling-chi, and Gungwu Wang, *The Chinese Diaspora: Selected Essays*. Singapore: Times Academic Press, 1998.

Wang, Xiang-yuan 王向远, 日本对华教育侵略 *Ri Ben Dui Hua Jiao Yu Qin Lue* (Japanese Invasion of Chinese Education.) China, 2005. http://lz.book.sohu.com/chapter-2408-2-4.html (accessed September 16, 2005).

Ward, Robert, *Asia for the Asiatics: The Techniques of Japanese Occupation*. Chicago: Univ. of Chicago Press, 1945.

Warren, Allen, "Baden-Powell: A Final Comment," *The English Historical Review*, 102/405, Apr. 1986, 948-950.

Warren, Allen, "Popular Manliness: Baden-Powell, Scouting, and the Development of Manly Character," in J. A. Mangan and James Walvin (eds.), *Manliness and Morality: Middle Class Masculinity in Britain and America, 1800-1940*. Manchester: Manchester Univ. Press, 1987, 199-219.———

Warren, Allen, "Sir Robert Baden-Powell, the Scout Movement and Citizen Training in Great Britain, 1900-1920," *The English Historical Review*, 101/399, Apr. 1986, 376-398.

Watt, Carey A., "The Promise of 'Character' and the Spectre of Sedition: The Boy Scout

Movement and Colonial Consternation in India, 1908-1921," *South Asia*, XII.2, 1999, 37-62.

Welsh, Frank, *A Borrowed Place: the History of Hong Kong*. New York: Kodansha International, 1993.

Wilkinson, Paul, "English Youth Movements, 1908-1930," *Journal of Contemporary History*, 4, April 1969.

Williams, S. Wells, *A Syllabic Dictionary of the Chinese Language*. Tung Chou: North China Union College, 1909.

Winterdyk, John, *Juvenile Justice Systems: International Perspectives*. Canadian Scholars' Press, 2002.

Wong, Cheuk Yin, "The Communist-inspired Riots in Hong Kong, 1967: A Multi-Actors Approach," Master's thesis, the Univ. of Hong Kong, August 2000.

Wong, Chung Leung, "School Leadership in the Context of Change: A Case Study of 'Patriotic Schools' in Hong Kong," thesis, the Chinese Univ. of Hong Kong, 2006.

Wong, George 黃奇仁, *The Lighter Side of a Hong Kong Police Inspector's Career in the 1960s* 警官手記: 六十年代香港警隊的日子. Hong Kong: Joint Publishing, 2008.

Wong, Ting-hong, *Hegemonies Compared: State Formation and Chinese School Politics in Postwar Singapore and Hong Kong*. Routledge, 2002.

Wong, Ting-hong, State Formation and Chinese School Politics in Singapore and Hong Kong, 1945 to 1965, Ph. D. dissertation, Univ. of Wisconsin—Madison, 1999.

Wong, Wendy Siu-yi, *Hong Kong Comics: A History of Manhua*. New York: Princeton Architectural Press, 2002.

Worboys, Michael, "The Colonial World as Mission and Mandate: Leprosy and Empire, 1900-1940," *Osiris*, 2nd Series, 15, 2000.

"World Atlas," http://www.worldatlas.com/ (accessed April 5, 2011).

Xiao, Hong (née Zhang Naiying 張乃瑩), "Yi Tiao Tie Lu De Wan Cheng 一條鐵路的完成 (The Completion of a Railroad)," in Zhang, Yumao, and Zhihong Yan (eds.), *Xiao Hong Wenji* 蕭紅文集(The Collected Works of Xiao Hong*)*. Anhwei: Anhwei Wenyi Chubanshi, 1996, 208-209.

Xing, Jun, *Baptized in the Fire of Revolution: the American Social Gospel and the YMCA in China: 1919-1937*, Ph. D. dissertation, Univ. of Michigan, 1995.

Xu, Guoqi, *Olympic Dreams: China and Sports, 1895-2008*. Cambridge, MA: Harvard Univ. Press, 2008.

Yamamoto, Sumiko, *History of Protestantism in China: The Indigenization of Christianity*. Tokyo: The Toho Gakkai, 2000.

Yep, Ray, "The 1967 Riots in Hong Kong: The Diplomatic and Domestic Fronts of the Colonial Governor," *The China Quarterly*, 2008, volume 193, 122-139.

Zeiger, Hans, *Get Off My Honor!: The Assault on the Boy Scouts of America*. Nashville: Broadman & Holman, 2005.

Zhang, Peng-yuan 張鵬雲, "Wo Zai Dong Bei Lun Xian Qu Qin Li De Ri Ben Nu Hua Jiao Yu 我在東北淪陷區親歷的日本奴化教育 (My Experience with Japanese Slavish Education in the Occupied Northeastrn Region)," http://news.china.com/zh_cn/histoyr/all/11025807/20050427/12275615.html (accessed Sept. 15, 2005).

Index

Notes: Entries in this index cover Introduction to the Appendices, i. e. 15-431; page no. indicates appearance(s) in body texts or captions and possibly also footnote(s); "n" behind page no. means appearance(s) only in footnote(s) (e. g., 255–6n = only in footnotes in pp. 255+256); and entries starting with a no. are listed alphabetically (e. g., "1946 Outlook" is listed as Nineteen Forty-nine Outlook).

About the author

Paul Kua holds a Ph. D. in history and is a Fellow of the Royal Historical Society. He has published books, chapters and papers in English/Chinese on history of East-West encounters, mission history in Asia, Chinese numismatics, and history of education and Scouting. Recent works incl. *Scouting in Hong Kong, 1910-2010*, 2nd ed. (London: Propius, 2024), *Europe meets Formosa, 1510-1662* (London: Propius, 2023), *Two Centuries of Excellence* (H.K.: Joint Publishing, 2022, 69-211), 香港童軍故事(香港:三聯, 2019), 皕載英華(香港:三聯, 2018, 88-232), and peer-reviewed articles in academic journals issued by Academia Sinica, Brill, OUP, Routledge and several universities (see https://hku-hk.academia.edu/PaulKua or https://www.researchgate.net/profile/Paul-Kua-2).

Paul joined the Hong Kong Scout Movement in 1966, and has been involved since then as a youth member/volunteer leader/supporter. He had served as Deputy Chief Commissioner, Association Archivist, etc. of Scout Association of Hong Kong and on Management Sub-Committee of the Asia Pacific Scout Region. He is also a Baden-Powell Fellow of the World Scout Foundation.

Made in the USA
Columbia, SC
26 July 2024

38943700R00261